Lecture Notes in Computer Science 3582

Commenced Publication in 1973
Founding and Former Series Editors:
Gerhard Goos, Juris Hartmanis, and Jan van Leeuwen

Lecture Notes in Computer Science 3582

Commenced Publication in 1973
Founding and Former Series Editors:
Gerhard Goos, Juris Hartmanis, and Jan van Leeuwen

Editorial Board

David Hutchison
Lancaster University, UK
Takeo Kanade
Carnegie Mellon University, Pittsburgh, PA, USA
Josef Kittler
University of Surrey, Guildford, UK
Jon M. Kleinberg
Cornell University, Ithaca, NY, USA
Friedemann Mattern
ETH Zurich, Switzerland
John C. Mitchell
Stanford University, CA, USA
Moni Naor
Weizmann Institute of Science, Rehovot, Israel
Oscar Nierstrasz
University of Bern, Switzerland
C. Pandu Rangan
Indian Institute of Technology, Madras, India
Bernhard Steffen
University of Dortmund, Germany
Madhu Sudan
Massachusetts Institute of Technology, MA, USA
Demetri Terzopoulos
New York University, NY, USA
Doug Tygar
University of California, Berkeley, CA, USA
Moshe Y. Vardi
Rice University, Houston, TX, USA
Gerhard Weikum
Max-Planck Institute of Computer Science, Saarbruecken, Germany

John Fitzgerald   Ian J. Hayes
Andrzej Tarlecki (Eds.)

FM 2005:
Formal Methods

International Symposium of Formal Methods Europe
Newcastle, UK, July 18-22, 2005
Proceedings

 Springer

Volume Editors

John Fitzgerald
University of Newcastle upon Tyne
Centre for Software Reliability
Newcastle upon Tyne, NE1 7RU, UK
E-mail: john.fitzgerald@ncl.ac.uk

Ian J. Hayes
University of Queensland
School of Information Technology and Electrical Engineering
Brisbane, QLD 4072, Australia
E-mail: Ian.Hayes@itee.uq.edu.au

Andrzej Tarlecki
Warsaw University
Faculty of Mathematics, Informatics and Mechanics
Banacha 2, 02-097 Warszawa, Poland
E-mail: tarlecki@mimuw.edu.pl

Library of Congress Control Number: 2005928720

CR Subject Classification (1998): D.2, F.3, D.3, D.1, J.1, K.6, F.4

ISSN   0302-9743
ISBN-10   3-540-27882-6 Springer Berlin Heidelberg New York
ISBN-13   978-3-540-27882-5 Springer Berlin Heidelberg New York

Springer is a part of Springer Science+Business Media

springeronline.com

© Springer-Verlag Berlin Heidelberg 2005
Printed in Germany

Typesetting: Camera-ready by author, data conversion by Scientific Publishing Services, Chennai, India
Printed on acid-free paper   SPIN: 11526841   06/3142   5 4 3 2 1 0

Preface

This volume contains the proceedings of Formal Methods 2005, the 13th International Symposium on Formal Methods held in Newcastle upon Tyne, UK, during July 18–22, 2005. Formal Methods Europe (FME, www.fmeurope.org) is an independent association which aims to stimulate the use of, and research on, formal methods for system development. FME conferences began with a VDM Europe symposium in 1987. Since then, the meetings have grown and have been held about once every 18 months. Throughout the years the symposia have been notably successful in bringing together researchers, tool developers, vendors, and users, both from academia and from industry. Formal Methods 2005 confirms this success.

We received 130 submissions to the main conference, from all over the world. Each submission was carefully refereed by at least three reviewers. Then, after an intensive, in-depth discussion, the Program Committee selected 31 papers for presentation at the conference. They form the bulk of this volume. We would like to thank all the Program Committee members and the referees for their excellent and efficient work.

Apart from the selected contributions, the Committee invited three keynote lectures from Mathai Joseph, Marie-Claude Gaudel and Chris Johnson. You will find the abstracts/papers for their keynote lectures in this volume as well.

An innovation for the FM 2005 program was a panel discussion on the history of formal methods, with Jean-Raymond Abrial, Dines Bjørner, Jim Horning and Cliff Jones as panelists. Unfortunately, it was not possible to reflect this event in the current volume, but you will find the material documenting it elsewhere (see the conference Web page).

An Industry Day was organized by the Formal Techniques Industrial Association (ForTIA) alongside the main symposium. This was directly related to the main theme of the FM symposia: the use of well-founded formal methods in the industrial practice of software design, development and maintenance. We have therefore included abstracts of the invited presentations in this volume as well.

The main FM 2005 conference was accompanied by 9 workshops and 11 tutorials.

The electronic submission, refereeing and Program Committee discussions would not have been possible without software support. We worked with the OCS system developed at the University of Dortmund — our thanks to the staff there for their support.

Finally, we would like to thank all those who helped to create and run the symposium in Newcastle, and in particular Claire Smith, Jon Warwick, Joan Atkinson, Sarah Davidson, Nigel Jefferson, Joey Coleman, Jeremy Bryans, Neil Henderson and Juan Bicarregui for their help in bringing the program, and these proceedings, together.

July 2005   John Fitzgerald, Ian Hayes, Andrzej Tarlecki

Organization

FM 2005 was organized by the Centre for Software Reliability at the University of Newcastle upon Tyne (www.csr.ncl.ac.uk) and Formal Methods Europe. We are grateful for the support of the University of Newcastle and its School of Computing Science. Within Formal Methods Europe, we are particularly grateful to Kees Pronk and Stefania Gnesi for their help with budgeting and organization. We also gladly acknowledge direct sponsorship from SAP Research and the British Computer Society Specialist Group on Formal Aspects of Computing Science (BCS-FACS).

Conference Chairs

General Chair	John S. Fitzgerald, University of Newcastle, UK
Program Co-chairs	Ian Hayes, University of Queensland, Australia
	Andrzej Tarlecki, Warsaw University, Poland
Conference Organizer	Claire Smith, University of Newcastle, UK
Finance Chair	Jon Warwick, University of Newcastle, UK
Tools Exhibition Chair	Joan Atkinson, University of Newcastle, UK
Workshops Chair	Juan Bicarregui, Rutherford Appleton Laboratory, UK
Tutorials Chair	Neil Henderson, University of Newcastle, UK

Program Committee

Bernhard Aichernig, UNU-IIST, Macau, China
Keijiro Araki, Kyushu University, Japan
Juan Bicarregui, Rutherford Appleton Laboratory, UK
Michel Bidoit, LSV, CNRS and ENS de Cachan, France
Ed Brinksma, University of Twente, The Netherlands
Luca Cardelli, Microsoft Research, UK
Ernie Cohen, Microsoft, USA
Jin Song Dong, National University of Singapore, Singapore
José Luiz Fiadeiro, University of Leicester, UK
John S. Fitzgerald, Centre for Software Reliability, UK
Stefania Gnesi, CNR, Italy
Anthony Hall, UK
Anne E. Haxthausen, Technical University of Denmark, Denmark
Ian Hayes, University of Queensland, Australia (Co-chair)
Thomas A. Henzinger, EPFL and University of California, Berkeley, USA
He Jifeng, UNU-IIST, Macau, China
Cliff Jones, University of Newcastle, UK

Shaoying Liu, Hosei University, Japan
Mícheál Mac an Airchinnigh, Trinity College Dublin, Ireland
Tom Maibaum, McMaster University, Canada
Dino Mandrioli, Politecnico di Milano, Italy
Tobias Nipkow, Technische Universität München, Germany
José Oliveira, Universidade do Minho, Portugal
Sam Owre, CRI, USA
Alexander Petrenko, ISPRAS, Russia
Nico Plat, West Consulting, The Netherlands
Ken Robinson, University of New South Wales, Australia
Mark Saaltink, ORA Canada, Canada
Shin Sahara, JFITS, Japan
Steve Schneider, University of Surrey, UK
Kaisa Sere, Åbo Akademi, Finland
Ketil Stølen, SINTEF, Norway
Andrzej Tarlecki, Warsaw University, Poland (Co-chair)
Mark Utting, Waikato University, New Zealand
Marcel Verhoef, Chess IT and Radboud University, Nijmegen, Netherlands
Alan Wassyng, McMaster University, Canada
Martin Wirsing, Ludwig-Maximilians-Universität, München, Germany

Referees

Carlos Bacelar Almeida	Gyrd Brændeland	Martin Fränzle
Paulo Sergio Almeida	Bettina Buth	Laurent Fribourg
Matthias Anlauff	Jens Bæk Jørgensen	Carlo Furia
Alvaro Arenas	Jacques Carette	Peter Gorm Larsen
Alexei Barantsev	David Carrington	Jean Goubault-Larrecq
Luis Barbosa	Arindam Chakrabarti	Adriaan de Groot
Leonor Barroca	Michel Chaudron	Stefan Gruner
Hubert Baumeister	Chunqing Chen	Moritz Hammer
Marek A. Bednarczyk	Jacek Chrząszcz	Ping Hao
Maurice ter Beek	David Clark	Neil Henderson
Axel Belinfante	Joey Coleman	Martijn Hendriks
Dirk Beyer	Phil Cook	Thai Son Hoang
Machiel van der Bijl	Véronique Cortier	Martin Hofmann
Henrik Bohnenkamp	Jorge Cuellar	Jozef Hooman
Pontus Boström	Roberto Delicata	Dang Van Hung
Ahmed Bouajjani	Dubravka Ilic	Wilson Ifill
Patricia Bouyer	Bruno Dutertre	Ryszard Janicki
Folker den Braber	Neil Evans	Tomasz Janowski
Laura Brandan Briones	Alessandro Fantechi	Einar Broch Johnsen
Phil Brooke	Gianluigi Ferrari	Wolfram Kahl
Roberto Bruni	Paul Fischer	Alexander Kamkin
Hans Bruun	Oana Florescu	Ridha Khedri

Victor Khomenko
Alexander Knapp
Erwin van der Koogh
Evgeny Kornykhin
Piotr Kosiuczenko
Fred Kröger
Steve Kremer
Victor Kuliamin
Alexander Kurz
Linas Laibinis
Christian Lange
Rom Langerak
Franiçois Laroussinie
Diego Latella
Timo Latvala
Christian Lengauer
Yuan Fang Li
Quan Long
Mass Soldal Lund
Volkmar Lotz
Hans Henrik Løvengreen
Tom Lysemose
Qaisar Ahmad Malik
Tiziana Margaria
Nicolas Markey
Mieke Massink
Brian Matthews
Franco Mazzanti
Alistair McEwan
Robert Meolic

Stephan Merz
Ali Mesbah
Tim Miller
Leonardo de Moura
Henry Muccini
Damian Niwiński
David von Oheim
Nickolay Pakulin
Jun Pang
Dirk Pattinson
Jan Peleska
Luigia Petre
Laure Petrucci
Nir Piterman
David Pitt
Matteo Pradella
Kees Pronk
Axel Rauschmayer
Atle Refsdal
Brian Ritchie
Markus Roggenbach
Judith Rossebø
Matteo Rossi
Ragnhild Kobro Runde
John Rushby
Theo Ruys
Denis Sabatier
Hassen Saidi
Thomas Santen
Bernhard Schätz

Norbert Schirmer
Aleksy Schubert
Fredrik Seehusen
Emil Sekerinski
Natarajan Shankar
Mike Shields
Graeme Smith
Monika Solanki
Bjørnar Solhaug
Jorge Sousa Pinto
Simao Melo de Sousa
Pieter van der Spek
Paola Spoletini
Mariëlle Stoelinga
Asuman Suenbuel
Jun Sun
Helen Treharne
Jan Tretmans
Leonidas Tsiopoulos
Irek Ulidowski
Neeraj Verma
Joost Visser
Peter Visser
Fredrik Vraalsen
Marina Waldén
Burkhart Wolff
Lu Yan
Yuwen Yang

Sponsors

Table of Contents

Timing and Testing

CSP, B and Circus

Security

Networks and Processes

Abstraction, Retrenchment and Rewriting

Scenarios and Modeling Languages

Model Checking

Industry Day: Abstracts of Invited Talks

Formal Aids for the Growth of Software Systems

Mathai Joseph

Tata Research Development & Design Centre,
A Division of Tata Consultancy Services
mathai.joseph@tcs.com

Abstract. The use of formal techniques has for a long time been focused on relatively small and complex applications. The hardware domain lends itself well to this and it has therefore been the target of some of the most significant applications of formal techniques. The software applications that have typically been considered were for small, safety-critical systems.

This restricted focus was understandable and necessary while formal techniques were evolving and practical considerations limited the size of the system that could be specified and verified. However, there are now compelling demands for the use of more precise techniques for a variety of large-scale applications, ranging from smart cards to financial systems.

So there are now new reasons to extend the use of formal methods for all phases of software development: from requirements and software modeling to coding and testing. Problems of scale still remain so it is important to focus the use of formal techniques in areas where their impact will be most important.

Different formal techniques can be used for solving different problems. For example, use of model-checking during requirements modeling can identify incomplete or inconsistent specifications, while use of transformational techniques can be very effective for software modeling and enable generation of code directly from models. Program analysis techniques can be used to generate tests that will greatly improve functional coverage during testing.

The use of formal techniques continues during *software maintenance* through the following kinds of activities:

a. **Remedial**: correction of errors discovered during use;
b. **Adaptive**: making changes to cater to changes in the operating environment;
c. **Enhancing**: adding new features or capabilities; and
d. **Improving**: making the software more robust and easier to maintain.

It is estimated that the cost of software maintenance amounts to as much as 90% of the life-cycle cost of a software system. While this calls for major improvements in maintenance techniques, changes in software development methods can also help to reduce the need for, and therefore the cost of, making remedial improvements (i.e. bug fixing).

In this talk, I will describe the use of formal techniques for different areas of the software life-cycle and relate this to evidence obtained through the analysis of a large number of actual software development and maintenance projects.

J.S. Fitzgerald, I.J. Hayes, and A. Tarlecki (Eds.): FM 2005, LNCS 3582, p. 1, 2005
© Springer-Verlag Berlin Heidelberg 2005

Formal Methods and Testing: Hypotheses, and Correctness Approximations

Marie-Claude Gaudel

LRI, Paris-Sud University & CNRS, Orsay, France
mcg@lri.fr

Abstract. It has been recognised for a while that formal specifications can bring much to software testing. Numerous methods have been proposed for the derivation of test cases from various kinds of formal specifications, their submission, and verdict. All these methods rely upon some hypotheses on the system under test that formalise the gap between the success of a test campaign and the correctness of the system under test.

1 Introduction

It has been recognised for a while that formal specifications and models can bring much to software testing [16], [10]. In this extended abstract, we first precisely introduce the distinction between specification testing, model checking, and implementation testing based on formal specifications. Then we focus on the specificities of the latter one.

Actually, embedding implementation testing within a formal framework is far from being obvious. One tests a system. A system is a dynamic entity. It raises tricky issues such as observability and controllability, and sometimes specific physical constraints. A system is not a formula, even if it can be partially described as such. Thus, testing is very different from program proving, even if it is related. Similarly, testing is different from model checking, where verifications are performed on a known model: when testing, the model corresponding to the system under test is unknown (if it was known, testing would not be necessary...) and it is sometimes difficult to observe in what state it is [20], [22]. These points have been successfully circumvented in several testing methods based on formal specifications (or models) that use various and diverse techniques such as graph theory, symbolic evaluation, proof techniques, constraint solving, static analysis or model checking.

Explicitly or not, all these methods rely upon hypotheses on the system under test. They provide some approximation of correctness that is correlated to these hypotheses. In this talk we recall the notions of testability hypotheses and selection hypotheses that were introduced in [4], and we show how they have been used or could be used on various kinds of formal methods. We also address the issues of observation and control of the system under test.

J.S. Fitzgerald, I.J. Hayes, and A. Tarlecki (Eds.): FM 2005, LNCS 3582, pp. 2–8, 2005.

2 Testing Specifications, Checking Models, or Testing Implementations?

Before starting some discussion on formal methods and testing, it is necessary to introduce some terminology. Unfortunately, there is no consensus on these issues among the various research communities working in the area of software.

There is not even an agreement on the meanings of the words "validation" and "verification" [7] [3]. Similarly, the word "testing" is often used with different meanings.

Looking in a dictionary, one gets definitions such as:
"*subjecting somebody or something to challenging difficulties*"
In the case of software and formal methods, the "somebody or something" and the "challenging difficulties" are sometimes understood in different ways.

In most cases, the entity under test is a system, and the "challenging difficulties" are inputs, or sequences of inputs, aiming at revealing some dysfunctions [4], [8], [12] [13], [15], etc. In such cases, formal descriptions of the system are mainly used as guidelines for the selection of (sequences of) inputs and for the verdict. We focus on these approaches in Sections 3, 4 and 5.

2.1 Debugging or Testing Formal Specifications

In some other cases, testing is understood as debugging of formal descriptions or models. The formal description is the subject of the test. The challenges are either properties to be satisfied or refuted [14], or inputs for some simulation of the future system, based on the formal description [19], [11].

As the main characteristic of formal specifications is the ability of reasoning, theorem proving is used either to prove that a required property is a consequence of the specification, or to refute a property that corresponds to a forbidden situation. The choice of such challenges is far from being simple. It requires a very good expertise in the application domain. As the specification may be wrong, is probably a good idea to make this choice as independent of it as possible [2], even if some positive experiments have been performed on mutation of formal specifications [6].

2.2 Checking Models ... or Testing Them?

Model checking is similar in purpose: it aims at finding faults in so-called models of software systems. These models are behavioural (Kripke Structures, Finite Automata, Finite State Machine, Labelled Transition Systems, or even program control graphs), with a finite (but often huge) number of states labelled by atomic propositions. A model checker checks properties written in some temporal logic via an exhaustive exploration of the model, or some equivalent technique. Here also, the choice of the temporal properties to be checked is far from being obvious.

Model checking could be seen as a special kind of testing where the subject is a model and the challenges are temporal properties. Actually, there is some evolution in this direction. Due to the state explosion problem new techniques have been proposed that somewhat give up exhaustiveness: for instance, bounded model checking [5] where only finite prefixes of traces are considered; or randomised exploration of models until a target coverage quality is reached [17].

2.3 Testing Implementations

When testing implementations against a formal specification, the situation is different. As said in the introduction, the subject of the test is an executable system, whose internal state is often unknown. The system under test is not a formal entity. The only way to observe it is to interact via some specific (and often limited) interface, submitting inputs and collecting outputs.

3 Specifications, Implementations, and Testing

Given a specification *SP* and a system under test *SUT*, any testing activity must be based on a *relation of satisfaction* (sometimes called conformance relation) that we note *SUT sat SP*. This relation is usually defined on a semantic domain common to implementations and specifications (i.e. there is some domain *D* such that $sat \subseteq D \times D$) [4], [9], [20], but in some cases they may be different ($sat \subseteq D1 \times D2$) [9].

3.1 Test Experiments, Exhaustiveness, and Testability

The satisfaction relation *SUT sat SP* is generally a large conjunction of elementary properties (for instance it may begin by "for all traces in the specification...""). These elementary properties are the basis for the definition of what is a *test experiment*, a test data, and the *verdict* of a test experiment, i.e. the decision whether *SUT* passes a test *t*. The satisfaction relation as a whole is used for the definition of an *exhaustive test set, Exhaust(SP)*.

However, an implementation's passing all the tests in the exhaustive test set does not necessarily mean that it satisfies the specification. This is true for a class of reasonable implementations. But a totally erratic system, or a diabolic one, may pass the exhaustive test set and then fail. More formally, the implementation under test must fulfil some basic requirements coming from the semantic domain considered for the implementations. As an example, in the case of finite state machines [20], the implementation must behave without memory of its history. Or when faced to non-deterministic *SUT*, some reasonable assumptions on the way of controlling it, or on the way of covering all the possible behaviours, are needed. We call such properties of the implementation the *testability hypothesis*, or the *minimal hypothesis*. We will note it *Hmin(SUT)*.

Hmin, Exhaust, and *sat* must satisfy:

$$Hmin(SUT) \Rightarrow (SUT \ passes \ Exhaust(SP) \Leftrightarrow SUT \ sat \ SP) . \tag{1}$$

There are cases where several choices are possible for the pair *<Hmin, Exhaust>* . When restricting the class of implementations under test, using for instance some knowledge on the way it was developed, it is possible to lessen *Exhaust(SP)*.

3.2 Selection Hypotheses, Uniformity, Regularity

A black-box testing strategy can be formalised as the selection of a finite subset of *Exhaust(SP)*. Let us consider as an example the classical partition testing strategy (more exactly, it should be called sub-domain testing strategy). It consists in defining a collection of (possibly non-disjoint) subsets that covers the exhaustive test set. Then a representative element of each subset is selected and submitted to the implementation under test.

The choice of such a strategy corresponds to stronger hypotheses than *Hmin* on the system under test. We call such hypotheses *selection hypotheses*. In this case, it is a *uniformity hypothesis*. The system is assumed to uniformly behave on the test subsets UTS_i:

$$UTS_1 \cup ... \cup UTS_p = Exhaust(SP), \quad and$$

$$\forall i = 1, ..., p, \ \forall t \in UTS_i, \ SUT \ passes \ t \Rightarrow SUT \ passes \ UTS_i \tag{2}$$

Various selection hypotheses can be formulated and combined depending on some knowledge of the program, some coverage criteria of the specification and ultimately cost considerations. A *regularity hypothesis* uses a size function on the tests and has the form "if the subset of *Exhaust(SP)* made up of all the tests of size less than or equal to a given limit is passed, then *Exhaust(SP)* also is" (there is some similarity with bounded model checking).

All these hypotheses are important from a theoretical point of view because they express the gap between the success of a test strategy and correctness. They are also important in practice because exposing them makes clear the assumptions made on the implementation. It gives some indication of complementary verifications.

Weak selection hypotheses lead, via formula (1), to large test sets. Strong selection hypotheses lead to smaller, more practicable test sets, with the risk that they may not be fulfilled. The strongest selection hypothesis is the correctness assumption: in this case, an empty test set is sufficient...

There exist various ways to select test sets in the framework of specification-based testing. The most used are coverage criteria based on the specification. A well-known example in the case of finite state machines is transition coverage [10]. It corresponds to a testability hypothesis that the SUT is some deterministic FSM. Another approach is to select tests via a finite number of test purposes describing some behaviours that are considered to be important to test. Combining the specification and the tests purposes, a finite number of test cases are generated. This kind of selection is used for example in the TGV tool [9]. It can be formalised as some restriction of the conformance relation combined with some selection hypotheses.

3.3 The Oracle Problem

The interpretation of the results of a test is often very difficult. This difficulty is known as the *oracle problem*. The problem may be difficult for various causes.

The *SUT* may yield the results in a way that depends on some representation choices and makes the comparison with the specified results difficult. The test is based on a specification that is (normally) more abstract than the program. Thus program results may appear in a form that is not obviously equivalent to the specified results. This contradicts a common belief that the existence of a formal specification is sufficient to directly decide whether a test is a success. In presence of complex data types, it may be necessary to embed the tests into observable contexts, or to enrich the *SUT* with some concrete equivalence function [22].

Similarly, when the specification is based on states and transitions, it may be difficult to check that the *SUT* is in an acceptable state after a test. It may require complementing the test itself by some other tests for identifying the internal state [20].

4   Axioms, Pre-conditions and Post-conditions

Historically the above framework has been developed for algebraic specifications [4], [22]. Test data are just instantiated axioms of the specification and test experiments consist in their evaluation by the *SUT* to check that they are satisfied. The exhaustive test set is the set of all closed instances of the axioms of the specification. The testability hypothesis on the *SUT* is that all the functions of the signature are implemented in a deterministic way, and that there is no junk (no unspecified values). A basic testing strategy is to cover once every axiom. It corresponds to uniformity hypotheses on the domains of their variables. This strategy can be refined by composing axioms (unfolding functions) in order to get a better coverage of sub-cases, i.e. weaker uniformity hypotheses. In the case of positive conditional axioms, this method has been automated by the LOFT constraint solver [4].

In the case of VDM, Jeremy Dick and Alain Faivre [12] have proposed to reduce the pre conditions and post conditions into disjunctive normal forms (DNF), creating a set of disjoint input sub-domains for each operation of the specification. This provides a nice way of discovering uniformity hypotheses. As VDM is state-based, it is not enough to partition operations domains: thus the authors give a method of extracting a finite state automaton from the specification. It uses the uniformity sub-domains of the operations to perform a partition of the states. Given this finite state automaton one can use one of the testing methods mentioned in the next section. This work has been influential on several researches on testing based on formal methods close to VDM, such as Z, or B, that are too numerous to be all cited here.

More recently, similar ideas have been used in the KORAT framework for testing Java methods specified by JML preconditions and post conditions [8]. KORAT derives from the precondition "all non isomorphic test cases up to a given small size", i.e. the selection is based on a combination of uniformity and regularity hypotheses.

5   Behavioural Models, FSM, LTS, etc

Historically, finite state machines (FSM) have been the first formal descriptions used as basis for automatic test derivation [10]. Originally, there was a testability hypothesis that the SUT behaves as a FSM with the same number (or a larger known number) of states as the specification FSM. The conformance relation was equivalence. These choices were adequate for hardware testing, which was the original motivation. The excellent survey by Lee and Yannakakis presents extensions to more elaborated conformance notions, and to extended state machines [20]. Similar approaches have been developed in the area of communication protocols, based on labelled transition systems (LTS) or variants of them [9]. In [15] and [21] we have stated the underlying notions of testability hypotheses, exhaustive test sets, and selection hypotheses for these approaches.

For some years, there is a fruitful cross-fertilisation between these so-called model-based testing methods and model checking techniques (cf. [1] [18], [23] among many others). For instance, the ability of model checker to provide counterexamples can be used to produce test sequences that satisfy a property *P* by model-checking the property *"always not P"*. Model checkers are now among the major tools for testing based on formal specification, together with constraint solvers, theorem provers, and symbolic interpreters.

6 Conclusion

There has been a lot of work on test cases derivation from formal descriptions. It is our claim that formal approaches bring more than that to testing. They make it possible to state the underlying hypotheses associated with test strategies and thus to express the correctness approximation they introduce. This open a lot of possibilities, first for identifying complementary verifications, second for assessing these approximations.

References

1. Ammann, P. E., Black, P.E., Majurski, W. : Using model checking to generate tests from specifications. IEEE International Conference on Formal Engineering Methods (ICFEM'98), IEEE , (1998) 46-54.
2. Arnold, A., Gaudel, M.-C., Marre B.: An experiment on the validation of a specification by heterogeneous formal means. 5th IFIP working conference on Dependable Computing for Critical Applications, Urbana Champaign, (1995) 24-34.
3. Avizienis, A., Laprie, J-C., Landwehr, C., Randell, B.: Basic Concepts and Taxonomy of Dependable and Secure Computing. IEEE Trans. on Dependable and Secure Computing, vol. 1, n° 1, (2004) 11-33.
4. Bernot, G., Gaudel, M.-C., Marre B.: Software Testing based on Formal Specifications : a theory and a tool. Software Engineering Journal, vol. 6, n° 6, (1991) 387-405.
5. Biere, A., Cimatti, A., Clarke, E., Zhu, Y. : Symbolic model checking without BDDs. TACAS'99, LNCS n° 1579, Springer-Verlag (1999) 193–207
6. Black, P.E., Okun, V., Yesha, Y. : Mutation Operators for Specifications. IEEE International Conference on Automated Software Engineering (ASE2000), IEEE (2000) 81-88.
7. Boehm, B. W.: Software Engineering Economics, Prentice Hall (1981).
8. Boyapati, C., Khurshid, S., Marinov, D.: KORAT: automated testing based on Java predicates. ACM International Symposium on Software Testing and Analysis, (2002) 123-133.
9. Brinksma, E., Tretmans, J.: Testing Transition Systems, an annotated bibliography. Lecture Notes in Computer Science n° 2067, Springer-Verlag (2001) 187-195.
10. Chow, T. S.: Testing Software Design Modeled by Finite-State Machines. IEEE Transactions on Software Engineering, vol. SE-4, n° 3, (1978) 178-187.

11. Desovski, D.: Combining Testing and Model Checking for Verification of High Assurance Systems. IEEE Int. Symp. on High Assurance Software Engineering, IEEE (2004).
12. Dick, J., Faivre, A.: Automating the Generation and Sequencing of test cases from model-based specifications. International Symposium of Formal Methods Europe, Lecture Notes in Computer Science n°670, Springer-Verlag (1993) 268-284.
13. Farchi, E., Hartman, A., Pinter, S. S.: Using a model-based test generator to test for standard conformance. IBM Systems Journal, vol. 41, n° 1, (2002) 89-110.
14. Garland, S.J, Guttag, J.V.: Using LP to Debug Specifications. IFIP TC2 Working Conference on Programming Concepts and Methods, North-Holland (1990).
15. Gaudel, M.-C., James, P. R.: Testing Algebraic Data Types and Processes : a unifying theory. Formal Aspects of Computing, 10(5-6), (1999) 436-451.
16. Goodenough, J. B., Gerhart, S.: Toward a Theory of Test Data Selection. IEEE Transactions on Software Engineering, vol. SE-1, n° 2, (1975) 156-173.
17. 17. Grosu, R., Smolka, S. A.: Monte Carlo Model Checking. TACAS 2005, Lecture Notes in Computer Science n° 3440, Springer-Verlag, (2005) 271–286.
18. Hamon, G., de Moura, L, Rushby, J.: Generating Efficient Test Sets with a Model Checker. IEEE Int. Conf. on Software Engineering and Formal Methods, IEEE, (2004) 261-270.
19. Kemmerer, R.A.: Testing Formal Specifications to Detect Design Errors. IEEE Transactions on Software Engineering, vol. SE-11, no 1 (1985) 32-43.
20. Lee, D, Yannakakis, M.: Principles and methods of Testing Finite State Machines – a survey. The Proceedings of IEEE, vol. 84, n° 8, (1996)1089-1123.
21. Lestiennes, G., Gaudel, M.-C.: Testing Processes from Formal Specifications with Inputs, Outputs, and Data Types. 13th IEEE Int. Symp. on Software Reliability Engineering (ISSRE-2002), IEEE, (2002) 3-14.
22. Machado, P. D. L,: On Oracles for Interpreting Test Results against Algebraic Specifications. Lecture Notes in Computer Science n° 1548, Springer-Verlag (1998) 502-518.
23. Peled, D., Vardi, M., Yannakakis, M.: Black Box Checking. Proceedings of FORTE/PSTV, Kluwer (1999) 225-240.

The Natural History of Bugs:
Using Formal Methods to Analyse Software Related Failures in Space Missions

C.W. Johnson

Department of Computing Science, University of Glasgow, Glasgow, G12 9QQ
johnson@dcs.gla.ac.uk

Abstract. Space missions force engineers to make complex trade-offs between many different constraints including cost, mass, power, functionality and reliability. These constraints create a continual need to innovate. Many advances rely upon software, for instance to control and monitor the next generation 'electron cyclotron resonance' ion-drives for deep space missions.Programmers face numerous challenges. It is extremely difficult to conduct valid ground-based tests for the code used in space missions. Abstract models and simulations of satellites can be misleading. These issues are compounded by the use of 'band-aid' software to fix design mistakes and compromises in other aspects of space systems engineering. Programmers must often re-code missions in flight. This introduces considerable risks. It should, therefore, not be a surprise that so many space missions fail to achieve their objectives. The costs of failure are considerable. Small launch vehicles, such as the U.S. Pegasus system, cost around $18 million. Payloads range from $4 million up to $1 billion for security related satellites. These costs do not include consequent business losses. In 2005, Intelsat wrote off $73 million from the failure of a single uninsured satellite. It is clearly important that we learn as much as possible from those failures that do occur. The following pages examine the roles that formal methods might play in the analysis of software failures in space missions.

1   The Challenges of Software Engineering in Space

Space is unforgiving. The following sections briefly review some of the challenges that complicate software development in this environment.

1.1   The Usual Suspects

'Rocket science' is often seen as the pinnacle of scientific and technological progress. For instance, it has been estimated that there are more than 1.5 million lines of code in the onboard command and control computers on the International Space Station.However, such figures are commonplace in several other industries. The day-to-day reality of maintaining space-related code would also be familiar to other software engineers. For example, the Expedition 10 crew is on the International Space

J.S. Fitzgerald, I.J. Hayes, and A. Tarlecki (Eds.): FM 2005, LNCS 3582, pp. 9–25, 2005.

Station as I write this article. Part of their six-month stay will be used to install software upgrades. These are intended to eliminate the 300 workarounds, 'Station Program Notes', that are used by ground flight controllers [15].

The causes of many failures in space missions will also be familiar to software engineers. These include the under-specification of complex systems, lack of resources for validation and verification, poor communication between multidisciplinary teams and so on. One consequence of this is that many academic computer scientists cite software failures from space missions as warnings to their students about what can go wrong in their own programs. The most familliar examples include the Ariane 5 code re-use [14] and the confusion over metric and imperial units of thrust in the Mars Climate Orbiter [16]. In contrast, the following pages delve a little more deeply into the challenges that distinguish software engineering for space systems from a mass of other applications.

1.2 Remoteness of Space

One of the first issues to confront a programmer is that many space missions must travel thousands of miles from Earth. This creates a peculiar form of batch processing where code will not be executed until months or even years after launch. Further complexity is created by the possibility of reprogramming these missions in flight. Such reprogramming is widely acknowledged to be both difficult and error prone. For example, some telemetry configurations may not enable programmers to verify that a spacecraft has successfully received instruction sequences. In other words, the target machines are often 'write-only'.

There are significant pressures associated with recoding a space mission as it travels towards a rendez-vous with a distant planet. In consequence, programming teams will often develop coding strategies to reduce the chances for an error.   One technique is to program a range of different options before launch. Once the mission is in flight, the team accepts self-imposed limits on the admissible reprogramming that may be attempted. Often the choice will be restricted to one of the pre-scripted instruction sequences planned and loaded before launch [19].   Other missions have adopted hybrid strategies where programmers can only upload new code after multiple reviews and at a small number of key stages in the mission. At all other times, they must rely on prescripted command sequences.

The differences that physical distance impose on the programming of space missions can be illustrated by events involving NASA's Spirit and Opportunity Mars Rovers during September 2004 [20]. Programmers had to transfer Spirit and Opportunity back from 'conjunction' to normal mode. During a conjunction, communications are disrupted because Mars and Earth are on opposite sides of the Sun. During the conjunction, pre-loaded command sequences were used to perform daily science missions, for instance using a Mössbauer spectrometer and a magnet array to analyze dust particles. The Rovers transmitted the data from these experiments to the Mars Odyssey orbiter. Odyssey then retransmitted the data back to Earth each afternoon. This link was extremely error prone. This created a bottleneck that reduced Spirit's memory available for science data storage from approximately 400 to 100 megabits. The problems were compounded when the mission team began to transmit 'no operation' commands to test direct communications with the Rovers during the conjunction. One of these commands triggered a software 'reset' on Opportunity.

Reprogramming arguably offers greatest benefits to programmers when they correct for problems with their own code. For example, Spirit and Opportunity had to be reprogrammed shortly after they landed on Mars in January 2004 and have been reprogrammed many times since. Spirit suffered a software fault during its navigation of the 'Columbia Hills'. The flight software team identified that an error occurred within a 3-microsecond window of vulnerability when a 'write' command was permitted and attempted on a 'write-protected' area of RAM [20]. The error was subsequently corrected in a software upgrade that was also communicated to Opportunity. Significant changes have been made to their code in order to extend their mission life beyond Summer 2004. For example, Spirit was commanded to avoid using a faulty brake relay on its steering motor. Both Rovers have been reprogrammed to alternate their drive direction to maintain the long-term health of their wheel drives.

Similarly, the Solar and Helioscopic Observatory (SOHO) was reprogrammed in-flight to de-spin one of its three gyroscopes. The gyros were identified as a 'life limiting' factor for the mission as a whole. Of course, such benefits carry risks as well. The de-spun 'A' gyroscope was involved in the SOHO mission interruption as controllers tried to work out which one of the three systems was providing reliable information [18].

1.3 Non-standard Hardware

Software development is complicated because many space applications require specialist hardware. As a minimum requirement, processors must be 'radiation hardened'. For example, the RAD 6000 processor has been tested to demonstrate 0.2 errors per year GCR – Galactic Cosmic Ray background [6]. If the radiation exposure is increased to a level similar to the flare events seen in October 1982 and January 1972 then the rate rises to 0.6 errors per flare.

Space programmers are caught between a 'rock and a hard place'. They must understand the unique features of 'rad-hard' processors. They must also cope with reduced tool support. Specialist devices lack the wide range of software development applications that support Commercial Off The Shelf (COTS) processors. The limited market for space rad-hard devices often does not justify the development of computer-aided software engineering tools. The additional validation criteria imposed on space-rated processors can also exacerbate the 'generation gap' between the facilities provided by this hardware compared to COTS processors.

Many of these problems can be illustrated by the General Purpose Computer configuration on the Shuttle. A five processor redundant architecture is used to perform critical guidance, navigation and control functions. However, the detailed analysis and design necessary to approve both the hardware and software on the GPC array prevented any updates to the processors for over fifteen years. During which time it became increasingly difficult to find vendors and suppliers for this technology. These are not isolated comments. For example, the minutes of subsystems groups reveal similar concerns throughout the Shuttle programme. The Extra-Vehicular Activities equipment board looking at the Caution and Warning System has continued to experience difficulties in supplying the "100 pieces of the EEPROM for the CPU board, which are becoming obsolete" [21]. It is difficult to underestimate the consequences of such supply problems. Storage and re-commissioning procedures must often be considered when utilizing stocks that were not initially acquired by the eventual end-user. Similarly, there are significant training issues associated with obsolete and non-standard hardware platforms.

Pilot projects have begun to develop specialist versions of commercial microprocessors. For instance, the US Defence Technology Program has invested over $50 million in providing a space-rated version of the PowerPC 750 processor. The resulting SCS750 processors can reduce the flare error rate from 0.6 per event, cited above, to 0.36 errors per flare. These individual heavy-ion irradiation errors can be detected and mitigated by the SCS750 processor [6]. However, the application of these hybrid platforms is still in its infancy.

1.4 Limitations of Re-use

There is a surprising degree of re-use in other forms of space engineering. For example, the design of the heat shields and the parachutes on the Mars Surveyor missions were based on designs from the Pathfinder missions. This provides important benefits to engineers in the aftermath of a mission failure. Investigators quickly dismissed these subsystems as causes of the Polar Lander loss because "the high degree of heritage to the successful Mars Pathfinder design, fabrication, test, and flight results (suggests) that the failure of an undamaged heat shield is implausible" [19]. These arguments can be based on limited evidence "there was not an extensive qualification program as part of the Pathfinder design phase, the Pathfinder chute did, in fact, work, thus providing at least one successful occurrence".

In contrast, space missions offer limited opportunities for code re-use. The loss of Ariane 5 provided a salient example of the problems that can arise when software is ported between different space missions. It is important to acknowledge some of the reasons why code re-use is difficult. Command and control software is typically used to interface complex sub-systems. Any unidentified interactions between these components will most often be revealed in the form of software failure. Later sections will also describe an increasing trend to introduce 'band-aid' software that is intended to fix design deficiencies or to achieve cost savings in the wider engineering of space missions. 'Band aid' code necessarily involves bespoke programming because it provides a short-term fix for underlying problems in the design and development of complex systems.

1.5 Limitations of Ground-Based Testing

Much of the software used in space missions cannot easily be tested on the ground. For example, no test was made to establish that Ariane 5's Inertial Reference System (SRI) would behave as intended under the countdown and flight time sequence for the expected trajectory. The Lyons investigation found that "for reasons of physical law, it is not feasible to test the SRI as a 'black box' in the flight environment, unless one makes a completely realistic flight test" [14]. It was possible to conduct a limited form of ground testing by injecting simulated accelerometric signals based on predicted flight parameters using a turntable to simulate launcher angular movements. Only in retrospect was it argued, "Had such a test been performed by the supplier or as part of the acceptance test, the failure mechanism would have been exposed".

Similarly, the attempt to deliver two Deep Space 2 high-impact micro-probes into the surface of Mars, went ahead in spite of concerns by mathematical modelers that they could not reliably analyze the potential impact forces acting on the devices. Their concerns were significant because of the problems involved in conducting other forms of testing. The mission validation exercises relied on an incremental build-test strategy. However, most of the communications system was only qualified with non-functioning brass-board and breadboard components. Issues of cost prevented a full impact test. In addition, delays in the schedule meant that a fully functioning probe was only available relatively late in the programme. To employ destructive testing would have involved a delay to the launch window [19].

1.6   Limitations of Executable and Abstract Modeling

The problems of software development for space missions are compounded because abstract models and simulations have often proven to be unreliable. It is common practice to enter into an iterative cycle where software is first developed and tested on a satellite or vehicle simulator [10]. The results from these evaluations are then compared with those results that can be obtained from the eventual platform. However, any discrepancies are just as likely to result in changes to the simulator as they are to changes in the command and control software. For example, both NASA and the European Space Agency operated their own simulators of the joint Solar and Helioscopic Observatory (SOHO) mission. During the mission interruption it was realized that the NASA model predicted some of the problems they were experiencing. However, the results could not be replicated for the ESA models; "analysis of the differing simulation results (ESA vs. NASA simulators) was continuing as the timeline execution was in process... this, in itself, was an indirect factor in the failure scenario since the technical support staff were distracted by the on-going simulation evaluation rather than focusing on the recovery efforts" [18]. The simulators had not been maintained with all on-board software changes that had been implemented on the spacecraft.

There has long been a debate in the formal methods communities about whether executable models can provide an appropriate level of abstraction to support reasoning about critical properties of complex software systems. However, there are aspects of space missions that stretch our ability to model interactions even at the highest level of abstraction. The investigation into the Mars Surveyor mission failures concluded that the "large modeling effort, however, may have not been enough to ensure success given the choice in the design phase of some of the system components, such as the propulsion system and the landing Radar, and given some aspects of the design of the Guidance and Control algorithms/software, which resulted in a system that was extremely difficult to model and more sensitive to model errors than it might have been" [19]. For example, the Polar Lander used pulse-width modulation (PWM) for controlling the thrust of the descent engines rather than the more conventional throttle based system. This reduced the costs of the Polar Lander hardware but greatly increased the complexity of software development for the programmers who had to calculate the exact duration of each engine pulse during the descent; "the complexity of the interactions between the feed system, the thrusters, the structure, the Guidance and Control sensors, and the Guidance and Control algorithms that the PWM approach creates, practically dictate that the only way of verifying the system with high confidence is with a full-scale closed-loop test of the system... this was prohibitive from a cost and schedule point of view and it was not done" [19].

1.7 Organizational Complexity and 'Band-Aid' Software

The use of software to compensate for the pulse-width modulation on the Polar Lander provides an example of 'band-aid' software. This code is introduced to fix design mistakes and compromises in other aspects of space systems engineering. Software is used to cover over design problems just as some mothers use sticking plasters to cover a host of injuries sustained by their children. Arguably the best example of band-aid software comes from the Mars Climate Orbiter mission. As mentioned previously many software engineers are aware that the probable cause of this mission failure stemmed from the use of Imperial rather than Metric units in the calculation of thrust for the rocket motors during the mission cruise phase. Few software engineers realize that the rockets were fired as part of Angular Momentum Desaturation (AMD) events. The software was called upon far more often than was originally intended, some estimates state that there were 10 to 14 times more AMDs than planned. AMD events were intended to desaturate the momentum that was built up on an internal flywheel. This momentum was, in turn, used to counteract solar induced momentum on an asymmetrical solar array. Previous missions had used symmetrical solar panels. The Climate Orbiter's novel design again reduced hardware costs but created problems because solar induced momentum skewed the cruise trajectory. In this way, the engineering decision to have asymmetrical solar arrays created the need to counteract the 'uneven' effects of solar induced momentum on the panels. This was done by spinning the flywheel in an equal and opposite direction to the momentum induced on the solar panels. However, the flywheel could only be used until its momentum threatened the stability of the vehicle. In order to desaturate the flywheel, programmers had to perform the complex calculations that controlled the rocket motors [16].

The problems created by band-aid software are increased by the organizational complexity of many space missions. For example, most of the team that worked on the software and hardware development of the Mars Climate Orbiter was transferred to the design of the Mars Polar Lander. The mission staff that then had to operate the Orbiter during its cruise and orbit acquisition phases, therefore, lacked many of the insights that might have been provided by the original coders. In other missions, there are conflicts between the programmers who must maintain the integrity of the platform and those who have a primary interest in particular scientific objectives. For instance, the SOHO Flight Operations Team was encouraged to modify the stored sequences of ground-generated commands. These modifications reduced operational cost during the extended life of the mission; they also minimized science 'downtime' and conserved the gyro life. Some modifications proposed by the Science Team 'were not necessarily driven by any specific requirement changes' [18]. The modifications were not adequately managed, for example not all of them were considered by a Configuration Board. Many were poorly documented. Verification relied on the NASA computer-based simulator, mentioned previously. There were no code walk-throughs, no independent reviews by ESA or any other body not involved in the implementation of the change. No hard copy of the command procedure set on the satellite existed at the time of the mission interruption.

2 Formal Methods in the Development of Space-Related Software

There have been a number of notable attempts to use formal methods to address the problems of software engineering for space-related applications. SRI have used a range of theorem provers, such as PVS, and model checking tools, including Murφ to verify that there are no violations of desired properties in models of a system. One of the best-known examples of this work includes the analysis of the software for the Simplified Aid for Extra-Vehicular (EVA) Rescue, known as SAFER. This can be thought of as a form of jet-pack [17]. Other projects have looked at the Shuttle's contingency guidance system [3]. In Europe, the Picgal project has used VDM to analyze ground-based software for launch vehicles similar to Ariane 5 [4]. Relatively slow progress has been made towards the introduction of these techniques as tools for the development of space-related software. One reason for this is the relative immaturity of contemporary software engineering practices in space applications. A number of more basic software engineering processes provide greater benefits at lower costs.

The remainder of this paper looks at an alternate use of formal methods. Rather than focusing on the constructive use of formal methods during program development, these techniques can be used to help us analyze the causes of software failures in space missions.

3 Understanding Space-Related Software Failures

As mentioned, most previous work has focused on the use of formal methods to support the design of space-related software. In general terms, this approach relies upon the following semantic inconsistency:

$$\text{System, Environment, Requirements} \models \text{false} \tag{1}$$

In other words, we might wish to establish that a particular model of the system and the environment necessarily involve a violation of safety or liveness properties. This is the traditional role of model checking. These tools will provide a trace of system states and properties that violate particular theorems. This approach can be extremely frustrating. The identification of a semantic inconsistency may provide analysts with limited insights to guide their search for a system and an environment such that the requirements hold. This is not the only way in which formal methods might be used. For example, the following semantic entailment can be used in theorem proving to establish that a system and its environment satisfy a set of requirements:

$$\text{System, Environment} \models \text{Requirements} \tag{2}$$

In other words, a set of theorems can be shown to hold for a given model of a system operating in a particular environment. These theorems, typically, represent the safety and liveness properties that we might like to hold for our application. This framework is a simplification of the high-level approach to environmental specifications being proposed by Michael Jackson and Pamela Zave [8]. For instance, they have recently proposed the following formalization of 'Adequacy' where e and s represent environment and system models respectively. Environment models include information about the World and any Requirements. System models include information about Machines and Programs:

$$\forall e\, s\, .\, \text{World} \wedge \text{Machine} \wedge \text{Program} \Rightarrow \text{Requirements} \tag{3}$$

In design, these approaches have been used to demonstrate that particular theorems continue to hold, as system models, in other words programs and machines, are iteratively refined towards implementation. We can also use these technologies in a completely different way. For example, after an accident we might like to verify that we have understood the manner in which a failure occurred. For example, one hypothesis about the failure of the Mars Polar Lander mission was that it met a localized meteorological anomaly, such as areas of low pressure, during the parachute descent to the planet surface. In such a situation we might therefore wish to prove that there exists a revised world model, one in which there are localized low pressure regions, with a machine and program that implies the requirements do not hold:

$$\exists e'\, s\, .\, \text{World} \wedge \text{Machine} \wedge \text{Program} \Rightarrow \neg\, \text{Requirements} \tag{4}$$

Equally, an investigation might focus on potential misunderstandings about the manner in which a program will execute on a particular machine. For example, a software requirement of the Mars Polar Lander was that thrust should be cut to the engines if a signal was generated from the Hall effect sensors on each of the legs and the Doppler radar system detected that the planet surface was in range. However, the programmers failed to account for a global variable that retained a spurious signal that was retained once the legs initially deployed from the body of the Lander. In terms of formula (4) these insights would force us to revise our ideas about how a Program within the system, s, might perform in a particular environment. The key point here is that we can use theorem proving and model checking to demonstrate that changes in our environment or system models will lead to the violation of safety and liveness properties. If we cannot construct such a proof then we need to search for an alternate explanation of the reasons why an accident occurred.

This approach to formal accident verification can yield some interesting surprises. For example, the system and environment models are often correct. In space missions, considerable time and skill is devoted to understanding these issues. The need to understand gravitational influences is well known. Similarly, the bespoke nature of many space missions leads to a detailed understanding of these machines. Mishaps often occur because the safety and liveness requirements are not well understood. For example, the Polar Lander had a software sequence that was to be executed if it remained on the planet surface for 24 hours without receiving a command. The purpose of this software was to start testing alternate communications facilities. However, the Lander was placed into a 'sleep mode' to conserve battery resources with an interval of less than 24 hours. Software reset the timer back to 24 hours each time the Lander awoke and hence the alternate communications configuration was never used. In this example, the model of the world, the machine and the program would satisfy the individual requirements for the backup communications and for the sleep mode. However, the models do not imply the requirement for the backup communications to work in the presence of the sleep mode. This illustrates some of the complexities associated with a formal approach to accident verification by providing an example of the problems associated with the development of complete requirements. The development of a formal proof to identify the potential problem before launch is technically feasible. However, the real challenge is to identify those requirements that are necessary to ensure mission success. Unless we can first do this, there is little likelihood that we will identify the corresponding theorems.

There are few examples of this alternate use of formal methods as a tool to assist accident investigation. Ladkin and Loer have extended theorem-proving mechanisms as part of their Why-Because Analysis technique [12]. This is deliberately intended to support accident investigation. There are other notable examples. Zuojun Shen [22] has used the Murφ procedure in Figure 1 to model the Entry, Descent and Landing phase of the Mars Polar Lander. The model checker was used to search for sequences of states that led to the violation of a Murφ invariant. This stated that the PWM thrust should always be on above a certain altitude. Although Shen's work illustrates the feasibility of the approach, many unresolved questions remain to be addressed.

```
Procedure EDL_DESCENT
        (freeD_uncnty:FREESECENT_ACC_UNCNTY;supon_uncnty:SUPON_ACC_UNCNTY;
        subon_uncnty:SUBON_ACC_UNCNTY;
        subon_hshelloff_uncnty:SUPONHSELLOFF_ACC_UNCNTY;
        SupPyroSwitchHealth: boolean; AccelerameterHEalth: boolean;
        SubPyroSwitchHealth: boolean; AltimeterEalth: boolean);--: EDLstate;
Var ENTRY_OK,state2_OK,state3_OK,state4_OK: boolean;

Begin
        ENTRY_OK :=false; state2_OK:=false; state3_OK:=false; state4_OK:=false;
        if s = ENTRY then
                SupDply(SupPyroSwitchHealth,AccelerameterHEalth,freeD_uncnty);
                ENTRY_OK :=true;
        End;
        if s = state2 & ENTRY_OK then
                SupSepr(supon_uncnty);
                state2_OK:= true;
        End;
        if s = state3 & ENTRY_OK & state2_OK then
                SubDply(freeD_uncnty);
                state3_OK:= true;
        End;
        if s = state4 & ENTRY_OK & state2_OK & state3_OK then
                HeatshellOff(subon_uncnty);
                state4_OK:= true;
        End;
        if s = state5 & ENTRY_OK & state2_OK & state3_OK & state4_OK then
                SubSepr(SubPyroSwitchHealth,AltimeterEalth,subon_hshelloff_uncnty);
        End;
End;
```

Fig. 1. Excerpt from Shen's Model of the Mars Polar Lander Mishap [22]

3.1   Traditional Investigation and Identifying Theorems

The most obvious limitation of formal methods in accident investigation is that the benefits may not outweigh any associated costs. Typically, the budgets available to accident investigation teams are a tiny fraction of those devoted to the development of space missions. Added to this, there are usually tight deadlines by which a report has to be presented to the commissioning authorities. These deadlines are dictated by future launch windows. A number of factors might mitigate these costs. For example, the use of technology such as Murφ can greatly assist the general application of formal methods both in design and accident verification. By extension, if mathematical specification techniques were more widely used in the development of space systems then this would drastically reduce the costs associated with accident modeling. In other words, we might already have the program, machine and environmental models identified in formula (4).

There are further problems. The application of formal methods would seem to require that we already have some idea about the potential failure mode for the space system. If an existing mathematical model of a program, machine and environment can be shown to violate safety or liveness requirements then the mission should not have gone ahead. In practice many missions, including the Mars Climate Orbiter, have been launched with known bugs in their software. The meta-level point is, however, that we cannot simply set a model checker loose on a system and environmental description with the hope that it will identify a sequence of events leading to an accident. The formalization process necessarily involves a number of complex decisions about the scope of any models and these circumscribe the range of possible causal hypotheses. This problem is even more acute for theorem proving where we must identify the particular safety and liveness properties that are to be disproved. These theorems represent a significant commitment towards the putative causes of an accident. Equally, however, the process of formalization can force developers to ask questions about requirements that might not previously have been asked. This is especially important in the early stages of development before requirements can become intractable in the mass of detail that is associated with an eventual implementation. Unfortunately, the introduction of 'band-aid' software implies that these initial requirements will be subject to constant revision. We are, therefore, faced with a complex situation in which formalization can help both to uncover problems that were not anticipated and to reinforce existing prejudices by modeling those aspects that are already well understood.

It can be argued that a formal model of the symptoms of an accident might be used to support a form of backwards reasoning from the observed failed state. Such models help to narrow the search space of possible causes. However, further problems arise from what has been termed 'causal asymmetries' [10]. If we know that an event has occurred then we can predict its effects with a reasonably degree of confidence. However, if all we know are the consequences of an earlier event then we typically have a far worse ability to predict the causes of those effects. By analogy, if we know a program and its inputs we can reason about the likely outputs. However, if we have a program and its outputs it can be far harder to reason about the combinations of input values that led to the observed results.

The previous caveats undermine some of Shen's achievements in his application of Murφ to the Mars Polar Lander case study. He already knew what to include in his finite state model because he was working from the Casani report into the mission failure. In general, investigations into space mission failure are not so fortunate. It is worth considering the investigatory processes that did reveal the possible software failures in this mission. The failure mode in the PWM engine code was not found by the application of the Murφ model checker. Lockhead Martin engineers identified the bug during a test run on a second Lander that was intended for a future mission. An engineer pushed a button to indicate a touchdown too early in the test. He released the button when he realized his error and "was surprised when thrust termination occurred prematurely" [19]. This prompted a more formal failure analysis that uncovered the software problem. Similarly, the bug in the Polar Lander's uplink command string was not found during the initial code design walkthrough. The investigators argued that one reason for this was that logic flow diagrams were not used; "it is difficult to find logic errors by walking through the code without logic flow diagrams to help the process" [19]. The uplink design error was discovered after a fault-tree analysis led to the examination of the code and the preparation of code descriptions for reviews by outside reviewers. Such observations make it important to be careful in the claims that are made for the formal analysis of accidents. They can be used to add confidence in any analysis but, at present, it seems too optimistic to argue that they will automatically uncover failure modes. It seems likely that the use of mathematical reasoning will continue to depend upon insights provided by more traditional forms of software forensics [9].

3.2 Material Implication Does not Represent Causation

The previous section focused on some of the practical limitations to the formal verification of accident models. There are also a number of theoretical problems [11]. For example, many people would interpret formula (4) as representing a causal relationship. Changes in our environmental model can be used to explain why an accident occurred. Unfortunately, material implication cannot easily be used to represent and reason about the causes of an adverse event. Several paradoxes, including circular arguments, can confuse the unwary. The impact of these paradoxes and other features of material implication should not be underestimated. For instance, we can introduce an arbitrary true antecedent to implications that may convince non-mathematicians of causal relationships even though there is no direct relevance with the antecedent. 'If NASA's Faster, Better Cheaper programme reduced funds for the Mars Surveyor projects then software failures led to the loss of the Polar Lander'.

A number of logicians, philosophers and linguists have recognised the limitations of strict implication and have responded by constructing alternative logics, which avoid the problems of classical logic, or by analysing the ways in which people construct implicational statements using material conditions. Grice [5] and Jackson [7] have exploited this latter approach. They argue that material implication remains a valid form of argument for *indicative* conditionals. In particular, Grice and Jackson observe that most people use arguments to communicate information in the most 'cost effective' means possible. They are anxious to avoid the costly repair actions that are necessary whenever misunderstandings occur. One consequence of this is that people will not assert weaker forms of a proposition when they can assert a strong form. In particular, speakers do not say 'If P, then Q' when they know that P is false. It is simpler and more informative to say 'not P'. Grice and Jackson's analysis is important because it can be used to avoid some of the problems that arise from material implication between two arbitrary false statements. Recall that material implication would allow a statement of the form 'If snow is black, then grass is red' to be true. Grice and Jackson argue that people do not reject such statements because they believe them to be 'false'. nstead, they argue that our reservations stem from the impression that such arguments would misleadingly suggest that we are unsure about the colour of snow.

Lewis [see Lewis and Langford, 13] goes beyond the material implication of classical logic to develop the notion of strict implication. This is based upon the idea that a proposition *strictly implies* all others, which are true, in all possible circumstances where it is true. The semantics for this form of strict implication is based around that of modal logics. Hence, we have that $A \text{->>} B$ is true at world w if and only if for all w' such that w' is accessible to w, either A fails in w' or B obtains there. However, the Lewis semantics for strict implication still permit an antecedent that is irrelevant to the consequent. Logicians have responded by developing what are known as relevance logics. One approach builds on a notion of 'relevant' proof [1]. This requires that premises and conclusion must share a variable in valid conditionals. This requirement can help to ensure that the antecedent and consequent refer to the same object in an assertion. Alternatively, the proof theory of relevance logics can require that conclusions can be directly derived from a premise without the introduction of arbitrary antecedents and consequents. This is intended to ensure that any premises really are used to obtain a valid conclusion.

Further problems also arise because the material implication of classical logic cannot convey different and varied interpretations of causal information. For example, mishap investigators often distinguish between necessary and sufficient causes. A necessary cause is often identified using counter-factual arguments of the form 'the mishap would not have occurred if this cause(s) had not also occurred'. A sufficient cause can be distinguished by arguments of the form 'the mishap could have occurred if this cause(s) had taken place irrespective of any other of the other circumstances surrounding the incident'. Similarly, many causal arguments are constructed using a form of subjunctive conditional that is not characterized by material implication. In particular, counterfactual conditionals rely upon an antecedent, which represents a past tense subjunctive sentence of the form "If X *had been the case* ...then Y would have happened. These sentences are known as counterfactuals because there is an assumption that the antecedent is false. In other words that X is known not to have been the case. For example, an investigator might assert that 'If he had been further away, then he would not have been hurt'. There is an implication that he was NOT further away and also that he was, in fact, hurt. Most incident investigation guidelines explicitly recommend that investigators use counterfactual arguments to guide their analysis [11]. The Lewis semantics for strict implication can be used to form counterfactual arguments. However, the interpretation of the accessibility relation between possible worlds still relies on the subjective judgment of domain experts. In other words, disagreements can arise over whether it is plausible that an accident would have been avoided if only a cause had been prevented.

The key meta-level issue here is that many of the logics that are used to support the formal analysis of complex systems have serious limitations if they are to model the causes of incidents and accidents. Instead, we have been forced to rely on modal logics and non-standard proof techniques. The identification of a tractable alternative to first order classical logic remains a topic of considerable debate amongst the small number of researchers in this area. It also remains the focus of several funding initiatives from the potential end-users of this technology.

3.3 Can We Model the System and the Environment?

The opening sections of this paper described how many academic software engineers use space mission failures to warn students about the hazards of programming. Many of these talks omit critical details. For example, they focus on the confusion between imperial and metric units in the Mars Climate Orbiter code. They overlook the ways in which software was used as a 'band aid' for the asymmetrical solar arrays. Similarly, I have attended research talks where software engineers construct elaborate counterfactual arguments of the form 'if only ESA/NASA/ISRO had followed software engineering technique X then the mishap would have been avoided'. Such counterfactuals are by their very nature non-truth functional. We have no accessible world in which the mishap did not occur so we can never really be sure that the software engineering technique X would have prevented the mission failure.

In contrast, I would urge software engineers to watch more natural history programmes on television. These programmes help to show how the animals' environment helps to shape behavior. By analogy, in order to understand the causes of software failure in space missions we need to look beyond the immediate causes of bugs to look at the organizational context that created them. It is extremely fashionable to talk about accidents as the result of 'emergent properties' or unanticipated outcomes from interaction between subsystems. I do not support this view. All of the failures mentioned in this report had precursors; the agencies either had experienced previous similar failures or their own employees and sub-contractors had described potential concerns through incident reporting systems.

It is also important to stress that analytical techniques can be applied to represent and reason about the environment in which bugs occur. For example, Figure 2 represents an Event and Causal Factor (ECF) analysis for the pre-launch phase of the Mars Polar Lander [10]. The US National Transportation Safety Board and the US Department of Energy pioneered ECF for use in accident investigation. Rectangles denote events while ellipses are used to represent those causal factors that make events more likely.

The 'Faster, Better, Cheaper' initiative placed the entire Surveyor programme under pressure to push the boundaries of cost and technology. This in turn led to a number of contextual factors that helped shape the programming effort. It was hard for contractors to meet the mission requirements with the available resources. As we have seen, opportunities for testing and validation were restricted as tight deadlines prevented access to hardware platforms and costs prevented many forms of destructive testing. Analysis and modeling were proposed as lower cost alternatives and so on. These influences led to the decision to use pulse mode control and a 4 by 3

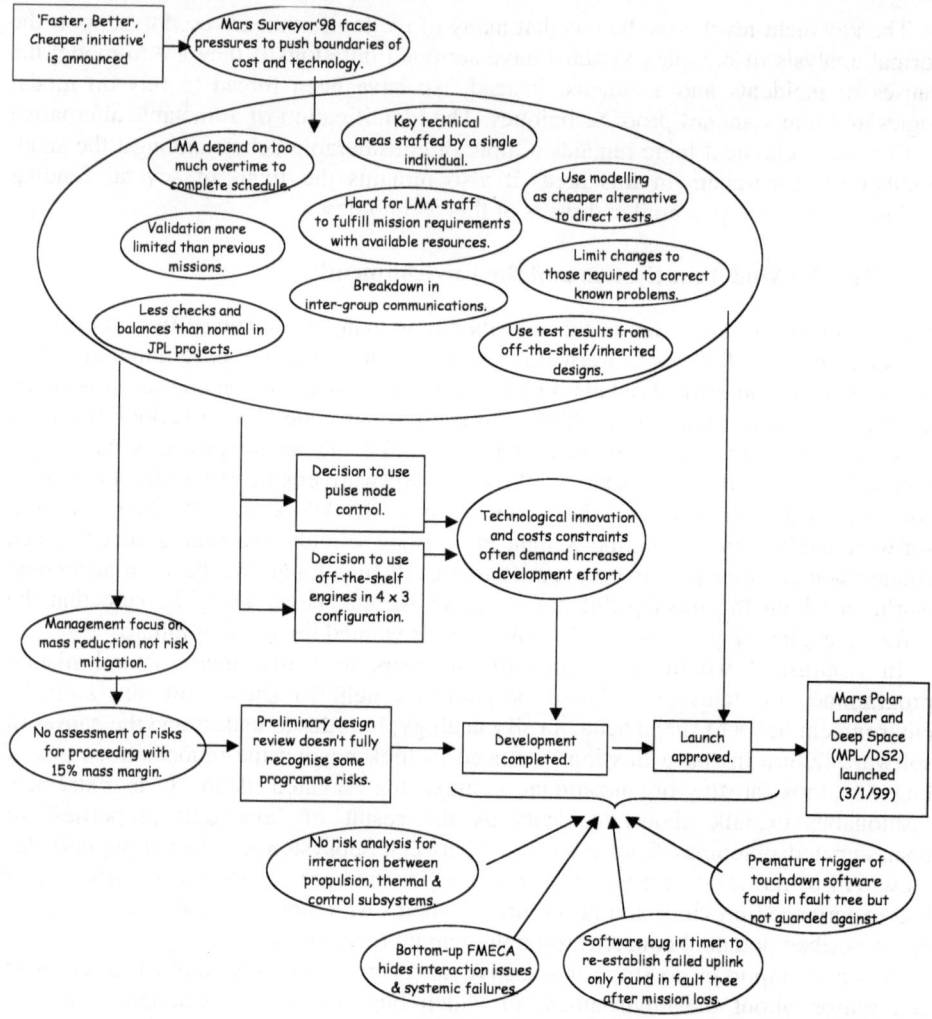

Fig. 2. Events and Causal Factor Overview of the Mars Polar Lander, Pre-Lauch [10]

array of off the shelf engines in preference to previous missions that had used a more gradual form of throttle control. The outcome of these decisions was to increase the complexity of software development to control the platform. At the same time, management focused on the problems of mass reduction so that the Polar Lander would meet the performance profile of the launch vehicle and cruise resources. This arguably took their attention away from the wider engineering risks created by cost reduction across the programme. The contextual factors at the bottom of Figure 2 show that fault tree analysis revealed the hazard from premature shutdown of the Lander engines, possibly triggered by a software bug. However, this risk was not adequately guarded against.

Figure 2 characterizes the growing pressures on investigators to look beyond the immediate or catalytic events that lead to mission failures. It has been argued by government organizations, by researchers and by a mass of other public bodies that accident and mishap analysis should instead look for root causes [10]. Unfortunately, software engineering has a tendency to focus on the immediate events that trigger particular failures. We remember the code re-use in Ariane 5 or the metric and imperial confusion with the Mars Climate Orbiter or even the uplink timer commands on the Polar Lander. Instead, we should look at the underlying causes. For instance, the Faster, Better Cheaper initiative arguably fostered a culture in which engineers took considerable risks to innovate with new design. These included the asymmetrical solar arrays on the Climate Orbiter and the pulse controlled engines on the Polar Lander. These innovative engineering decisions saved costs but relied on 'band aid' software. Programmers were forced to calculate the de-saturation parameters that would compensate for momentum induced by the innovative solar arrays. Programmers had to develop control software for the pulse times needed by the Polar Lander.

4 Conclusions and Further Work

The rise of 'systemic' approaches to accident investigation has clear implications for the use of formal methods in mishap analysis. One option is to follow the route taken by many others in the formal methods communities by looking for niche applications. Mathematical reasoning might be confined to the early stages of an investigation where it is important to understand precisely what happened. In this view, techniques such as model checking would provide simple extensions of their more conventional role in software engineering following the model outlined by Shen's use of the Murφ system. The challenges of this work should not be underestimated. In particular, we must find ways of using the results from theorem proving and model checking to inform the wider analytical techniques, such as ECF analysis, that will retain the primary role in identifying the managerial and organizational root causes of any mishap. This use of formal methods in forensic software engineering raises a host of further technical barriers. Space-related software continues to become more complex as it controls increased functionality and provides a vehicle for highly integrated systems, including satellite arrays.

An alternative future is one in which the scope of formal methods is expanded to reason about the root causes of software-related failures. Such a route follows the vision of Jackson and Zave where we begin to model many features of the environment that are not traditionally considered within formal areas of software engineering. Again this poses enormous technical challenges. A key question is what might be included within a formal model of a mishap. For interactive systems, such as the Shuttle's General Purpose Computing system, our model may be forced to consider cognitive, perceptual and physiological attributes of the crew. This, in turn, raises profound questions about the abstractions that might support such modeling. There has been work on formal aspects of human computer interaction but the results are limited and can often be disappointing when applied to applications such as the Shuttle or Rovers. Even if formal modeling were expanded in this way, it would still not capture the organizational and managerial issues that are increasingly being identified as the root causes of software failure. The use of epistemic and deontic notations to model such decision-making now forms part of the heritage of formal methods. Studies in the 1980s and 1990s showed how these techniques might be used, for instance to model legislative requirements. Again, however, the results do not seem to scale well and there are considerable problems in developing suitable proof theories. These problems are compounded when one remembers the host of problems in developing discrete mathematics to provide a satisfactory model of causal arguments.

To summarize, this paper has introduced some of the demands that are created by software development for space-related applications. These include the usual suspects that complicate all forms of software engineering. However, the physical properties of space environments create novel problems. For example, data and software updates must often be communicated over vast distances and this creates novel forms of batch processing. High-levels of radiation as well as mass and power limitations also create problems because they typically force programmers to rely on specialist hardware. Additional verification requirements and the limited sales of these processors often imply that they are obsolete in terms of mass-market applications long before they reach the launch pad. Later sections have also described the problems created by 'band aid' software. There is a growing tendency to rely on code to mitigate problems created by engineering decisions that are made elsewhere in the development of a space mission. One consequence of this is that software seems to be playing an increasingly prominent role in space-related mission failures.

The traditional role of formal methods can be expanded beyond design to analyze software failures. Existing models of software development, such as that proposed by Jackson and Zave, can easily be adapted to support this endeavor. Others have used a range of theorem proving and model-checking technology to represent and reason about space-related software failures [10, 22]. However, there are many technical and conceptual challenges that remain to be addressed. In particular, software bugs often form part of more complex problems that permeate through many different aspects of the engineering of space missions. The technical challenges also include basic issues with the representation of causal arguments given the limitations of classical material implication. The conceptual issues relate to the scope of the modeling activity. Do we focus narrowly on the behavior of a machine and its program? Or do we consider the managerial and organization precursors that are the root causes of software failure? Until these issues are resolved we remain even less equipped to identify the causes of software failure than we are to support the development of space related systems.

References

[1] A.R. Anderson and N.D. Belnap, Entailment: The Logic of Relevance and Necessity, Princeton, Princeton University Press, Volume I, 1975.
[2] J.Blum, Intelsat Loses Use of Satellite: Spacecraft Failure Could Jeopardize Sale of Company, Washington Post, Tuesday, January 18, 2005; Page E01.
[3] J. Crow and B. L. Di Vito. Formalizing space shuttle software requirements. In Proceedings of the ACM SIGSOFT Workshop on Formal Methods in Software Practice, pages 40-48, January 1996.

[4] L. Devauchelle, PICGAL: Process Improvement Experiment of a Code Generator to the ARIANE Launcher, ESSI Project 21 710, Final Report, Aerospatiale, November 1997. http://www.esi.es/VASIE/Reports/All/21710/Report/21710.pdf

[5] H.P. Grice, Studies in the Way of Words. Harvard University Press, Cambridge MA, 1989.

[6] R. Hillman, M. Conrad, P. Layton, C. Thibodeau, G.M. Swift and F. Irom, Space Processor Radiation Mitigation and Validation Techniques for an 1800 MIPS Processor Board, Maxwell Technologies and Jet Propulsion Laboratory, California Institute of Technology, 2003. http://parts.jpl.nasa.gov/docs/radecs03_swift.pdf

[7] F. Jackson, On Assertion and Indicative Conditionals. Philosophical Review, (88):565-589, 1979.

[8] M. Jackson and P. Zave, Deriving Specifications from Requirements: An Example, Proceedings of the 17th International Conference on Software Engineering, pages 15-24, ACM Press, 1995.

[9] C.W. Johnson, Forensic Software Engineering: Are Software Failures Symptomatic of Systemic Problems? Safety Science (40)9:835-847, 2002.

[10] C.W. Johnson, A Handbook of Accident and Incident Reporting, Glasgow University Press, Glasgow, 2003. http://www.dcs.gla.ac.uk/~johnson/book

[11] C.W. Johnson and C.M. Holloway, A Survey of Causation in Mishap Logics, eliability Engineering and Systems Safety, (80)3:271-291, 2003.

[12] P. Ladkin and K. Loer, Why-Because Analysis: Formal Reasoning About Incidents, RVS-Bk-98-01, Technischen Fakultät der Universität, Bielefeld, Germany, 1988.

[13] C.I. Lewis and C.H. Langford, Symbolic Logic, The Century Co. New York and ondon, 1932.

[14] J.L. Lyons. Report of the inquiry board into the failure of Flight 501 of the Ariane 5 rocket. Technical report, European Space Agency, Paris, France, July 1996.

[15] NASA, Expedition 10: Paving the Road for the Return to Flight, International Space Station, Science Operations, Oct. 2004. http://www.scipoc.msfc.nasa.gov/expedition10.html

[16] NASA. Mars Climate Orbiter: Mishap Investigation Board, Phase I Report. Technical report, Mars Climate Orbiter, Mishap Investigation Board, NASA Headquarters, Washington DC, USA, 1999. ftp://ftp.hq.nasa.gov/pub/pao/reports/1999/MCO_report.pdf.

[17] NASA, Formal Methods Specification and Verification Guidebook for Software and Computer Systems, Report NASA-GB-002-95, NASA Office of Safety and Mission Assurance, Washington DC, 1995. http://eis.jpl.nasa.gov/quality/Formal_Methods

[18] NASA/ESA, SOHO Mission Interruption Joint NASA/ESA Investigation Board Final Report, 1998. http://umbra.nascom.nasa.gov/soho/SOHO_final_report.html

[19] NASA/JPL. Report on the loss of the Mars Polar Lander and Deep Space 2 Missions (The 'Casani' Report). JPL D-18709, NASA/Jet Propulsion Laboratory, 2000.

[20] NASA/JPL, Sol 243-262: Spirit Back to Normal Operations, Mars Exploration Rover Mission, NASA/Jet Propulsion Laboratory, California Institute of Technology, 29 September 2004, http://marsrover.nasa.gov/mission/status_spiritAll.html#sol243

[21] NASA/JSC EVA Project Office, EVA Equipment Board (EEB) Minutes of Meeting September 19, 2001, http://www.spaceref.ca/news/viewsr.html?pid=3821

[22] Z. Shen, Model Checking for the MPL Entry and Descent Sequence, Technical Report, Department of Aerospace Engineering, Iowa State University, December 2001, http://www.public.iastate.edu/~zjshen/ProjectReport.pdf

Modular Verification of Static Class Invariants

K. Rustan M. Leino[1] and Peter Müller[2]

[1] Microsoft Research, Redmond, WA, USA
leino@microsoft.com
[2] ETH Zürich, Switzerland
peter.mueller@inf.ethz.ch

Abstract. Object invariants describe the consistency of object-oriented data structures and are central to reasoning about the correctness of object-oriented software. But object invariants are not the only consistency conditions on which a program may depend. The data in object-oriented programs consists not just of object fields, but also of static fields, which hold data that is shared among objects. The consistency of static fields is described by *static class invariants*, which are enforced at the class level. Static class invariants can also mention instance fields, describing the consistency of dynamic data structures rooted in static fields. Sometimes there are even consistency conditions that relate the instance fields of many or all objects of a class; static class invariants describe these relations, too, since they cannot be enforced by any one object in isolation.

This paper presents a systematic way (a *methodology*) for specifying and verifying static class invariants in object-oriented programs. The methodology supports the three major uses of static fields and invariants in the Java library. The methodology is amenable to static, modular verification and is sound.

Keywords: Static class invariant, verification, object-oriented programming, static field.

1 Introduction

A central problem in reasoning about a computer program's correctness comes down to reasoning about which program states the program can ever reach. Programmers rely on that only some states are reached, most prominently by assuming that the program's data structures satisfy certain properties. These properties are called *invariants*. By declaring invariants explicitly, the programmer can get support from tools (like the tools for JML [4] or Spec# [2]) that make sure the program maintains the invariants. In this paper, we present a systematic way (a *methodology*) for specifying and reasoning about invariants in object-oriented programs. In particular, we consider invariants that are described and enforced at the level of each class, called *static class invariants*.

The main data structures in modern object-oriented programs are stored as the state of individual objects, in variables known as *instance fields*, and as the state of classes, in variables known as *static fields*. We have identified three major uses of static fields and invariants in the standard Java libraries (Java 2 Standard Edition version 5.0). First and foremost, static fields are used to store shared values. For example, the well-known static field *System.out* in Java provides an output stream whose characters flow to the

J.S. Fitzgerald, I.J. Hayes, and A. Tarlecki (Eds.): FM 2005, LNCS 3582, pp. 26–42, 2005.

console. Second, static fields are used to hold the roots of object data structures. For example, the implementation of the *String* class in Java has a shared pool of interned strings, storing canonical string references for certain character sequences. Third, static fields are occasionally used to reflect something about all instances of a class. For example, Java's *Thread* class assigns unique identifiers to its instances and uses a static field to keep track of which identifiers are in use. In all of these three cases, implicit or informally documented static class invariants describe the intended consistency conditions. The methodology we present in this paper enables the explicit specification and formal verification of these invariants.

Previous work on specifying and verifying invariants in object-oriented programs have developed methodologies for *object invariants*, which describe the consistent state of individual objects and aggregate objects, formations of individual objects into one logic unit [16, 1, 10, 3]. However, these methodologies do not apply to static class invariants, because the classes of a program build on each other in a way that is different from the principal way in which objects in an aggregate build on each other: whereas an object has a unique point of use in an aggregate, a class is used by many other classes.

Our basic methodology draws from the Boogie methodology for object invariants [1, 10, 3], but innovates in significant ways to handle static class invariants. First, to address the abstraction problem that arises when a class is used by several other classes, our methodology performs different bookkeeping for invariants, tailored to work with any partial order among classes. Second, our methodology introduces such a partial order on classes. This order makes it possible for a method override to rely on the static class invariant of the subclass even when the method specification in a superclass is not able to name the subclass. The order also prescribes how to initialize classes, which provides a way to avoid unexpected class initialization errors. Third, our methodology adds the ability for an invariant to quantify over objects (for example, specifying that no two linked-list nodes have the same successor), which involves a syntactic restriction on programs. We present our methodology for a programming language similar to the sequential subset of Java or C#. The only major semantic difference is how class initialization is performed, as explained later.

To support programming in the large, a crucial aspect of any specification and verification methodology is that it be *modular*. That is, it should be possible to reason about smaller portions of a program at a time, say a class and its imported classes, without having access to all pieces of code in the program that use the class or extend the class. Our methodology is modular.

To save space, we combine the three kinds of static class invariants into one running example, the *Service* and *Client* classes in Figs. 1 and 2. Objects of class *Service* represent instances of a system service. These instances share a common job cache, which is referenced from the static field *jobs*. The first class invariant in *Service* says that *jobs* is non-null, and the second says that the non-null elements of the cache are distinct. Objects of class *Client* represent users of the service. Each client has an ID and the static field *ids* keeps track of the number of IDs ever given out. The first class invariant says that *ids* is a natural number, the second says that *ids* exceeds all client IDs, and the third says that clients have unique IDs. Here and throughout, quantifications over objects range over allocated, non-null objects. The quantifications in the class invariants

```
class Service imports Client {
  static rep Client[ ] jobs ;
  static invariant Service.jobs ≠ null ;  // simple
  static invariant (∀int i,j  |  0 ≤ i < j < Service.jobs.length •
        Service.jobs[i] ≠ null ⇒ Service.jobs[i] ≠ Service.jobs[j] ) ;  // ownership
  static initializer {Service.jobs := new ⟨Service⟩Client[10] ;}
  static void cache(Client c)
    requires Service.sinv = tvalid ∧ c ≠ null ;
  {
    if (c ∉ Service.jobs) {
      int free := arbitrary value in { 0, . . . , Service.jobs.length − 1 } ;
      expose Service {
        expose Service.jobs for Client[ ] ;  Service.jobs[free] := c ;
        unexpose Service.jobs for Client[ ] ;
} } } }
```

Fig. 1. *Service* has a static field *jobs*, which references an array of *Client* objects. The class invariants guarantee that *jobs* is not **null** and that each *Client* object is stored at most once in the *jobs* array. Both invariants are established by the static initializer. The **rep** keyword in the declaration of *jobs* indicates an ownership relation between the *Service* class and the array referenced by *jobs*

in *Client* are also restricted to *valid Client* objects, indicated by $c.inv_{Client} = valid$ and explained later. Note that the third invariant in *Client* does not mention any static fields, but we nevertheless consider it a class invariant since individual objects cannot maintain this invariant. No previous methodology can handle these kinds of invariants in an object-oriented setting where the dynamic call order does not follow any statically determined order on the classes, but our methodology handles all of them.

In Sec. 2, we present our methodology for *simple class invariants*, which talk about the static fields of a class, handling the shared-values use of static fields. In Sec. 3, we extend this methodology to *ownership-based class invariants*, handling the roots-of-object-structures use of static fields. In Sec. 4, we further extend the methodology to *global class invariants*, which quantify over all valid objects of the class, handling the all-instances use of static fields and invariants. We formalize the methodology and state a soundness theorem in Sec. 5. We end the paper with related work and a conclusion.

2   Methodology

In this section, we introduce our methodology for class invariants, explain how we overcome the central problem of abstraction and information hiding, and prescribe class initialization. We focus on the general ideas, tightening up the details in Section 5.

As illustrated by the examples in Figs. 1 and 2, class invariants are declared by clauses of the form **static invariant** P; where P is a predicate that can mention fields. A class C can contain several invariant clauses. *The class invariant of C*, denoted by $ClassInv_C$, refers to the conjunction of all invariant clauses declared in C. In

```
class Client imports String {
   int id ;        static int ids ;
   static invariant 0 ≤ Client.ids ;  // simple
   static invariant ( ∀ Client c |  c.inv_Client = valid •  c.id < Client.ids ) ;  // global
   static invariant ( ∀ Client c |  c.inv_Client = valid •
            ( ∀ Client d |  d.inv_Client = valid •  c ≠ d  ⇒  c.id ≠ d.id )) ;  // global
   static initializer { Client.ids := 0 ; }
   Client()
      requires Client.sinv = tvalid ;
      ensures this.inv_Client = valid ;
   {
      expose Client {
         id := Client.ids ;    Client.ids := Client.ids + 1 ;
         unexpose this for Client ;
      }
   }
   static String debugMsg()
      requires Client.sinv = tvalid ;
   { result := "Client objects created : ".appendNat(Client.ids) ; }
}
```

Fig. 2. Every object of class *Client* has an ID. The next available ID is stored in the static field *ids*. Class invariants guarantee that *ids* has not been assigned to a *Client* object and that all *Client* objects have different IDs

this section, we focus on simple class invariants, that is, invariants where the only fields mentioned in P are static fields of C.

2.1   Basic Methodology

Two fundamental issues drive the design of a methodology for class invariants. First, in general, class invariants relate the values of several fields. Therefore, it is not possible to expect class invariants to hold at every program point; we must allow class invariants to be temporarily violated.

Second, it is not possible to completely free clients of the responsibility of making sure the class invariant holds when a method of the class is called. This is because of the possibility of reentrancy: a method m declared in class C can call methods that cause control to reenter C. A problem would occur if m makes such a call at a time C's invariant is temporarily violated and the method through which C is reentered expects the invariant to hold. It would be overly restrictive to forbid method calls while an invariant is temporarily violated. For example, one may want to invoke a method on the data structure rooted in a static field.

To deal with these two fundamental issues, the methodology must permit times when the class invariant becomes violated. For this reason, we introduce a special program statement, **expose** C { s }, which allows the invariant of class C to be violated for the duration of the sub-statement s, throughout which time we say that C is *mutable*. Any update of any static field $C.g$ must take place while C is mutable (but there are no restrictions on when variables can be read). The class invariant is checked to hold at the end of the **expose** block. We define **expose** blocks to be non-reentrant; that is, it is illegal to expose an already mutable class. (Non-reentrancy and condition J2, below, are what guarantee that the class invariant holds on entry to sub-statement s.)

When reasoning modularly about a program, it is important to know whether or not a class is mutable. For example, *Client*'s constructor in Fig. 2 needs to declare a precondition that says class *Client* is *valid*, that is, not mutable; otherwise, it would not be possible to prove that the program meets the non-reentrancy requirement of the **expose** block in the constructor's implementation. To facilitate mentioning the validity status of a class, we introduce for each class C a special static field $C.sinv$ (whose possible values we will describe later), which can be mentioned in method specifications. $C.sinv$ is an abstraction of the static class invariant in C: a specification can mention $C.sinv$ to require C to be valid, which in effect says that C's invariant holds but does not reveal the details of the invariant itself.

A program cannot update the static field $C.sinv$ directly. Instead, the value of $C.sinv$ is changed automatically on entry and exit of each **expose** statement. We postpone until Section 2.4 the issue of setting the initial value of $C.sinv$.

It is important to understand that our methodology does not use a *visible state semantics*, where methods can automatically assume all class invariants to hold in the pre-state. Instead, a method is allowed to rely only on those invariants whose validity follows from the explicit precondition. Conversely, one does not have to prove that all class invariants hold when the method terminates. Instead, we prove that (1) the only static fields that are assigned to are those of mutable classes, and (2) the class invariant of a class C holds at the end of each **expose** C statement.

2.2   Abstraction and Information Hiding

The special static field *sinv* makes it possible for a program to record, usually in preconditions of methods, when a class invariant is expected to hold. However, whenever one class uses another, it would be clumsy, at best, to have to mention explicitly in a precondition all classes whose validity is needed. For example, suppose the *String* class contains a global cache of integers and their *String* representations. Then, many methods of *String*, including *appendNat* which is called by *debugMsg* (Fig. 2), would have a precondition that requires the *String* class to be valid. Method *debugMsg*, in turn, would then need to declare the precondition that both *Client* and *String* are valid. And so on, for the methods of other classes that may transitively call *debugMsg*. As this example suggests, preconditions would become unwieldy. Moreover, if one class deep in a program one day is changed to call a method of *String*, then all transitive callers would have to be changed to add *String* validity as a precondition. Such a programming methodology would not respect good principles of information hiding.

To address this problem, we derive from the class declarations of a program a partial order on classes, the so-called *validity ordering*, and provide the ability, using the special static field *sinv*, to express the transitive validity of a class. A class C is *transitively valid* (or *t-valid* for short) if the invariant of C holds and all classes that precede C in the validity order are t-valid.

The most common edge in the validity ordering arises when one class is a client of another class. We require that if a class C refers to a class D or to an entity declared in

D, then either D is a superclass of C or C is declared explicitly to *import* D. (Note that in the latter case, the import declaration is mandatory, in contrast to Java's "import" construct, which is just a convenient alternative to writing fully qualified names.) If C imports D, then this import also gives rise to the edge $D \leftarrow C$ ("*D precedes* C") in the validity ordering. For instance, class *Client* imports *String*, which, in particular, allows *debugMsg* to call a method of *String*. The case where D is a superclass of C is handled conversely as explained below.

It is now time we introduce actual values for the *sinv* field:

- $C.sinv = tvalid$ says that C is transitively valid, that is, that the invariant of C holds and that all classes that precede C in the validity order are t-valid.
- $C.sinv = valid$ says that the invariant of C holds, but says nothing about the validity of C's predecessors.
- $C.sinv = mutable$ says that C's invariant may be violated and that the program is allowed to execute statements that assign to the static fields of C.

As suggested by these bullets, and as we later shall justify, our methodology guarantees that the following properties are *program invariants*, that is, that they hold at every control point in a program (here and throughout, quantifications over class names range over all classes of a program):

J1: $(\forall C, D \bullet D \leftarrow C \wedge C.sinv = tvalid \Rightarrow D.sinv = tvalid)$

J2: $(\forall C \bullet C.sinv = tvalid \vee C.sinv = valid \Rightarrow ClassInv_C)$

We can now spell out the preconditions of the methods involved in the Fig. 2 example. Since *Client* imports *String*, *String* precedes *Client* in the validity ordering. Assume the following declaration in class *String*:

String appendNat(**int** n)
  requires $0 \le n \wedge String.sinv = tvalid$;

Method *debugMsg* needs the precondition *Client.sinv* = *tvalid*, since it not only needs *Client*'s invariant in order to establish that the parameter passed to *appendNat* is non-negative, but also needs the t-validity of *String* in order to meet the precondition of *appendNat*. *Client*'s constructor can require *Client.sinv* = *tvalid*, *Client.sinv* = *valid*, or *Client.sinv* = *tvalid* $\vee$ *Client.sinv* = *valid*, since the implementation of the constructor does not depend on the validity of other classes. However, *Client.sinv* = *tvalid* is generally to be preferred, because that specification is general enough to allow the implementation to be changed to rely on the validity of other classes.

2.3   Subclasses

Since validity-ordering edges are introduced along with the imports relation, a declared class becomes a successor of all classes it imports. In this subsection, we show that subclassing has to be treated differently from other uses-relations between classes.

To illustrate with an example, consider a hierarchy of classes representing decision procedures for various theories, as may be used in the implementation of an automatic theorem prover. Each theory implements a method *assertLiteral* that adds a constraint to the decision procedure. Fig. 3 declares class *Theory*, the root of the hierarchy.

```
class Theory { void assertLiteral(Literal l) { ... } ... }
class LATheory extends Theory imports String {
  static String version ;
  static invariant LATheory.version ≠ null ;
  static initializer {LATheory.version := "Version ".appendNat(3) ;}
  override void assertLiteral(Literal l) { ... }
  ... }
```

Fig. 3. An example to illustrate the specification problem of a method override that relies on a static class invariant

Now, consider a particular theory, say the theory of linear arithmetic, represented by a subclass *LATheory*, see Fig. 3. Being a method override, *LATheory.assertLiteral* has the same specification as the overridden *Theory.assertLiteral*, and in particular, the override cannot strengthen the precondition of the overridden method.

Suppose the *LATheory* implementation of *assertLiteral* makes use of some static fields of *LATheory* and relies on the class invariant to hold of these static fields. This means that *LATheory.assertLiteral* relies on the t-validity of *LATheory*. Since this method override cannot strengthen the precondition for *assertLiteral* defined in *Theory*, the precondition of *Theory.assertLiteral* must imply that *LATheory* is t-valid. But how can such a precondition be declared in class *Theory* without explicitly mentioning *LATheory* (since *Theory* may not know about the existence of *LATheory*, which may be authored long after the authoring of *Theory*)?

If *LATheory* precedes *Theory* in the validity ordering, then we can solve the specification problem on account of program invariant J1. The method in class *Theory* then declares the precondition

> **requires** $Theory.sinv = tvalid$;

which by J1 implies $LATheory.sinv = tvalid$, as needed in the method override. In other words, a caller of method *assertLiteral*, which may not even know about the existence of *LATheory* but may nevertheless hold a reference to an object of allocated type *LATheory*, must establish the t-validity of *Theory* at the time of call, which allows the implementation of *LATheory* to determine that *LATheory* is t-valid, too.

To allow class *LATheory* to define the edge $LATheory \leftarrow Theory$ in the validity ordering, we use the *extends* relation that is already used to declare subclasses. That is, as part of our methodology, a subclass precedes its superclasses in the validity ordering. A class can extend one superclass (single inheritance) and import any number of other classes. However, we require that the resulting validity ordering is acyclic.

An acyclic validity ordering prevents mutually dependent classes (except when one class is a subclass of the other). Cyclic references between classes can be allowed by grouping classes into *modules* and declaring the validity ordering on modules instead of classes. Then, the classes in one module can mutually depend on each other. We explain and formalize this approach in our technical report [9].

2.4   Class Initialization

A static class invariant is first established by the static initializer of the class, a designated block of code that is invoked exactly once. Static initializers are invoked by the runtime system, so as to orchestrate the initialization of multiple classes. For brevity, we do not consider dynamic class loading here, but our methodology can handle it [9].

Since the static initializer of a class C may access fields and methods of imported classes, it requires C's predecessors in the validity ordering to be valid. This is achieved by initializing classes in the order of the validity ordering.

A program is executed by invoking the static method $main$ on a specified class, say M. Before $main$ is actually called, the runtime system loads M and all classes that M transitively imports or extends. The static fields of all classes are initialized to zero-equivalent values, in particular, $sinv$ is initialized to $mutable$. Next, the runtime system executes the static initializer of each class, according to the validity ordering. After executing the static initializer of a class C, $C.sinv$ is set to $tvalid$.

C's static initializer can, therefore, assume on entry that (1) C is mutable, which allows the initializer to assign to C's static fields, and (2) all predecessors of C are t-valid. That is, C's static initializer may assume that the following precondition holds:

$$C.sinv = mutable \land (\forall D \bullet D \leftarrow C \Rightarrow D.sinv = tvalid)$$

The initializer is responsible for making sure the implicit assertion **assert** $ClassInv_C$ holds on exit. For example, consider class $LATheory$ in Fig. 3. Because $String$ precedes $LATheory$, the second conjunct of the precondition implies $String.sinv = tvalid$; therefore, the initializer can meet the precondition of $appendNat$. Because of the first conjunct of the precondition, the assignment to $LATheory.version$ is permitted. Provided $appendNat$ returns a non-null value, the implicit assertion at the end of the initializer body will hold.

Note, by the way, that the $LATheory$ initializer cannot assume $Theory$ to be t-valid, since $Theory$ does not precede $LATheory$. This is different from the initialization order in Java, where superclasses are initialized before their subclasses. Most correct programs that require that superclass invariants are established before subclasses are initialized can be modeled or rewritten to follow Java's initialization ordering. The key idea is to separate out static fields and invariants of the superclass into a helper class, which is imported by both the superclass and the subclasses.

2.5 Summary

We summarize the steps that lead us to our methodology: Class invariants can state relations between multiple static fields, and thus the methodology must permit class invariants to be temporarily violated. To allow calls while a class invariant is violated and since such calls may reenter the class, we explicitly represent (by $sinv$) whether or not a class invariant might be violated, which allows preconditions to be explicit about which invariants are assumed to hold. The explicit representation reveals the central problem of abstraction, which we address by allowing classes to be ordered (by the validity ordering) and by representing transitive validity of classes along that ordering. Finally, the validity ordering has an impact on class initialization.

The methodology allows programmers to specify invariants on the state of each class. The programmer is assured that the invariant of a class C holds whenever $C.sinv$ is $valid$ or $tvalid$. Thus, by requiring that, for example, $C.sinv = tvalid$ holds on entry to a method, the implementation of the method can safely rely on C's class invariant to hold on entry. Dependencies between classes are indicated by edges in the validity ordering, which coupled with our initialization order avoids class initialization errors.

3   Ownership-Based Class Invariants

Simple class invariants refer only to static fields of the enclosing class, but not to instance fields. Preventing class invariants from depending on instance fields is too restrictive for many interesting programs. For instance, class *Service* (Fig. 1) uses a global cache, which is implemented by an array and rooted in the static field *jobs*. *Service* imposes restrictions on the elements stored in this array object.

Assume that the class invariant of a class C refers to the instance field f of an object X. The reason the methodology introduced so far cannot handle such class invariants is that a method m outside C that gets hold of a reference to X can update $X.f$, thereby potentially violating C's invariant. Since the invariant might not be known to m, it is not possible to determine modularly that this update has to be guarded by an assertion that C is mutable. In our example, any method that has a reference to the *Service.jobs* array can break the *Service* invariant by assigning to elements of the array.

In this section, we extend our methodology by the notion of *ownership*. This extension allows the invariant of a class C to depend on fields of objects *owned* by C without restricting where these fields are declared. The extended methodology ensures that a field of an object can be updated only if the object's owning class is mutable.

3.1   Ownership

Ownership organizes objects into a hierarchy of *contexts*, where the objects in each context have a common owner (see, *e.g.*, [5, 16]). In this paper, we use a restricted form of ownership where objects can be owned by a class, but not by other objects. This restriction allows us to focus on the methodology for class invariants without getting into details of the corresponding methodology for object invariants. An extension to ownership among objects is presented in our report [9]. We do not restrict references; classes and objects may have non-owning references to objects.

Following the encoding in our work on object invariants [10], we represent ownership by a special field *owner* for every object. The value of *owner* is a class name. It is set when an object is created. The allocation statement $x := \textbf{new} \langle C \rangle T$ creates a new object of class T owned by class C. In this paper, we assume *owner* to be immutable after object creation. We described how to handle a mutable *owner* field for objects (ownership transfer) in a previous paper [10].

We allow the *owner* field to be mentioned in class invariants. To specify ownership relations, we introduce a modifier **rep** that can be used in the declaration of any static field. A field declaration **static rep** S g; in a class C gives rise to the following implicit class invariant about ownership in C:

$$C.g \neq \textbf{null} \Rightarrow C.g.owner = C \; ;$$

The invariant of a class C is allowed to refer to fields of objects owned by C. In our example, the **rep** modifier of the static field *Service.jobs* indicates that the object referenced by *Service.jobs* is owned by *Service*, which allows the class invariant of

Service to refer to the fields (that is, array elements) of *jobs*. Accessing array elements is handled analogously to field access, as if each element were a field.

3.2 Mutability of Owned Objects

Analogously to the static field *sinv* and following our methodology for objects, each object type (class or array type) C declares a two-valued field inv_C that indicates whether the object invariant declared in C may be assumed to hold. If $X.inv_C = valid$, we say that object X *is valid for* C, or just X *is valid* if the object type is clear from the context. Conversely, we say X *is mutable for* C if $X.inv_C = mutable$. An instance field f declared in C can be assigned to only if the instance is mutable for C. That is, an update $X.f := E$ is guarded by the precondition $X.inv_C = mutable$.

Consider a class C that owns an object X. C's invariant is allowed to depend on $X.f$ even if f is declared in another class. Consequently, an update of $X.f$ may potentially violate C's invariant. Our methodology handles this situation by the following rule: If a class C is valid, then all objects owned by C are valid for their object type and all supertypes. That is, if X is mutable for D so that $X.f$ can be assigned to (where f is declared in class D), then X's owner, C, is also mutable, so violations of C's static class invariant are allowed.

This rule is enforced by manipulating the inv_D field according to a strict protocol: inv_D can be manipulated only by statements analogous in functionality to **expose** for classes. However, although exposing and unexposing objects typically is done in a block-structured way, it does not have to be. In particular, some constructors, like *Client*'s constructor in Fig. 2, unexpose the newly created object without previously exposing it. Therefore, instead of an **expose** block statement for objects, we use two separate statements, **expose** X **for** D and **unexpose** X **for** D, which expose and unexpose an object X for a class D, respectively. When applied to a valid object X and for a class D, **expose** X **for** D checks that X's owner is mutable and sets $X.inv_D$ to *mutable*. **unexpose** X **for** D checks that X is mutable and sets $X.inv_D$ to *valid*. When an object of class C is created, its inv_D fields start off as *mutable* for all superclasses D of C.

The *cache* method of class *Service* in Fig. 1 illustrates how ownership-based invariants are handled. It requires *Service* to be t-valid. To satisfy the precondition $Service.jobs.inv_{Client[\,]} = mutable$ of the update $Service.jobs[free] := c$, *Service* has to be mutable. The **expose** statement sets $Service.sinv$ to *mutable*, which makes the *jobs* array exposable and allows updates to temporarily violate *Service*'s class invariant. In our example, the invariant is not actually violated by the update, because we insert c only if it is not already contained in the array.

Because of lack of space and to focus on static class invariants, we do not present in this paper the complete object-centered methodology that allows a program to ensure its field updates apply only to mutable objects, but see [1, 10].

4 Global Class Invariants

In this section, we explain how our methodology allows class invariants to quantify over all valid objects of the enclosing class.

4.1 Quantification over Valid Objects

A class invariant of a class C is allowed to universally quantify over all C objects that are valid for C and to refer to those instance fields of these objects that are declared in C. For example, *Client*'s third invariant (Fig. 2) quantifies over valid *Client* objects and refers to the *id* field declared in *Client*. We only let a class invariant quantify over valid objects, because during the time when an object is being updated, which occurs when the object is mutable, the object cannot be expected to satisfy all invariants.

A global class invariant of a class C is potentially violated by unexposing C objects for C, since making a C object valid for C enlarges the range of the quantification in the invariant. Therefore, additional requirements for **unexpose** are needed to guarantee that a class C is mutable whenever one of its objects is unexposed for C. Note that updates of instance fields do not require additional proof obligations for global class invariants, because only fields of mutable objects can be updated.

For soundness, it is sufficient to guard the statement **unexpose** X **for** C by a precondition $C.sinv = mutable$. However, stronger requirements are necessary to achieve a practical solution, as we discuss next.

4.2 Practicality

Assume that class *Client* has a method *Client Foo*() and that we want to verify the statement **expose** *Client* { $v := X.Foo()$; }, where X is a valid *Client* object. To prove that *Client*'s class invariant holds at the end of the **expose** block, we have to show in particular that the call to *Foo* does not create new valid *Client* objects that violate the global class invariants. For instance, the following implementation of *Foo* does violate *Client*'s third invariant:

```
Client Foo()
    requires Client.sinv = mutable ∧ this.inv_Client = valid ;
{
    result := new ⟨Object⟩ Client() ;  result.id := this.id ;
    unexpose result for Client ;
}
```

Since allocation and initialization of objects is typically considered an implementation detail [8, 11], *Foo*'s specification will in general be too weak to determine whether *Foo* creates valid objects, which makes it impossible to verify the **expose** block above.

To be able to reason about the effects of a method call on a global class invariant, we impose a syntactic requirement that prevents methods and constructors from unexposing objects for C, if called in a state in which class C is mutable: each **unexpose** X **for** C operation has to be textually enclosed by C's static initializer or by an **expose** C block. This syntactic requirement guarantees that $C.sinv = mutable$ holds before making an object valid for C. That is, we do not have to impose this condition as a precondition for unexposing C objects explicitly.

This syntactic requirement prevents a method called from within an **expose** C block from unexposing objects for C, in particular, newly created objects. This property gives rise to an implicit postcondition that allows one to verify the **expose** C block. In our example above, *Foo* does not meet the requirement because it unexposes **result** outside an **expose** *Client* block.

5   Technical Treatment

In this section, we define precisely which invariants are admissible, explain the proof obligations that are necessary to maintain the program invariants J1 and J2 (Sec. 2.2), and present a soundness theorem.

5.1   Admissible Invariants

A class invariant of class C can refer to static fields of C, instance fields of objects owned by C, and, by quantification, instance fields of valid C objects:

Definition 1 (Admissible class invariant). *A class invariant declaration in class C is admissible if its subexpressions typecheck according to the rules of the programming language and if each of its field-access expressions has one of the following forms:*

1. *$C.g$.*
2. *$C.g.f$ where $C.g$ is declared **rep**.*
3. *$o.f$ where f is declared in C and o is bound by a quantification of the form $(\forall C\ o \mid o.inv_C = valid \bullet\ \ldots o.f \ldots)$*

The static field g must not be the predefined field sinv, and the instance field f must be different from all inv_T fields.

Simple class invariants contain only access expressions of Case 1. Access expressions of Case 2 allow ownership-based class invariants to depend on fields of objects owned by C. Invariants that contain access expressions of Case 3 are global.

5.2   Proof Rules

The methodology presented in this paper does not assume a particular programming logic to reason about programs and specifications. Special rules are required only for class initialization and those statements that deal with the $sinv$ and inv_T fields (static and instance field update, class **expose**, and object **expose** and **unexpose**) as well as *owner* (object creation). In this subsection, we present these rules and explain why they are necessary to maintain the program invariants J1 and J2 presented in Sec. 2.2.

The proof rules are formulated in terms of assertions, which cause the program execution to abort if evaluated to **false**. Proving the correctness of a program therefore amounts to statically verifying that the program does not abort due to a violated assertion. To do that, each assertion is turned into a proof obligation. One can then use an appropriate program logic to show that the assertions hold (*cf.* [18, 7]). All of the proof obligations can be generated and shown modularly. For the proof, one may assume that the program invariants J1 and J2 hold.

Class Loading and Initialization. The program invariants J1 and J2 are first established during class loading and initialization. Program execution starts with a class loading phase, followed by a class initialization phase. In the loading phase, each class of the program is loaded and its static fields are set to zero-equivalent values. The zero-equivalent value for $sinv$ is *mutable*. This guarantees that all classes are mutable after the loading phase, which implies that both J1 and J2 hold.

In the following initialization phase, classes are initialized according to the validity ordering, that is, a class C is initialized after its predecessors in the validity ordering. For each class C, C's static initializer is called before setting $C.sinv$ to $tvalid$. Since $C.sinv$ is set to $mutable$ by the loading phase and since C's predecessors in the validity ordering are initialized before C, the precondition of C's static initializer is established (see Sec. 2.4). In particular, all predecessors of C are t-valid. The postcondition of this initializer, $ClassInv_C$, guarantees that J2 is preserved when $C.sinv$ is set to $tvalid$. Since C's predecessors are tvalid, J1 is preserved as well. Consequently, both J1 and J2 hold after the initialization phase.

The static initializer of a class D can create valid objects only for D's predecessors in the validity ordering. Consider a class C that is *not* a predecessor of D. D's static initializer cannot expose C since C is mutable, that is, the precondition of **expose** C is not satisfied. Therefore, it cannot unexpose an object for C since the **unexpose** X **for** C statements can occur only within **expose** C blocks and C's static initializer. Consequently C's static initializer may assume the precondition $(\forall C\ X \bullet\ X.inv_C = mutable\ )$, which is important to prove that it establishes C's global class invariants.

Static Field Update. Updating a static field cannot affect program invariant J1. For J2, we have to ensure that a static field update does not break the invariant of a valid or t-valid class C. The only static fields C's class invariant can refer to are static fields of C (Def. 1). Consequently, we can maintain J2 by requiring C to be mutable, which is enforced by guarding each static field update of the form $C.f := E$ by the check **assert** $C.sinv = mutable$.

Instance Field Update. Program invariant J1 is trivially preserved. An update $X.f := E$ potentially breaks the class invariant of a class C if (1) X is owned by C (ownership-based invariants) or (2) f is declared in C and X is valid for C (global invariants). The check **assert** $X.inv_C = mutable$ guarantees that (1) X's owner class is mutable (see proof rule for **expose**) and (2) X is not valid for C.

Class Expose. As explained in Sec. 2.1, **expose** C { s } essentially sets $C.sinv$ to $mutable$, executes s, and restores the original value of $C.sinv$. To prevent reentrant **expose** blocks, an assertion checks that C is not already mutable before the statement. Program invariant J2 is maintained by asserting that C's class invariant holds before $C.sinv$ is restored.

Maintaining J1 is a bit more involved. Changing $C.sinv$ from $tvalid$ to $mutable$ implies that C's t-valid successors in the validity ordering are no longer t-valid, but just valid. Therefore, for each class D that transitively succeeds C (that is, $C \leftarrow D$), if $D.sinv = tvalid$, then the **expose** statement temporarily changes $D.sinv$ to $valid$. At the end of the **expose** block, the initial values of the $D.sinv$'s are restored. This results in the following pseudo code for **expose**:

```
expose C { s } ≡
    assert C.sinv ≠ mutable ;
    let Q = { D | C ← D ∧ D.sinv = tvalid } ;
    foreach D ∈ Q { D.sinv := valid ; }
```

$C.sinv := mutable$;

s ;

assert $ClassInv_C$;

foreach $D \in \{C\} \cup Q$ { $D.sinv := \mathbf{old}(D.sinv)$; }

Object Expose. **expose** and **unexpose** for objects do not modify *sinv* of any class, so J1 is preserved. Exposing an object cannot break a class invariant. **expose** X **for** C requires X's owner to be mutable before setting $X.inv_C$ to *mutable* to maintain the property that an object can be mutable only if its owner class is mutable. Since **unexpose** X **for** C modifies only the field $X.inv_C$, the only class invariant that can be potentially broken by this operation is a global class invariant in class C. As discussed in Sec. 4.2, a syntactic requirement guarantees that C is mutable at the time when X is unexposed for C, so no extra precondition is required. The Boogie methodology for object invariants requires X's object invariant to hold before X is unexposed. We omit this assertion since we do not consider object invariants in this paper. In summary, we have the following pseudo code for **expose** and **unexpose**:

expose X **for** C $\equiv$

  assert $X \neq \mathbf{null} \wedge X.inv_C = valid$;

  assert $X.owner.sinv = mutable$;

  $X.inv_C := mutable$

unexpose X **for** C $\equiv$

  assert $X \neq \mathbf{null} \wedge X.inv_C = mutable$;

  $X.inv_C := valid$

Object Creation. Again, program invariant J1 is trivially preserved. As explained in Sec. 3.2, the created object has its inv_T fields set to *mutable* and its *owner* field initialized with the class C given in the creation expression. These assignments have no impact on class invariants with field-access expressions of Forms 1 (no static field involved), 2 (the new object is not referenced from a static field), or 3 (the new object is not valid for its class) of Def. 1. Since the new object is mutable, its owner class, C, has to be mutable as well, which is checked by the precondition $C.sinv = mutable$.

5.3 Soundness

A program **P** is well-formed if **P** is syntactically correct and type correct, **P**'s invariants are admissible (Def. 1), and the syntactic requirement for **unexpose** (Sec. 4.2) is met.

Theorem 1. *In each reachable state of a well-formed program, J1 and J2 hold.*

For a lack of space, we do not present the soundness proof in this paper. We have explained the arguments of the soundness proof along with the presentation of the proof rules. The complete proof is found in our technical report [9].

6 Related Work

Classical proof systems for objects and invariants such as Meyer's work [15] or the approach of Liskov, Wing, and Guttag [13, 12] do not consider static fields or quantification over objects.

JML [8, 4] provides both object and class invariants (called instance and static invariants, respectively). Object invariants may refer to static fields, but class invariants cannot refer to the states of objects. In contrast to our work, JML applies a visible state semantics, where invariants have to hold in the pre- and post-states of all non-helper methods. It does not provide a sound modular proof system.

The use of static fields is sometimes considered bad programming style that can be avoided by using instance fields of a singleton object, u. Simple and ownership-based class invariants can then be expressed as an object invariant of u. However, such a programming model requires that all objects that need access to the shared state of u have references to u and can expose and modify u. Therefore, reasoning about the shared object, in particular, about the validity of u, is tedious. It is generally based on the fact that u is a singleton, which is difficult to express by standard object invariants.

Eiffel's *once methods* [14] provide a better abstraction mechanism for shared objects. A once method computes its result when it is called the first time. This result is cached and then returned upon succeeding calls. Therefore, each object can access shared data (in particular, a reference to the singleton u) through a once method instead of storing the reference in a field. Validity of u can then be guaranteed by the postcondition of the once method returning the reference. However, since u may not be valid in all execution states in which the method might be called, an additional flag is needed for each once method, indicating whether the object returned by the method is valid. The methodology required to maintain such a flag is identical to our methodology for class invariants and the *sinv* field.

The Boogie methodology for object invariants [1, 3, 10] does not admit class invariants. However, visibility-based object invariants [3, 10] can be generalized to allow object invariants to mention static fields. For instance, *Client*'s second class invariant can also be expressed by the object invariant $this.id < Client.ids$. With such object invariants, a static field update potentially violates the object invariant of many objects, all of which would have to be exposed before the update. Barnett and Naumann [3] show that *update guards* can be used to exploit monotonicity properties to avoid exposing all objects possibly affected by a field update. An update guard specifies a condition under which a field update is guaranteed not to break an invariant. For instance, increasing the value of *Client.ids* cannot violate the above invariant for any *Client* object.

Like our work, Pierik *et al.* [17] extend the Boogie methodology to class invariants. They handle simple class invariants in the same way as we do. Ownership-based class invariants are not supported. Therefore, class invariants can refer to instance fields only in a limited way. Invariants are allowed to quantify over all objects of a class, for example, to specify that a singleton object is the only instance of a class. Invariants that quantify over all objects of a class rather than over all *valid* objects can be broken by object creation. Therefore, one has to expose a class before creating an instance of it, an obligation that unfortunately falls on the client of a class. The client is then responsible for reestablishing the class invariant. Alternatively, a client can prove that it establishes a *creation guard*, which specifies a condition under which an object creation is guaranteed not to break an invariant. However, a creation guard cannot refer to the newly allocated object, so it is typically **false**. Pierik *et al.* do not address either the abstraction problem for class invariants or the initialization-order problem for classes.

Müller's thesis [16] also uses a visible state semantics for object invariants. It supports invariants over so-called abstract fields in a sound way, which we consider future work for the methodology presented here.

Leino and Nelson [11] developed a modular treatment of object invariants over abstract fields, which was used in the Extended Static Checker for Modula-3 [6]. Leino and Nelson treat some aspects of class invariants, but neither Müller's nor Leino and Nelson's work fully supports class invariants.

7   Conclusions

We have presented a verification methodology for class invariants, which allows class invariants to specify properties of static fields, of object structures rooted in static fields, and of all valid objects of a class. The methodology is sound and covers all typical applications of static fields we have found in programs. This work is part of a larger effort to advance programming theory to catch up with the current programming practice.

As future work, we plan to build on our previous work on visibility-based invariants [10] to support less common class invariants that refer to static fields and that quantify over objects of other classes. Moreover, we plan to implement our methodology as part of the .NET program checker Boogie, which is part of the Spec# programming system [2].

References

1. M. Barnett, R. DeLine, M. Fähndrich, K. R. M. Leino, and W. Schulte. Verification of object-oriented programs with invariants. *Journal of Object Technology*, 3(6), 2004. www.jot.fm.
2. M. Barnett, K. R. M. Leino, and W. Schulte. The Spec# programming system: An overview. In *CASSIS 2004*, volume 3362 of *LNCS*, pages 49–69. Springer-Verlag, 2004.
3. M. Barnett and D. A. Naumann. Friends need a bit more: Maintaining invariants over shared state. In *MPC 2004*, volume 3125 of *LNCS*, pages 54–84. Springer-Verlag, July 2004.
4. L. Burdy, Y. Cheon, D. R. Cok, M. D. Ernst, J. R. Kiniry, G. T. Leavens, K. R. M. Leino, and E. Poll. An overview of JML tools and applications. *Software Tools for Technology Transfer (STTT)*, 2004.
5. D. G. Clarke, J. M. Potter, and J. Noble. Ownership types for flexible alias protection. In *OOPSLA '98*, pages 48–64. ACM, October 1998.
6. D. L. Detlefs, K. R. M. Leino, G. Nelson, and J. B. Saxe. Extended static checking. Research Report 159, Compaq SRC, December 1998.
7. C. Flanagan, K. R. M. Leino, M. Lillibridge, G. Nelson, J. B. Saxe, and R. Stata. Extended static checking for Java. In *PLDI 2002*, pages 234–245. ACM, 2002.
8. G. T. Leavens, A. L. Baker, and C. Ruby. Preliminary design of JML: A behavioral interface specification language for Java. Technical Report 98-06-rev27, Iowa State University, 2003.
9. K. R. M. Leino and P. Müller. Modular verification of global module invariants in object-oriented programs. Technical Report 459, ETH Zürich, 2004.
10. K. R. M. Leino and P. Müller. Object invariants in dynamic contexts. In *ECOOP 2004*, volume 3086 of *LNCS*, pages 491–516. Springer-Verlag, 2004.
11. K. R. M. Leino and G. Nelson. Data abstraction and information hiding. *TOPLAS*, 24(5):491–553, September 2002.

12. B. Liskov and J. Guttag. *Abstraction and Specification in Program Development*. MIT Electrical Engineering and Computer Science Series. MIT Press, 1986.
13. B. Liskov and J. M. Wing. A behavioral notion of subtyping. *TOPLAS*, 16(6):1811–1841, 1994.
14. B. Meyer. *Eiffel: The Language*. Prentice Hall, 1992.
15. B. Meyer. *Object-Oriented Software Construction*. Prentice Hall, 1997.
16. P. Müller. *Modular Specification and Verification of Object-Oriented Programs*, volume 2262 of *LNCS*. Springer-Verlag, 2002. PhD thesis.
17. C. Pierik, D. Clarke, and F. S. de Boer. Controlling object allocation using creation guards. In *Formal Methods (FM 2005)*, LNCS. Springer-Verlag, 2005. In this volume.
18. A. Poetzsch-Heffter and P. Müller. A programming logic for sequential Java. In *ESOP 1999*, volume 1576 of *LNCS*, pages 162–176. Springer-Verlag, 1999.

Decoupling in Object Orientation

Ioannis T. Kassios

Dept. of Computer Science, University of Toronto,
BA5212, 40 St.George St. Toronto ON M5S 2E4 Canada
ykass@cs.toronto.edu

Abstract. In formal design, *decoupling* means to make the features of a formal system as independent as possible from each other. Decoupling tends to make the features semantically more primitive and the overall system more general. Quite opposite to decoupling, the tradition in object oriented refinement theories is to combine all features, such as specification, usage constraints, encapsulation and inheritance into a single formal construct, the *class*. We propose a decoupled formalization of object orientation, in which all those features are introduced independently from the class construct and from each other. Even though each of the features is significantly simpler than its standard counterparts, the overall system is more general: standard class-based object orientation is shown to be a special case of our system.

Keywords: object orientation, specification and refinement

1 Introduction

In a formal system, feature A is *coupled* with feature B, if the constructs of the system force the user to always use B when using A. In the opposite situation, we say that A is *decoupled* from (or orthogonal to) B. Decoupling enhances the expressiveness of a system, because it permits the independent use of the decoupled features. It also enhances the simplicity of the system, because decoupled features tend to be more primitive. Thus, from the point of view of generality and simplicity, it makes good sense to make the features of a formal system as decoupled from each other as possible.

Example 1. In Pascal, a defined function must always have a name: we say that Pascal functions are *coupled* with names. In contrast, in most functional languages, functions are decoupled from names, thanks to λ abstraction, a construct that creates nameless functions.

In the systems which decouple names from functions, it is still possible to create functions with names by using the two features together, but it is also possible to create and use nameless functions. For example, in

$$\text{let } f = \lambda x \cdot \big((\lambda y \cdot 2 \times y + 3)(3 \times x)\big) + 5$$

we have both a named and a nameless function. Decoupling makes these systems more general in that respect.

Decoupling also makes both features simpler. The naming feature (i.e. the **let** construct) by itself is extremely simple. We can use it to give names to

J.S. Fitzgerald, I.J. Hayes, and A. Tarlecki (Eds.): FM 2005, LNCS 3582, pp. 43–58, 2005.

functions as well as to other values and it has none of the complexity of the function construct. Similarly, the function feature (i.e. the λ construct) is more primitive than its Pascal counterpart. We can use it with or without a name and it has none of the complexity of the naming construct.

In object oriented refinement formal theories, designers usually overload a single formal construct with many different features: specification, encapsulation, usage constraints, inheritance are all supported by the class construct only (or, in some frameworks, the object construct). In other words, the traditional view of object orientation couples all those features with the class construct. This is especially true of model-based specification languages [15, 18, 1, 16, 17, 4, 3, 6, 19, 9], while languages with algebraic specification features [2, 8, 14, 13] tend to be less coupling (specifications are not coupled with classes).

In light of our discussion above, a way to generalize object orientation and to make all those features mathematically simpler is decoupling. This is the task undertaken by the present paper. Our approach is to introduce the notions of object specification, object refinement, usage constraints (including encapsulation) and inheritance independently from the class construct and from each other.

Thanks to decoupling, the semantics of each of the features that we introduce is mathematically primitive. This results in what we believe to be a very clean and easy to understand model. Despite the primitive mathematical basis, the theory fully covers the standard notions of object orientation as special cases. It is even somewhat more general than other theories, because it allows independent use of these features. The minimalism of the mathematics is a worthwhile goal of any formal system design: it means that the formulas that we manipulate do not have any unnecessary complexity and therefore reasoning is only as complicated as the problem we are trying to solve. Construct generality is another worthwhile goal: the more we can express formally, the smaller the formalization gap is likely to be.

This paper presents only part of the theory, omitting pointers. This limits its applicability compared to some other object oriented refinement theories, although some of the most important work in the area also has copy semantics, for example the ROOL project [6] and the object oriented extensions [18, 4, 3, 9] of [5, 11]. Pointers are supported in the full theory to be presented in the author's forthcoming Ph.D. thesis.

An extended version of this paper is [12]; the interested reader is referred there for more details, features that are not covered here and for the omitted proofs. Sect. 6.2 contains a small summary of some of the omitted features. The examples presented both here and in [12] are purposefully primitive, because their aim is to explain the theory as simply as possible.

2   Preliminaries

2.1   Notation

Meta-notation. If S and t are expressions and x is a variable, then $S(t/x)$ represents expression S with all free occurrences of x replaced by t.

Primitive Values. A *label* is a finite sequence of Latin letters. A constant label is written in sans serif font. For example, n, x and get are labels. The set of all labels is denoted $\mathbb{L}$. The set of boolean values is $\mathbb{B} = \{\top, \bot\}$. Boolean equivalence is not different from equality, so we use the same sign ($=$) for both. Symbols $=\wedge$ have the same semantics as $= \wedge$ respectively, but their precedence is lower than every other symbol in the notation and even the scope of quantifiers. They are used to reduce the number of parentheses in expressions.

Functions. Function application is denoted by juxtaposition. The domain of function f is denoted Δf. The set of all total functions from set A to set B is denoted $A \rightarrow B$.

For any x and a, function $x \mapsto a$ is defined by:

$$\Delta(x \mapsto a) = \{x\} \qquad (x \mapsto a)x = a$$

If f, g are functions then $f|g$ is a function defined by

$$\Delta(f|g) = \Delta f \cup \Delta g$$
$$y \in \Delta(f|g) \;\Rightarrow\; (f|g)y \;=\; \textbf{if } y \in \Delta f \textbf{ then } f\,y \textbf{ else } g\,y$$

A function in $S \rightarrow \mathbb{B}$ is called a *predicate* on S. Implication ($\Rightarrow$) is pointwise extended on predicates. If $F \in (S \rightarrow \mathbb{B}) \rightarrow S \rightarrow \mathbb{B}$ is monotonic with respect to $\Rightarrow$, then νF is the weakest fixpoint of F, i.e.

$$F(\nu F) = \nu F \qquad f \in S \rightarrow \mathbb{B} \,\wedge\, F\,f = f \;\Rightarrow\; (f \Rightarrow \nu F)$$

Predicate *even* returns $\top$ if and only if its argument is an even number.

A function whose domain is a set of labels is called a *record*. If S is a set, then the set of all records that return elements in S is denoted rec S. In this paper, the set of all data values is denoted $\mathcal{U}$ and includes rec $\mathcal{U}$. If $S \subseteq \mathcal{U}$, and l is a label, then $l \rightharpoonup S$ is a the set of records whose domain contains l and whose application to l returns an element of S:

$$l \rightharpoonup S \;=\; \{r \in \text{rec } \mathcal{U} \mid l \in \Delta r \,\wedge\, r\,l \in S\}$$

If the l_i are mutually disjoint labels and the S_i are non-empty sets of values, and $R = \bigcap i \cdot l_i \rightharpoonup S_i$, then R is called a *record space*. Set $\bigcup i \cdot l_i$ is called the *domain* of R. Notice that record spaces are contravariant in their domain. Adding a label in the domain adds a further restriction. For example, record $x \mapsto 3$ is contained in $x \rightharpoonup \mathbb{Z}$ but not in $x \rightharpoonup \mathbb{Z} \cap y \rightharpoonup \mathbb{B}$.

A function whose domain is $\{0, .., n-1\}$, for some natural n, is called a *list*. If S is a set, the set of all lists of elements of S is denoted list S. List catenation is denoted $^+$. Operator *tail* takes a non-empty list and removes its first item.

Strings. A number, boolean, label or function is an *item*. A *string* is a sequence of zero or more items separated by the string catenation operator (;). The catenation operator is associative. A one-item string coincides with that item. The empty string is denoted *nil*. The length of string s (the number of items it contains) is denoted ℓs. Item i of string s is denoted s_i (starting from item 0). The suffix of string s starting from item i (incl.) is denoted $s_{i;..}$.

Let S be a set. The set of all strings of elements of S is denoted S^*. The set of all strings of elements of S whose length is exactly n is denoted $n*S$.

Given a string s we can form a list $[s]$ such that for all $i \in \{0,..,\ell s - 1\}$, it is $[s]i = s_i$. The difference between lists and strings is packaging: a one-item list $[x]$ does not coincide with that item x. In this paper we use both strings and lists. We use strings when we want items to be treated as special cases of sequences. We use lists when we want packaging so that we can form sequences of sequences.

2.2   Predicative Programming

We use [10] as an underlying programming theory. In [10], an *imperative specification* is a boolean expression on the initial and the final values of the program variables. Thus a *program variable* x is a pair of mathematical variables: its plain version x that represents the initial value and its primed version x' that represents the final value. An example of imperative specification is $x' > x$, which specifies that the value of program variable x must be increased. Programming constructs are introduced as abbreviations for boolean expressions.

Let P be an imperative specification on program variables $x, y, z, ...$ and T be a set of values. Then **var** $x : T \cdot P$ is an imperative specification on program variables $y, z, ...$, called *local declaration* and defined as follows:

$$\textbf{var } x : T \cdot P \;=\; \exists x \in T \cdot \exists x' \in T \cdot P$$

Set T is called the *type* of x in P.

Let P and Q be imperative specifications on program variables $x, y, ...$ of types $X, Y, ...$ resp. Then the *sequential composition* of P and Q is an imperative specification $P;Q$ defined as follows:

$$P;Q \;=\; \exists x'' \in X \cdot \exists y'' \in Y \cdot ... \cdot \; P(x''/x')(y''/y')... \;\wedge\; Q(x''/x)(y''/y)...$$

Let P be an imperative specification on program variables $x, y, ...$ and $a, b, ...$ Then **frame** $x, y, ... \cdot P$ is an imperative specification that asserts P and that all the program variables other than $x, y, ...$, remain unchanged:

$$\textbf{frame } x, y, ... \cdot P \;=\; P \wedge a' = a \wedge b' = b \wedge \; ...$$

Let E be an expression without primed variables and let x be a program variable. Then *assignment* of E to x is an imperative specification $x := E$ defined as follows:

$$x := E \;=\; \textbf{frame } x \cdot x' = E$$

If the type T of x is a record space and y belongs to the domain of T, then $x\,y$ may be used as a left operand of $:=$

$$x\,y \;:=\; E \;=\; x \;:=\; y \mapsto E \mid x$$

Imperative specification ok preserves the state

$$ok \;=\; \mathbf{frame} \cdot \top$$

3 Specification

In this section, we introduce object specifications independently of classes and we show an object specification that is not expressible as a class. Then we define classes as a special case of object specifications.

3.1 Basic Definitions

Denote by $\mathcal{U}$ the set of all possible values. $\mathcal{U}$ contains at least integers, booleans, records and lists. It also includes a set $\mathcal{O}$ of *objects*. The axiomatization of $\mathcal{O}$ is left to the makers of object specifications.

A *message* is a list whose first item is a label and all the subsequent items are data values. The set of all messages is $\mathcal{M} \;=\; \{[m; w] \mid m \in \mathbb{L} \,\wedge\, w \in \mathcal{U}^*\}$.

Let x be a program variable whose value is an object, m a label, $y, z, \ldots$ other program variables and w a string of data expressions. Then, expression $y; z; \ldots \;:=\; x.m(w)$ in an imperative specification called *invocation of message* $[m; w]$ *on* x *assigned to* $y; z; \ldots$. If there are no variables $y, z, \ldots$ then $:=$ is omitted. If $w = nil$, then (w) is omitted.

Invocation $y; z; \ldots \;:=\; x.m(w)$ changes the values of $x, y, z \ldots$ only[1]. The list $[y'; z'; \ldots]$ of the values of variables $y; z; \ldots$ *after* the invocation is called the *result* of the invocation. Denote by $x \hookleftarrow \varsigma$ the value of x *after* the invocation of ς on x (i.e. the object at its new state) and by $x@\varsigma$ the result of the invocation. Then invocation is defined as follows:

$$
\begin{aligned}
& y; z; \ldots \;:=\; x.m(w) \\
={}& \mathbf{frame}\; x, y, z, \ldots \cdot\; [y'; z'; \ldots] \;=\; x@[m; w] \;\wedge\; x' \;=\; x \hookleftarrow [m; w]
\end{aligned}
$$

A *scenario* is a string of messages. A *scenario result* is a string of results (i.e. lists of data values). Set $\mathcal{S} \;=\; \mathcal{M}^*$ is the set of all scenarios and set $\mathcal{R} \;=\; (\text{list } \mathcal{U})^*$ is the set of all scenario results.

We can extend operators $\hookleftarrow$ and $@$ to apply to general scenarios instead of just messages. If ς is a scenario, then $x \hookleftarrow \varsigma$ is object x after invoking all messages in ς (in the order they appear in ς) and $x@\varsigma$ is the string of all the results that we get by making these invocations. Formally:

$$
\begin{aligned}
x \hookleftarrow nil &= x & x \hookleftarrow (\varsigma; \tau) &= (x \hookleftarrow \varsigma) \hookleftarrow \tau \\
x@nil &= nil & x@(\varsigma; \tau) &= (x@\varsigma)\; ;\; ((x \hookleftarrow \varsigma)@\tau)
\end{aligned}
$$

---

[1] All parameter passing is by value. For simplicity, any observation of the global state must be an explicit input and any side-effect must be an explicit output of the invocation.

3.2   Object Specifications and Object Refinement

An *object specification* is a subset of $\mathcal{O}$. An object specification can be created by specifying $x@\varsigma$ for any conforming object x and any scenario ς. To do that, we use a predicate on $\mathcal{S}$ and $\mathcal{R}$ called a *value specification*. Set $\mathcal{VS} = \mathcal{S} \rightarrow \mathcal{R} \rightarrow \mathbb{B}$ contains all value specifications. Operator **o** applies to a value specification V and returns the corresponding object specification:

$$\mathbf{o}V = \{x \in \mathcal{O} \mid \forall \varsigma \in \mathcal{S} \cdot V \varsigma (x@\varsigma)\}$$

Usually, we use mutual recursion to define a whole family of value specifications. Let Σ be a non-empty set of values. Let $F \in (\Sigma \rightarrow \mathcal{VS}) \rightarrow \Sigma \rightarrow \mathcal{VS}$ be a monotonic function. From F, we get a family of value specifications $V \in \Sigma \rightarrow \mathcal{VS}$ as the weakest fix-point of F and then an object specification S:

$$V = \nu F \qquad S = \bigcup \sigma \in I \cdot \mathbf{o}(V \sigma)$$

for some I such that $\emptyset \neq I \subseteq \Sigma$. Function F is called a *pre-specification*. Set Σ is called the *abstract state space* of S and F. Set I is called the *initialization space* of S. A further axiom that we need is $S \neq \emptyset$, which guarantees that a client can introduce objects that conform to S.

Example 2. Consider the following abstract requirements for stacks of integers:

(a) If the top value is n and we invoke top, then the result is n.
(b) Invoking push with parameter x sets the top value to x.
(c) If we make a series of invocations of push, pop and top, in which push and pop invocations balance out, then the top value is preserved.

Requirements (a,b,c) are more abstract than the standard model-based specification for stacks and closer to the standard algebraic specification. However, they are even weaker than the standard algebraic specification in that they do not require that a push followed by a pop return back the same stack.

To formalize Requirements (a,b,c) as an object specification, we first define the set *Balance* of all scenarios in which push and pop invocations balance out. This is the smallest set that satisfies the following axioms:

$$nil \in Balance \qquad [\text{top}] \in Balance$$
$$x \in \mathbb{Z} \wedge s \in Balance \quad \Rightarrow \quad [\text{push}; x]; s; [\text{pop}] \in Balance$$

Since our requirements only talk about the top value, our abstract state space must contain enough information to store the top value. We must also reserve an abstract state for the situation when the stack is empty. Define:

$$\Sigma_{Stack} = \mathbb{Z} \cup \{\bot\}$$

An abstract state $\sigma \in \Sigma$ is either an integer n, indicating that the top value is equal to n, or the special value $\bot$, indicating that the stack is empty.

Define pre-specification $F_{Stack} \in (\Sigma_{Stack} \to \mathcal{VS}) \to \Sigma_{Stack} \to \mathcal{VS}$ as follows

$$
\begin{aligned}
& F_{Stack}\ V\ \sigma\ \varsigma\ \rho \\
& = (\quad \varsigma = [\mathsf{top}] \ \wedge\ \sigma \neq \bot \ \Rightarrow\ \rho = [\sigma] \\
& \quad \wedge\ \forall x \in \mathbb{Z} \cdot \forall t \in \mathcal{S} \cdot \quad \varsigma = [\mathsf{push}; x]; t \ \Rightarrow\ V\ x\ t\ \rho_{1;..} \\
& \quad \wedge\ \forall s \in Balance \cdot \forall t \in \mathcal{S} \cdot \quad \varsigma = s; t \ \Rightarrow\ V\ \sigma\ t\ \rho_{\ell s;..}\quad)
\end{aligned}
$$

This axiom specifies the behavior of a stack that is in abstract state σ as follows. The first conjunct says that if we invoke message [top], and the stack is not empty, then the result is σ (Requirement (a)). The second conjunct says that if the first message is [push; x], then the behavior for the rest of the scenario is that of a stack whose top value is x (Requirement (b)). The last conjunct says that if the first part of the scenario is in *Balance*, then the behavior for the rest of the scenario is that of a stack in abstract state σ (i.e. the top value or its non-existence is preserved – Requirement (c)).

The rest of the axioms are (using $\{\bot\}$ as the initialization space):

$$
V_{Stack} = \nu F_{Stack} \qquad Stack = \mathbf{o}(V_{Stack}\bot) \neq \emptyset
$$

To use an object x that conforms to object specification S, we introduce it in the client using syntax **new** $x : S$, which is defined as follows:

$$
\textbf{new } x : S \quad = \quad \textbf{frame } x \cdot\ x' \in S
$$

Example 3. Here is a client for *Stack* of Example 2:

$$
\begin{aligned}
& P \\
& = \textbf{new }\ x : Stack\ ;\ x.\mathsf{push}(3)\ ;\ x.\mathsf{push}(4)\ ;\ z := x.\mathsf{top}\ ;\ x.\mathsf{pop}\ ;\ y := x.\mathsf{top}
\end{aligned}
$$

We can prove [12] that P sets variable z to 4 and variable y to 3:

$$
P \ \Rightarrow\ z' = 4 \ \wedge\ y' = 3
$$

An object specification S *refines* an object specification Q, if and only if $S \subseteq Q$. Relation $\subseteq$ on object specifications is called *object refinement*.

3.3   Classes

Class Basics. A *class* is a special kind of object specification in which we specify the result of one invocation at a time. To formalize self-invocation later on, we also assert that invocation of message [state] returns the whole state of the object without changing it. This does not contradict encapsulation, as explained in Sect. 4. When we talk about classes, set Σ is called the *concrete state space* (or simply *state space*) and function F is called the *pre-class*.

Formally, a class C is defined as follows. First we pick the state space Σ_C. The state space is a record space. The elements of the domain of Σ_C are called the *attributes* of C. We define pre-class $F_C \in (\Sigma_C \to \mathcal{VS}) \to \Sigma_C \to \mathcal{VS}$ as follows:

$$F_C\, V\, \sigma\, \varsigma\, \rho\ =\ (\quad \varsigma = nil\ \Rightarrow\ \rho = nil \tag{1}$$
$$\wedge\ \varsigma_0 = [\text{state}]\ \Rightarrow\ \rho_0 = [\sigma]\ \wedge\ V\, \sigma\, \varsigma_{1;..}\ \rho_{1;..}$$
$$\wedge\ P\ )$$

where P is a boolean expression that describes the methods of the class called the *class body*.

The class body is a conjunction of method specifications. A *method specification* is a boolean expression of the form:

$$\forall x \in X \cdot \forall y \in Y \cdot ... \cdot \exists \sigma' \in \Sigma_C \cdot \exists r' \in R \cdot \exists q' \in Q \cdot ...\cdot \tag{2}$$
$$\varsigma_0 = [m; x; y; ...]\ \Rightarrow\ S\ \wedge\ \rho_0 = [r'; q'; ...]\ \wedge\ V\, \sigma'\, \varsigma_{1;..}\ \rho_{1;..}$$

where m is a label, $X, Y, ..., R, Q, ...$ are sets of data values and S is an imperative specification on program variable σ and mathematical variables $x, y, ...$ and $r', q', ...$ and V.

If method specification (2) appears in the body of C, and the number of variables $x, y, ...$ is a, we say that C *supports method m with arity a* (or method m/a). Imperative specification S is called the *body* of m/a in C. Two different methods of C must have either different names or different arities and no method with arity 0 can have name state .

Finally, we pick an initialization space I_C. The rest of the axioms are the usual:

$$V_C\ =\ \nu F_C \qquad C = (\bigcup \sigma \in I_C \cdot \mathbf{o}(V\, \sigma)) \neq \emptyset \tag{3}$$

Abbreviations. The **class** construct is introduced as an abbreviation for the class definition axioms presented above. In particular, syntax

$$C\ =\ \mathbf{class}(\Sigma)(I) \cdot P$$

abbreviates axioms $\Sigma_C = \Sigma$, $I_C = I$, (1), (3). The **method** construct

$$\mathbf{method}\ m(x : X\ ,\ y : Y\ ,\ ...)(r : R\ ,\ q : Q\ ,\ ...) \cdot S$$

abbreviates method specification (2).

Self-invocation. Imperative specification $y; z; ... := \mathbf{this}.m(w)$ represents *self-invocation of message $[m; w]$ assigned to $y; z; ....$* Its definition is:

$$y; z; ... := \mathbf{this}.m(w)$$
$$= \mathbf{frame}\ y, z, ..., \sigma \cdot\ V\, \sigma\, ([m; w]; [\text{state}])\ ([y'; z'; ...]; [\sigma'])$$

where σ is the program variable that represents the state within the method, and V is the value specification family that is being currently defined. We can prove [12] that if C supports a method with specification (2), then self-invocation of that method is the same as executing S. Formally:

$$V_C\, \sigma\, ([m; w]; [\text{state}])\ ([v']; [\sigma'])\ =\ S(w_0/x)(w_1/y)...(v_0'/r')(v_1'/q')...$$

The following example shows the classical model-based specification for stacks in our notation.

Example 4. Here is a class *StackC* that specifies stacks of integers, using lists of integers as the state space.

$$StackC$$
$$= \mathbf{class}(\mathsf{c} \rightharpoonup \text{list } \mathbb{Z})(\mathsf{c} \rightharpoonup \{[nil]\})\cdot$$
$$(\quad \mathbf{method} \text{ push}(x : \mathbb{Z})()\cdot \ \sigma\mathsf{c} := [x]^{+}\sigma\mathsf{c}$$
$$\wedge \ \mathbf{method} \text{ pop}()()\cdot \mathbf{var} \ b : \mathbb{B}\cdot$$
$$b := \mathbf{this}.\text{isempty} \ ; \ \mathbf{if} \ b \ \mathbf{then} \ ok \ \mathbf{else} \ \sigma\mathsf{c} := tail(\sigma\mathsf{c})$$
$$\wedge \ \mathbf{method} \text{ top}()(r : \mathbb{Z})\cdot \mathbf{var} \ b : \mathbb{B}\cdot$$
$$b := \mathbf{this}.\text{isempty} \ ; \ \mathbf{if} \ b \ \mathbf{then} \ ok \ \mathbf{else} \ r := \sigma \ \mathsf{c} \ 0$$
$$\wedge \ \mathbf{method} \text{ isempty}()(e : \mathbb{B})\cdot \ e := \ \sigma\mathsf{c} = [nil] \quad)$$

We can prove [12] that *StackC* refines *Stack* of Example 2. Since *StackC* is written entirely using executable constructs, it is an implementation[2] of object specification *Stack*.

Model-based theories define specifications to be classes and refinement to be pointwise method refinement. Pointwise method refinement is a special case of object refinement. Although it is more complex than object refinement, pointwise method refinement is known to be incomplete, while object refinement does not have this problem. This is demonstrated in the following example.

Example 5. Define:

$$C = \mathbf{class}(\mathsf{n} \rightharpoonup \mathbb{Z})(\mathsf{n} \rightharpoonup \mathbb{Z})\cdot \ \mathbf{method} \text{ m}()()\cdot even(\sigma'\mathsf{n})$$
$$D = \mathbf{class}(\mathsf{n} \rightharpoonup \mathbb{Z})(\mathsf{n} \rightharpoonup \{0\})\cdot \ \mathbf{method} \text{ m}()()\cdot \sigma'\mathsf{n} = \sigma\mathsf{n} + 2$$

We can prove that $D \subseteq C$, even though D does not refine C in the standard sense of pointwise method refinement.

4 Encapsulation and Usage Constraints

In this section, we introduce *usage schemes* as a feature that plays the role that usage constraints (also known as "history clauses") play in some specification languages. Usage schemes are stand-alone and independent of classes, so they can be applied incrementally and they can be applied to general object specifications. We show an example of such an application. We then introduce standard encapsulation as a special case of the use of usage schemes and data refinement as its application.

---

[2] Not all classes are implementations; non-deterministic method specifications are also possible.

4.1 Usage Schemes

Sometimes the client of an object specification is required to obey certain rules when invoking methods on its conforming objects. Such rules are captured by our notion of *usage scheme*. A *usage scheme* is a predicate on S. Given a value specification V and a usage scheme E, the *encapsulated version of V with respect to E* is value specification $V \backslash E$ defined as follows:

$$(V \backslash E) \varsigma \, \rho \;\; = \;\; E \, \varsigma \;\Rightarrow\; V \, \varsigma \, \rho$$

Value specification $V \backslash E$ insists that the behavior of an object value agrees with V as long as the client obeys E, but makes no promise about what happens if the client does not obey E. Because of that, $V \backslash E$ is weaker than V and consequently the implementer of $\mathbf{o}(V \backslash E)$ has an easier job than the implementer of $\mathbf{o}V$.

Example 6. Consider the *Stack* specification of Example 2. If we assume that the client does not need to store more than N items in the stack at any given time, we have the freedom to implement *Stack* using a fixed-size list.

In this example, we create object specification *LimStack* that only allows storage of N items in the stack. Instead of creating *LimStack* from scratch, we create it incrementally, by first devising a usage scheme and then defining *LimStack* as the encapsulated version of *Stack* with respect to that scheme. In fact, we define a family of usage schemes $E \in \{-1, .., N+1\} \to S \to \mathbb{B}$, with mutual recursion as follows: for any $n \in \{0, .., N\}$ and scenario ς:

$$
\begin{aligned}
E \, n \, \varsigma \;=\;\; & \varsigma = nil \;\vee\; (\exists x \in \mathbb{Z} \cdot \; \varsigma_0 = [\mathsf{push}; x] \;\wedge\; E(n-1)\varsigma_{1;..}) \\
& \vee \; (\varsigma_0 = [\mathsf{pop}] \;\wedge\; E(n+1)\varsigma_{1;..}) \;\vee\; (\varsigma_0 = [\mathsf{top}] \;\wedge\; E \, n \, \varsigma_{1;..}) \\
\neg E(-1)\varsigma \quad\quad & \neg E(N+1)\varsigma
\end{aligned}
$$

Intuitively, $E \, n$ allows at most another n items to be pushed and at most another $N - n$ items to be popped (for $n \in \{0, .., N\}$).

The definition of *LimStack* is now incremental:

$$V_{LimStack} \, \sigma \;=\; V_{Stack} \, \sigma \setminus E \, N \quad\quad\quad LimStack \;=\; \mathbf{o}(V_{LimStack}\bot)$$

Unlike *Stack,* we can implement *LimStack* with a list of fixed size N. An implementation is shown in [12].

4.2 Encapsulation

Let C be a class and E a usage scheme. The *encapsulated version of C with respect to E* is object specification $C \backslash E$ defined as follows:

$$C \backslash E \;=\; \bigcup \sigma \in I_C \cdot \mathbf{o}(V_C \, \sigma \setminus E)$$

Applying a usage scheme to a class corresponds to the *history clauses* that the class constructs of certain model-based specification languages support.

Standard encapsulation is another special case of the use of usage schemes. When we encapsulate a class, we do not allow the client to access the state. This is expressed by usage scheme *StdEnc,* which is defined as follows:

$$StdEnc \, \varsigma \;=\; \forall i \in \{0, .. \ell\varsigma - 1\} \cdot \varsigma_i \neq [\mathsf{state}]$$

Scheme *StdEnc* allows the implementer to change the representation of the class data in such a way that the rest of the behavior of the class is preserved. This is called *data refinement*. A methodology[3] to data-refine class C into class D is to decide on a new state space Σ_D and a transformer $G \in \Sigma_C \to \Sigma_D \to \mathbb{B}$ that relates the two state spaces. The transformer must be such that

$$\forall \sigma_D \in \Sigma_D \cdot \exists \sigma_C \in \Sigma_C \cdot G \, \sigma_C \, \sigma_D$$

The initialization space of C is transformed into I_D as follows:

$$I_D \; = \; \{\sigma \in \Sigma_D \mid \exists \sigma_C \in I_C \cdot G \, \sigma_C \, \sigma\}$$

The body S of each method of C is transformed into:

$$\forall \sigma_C \in \Sigma_C \cdot G \, \sigma_C \, \sigma \;\; \Rightarrow \;\; \exists \sigma'_C \in \Sigma_C \cdot G \, \sigma'_C \, \sigma' \, \wedge \, S(\sigma_C/\sigma)(\sigma'_C/\sigma')$$

Example 7. Let

$$C = \mathbf{class}(\mathsf{n} \to \mathbb{Z})(\mathsf{n} \to \{0\}) \cdot \mathbf{method} \; \mathsf{inc}()(r : \mathbb{B}) \cdot \sigma'\mathsf{n} = \sigma\mathsf{n}{+}1 \wedge r' = even(\sigma'\mathsf{n})$$

We can change the wasteful internal representation of C because the only information that is observed by a client that does not invoke [state] is whether the value of attribute n is even or not. The new attribute space is $\mathsf{b} \to \mathbb{B}$ and the transformer is defined by:

$$G \; \sigma_C \; \sigma_D \;\; = \;\; even(\sigma_C\mathsf{n}) = \sigma_D\mathsf{b}$$

The transformation gives us class D, which is defined as follows:

$$D = \mathbf{class}(\mathsf{b} \to \mathbb{B})(\mathsf{b} \to \{\top\}) \cdot \mathbf{method} \; \mathsf{inc}()(r : \mathbb{B}) \cdot \; r' = \neg\sigma\mathsf{b} \, \wedge \, \sigma'\mathsf{b} = \neg\sigma\mathsf{b}$$

By the soundness of data refinement, we know that $D \subseteq C\backslash StdEnc$.

5   Inheritance

In this section, we introduce inheritance as an operation on pre-specifications and subclassing as the application of inheritance to pre-classes.

Inheritance is sometimes understood as a kind of refinement: if class D inherits from class C, then we should be able to use objects of D when objects of C are wanted (this is for example the philosophy of Eiffel [16]). An alternative view decouples code reuse from object substitutability (see for example [4]). In that view, objects of D can be used where objects of C are expected if and only if D is a refinement of C regardless of whether D was created incrementally from C. Also, a class D can be created incrementally from another class C, regardless of whether D is a refinement of C. We subscribe to the latter more liberal view and generalize it to object specifications: by the term "inheritance" we mean the creation of an object specification incrementally from other object specifications, regardless of whether the new object specification is a refinement of the old ones.

---

[3] The outlined methodology is called L^{-1} data refinement in [7].

5.1   General Inheritance

Let F be a pre-specification. We can create a new pre-specification G incrementally from F by adding and/or excluding functionality. We add functionality by conjoining a boolean expression N that describes the new functionality:

$$G \, V \, \sigma \, \varsigma \, \rho \quad = \quad F \, V \, \sigma \, \varsigma \, \rho \wedge N \tag{4}$$

We exclude functionality as follows:

$$G \, V \, \sigma \, \varsigma \, \rho \quad = \quad \neg E \, \varsigma \ \Rightarrow \ F \, V \, \sigma \, \varsigma \, \rho \tag{5}$$

where E is a usage scheme that describes the excluded scenarios.

   Inheritance is the use of operations that add functionality, such as (4), and operations that exclude functionality, such as (5) to create a pre-specification G incrementally from other pre-specifications F whose abstract state space is greater than or equal to that of G. If more than one pre-specifications F are involved, then we have *multiple inheritance*. *Overriding* of functionality is a combination of operations: first we exclude the old functionality and then we add the new one.

   Notice that our notion of overriding ensures dynamic dispatch of the messages invoked by the client (the related behavior is re-specified). In Sect. 5.2, we see that dynamic dispatch of self-invocations is also supported.

Example 8. Suppose that we want to write an object specification *VarStack* that describes stacks. A stack conforming to *VarStack* behaves according to *Stack* of Example 2 but is different in that method **top** allows only one observation of the top value. In particular, after the invocation of [top], the top value is set to 0.

   Since our requirement is incremental, it is a good idea to create *VarStack* incrementally. To do that, we use our mechanism of inheritance. We keep the same abstract state space Σ_{Stack}.

   Our requirement is an overriding requirement. We must exclude the functionality that has to do with what happens *after* the invocation of **top** . So we exclude scenarios [top]; t where $t \neq nil$. We must then add the new functionality. The new pre-specification $F_{VarStack} \in (\Sigma_{Stack} \rightarrow \mathcal{VS}) \rightarrow \Sigma_{Stack} \rightarrow \mathcal{VS}$ is defined as follows:

$$\begin{aligned}
&F_{VarStack} \, V \, \sigma \, \varsigma \, \rho \\
= (\ &\neg(\exists t \in \mathcal{S} \cdot t \neq nil \ \wedge \ \varsigma = [\text{top}]; t) \ \Rightarrow \ F_{Stack} \, \sigma \, \varsigma \, \rho \\
\wedge \ &\forall t \in \mathcal{S} \cdot \ t \neq nil \ \wedge \ \varsigma = [\text{top}]; t \ \Rightarrow \ V \, 0 \, t \, \rho_{1;..}\ )
\end{aligned}$$

The first line inherits the behaviors of *Stack* excluding the above stated scenarios. The second line defines the new functionality for exactly those scenarios. Notice that the behavior for a single [top] invocation is inherited. This guarantees that an invocation of [top] still returns the top value. The "balance" behaviors (except for scenarios that start with [top]) are also inherited, so for example [push; 6]; [top]; [top]; [pop] still preserves the top value.

The rest of the axioms are the usual:

$$V_{VarStack} = \nu F_{VarStack} \qquad\qquad VarStack = \mathbf{o}(V_{VarStack}\bot) \neq \emptyset$$

The fact that the state space of F is greater than or equal to that of G might seem counter-intuitive when one considers standard inheritance in which the state of the subclass "grows" by adding more attributes. This intuition is wrong: in fact adding attributes makes the state space smaller, because record spaces are contravariant in their domain.

5.2   Subclassing

Subclassing is a restricted form of inheritance in which:

- The pre-specifications involved are pre-classes.
- The state space is restricted only by adding attributes and intersecting an initialization space related to the new attributes.
- We add functionality only by conjoining new method specifications.
- We only override methods.
- There is no name clash between any of the inherited attributes and the new attributes or any of the inherited methods and the new methods.

The formula below makes all the above formal. It creates a new class D incrementally from classes C_i, provided that there is no name clash:

$$D = \mathbf{class}(\Sigma \cap \bigcap i \cdot \Sigma_{C_i})(I \cap \bigcap i \cdot I_{C_i}) \cdot \quad P \wedge \forall i \cdot \neg E_i \varsigma_0 \Rightarrow F_{C_i} \ V \ \sigma \ \varsigma \ \rho$$

$$(6)$$

where Σ is the state space for the new attributes, I is the initialization space for the new attributes, P is a class body that describes the new methods and for all i, E_i is a usage scheme that describes the methods that are overridden from class C_i. Every usage scheme E_i has a special form:

$$E_i \varsigma \quad = \quad \exists j \cdot \exists x \in a_{i;j} * \mathcal{U} \cdot \varsigma = [m_{i;j}; x]$$

where the $m_{i;j}/a_{i;j}$ are the methods of C_i to be excluded.

Note that, all self-invocations in the C_i refer to the family V under definition and thus, they become self-invocations in D. This means that our notion of inheritance supports dynamic dispatch not only of client invocations, but of self-invocations as well.

Definition (6) can be abbreviated by the following syntax:

$$D = \mathbf{class}(\Sigma)(I)$$
$$\qquad \mathbf{inherit} \ C_0 \ \mathbf{without} \ m_{0;0}/a_{0;0} \ ; \ m_{0;1}/a_{0;1} \ ; \ \cdots$$
$$\qquad \mathbf{inherit} \ C_1 \ \mathbf{without} \ m_{1;0}/a_{1;0} \ ; \ m_{1;1}/a_{1;1} \ ; \ \cdots$$
$$\qquad \cdots$$
$$\qquad \cdot P$$

Keyword **without** is omitted if there is no overridden method.

Some languages allow the invocation of an overridden method m from class C within the body of the inheriting class D, bypassing dynamic dispatch (for example Java uses keyword **super**). This is possible in our language too: the idea is to replace V with V_C in the definition of self-invocation. The syntax we use is $y; z; ... := (\textbf{this as } C).m(w)$:

$$y; z; ... := (\textbf{this as } C).m(w)$$
$$= \textbf{frame } y, z, ..., \sigma \cdot V_C \ \sigma \ ([m; w]; [\text{state}]) \ ([y'; z'; ...]; [\sigma'])$$

Example 9. We create a class *CountStackC* that inherits from *StackC,* of Example 4 but also provides a counter that counts invocations of push. To do that, we add an attribute n, a method getCount and we override method push. The new method specification for push invokes the old method. We initialize the value of n to 0.

CountStackC
$= \textbf{class}(n \rightharpoonup \mathbb{Z})(n \rightharpoonup \{0\}) \ \textbf{inherit } StackC \ \textbf{without } \text{push}/1 \cdot$
(**method** push$(x : \mathbb{Z})()\cdot$
$\qquad \sigma n := \sigma n + 1 \ ; \ (\textbf{this as } StackC).\text{push}(x)$
$\wedge$ **method** getCount$()(r : \mathbb{N}) \cdot r := \sigma n$)

6 Discussion

6.1 Contribution

In this paper, we have presented part of the object oriented refinement theory of [12]. Our focus here is the decoupling aspect of the theory. We have shown that decoupling makes all our features very primitive. For example, our notions of object specification and refinement are as primitive as they can be, having none of the complexity of classes, encapsulation or usage constraints.

We have also shown that the overall system is more general than standard systems, because the decoupled features can apply independently. In particular, object specifications are more general than classes, as shown in Example 2, encapsulation and usage constraints are applicable incrementally as shown in Example 6, and both usage constraints and inheritance are applicable to general object specifications, as shown in Examples 6 and 8. Object refinement is more general than pointwise method refinement, as shown in Example 5. Examples 4, 7 and 9 show standard object orientation as a special case of our theory.

6.2 Features not Covered Here

There are significant parts of the theory of [12] that we do not have space to discuss here. The other major underlying design principle behind the theory is *unification*. The theory shows that the concept of object specification alone formalizes all object oriented entities (interfaces, classes, objects) and that object refinement alone formalizes all object oriented relations (instantiation, type compliance, subtyping, the sub-object relation, class refinement, implementation etc.). The theory also provides algebraic laws like those in [10], to make reasoning practical. The use of these laws is demonstrated in refinement proofs that had to be omitted here. Finally, the theory provides a formalism that avoids referring to the state σ when writing object specifications. This, and other syntactic sugar, makes specifications easier to read.

6.3   Restrictions of the Theory and Future Work

The theory of [12] does not support delegation-based object orientation, and it is relational. We do not treat features like parallelism and distributed computation, but these are directly supported by [10].

We think that the main disadvantage of the theory presented here is that it has a copy semantics. The extension to cover pointers requires a further decoupling: value specifications are separated from state. Other than that, the extension is orthogonal to the theory.

We have argued that mathematical simplicity and construct generality are important goals in their own right. We have shown how our theory achieves those goals. However, this paper does not show how these goals translate into concrete practical advantages for the user of the theory. That requires more pragmatic examples than the ones presented here (whose purpose is the explanation of the theory and not the demonstration of its practicality).

Both the extension of the theory with pointers and the validation of the theory with pragmatic examples will be included in the author's forthcoming Ph.D. thesis.

Acknowledgment. This paper has benefited greatly from the criticisms by anonymous reviewers of this and an earlier version.

References

[1] M. Abadi and K. R. M. Leino. A logic of object-oriented programs. In M. Bidoit and M. Dauchet, editors, *Proceedings of TAPSOFT'97: Theory and Practice of Software Development*, volume 1214 of *Lecture Notes in Computer Science*, pages 682–696. Springer-Verlag, 1997.

[2] A. J. Alencar and J. A. Goguen. OOZE: An object-oriented Z environment. In P. America, editor, *Proceedings of ECOOP'91: European Conference on Object-Oriented Programming*, volume 512 of *Lecture Notes in Computer Science*, pages 180–199. Springer-Verlag, 1991.

[3] R. Back, L. Mikhajlov, and J. vonWright. Formal semantics of inheritance and object substitutability. Technical Report 337, Turku Centre for Computer Science, Lemminkäisenkatu 14, FIN-20520, Turku, Finland, 2000.

[4] R. Back, A. Mikhajlova, and J. vonWright. Class refinement as semantics of correct object substitutability. Technical Report 333, Turku Centre for Computer Science, Lemminkäisenkatu 14, FIN-20520, Turku, Finland, 2000.

[5] R. Back and J. vonWright. *Refinement Calculus. A Systematic Introduction.* Graduate Texts in Computer Science. Springer-Verlag, 1998.

[6] A. Cavalcanti and D. A. Naumann. A weakest precondition semantics for an object-oriented language of refinement. In J. M. Wing, J. Woodcock, and J. Davies, editors, *Proceedings of the FM'99 World Congress on Formal Methods*, volume 1709 of *Lecture Notes in Computer Science*, pages 1439–1459. Springer-Verlag, 1999.

[7] W. P. deRoever and K. Engelhardt. *Data Refinement: Model Oriented Methods and their Comparison*. Cambridge Tracts in Theoretical Computer Science. Cambridge University Press, 1998.

[8] J.A Goguen and J. Meseguer. Unifying functional, object-oriented and relational programming with logical semantics. In B. Shriver and P. Wegner, editors, *Research Directions in Object-Oriented Programming*, Series in Computer Systems, pages 417–477. MIT Press, 1987.

[9] J. He, Z. Liu, and X. Li. Towards a refinement calculus for object systems. In *Proceedings of ICCI2002*, pages 69–77. IEEE Computer Society, 2002.

[10] E. C. R. Hehner. *A Practical Theory of Programming*. Current edition, 2004. Available on-line: http://www.cs.toronto.edu/~hehner/aPToP/ First edition was published by Springer-Verlag in 1993.

[11] C. A. R. Hoare and J. He. *Unifying Theories of Programming*. Prentice Hall Series in Computer Science. Prentice Hall, 1998.

[12] I. T. Kassios. Object orientation in predicative programming, unification and decoupling in object orientation. Technical Report 500, Computer Systems Research Group, University of Toronto, 2004. Available on-line: http://www.cs.toronto.edu/~ykass/work/oopp.ps.gz.

[13] K. Lano. *Formal Object-Oriented Development*. Springer-Verlag, 1995.

[14] G. T. Leavens. An overview of Larch/C++. behavioral specifications for C++ modules. Technical Report TR96-01e, Department of Computer Science, Iowa State University, 1996.

[15] S. Meira and A. Cavalcanti. Modular object-oriented Z specifications. In *Z User Meeting 1990*, Workshops in Computing, pages 173–192. Springer-Verlag, 1990.

[16] B. Meyer. *Object-Oriented Software Construction*. The Object-Oriented Series. Prentice Hall, 2nd edition, 1997.

[17] R. F. Paige and E. C. R. Hehner. Bunches for object-oriented, concurrent and real time specification. In J. M. Wing, J. Woodcock, and J. Davies, editors, *Proceedings of the FM'99 World Congress on Formal Methods*, volume 1708 of *Lecture Notes in Computer Science*, pages 530–550. Springer-Verlag, 1999.

[18] E. Sekerinski. A type-theoretic basis for an object-oriented refinement calculus. In S. J. Goldsack and S. J. H. Kent, editors, *Formal Methods and Object Technology*. Springer-Verlag, 1996.

[19] G. Smith. *The Object Z Specification Language*. Advances in Formal Methods. Kluwer Academic Publishers, 2000.

Controlling Object Allocation Using Creation Guards

Cees Pierik[1], Dave Clarke[2], and Frank S. de Boer[1,2,3]

[1] ICS, Utrecht University, The Netherlands
[2] CWI, Amsterdam, The Netherlands
[3] LIACS, Leiden University, The Netherlands
cees@cs.uu.nl, {dave, frb}@cwi.nl

Abstract. Sharing of objects between different modules is often necessary to meet speed and resource demands. The invariants that describe properties of shared objects are difficult to maintain because they can be falsifiable by object allocation. This paper introduces creation guards to obtain a sound and modular methodology that supports such invariants.

Keywords: invariants, object allocation, specification, verification, object-oriented programming.

1 Introduction

Sharing of objects is often necessary to increase the speed and reduce the resource demands of programs. A system that allocates too many objects is prone to be slow. This phenomenon forces modules to share objects whenever possible.

Fortunately, many objects can safely be shared. This holds, for example, for simple immutable objects like strings and classes that encapsulate primitive data like integers or floating-point values. More complex examples include objects that represent key strokes, and borders of graphical user interface elements.

The resource demands of a program can be reduced by means of a mechanism that handles requests of client code for new objects by returning existing, shared objects whenever possible. Moreover, clients should be discouraged (or downright precluded) from allocating such objects directly. The flyweight pattern [6] supports object sharing by means of *factories* that maintain pools of shared objects. It is interesting to see that many variants of this pattern appear in version 1.4 and later versions of the Java API.

In this paper, we formally analyze this type of object sharing by studying the invariants that describe such object pools. A common feature of these invariants is that they are falsifiable by the allocation of new objects. This is a disturbing observation because object allocation is possible in every context in which a constructor method of the class is visible. Therefore almost every code fragment may potentially falsify the invariant. We show how such invariants can nevertheless be maintained by means of *creation guards*. A creation guard for a

J.S. Fitzgerald, I.J. Hayes, and A. Tarlecki (Eds.): FM 2005, LNCS 3582, pp. 59–74, 2005.

particular class is a formula that should hold in each state in which a new object of that class is allocated.

Invariants are commonly used to describe properties of the encapsulated representation of a single object following an influential paper by Hoare [8]. Barnett and Naumann recently proposed a friendship system with update guards for maintaining invariants over shared state [2]. In this paper, we show how to extend their system with creation guards in order to control object allocation. A preliminary version [15] of this paper has been presented at a workshop.

This paper is organized as follows. Sect. 2 presents an example involving a border factory that enables clients to share border objects. In the following section we give the syntax of the (static) invariants that we consider in this paper, along with some new results concerning the relationship between object creation and invariants. Sect. 4 summarizes the invariant framework on which we build. In Sect. 5 we introduce creation guards, and the corresponding invariant methodology. Sect. 6 generalizes the methodology in order to handle subclassing. We provide a sketch of the soundness proof of our methodology in Sect. 7. The last two sections are devoted to related work and conclusions.

2   An Example: Sharing Borders

In this section, we describe an example factory class that enables clients to share bevel borders. Fig. 1 shows the two classes of the example. The example is derived from the corresponding classes in Java's `javax.swing` package. More complex examples are possible, but this example suffices to illustrate our approach.

The example is written in a simple class-based object-oriented Java-like language. For convenience, we will assume that our examples behave according to the semantics of Java. However, this does not imply that the techniques that we will describe cannot be applied to other object-oriented languages like C#.

A bevel border can either be lowered or raised. The `type` field in class `BBorder` stores the type of the border. The factory class has two static fields (`LOWERED` and `RAISED`) that represent the two types.

Factory methods handle request for specific objects. They ensure that only one object is created for each value (or type). The `getBBorder` method in the `BorderFactory` class is an example of a factory method; it returns `BBorder` objects. The border factory class typically provides a factory method for each available border type.

To enable object sharing, references to the existing instances of a class should be maintained in a global object pool. In our example two static variables (`raised` and `lowered`) are used to build such a pool; more complex examples usually involve a hash table.

The constructor method of class `BBorder` is public. This is necessary because the factory method must have access to it. However, this also implies that client code is able to ignore the factory method by directly instantiating the class. That is, the implementation does not effectively impose object sharing on clients. This kind of situation is often accompanied by strong warnings in the class

```
class BBorder {
  private boolean type ;

  public BBorder(boolean type) { this.type := type ; }

  /* methods for drawing the border omitted */
}
class BorderFactory {
  public static final boolean RAISED := true, LOWERED := false ;
  private static BBorder raised, lowered ;

  public static BBorder getBBorder(boolean type) {
    if (type = RAISED) {
      if (raised = null) { raised := new BBorder(RAISED) ; }
      return raised ;
    }
    else {
      if (lowered = null) { lowered := new BBorder(LOWERED) ; }
      return lowered ;
    }
  }

  /* fields and factory methods for other border types omitted */
}
```

Fig. 1. A class that represents bevel borders, and a factory class that maintains a border pool

documentation not to exploit this leak. We will show how creation guards can repair this weak spot.

In situations where a factory only controls one class, it is best to place the factory method in the same class; the problem can then be avoided by declaring the constructor to be private (see, e.g., class `java.util.Currency` in version 1.4 of the Java API). However, one still needs a way to check whether statements in that class do not inadvertently falsify invariants by allocating new objects. Our example addresses the more general situation where the factory method resides in a different class.

The code of the factory class facilitates (but does not impose) an invariant regarding BBorder objects: each object occurs in the object pool, and each bevel border has a unique type. That situation is described by the following invariant.

$$(\forall b : \texttt{BBorder} \bullet b = \texttt{lowered} \vee b = \texttt{raised})$$
$$\wedge\ \texttt{lowered} \neq \texttt{null} \rightarrow \texttt{lowered.type} = \texttt{LOWERED} \qquad (\texttt{BorderFactory.}Inv)$$
$$\wedge\ \texttt{raised} \neq \texttt{null} \rightarrow \texttt{raised.type} = \texttt{RAISED} \ .$$

(Here, and throughout this paper, we assume that quantification ranges over allocated non-null objects.) We assign this invariant to class BorderFactory, which makes it a static invariant. We will assume that static invariants are invariants that belong to a class, and not to the instances of a particular class.

Non-static (object) invariants describe the representation of *instances* of a class, and are allowed to refer to their receiver by means of `this`. The first part of the above invariant could be rephrased as the object invariant

$$\texttt{this} = \texttt{lowered} \vee \texttt{this} = \texttt{raised} \ .$$

However, this object invariant has the flaw that it makes the instances responsible for assigning themselves to the proper location in the object pool. This is impossible in our example due to the visibility restrictions. We will therefore focus on static invariants in this paper.

Invariants reveal important design choices regarding a class that may justify code optimizations. For example, if invariant (`BorderFactory.`*Inv*) holds, then the following efficient implementation of the `equals` method is sufficient to check if two instances of the class represent the same border type.

```
public boolean equals(Object obj) {  return this = obj ;  }
```

3   The Syntax of Invariants

In this section, we define the syntax of invariants, and describe a syntactical criterion for determining whether invariants are falsifiable by the creation of new objects of a particular class. This criterion will later be used to determine which invariants are admissible.

We will assume that invariants are expressed in terms of the expressions of the underlying (Java-like) programming language. That is, they should be based on the following set of expressions:

$$e \in \text{Expr} ::= \texttt{undefined} \mid \texttt{null} \mid C.x \mid z \mid e.f \mid (C)e \mid e \ ? \ e : e \mid e = e$$
$$\mid \ \texttt{type}(e) \mid e \ \texttt{instanceof} \ C \mid \text{op}(e_1, \ldots, e_n)$$

The keyword `undefined` denotes the value of expressions whose values would normally be undefined because they result in an exception. For example, it would have the same value as the expression $e.f$ if e were equal to `null` (where $e.f$ denotes the value of field f of object e). We will assume that x is a static variable declared in class C, whereas z always denotes a logical variable. By $\texttt{type}(e)$ we denote the dynamic (allocated) type of object e. Finally, op denotes an arbitrary operator on elements of a primitive type. The meaning of other expressions should be clear.

Invariants are simply formulas over the set of expressions that we have defined above:

$$I \in \text{Inv} ::= e \mid \neg I \mid I \wedge I \mid (\forall z : t \bullet I)$$

A formula $(\forall z : C \bullet I)$ means that I holds for all *existing* objects of (each subclass of) class C. The type t is either a primitive type or a class name; we usually omit it if it is clear from the context. Invariants are not allowed to have unbound occurrences of logical variables. The standard abbreviations like $I_1 \vee I_2$ for $\neg(\neg I_1 \wedge \neg I_2)$ and $(\exists z \bullet I)$ for $\neg(\forall z \bullet \neg I)$ are valid.

The formal semantics of the introduced set of formulas is fairly standard (see, e.g., [16]).

3.1   Invariants, Object Allocation and Quantification

The static invariant of class BorderFactory (BorderFactory.*Inv*) is an example of an invariant that is falsifiable by object creation. It is clear that (BorderFactory.*Inv*) is falsified by the allocation of a new instance of class BBorder whenever the static variables raised and lowered already reference existing objects.

In general, we will use a weakest precondition operation of object allocation to check whether invariants are falsifiable by object allocation. Let $[\text{new}_C/u]$ denote the weakest precondition of the allocation of a new instance of class C, and its assignment to a fresh local variable u that temporarily stores a reference to the object. (The weakest precondition operation of object allocation has to take the change scope of quantifiers into account. A formal definition of the operation can be found in previous work of the first and third authors [16].)

The operation does not model the execution of a constructor method. It merely models the effect of the heap extension that is caused by the allocation of a new object, which is the first effect of the execution of a statement new $C(e_1, \ldots, e_n)$ in Java [7]. Whether the constructor method preserves the invariant should be checked in the constructor method itself.

The following theorem describes the correspondence between falsifiability by object creation of an invariant and the validity of a formula.

Theorem 1. *An invariant I is falsifiable by the allocation of a new instance of class C if $I \rightarrow (I[\text{new}_C/u])$ does not hold.*

It follows from the assumption that $[\text{new}_C/u]$ computes the weakest precondition of the allocation of a new instance of class C [16].

In most cases one can also directly deduce from the syntax of an invariant that it cannot be falsified by the allocation of a new instance. The following result states that only invariants that quantify over a domain that includes the new object may be falsified by its allocation.

Theorem 2. *If an invariant I has no subformula of the form $(\forall z : C \bullet I')$, for some superclass C of class D, then it cannot be falsified by the allocation of a new instance of class D.*

We assume here that each class is also a sub- or superclass of itself. Invariants that have a subformula of the form $(\exists z : C \bullet I)$ may also be falsifiable by object creation (recall that a formula of the form $(\exists z \bullet I)$ abbreviates the formula $\neg(\forall z \bullet \neg I)$). The result can be proved by structural induction on the invariants using Theorem 1. Note that the implication is not valid in the opposite direction.

4   The Boogie Approach to Invariants

Invariants are commonly expected to hold in all 'visible' states. This implies that the invariants must hold every time control leaves a method of a class [9, 10]. The Boogie approach to invariants [1, 11] weakens this restriction while still preventing scenarios in which one wrongfully assumes that an invariant holds.

For this purpose, an auxiliary field inv is introduced to signal which invariants hold for a particular object. Its value is always a superclass of the dynamic type of an object. The methodology ensures that if the value of the inv field of an object is class C, then the object satisfies all object invariants declared in superclasses of C (including the invariant in class C). The following system invariant (for each class C) formally describes the relation between this field and the object invariant Inv_C of class C.

$$(\forall o : C \bullet o.\text{inv} \preceq C \rightarrow (Inv_C[o/\text{this}])) \tag{1}$$

Here, $\preceq$ denotes the reflexive and transitive subclass-relation, and $[o/\text{this}]$ is the capture-avoiding substitution of this by o.

The default value of field inv is the root class Object, which implies that the object invariant of this class must hold for each fresh object. The value of the inv is controlled by two special statements, pack and unpack, which are defined as follows for a class D with immediate superclass C.

> pack e as $D \equiv$
>   assert $e \neq$ undefined $\land e \neq$ null $\land e.\text{inv} = C \land (Inv_D[e/\text{this}])$;
> $e.\text{inv} := D$;
>
> unpack e from $D \equiv$
>   assert $e \neq$ undefined $\land e \neq$ null $\land e.\text{inv} = D$;
> $e.\text{inv} := C$;

The formulas that follow the assert keyword should be seen as preconditions for these statements. The program logic in which they are used should guarantee that they hold whenever these statements are executed (e.g., by adding them to the weakest preconditions of these statements). A runtime assertion checker can simply check if the assertion holds upon reaching the statement.

These statements enable a discipline whereby each object is sufficiently unpacked before its fields may be modified. This can be achieved by placing the additional precondition $e.\text{inv} \npreceq C$ on all field assignments of the form $e.f := e'$, where C is the class in which field f is declared.

The above mentioned discipline suffices for object invariants that only depend on the fields of their receiver. Other invariants can be allowed by using ownership [4] in order to extend the range of invariants to objects beyond of the original object, to owned objects and objects with the same owner [1, 11].

The Boogie approach to invariants can also be used to handle static invariants. For this purpose, we assign to each class an auxiliary boolean field stable that indicates whether the class is stable, i.e., whether its static invariant holds. Assignments to static fields of a class will only be allowed if it is unpacked. A class is unpacked if its stable field has the value false. The following statements control this field.

> pack_class $C \equiv$ assert $C.Inv$; $C.\text{stable} :=$ true ;
> unpack_class $C \equiv C.\text{stable} :=$ false ;

Thus we maintain the following system invariant, for each class C.

$$C.\text{stable} \rightarrow C.Inv \tag{2}$$

4.1   The Friendship System

Barnett and Naumann [2, 14] extended the set of admissible invariants by allowing object invariants to depend on fields of unowned (shared) objects. The classes of these objects are called *friend* classes. Translated to our setting, this allows the invariant of the factory class to depend on instance fields of objects of (friend) class BBorder. Note that BorderFactory.*Inv* depends on field type declared in class BBorder. We will describe in this section how their proposal can be applied to static invariants.

Their *friendship system* uses update guards to describe permitted updates to shared fields. An update is permitted if it occurs in a state in which the guards of the field hold, or if the factory class is unpacked. We will use the following syntax to declare an update guard U in class C for an instance field f of class C.

static guard U guards f for F ;

The keyword static indicates that the guard protects a static invariant; the guard U protects the static invariant of class F against updates of field f of C-objects that would falsify F's invariant. The guard itself should be a valid formula that does not mention fields that are invisible to clients of the class. It may additionally refer to two keywords: this denotes the object whose field is modified, and val denotes the value that is assigned to the field. A field may have several update guards.

A static invariant $F.Inv$ that depends on a field f of some other class C is only allowed if it is sufficiently protected by the update guard of that field. An update guard U for field f protects the static invariant of class F if

$$F.Inv \land U \to (F.Inv[\text{val}/\text{this}.f]) \qquad (3)$$

holds. By [val/this.f] we denote the weakest precondition operation of the assignment this.f := val (see, e.g., [16]).

As mentioned above, updates to guarded fields are only allowed in states in which either the guards hold or in which the class of the invariant is unpacked. This is checked by giving each assignment of the form $e.f := e'$ the (additional) precondition $\neg F.\text{stable} \lor (U[e, e'/\text{this}, \text{val}])$. Here $[e, e'/\text{this}, \text{val}]$ is the simultaneous substitution of this by e, and val by e'. Thus we ensure that all updates to this field maintain (2).

Note that guards are always placed in the class in which the field is declared. This is necessary in a modular proof system. It ensures that a proof of correctness for a method cannot be falsified by adding additional classes that declare new guards for arbitrary fields of other classes.

We can also use this mechanism to allow static invariants that depend on static variables declared in other classes. A guard declaration

static guard U guards x for F ;

protects the static invariant of class F against updates of static variable $C.x$ in states in which the guard does not hold. The keyword this does not make sense in update guards of static fields and is therefore not permitted.

One can check whether an update guard U for a static field $C.x$ protects the invariant by replacing $[\mathtt{val}/\mathtt{this}.f]$ in (3) by the weakest precondition operation $[\mathtt{val}/C.x]$ of the assignment $C.x := \mathtt{val}$. An assignment $C.x := e$ is only allowed in states in which $\neg F.\mathtt{stable} \lor (U[e/\mathtt{val}])$ holds.

In the following section we introduce creation guards in order to enable static invariants that are falsifiable by object creation. The definition of the set of admissible static invariants will therefore also be deferred to that section.

5   Creation Guards

Theorem 2 states that only invariants that quantify over a domain that includes new objects can be falsified by object creation. It would therefore be safe to allow static invariants to quantify over the instances of the class in which they are declared if that class has only private constructors. Thus creation of instances of the class would be restricted to methods of the class, and it would suffice to check that the methods of the class ensure that the invariant holds in all visible states.

However, as we have argued in Sect. 2, it is often not the case that the factory methods are part of the same class. Moreover, we often find protected or even public constructors for shareable objects. We will use creation guards to grant the class of the factory method the right to quantify over shared objects. A creation guard for some class C is a formula that should hold in each state in which a new object of class C is allocated.

Let F be the class that contains the factory method(s) for objects of class C. Class C can protect the static invariant of its factory class by declaring a creation guard. Such a declaration could have the following form.

static creation guard G for F ;

The creation guard G is an arbitrary formula over the part of the program state that is visible to clients; it should not reveal hidden implementation details of class C.

The most commonly used creation guard is **false**. This creation guard seems to prohibit creation of objects of class C, but that is not the case. The effect of such a creation guard is that objects of that class can only be created if the factory class is unpacked. That is, we require that $\neg F.\mathtt{stable} \lor G$ holds prior to the execution of each statement of the form **new** $C()$.

The invariants that are enabled by a creation guard depend on the strength of the guard. The only invariants that are allowed are those that cannot be inadvertently falsified by the allocation of a new object as a consequence of the creation guard. A creation guard G protects the static invariant $F.Inv$ of a factory class F against allocation of instances of class C if

$$F.Inv \land G \rightarrow (F.Inv[\mathbf{new}_C/u])$$

holds, where u is a fresh local variable. Only invariants that are protected by guards in the above sense will be allowed to quantify over the shared objects.

5.1   Admissible Invariants

In this subsection, we briefly summarize the methodology that we have proposed thus far. In particular, we give a precise definition of the set of admissible invariants that is supported by the guards that have been introduced up to now. The definition avoids possible complications that may arise due to subclassing; we discuss subclassing in Sect. 6.

Definition 1 (admissible invariant). *A static invariant F.Inv is admissible if the following conditions are met:*

- *each static variable $C.x$ that occurs in F.Inv is syntactically distinct from C.*stable*, and either belongs to class F ($C \equiv F$), or class C has a static update guard U for $C.x$ and class F such that $F.Inv \wedge U \rightarrow (F.Inv[\text{val}/C.x])$;*
- *each subformula of the form $e.f$ concerns a field f that is syntactically distinct from* inv*, and the class C in which it has been declared has a static update guard U for f and class F such that $F.Inv \wedge U \rightarrow (F.Inv[\text{val}/\text{this}.f])$;*
- *each subformula of the form $(\forall z : C \bullet I)$ concerns a class C that has a creation guard G for class F such that $F.Inv \wedge G \rightarrow (F.Inv[\text{new}_C/u])$; moreover, class C is either final, or has at least one private constructor, and no public or protected constructors.*

Note that quantification over the values of a primitive type is never a problem. Such formulas are not falsifiable by object creation (as follows from Theorem 2). The last clause ensures that the class over which the invariant quantifies has no subclasses. Classes that have at least one private constructor, and no public or protected constructors, cannot have subclasses in Java. Thus the quantification domain of a formula in an invariant never includes instances of subclasses. This prevents invariants from depending on the creation of such objects. We will weaken this restriction in Sect. 6, where we address subclassing.

5.2   The Border Example Revisited

In this subsection we revisit the example described in Sect. 2. A proof outline of the example classes can be found in Fig. 2. It shows what annotation is needed to ensure that the required invariant is maintained, and how the invariant can be used to guarantee that methods behave according to their specification.

The static invariant of class BorderFactory is introduced by the keywords static and invariant on three succesive lines; the actual invariant is the conjunction of its three parts. The first part of the invariant is protected by a creation guard in class BBorder. However, the given invariant is only admissible if the class BBorder would have been declared to be final; we will explain in the following section why the invariant is also admissible without finalizing class BBorder.

Note that the references to the static variables in the invariant do not require update guards; a static invariant is always allowed to depend on static fields of the class in which it is declared. The following two parts are protected by the update guard for field type in the code of class BBorder.

```
class BBorder {
  private boolean type ;

  static creation guard false for BorderFactory ;
  static guard false guards type for BorderFactory ;

  requires ¬BorderFactory.stable ;
  ensures this.type = type ;
  public BBorder(boolean type) { this.type := type ; }

  requires BorderFactory.stable ;
  ensures result = (obj instanceof BBorder
                    && ((BBorder)obj).type = this.type) ;
  public boolean equals(Object obj) { return this = obj ; }
}

class BorderFactory {
  public static final boolean RAISED := true, LOWERED := false ;
  private static BBorder raised, lowered ;

  static invariant (∀b : BBorder • b = raised ∨ b = lowered) ;
  static invariant raised ≠ null → raised.type = RAISED ;
  static invariant lowered ≠ null → lowered.type = LOWERED ;

  requires stable ;
  ensures result.type = type ∧ stable ;
  public static BBorder getBBorder(boolean type) {
    if (type = RAISED) {
      if (raised = null) {
        unpack_class BorderFactory ;
        assert type = RAISED ∧ raised = null ∧ (∀c : BBorder • c = lowered)
          ∧¬stable ∧ (lowered ≠ null → lowered.type = LOWERED) ;
        raised := new BBorder(RAISED) ;
        pack_class BorderFactory ;
      }
      return raised ;
    }
    else {
      if (lowered = null) {
        unpack_class BorderFactory ;
        assert type = LOWERED ∧ lowered = null ∧ (∀c : BBorder • c = raised)
          ∧¬stable ∧ (raised ≠ null → raised.type = RAISED) ;
        lowered := new BBorder(LOWERED) ;
        pack_class BorderFactory ;
      }
      return lowered ;
    }
  }
}
```

Fig. 2. A proof outline of the shared borders example

The proof outline does not restrict the values of the static fields RAISED and LOWERED with e.g., the invariant RAISED = true ∧ LOWERED = false. Instead, we assume that the proof method replaces occurrences of these variables by their initializer expressions, which would make the above invariant trivially true. This preprocessing step corresponds to the way Java compilers handle final static variables with initializer expressions that are compile-time constants [7–§ 12.4.1].

The constructor method of class BBorder is listed with its precondition (requires clause) and postcondition (ensures clause). It assigns to field type, and must therefore require that the factory class is unpacked due to the update guard of the field. Note that we assume that an occurrence of a parameter in a postcondition denotes its value in the initial state.

The equals-method of class BBorder depends on the static invariant of BorderFactory as signalled by its precondition. It uses the fact that the class is packed and the system invariant (2) to prove its postcondition, which would otherwise be too strong.

The factory method preserves the invariant of the class according to its specification. It temporarily unpacks the class if it has to allocate a new instance of the class. For clarity, we have inserted assert statements that describe what holds immediately after the class is unpacked. The invariant is restored in the factory method by assigning the fresh object to the proper static variable after completion of the constructor method.

6   Subclassing

The set of admissible invariants that we defined in Sect. 5.1 does not allow quantification over a range that includes instances of subclasses. This may seem a strong restriction, but it actually matches well with many variants of the flyweight pattern that we found in the Java API. These sharing facilities do not cater for subclasses because the creation statements in the factory methods fix the classes of the objects in the pool.

However, it is not difficult to conceive a more flexible factory based on the prototype pattern [6] that would not statically fix the class of its objects. Such a factory method would have to be initialized with a prototype object. From that point on, the factory method should clone the prototype object each time a new object is required, thus ensuring that all objects have the same type. We therefore investigate the use of creation guards in the presence of subclassing in this section.

Assume that we have a static invariant in class F that quantifies over the instances of class C. In closed programs, one can check for each subclass D of C if its creation guards protect the invariant. However, this solution cannot be applied if some of the (future) subclasses are unavailable. Therefore we will have to rely on a system in which the creation guards of a subclass are restricted by the creation guards of its superclass.

At first glance, one is tempted to think that it suffices to let subclasses inherit the guards of their superclass, but that is not the case. Assume, for example, that we have a static invariant $(\forall o : C \bullet \text{type}(o) = C)$. This invariant is not falsifiable by creation of instances of class C, so we could give class C the creation guard **true** for this invariant. However, if class C has a subclass D, then we can easily break the invariant by allocating an instance of class D. The inherited creation guard does not prevent this scenario. The problem with this invariant is that it depends on a property of objects that is not inherited by subclasses. Instances of a subclass belong to a different class than instances of their superclass. The **type** operator may be used to discriminate between objects that differ in this sense, and should therefore not be allowed inside quantified formulas.

The **instanceof** operator and the cast operator are operations that also depend on the class of the objects to which they are applied, but their second operand (a class name) always reveals the criterion that is used. These operators cannot discriminate between instances of that class and its subclasses, and may therefore be used inside quantified formulas, provided that one checks whether the creation guard of the second operand protects the invariant. This latter restriction needs only be checked if the class occurs in a formula that quantifies over the instances of some superclass of that class.

The above mentioned restrictions suffice to protect invariants provided that creation guards are inherited by subclasses. A subclass may override a creation guard that it inherits if the new creation guard is stronger than the inherited guard. The above considerations lead to the following refinement of Def. 1.

Definition 2 (admissible invariant). *A static invariant F.Inv is admissible if the first two conditions of Def. 1 are met, and moreover, each subformula of the form $(\forall z : C \bullet I)$ of F.Inv concerns a class C with a creation guard G for class F such that the implication $F.Inv \land G \to (F.Inv[\text{new}_C/u])$ holds, and*

- *class C is either final, or has at least one private constructor, and no public or protected constructors, or*
- *operator* **type** *does not occur in I, and each subclass D of class C that occurs in I has a creation guard G' for F such that $F.Inv \land G' \to (F.Inv[\text{new}_D/u])$.*

7   Soundness

Soundness of our methodology means that system invariant (2) holds in each reachable state of a properly annotated program in which all invariants are admissible according to Def. 2. Our soundness proof presupposes a sound proof system which ensures that the explicated preconditions of program statements hold. We show that these preconditions suffice to ensure that the various statements in the program maintain the system invariant.

A full soundness proof would require more space than is available to us here. Fortunately, many details of the proof would correspond to similar steps in the soundness proof of the friendship system [14]. The results that we prove below cover the part of the proof that checks if object allocation preserves (2).

A program state $\langle H, \sigma \rangle$ consists of a heap H and a store σ (see [14, 16]). The heap map objects to object states. The store σ is a map that assigns values to all local, static, and logical variables. A state $\langle H, \sigma \rangle$ is valid if H and σ have no dangling references, i.e., if their range does not include objects that do not exist in H. By $\mathsf{val}(e)(\langle H, \sigma \rangle)$ we denote the value of expression e in state $\langle H, \sigma \rangle$. The validity of an invariant I in a state $\langle H, \sigma \rangle$ is written $\langle H, \sigma \rangle \models I$.

A statement $\mathbf{new}\ C(e_1, \ldots, e_n)$ first allocates a new instance of class C, and then initializes the object by calling the corresponding constructor method with parameters e_1 to e_n [7]. For simplicity, we assume that parameter evaluation has no side effects. The methodology must ensure that the system invariant is maintained by the allocation to prevent scenarios in which the specifier of the constructor method wrongfully assumes that the invariant holds. We will denote the heap that results from the allocation of a new instance of some class C in H by H_C. The fields of the new object have their default values after allocation.

The following definitions play an important role in the proof. Let $\mathsf{classes}(I)$ denote the least set such that $C \in \mathsf{classes}(I)$ whenever invariant I has a subformula $(\forall z : C \bullet I')$, or a subexpression of the form $(C)e$ or $e\ \mathbf{instanceof}\ C$. By the *most specific superclass* of a class D in an invariant I we mean the most specific superclass C of D such that $C \in \mathsf{classes}(I)$, if any. Formally, $C \in \mathsf{classes}(I)$ is the most specific superclass of D in invariant I if $D \preceq C$, and there exists no other class $E \in \mathsf{classes}(I)$ such that $D \preceq E \preceq C$.

The following lemma shows that allocation of an instance of an arbitrary subclass has the same effect on an invariant as the allocation of an object of its most specific superclass.

Lemma 1 (equality formulas). *Let I be a formula in which the $\mathbf{type}$ operator does not occur. Let class C be a superclass of class D such that C is the most specific superclass of D in I if it exists. Let H and σ be a heap and a store such that $\langle H_C, \sigma \rangle$ is a proper state. We assume that the identity of the new object does not depend on its class. Then $\langle H_D, \sigma \rangle \models I \Leftrightarrow \langle H_C, \sigma \rangle \models I$.*

Proof. By structural induction on I. The base case requires us to prove that $\mathsf{val}(e)(\langle H_D, \sigma \rangle) = \mathsf{val}(e)(\langle H_C, \sigma \rangle)$ for any expression e in which the $\mathbf{type}$ operator does not occur.

The main result of this section implies that any admissible invariant cannot be falsified by object allocation in a state in which all relevant creation guards hold. It is necessary to prove a slightly stronger result to be able to prove the claim by structural induction.

Lemma 2 (immutability invariants). *Let $C.Inv$ be an admissible invariant according to the additional requirements stated in Def. 2 (i.e., without the requirements of Def. 1 concerning update guards). Let D be an arbitrary class. Let $\langle H, \sigma \rangle$ be a state such that $\langle H, \sigma \rangle \models C.Inv$, and moreover, for each creation guard G declared in some class $E \in \mathsf{classes}(C.Inv)$ that protects friend class C we have $\langle H, \sigma \rangle \models G$. Then $\langle H_D, \sigma \rangle \models C.Inv$.*

Proof. By structural induction on I. We first prove for the base case that $\mathsf{val}(e)(\langle H_D, \sigma \rangle) = \mathsf{val}(e)(\langle H, \sigma \rangle)$ by structural induction on e.

The most interesting case of the lemma concerns an invariant $C.Inv$ such that $C.Inv \equiv (\forall z : E \bullet I)$ for some class E such that $D \preceq E$. Let S be the most specific superclass of D in $C.Inv$. Note that S exists because E is already a valid candidate. We have by Def. 2 that $C.Inv \wedge G \rightarrow (C.Inv[\mathtt{new}_S/u])$, where G is the creation guard declared in class S for friend class C. From $\langle H, \sigma \rangle \models C.Inv[\mathtt{new}_S/u]$ follows by the definition of the weakest precondition that $\langle H_S, \sigma \rangle \models C.Inv$. The required validity of $\langle H_D, \sigma \rangle \models C.Inv$ then follows from Lemma 1.

8 Related Work

The problem of maintaining invariants that are falsifiable by object creation has not been solved before. This is somewhat surprising because it is quite common to allow quantification in program annotations, and quantification is the (potential) source of the issue. Leino and Nelson also identified the problem [13], but they responded to it by forbidding this kind of invariant.

Calcagno et al. [3] studied the consequences of garbage collection (object deallocation) on program specifications. They rightly pointed out that certain formulas that are similar to the set of invariants that we studied are vulnerable to object deallocation. Their remedy is to weaken the semantics of quantification such that non-existing objects are also included. However, the invariants that we studied are not valid in their semantics. Consequently, one has no means to prove the correctness of method specifications that rely on such invariants. It is more common to ignore garbage collection in the semantics of garbage-collected languages without pointer arithmetics such as Java and C#. Note that our example invariants are invulnerable to garbage collection because the references retained by each factory ensure that the objects are always reachable.

The Boogie approach to invariants was initially designed to handle reentrant calls to objects that are not in a stable state [1]. Several later extensions showed that the initial extended state approach could be stretched to cope with other object-oriented specification patterns. In this paper, we have focussed on the use of creation guards, and have therefore ignored some of the orthogonal extensions such as the use of ownership.

Leino and Müller [11] proposed a new ownership model to support object invariants that depend on fields of owned objects that are not statically reachable from their owner, which allows, e.g., the invariant of a List object to depend on the fields of all the Node objects in its representation. They later also explored the use of ownership in static invariants [12]. However, quantification over owned objects is too weak to fully express the properties obtained by factory methods. They also explore quantification over packed objects, which turns out to be difficult to handle in a general way [12].

Barnett and Naumann [2] introduced update guards to protect object invariants that depend on fields of *friend* objects. They show how the set of friends can be managed using auxiliary state. Their friendship system protects invariants over shared state in circumstances where the ownership relation would be too rigid. They give a semantical characterization of the set of admissible invariants that rules out invariants that can be invalidated by object creation. An elaborate soundness proof of the system appeared in a companion paper [14].

The Java specification language JML [10] defines static invariants in terms of visible states. Such a definition seems incompatible with invariants that are falsifiable by object creation, because objects can be created in every state.

The preliminary version [15] of this paper does not contain a precise definition of the set of admissible invariants, and it also does not address subclassing and the soundness of our proposal.

9   Conclusions

Object sharing is an important technique to overcome some of the potential resource demands and speed limitations of object-oriented programs. This is witnessed by the amount of examples of patterns that manage object allocation that we found in the Java API. However, as we have shown in this paper, the invariants that describe pools of shared objects are falsifiable by object alloca-tion. The singleton pattern [6] is another example of a pattern that leads to an invariant that is falsifiable by object creation [15].

The main contribution of this paper is a sound and modular methodology for static invariants which could be falsified by both states updates and object allocation. We introduced creation guards to maintain such invariants. The ex-amples that we studied are best described using static invariants, but creation guards can also be used to protect object invariants.

The invariant methodology can be applied in both a static-checking and in a full program verification context. It also seems useful to check creation guards using a runtime assertion checker. The methodology is not tied to a specific program logic, although we have partly expressed it in terms of our previous work on program logics for object-oriented programs. The formulas that use the weakest precondition operation for object allocation can be rephrased in terms of the semantics of object allocation. We employed a syntactical description to be more specific about the set of admissible invariants.

We have implemented the invariant methodology in a successor of the tool described in [5] that computes the proof obligations of proof outlines of sequential Java programs. Future work includes a study of the use of creation guards in a concurrent setting.

References

1. M. Barnett, R. DeLine, M. Fähndrich, K. R. M. Leino, and W. Schulte. Verification of object-oriented programs with invariants. *Journal of Object Technology*, 3(6):27–56, June 2004.
2. M. Barnett and D. A. Naumann. Friends need a bit more: Maintaining invariants over shared state. In *Mathematics of Program Construction (MPC 2004)*, volume 3125 of *LNCS*, pages 54–84, 2004.
3. C. Calcagno, P. O'Hearn, and R. Bornat. Program logic and equivalence in the pres-ence of garbage collection. *Theoretical Computer Science*, 298(2):557–581, 2003.

4. D. Clarke, J. Potter, and J. Noble. Ownership types for flexible alias protection. In *Proceedings of the 13th ACM SIGPLAN conference on Object-oriented programming, systems, languages, and applications*, pages 48–64, 1998.
5. F. de Boer and C. Pierik. Computer-aided specification and verification of annotated object-oriented programs. In *Proc. of Formal Methods for Open Object-Based Systems V (FMOODS 2002)*, pages 163–177. Kluwer Academic Publishers, 2002.
6. E. Gamma, R. Helm, R. Johnson, and J. Vlissides. *Design Patterns: Elements of Reusable Object-Oriented Software*. Addison-Wesley, 1994.
7. J. Gosling, B. Joy, G. Steele, and G. Bracha. *The Java Language Specification*. Addison-Wesley, second edition, 2000.
8. C. Hoare. Proof of correctness of data representations. *Acta Informatica*, 1:271–281, 1972.
9. K. Huizing and R. Kuiper. Verification of object oriented programs using class invariants. In *Fundamental Approaches to Software Engineering (FASE 2000)*, volume 1783 of *LNCS*, pages 208–221, 2000.
10. G. T. Leavens, A. L. Baker, and C. Ruby. Preliminary design of JML: A behavioral interface specification language for Java. Technical Report 98-06y, Department of Computer Science, Iowa State University, June 2004.
11. K. R. M. Leino and P. Müller. Object invariants in dynamic contexts. In *Proc. of the European Conference on Object-Oriented Programming (ECOOP 2004)*, volume 3086 of *LNCS*, pages 491–516. Springer, 2004.
12. K. R. M. Leino and P. Müller. Modular verification of static class invariants. In: Formal Methods (FM 2005). LNCS, Springer, 2005. In this volume.
13. K. R. M. Leino and G. Nelson. Data Abstraction and Information Hiding. *ACM Transaction on Programming Languages and Systems*, 24(5):491–553, 2002.
14. D. A. Naumann and M. Barnett. Towards imperative modules: Reasoning about invariants and sharing of mutable state. In *Proc. of Logic in Computer Science (LICS 2004)*, pages 313–323. IEEE, 2004.
15. C. Pierik, D. Clarke, and F. S. de Boer. Creational invariants. In *Formal techniques for Java-like Programs (Proceedings of the ECOOP Workshop FTfJP '2004)*, 2004. The proceedings appeared as technical report nr. NIII-R0426, University of Nijmegen, 2004.
16. C. Pierik and F. S. de Boer. A syntax-directed Hoare logic for object-oriented programming concepts. In *Formal Methods for Open Object-Based Distributed Systems (Proc. of FMOODS 2003)*, volume 2884 of *LNCS*, pages 64–78, 2003.

Symbolic Animation of JML Specifications[*]

Fabrice Bouquet, Frédéric Dadeau, Bruno Legeard, and Mark Utting

Laboratoire d'Informatique (LIFC),
Université de Franche-Comté, CNRS - INRIA,
16, route de Gray - 25030 Besançon cedex, France
{bouquet, dadeau, legeard, utting}@lifc.univ-fcomte.fr

Abstract. This paper presents a model-based framework for the symbolic animation of object-oriented specifications. A customized set-theoretic solver is used to simulate the execution of the system and handle constraints on state variables. We define a framework for animating object-oriented specifications with dynamic object creations, interactions and inheritance. We show how this technique can be applied to Java Modeling Language (JML) specifications, making it possible to animate Java programs that only contain method interfaces and no code!

Keywords: Java Modeling Language, JML, model-based, object-oriented, symbolic animation.

1 Introduction

The use of formal models is a common practice in the software design process. A variety of modeling languages, such as B [1], Z [15], and UML [14] enriched with OCL [17] constraints, are available for specifying and analyzing systems before they are implemented.

JML (Java Modeling Language) [9] is a relatively recent modeling language that is targeted at specifying Java classes and interfaces. It is an extension of Java which allows formal specifications to be written within the Java comment syntax. It allows invariants to be added to constrain the class variables and preconditions and postconditions to be added to Java methods to describe their behavior. This paper describes an animation framework for JML, implemented in a tool, which can assist specifiers to validate their JML specifications.

When developing a formal model of a system, it is important to be able to both *verify* and *validate* the model. *Verification* involves checking various properties of the model itself, to ensure that it is consistent, well-typed, that invariants are preserved, etc. On the other hand, *validation* involves checking the model against the informal system requirements, to ensure that the desired behavior has been specified. Animation is one of the most important techniques for validating models. Animation consists of simulating the execution of the system, by

---

[*] This work has been realized within the GECCOO project of program "ACI Sécurité Informatique" supported by the French Ministry of Research and New Technologies.

J.S. Fitzgerald, I.J. Hayes, and A. Tarlecki (Eds.): FM 2005, LNCS 3582, pp. 75–90, 2005.

activating the different behaviors described in the model. Whereas verification can be automated with proof or model-checking techniques, validation is at best a semi-automated process, because it requires human assistance to compare the model with the initial requirements. Animation is also semi-automated in the sense that it requires human assistance to choose the input values of methods, and thus, which behavior the user wants to activate. However, the computation of the resulting system states can be done automatically, based on the formal model.

Symbolic animation increases the power and flexibility of animation as a validation tool. A symbolic animator simulates of the execution of a system using abstract states rather than concrete values. A symbolic solver is used to manipulate these abstract states during execution. Our symbolic solver uses Constraint Logic Programming (CLP) techniques, which treat the execution of an operation as a Constraint Satisfaction Problem (CSP). This means that one abstract (constrained) state can represent a large number of actual system states. This significantly decreases the size of the reachability graph. Moreover, it becomes possible to handle data non-determinism, which allows users to leave input parameters undefined, in order to create constrained states.

The major contributions of this paper are that it describes how we modified an existing non-modular specification animator to support multiple interacting objects, inheritance with behavioral subtyping, dynamic object creation, frames and invariant and history checking with counter-example generation. One of the strengths of the approach is that it supports *constrained* animation, which allows many possible behaviors to be explored within a single animation sequence. The techniques described here have been implemented in the JML-TT tool, which to our knowledge is the first animation tool for JML.

The paper is organized as follows. Section 2 presents the Java Modeling Language and introduces the example that will be used in the remainder of the paper. Section 3 presents the symbolic animation of specifications as realized in our framework. Section 4 explains how we express object concepts, such as class representation and inheritance, within our framework. Section 5 shows the application of these techniques to JML. Section 6 illustrates the possibilities of our approach with an animation of the example. Section 7 discusses the related work. Finally, Section 8 concludes and describes our future work.

2   The Java Modeling Language

The Java Modeling Language (JML) is an object-oriented specification language used to describe Java modules, i.e. classes or interfaces. JML was introduced recently by Leavens et al. at the Iowa State University who wanted to create an object-oriented modeling language that may be easily understood and practiced by developers. Therefore, the syntax of JML is based on Java syntax and JML annotations are directly integrated within the Java code of a program, in a transparent way, so that standard Java compilers can be run unchanged. The

JML annotations are inserted using //@ for one-line annotations or /*@ ... @*/ for multiple-line annotations.

2.1   General Description

JML makes it possible to describe the behavioral interface specification of a Java class, by adding annotations describing several kind of properties, such as class invariants or history constraints, and by specifying the behavior of the methods. Method specifications may contain various specification clauses, the most common being the precondition and the postcondition. Preconditions describe the requirements that the class attributes and the method parameters have to fulfill in order to execute the method. If the precondition is not satisfied, the method should not be executed, according to the concept of Design By Contract (DBC) introduced by Eiffel [12]. Postconditions are written using before-after predicates, which link the *after* values of fields with their *before* values (represented by a \old expression). By default, an expression which is not surrounded by \old is evaluated, in a before-after predicate, as its value in the after-state.

First order logic predicates are written using Java boolean operators (e.g. && for logical and, || for logical or, ! for logical not), plus new symbols such as <==> for equivalence, <=!=> for non-equivalence, or \forall (resp. \exists) for the universal (resp. existential) quantifier. New keywords extend the expressiveness of Java, such as \result, which represents the return value of a method.

JML also introduces ways to express the dynamic of objects, such as object creation, specified using the \fresh(o) keyword, which expresses, in a postcondition, that the object o has been freshly allocated during the execution of the method.

2.2   Illustrating JML with an Example

The example we will use in the remainder of the paper is shown in figure 1. It is a specification of a simplified electronic purse. This example is used to illustrate the main concepts of JML.

This specification illustrates the main clauses of JML, such as the class invariant (invariant), specifying that the balance should always be greater or equal to zero. History constraints (constraints) can be used to describe a property that should hold after each method execution.

Each clause is described by a keyword indicating its kind (e.g. requires for preconditions, ensures for normal postcondition (normal_behavior), signals for exceptional postcondition (exceptional_behavior), etc.), followed by a first-order logic predicate or an explicit keyword (e.g. \nothing, \not_specified, etc.). The assignable clause in the method specifications is used to list the fields which may be modified by the execution of the method. This is called the *frame*. The signals clause is used to describe the postcondition the method establishes when the considered method throws an exception of the given type. In our example, the exception NoCreditException is raised when the amount to withdraw is greater than the value of the balance.

```
class Purse {

  //@ invariant balance >= 0;
  protected short balance;

  /*@ public normal_behavior
    @    requires b >= 0;
    @    assignable balance;
    @    ensures balance == b;
    @*/
  public Purse(short b) { ... }

  /*@ behavior
    @    requires a > 0;
    @    assignable balance;
    @    ensures balance == \old(balance) + a;
    @*/
  public void credit(short a) { ... }

  /*@ behavior
    @    requires a > 0;
    @    assignable balance;
    @    ensures balance == \old(balance) - a;
    @    signals (NoCreditException e)
    @             (\old(balance) < a) ==>
    @             balance == \old(balance);
    @*/
  public void withdraw(short a)
             throws NoCreditException { ... }

  /*@ normal_behavior
    @    assignable \nothing;
    @    ensures \result == balance;
    @*/
  public /*@ pure */ short getBalance() { ... }

  /*@ normal_behavior
    @    assignable \nothing;
    @    ensures \fresh(\result) &&
    @             \result.equals(this);
    @*/
  public /*@ pure @*/ Purse duplicate() { ... }
```

```
  /*@ normal_behavior
    @    assignable \nothing;
    @    ensures \result <==>
    @       (this.getBalance() == p.getBalance())
    @*/
  public /*@ pure @*/ boolean equals(Purse p){...}

}

class LimitedPurse extends Purse {

  //@ invariant balance <= max;
  //@ constraint \not_modified(max);
  static short max = 10000;

  /*@ normal_behavior
    @    requires b >= 0 && b <= max;
    @    assignable balance;
    @    ensures balance == b;
    @*/
  public LimitedPurse(short b) { ... }

  /*@ also
    @    requires a > 0;
    @    {|
    @      requires \old(balance)+a <= max;
    @      assignable balance;
    @      ensures balance == \old(balance) + a;
    @    also
    @      requires \old(balance)+a > max;
    @      assignable \nothing;
    @      signals (MaxReachedException e)
    @             balance == \old(balance);
    @    |}
    @*/
  public void credit(short a) { ... }

}
```

Fig. 1. The JML specification of the Purse example

JML also introduces new kinds of method declaration modifiers, including the notion of *purity*, meaning that a method specified as `pure` does not change the value of any field of the considered class. In our example, method `getBalance()` is described to observe the value of the field `balance`.

Method specifications may contain method calls, if and only if these methods are described as *pure*, in order to avoid side-effects. The use of the `\fresh` operator is illustrated by the specification of method `duplicates` which *creates* a new Purse, whose attributes have the same values as the current Purse.

3   Symbolic Animation

This section presents the symbolic animation using constraint systems, as realized in the current framework. Constrained animation makes it possible to keep the non-determinism on data, and also lets the user constrain input parameters to specific values or leave them unconstrained in order to represent a large subset of the possible resulting system states. Firstly, we introduce the framework architecture, the internal format and the environment representation. Secondly we present the animation itself, beginning with an initial state, then showing the effects of the operations.

3.1   General Framework

Each input JML class is translated into an equivalent set of PROLOG clauses in an intermediate format. We briefly describe several aspects of this format, which are useful to understand the rest of the paper. Each clause represents one JML construct (method, precondition, variable etc.), and is tagged with the name of the class from which it originated. Specification variables may be either constants (const), variables (variable) or primed variable (prime), designating the specification variable after an operation has been invoked. Each specification variable has a domain, which is a subset of the solver's computation domain. Operations are related to modules, and are applied to specification variables to change their values. They are described with local variables, i.e. inputs (input(op)), or outputs (output(op)), which are used within preconditions and postconditions. Postconditions are expressed with before-after predicates displaying at the same time state variables at the before state and at the after state, expressed using a specific function: prime. Finally, initialization clauses, related to a module and expressed with "after predicates only", are used to describe the initial state of the system. The dot operator is used to reference data from another module, by using the syntax: *module* dot *variable*.

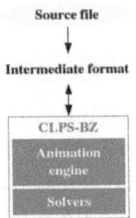

The animation itself is realized from this internal format, within a PROLOG module named CLPS-BZ. This module contains an animation engine and a constraint solver. In order to animate the specification, we need to maintain an environment that represents the variables and their values during the execution. The environment maps each specification variable to a CLPS-BZ variable, on which it is possible to define constraints.

Definition 1 (Multi-module constrained environment). *Let $\mathcal{M}$ be the set of modules, $\mathcal{S}_V$ the set of specification variables, $\mathcal{V}$ the set of CLPS-BZ variables, $\mathcal{K}$ the set of data kinds, $\mathcal{D}_V$ the union of data domains, and C_S a constraint store. The multi-module constrained environment $\mathcal{CE}$ managed by CLPS-BZ is defined by:*

$$\mathcal{CE} = \langle C_S, \ \mathcal{M} \times \mathcal{S}_V \rightarrowtail \mathcal{V} \times \mathcal{K} \times \mathcal{D}_V \rangle \tag{1}$$

The constraint store is managed by the CLPS-BZ solver, which makes it possible to (*i*) add constraints to the store, (*ii*) check the store's consistency, and (*iii*) perform labeling (enumeration of all possible solutions) to assign to CLPS-BZ variables a value of their domain.

The types managed by the internal format ($\mathcal{T}$) are defined by the following abstract grammar: int, atom, set($\mathcal{T}$), pair($\mathcal{T},\mathcal{T}$). The solver works with finite domains, and its computation structures have to be hereditary finite.

3.2 Animating Specifications

Our animation approach is based on the decomposition of predicative specifications into Disjunctive Normal Form (DNF). As a result, *effects* are identified, that are expressed with before-after predicates [10]. We use our internal format as a predicative specification representing the original specification language.

Example 1. Considering the before-after predicate describing an operation applying on the state variable x:

$$x \in [-10\ldots 10] \wedge ((x > 0 \Rightarrow x' = x - 5) \vee (x \leq 0 \Rightarrow x' = x + 5))$$

This operation can be decomposed in two effects, separated by the symbol [] expressing a disjunction of effects:

$$x \in [-10\ldots 10] \wedge x > 0 \wedge x' = x - 5 \; [] \; x \in [-10\ldots 10] \wedge x \leq 0 \wedge x' = x + 5$$

The animation engine performs the activation of effects. Therefore, it has two tasks. First of all, it creates new variables in the environment, which are the primed versions of the current variables, representing the variables in the after state of the effect. Secondly, it adds constraints corresponding to the effect to the store, which changes their values, or reduces their set of solutions.

Definition 2 (Activation of an effect). *An effect is called "enabled" if and only if the store remains consistent after the adding the before-after predicates of the effect.*

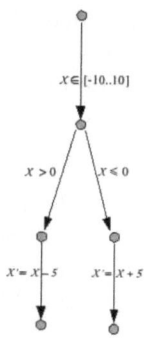

The activation of an effect is done by adding corresponding before-after predicates to the store, after having added to the environment the local variables of the corresponding operation, whether instantiated by an user or left constrained. The environment manager is used to access CLPS-BZ variables to be computed with the solver. The executability of an effect is deduced from the consistency of the constraints store after the effect's activation.

In practice, the behavior decomposition of an operation and the effect activation are done simultaneously by a PRO-LOG module which creates choice-points when a disjunction of effects is met. A simple PROLOG backtracking technique makes it possible to fail with the current effect and try the activation of the next effect.

The environment is initialized by creating an entry in the environment for each declared specification variable. The activation of the effects extracted from the initialization predicates is used to determine the initial values of the variables.

This environment can only represent before and after versions of the specification variables. Therefore, in order to execute successive operations, it is necessary to remove primed variables, and local variables of the operation. For the environment to be ready for the next execution, a specific function named *unprime*, overrides modified variables (i.e., existing in a primed version) by assigning them their after value. Obviously their corresponding CLPS-BZ variables and constraints are still stored in the environment.

4   Expression of Object Concepts

This section focuses on the expression of object concepts in our framework. We firstly describe the general expression of classes and instances, then we present how inheritance can be handled.

4.1   Class Representation

We consider classes to be modules. Instances of classes are represented by distinct atoms. Each class manages its instances with a variable named `instances` of type `set(atom)`, indicating the created instances of the considered class.

Methods (static and non-static) are represented as module operations. Each non-static operation has an input parameter named `this`, representing the instance to which the method is applied. A precondition is added to the operation to require that the parameter `this` is a member of the set of instances of the class. Non-static attributes are modeled as partial functions, which map instances of the class to their corresponding value.

Example 2. Considering the example described in figure 1, the creation of two instances p_1 and p_2 with a respective initial balance of 200 and 1000, leads to `balance` $= \{p_1 \mapsto 200, p_2 \mapsto 1000\}$.

In reality, we also record module names, and extra typing information as described in the following definition.

Definition 3 (Non-static attributes representation). *Let C be the set of class names, $\mathcal{A}$ be the set of non-static attribute names, $\mathcal{V}$ a set of CLPS-BZ variables, $\mathcal{K}$ the set of data kinds, $\mathcal{I}_c$ the set of created instances from the class $c \in C$, and $\mathcal{D}_\mathcal{A}$ the domain of the attributes translated to be handled by CLPS-BZ. An object-oriented representation for non-static attributes is defined by:*

$$C \times \mathcal{A} \twoheadrightarrow \mathcal{V} \times \mathcal{K} \times (\mathcal{I}_c \to \mathcal{D}_\mathcal{A}) \tag{2}$$

Likewise, static attributes, which have the same value for all instances, are translated as a variable whose domain is not indexed by the instances ($\mathcal{I}_c$). That is, ($\mathcal{I}_c \to \mathcal{D}_\mathcal{A}$) in Definition 3 becomes just $\mathcal{D}_\mathcal{A}$.

So each name of each class is mapped to a triple ($\mathcal{V}, \mathcal{K}, Domain$), where $\mathcal{V}$ is a CLPS-BZ constrained variable that represents all the possible values of the name (this is usually a function from instance names to values), $\mathcal{K}$ gives the role that the name plays (input, output, variable, primed variable etc.), and *Domain* specifies the maximum possible set of values (that is, the type) of the name within each instance. Example 3 in the next subsection illustrates these principles in addition to inheritance.

4.2 Inheritance Representation

Inheritance is expressed by considering that subclass instances are a subset of the superclass instances. If B is a subclass of A, then $instances_B \subseteq instances_A$.

An attribute is always associated with the class, i.e, the module, in which it is first declared. There is no copy of inherited fields within the subclasses, unless the fields are redefined. Fields and methods that are inherited without redefinition are not copied into the subclasses. Instead, we directly use the definitions from their original superclass. When the user invokes a method like `p.credit(100)`, a dynamic dispatch is performed by using the runtime type of `p` to determine which specification of `credit(short)` is used.

Example 3. Consider the two classes `Purse` and `LimitedPurse`, described in the example in Fig. 1. Given an animation sequence that has created one instance of each class `Purse` and `LimitedPurse` (respectively named p_1 and lp_1), by invoking their respective constructors with an unspecified initializing value, the resulting constrained multi-modules environment $\mathcal{CE}_{ex}$ managing the execution is the following:

$$\mathcal{CE}_{ex} = \langle\{V_1 \in 0..32767\}, V_2 \in 0..10000\}, \{(\text{b\_Purse, instances}) \mapsto (\{p_1, lp_1\}, \text{variable}, \{\{p_1, lp_1\}\}),$$
$$(\text{b\_Purse, b\_balance}) \mapsto (\{p_1 \mapsto V_1, lp_1 \mapsto V_2\}, \text{variable}, \{p_1, lp_1\} \to -32768..32767),$$
$$(\text{b\_LimitedPurse, instances}) \mapsto (\{lp_1\}, \text{variable}, \{\{lp_1\}\}),$$
$$(\text{b\_LimitedPurse, b\_max}) \mapsto (10000, \text{variable}, -32768..32767)\})$$

Notice that names extracted from the original specification are systematically prefixed with `b_` to create PROLOG atoms, to prevent problems with capital letters being reserved for PROLOG variables.

We will now explain the meaning of this environment. The instance p_1 has been created using the `Purse(short)` constructor, leaving the value of the parameter unspecified, i.e., constrained by the precondition of the constructor, thus its domain has been reduced to 0..32767. The second instance lp_1 has been created using the `LimitedPurse(short)` constructor with a constrained parameter, whose domain has been reduced to 0..10000 according to the constructor's preconditions. Both of these instances are member of the set of `Purse` instances, whereas lp_1 only is a specific member of the set of `LimitedPurse` instances. Since `max` is a static field, its value is not related to any instance, contrary to balance, which is a total function mapping p_1 and lp_1 to their values.

5   Application to JML Specifications

Animating JML specifications is different from animating B machines, as performed in BZ-Testing-Tools [2]. In order to animate a B machine, we need to express it as pre- and postconditions by rewriting the generalized substitutions with before-after predicates according to the rules given in [1]. Unlike B, JML is well-suited to the possibilities of our approach. Indeed, the postconditions of the Java/JML methods are expressed using before-after predicates, which represents constraints over the class fields. Moreover, the frame condition is explicitly given for each method, describing the exhaustive list of fields modified by the method invocation. Thus, the expression of JML within our framework is quite straightforward as shown in [3].

This section firstly presents the way JML is handled within our framework and secondly we introduce the way we consider the dynamic creation of objects. Finally, we introduce the way properties are checked for a specific execution state.

5.1   Expressing Java/JML Within Our Framework

Expressing Types. In our translation, the supported types are integers (to represent all built-in Java types, except `long` and floats), and atoms (for object references). Domain definitions are distinguished to differentiate the different types. For example, $Range(\texttt{byte}) = -128..127$, $Range(\texttt{char}) = 0..65535$, and $Range(C) = \texttt{b\_}C$ `dot instances` $\cup$ `{null}` respectively give the range of values for bytes, characters and objects of class C. We represent arrays by functions mapping the indexes to the values. Basic integers (`int`) are restricted according to the limitation of the underlying SICStus CLP(FD) library.

These data domains are used to specify the domain of variables representing the class attributes in the internal format. They appear in the internal format as an `invariant`, used to type data, and also in the preconditions of operations to type the method parameters.

Expressing JML Clauses. JML clauses are expressed in our internal format with only minor changes, because our internal format supports first-order logic predicates. Moreover, its expressiveness, based on B, is sufficient to express JML predicates without major modifications. The JML before-after predicates are written using the special `\old` symbol to represent *before* values, whereas our internal format uses the `prime` symbol to distinguish *after* values. Thus, we rely on static analysis to determine in the expressions, whether attributes have to be considered at their before or after values.

In order to handle JML specification clauses, our internal format is enriched with new kind of predicates, named `jml_invariant` and `jml_constraints` to respectively express invariant and history constraints. In order to be able to check history constraints, we store in an execution environment both current and previous values of the state variables representing the JML fields. Current state variable are those whose kind is `prime` whereas previous values have the `variable` kind.

Method Specification Clauses. As described in the previous section, class methods are expressed with module operations. Return values of the operations, symbolized by the \result keyword in JML predicates, are declared as an operation output parameter, named b_result. Preconditions and postconditions are both natively supported by our format, but we need to distinguish normal and exceptional JML postconditions. To do this, the exception that is thrown is bound to a parameter named exc, which is no_exc for normal returns, or the exception object when exceptions are thrown, as shown in the example 4 below.

Example 4 (Distinction of effects). Considering the following JML method specification:

```
/*@ behavior
 @      requires P;
 @      assignable A;
 @      ensures Q;
 @      signals (Ex1) S1;
 @      ...
 @      signals (ExN) SN;
 @*/
void m() throws Ex1,...,ExN { ... }
```

The following $(N + 1)$ effects are identified:

$$(P \wedge Q \wedge \texttt{exc} = \texttt{no\_exc}) \; [] \; (P \wedge S1 \wedge \texttt{exc} = \texttt{Ex1}) \; [] \; \ldots \; [] \; (P \wedge SN \wedge \texttt{exc} = \texttt{ExN})$$

5.2   Dynamic Objects Management

Java objects can be seen as pointers on memory addresses at which structures are defined. Firstly, we define the heap representation we have considered. Secondly, we explain how we handle dynamic object creation.

Heap Representation. The heap structure is represented by a set of atoms, describing the set of addresses that may be used during the animation. Since our solver works with finite domains, this set is bounded but its size can be user-defined. It is represented by a constant, named all_addresses, linked with a general module named system. In addition, we consider a set of addresses, the subset of created instances, which is a subset of all_addresses, also linked with the system module. This set, named allocated, represents the union of all the instances variables of the different modules. This makes it possible to use a non-deterministic choice among the possible addresses, each time an object is created, either when a constructor is invoked, or when a field is freshly allocated.

Frames and Dynamic Object Creation. For precisely animating a specification we need to know which fields are modified or not. Therefore, we use the assignable clause to determine which field are supposed to be modified, and by extension which ones are supposed to remain unchanged. The main difficulty in animating an object oriented specification is to "detect" the creation of objects during the execution of a method. Using the \fresh(o) JML operator in addition to the assignable clause, we are able to identify among the modified fields, which ones are assigned to an already-existing object, and which ones are assigned to a new object. If the postcondition does not explicitly specify that a field is assigned to a newly-created object, then the after value of this latter is computed among the already existing object of the considered type.

The presence of the \fresh operator causes a new object identifier to be allocated and returned. This new object identifier is chosen from the set of unallocated addresses, given by the set-difference between all_addresses and allocated in the system module. Since this local variable is constrained, we have chosen to immediately perform a labeling on it, so that a value is directly assigned to it. Thus, there are no choice-points related to the new object's addresses. In addition, we have to consider all the instance fields to make them appear in the domain of the CLPS-BZ variables representing the corresponding fields. Recursively, if one of the fields is specified as being *fresh*, the same process is applied. If the new object's class has subclasses, a choicepoint is created to select one of these possible (sub)types. This choicepoint may be discarded by the use of the JML \typeof operator which specifies the dynamic type of an object.

5.3   Checking Model Properties On-the-Fly

Our framework makes it possible to check predicates within an execution state. When the execution sequence does not introduce any constrained variables, the property can be evaluated to true or false. On the contrary, if constrained variables have been introduced, the property can be evaluated either to satisfiable –if the property can be true for at least one of the variables values– or valid, if the property is true for all possible values of the variables. Our technique for checking predicates is describe hereafter.

The validity of the predicate is checked by adding its negation to the constraint store. If it produces an inconsistency, the predicate is declared as valid. Otherwise, the store is still consistent and its valuation presents a counter-example to the predicate. Similarly, the satisfiability of the predicate is checked by adding the predicate itself to the store. If it produces an inconsistency, then we can conclude that the predicate is unsatisfiable, and a valuation of the store before adding the predicate is a counter-example.

This ability to produce precise counter-examples gives very useful concrete feedback to users, and is one of the strengths of our approach.

6   Animating the Example

Considering the example described in figure 1, we will describe its animation step by step to illustrate our approach. At each step, we present the resulting environment. In order to lighten the display, after values of variables are not displayed if they are equal to the before value. Some details of how these object states and constraints are actually displayed to the user are given in [4].

Suppose we consider a heap of size 5 for the needs of the animation. The initial state describing the execution of the Purse specification is:

$$\mathcal{CE}_0 = \langle \{\}, \{(\text{system}, \text{all\_addresses}) \mapsto (\{a_1, a_2, a_3, a_4, a_5\}, \text{const}, ...),$$
$$(\text{system}, \text{allocated}) \mapsto (\{\}, \text{variable}, \{\{\}\}), (\text{b\_Purse}, \text{instances}) \mapsto (\{\}, \text{variable}, \{\{\}\}),$$
$$(\text{b\_Purse}, \text{b\_balance}) \mapsto (\{\}, \text{variable}, \{\{\}\}), (\text{b\_LimitedPurse}, \text{instances}) \mapsto (\{\}, \text{variable}, \{\{\}\}),$$
$$(\text{b\_LimitedPurse}, \text{b\_max}) \mapsto (10000, \text{variable}, -32768..32767)\}\rangle$$

The creation of an instance a_1 from class `LimitedPurse` using the constructor `LimitedPurse(?)`, leaving the initial amount of money unspecified, leads to the following environment.

$$\mathcal{CE}_1 = \langle\{V_1 \in [0..10000]\}, \{(\texttt{system}, \texttt{all\_addresses}) \mapsto (\{a_1, a_2, a_3, a_4, a_5\}, \text{const}, ...),$$
$$(\texttt{system}, \texttt{allocated}) \mapsto (\{\}, \text{variable}, \{\{\}\}), (\texttt{b\_Purse}, \texttt{instances}) \mapsto (\{\}, \text{variable}, \{\{\}\}),$$
$$(\texttt{b\_Purse}, \texttt{b\_balance}) \mapsto (\{\}, \text{variable}, \{\{\}\}), (\texttt{b\_LimitedPurse}, \texttt{instances}) \mapsto (\{\}, \text{variable}, \{\{\}\}),$$
$$(\texttt{b\_LimitedPurse}, \texttt{b\_max}) \mapsto (10000, \text{variable}, -32768..32767),$$
$$(\texttt{b\_Purse}, \texttt{this}) \mapsto (a_1, \text{input}(\texttt{b\_Purse\_short}), -32768..32767),$$
$$(\texttt{b\_Purse}, \texttt{b\_b}) \mapsto (V_1, \text{input}(\texttt{b\_Purse\_short}), -32768..32767),$$
$$(\texttt{system}, \texttt{allocated}) \mapsto (\{a_1\}, \text{prime}, \{\{a_1\}\}), (\texttt{b\_Purse}, \texttt{instances}) \mapsto (\{a_1\}, \text{prime}, \{\{a_1\}\}),$$
$$(\texttt{b\_LimitedPurse}, \texttt{instances}) \mapsto (\{a_1\}, \text{prime}, \{\{a_1\}\}),$$
$$(\texttt{b\_Purse}, \texttt{b\_balance}) \mapsto (\{a_1 \mapsto V_1\}, \text{prime}, \{a_1\} \to -32768..32767)\}\rangle$$

This introduces a constrained value V_1, whose domain is reduced by the precondition `b >= 0 && b <= max` to $0..10000$.

The dynamic creation of object can be illustrated when calling method `duplicate()` on the previously created instance. The first possible address is chosen to represent the new instance. By default, this instance is added to the set of created instances of the class representing the return type of the module. This is shown in the environment below.

$$\mathcal{CE}_2 = \langle\{V_1 \in 0..10000, V_2 = V_1\}, \{(\texttt{system}, \texttt{all\_addresses}) \mapsto (\{a_1, a_2, a_3, a_4, a_5\}, \text{const}, ...),$$
$$(\texttt{system}, \texttt{allocated}) \mapsto (\{a_1\}, \text{variable}, \{\{a_1\}\}),$$
$$(\texttt{b\_Purse}, \texttt{instances}) \mapsto (\{a_1\}, \text{variable}, \{\{a_1\}\}),$$
$$(\texttt{b\_Purse}, \texttt{b\_balance}) \mapsto (\{a_1 \mapsto V_1\}, \text{variable}, \{a_1\} \to -32768..32767),$$
$$(\texttt{b\_LimitedPurse}, \texttt{instances}) \mapsto (\{a_1\}, \text{variable}, \{\{a_1\}\}),$$
$$(\texttt{b\_LimitedPurse}, \texttt{b\_max}) \mapsto (10000, \text{variable}, -32768..32767),$$
$$(\texttt{b\_Purse}, \texttt{this}) \mapsto (a_1, \text{input}(\texttt{b\_duplicate}), -32768..32767),$$
$$(\texttt{system}, \texttt{allocated}) \mapsto (\{a_1, a_2\}, \text{prime}, \{\{a_1, a_2\}\}),$$
$$(\texttt{b\_Purse}, \texttt{instances}) \mapsto (\{a_1, a_2\}, \text{prime}, \{\{a_1, a_2\}\}),$$
$$(\texttt{b\_Purse}, \texttt{b\_balance}) \mapsto (\{a_1 \mapsto V_1, a_2 \mapsto V_2\}, \text{prime}, \{a_1, a_2\} \to -32768..32767)\}\rangle$$

Notice that `prime` variables of the previous environment have become the current `variable` of this environment. Suppose now we perform a labeling so that V_2 is assigned to 200. By constraints propagation, V_1 will also be assigned to 200.

We now applying the method `withdraw` on instance a_2, without specifying which exception will be thrown or which amount should be removed. This induces two possible effects, which produce two different environments. The first one, $\mathcal{CE}_{3a}$, is established when no exception is raised. The second one, $\mathcal{CE}_{3b}$, corresponds to the throwing of exception `NoCreditException`.

$$\mathcal{CE}_{3a} = \langle\{V_3 \in 1..32767, V_4 = 200 - V_3\}, \{(\texttt{system}, \texttt{all\_addresses}) \mapsto (\{a_1, a_2, a_3, a_4, a_5\}, \text{const}, ...),$$
$$(\texttt{system}, \texttt{allocated}) \mapsto (\{a_1, a_2\}, \text{variable}, \{\{a_1, a_2\}\}),$$
$$(\texttt{b\_Purse}, \texttt{instances}) \mapsto (\{a_1, a_2\}, \text{variable}, \{\{a_1, a_2\}\}),$$
$$(\texttt{b\_Purse}, \texttt{b\_balance}) \mapsto (\{a_1 \mapsto 200, a_2 \mapsto 200\}, \text{variable}, \{a_1, a_2\} \to -32768..32767)),$$
$$(\texttt{b\_LimitedPurse}, \texttt{instances}) \mapsto (\{a_1\}, \text{variable}, \{\{a_1\}\}),$$
$$(\texttt{b\_LimitedPurse}, \texttt{b\_max}) \mapsto (10000, \text{variable}, -32768..32767),$$
$$(\texttt{b\_Purse}, \texttt{this}) \mapsto (a_2, \text{input}(\texttt{b\_withdraw\_short}), -32768..32767),$$
$$(\texttt{b\_Purse}, \texttt{exc}) \mapsto (\texttt{no\_exc}, \text{input}(\texttt{b\_withdraw\_short}), \{\texttt{no\_exc}, \texttt{b\_NoCreditException}\}),$$

$(\texttt{b\_Purse}, \texttt{b\_a}) \mapsto (V_3, \texttt{input}(\texttt{b\_withdraw\_short}), -32768..32767),$

$(\texttt{b\_Purse}, \texttt{b\_balance}) \mapsto (\{a_1 \mapsto 200, a_2 \mapsto V_4\}, \texttt{prime}, \{a_1, a_2\} \rightarrow -32768..32767)\})$

$\mathcal{CE}_{3b} = \langle \{ V3 \in 201..32767 \}, \{ (\texttt{system}, \texttt{all\_addresses}) \mapsto (\{a_1, a_2, a_3, a_4, a_5\}, \texttt{const}, ...),$

$\quad (\texttt{system}, \texttt{allocated}) \mapsto (\{a_1, a_2\}, \texttt{variable}, \{\{a_1, a_2\}\}),$

$\quad (\texttt{b\_Purse}, \texttt{instances}) \mapsto (\{a_1, a_2\}, \texttt{variable}, \{\{a_1, a_2\}\}),$

$\quad (\texttt{b\_Purse}, \texttt{b\_balance}) \mapsto (\{a_1 \mapsto 200, a_2 \mapsto 200\}, \texttt{variable}, \{a_1, a_2\} \rightarrow -32768..32767)),$

$\quad (\texttt{b\_LimitedPurse}, \texttt{instances}) \mapsto (\{a_1\}, \texttt{variable}, \{\{\}\}),$

$\quad (\texttt{b\_LimitedPurse}, \texttt{b\_max}) \mapsto (10000, \texttt{variable}, -32768..32767),$

$\quad (\texttt{b\_Purse}, \texttt{this}) \mapsto (a_2, \texttt{input}(\texttt{b\_withdraw\_short}), -32768..32767),$

$\quad (\texttt{b\_Purse}, \texttt{exc}) \mapsto (\texttt{b\_NoCreditException}, \texttt{input}(\texttt{b\_withdraw\_short}), \{\texttt{no\_exc}, \texttt{b\_NoCreditException}\}),$

$\quad (\texttt{b\_Purse}, \texttt{b\_a}) \mapsto (V_3, \texttt{input}(\texttt{b\_withdraw\_short}), -32768..32767),$

$\quad (\texttt{b\_Purse}, \texttt{b\_balance}) \mapsto (\{a_1 \mapsto 200, a_2 \mapsto 200\}, \texttt{prime}, \{a_1, a_2\} \rightarrow -32768..32767)\})$

In the first case, no exception is raised, and the new value of the balance is computed, depending on the input value. In the second case, an exception is thrown, and the value of the balance is unchanged.

If we consider the first environment ($\mathcal{CE}_{3a}$), the verification of the validity of the class invariant of instance a_1 (i.e., class `Purse`) is performed by adding its negation to the store. This leads to the following set of constraints:

$$\{ V_3 \in 1..32767, V_4 = 200 - V_3, V_4 < 0 \}$$

which is still consistent. Performing a labeling displays a reachable counter-example to the validity of the invariant $\{ V_3 = 201, V_4 = -1 \}$. This exhibits an error in the specification of the `withdraw(short)` method. Indeed, the model makes it possible to withdraw more money than the purse contains, since the normal postcondition does not take this fact into account. This mistake can be corrected by rewriting the method specification to:

```
/*@ behavior
  @     requires a > 0;
  @     assignable balance;
  @     ensures (a <= \old(balance)) ==> (balance == \old(balance) - a);
  @     signals (NoCreditException e)
  @             (a > \old(balance)) ==> (balance == \old(balance));
  @*/
public void withdraw(short a) throws NoCreditException { ... }
```

Note how powerful the constrained animation was in this example – we effectively executed the `withdraw` method with *all* possible input values, then *after* executing the method we determined which of those input values could result in a contradiction (thus showing that the postcondition was not precise enough, or the precondition was too weak). This ability to delay choosing input values makes constrained animation a much more powerful validation tool than traditional value-based animation.

7   Related Work

Animating a specification is a simple and direct way for an user to validate the specification he has written. Most of the animation work deals with the trade-off between expressiveness of the notation and its executability, especially with the Z notation. For example, Possum [8] executes Z and uses Cogito to test the specification before refining. Works about Object-Z animation with a Z animation environment has been described in [11].

UML/OCL presents a higher abstraction level that JML, which can be seen as a refinement step from UML. In UML the interaction between objects are represented through associations, which make step-by-step animation easier to perform. The USE tool [6] for UML/OCL makes it possible to perform the animation of an UML description of a system. On the same principle, in the domain of symbolic animation, [7] describes the animation of UML diagrams enriched with OCL constraints by expressing it into them into the PROLOG++ declarative language, but this work only focuses on invariant constraints and does not take into account the pre- and postconditions for the animation.

One of the closest work related to ours is the approach presented by Wahls et al. for executing formal model-based specifications in [16]. As for the latter, specifications are translated to the concurrent constraints language AKL (Agents Kernel Language). An application is made on the SPECS/C++ language, which is a JML-like specification language based on C++ with pre- and postconditions annotations for each method. The main difference is that both approaches rely on AKL or PROLOG++ to perform the animation.

Efforts have also been made for checking JML specifications by relying on the model-checker Bogor, as implemented within the SpEx-JML tool [13]. As for our approach, this tools performs verifications dynamically, but as for every model-checker, it suffers from state-space-explosion, even if Bogor is powerful enough to delay it. Although it does not have the same goals –verification vs. validation– this approach is similar to ours, but we use constrained values to represent Java values and therefore avoid the state-explosion phenomenon.

The existing object-oriented model-based animators rely on common constrained languages and built-in virtual machines for interpretation and so, animation. Our approach is different. We rely on an intermediate language, interpreted by a customized virtual machine, which combines constraint solvers, to handle state variable values, and backtracking techniques, to enable the different effects of the operations. Thus, our framework is fully independent and may be extended at will. Although it does not directly integrate object concepts, we are able to express and to handle them easily, as shown in this application to JML, which does not seem to have been targeted before.

8 Conclusion and Future Work

This paper has presented a technique for animating object-oriented specifications. It relies on an existing non-modular framework extended to take into account object-oriented specifications. We have chosen to apply this translation on JML specifications and we have implemented it into a tool-set named JML-Testing-Tools [4]. This tool handles, in addition to the previously described features, precondition checking and property verification with counter-example display. The tool also allows animation sequences to be saved and rerun. This is useful for regression testing, when the JML specifications evolve. To our knowledge, this is the first specification animation tool for JML specifications.

The use of our animation tool is a very important part of the design of formal models, since it makes it possible to detect model inconsistencies and unintended behaviors, early in the software lifecycle. Nevertheless, our approach requires the specification to be detailed enough to perform a "realistic" symbolic execution. Anyway, a detailed modeling is still very useful, since the more precise the specification is, the more accurate are the results, whatever the purpose is: validating a model, or validating the implementation w.r.t. the model.

In the future, we plan to extend the computation domain of the CLPS-BZ solver, to handle sequences and floats. These extensions will allow us to express a larger subset of JML/Java, with a better management of arrays and the integration of floats. In parallel, we plan to use our technology to generate Java test sequences to ensure the conformance of the implementation with respect to the specification. Our tool already allows user-defined animation sequences to be saved as Java code sequences, so that they can be used as test cases for implementations that can be verified with the JML Runtime Assertion Checker, as described in [5]. But, we would like to adapt the boundary test generation method implemented in BZ-Testing-Tools [2] and therefore produce boundary test cases from JML specifications for Java programs.

References

1. J.-R. Abrial. *The B-book: Assigning Programs to Meanings*. Cambridge University Press, 1996.
2. F. Ambert, F. Bouquet, S. Chemin, S. Guenaud, B. Legeard, F. Peureux, N. Vacelet, and M. Utting. BZ-TT: A Tool-Set for Test Generation from Z and B using Contraint Logic Programming. In Robert Hierons and Thierry Jerron, editors, *Formal Approaches to Testing of Software, FATES 2002 workshop of CONCUR'02*, pages 105–120. INRIA Report, August 2002.
3. F. Bouquet, F. Dadeau, and J. Groslambert. Checking JML Specifications with B Machines. In *Proceedings of the International Conference on Formal Specification and Development in Z and B (ZB'05)*, volume 3455 of *Lecture Notes in Computer Science*, pages 435–454, Guildford, United Kingdom, April 2005. Springer-Verlag.
4. F. Bouquet, F. Dadeau, B. Legeard, and M. Utting. JML-Testing-Tools: a Symbolic Animator for JML Specifications using CLP. In Nicolas Halbwachs and Lenore Zuck, editors, *Proceedings of 11th Int. Conf. on Tools and Algorithms for the Construction and Analysis of Systems, Tool session (TACAS'05)*, volume 3440 of *Lecture Notes in Computer Science*, pages 551–556, Edinburgh, United Kingdom, April 2005. Springer-Verlag.
5. Yoonsik Cheon and Gary T. Leavens. A Runtime Assertion Checker for the Java Modeling Language (JML). In Hamid R. Arabnia and Youngsong Mun, editors, *Proceedings of the International Conference on Software Engineering Research and Practice (SERP '02), Las Vegas, Nevada, USA, June 24-27, 2002*, pages 322–328. CSREA Press, June 2002.

6. M. Gogolla and M. Richters. Development of UML Descriptions with USE. In Hassan Shafazand and A Min Tjoa, editors, *Proc. 1st Eurasian Conf. Information and Communication Technology (EURASIA'2002)*, volume 2510 of *LNCS*, pages 228–238. Springer, 2002.

7. J. Gray and S. Schach. Constraint Animation Using an Object-Oriented Declarative Language. In *Proceedings of the 38th Annual ACM SE Conference*, Clemson, April 2000.

8. D. Hazel, P. Strooper, and O. Traynor. Possum: An Animator for the SUM Specification Language. In *Proceedings of the Fourth Asia-Pacific Software Engineering and International Computer Science Conference*, pages 42–51, 1997.

9. G.T. Leavens, A.L. Baker, and C. Ruby. JML: a Java Modeling Language. In *Formal Underpinnings of Java Workshop (at OOPSLA '98)*, October 1998.

10. B. Legeard, F. Peureux, and M. Utting. Controlling Test Case Explosion in Test Generation from B Formal Models. *The Journal of Software Testing, Verification and Reliability*, 14(2):to appear, 2004.

11. T. McComb and G. Smith. Animation of Object-Z Specifications Using a Z Animator. In IEEE Computer Society, editor, *International conference on Software Engineering and Formal Methods (SEFM 2003)*, 2003.

12. B. Meyer. *Object-Oriented Software Construction*. Prentice Hall, 2 edition, 1997.

13. Robby, E. Rodríguez, M. Dwyer, and J. Hatcliff. Checking Strong Specifications Using an Extensible Software Model Checking Framework. In Kurt Jensen and Andreas Podelski, editors, *Tools and Algorithms for the Construction and Analysis of Systems, 10th International Conference, TACAS 2004*, volume 2988 of *Lecture Notes in Computer Science*, pages 404–420. Springer, 2004.

14. J. Rumbaugh, I. Jacobson, and G. Booch. *The Unified Modeling Language Reference Manual*, addison-wesley edition, 1999.

15. J.M. Spivey. *The Z Notation: A Reference Manual*. Prentice-Hall, 2nd edition, 1992. ISBN 0 13 978529 9.

16. T. Wahls, G.T. Leavens, and A.L. Baker. Executing Formal Specifications with Concurrent Constraint Programming. *Automated Software Engineering*, 7(4):315 – 343, December 2000.

17. J. Warmer and A. Kleppe. *The Object Constraint Language: Precise Modeling with UML*. Addison-Wesley, 1998.

Certified Memory Usage Analysis[*]

David Cachera[1], Thomas Jensen[2], David Pichardie[1], and Gerardo Schneider[2,3]

[1] IRISA/ENS Cachan (Bretagne), Campus de Ker Lann, 35170 Bruz, France
[2] IRISA/CNRS, Campus de Beaulieu, 35042 Rennes cedex, France
[3] Dept. of Informatics, Univ. of Oslo, PO Box 1080 Blindern, N-0316 Oslo, Norway

Abstract. We present a certified algorithm for resource usage analysis, applicable to languages in the style of Java byte code. The algorithm verifies that a program executes in bounded memory. The algorithm is destined to be used in the development process of applets and for enhanced byte code verification on embedded devices. We have therefore aimed at a low-complexity algorithm derived from a loop detection algorithm for control flow graphs. The expression of the algorithm as a constraint-based static analysis of the program over simple lattices provides a link with abstract interpretation that allows to state and prove formally the correctness of the analysis with respect to an operational semantics of the program. The certification is based on an abstract interpretation framework implemented in the Coq proof assistant which has been used to provide a complete formalisation and formal verification of all correctness proofs.

Keywords: Program analysis, certified memory analysis, theorem proving, constraint solving.

1   Introduction

This paper presents a certified algorithm for resource usage analysis, aimed at verifying that a program executes in bounded memory. Controlling the way that software consumes resources is a general concern to the software developer, in particular for software executing on embedded devices such as smart cards where memory is limited and cannot easily be recovered. Indeed, for Java Card up to version 2.1 there is no garbage collector and starting with version 2.2 the machine includes a garbage collector which may be activated invoking an API function at the end of the execution of the applet. This has lead to a rather restrictive programming discipline for smart cards in which the programmer must avoid memory allocation in parts of the code that are within loops. We provide a certified analysis that automatically and efficiently can check that such a programming discipline is respected on a Java Card. This analysis can be deployed in two contexts:

1. As part of a software development environment for smart cards. In that case, it will play a role similar to other program analyses used in type checking and optimisation.

---

[*] This work was partially supported by the French RNTL project "Castles".

J.S. Fitzgerald, I.J. Hayes, and A. Tarlecki (Eds.): FM 2005, LNCS 3582, pp. 91–106, 2005.
© Springer-Verlag Berlin Heidelberg 2005

2. As part of an extended *on-card* byte code verifier that checks applets and software down-loaded on the card after it has been issued.

In both scenarios, there is a need for certification of the analysis. In the first case, the analysis will be part of a software development process satisfying the requirements of the certification criteria. In the second case, the analysis will be part of the card protection mechanisms (the so-called Trusted Computing Base) that have to be certified. The current implementation has a time complexity that is sufficiently low to integrate it in a development tool. However, we have not yet paid attention to the space complexity of the algorithm and current memory consumption excludes any analysis to take place on-device.

The analysis is a constraint-based static analysis that works by generating a set of constraints from the program byte code. These constraints define a number of sets that describe *a)* whether a given method is (mutually) recursive or can be called from (mutually) recursive methods, and *b)* whether a method can be called from intra-procedural cycles. This information is then combined to identify memory allocations (or any other type of resource-sensitive instructions) that could be executed an unbounded number of times. By casting the analysis as a constraint-based static analysis we are able to give a precise semantic definition of each set and use the framework of abstract interpretation to prove that the analysis provide correct information for all programs. The paper offers the following contributions:

- A constraint-based static analysis that formalises a loop-detecting algorithm for detecting methods and instructions that may be executed an unbounded number of times.
- A formalisation based on abstract interpretation of the link between the analysis result and the operational semantics for the underlying byte code language.
- A certification of the analysis in the form of a complete formalisation of the analysis and the correctness proof within the Coq theorem prover.

The paper is organised as follows. Section 2 briefly introduces the byte code language of study. Section 3 gives an informal presentation of the algorithm and its relation to an operational trace semantics. In Section 4 we formalise the correctness relationship. In Section 5 we give a general description of the structure of the Coq proof. Section 6 exposes some complexity considerations and presents some benchmarks. Section 7 describes the background for this work and compares with existing resource analyses. Section 8 concludes.

2   Java Card Byte Code

Our work is based on the Carmel intermediate representation of Java Card byte code [11]. The Carmel language consists of byte codes for a stack-oriented machine whose instructions include stack operations, numeric operations, conditionals, object creation and modification, and method invocation and return. We do not deal with subroutines (the Java jsr instruction) or with exceptions. These instructions can be treated in our framework but complicates the control flow and may lead to inferior analysis results.

$$\frac{\text{instructionAt}_P(m, pc) = \text{instr}}{\langle\!\langle h, \langle m, pc, l, s\rangle, sf\rangle\!\rangle \rightarrow_{\text{instr}} \langle\!\langle h, \langle m, pc+1, l', s'\rangle, sf\rangle\!\rangle}$$

$$\frac{\substack{\text{instructionAt}_P(m, pc) = \text{if } pc' \\ n = 0}}{\langle\!\langle h, \langle m, pc, l, n :: s\rangle, sf\rangle\!\rangle \rightarrow_{\text{if } pc'} \\ \langle\!\langle h, \langle m, pc', l, s\rangle, sf\rangle\!\rangle}$$

$$\frac{\substack{\text{instructionAt}_P(m, pc) = \text{if } pc' \\ n \neq 0}}{\langle\!\langle h, \langle m, pc, l, n :: s\rangle, sf\rangle\!\rangle \rightarrow_{\text{if } pc'} \\ \langle\!\langle h, \langle m, pc+1, l, s\rangle, sf\rangle\!\rangle}$$

$$\frac{\text{instructionAt}_P(m, pc) = \text{goto } pc'}{\langle\!\langle h, \langle m, pc, l, s\rangle, sf\rangle\!\rangle \rightarrow_{\text{goto } pc'} \\ \langle\!\langle h, \langle m, pc', l, s\rangle, sf\rangle\!\rangle}$$

$$\frac{\substack{\text{instructionAt}_P(m, pc) = \text{new } cl \\ \exists c \in \text{classes}(P) \text{ with nameClass}(c) = cl \\ (h', loc) = \text{newObject}(cl, h)}}{\langle\!\langle h, \langle m, pc, l, s\rangle, sf\rangle\!\rangle \rightarrow_{\text{new } cl} \\ \langle\!\langle h', \langle m, pc+1, l, loc :: s\rangle, sf\rangle\!\rangle}$$

$$\frac{\substack{\text{instructionAt}_P(m, pc) = \text{invokevirtual } M \\ h(loc) = o \quad m' = \text{methodLookup}(M, o) \quad f = \langle m, pc, l, loc :: V :: s\rangle \\ f' = \langle m', 1, V, \varepsilon\rangle \qquad\qquad f'' = \langle m, pc, l, s\rangle}}{\langle\!\langle h, f, sf\rangle\!\rangle \rightarrow_{\text{invokevirtual } M} \langle\!\langle h, f', f'' :: sf\rangle\!\rangle}$$

$$\frac{\text{instructionAt}_P(m, pc) = \text{return} \quad f' = \langle m', pc', l', s'\rangle}{\langle\!\langle h, \langle m, pc, l, v :: s\rangle, f' :: sf\rangle\!\rangle \rightarrow_{\text{return}} \langle\!\langle h, \langle m', pc'+1, l', v :: s'\rangle, sf\rangle\!\rangle}$$

Fig. 1. Carmel operational semantics

The formal definition of the language is given as a small-step operational semantics with a state of the form $\langle\!\langle h, \langle m, pc, l, s\rangle, sf\rangle\!\rangle$, where h is the heap of objects, $\langle m, pc, l, s\rangle$ is the current *frame* and sf is the current call stack (a list of frames). A frame $\langle m, pc, l, s\rangle$ contains a method name m and a program point pc within m, a set of local variables l, and a local operand stack s (see [15] for details). Let State$_P$ be the set of all the states of a given program P. We will write simply State if P is understood from the context. The transition relation $\rightarrow_I$ describes how the execution of instruction I changes the state. This is extended to a transition relation $\rightarrow$ on traces such that $tr ::: s_1 \rightarrow tr ::: s_1 ::: s_2$ if there exists an instruction I such that $s_1 \rightarrow_I s_2$[1].

The instructions concerned with control flow and memory allocation: if, goto, invokevirtual, return and new, need a special treatment in our analysis. The rest of the instructions may have different effects on the operand stack and local variables but behave similarly with respect to memory and control flow (move to the next instruction without doing any memory allocation). For clarity and in order to focus on the essentials, these instructions have been grouped into one generic instruction instr with this behaviour. Fig. 1 shows the rules describing the operational semantics of Carmel.

The rule for the generic instruction instr is formalised as a (non-deterministic) transition from state $\langle\!\langle h, \langle m, pc, l, s\rangle, sf\rangle\!\rangle$ to any state of form $\langle\!\langle h, \langle m, pc+1, l', s'\rangle, sf\rangle\!\rangle$. Instructions if and goto affect the control flow by modi-

---

[1] Here and everywhere in the paper, "$:::$" denotes the "cons" operation for traces (appending an element to the right of the trace). We will use "$::$" as the "cons" operation of the operand stack (the top of the stack being on the left).

fying the pc component of the state. The $\texttt{if}$ instruction produces a jump to an indicated program point pc' if the top of the operand stack is 0; otherwise it moves to the instruction $pc + 1$. The $\texttt{goto}\ pc'$ unconditionally jumps to pc'. The $\texttt{new}$ instruction modifies the heap (h') creating an object of class cl on location loc; loc is added to the stack and the pc is incremented.

The rule for $\texttt{invokevirtual}$ is slightly more complicated. Let M be a method name. The instruction $\texttt{invokevirtual}\ M$ at address (m, pc) of state $\sigma = \langle\!\langle h, f, sf \rangle\!\rangle$ may only occur if the current frame f of σ has an operand stack of the form $loc :: V :: s$, i.e., it starts with a *heap location* denoted by loc, followed by a vector of values V. The actual method that will be called is to be found in the object o that resides in the heap h at the address $h(loc)$, and the actual parameters of that method are contained in the vector V. Then, the $\texttt{methodLookup}$ function searches the class hierarchy for the method name M in the object o, and returns the actual method to which the control will be transferred. The new method, together with its starting point $pc = 1$, its vector V of actual parameters, and an empty operand stack ε, constitute a new frame f' pushed on top of the call stack of the resulting state $\sigma' = \langle\!\langle h, f', f'' :: sf \rangle\!\rangle$, where $f'' = \langle m, pc, l, s \rangle$ is the frame to be taken into account after the completion of the method invocation. Finally, the $\texttt{return}$ instruction pops the control stack and execution continues at the program point indicated in the frame that is now on top of the control stack.

The *partial trace semantics* $[\![P]\!]$ of a Carmel program P is defined as the set of reachable partial traces:

$$[\![P]\!] = \left\{ s_0 :: s_1 :: \cdots :: s_n \in \text{State}^+ \;\middle|\; \begin{array}{l} s_0 \in \mathcal{S}_{init} \wedge \\ \forall k < n,\ \exists i,\ s_k \to_i s_{k+1} \end{array} \right\} \in \wp(\text{State}^+)$$

where $\mathcal{S}_{init}$ is the set of initial states.

3   Specification of the Analysis

The memory usage analysis detects inter- and intra-procedural loops and checks if the creation of new objects may occur inside such loops, leading to unbounded memory consumption. Intuitively, the algorithm consists of the following steps:

1. Compute the set of potential ancestors of a method m in the call graph: $Anc(m)$;
2. Determine the set of methods that are reachable from a mutually recursive method: $MutRecR$;
3. Compute the set of potential predecessors of a program point pc in a method m: $Pred(m, pc)$;
4. Determine the set of methods that may be called from intra-procedural loops: $LoopCall$;
5. Combining all these results ($Unbounded(P)$): phases 1 to 4 are used to detect if a new object creation may occur in a loop, leading to a potentially unbounded memory usage.

Notice that step 3 is the only intra-procedural computation. In the following, we describe the rules for obtaining each of the above-mentioned sets and explain informally how they are related to the operational semantics. This relationship is formalised in Section 4 which proves the correctness of the analysis.

$$\frac{(m, pc) : \texttt{invokevirtual}\ m_{\text{ID}} \qquad m' \in \text{implements}(P, m_{\text{ID}})}{Anc(m) \cup \{m\} \subseteq Anc(m')}$$

Fig. 2. Rule for Anc

$$\frac{m \in Anc(m)}{\{m\} \subseteq MutRecR} \qquad \frac{Anc(m) \cap MutRecR \neq \emptyset}{\{m\} \subseteq MutRecR}$$

Fig. 3. Rules for $MutRecR$

3.1 Computing Ancestors of a Method (Anc)

Anc associates to each method name the set of potential ancestors of this method in the call graph. The type of Anc is thus methodName $\rightarrow$ $\wp$(methodName). Fig. 2 shows the rule corresponding to the `invokevirtual` instruction for computing the set $Anc(m')$: for each method m' which may be called by a method m, it determines that the set of ancestors of m' must contain m as well as all the ancestors of m. The function *implements* is a static over-approximation of the dynamic method lookup function. It returns all possible implementations of a given method with name m_{ID} relative to a program P. We do not specify it in further detail. No constraint is generated for any other instruction different from `invokevirtual` since we are here interested only in the method call graph.

Intuitively, given a trace, if the current method being executed is m, then $Anc(m)$ contains all the methods appearing in the current stack frame.

3.2 Determining Mutually Recursive Methods ($MutRecR$)

$MutRecR$ contains the mutually recursive methods as well as those reachable from a mutually recursive method. Fig. 3 shows the rules used to compute the set $MutRecR$: if m is in the list of its ancestors, then it is mutually recursive, and all the descendants of a mutually recursive method are reachable from a mutually recursive method. The result of the computation of $MutRecR$ can be seen as a marking of methods: methods reachable from mutually recursive methods may be called an unbounded number of times within the execution of an inter-procedural loop. Instructions in these methods may be executed an unlimited number of times. For an example, see Fig. 4: methods are represented with rectangles, thin arrows represent local jumps (`goto`), and thick arrows represent method invocations. Shaded methods are those in $MutRecR$.

Intuitively, given a trace where the current method being executed is m, if $m \notin MutRecR$, then m does not appear in the current stack frame, and all methods in this stack frame are distinct.

3.3 Computing Predecessors of a Program Point ($Pred$)

Given a method m, $Pred(m, pc)$ contains the set of predecessors of the program point pc in the intra-procedural control flow graph of method m. The type of $Pred$ is thus methodName $\times$ progCount $\rightarrow$ $\wp$(progCount). Fig. 5 shows the rules (one for each

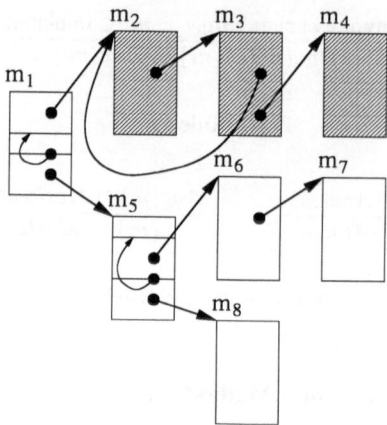

Fig. 4. Example of mutually recursive reachable methods

$$\frac{(m, pc) : \texttt{instr}}{Pred(m, pc) \cup \{pc\} \subseteq Pred(m, pc + 1)} \qquad \frac{(m, pc) : \texttt{if } pc'}{\begin{array}{c} Pred(m, pc) \cup \{pc\} \subseteq Pred(m, pc + 1) \\ Pred(m, pc) \cup \{pc\} \subseteq Pred(m, pc') \end{array}}$$

$$\frac{(m, pc) : \texttt{goto } pc'}{Pred(m, pc) \cup \{pc\} \subseteq Pred(m, pc')}$$

Fig. 5. Rules for *Pred*

instruction) used for defining *Pred*. For instructions that do not induce a jump (`instr` stands for any instruction different from `if` and `goto`), the set of predecessors of a program point pc, augmented with pc itself, is transferred to its direct successor $pc + 1$. For the `if` instruction, the two branches are taken into account. For a `goto` instruction, the set of predecessors of the current program point pc, augmented with pc itself, is transferred to the target of the jump.

To relate *Pred* to the execution traces, we need to define the notion of *current execution* of a method: the current execution of a method m in a trace $tr' = tr ::: \langle\langle h, \langle m, pc, l, s \rangle, sf \rangle\rangle$ is the set of all program points (m, pc') appearing in a maximal suffix of tr' that does not contain a program point where a call to m is performed. Intuitively, given a trace, $Pred(m, pc)$ represents the set of all programs points pc' appearing in the current execution of m.

3.4   Determining Method Calls Inside Loops (*LoopCall*)

The *LoopCall* set contains the names of the methods susceptible to be executed an unbounded number of times due to intra-procedural loops. Fig. 6 shows the rules used for computing *LoopCall*. The first rule says that if a method m' is possibly called by a method m at program point pc, and if pc is within an intra-procedural loop of m (pc is in the set of its predecessors), then m' may be called an unbounded number of times.

$$\frac{(m, pc) : \texttt{invokevirtual}\ m_{\text{ID}} \quad m' \in \text{implements}(P, m_{\text{ID}}) \quad pc \in Pred(m, pc)}{\{m'\} \subseteq LoopCall}$$

$$\frac{(m, pc) : \texttt{invokevirtual}\ m_{\text{ID}} \quad m' \in \text{implements}(P, m_{\text{ID}}) \quad m \in LoopCall}{\{m'\} \subseteq LoopCall}$$

Fig. 6. Rules for *LoopCall*

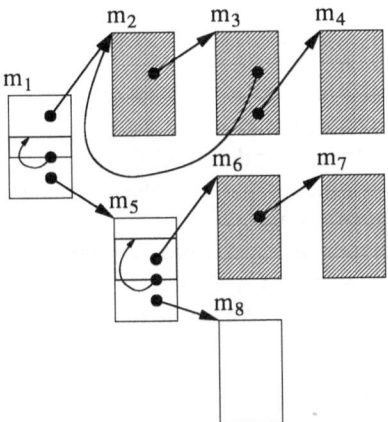

Fig. 7. Marking methods called from inside an intra-procedural loop

Furthermore, if m may be called an unbounded number of times and m calls m', then this property is inherited by m'.

Intuitively, given a trace tr where the method currently being executed is m, if $m \notin LoopCall$ then for each method m' at point pc' performing a call to m, (m', pc') appears only once in the current execution of m'. For an example of the result of this phase of the algorithm, see Fig. 7. The newly shaded methods m_6 and m_7 are in *LoopCall* because of the call from within the loop in method m_5.

3.5   The Main Predicate (*Unbounded(P)*)

So far, the constraints we defined yield an algorithm that detects inter- and intra-procedural loops of a given program P. We now can specialise this algorithm for determining if the memory usage of our program is certainly bounded. The final result consists in a predicate *Unbounded(P)* which is computed by the rule depicted in Fig. 8. This rule sums up the previous results, by saying that if a new object creation may

$$\frac{(m, pc) : \texttt{new}_o\ cl \quad m \in MutRecR \lor m \in LoopCall \lor pc \in Pred(m, pc)}{Unbounded(P)}$$

Fig. 8. Rule for *Unbounded(P)*

occur inside a loop (directly or indirectly, as described by the sets *Anc*, *LoopCall*, *MutRecR* and *Pred*) then *Unbounded*(P) is true.

4   Correctness

The correctness proof follows a classic abstract interpretation approach in which we show that the information computed by the constraints is an invariant of the trace semantics of a program P. For each previously defined function or set X (*Anc*, *MutRecR*, *LoopCall*, *Pred* and *Unbounded*(P)) we use the following schema:

1. Prove that all the domains are lattices and that they have no infinite, strictly increasing chains (ascending chain condition).
2. Determine a set of constraints for defining X.
3. Define a concretisation function γ_X in order to relate concrete domains (sets of traces) and abstract domains (X).
4. Prove that all partial traces of a given program are correctly approximated by X, i.e., that $\forall t \in [\![P]\!]$, $t \in \gamma_X(X)$. This result is a consequence of the classical characterisation of $[\![P]\!]$ as the least element of the following set:

$$\left\{ S \in \wp(\text{Trace}) \; \middle| \; \begin{array}{l} \forall t_1, t_2 \in \text{Trace}, \\ \mathcal{S}_{init} \subseteq S \; \wedge \; \text{if } t_1 \in S \text{ and } t_1 \to t_2 \\ \text{then } t_2 \in S \end{array} \right\}$$

We must prove the following two intermediary lemmas:

For any trace $t_1 \in [\![P]\!]$*, if* $t_1 \in \gamma_X(X)$ *and* $t_1 \to t_2$*, then* $t_2 \in \gamma_X(X)$.   (1)

For any trace $t \in \mathcal{S}_{init}$*,* $t \in \gamma_X(X)$.   (2)

5. Analyse a given applet P, which consists then of 1) constructing the set of constraints associated to the program 2) solving this system with a classic fixed point iteration whose termination is ensured by the lattice ascending chain condition.

Steps 1 to 4 are proof-theoretical while step 5 is algorithmic. All these steps are performed in the Coq proof assistant. Steps 1, 2 and 5 benefit from the framework proposed in [3] and thus no new proof is required. We only need to prove steps 3 and 4, for which the property (1) represents the core of the work:

Lemma 1. *For any trace* $t_1 \in [\![P]\!]$*, if* $t_1 \in \gamma_X(X)$ *and* $t_1 \to t_2$*, then* $t_2 \in \gamma_X(X)$.

We now define the concretisation functions γ_X for *Anc*, *MutRecR*, *Pred* and *LoopCall*.

Anc. The concretisation function for *Anc* formalises the fact that m' calls m (directly or indirectly) in a trace t by examining the call stack of each element in t:

$$\gamma_{Anc} : (\text{methodName} \to \wp(\text{methodName})) \longrightarrow \wp(\text{State}^+)$$
$$X \mapsto \left\{ t \in \text{State}^+ \; \middle| \; \begin{array}{l} \text{for all } \langle\!\langle h, \langle m, pc, l, s \rangle, sf \rangle\!\rangle \text{ in } t \\ \text{for all } m' \text{ appearing in } sf, m' \in X(m) \end{array} \right\}$$

MutRecR. Given a method name m and a partial trace t, we say that "*m is ever executed with a safe callstack in t*" (which is denoted by the SafeCallStack(m, t) predicate) iff for all $\langle\langle h, \langle m, pc, l, s\rangle, sf\rangle\rangle$ in t, m does not appear in sf and all methods in sf are distinct.

The concretisation function for *MutRecR* is then defined by:

$$\gamma_{MutRecR} : \wp(\text{methodName}) \longrightarrow \wp(\text{State}^+)$$
$$X \mapsto \left\{ t \in \text{State}^+ \;\middle|\; \begin{array}{l} \text{for all } m \in \text{methodName, if } m \notin X, \\ \text{then SafeCallStack}(m, t) \text{ holds} \end{array} \right\}$$

Pred. The associated concretisation function is

$$\gamma_{Pred} : (\text{methodName} \times \text{progCount} \to \wp(\text{progCount})) \longrightarrow \wp(\text{State}^+)$$
$$X \mapsto \left\{ t \in \text{State}^+ \;\middle|\; \begin{array}{l} \text{for all prefix } t' ::: \langle\langle h, \langle m, pc, l, s\rangle, sf\rangle\rangle \text{ of } t, \\ \text{if SafeCallStack}(m, t) \text{ then } current(t', m) \subseteq X(m, pc) \end{array} \right\}$$

where $current(t', m)$ is the set of program points which appear in the current execution of m relative to the trace t'.

LoopCall. Given two method names m and m', and a partial trace t, we use the predicate OneCall to state that m is called at most once within each invocation of m'. Formally, OneCall is defined by OneCall(m, m', t) iff for all prefix t' ::: $\langle\langle h, \langle m, pc, l, s\rangle, sf\rangle\rangle$ of t, and for all positions (m', pc') where a call to m is performed, pc' occurs only once in the corresponding current execution of m'.

The concretisation function for *LoopCall* is then defined by:

$$\gamma_{LoopCall} : \wp(\text{methodName}) \longrightarrow \wp(\text{State}^+)$$
$$X \mapsto \left\{ t \in \text{State}^+ \;\middle|\; \begin{array}{l} \text{for all prefix } t' ::: \langle\langle h, \langle m, pc, l, s\rangle, sf\rangle\rangle \text{ of } t, \\ \text{if SafeCallStack}(m, t) \text{ and } m \notin X, \\ \text{then for all } m' \text{ in methodName,} \\ \text{OneCall}(m, m', t) \text{ holds} \end{array} \right\}$$

To prove the correctness of *Unbounded*(P) we need to prove the following lemma:

Lemma 2. *If for all program point (m, pc) where an instruction new is found we have $m \notin MutRecR \cup LoopCall$ and $pc \notin Pred(m, pc)$, then there exists a bound Max_{new} so that*

$$\forall t \in [\![P]\!], \; |t|_{new} < Max_{new}$$

where $|t|_{new}$ counts the number of new instructions which appear in the states of the trace t.

To establish the above result we first prove an inequality relation between the number of executions of the different methods. We write $Exec(m, t)$ for the number of executions of a method m found in a trace t. Similarly, $Max_{invoke}(m)$ is the maximum number of invokevirtual instructions which appear in a method m. Let $m \in Call(m')$ denote that m' calls m.

Lemma 3. *For all methods m, if $m \notin MutRecR \cup LoopCall$ then for all $t \in [\![P]\!]$,*

$$Exec(m, t) \leq \sum_{m \in Call(m')} Exec(m', t) \cdot Max_{invoke}(m').$$

Using this lemma we prove that the number of executions of the method m in the trace t is bounded, as expressed in the following lemma.

Lemma 4. *There exists a bound Max_{exec} such that for all methods m which verify $m \notin LoopCall \cup MutRecR$, we have*

$$\forall t \in \llbracket P \rrbracket, \; Exec(m,t) \le Max_{exec}.$$

To conclude the proof of Lemma 2 we need to prove the following result, establishing that if a method is not (mutually) recursive, nor reachable from a mutually recursive one and it is not in a intra-method cycle, then the number of new instructions is bounded.

Lemma 5. *Given a method m which verifies $m \notin MutRecR \cup LoopCall$, if for all program points (m, pc) in m where an instruction new is found, $pc \notin Pred(m, pc)$ holds then*

$$\forall t \in \llbracket P \rrbracket, \; |t|_{new}^{m} \le Exec(m,t)$$

where $|t|_{new}^{m}$ counts the number of instructions new which appears in the states of the trace t in the method m.

Lemma 2 follows then from the following inequality:

$$\forall t \in \llbracket P \rrbracket, \; |t|_{new} = \sum_{m} |t|_{new}^{m} \le MethodMax_{P} \cdot Max_{invoke}$$

where $MethodMax_{P}$ is the number of methods in program P.

The correctness of our analysis is a corollary of Lemma 2:

Theorem 1. $\neg Unbounded(P) \Rightarrow \exists Max_{new}, \; \forall t \in \llbracket P \rrbracket, \; |t|_{new} < Max_{new}.$

5   Coq Development

The following section gives an overview of the structure of the Coq development. It is meant to give an intuition for how the development of a certified analyser can be done methodologically [3] and to serve as a first guide to the site [13] from which the analyser and the Coq specification and proofs can be downloaded, compiled and tested.

The formalisation of Java Card syntax and semantics is taken form an existing data flow analyser formalised in Coq [3]. The analysis consists in calculating the sets Anc, $MutRecR$, $Pred$ and $LoopCall$ that are indexed by program methods and program points. This naturally leads to a representation as arrays of sets, defined in the following way using Coq modules:

```
Module MAnc := ArrayLattice(FiniteSetLattice).
Module MMutRec := FiniteSetLattice.
Module MPred := ArrayLattice(ArrayLattice(FiniteSetLattice))
Module MLoopCall := FiniteSetLattice.
Module MUnbounded := BoolLattice.
```

This leads to a type for *eg. Pred* that is dependent on the actual program P to analyse. Once the program P is supplied, we construct the actual set *Pred*, properly indexed by the methods and program points of P.

Each of the four type of sets gives rise to a specific kind of constraints. For example, the constraints defining the set *Pred* are given the following definition

Inductive `ConstraintPred : Set :=`
`  C4: MethodName -> progCount -> progCount   ->`
`      (FiniteSetLattice.Pos.set -> FiniteSetLattice.Pos.set)`
`        -> ConstraintPred.`

Thus, each constraint is constructed as an element of a data type that for a given method m and two instructions at program points pc and pc' provides the transfer function that links information at one program point to the other. The actual generation of constraints is done via a function that recurses over the program, matching each instruction to see if it gives rise to the generation of a constraint. The following definition corresponds to the Coq formalisation of the constraint rules depicted on Fig. 5.

Definition `genPred (P:Program) (m:MethodName) (pc:progCount)`
`                   (i:Instruction) : list ConstraintPred :=`
`    match i with`
`    return_v => nil`
`  | goto pc' => (C4 m pc pc' (fun s => (add_set pc s)))::nil`
`  | If pc' => (C4 m pc pc' (fun s => (add_set pc s)))::`
`            (C4 m pc (nextAddress P pc)`
`                    (fun s => (add_set pc s)))::nil`
`  | _ => (C4 m pc (nextAddress P pc)`
`                    (fun s => (add_set pc s)))::nil`

The result of the constraint generation is a list of constraints that together specify the sets *Anc*, *Pred*, *MutRecR* and *LoopCall*. When calculating the solution of the constraint system, we use the technique that the resolution of a constraint system can be done by interpreting each constraint as a *function* that computes information to add to each state and then increment the information associated with the state with this information. Formally, for each constraint of the form $f(X(m, pc_1)) \sqsubseteq X(m, pc_2)$ over an indexed set X (such as *Pred*), we return a function for updating the indexed set by replacing the value of X at (m, pc_2) by the value $f(X(m, pc_1))$.

Definition `F_Pred (c:ConstraintPred) :`
`                   MPred.Pos.set -> MPred.Pos.set :=`
`    match c with`
`    (C4 m pc1 pc2 f) => fun s => update s m pc2 (f (s m pc1))`

The resolution of the constraints can now be done using the iterative fix-point solver, as explained in [3]. The fix-point solver is a function of type

`(l: (L -> L) list) -> (∀f ∈ l, (monotone L f)) ->`
`   ∃x:A, (∀f ∈ l, (order L (f x) x)) ∧`
`        (∀ y:A (∀f ∈ l, (order L (f y) y)) ⇒ (order L x y))`

Subject	number of lines
syntax + semantics	1000
lattices + solver	3000
Anc, MutRecR, Pred, LoopCall correctness	1300
Unbounded(P)correctness	2500
constraint collecting, monotonicity	1200
total	9000

Fig. 9. Proof effort for the development

that will take a list of monotone functions over a lattice L and iterate these until stabilisation. The proof of this proposition (*ie.* the inhabitant of the type) is a variant of the standard Knaster-Tarski fix-point theorem on finite lattices that constructs (and hence guarantees the existence of) a least fix-point as the limit of the ascending chain $\bot, f(\bot), f^2(\bot), \ldots$.

5.1 Correctness Proof in Coq

The remaining parts of the proof effort are dedicated to the correctness of the memory usage analysis. Two particular points connected with the correctness proof are worth mentioning:

- The correctness of *Unbounded*(P) requires much more work than the proof of the various partial analyses. This is not surprising because of the mathematical difficulties of the corresponding property: counting proofs are well-known examples of where big gaps can appear between informal and formal proofs.
- In many of the proofs involved in the construction of the analyser, there is one case for each byte code instruction. Most of the cases are dealt with in the same way. For the methodology to scale well, the proof effort should not grow proportional to the size of the instruction set. This is true already for the relatively small Carmel instruction set (15 instructions) and in particular for the real Java Card byte code language (180 instructions).

For the latter point, it was essential to use the Coq tactic language of proof scripts (called *tactics* in Coq) which allows to apply the same sequence of proof steps to different subgoals, looking in the context for adequate hypothesis. In this way, most of our proofs are only divided in three parts: one case for `invokevirtual`, one case for `return` and one case (using an appropriate tactics applied on several subgoals) for the other instructions. With such a methodology, we can quickly add simple instructions (like operand stack manipulations) without modifying any proof scripts.

The extracted analyser is about 1000 lines of OCaml code while the total development is about 9000 lines of Coq. The following table gives the breakdown of the proof effort measured in lines of proof scripts[2]. Fig. 9 summarises the proof effort for each part of the certified development of the analyser.

6 Complexity and Benchmarks

The computation of the final result of the algorithm from the constraints defined above is performed through well-known iteration strategies. Let N denote the number of methods and I_m the number of instructions in method m. The computation of the sets Anc, $MutRecR$ and $LoopCall$ consists in a fix-point iteration on the method call graph, that is at most quadratic in N. The computation of $Pred$ for a given method m requires at most $I_m \times (|$ number of jumps in $m | +1)$ operations. The computation of $Unbounded(P)$ requires $\sum_m I_m \leq N \times \max\{I_m\}$ operations and in the worst case to save I_m line numbers for each instruction (i.e., I_m^2). The algorithm may be further optimised by using a more compact representation with intervals but we have not implemented this.

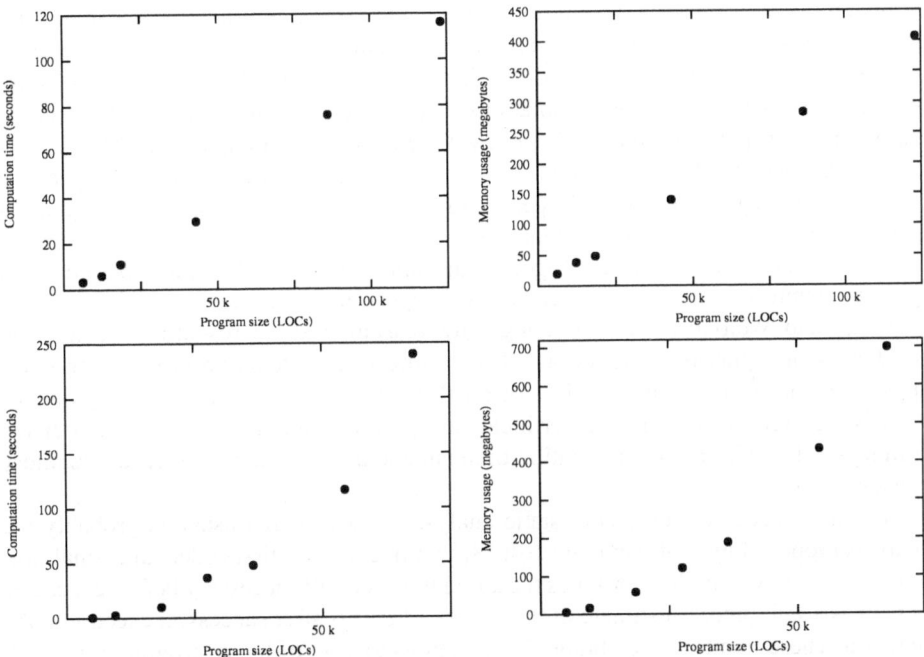

Fig. 10. Performance measures. The first row corresponds to a variable number of methods with a fixed number of lines per method, while the second corresponds to a fixed number of methods with a variable number of lines per method

---

[2] Note that the size of a Coq development can change significantly from one proof script style to another. The same proofs could have consumed two or three times more script lines if the capabilities of the proof tactics language were not exploited. Thus, it is the relative size of the proofs that is more important here.

Fig. 10 gives benchmarks for the performance of the extracted program. These measure have been performed with a randomly byte code program generator. Given two parameters N and l, this program generates a well formed Carmel program with N methods, each of them containing $6 \cdot l$ lines of byte code. Each group of 6 lines handles a call to a randomly chosen method, a `goto` and a `if` instruction with an apparition probability of $1/5$. Hence we can easily measure the performance of our extracted program on big Carmel programs. The first row of Fig. 10 corresponds to a variable number of methods with a fixed number of lines per method, while the second corresponds to a fixed number of methods with a variable number of lines per method. These benchmarks show a linear performance in the first case (both in computation time and memory requirements), and a quadratic performance in the latter.

As the benchmarks show, the extracted program performs very well, in particular when taking into account that no modification on the extracted code was necessary.

7   Related Work

Hofmann [7] has devised a type system for bounded space and functional in-place update. In this system, a specific ◇-type is used to indicate heap cells that can be overwritten. A type system for a first-order functional language defines when the reuse of heap cells due to such type annotations is guaranteed not to alter the behaviour of the program. Inspired by this work and by Typed Assembly Language of Morrisett et al. [12], Aspinall and Campagnoni [1] have defined heap-bounded assembly language, a byte code language equipped with specific *pseudo-instructions* for passing information about the heap structure to the type system. The type system use linearity constraints to guarantee absence of aliasing. Together, this allows to prove the sound reuse of heap space in the presence of kinds of heap cells (integers, list cells, *etc*).

Crary and Weirich [5] define a logic for reasoning about resource consumption certificates of higher-order functions. The certificate of a function provides an over-approximation of the execution time of a call to the function. The logic only defines what is a correct deduction of a certificate and has no inference algorithm associated with it. The logic is about computation time but could be extended to measure memory consumption.

The most accurate automatic, static analysis of heap space usage is probably the analysis proposed by Hofmann and Jost [8] that operates on first-order functional programs. The analysis both determines the amount of free cells necessary before execution as well as a safe (under)-estimate of the size of a *free-list* after successful execution of a function. These numbers are obtained as solutions to a set of linear programming (LP) constraints derived from the program text. Automatic inference is obtained by using standard polynomial-time algorithms for solving LP constraints. The correctness of the analysis is proved with respect to an operational semantics that explicitly keeps track of the memory structure and the number of free cells.

The Hofmann-Jost analysis is more precise than the analysis presented here but is too costly to be executed on most embedded devices, in particular smart cards. Rather, its use lies in the generation of certificates that can then be checked on-card. A similar distinction can been observed in on-card byte code verification where the on-card verifier of Casset et al. [4] relies on certificates generated off-card, whereas the verifier described by Leroy [10] imposes slight language restrictions so that the verifier can execute on-card.

A similar (but less precise) analysis to ours is presented in [14]. The analysis is shown to be correct and complete w.r.t. an abstraction of the operational semantics. One difference with our work is the computation of *Pred*, which keeps track only of the program points *pc* of the branching commands instead of all the visited method program points, decreasing the space complexity. However, in such work the proofs are done manually and the semantics being considered is *total* in contrast with the *partial* semantics used in our work; this could make the formal proof in Coq much more difficult.

The certification of our analysis was done by formalising the correctness proof in the proof assistant Coq. Mechanical verification of Java analysers have so far mainly dealt with the Java byte code verifier [2, 9, 4]. The first exception is the work reported in [3] on formalising an interprocedural data flow analyser for Java Card, on which part of the formalisation of the present analysis is based. The framework proposed in [3] allows us to concentrate on the specification of the analysis as a set of constraints and on the correctness of this system with respect to the semantics of the language (see Section 4). The lattice library and the generic solver of [3] were reused *as is* to extract the certified analyser.

8   Conclusion

We have presented a constraint-based analysis for detecting unbounded memory consumption on embedded devices such as Java Card smart cards. The analysis has been proved correct with respect to an operational semantics of Java byte code and the proof has been entirely formalised in the theorem prover Coq, providing the first certified memory usage analysis. The analysis can be used in program processing tools for verifying that certain resource-aware programming styles have been followed. An important contribution of the paper is to demonstrate how such an analysis can be formalised entirely inside a theorem prover. To the best of our knowledge, this is the first time that a resource usage analysis has undergone a complete formalisation with machine-checkable correctness proof. Still, several aspects of the analysis merit further development:

- By using the formula established in Lemma 3, we could in principle compute an over-approximation of the number of new instructions performed during any execution of the program and thereby produce an estimation of the memory usage. However, it is unclear whether this algorithm can be expressed in the constraint-based formalism used here; a specific proof effort would be required for this extension.
- From a programming language perspective, it would be interesting to investigate how additional restrictions on the programming discipline could be used to lower the complexity of the analysis, in the style of what was used in [10]. For example, knowing that the byte code is a result of a compilation of Java source code immediately gives additional information about the structure of the control flow graph.

– A challenge in the smart card setting would be to refine the algorithm to an implementation of a certified on-device analyser that could form part of an enhanced byte code verifier for protecting the device against resource-consumption attacks. The main challenge here is to optimise the memory usage of the analysis which is currently too high. Recent work on verification of C code in Coq [6] could be of essential use here. Techniques for an actual implementation can be gleaned from [10] as well as from [14] in order to optimise the computation of *Pred*.

References

1. David Aspinall and Andrea Compagnoni. Heap bounded assembly language. *Journal of Automated Reasoning*, 31(3–4):261–302, 2003.
2. Gilles Barthe, Guillaume Dufay, Line Jakubiac, Bernard Serpette, and Simão Melo de Sousa. A Formal Executable Semantics of the JavaCard Platform. In *Proc. ESOP'01*. Springer LNCS vol. 2028, 2001.
3. David Cachera, Thomas Jensen, David Pichardie, and Vlad Rusu. Extracting a data flow analyser in constructive logic. In *Proc. ESOP'04*, number 2986 in Springer LNCS, pages 385–400, 2004.
4. Ludovic Casset, Lilian Burdy, and Antoine Requet. Formal Development of an embedded verifier for Java Card Byte Code. In *Proc. of IEEE Int. Conference on Dependable Systems & Networks (DSN)*, 2002.
5. Karl Crary and Stephanie Weirich. Resource bound certification. In *Proc. 27th ACM Symp. on Principles of Programming Languages (POPL'00)*, pages 184–198. ACM Press, 2000.
6. Jean-Christophe Filliâtre and Claude Marché. Multi-Prover Verification of C Programs. In *Proc. ICFEM 2004*, number 3308 in Springer LNCS, pages 15–29, 2004.
7. Martin Hofmann. A type system for bounded space and functional in-place update. *Nordic Journal of Computing*, 7(4):258–289, 2000.
8. Martin Hofmann and Stefan Jost. Static prediction of heap space usage for first-order functional programs. In *Proc. of 30th ACM Symp. on Principles of Programming Languages (POPL'03)*, pages 185–197. ACM Press, 2003.
9. Gerwin Klein and Tobias Nipkow. Verified Bytecode Verifiers. *Theoretical Computer Science*, 298(3):583–626, 2002.
10. Xavier Leroy. On-card bytecode verification for Java card. In I. Attali and T. Jensen, editors, *Smart card programming and security, (E-Smart 2001)*, pages 150–164. Springer LNCS vol. 2140, 2001.
11. Renaud Marlet. Syntax of the JCVM language to be studied in the SecSafe project. Technical Report SECSAFE-TL-005, Trusted Logic SA, May 2001.
12. Greg Morrisett, David Walker, Karl Crary, and Neal Glew. From System F to typed assembly language. *ACM Trans. Program. Lang. Syst.*, 21(3):527–568, 1999.
13. David Pichardie. Coq sources of the development. http://www.irisa.fr/lande/pichardie/MemoryUsage/.
14. Gerardo Schneider. A constraint-based algorithm for analysing memory usage on Java cards. Technical Report RR-5440, INRIA, December 2004.
15. Igor Siveroni. Operational semantics of the Java Card Virtual Machine. *J. Logic and Algebraic Programming*, 58(1-2), 2004.

Compositional Specification and Analysis of Cost-Based Properties in Probabilistic Programs

Orieta Celiku[1] and Annabelle McIver[2]

[1] Åbo Akademi University and Turku Centre for Computer Science,
Lemminkäisenkatu 14 A, 20520 Turku, Finland
oceliku@abo.fi
[2] Department of Computer Science and Mathematics,
Macquarie University, Sydney 2109, Australia
anabel@ics.mq.edu.au

Abstract. We introduce a formal framework for reasoning about performance-style properties of probabilistic programs at the level of program code. Drawing heavily on the refinement-style of program verification, our approach promotes abstraction and proof re-use. The theory and proof tools to facilitate the verification have been implemented in HOL.

1 Introduction

The importance of a timely consideration of performance-style properties has been noted by several authors [6], and recent research has produced a number of modelling and verification tools based on formal principles — the model checkers PRISM [12] and the Erlangen-Twente checker [3], and performance evaluation tools such as PEPA [6] are just a few examples of the impressive work in this area. However all these tools are based on concrete model realisation rather than at the level of program code. The contribution of this paper is to introduce language constructs to specify performance-style properties, together with a toolkit of formal techniques to enable the construction of mechanised tool support for verifying those properties at varying levels of abstraction, including at the level of program code.

Our point of departure is Morgan's pGCL [14], the extension of the guarded command language [2] to include probabilistic program statements; crucially for us the semantics leaves intact the refinement structure of the original framework giving access to abstraction, which is fundamental for practical specification and development tasks, encouraging the verifier to move between levels of abstraction as appropriate. Moreover pGCL's innovative program logic (originally suggested by Kozen [11]), and its combination of "nondeterminism" and "probabilistic choice" make it ideal for the specification of performance-style properties of probabilistic programs. Terms in the logic are interpreted as real-valued functions — originally conceived to give access to pure probabilistic events, they can

J.S. Fitzgerald, I.J. Hayes, and A. Tarlecki (Eds.): FM 2005, LNCS 3582, pp. 107–122, 2005.

be used equally effectively for general quantitative properties such as "delays" or other performance-style costs. The presence of nondeterminism, as distinct from probabilistic choice, represents genuine unquantifiable uncertainty in the system; as well as being fundamental for a theory of program refinement, in practice, it turns out to be very useful for specifying ranges in input data, which often becomes necessary in performance-style analyses where delays present in the system are only known up to some margin of error [17].

In this paper we use the formal mechanisms provided by pGCL to propose methods based on a novel refinement order. That leads to a compositional style of code-level performance verification via a combination of abstraction and dividing the work of a complete verification into smaller, more palatable fragments, whilst maintaining the integrity of the entire verification task. Our specific contributions include the following:

- A delay statement and semantics for the specification of performance-style properties (Sec. 3);
- An augmented refinement relation between programs and a "calculus of delays" to allow simplification of performance-style properties (Sec. 4);
- Mechanised tool support which uses the delay semantics to provide machine assistance for the many small proofs required for analysis (Sec. 3.1 and Sec. 4).

We also include a range of examples to illustrate and explain the proposed methods. We begin in Sec. 2 by reviewing pGCL.

The mechanised tool support was developed in the HOL proof environment [5]. It provides a high degree of assurance for program verification as well as supports the creation of mechanised tools so that many proofs can be carried out automatically. We have not included any detailed proofs of theorems and lemmas stated in this paper as they have all been developed and proved within the HOL system. We have sometimes however described how a particular verification has been achieved whenever we wish to indicate how the mathematical results have been used.

Throughout the following notational conventions and definitions will be used. We use "." for function application. We write S for a (fixed) underlying state space, and $\overline{S}$ for the set of *discrete probability distributions* over S, where a probability distribution is a function from S to the interval $[0, 1]$ which is normalised to 1. Functions from S to the non-negative reals are called *expectations*; they are ordered by lifting pointwise the order $\leq$ on the reals, which we denote by $\Rrightarrow$. Given two expectations A and B, they are equivalent, denoted $A \equiv B$ exactly when $A \Rrightarrow B$ and $B \Rrightarrow A$. Operations on expectations are pointwise liftings of those on the reals. We write $\underline{c}$ for the constant function returning c for all states. cA denotes $\underline{c} \times A$, where A is an expectation. If f is a probability distribution and A is a measurable function then $\int_f A$ denotes the expected value of A with respect to f. When f is in $\overline{S}$ and A is a real-valued function over S, this reduces to $\sum_{s \in S}(f.s) \times (A.s)$ (if defined). If pred is a predicate, then we write [pred] for the *characteristic function* which takes states satisfying pred to 1, and to 0 otherwise. Other notation will be introduced as we need it.

2   Cost-Analysis of Sequential Programs

When programs incorporate probability, their properties can no longer be guaranteed "with certainty", but only "up to some probability". For example the program

$$b := \mathsf{T} \;_{2/3}\oplus\; b := \mathsf{F} \;, \tag{1}$$

sets the Boolean-valued variable b to T only with probability $2/3$ — in practice this means that if the statement were executed a large number of times, and the final values of b tabulated, roughly $2/3$ of them would record b having been set to T (up to well-known statistical error).

The language pGCL and its associated *quantitative logic* [13] were developed to express such programs and to derive their probabilistic properties by extending the classical assertional style of programming [15]. Programs in pGCL are modelled (operationally) as functions (or transitions) which map *initial states* in S to (sets of) probability distributions over *final states* — the program at (1) for instance operates over a state space of size 2, and has a single transition which maps any initial state to a (single) final distribution; we represent it as a normalised function d, evaluating to $2/3$ when $b = \mathsf{T}$ and to $1/3$ when $b = \mathsf{F}$.

Since properties are now quantitative we express them via a logic of (non-negative) *real-valued functions*, or *expectations*. For example the property "the final value of b is T with probability $2/3$" can be expressed as $\int_d [b = \mathsf{T}]$, the *expected value* of the function $[b = \mathsf{T}]$ with respect to d, which evaluates to $2/3 \times 1 + 1/3 \times 0 = 2/3$. Direct appeal to the operational semantics is however unwieldy — better is the equivalent transformer-style semantics which is obtained by rationalising the above calculation in terms of expectations rather than transitions. The expectation $[b = \mathsf{T}]$ has been transformed to the expectation $2/3$ by the program (1) above so that they are in the relation "$2/3$ is the expected value of $[b = \mathsf{T}]$ with respect to the program's result distribution". More generally given a program P, an expectation A and a state $s \in S$, we define wp.$P.A.s$ to be the expected value of A with respect to the result distribution of program P if executed initially from state s [13]. We say that wp.P is the *expectation transformer* relative to P. In our example that allows us to write

$$2/3 \quad \equiv \quad \mathsf{wp}.(b := \mathsf{T} \;_{2/3}\oplus\; b := \mathsf{F}).[b = \mathsf{T}] \;.$$

In the case that *nondeterminism* is present, execution of P results in a set of possible distributions and we modify the definition of wp to take account of this — in fact we may define wp.$P.A.s$ so that it delivers either the *greatest-* or *least-* expected value with respect to all distributions in the result set. Those choices correspond respectively to an *angelic* or *demonic* resolution of the nondeterminism — which interpretation is used depends very much on the application, and we explain the alternatives in the next section, where we also set out in full the details of the expectation transformer semantics.

Continuing informally for the time being, with the transformer approach we see that having access to *real-valued* functions makes it possible to express a great range of quantitative properties other than just "plain probabilities".

More precisely we can specify a property as some "random variable" of interest and investigate a program's behaviour relative to it, where a random variable is just a real-valued function of S (not necessarily normalised), and for us they are synonymous with expectations.

The property we investigate in this paper was inspired by the need to analyse the efficiency of probabilistic programs. To motivate the idea, suppose we have an iterative program whose termination depends on the result of a coin flip, for example the iterative program

$$\mathsf{do}\ (b = \mathsf{F}) \ \rightarrow \ b := \mathsf{T}\ _{2/3}\oplus\ b := \mathsf{F}\ \mathsf{od}\ , \tag{2}$$

has termination occurring after a random number of iterations, whenever b is set to T. Clearly the precise moment of termination of program (2) cannot be determined exactly since the result of the flip cannot be predicted in advance: the best that can be done is to estimate the *expected* number of required iterations. Put another way, the property we wish to investigate is the expected value of a random variable which records the number of iterations until termination.

Fortunately the quantitative program logic can cope with this — we add a fresh variable n to the program and increment it on each iteration,

$$\mathsf{flips}_n \ \ \hat{=} \ \ n := 0;\ \mathsf{do}\ (b = \mathsf{F}) \ \rightarrow \ (b := \mathsf{T}\ _{2/3}\oplus\ b := \mathsf{F});\ n := n+1\ \mathsf{od}\ . \tag{3}$$

The effect of this is to produce an output distribution over final values of n at termination. For example $n = 1$ finally if the loop terminates on the first step, which occurs with probability 2/3; more generally $n = k$ finally if the loop terminates on the k'th step, which occurs with probability $2/3 \times (1/3)^{k-1}$. This means that the expected final value of n with respect to that distribution is precisely the expected number of iterations until termination. In our logical framework we define n to be the real-valued function which returns the current value of the variable n — its expected value relative to the program's result probability distribution (over n) is now just

$$\mathsf{wp.flips}_n.\mathsf{n} \ \ \equiv \ \ 3[b = \mathsf{F}]/2\ , \tag{4}$$

indicating that on *average* there will be 3/2 iterative steps before termination, when $b = \mathsf{F}$ initially.

Although at first glance this is an appealingly simple way to estimate expected efficiency, several technical difficulties arise in attempts to extend it to programs generally. First, it gives an unintuitive answer in the case when programs only terminate with some probability. For example if the probabilistic choice in (3) above were changed from "$_{2/3}\oplus$" to "$_0\oplus$" (that is to say that there is no chance of b's ever being set to T) then intuitively one might think that the expected time to achieve termination would be infinite; however the wp-(total-correctness) semantics for non-terminating programs gives 0. [1]

---

[1] There are similar problems associated with using a "partial-correctness" interpretation for iterative programs.

More serious however is that in practice its application to more intricate programs is somewhat cumbersome, a situation which cannot be relieved by developing simplification rules within the current pGCL theory. [2]

Celiku and McIver [1] overcame some of these problems by formalising a transformer that accomplishes the task of efficiency analysis without the need to introduce a fresh "n" at all. That approach deals properly with non-terminating programs, and considerably simplifies the mechanised tools implemented to aid with the many small proofs required for the formal analysis. Unfortunately it is limited to un-nested iterations, and can only express the expected *number* of iterations, rather than a range of cost-based performance properties. In the remainder of the paper we propose a *calculus of delays* which distinguishes functional and performance properties, in order to develop a fully compositional verification method. That idea requires a theory which can handle non-constant costs associated with each iteration, together with a novel *program refinement* augmenting standard refinement's functional properties with expected costs. We address those topics below.

3   The Delay Statement

In this section we introduce a new programming statement $\langle X \rangle$ which we will use to specify "delays" at various points in a program. Here X is an expectation, and the idea is that when $\langle X \rangle$ "executes" from initial state s, it does nothing at all, except to wait for $X.s$ "time steps". (Note that we are not assuming that the delay is governed by some underlying exponential distribution as in traditional theories of performance analysis [6].)

As a simple example we consider how delay statements can be used to express the expected number of iterations to termination — we re-write flips_n at Eqn. 3 using a delay statement rather than a fresh n,

$$\mathsf{flips} \quad \hat{=} \quad \mathsf{do}\ (b = \mathsf{F})\ \rightarrow (b := \mathsf{T}\ _{2/3}\oplus\ b := \mathsf{F}); \langle \underline{1} \rangle\ \mathsf{od}\ . \tag{5}$$

Operationally we think of a "delay" of 1 time step after every iteration. Our aim is to introduce a transformer-style semantics which will allow analysis of all specified delays so that, for example, applied to flips will give a total expected delay of $3[b = \mathsf{F}]/2$, agreeing with Eqn. 4. Before we can do that, we must review the analysis of probabilistic functional properties, as it is fundamental to the analysis of cost-based properties.

As indicated in Sec. 2, the **functional properties** of probabilistic programs are based on a wp-style transformer; here we formalise two interpretations, which differ only in their treatment of nondeterminism; recall that a nondeterministic choice represents genuine unquantifiable variation in program behaviour. In the

---

[2] The standard pGCL is based on a program equivalence defined at the distribution level; simplification rules for cost-based properties need an equivalence based directly on expected costs.

awp-semantics we interpret nondeterministic choice angelically, that is *maximal* seeking; in the dwp-semantics it is interpreted demonically, that is *minimal* seeking. Both interpretations are useful depending on the application — a demonic style is best for reasoning about *total correctness* as it provides guarantees on lower bounds on probabilistic behaviour. Alternatively the angelic style guarantees a least upper bound on *possible* probabilistic behaviour, and is therefore ideal for bounding from above *worst-case* expected efficiency. For our calculus of delays we will need both — the details are set out in Fig. 1 below for a small programming language which augments pGCL with delay statements.

---

skip	$\text{awp.skip.}A \mathrel{\hat=} A$,
delay	$\text{awp.}\langle X \rangle.A \mathrel{\hat=} A$,
assignment	$\text{awp.}(x := E).A \mathrel{\hat=} A[x := E]$,
sequential composition	$\text{awp.}(r; r').A \mathrel{\hat=} \text{awp.}r.(\text{awp.}r'.A)$,
probabilistic choice	$\text{awp.}(r \;_p\!\oplus r').A \mathrel{\hat=} p \times \text{awp.}r.A + (\underline{1}{-}p) \times \text{awp.}r'.A$,
nondeterministic choice	$\text{awp.}(r \parallel r').A \mathrel{\hat=} \text{awp.}r.A \sqcup \text{awp.}r'.A$,
Boolean choice	$\text{awp.}(\text{if } B \text{ then } r \text{ else } r').A \mathrel{\hat=} [B] \times \text{awp.}r.A + [\neg B] \times \text{awp.}r'.A$,
iteration	$\text{awp.}(\text{do } B \to r \text{ od}).A \mathrel{\hat=} (\mu X \bullet [B] \times \text{awp.}r.X + [\neg B] \times A)$.

X is an expectation, E is an integer-valued state function, p is an expectation bounded by $\underline{1}$, and the term $(\mu X \ldots)$ refers to the least fixed point with respect to $\Rightarrow$; it is guaranteed to exist since the expectations (augmented with a "top" element) form a complete partial order [8]. $\sqcup$ denotes the pointwise lifting of the max operator from the non-negative reals; similarly, $\sqcap$ below denotes the lifting of min.

The dwp-interpretation can be rendered directly from the above structural definition by replacing awp with dwp everywhere except for nondeterministic choice, whose definition is instead

$$\text{dwp.}(r \parallel r').A \mathrel{\hat=} \text{dwp.}r.A \sqcap \text{dwp.}r'.A .$$

These definitions are dual to an operational model based on the state-to-distribution semantics [13].

Fig. 1. Structural definitions of awp and dwp for pGCL with delays

---

From Fig. 1 we see that the awp/dwp-semantics are almost identical to the standard weakest-precondition semantics — the extra construct $_p\!\oplus$ *averages* the results of its operands, whereas the nondeterministic choice seeks to maximise/minimise the results corresponding to the angelic/demonic execution described above. Notice that the functional behaviour of the new $\langle X \rangle$ statement is identical to skip.

We can appreciate the difference between the angelic and demonic styles, by considering the program fragment

$$(b := \mathsf{T} \;_{2/3}\!\oplus b := \mathsf{F}) \parallel \text{skip} ,$$

which elects either to set b probabilistically, or to do nothing. Suppose we wish to investigate termination in a state satisfying $b = \mathsf{T}$. A "demon" executing "$\|$" would be able to avoid this outcome every time provided that $b = \mathsf{F}$ holds initially, since he would choose to execute the skip option. On the other hand if $b = \mathsf{T}$ initially then the demon could only avoid remaining in that state with probability "at most" $1/3$, by choosing to execute the probabilistic option. Thus

$$\mathsf{dwp}.((b := \mathsf{T}\ {}_{2/3}\!\oplus b := \mathsf{F}) \| \mathsf{skip}).[b = \mathsf{T}] \quad \equiv \quad 2[b = \mathsf{T}]/3 \ ,$$

since the program must, after all, satisfy $b = \mathsf{T}$ with probability "at least $2/3$", but only from the initial state where $b = \mathsf{T}$. An "angel" executing $\|$, on the other hand, would do the opposite, and strive to satisfy $b = \mathsf{T}$ finally, thus would choose to skip when $b = \mathsf{T}$ initially and execute the probabilistic statement otherwise. Hence

$$\mathsf{awp}.((b := \mathsf{T}\ {}_{2/3}\!\oplus b := \mathsf{F}) \| \mathsf{skip}).[b = \mathsf{T}] \quad \equiv \quad 2[b = \mathsf{F}]/3 \ \sqcup\ [b = \mathsf{T}] \ .$$

We can see from this small example that it is possible to express ranges of probabilistic behaviour using $\|$ — that will be useful in examples where precise quantitative values are only known up to some margin of error.

Next we recall the definition of standard program refinement. It is defined by preservation of functional properties: a program $Prog$ is refined by $Prog'$ if $Prog'$ exhibits less nondeterminism. That corresponds to reducing the range of choice available whilst maintaining the functional properties, and is equivalent to *increased* dwp results.

Definition 1 (Program refinement [13]). *Program Prog is refined by program Prog', or Prog $\sqsubseteq$ Prog', if and only if,*

$$\forall A \bullet \mathsf{dwp}.Prog.A \quad \Rightarrow \quad \mathsf{dwp}.Prog'.A \ .$$

As a total-correctness semantics, we can use dwp to express program termination. An iterative program terminates only if there is no chance of iterating forever, i.e. the chance that the loop guard is eventually not satisfied must be 1. An equivalent, but simpler property is that terminating programs have no effect on constant-valued expectations.

Definition 2 (Program termination [13]). *We say program Prog terminates (with probability 1), if and only if, for all non-negative reals k,*

$$\mathsf{dwp}.Prog.\underline{k} \quad \equiv \quad \underline{k} \ .$$

As expected there is a duality between awp and dwp in the context of program refinement, but only for terminating programs — as dwp results increase, awp results decrease.

Theorem 3 (Dual refinement). *If programs Prog and Prog' terminate, then Prog $\sqsubseteq$ Prog', if and only if,*

$$\forall A \bullet \mathsf{awp}.Prog'.A \quad \Rightarrow \quad \mathsf{awp}.Prog.A \ .$$

Next we set out a semantics which takes account of the **specified delays**. Given a program P we write $\Delta(P)$ for the expectation which, when evaluated at an initial state s, gives the expected *accumulated delays* specified by the delay statements if execution begins at s. The structural semantics of Δ is set out in full at Fig. 2.

skip	$\Delta(\mathsf{skip}) \triangleq \underline{0}$,
delay	$\Delta(\langle X \rangle) \triangleq X$,
assignment	$\Delta(x := E) \triangleq \underline{0}$,
sequential composition	$\Delta(r; r') \triangleq \Delta(r) + \mathsf{awp}.r.\Delta(r')$,
probabilistic choice	$\Delta(r \,_p{\oplus}\, r') \triangleq p \times \Delta(r) + (\underline{1} - p) \times \Delta(r')$,
nondeterministic choice	$\Delta(r \parallel r') \triangleq \Delta(r) \sqcup \Delta(r')$,
Boolean choice	$\Delta(\text{if } B \text{ then } r \text{ else } r') \triangleq [B] \times \Delta(r) + [\neg B] \times \Delta(r')$,
iteration	$\Delta(\text{do } B \rightarrow r \text{ od}) \triangleq (\mu X \bullet [B] \times (\Delta(r) + \mathsf{awp}.r.X))$.

Fig. 2. Delay semantics of pGCL with $\langle X \rangle$

We note that only the $\langle X \rangle$ statement introduces actual delays; the other operators combine the delays of their operands, taking account of the intervening probabilistic transitions. The choice operators — $r \parallel r'$, $r \,_p{\oplus}\, r'$ and (if B then r else r') — take (in the worst case) the maximum, the average and the Boolean combination of their operands. The rule for a sequential composition $r; r'$ corresponds to the sum of the two expected delays, although $\Delta(r')$ must be averaged over the distribution of intermediate states as a result of r's execution. The definition reflects the idea that subsequent delays are independent of earlier ones.

As for the functional properties, the delay semantics has a similar operational interpretation based on a state-to-distributions model where some of the transitions are "weighted" with delays. However we can appreciate informally the definitions of Fig. 2 by returning briefly to the "variable counter" approach suggested in Sec. 2. Given a program P containing delay statements, we imagine replacing each delay $\langle X \rangle$ with the assignment $n := n + X.s$, where as before n is a fresh variable; next we imagine executing the statement $n := 0$ immediately before the revised P. We write P_n for the resulting program — flips and flips$_n$ at Eqns. 5 and 3 above illustrate the conversion from P to P_n. It is possible to show that $\mathsf{awp}.P_n.n \Rightarrow \Delta(P)$, and thus that the Δ semantics is correctly giving the required upper bound on the running time. The details for $\Delta(\mathsf{flips})$ are as follows, where we write flip for $b := \mathsf{T} \,_{2/3}{\oplus}\, b := \mathsf{F}$:

$$
\begin{array}{lll}
& \Delta(\mathsf{flips}) & \\
\equiv & (\mu X \bullet [b = \mathsf{F}] \times (\Delta(\mathsf{flip}; \langle \underline{1} \rangle) + \mathsf{awp}.(\mathsf{flip}; \langle \underline{1} \rangle).X)) & \text{Fig. 2} \\
\equiv & (\mu X \bullet [b = \mathsf{F}] \times (\underline{1} + \mathsf{awp}.(\mathsf{flip}; \langle \underline{1} \rangle).X)) & \text{Fig. 1} \\
\equiv & 3[b = \mathsf{F}]/2 \; ,
\end{array}
$$

in agreement with Eqn. 4 above.

In general the analysis of iterations is not computed directly as above, but rather relies on an invariant-style rule in the same way that correctness arguments for loops rely on program invariants [15]. The details are set out in the next lemma.

Lemma 4 (Δ-iteration).

$$\forall A, r, B \bullet [B] \times (\Delta(r) + \mathsf{awp}.r.A) \Rrightarrow A \quad \Rightarrow \quad \Delta(\mathsf{do}\ B \to r\ \mathsf{od}) \Rrightarrow A \ .$$

We call any expectation A satisfying the antecedent a weak invariant.

There is a nice relationship between expected delays and termination: if the expected cost for a single (iterative) step is bounded away from zero, and the (worst-case) accumulated expected cost is finite, then the program is guaranteed to terminate.

Lemma 5 (Δ-reasoning and termination).

$$\forall B, r \bullet \ \mathsf{terminates}\ (r) \ \wedge$$
$$(\exists c \bullet 0 < c \ \wedge \ c \neq \infty \ \wedge \ c[B] \Rrightarrow \Delta.r) \ \wedge$$
$$(\exists c' \bullet 0 < c' \ \wedge \ c' \neq \infty \ \wedge \ \Delta(\mathsf{do}\ B \to r\ \mathsf{od}) \Rrightarrow \underline{c'})$$
$$\Rightarrow \quad \mathsf{terminates}\ (\mathsf{do}\ B \to r\ \mathsf{od}) \ .$$

This result allows us to reduce the burden of analysis as we can deduce termination immediately from the efficiency analysis.

3.1   An Automated Verification Condition Generator

To support the practical analysis of delays we implemented a verification condition generator (VCG) which takes a goal of the form $\Delta(r) \Rrightarrow X$, systematically transforms "Δ" and "awp", and reduces the goal to checking relationships between explicit expectations. The VCG works with Prolog-like rules derived from the definitions set out in Fig. 1 and Fig. 2, and monotonicity of awp [13]. In the case of iterations Lem. 4 justifies a verification style based on user-defined weak invariants in much the same way that the application of standard loop rules requires user-defined program invariants.

If r contains no loops an exact (although not necessarily fully simplified) result for $\Delta(r)$ can be produced automatically, whereas in the case loops are present, the weak-invariant approach limits the automatic calculation to the calculation of upper bounds on $\Delta(r)$. Exact results can be verified for loops too, however that requires interactive algebraic reasoning as demonstrated in the calculation of flips.

To illustrate we consider the analysis of a standard geometric probability distribution generated by sampling from a source of random bits [10, 7]. A Geometric(p) random variable is defined to be the index of the first success in an infinite sequence of Bernoulli(p) trials, where a Bernoulli(p) trial is just a flip of a p-biased coin. The Geometric($\frac{1}{2}$) distribution can be sampled by recording the number of leading "heads" in a potentially infinite sequence of coin flips, which we model in the program below using a variable m, incremented whenever the loop guard is true.

$$
\text{Geometric} \,\hat{=}\, \left.
\begin{array}{l}
m := 0; \\
\text{do } (b = \mathsf{T}) \rightarrow \\
\quad m := m + 1; \\
\quad b := \mathsf{T} \,_{1/2}\oplus (b := \mathsf{F}; \langle [m = k] \rangle) \\
\text{od}
\end{array}
\right\} \; loop
$$

The delay statement $\langle [m = k] \rangle$ depends on the value of the program variables, and is only nonzero when m is equal to k, and b is set to F, at which point the loop terminates. Thus $\Delta(\text{Geometric})$ gives the expected cost of that event which, by a fact of basic probability theory, is the same as the probability that the program terminates with m equal to k.

To verify the total delay, we provide $[m < k \wedge b = \mathsf{T}]/2^{k-m}$ as weak invariant for $loop$. Since $\Delta(\text{Geometric}) \equiv \mathsf{awp}.(m := 0).\Delta(loop)$, we expect

$$
[0 < k \wedge b = \mathsf{T}]/2^k
$$

to be (an upper bound on) the total expected delay, a fact which is verified from the VCG and expressed in the following theorem:

$$
\Delta(\text{Geometric}) \quad \Rightarrow \quad [0 < k \wedge b = \mathsf{T}]/2^k \,. \tag{6}
$$

Indeed in this case we can verify an equality, because there is no nondeterminism in the program, and it terminates.

To give an idea of the verification effort involved, we recorded the number of primitive inference steps HOL took to prove the theorem at (6) above: it took 83,922 such steps. The VCG generated 4 verification conditions and around 30 lines of interactive proof were needed to discharge them. On the other hand, the VCG could automatically verify (in 9,582 primitive inference steps) that $loop$ iterates on average (at most) twice. In the next section we examine techniques to mitigate the effort of interactive proof.

4   Cost-Based Program Refinement

Although in theory the basic HOL verification condition generator outlined above has sufficient implemented theory to verify programs' expected delays, unfortunately in practice it requires too much guidance from the prover for programs of any intricacy. In this section we investigate more sophisticated techniques for simplifying analysis in order to increase the efficiency of tool support in practice.

Our approach is to augment the standard equivalence between programs based on functional properties with expected delays. That will allow us to simplify programs using refinement-like techniques.

Definition 6 (Δ-refinement). *We say program Prog is "delay-refined by program Prog'", or Prog $\trianglelefteq$ Prog', if and only if,*

$$Prog \sqsubseteq Prog' \quad \wedge \quad \Delta(Prog') \Rightarrow \Delta(Prog) .$$

In other words, *Prog'* $\trianglelefteq$-refines *Prog* only if *Prog'* preserves both the functional properties of *Prog*, and is at least as efficient. The next theorem shows that this definition does indeed lead to a compositional equivalence, in the sense that $\trianglelefteq$-refinement is preserved by contexts.

Theorem 7 ($\trianglelefteq$-monotonicity).

$$\forall Prog, r, r' \bullet r \trianglelefteq r' \quad \wedge \quad \text{terminates } (r) \quad \Rightarrow \quad Prog \trianglelefteq Prog[r \backslash r'] .$$

The extra condition in Thm. 7 — that r terminates [3] — is needed to be able to appeal to Thm. 3, the duality between awp- and dwp-results, since both awp and dwp are used in the proof.

Now that we have access to the $\trianglelefteq$-refinement, we are in a position to develop a calculus of delays; in Fig. 3 we set out some $\trianglelefteq$-refinement rules. Rules (7–9) illustrate some simple ways to combine delay statements directly, whereas rules (10–13) promote the technique of separating the delays from the standard program statements. Rule (13), for example, suggests a proof method based on a gradual simplification of both the functional properties — using standard program refinement — and of the delay analysis.

$$\langle X \rangle \parallel \langle Y \rangle \quad \equiv \quad \langle X \sqcup Y \rangle \tag{7}$$
$$\langle X \rangle; \langle Y \rangle \quad \equiv \quad \langle X + Y \rangle \tag{8}$$
$$\langle X \rangle \,_p\oplus \langle Y \rangle \quad \equiv \quad \langle p \times X + (\underline{1} - p) \times Y \rangle \tag{9}$$
$$P; \langle X \rangle \quad \equiv \quad \langle \text{awp}.P.X \rangle; P \tag{10}$$
$$P; \langle \underline{a} \rangle \,_p\oplus \; Q; \langle \underline{b} \rangle \quad \equiv \quad (P \,_p\oplus Q); \langle p \times \underline{a} + (\underline{1} - p) \times \underline{b} \rangle \tag{11}$$
$$(P \parallel Q); \langle X \sqcup Y \rangle \quad \trianglelefteq \quad P; \langle X \rangle \parallel Q; \langle Y \rangle \tag{12}$$
$$Q \sqsubseteq P \wedge \Delta(Q) \equiv \underline{0} \quad \Rightarrow \quad \langle \Delta(P) \rangle; Q \trianglelefteq P \tag{13}$$

In the above definitions, a and b are non-negative reals, X and Y are expectations, and P and Q are pGCL programs with delays. The equivalence symbol means that the $\trianglelefteq$-refinement holds in both directions.

Fig. 3. A calculus of delays

Turning now to the application of the rules in Fig. 3 we observe that, as well as needing to determine Δ-results, we also need to establish $\sqsubseteq$-refinements

---

[3] Termination of r' follows from termination of r, and $r \sqsubseteq r'$.

between program fragments. Unfortunately direct appeal to Def. 1 for accomplishing the latter task implies consideration of all expectations, clearly an infeasible approach in practice. As for standard programs, we need to derive instead "first order" rules to determine ⊑-refinements — but for probabilistic programs however, this is not a straightforward matter [13]. In some important cases however, such as sampling from randomly-generated bits, "almost" first-order rules are indeed available, and the next lemma sets out a rule for one such simple case. Essentially, any program ⊑-refines a probabilistic choice provided that the probabilities are preserved.

Lemma 8. *Let* $P \mathrel{\hat{=}} x := 0 \ {}_p\oplus x := 1$. *For any* pGCL *program* Q, *if*

$$p \quad \Rightarrow \quad \mathsf{dwp}.Q.[x = 0]$$
$$and \quad 1 - p \quad \Rightarrow \quad \mathsf{dwp}.Q.[x = 1] \ ,$$

then $P \sqsubseteq Q$.

To illustrate Lem. 8 we consider the cost of simulating a biased coin by sampling from a stream of uniformly-generated random bits. Let m and n be natural numbers such that $0 \leq m/n \leq 1$ (and $n \neq 0$). The program Bernoulli$(m/n, x)$ uses only "$_{1/2}\oplus$" choices to simulate a "$_{m/n}\oplus$" choice, which we prove formally below.

$$
\begin{aligned}
\text{Bernoulli}(m/n, x) \ \mathrel{\hat{=}} \ \lVert \ &\textbf{var } s, b \bullet \\
&s := m; \\
&(b := \mathsf{T} \ {}_{1/2}\oplus b := \mathsf{F}); \ \langle \underline{k} \rangle \\
&\textbf{do } (b = \mathsf{T}) \to \\
&\quad s := 2s; \\
&\quad \textbf{if } s > n \textbf{ then } s := s - n \textbf{ else skip}; \\
&\quad (b := \mathsf{T} \ {}_{1/2}\oplus b := \mathsf{F}); \ \langle \underline{k} \rangle \\
&\textbf{od}; \\
&\textbf{if } 1/2 \leq s/n \textbf{ then } x := 0 \textbf{ else } x := 1 \\
\rVert &
\end{aligned}
$$

with *bloop* bracketing the loop body.

Informally however, Bernoulli$(m/n, x)$'s correctness relies on the fact from probability theory that for any fraction $0 \leq p \leq 1$ the equality $p = \sum_{i \geq 0} p_i/2^i$ is valid, where $0.p_0 p_1 p_2 \ldots$ is the binary expansion of p [7]. But the infinite sum is just the expected value with respect to the geometric distribution of the random variable which returns the i'th bit in the binary expansion of p. Focusing on the variable b, and comparing with the program Geometric above, we see that *bloop* below does indeed compute a geometric distribution over, so-to-speak, leading "heads". The additional variable s computes *in situ* the i'th bit in the binary expansion of m/n. Observe that the variables s and b are introduced as local variables so that overall the program can be considered to operate over the single (public) variable x. Local variables are handled in the usual way [15]: they are introduced via a nondeterministic choice over their type, thus $\mathsf{awp}.(\lVert \textbf{var } y \cdot P \rVert) \equiv \mathsf{awp}.(y \in Y; P)$ for local variable y, and the introduction is instantaneous, i.e. $\Delta(\llbracket \textbf{var } y \cdot P \rrbracket) \triangleq \Delta(P)$. [4] We attach a delay of k to each call to the random bit, modelled with a "$_{1/2}\oplus$" choice, so that the performance property effectively determines the expected number of coin flips, with a cost of k per flip.

To verify that Bernoulli$(m/n, x)$ does indeed simulate a "$_{m/n}\oplus$" flip, using a total delay of no more than $2k$, we prove the $\trianglelefteq$-refinement,

$$\langle \underline{2k} \rangle ; (x := 0 \,_{m/n}\oplus\, x := 1) \quad \trianglelefteq \quad \text{Bernoulli}(m/n, x) , \tag{14}$$

which, according to Def. 6, we do by considering the delay- and functional analyses separately.

The delay-analysis proceeds in two steps. First we show that

$$\Delta(bloop) \quad \Rightarrow \quad 2k[b = \mathsf{T}] ,$$

using the weak invariant $2k[b = \mathsf{T}]$; next we use rule (13) of Fig. 3 establishing the inequality

$$\langle 2k[b = \mathsf{T}] \rangle ; bloop' \quad \trianglelefteq \quad bloop ,$$

where $bloop'$ is the delay-free version of $bloop$. Finally we use rules (8) and (10), first to combine the two remaining delay statements (adding the delays together), and then to bring all the delays to the front through the various assignments to b and s. The result of the analysis is that indeed

$$\Delta(\text{Bernoulli}(m/n, x)) \quad \Rightarrow \quad \langle \underline{2k} \rangle .$$

The delay-analysis is also used to establish termination for $bloop$ (and hence Bernoulli$(m/n, x)$). Note that it is sufficient to prove that $bloop$ satisfies the conditions of Lem. 5 for a particular (suitable) instance of k, since dwp.$bloop$ is not affected by k. It is easy to see that any finite positive value for k would do.

To establish the $\sqsubseteq$-refinement we verify that two conditions

$$\underline{m/n} \quad \Rightarrow \quad \text{dwp.Bernoulli}(m/n, x).[x = 0] \;\; and$$
$$\underline{1 - m/n} \quad \Rightarrow \quad \text{dwp.Bernoulli}(m/n, x).[x = 1] ,$$

are satisfied, which suffices by Lem. 8. The inequalities follow using standard probabilistic invariant-based techniques [13] and and their HOL implementation [8].

5   The IEEE FireWire

In this section we illustrate our techniques further by considering the root contention mechanism present in the IEEE High Performance serial bus ("FireWire")

---

[4] The actual HOL implementation achieves the same effect differently, but we omit the details here; a nice way of implementing local variables is shown in [16].

standard [9], which is used to transport digitised video and audio signals within a network of multimedia systems and devices.

As part of the protocol, a leader must be elected whenever there is a bus reset in the network. The election protocol first constructs a spanning tree over the network nodes with the tree root becoming the leader. To do this, nodes engage in a series of negotiations in which they send "be my parent" requests to their neighbours who are not already their children. Contention can arise when two nodes simultaneously send requests to each other; to break the stalemate situation when such a contention is detected, the contending nodes flip coins to determine whether to wait either a short or a long delay before backing off and trying again.

In this paper we only consider the contention mechanism, and our specification is based on that of Fidge and Shankland [4], who used pGCL to analyse the expected number of "back-off-and-retry" rounds until the contention is resolved. Here we do something rather different, and use our delay-statements to incorporate specific times attached to the short and long delays specified by the IEEE standard [9]. We then analyse the total expected *time delay* for the contention to resolve (rather than the expected total number of rounds). Nondeterminism is important here as the delays for the "long/short" delays are only specified as ranges.

Fidge and Shankland's specification of the contention mechanism is very simple: once two nodes are in a "contention state" they repeatedly flip for "long" or "short" delay. We write x and y for the variables corresponding to the two contending nodes, and these are set probabilistically; an outcome of 0 represents a short delay, and 1 a long delay. Thus in any round there are three possible outcomes: either both nodes choose short, both choose long, or one chooses short and the other long. A short delay is specified to be in the range $240 - 260$ ns, and a long delay in the range $570 - 600$ ns; we assume that the time to send packets is negligible and that in the case that the nodes choose differently the time is dominated by the long delay. In the program below we use $\|$ to incorporate the above delay ranges. We also use the Bernoulli(p, x) program above to simulate a "$_p\oplus$" choice, whose optimal value we determine formally below.

$$\text{FireWire} \; \hat{=} \; \text{do } x = y \rightarrow$$
$$\text{Bernoulli}(p, x);$$
$$\text{Bernoulli}(p, y);$$
$$\left. \begin{array}{l} \text{if } (x = 0 = y) \text{ then } \langle \underline{240} \rangle \; \| \; \langle \underline{260} \rangle \\ \text{else if } (x = 1 = y) \text{ then } \langle \underline{570} \rangle \; \| \; \langle \underline{600} \rangle \\ \text{else } \langle \underline{570} \rangle \; \| \; \langle \underline{600} \rangle \end{array} \right\} delays$$
$$\text{od}$$

The formal analysis proceeds in several simplification steps. First we simplify both Bernoulli-procedures using the analysis of Sec. 4, for example from Eqn. 14 we have

$$\langle \underline{2k} \rangle; (x := 0 \;_p\oplus\; x := 1) \quad \trianglelefteq \quad \text{Bernoulli}(p, x) \; .$$

As each Bernoulli-procedure supplies a delay of $2k$, that makes $4k$ in all, and we can move the $\langle \underline{4k} \rangle$-statement to the front of the FireWire outer loop body. Next we take into account the *delays* involved in the long/short waits as follows:

$$\Delta(x := 0\, _p\oplus x := 1; y := 0\, _p\oplus y := 1; delays)$$
$$\equiv \quad \mathsf{awp}.(x := 0\, _p\oplus x := 1; y := 0\, _p\oplus y := 1).\Delta(delays) \qquad \text{Fig. 2}$$
$$\equiv \quad \underline{\langle 600 - 340p^2 \rangle} \,. \qquad\qquad\qquad\qquad\qquad\qquad\qquad\qquad \text{Fig. 1}$$

Next moving the $\langle 600 - 340p^2 \rangle$ statement through the probabilistic choices using rule (13), and combining it with the $\langle \underline{4k} \rangle$-statement using (8) we have verified the $\trianglelefteq$-refinement:

$$\begin{aligned}
&\mathsf{do}\ x = y \rightarrow \\
&\qquad \langle 4k + 600 - 340p^2 \rangle; \\
&\qquad (x := 0\, _p\oplus x := 1); \quad \trianglelefteq \quad \text{FireWire} \\
&\qquad (y := 0\, _p\oplus y := 1) \\
&\mathsf{od}
\end{aligned}$$

Finally using a direct Δ-analysis on the simplified loop with weak invariant $[x = y](2k + 300 - 170p^2)/(p(1-p))$ by $\trianglelefteq$-refinement we deduce that

$$\Delta(\text{FireWire}) \quad \Rightarrow \quad [x = y](2k + 300 - 170p^2)/(p(1-p)) \,. \qquad (15)$$

As a corollary to this, using Lem. 5, since the total expected delay until conflict is resolved is finite (for $0 < p < 1$ and finite k), we deduce that the protocol terminates with probability 1, for $0 < p < 1$.

A number of researchers have investigated the expected time delay of the contention stage using a wide variety of methods, though most of them are based on some form of model checking; Stoelinga [17] gives a nice survey of those results. Of those that investigate the effect of biasing the probability of selecting between long and short delays, all conclude that there should be a bias in favour of a short delay, for although this results in more rounds until the conflict is resolved, overall the total time delay is still minimised. Assuming that k is small compared to the back-off delays, examining Eqn. 15 we see that the right-hand side takes a minimal value (for $0 \leq p \leq 1$) ranging between 0.598 and 0.603 for various values of k. This compares almost precisely with results reported by Stoelinga.

6 Conclusions

In this paper we have provided a formal framework for reasoning about performance-style properties at the level of program code; we have also implemented a tool which provides a high assurance of correctness. Our approach draws heavily on the refinement-style of program verification, which promotes abstraction and proof re-use, the latter was borne out by our practical experience where we made many small changes to the specifications of the delay statements. Other approaches, whilst also being compositional, do not exploit program refinement to simplify performance-style analysis.

In the future we would like to explore the possibility of finding weak invariants using tools such as constraint solvers, reducing even further the burden on the human prover.

References

1. O. Celiku and A. McIver. Cost-based analysis of probabilistic programs mechanised in HOL. *Nordic Journal of Computing*, 11(2):102–128, 2004.
2. E. W. Dijkstra. *A Discipline of Programming*. Prentice-Hall, 1976.
3. Erlangen-Twente Markov Chain Checker. *http://www.informatik.uni-erlangen.de/etmcc/*.
4. C. J. Fidge and C. Shankland. But what if I don't want to wait forever? *Formal Aspects of Computing*, 15(2-3):258–279, 2003.
5. M. J. C. Gordon and T. F. Melham. *Introduction to HOL (A theorem-proving environment for higher order logic)*. Cambridge University Press, 1993.
6. J. Hillston. *A Compositional Approach to Performance Modelling*. Cambridge University Press, 1996.
7. J. Hurd. *Formal Verification of Probabilistic Algorithms*. PhD thesis, University of Cambridge, 2002.
8. J. Hurd, A. McIver, and C. Morgan. Probabilistic guarded commands mechanized in HOL. In *Proc. of QAPL 2004*, Mar. 2004.
9. Institute of Electrical and Electronics Engineers. *IEEE Standard for a High Performance Serial Bus (Ammendment). Std 1394a-2000*. June 2000.
10. D. E. Knuth and A. C. Yao. The complexity of nonuniform random number generation. In J. F. Traub, editor, *Algorithms and Complexity: New Directions and Recent Results*. Academic Press, 1976.
11. D. Kozen. A probabilistic PDL. In *Proceedings of the 15th ACM Symposium on Theory of Computing*, 1983.
12. M. Kwiatkowska, G. Norman, and D. Parker. PRISM: Probabilistic symbolic model checker. In *Proceedings of TOOLS 2002*, volume 2324 of *Lecture Notes in Computer Science*, pages 200–204. Springer, Apr. 2002.
13. A. McIver and C. Morgan. *Abstraction, refinement and proof for probabilistic systems*. Springer, 2004.
14. C. Morgan and A. McIver. pGCL: Formal reasoning for random algorithms. *South African Computer Journal*, 22:14—27, 1999.
15. C. C. Morgan. *Programming from Specifications*. Prentice-Hall, 1990.
16. T. Nipkow. Hoare logics in Isabelle/HOL. In H. Schwichtenberg and R. Steinbrüggen, editors, *Proof and System-Reliability*, pages 341–367. Kluwer, 2002.
17. M. Stoelinga. Fun with FireWire: A comparative study of formal verification methods applied to the IEEE 1394 root contention protocol. *Formal Aspects of Computing*, 4(3):328–337, 2003.

Formally Defining and Verifying Master/Slave Speculative Parallelization*

Pierre Salverda, Grigore Roşu, and Craig Zilles

University of Illinois at Urbana-Champaign
{salverda, grosu, zilles}@cs.uiuc.edu

Abstract. Master/Slave Speculative Parallelization (MSSP) is a new execution paradigm that decouples the issues of performance and correctness in microprocessor design and implementation. MSSP uses a fast, not necessarily correct, master processor to speculatively split a program into tasks, which are executed independently and concurrently on slower, but correct, slave processors. This work reports on the first steps in our efforts to formally validate that overall correctness can be achieved in MSSP despite a lack of correctness guarantees in its performance-critical parts. We describe three levels of an abstract model for MSSP, each refining the next and each preserving equivalence to a sequential machine. Equivalence is established in terms of a jumping refinement, a notion we introduce to describe equivalence at specific places of interest in the code. We also report on experiences and insights gained from this exercise. In particular, we show how formalizing MSSP facilitated a deeper understanding of performance-correctness decoupling and its attendant trade-offs, all key features of the MSSP paradigm. Moreover, formalization revealed all assumptions underpinning correctness, which, being specified abstractly, can be understood in an implementation-independent way. We found these results so valuable that we plan to advance MSSP's formalization in parallel with its subsequent design iterations.

1   Introduction

Technology advances have reached the point where it is now possible to engineer multiple processor cores onto a single chip. While this capability lends itself to throughput-oriented workloads, latency-critical sequential applications do not see any benefit. The traditional approach of relying on the programmer to find and extract parallelism in such programs has met with little success, primarily because manual parallelization is complicated and error-prone. Thus, a fundamental challenge facing computer architects today is bringing the benefits of multiple cores to bear on the performance of sequential programs.

Master/Slave Speculative Parallelization (MSSP) [14] is a recent proposal for automatically extracting parallelism from sequential programs. The paradigm

---

* This work was supported in part by a grant from Intel and National Science Foundation grants CCR-0311340 and CCF-0347260.

J.S. Fitzgerald, I.J. Hayes, and A. Tarlecki (Eds.): FM 2005, LNCS 3582, pp. 123–138, 2005.

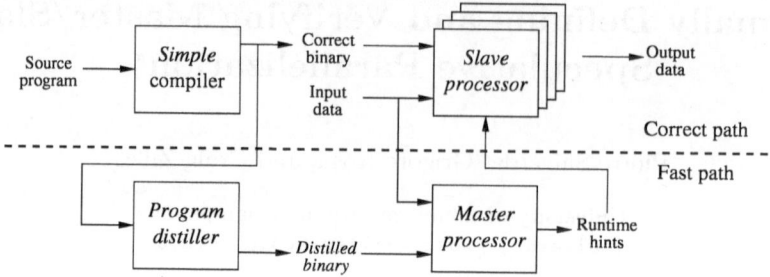

Fig. 1. Conceptual organization of MSSP. On the fast path, the master executes an approximate program (distilled binary) to run ahead of the slaves, providing hints (live-ins) of where execution is likely to be headed. On the slower correct path, the slave processors use the hints to concurrently compute their tasks

uses a *master* processor to divide the dynamic instruction stream into pieces, called *tasks*, which are executed in parallel on multiple *slave* processors. Dataflow dependences between the tasks are resolved by the master, which predicts *live-in* values for each task by executing an *approximate* version of the original program. Slaves use the original program code when executing their tasks, but operate on the speculative live-in data supplied to them by the master. The results computed by slaves are committed to the machine's non-speculative state only if the corresponding live-ins are consistent with that state. If inconsistencies are detected, the results are discarded and the machine resumes its operation using the pristine non-speculative state as a starting point. Because slaves operate concurrently, overall performance is determined largely by the master processor. In turn, because the master executes an approximate (shorter) version of the original program, MSSP is able to achieve significant speed-ups over speculative, out-of-order superscalar machines [14].

The potential for high performance in MSSP is underpinned by its ability to *decouple* performance and correctness concerns, in so doing facilitating the simultaneous pursuit of these otherwise conflicting goals. *Complexity* lies at the root of the tension between performance and correctness: pursuit of the former incurs complexity (out-of-order superscalar architectures and optimizing code transformations are complex), which, in turn, compromises our ability to ensure the latter (complex systems are hard to verify). MSSP decouples the two by separating the parts of the system that produce output — and are thereby constrained to be correct — from the parts that determine the rate at which output is produced. Figure 1 depicts this idea.

Decoupling in such a framework is successful if neither subsystem can compromise the objectives of the other. That is, the fast path should not compromise correctness and the correct path should not determine overall performance. As noted already, the latter property does indeed hold in MSSP because the master processor resides on the critical path, not the slaves. The former requirement — that of correctness in spite of the potential for errors on the fast path — is the focus of this paper.

Thus, our primary goal here is to demonstrate that correctness in MSSP cannot be influenced by how the master operates, nor by the instructions contained in the distilled binary it executes. In so doing, we conclusively demonstrate that the correct path is properly decoupled from the fast path. This provides a formal basis for a central theme in our work: correctness need not be compromised by the pursuit of performance.

The formalization of MSSP also served a secondary goal of obtaining an abstract model for the new execution paradigm. In developing that model, we have exposed the fundamental aspects of MSSP that underpin its correctness. Specifically, we isolated the notion of *task safety* (Section 4) as the principal condition upon which correct operation rests. That we could distill the correctness requirement so precisely and succinctly was simultaneously surprising and encouraging. Indeed, the mere process of formalizing MSSP has been fundamental to our gaining a deeper understanding of an execution paradigm we previously understood only "intuitively." The lack of implementation-specific detail in the abstract model will also facilitate reasoning about correctness in subsequent iterations of the MSSP design, each of which is likely to be encumbered by the artifacts of technology-driven design trade-offs. These benefits accrue because we embarked on the formal study early on in our research, in contrast to much formal work, which tends to be a "post-mortem" exercise whose sole goal is to find errors in an extant design. In this respect, our experiences are in agreement with previous assertions (see, for example, [5]) that formal verification should be a part of the design process.

In terms of the formalization itself, we report on our use of rewriting logic [7], as supported by Maude [3]. We establish correctness by proving MSSP's equivalence to a conventional sequential execution model. In this respect, our work is similar to the extensive studies of microarchitecture verification, where correctness is proven by comparing a microarchitectural specification to the specification of an instruction set architecture (ISA). The work of Burch and Dill [2], Hunt and Sawada [10, 11] and Arvind and Shen [1] are notable examples in this area. However, we differ from those studies in that we are *not* trying to establish that a refinement — in the usual sense of the word — of an ISA is correct, since MSSP is *not* a standard refinement of an ISA.

Although an MSSP machine implements a conventional sequential ISA, it differs from a sequential machine in terms of the granularity at which updates the architected state[1] occur — MSSP updates state at task boundaries rather than at instruction boundaries. Thus, a key property of MSSP is that it "jumps" over sequences of states in the sequential model. In fact, if one ignores MSSP transitions that do not change architected state, then the sequential model can be regarded as a stuttering refinement [6] of MSSP. But this is somewhat counterintuitive because our objective is to reason about MSSP in terms of the sequential

---

[1] By this we mean the ISA-visible state — the set of all registers and memory cells accessible via the instruction set. Internal state, such as that held speculatively by the master and all slave processors, is not included in this set.

model, not the other way round. To capture the desired relationship between MSSP and the sequential model, we define the notion of *jumping refinement* in Section 3 and then show formally that MSSP is a jumping refinement of the sequential model.

We tackled the formalization process iteratively, beginning with a high-level abstract model in which we make a number of simplifying assumptions. Section 4 describes this work. Sections 5 and 6 show successive refinements of the abstract model, identifying low-level requirements from which our initial assumptions can be inferred. Throughout, we present only the most important and interesting results at an abstract, mathematical level, rather than our particular formalization in Maude. Even though Maude provides a suite of useful tools for our project, we would like to avoid giving the reader the impression that it was a crucial part of our formalization. We believe that one can relatively easily adapt our work to other formal systems and tools. Section 7 concludes the paper and summarizes some of our main observations and lessons learned during this work.

2   An Overview of MSSP

In this section, we present an overview of MSSP. This high-level description is meant to provide the contextual knowledge necessary to understand the formal work that follows in the remainder of the paper. A more extensive treatment of MSSP can be found in [13] and [14].

2.1   High-Level Operation

Consider again Figure 1. An MSSP machine has two execution paths: the fast path and the correct path. The fast path is composed of a single, complex *master* processor that executes a speculatively optimized executable called the *distilled program*. The master processor runs ahead of the correct path execution to produce hints of where the execution is headed. The correct path is implemented by multiple *slave* processors, which lag behind the master. Because the individual slave processors are slower than the master, we need a means for the correct path to keep up. MSSP uses *speculative parallelization* [12] for this purpose. Execution of the correct path program is split into segments, called *tasks*, that are executed concurrently on the slaves.

To enable these tasks to execute independently and in parallel, the master execution is used to predict the sequence of tasks — that is, the starting program counter (PC) of each task, and the values that are live-in to each of them. The predictions are generated by logically taking a checkpoint of the master's (speculative) state at the point corresponding to the beginning of the task.

Because the master's predictions are not guaranteed to be correct, the results computed by slaves are themselves speculative, and must be checked before they can be made architecturally visible. To enable this, each task's inputs (live-ins) and outputs (live-outs) are recorded and sent to a *verification/commit unit*. When a completed task becomes the oldest (*i.e.*, the next to commit), a

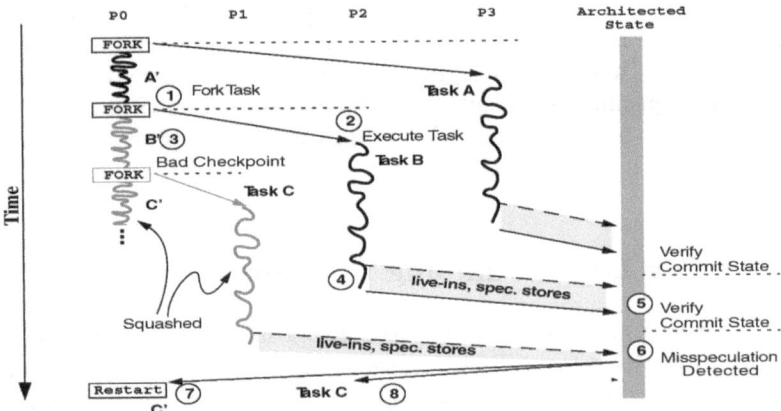

Fig. 2. Master processor distributes checkpoints to slaves. The master, executing the distilled program on processor P0, assigns tasks to slave processors, providing
them with predicted live-in values

memoization-like operation is performed that commits the outputs if the inputs
match the machine's current architected state.

2.2   MSSP Example

To facilitate a conceptual understanding of MSSP, we provide an example that
outlines its basic behavior. Figure 2 illustrates an MSSP execution with four
processors: one master (P0) and three slaves (P1, P2, and P3) that begin the
example idle. Each processor has its own register file and local first-level cache;
values held there are speculative. The machine's architected state appears on
the right in the figure. This holds the current (correct) values of all ISA-visible
registers and memory addresses. In an MSSP machine, this is maintained in the
shared second-level cache, which is backed by DRAM.

At annotation (1) in the figure, the master processor spawns Task B onto
processor P2, which then begins executing (2). P0 continues executing (3) the
distilled program segment that corresponds to Task B, which we refer to as
Task B'. As the slave executes Task B, it reads values that it did not write (the
live-in values supplied by the master) and performs writes of its own (the live-out
values). When Task B completes (4), P2 sends its live-in and live-out values to
a verify/commit unit, which checks that the live-ins exactly correspond to the
architected state; if so, the live-outs can be committed to architected state (5).
The commit is implemented so that it appears atomic to all processors in the
system [14]. This avoids potential problems with memory coherence if MSSP is
used in a multiprocessor system.

If the master generates an incorrect value (3), one of the recorded live-in
values will differ from the corresponding value in the architected state, and a
mismatch will be detected at verification (6). When this occurs, the master
and all other in-flight tasks are *squashed* — the speculative data they hold in

their registers and caches is discarded. The architected state of the machine is not affected by the misspeculation, so it holds the state the program was in at the completion of Task B. At this time, the master is restarted at C′ (7) and, in parallel, non-speculative execution of the corresponding task in the original program (Task C) begins on P2 (8). In both cases, the processors have their state seeded with the correct values currently held in architected state.

3   Rewriting Logic, Jumping Refinements and Maude

We chose rewriting logic as the formal framework in which to define and reason about MSSP. Rewriting logic (RL) has been introduced as a unifying framework for concurrency [7], making it quite appealing for a complex and highly concurrent architecture like MSSP. As a tool supporting RL, we chose the Maude system [3]. Maude provides a series of formal analysis tools for rewriting logic theories, including: (1) a highly-efficient rewriting engine; (2) a search procedure exploring the (potentially unbounded) state space using a breadth-first strategy; (3) a linear temporal logic (LTL) model checker; and (4) an inductive theorem prover and proof assistant (ITP) [4]. While our present work does not require all of these features, the potential to expand without changing tools makes Maude a compelling choice.

RL extends equational logic by adding rewriting rules as parameterized state transitions. Briefly, a rewriting theory $\mathcal{R}$ is a triple (Σ, E, R), where Σ contains all the type and operator declarations, E contains a set of equations, and R is a set of rewriting rules. Equations in E are used to define the computational infrastructure of a system specification (such as predicates and sets of tasks, in the case of MSSP), while the rewriting rules in R are used to specify the *concurrent* aspects (such as committing a slave processor's live-outs). Equations and rules can contain variables, and they are applied to a given term at any position where they match. Given $\mathcal{R} = (\Sigma, E, R)$, we let $\equiv_\mathcal{R}$ and $\Rightarrow_\mathcal{R}$ denote the binary relations on terms derived by applying the equations and the rewriting rules, respectively; $\Rightarrow_\mathcal{R}^*$ denotes the reflexive, transitive, and $\equiv_\mathcal{R}$-closure (*i.e.* modulo equations in E) of $\Rightarrow_\mathcal{R}$. The subscript $\mathcal{R}$ is omitted whenever apparent from context.

Any transition system can be defined as a rewrite theory. In particular, both the sequential model and the various versions of MSSP are rewrite theories, each having a special *state* type (or sort); the rewrite sequences on state terms correspond to state transitions. The standard notion of (stuttering) refinement of rewrite theories states that a step in the abstract theory can be simulated by a sequence of steps in the refined theory. We would clearly want MSSP to refine the sequential model, but note that this is not true within the standard meaning of (stuttering) refinement — and this has nothing to do with our choice of using rewriting logic for our formal framework — because MSSP deliberately does not reproduce all the steps of the sequential model. To formally capture this relationship, we introduce the notion of *jumping refinement*, as follows.

Definition 1. *Given* $\mathcal{R} = (\Sigma, E, R)$ *and* $\mathcal{R}' = (\Sigma', E', R')$ *with rewrite relations* $\Rightarrow_{\mathcal{R}}$ *and* $\Rightarrow_{\mathcal{R}'}$, *respectively, and containing some designated sorts State and State', respectively, together with a map* ψ *associating terms of sort State to terms of sort State', we say* $\mathcal{R}'$ **is a jumping** ψ**-refinement of** $\mathcal{R}$ *iff for any transition* $t \Rightarrow_{\mathcal{R}'} u$ *in* $\mathcal{R}'$ *there is a sequence* $\psi(t) \Rightarrow_{\mathcal{R}}^* \psi(u)$ *of transitions in* $\mathcal{R}$.

The intuition here is that the states in $\mathcal{R}'$ contain more information than those in $\mathcal{R}$, and ψ is a projection extracting a state of $\mathcal{R}$ from a state of $\mathcal{R}'$. It may therefore be the case that several transitions take place in $\mathcal{R}'$ without changing the corresponding state in $\mathcal{R}$. In other words, it may be the case that $t \Rightarrow_{\mathcal{R}'} t'$ while $\psi(t) \equiv_{\mathcal{R}} \psi(t')$, but it is also possible that $\psi(t) \Rightarrow_{\mathcal{R}}^+ \psi(t')$ for a large number of transitions in $\mathcal{R}$. In the first case we metaphorically say that the transition in $\mathcal{R}'$ "accumulates energy" with respect to $\mathcal{R}$, and in the second that the transition in $\mathcal{R}'$ "jumps" with respect to $\mathcal{R}$. In our case, $\mathcal{R}'$ will specify MSSP, $\mathcal{R}$ the sequential model, and ψ will return the architected state of MSSP. Note that the slave execution steps in MSSP do not modify the architected state, so their execution "accumulates energy"; but once a slave computation is committed, the MSSP machine "jumps" several sequential states.

4   First Iteration

We next introduce abstract models for sequential and MSSP execution, and then show that the latter is a jumping refinement of the former. Since the sequential machine model under consideration is deterministic, its executions can safely be considered atomic. This implies the rewrite rules (transitions) in the sequential model can be regarded as equations, so we will often say, by slight abuse of language, that MSSP is *equivalent* to the sequential model instead of a jumping refinement of it.

The formalisms presented here are abstracted from our original *Maude* source, which is harder to read but available online in complete form at [8]. The reader is encouraged to refer to that source for a mechanical formalization, both of the execution model specifications and of the proofs of the main results, the details of which we must necessarily omit here.

4.1   The Sequential Execution Model

The sequential execution model, which we denote by SEQ, serves as a reference against which correctness of MSSP is measured. Since we do not wish to couple ourselves to any particular sequential ISA, we avoid specifying one for SEQ. We can afford to do so because we assume that the slaves implement the same ISA as the "reference" sequential machine.

The SEQ model is centered on the notion of machine state. Although we have defined machine state precisely in other work [9], the abstractions we present in this paper are at a sufficiently high level for us to avoid having to impose a structure on it. Thus, machine state is defined simply as the domain, denoted by $\mathcal{S}$, in which execution occurs. That said, it is useful, in this and subsequent sections, to understand — if only informally — that a member of $\mathcal{S}$ captures the values held in a machine's ISA-visible storage cells (registers and memory locations). We will see in Section 5 that the live-in and live-out data processed by MSSP slaves also constitute machine states, but that these sets will generally contain members for only a subset of all ISA-visible cells. That is, a machine state need not hold members for *all* ISA-visible cells.

Executing an instruction results in updates to a machine's storage cells, so an instruction's execution constitutes a transformation of machine state. Sequential execution of more instructions is then defined as follows.

Definition 2 (Sequential execution). *Function* $seq : \mathcal{S} \times \mathbb{Z}^+ \mapsto \mathcal{S}$ *models the sequential execution of multiple instructions, and is defined:*

$$seq(S, n) = \begin{cases} S & \text{if } n = 0 \\ seq(next(S), n-1) & \text{otherwise} \end{cases}$$

Function $next : \mathcal{S} \mapsto \mathcal{S}$, *which is uninterpreted, models the execution of a single instruction.*

Note that $seq(S_0, n) = S_1$ states only that S_1 is the state that results after executing n instructions in state S_0. S_0 determines those instructions implicitly, since a machine's state holds both instructions and data. The program counter, itself a member of S_0, identifies the cell in which the next instruction is held.

4.2   The MSSP Execution Model

The design of a realistic MSSP machine is encumbered by numerous performance-mandated features, none of which have any bearing on the processes that underly its correct operation. Thus, our formalisms are based not on the operation of a real MSSP machine, but on a more abstract model [9] that eliminates all of the performance-related complexities. A few differences between the abstract model and the real machine are worth noting.

First, we view the master as a "black box" that is capable of generating *arbitrary* live-in data. This is of course key to our objective of ensuring that correctness in MSSP is entirely independent of how the fast path operates. This view does, however, expose a limitation of the model: we cannot guarantee forward progress if we cannot guarantee anything about live-in data. But this is an artifact of our model, not of the real MSSP machine, which can make guarantees about forward progress because it has the capability to revert, at any time, to normal sequential execution. In the interests of keeping our formalisms simple, we choose not to model this dual-mode operation in MSSP, and thus treat forward progress as a property that can be verified separate from this work.

Second, rather than have each task's boundaries specified in terms of start and end program counter values, the abstract model assumes tasks are delineated by means of an instruction count — a task is complete when the specified number of instructions have been executed. This simplifies our work because it eliminates the need to expose the notion of program counter in the formal models.

Finally, a real MSSP machine permits slaves to read (but *not* to write) architected state, which, in turn, allows the master to supply as live-in data only that which has been modified by it; values not modified recently are fetched by a slave direct from architected state.[2] Rather than encumber our model with these details, we assume the master supplies *all* data that it assumes a slave will need; slaves are wholly isolated from architected state (and one another) in our abstract model.

Analogous to the sequential model, MSSP's execution is defined in terms of state transitions, but now manipulation of state occurs at the granularity of *tasks* rather than instructions. MSSP contains a collection of "active" tasks. At each step, the machine selects one task from this collection and, if certain conditions are met (the *task safety* requirement), "commits" it to the architected state. In this section, we do not specify a structure for tasks, nor do we define how the commit process is effected. We state only that if a task satisfies the commit requirement, then committing it has the same effect as advancing the architected state according to the sequential model; we use $\#t$ to denote the number of instructions by which this advancing occurs.

In this section, *task safety* is not interpreted; we define it only as a necessary condition for committing a task, and hence for advancing the architected state. Task safety is a property both of the task to be committed and the machine state to which the commit is to occur. Changes to machine state can thus establish or violate the safety of a given task. Hence, committing one task can affect the safety of another.

We let T denote the set of all MSSP tasks, T^* *the set* of all finite sets of tasks, and use operator $|: T^* \times T^* \mapsto T^*$ to construct new task sets; it is both associative and commutative.[3] $|$ is overloaded to also permit construction of task sets from individual tasks.

Definition 3 (MSSP execution). *Function* $mssp : S \times T^* \mapsto S$ *models a single step in the operation of an MSSP machine. For* $t \in T$, $\tau \in T^*$ *and* $S \in S$ *such that t is safe for S, we define the rule* $mssp(S, t|\tau) \Rightarrow mssp(seq(S, \#t), \tau)$. *To define MSSP operation on the empty task set, we add rule* $mssp(S, \emptyset) \Rightarrow S$.

Note that the above rule is *conditional* — t must be safe for S for the state transition to apply, so at this point MSSP's behavior is left undefined for tasks that are not safe. Note also that the task that is selected for committing is not prescribed, since $|$ is associative and commutative. Indeed, a key property of our model is that *we do not impose an ordering* on the sequence of task commits.

That ordering of commits is not important was initially surprising to us, mainly because the extant MSSP design does impose an order. In fact, we discovered this as a direct result of formalizing MSSP, which thus helped us discover that task safety is the single requirement for correct operation. Further, in

---

[2] This is merely a performance-driven design choice: the master could equally supply all data, but that would demand too much bandwidth between it and each slave.

[3] We distinguish $|$ from set union ($\cup$) because, in our Maude framework, T is not a set, but a multiset — it can contain duplicate members.

eliminating ordering from our model, we impose minimal constraints on implementations while still allowing for reasoning about correctness.

We point out again that our model for MSSP is devoid of any mention of the master processor. The omission is deliberate — correct operation of the MSSP machine is not dependent on what the master does. Correctness depends only on the slaves and the manner in which the results of their execution are committed.

4.3 Equivalence

We need to show that any transformation of state that can be effected by MSSP can also be achieved in SEQ. In what follows, we first show how we used Maude to arrive at a slightly weaker result — that MSSP *can* effect sequential transformations of machine state — and then a stronger result — that *all* transformations that can be achieved by MSSP are also possible in SEQ.

Equivalence on Safe Task Sets. We can extend Definition 3 to describe MSSP operation at the more coarse granularity of a task set. This requires an extension of our notion of task safety: a task set is considered safe for a given machine state if *there exists* some enumeration of its members such that each is safe for the machine state resulting from committing its predecessor. A simple inductive argument then gives us the following.

Lemma 1. *If $\tau \in T^*$ is safe for S, then $mssp(S, \tau) \Rightarrow^* mssp(seq(S, \#\tau), \emptyset) \Rightarrow seq(S, \#\tau)$.*

The above lemma states that an MSSP machine starting out in state S and with an active set of tasks τ, which is safe for S, *can* attain the same configuration as a sequential machine executing $\#\tau$ instructions from the same S. This is because safety of a task set is defined in terms of the *existence* of a safe enumeration of its members, yet MSSP operation is not constrained to follow the order of such an enumeration. We therefore cannot infer that MSSP necessarily commits all members of a safe set of tasks; it will do so only if it chooses the right commit order. If it chooses poorly, it can commit some task which, despite being safe, is not the next task in any safe enumeration of τ. In such a case, the remaining members of τ can be rendered unsafe.

It is important to realize that even though our model permits MSSP to pick an inappropriate task, it is never wrong for that task to be committed — since it was safe, committing it, by definition, advances architected state as per SEQ. Choosing an inappropriate task affects only the *efficiency* of the machine, not its correctness, as shown next.

Equivalence for All Task Sets. We can easily extend the above result to cater for any collection of tasks in the active set. To do so, we define $mssp(S, \tau) = mssp(S, \emptyset)$ for all $\tau \in T^*$ that contain no tasks safe for S. Thus, if the machine chooses to commit a task that renders the remainder of its active task set unsafe, it simply discards what remains. Hence our earlier claim that inappropriate choices affect only the machine's efficiency: the order in which tasks are committed determines the fraction of the active set that can be committed before the remainder is discarded.

We are now in a position to define MSSP operation on any given task set. Our main result rests on the claim that any given task set can be partitioned into two disjoint subsets, one that is safe for the current architected state and one that contains *no* safe members.

Theorem 1. *If τ is safe for machine state S, and τ' contains no members that are safe for $seq(S, \#\tau)$, then $mssp(S, \tau|\tau') \Rightarrow^* mssp(seq(S, \#\tau), \emptyset) \Rightarrow seq(S, \#\tau)$.*

In the above, we assert the existence of a sequence of transitions; we do *not* claim that, given task set $\tau|\tau'$, the MSSP machine will necessarily reach state $seq(S, \#\tau)$. However, we can invoke a "meta-argument" about our specification to prove that any trace of MSSP execution on a given set of tasks effects a bisection of that set into a safe subset and a subset that contains no safe members, so Theorem 1 applies to any execution of the MSSP machine. In other words, all executions in MSSP are possible in SEQ.

5   Second Iteration

In the previous section, tasks were uninterpreted and effectively treated as the atomic units on which execution of an MSSP machine is based. Likewise, task safety and the commit operation were uninterpreted and treated as basic capabilities of the machine. In this section, we zoom in on the domain $\mathcal{T}$ by imposing a structure on tasks, which yields a *stuttering refinement* [6] of the MSSP execution model. Thus, we now describe MSSP's execution at an instruction rather than at a task granularity. In so doing, we also partially interpret both task safety and the commit process; Section 6 further refines those concepts.

Once again, we point out that the results presented here are distilled from the original Maude specifications [8], to which we refer the interested reader.

5.1   Tasks

In the existing MSSP implementation, a task is constructed by the master processor, then transferred to a slave where it executes to completion, and finally checked by the verification unit, which either commits or discards the results. Consequently, we define a task as a tuple comprising input and output data, plus information about the current state of the execution at a slave processor.

Definition 4 (Task). *A task is a 4-tuple contained in $\mathcal{T} = S \times \mathbb{Z}^+ \times S \times \mathbb{Z}^+$. The tuple $\langle S_{in}, n, S_{out}, k \rangle \in \mathcal{T}$ denotes a task with live-in set S_{in} and live-out set S_{out}. The value n is the number of sequential instructions that constitute complete execution of this task; k is the number of instructions that have been executed by a slave so far ($0 \leq k \leq n$).*

A newly created task has form $\langle S_{in}, n, S_{in}, 0 \rangle$; at its completion, it has form $\langle S_{in}, n, S_{out}, n \rangle$. We will relate S_{in} and S_{out} later in this section.

We define a number of functions on $\mathcal{T}$ for the sake of notational convenience. Let $t = \langle S_{in}, n, S_{out}, k \rangle$. Functions $live\_in : \mathcal{T} \mapsto S$ and $live\_out : \mathcal{T} \mapsto S$

produce the live-in and live-out sets for a given task. Thus, $live\_in(t) = S_{in}$ and $live\_out(t) = S_{out}$. Function $\# : \mathcal{T} \mapsto \mathbb{Z}^+$, which we introduced in the previous section, yields the second component of a task: $\#t = n$.

5.2 Task Evolution

We use *task evolution* as a means for modeling the manner in which a task is processed by a slave processor. It is defined as follows.

Definition 5 (Task evolution). *Let* $\langle S_{in}, n, S_{out}, k \rangle \in \mathcal{T}$ *be a task in an MSSP machine's active task set. Then the following transition rule applies.*

$$\langle S_{in}, n, S_{out}, k \rangle \Rightarrow \begin{cases} \langle S_{in}, n, next(S_{out}), k+1 \rangle & \text{if } k < n \\ \langle S_{in}, n, S_{out}, n \rangle & \text{otherwise} \end{cases}$$

Note that this rule is decoupled from the specification of the MSSP machine itself, so tasks evolve independent of, and concurrent with, the task commit process defined in the previous section. From the above definition it is also clear that slaves execute according to the sequential model. More precisely, the first step in slave execution simply advances the live-outs as per SEQ: $live\_out(t)$, which is initially the same as $live\_in(t)$, is transformed to $next(live\_in(t))$. Extrapolating, we arrive at the following transition rule.

Lemma 2. $\langle S_{in}, n, S_{in}, 0 \rangle \Rightarrow^* \langle S_{in}, n, seq(S_{in}, n), n \rangle$.

In fact, we can say something stronger: since we specify no transition rules other than those in Definition 5, the *only* way in which a task can reach completion is through the sequential advancing of its live-in set. That is, if t is a completed task, then $live\_out(t) = seq(live\_in(t), \#t)$.

5.3 Task Safety and Commit

Having introduced task evolution, we can now partially interpret task safety. To do so, we introduce the notion of superimposition, which models the commit process. Operator $\_ \leftarrow \_ : \mathcal{S} \times \mathcal{S} \mapsto \mathcal{S}$ denotes the superimposition of one machine state onto another. We do not interpret this operation formally, simply because the domain $\mathcal{S}$ itself remains uninterpreted. However, the intuition behind its operation should be clear: $S_0 \leftarrow S_1$ is the machine state that results when S_0 is *overwritten* by S_1.[4]

Definition 6 (Task safety). $t \in \mathcal{T}$ *safe for* S *if* $seq(S, \#t) = S \leftarrow live\_out(t)$.

Since $live\_out(t) = seq(live\_in(t), \#t)$ at the completion of t (Lemma 2), task safety is equivalently characterized by $seq(S, \#t) = S \leftarrow seq(live\_in(t), \#t)$.

---

[4] Recall that live-in and live-out sets need not represent the state of a *whole* machine. It can therefore be the case that S_0 refers to storage cells not covered by S_1. Those cells will appear, unchanged, in the superimposition.

5.4   MSSP Operation, Refined

We can now replace Definition 3 with the following.

Definition 7 (MSSP operation, refined). *Let $t \in \mathcal{T}$ and $\tau \in \mathcal{T}^*$. If S is a state for which t is safe, then $mssp(S, t|\tau) \Rightarrow mssp(S \leftarrow live\_out(t), \tau)$.*

We have argued that at the completion of task t, $live\_out(t) = seq(live\_in(t), \#t)$. Since t is safe for S, $S \leftarrow seq(live\_in(t), \#t) = seq(S, \#t)$, so the above refinement implies $mssp(S, t|\tau) \Rightarrow mssp(seq(S, \#t), \tau)$, which is precisely Definition 3.

6   Third Iteration

We have not yet specified what the check for task safety entails. We now refine our formal models to prove that a more low-level set of checks, which have feasible hardware implementations, are sufficient to ensure task safety. To do so, we first introduce a number of constraints on the superimposition operator and then refine our SEQ model to incorporate superimposition.

6.1   Superimposition

In this subsection, we persist with an informal view of superimposition, but we now impose a number of constraints on its behavior. In order to do so, we must first refine knowledge about machine state. We introduce an uninterpreted "consistency" operator $\_ \subseteq \_ : \mathcal{S} \times \mathcal{S} \mapsto \{\texttt{true}, \texttt{false}\}$, understanding informally that $S_1 \subseteq S_2$ implies that S_1 is consistent with S_2 in the sense that all of the storage cells of S_1 are also available in S_2 and, further, that both agree on the values held in those cells.

Definition 8 (Superimposition properties). *Superimposition satisfies*

1. *Associativity: $(S_1 \leftarrow S_2) \leftarrow S_3 = S_1 \leftarrow (S_2 \leftarrow S_3)$;*
2. *Containment: $S_1 \subseteq S_2$ implies $(S_1 \leftarrow S_3) \subseteq (S_2 \leftarrow S_3)$;*
3. *Idempotency: $S_2 \subseteq S_1$ implies $(S_1 \leftarrow S_2) = S_1$.*

6.2   Sequential Execution, Refined

A sequential machine operates by fetching an instruction, decoding and executing it, and then writing the results back to machine state. This view leads to a definition of instruction execution in terms of superimposition. Before that, however, we must address a problem incurred by SEQ in the context of MSSP slave execution. Tasks evolve by sequentially advancing their live-in sets (as per Definition 5). Since those live-in sets are produced by the master, they are potentially unsuitable for the purposes of executing the next instruction (we make no assumptions about the live-ins produced by the master). To serve as a precondition for well-defined sequential execution, we introduce an uninterpreted notion of machine state *completeness*. Completeness is largely ISA-specific, but we can understand it in a general sense as follows. A machine state is complete for an instruction's execution if it contains a cell for the program counter, the memory cell pointed to by that program counter (the instruction itself), and all other cells (registers and/or memory locations) that the instruction will read during its execution.

Definition 9 (Instruction execution). *If $S \in \mathcal{S}$ is complete, then we define $next(S)$ to be $S \leftarrow \delta(S)$. Thus, $\delta(S) \in \mathcal{S}$ constitutes the changes to state that will result from executing the next instruction.*

Effectively, the function $\delta : \mathcal{S} \mapsto \mathcal{S}$, which is defined only if its argument is complete, performs the fetch-decode-execute steps alluded to above; the superimposition "commits" the results.

A key property of sequential execution upon which our results depend is *determinism*. Specifically, we require that advancing two *consistent* machine states by the same number of steps must yield consistent results. Formally, $S_1 \subseteq S_2$ must imply $seq(S_1, n) \subseteq seq(S_2, n)$. This can be inferred from the more basic requirement that execution of a single instruction be deterministic: $S_1 \subseteq S_2$ must imply $\delta(S_1) = \delta(S_2)$. That is, two consistent, complete states, which will execute the same instruction on the same data when advanced one step, must produce the same set of outputs.

Of course, sequential execution of n instructions is well-defined only if, at each step along the way, the machine state is complete. When this is the case for a given machine state, we will say that state is n-complete. More formally, S is n-complete if it is complete (for one instruction) and $next(S)$ is $(n-1)$-complete.

In order to define sequential execution in terms of superimposition, we introduce the notion of *cumulative writes*, which are the results that accrue from the sequential execution of multiple instructions.

Definition 10 (Cumulative writes). *The cumulative writes generated by sequential execution are given by $\Delta : \mathcal{S} \times \mathbb{Z}^+ \mapsto \mathcal{S}$. For all $n \geq 0$, we define*

$$\Delta(S, n) = \left\{ \begin{array}{ll} \emptyset & \text{if } n = 0 \\ \Delta(S, n-1) \leftarrow \delta(seq(S, n-1)) & \text{otherwise} \end{array} \right]$$

From properties of superimposition, determinism and cumulative writes we obtain the following important result.

Lemma 3. *For all $n \geq 0$, the following hold.*

- *If $S \in \mathcal{S}$ is n-complete, then $seq(S, n) = S \leftarrow \Delta(S, n)$.*
- *For $S_1, S_2 \in \mathcal{S}$ n-complete, $S_1 \subseteq S_2$ implies $\Delta(S_1, n) = \Delta(S_2, n)$.*

6.3   Establishing Task Safety

We can now show that checking for task safety, which we have assumed is a basic capability of the MSSP machine, is equivalently performed through two low-level checks. This result is expressed formally as follows.

Theorem 2. *If $S_1 \subseteq S_2 \in \mathcal{S}$ are n-complete then $seq(S_2, n) = S_2 \leftarrow seq(S_1, n)$.*

This result follows from Lemma 3 and the properties of superimposition that we enumerated in Definition 8. Specifically, since S_1 is n-complete, $seq(S_1, n) = S_1 \leftarrow \Delta(S_1, n)$. Hence, $S_2 \leftarrow seq(S_1, n) = S_2 \leftarrow (S_1 \leftarrow \Delta(S_1, n))$. Since superimposition is associative, the right hand side is the same as $(S_2 \leftarrow S_1) \leftarrow \Delta(S_1, n)$. But $S_1 \subseteq S_2$, so $S_2 \leftarrow S_1 = S_2$. Thus, $S_2 \leftarrow seq(S_1, n) = S_2 \leftarrow \Delta(S_1, n)$. But we also know that $\Delta(S_2, n) = \Delta(S_1, n)$, and hence that $S_2 \leftarrow seq(S_1, n) = S_2 \leftarrow \Delta(S_2, n)$. The latter expression is exactly $seq(S_2, n)$.

The obvious implication of this result is that completeness and consistency imply task safety: if S is the architected state of an MSSP machine, and $t \in T$ is some task such that $live\_in(t) \subseteq S$ and $live\_in(t)$ is $\#t$-complete, then $seq(S, \#t) = S \leftarrow seq(live\_in(t), \#t)$. That is, t is safe for S.

7   Conclusion

We have shown that MSSP achieves the equivalent of a sequential execution, albeit at the coarser granularity of tasks rather than instructions. Through our formalization of its operation, we isolated the concept of *task safety* as the principal factor that underpins correctness. We proved that safety follows from *completeness* and *consistency* of live-ins with respect to architected state, two requirements that the existing MSSP architecture can easily be shown to satisfy.

In establishing the above results, we also discovered a number of unexpected properties of MSSP. Good examples are the associativity of superimposition (commits) and our dependence on determinism in SEQ. In a sense, these results are merely artifacts of the formalization process itself — superimposition's associativity, for example, was needed in the proof of one of our lemmas. In this respect, we feel the process of deriving the formal model was as beneficial to our understanding as was the final model itself. On those grounds alone, the exercise proved its worth.

In general, all the benefits we reaped in this work are a result of the systematic, rigorous thinking necessitated by formalization. The computer architects involved in this work found such rigor particularly liberating because it permitted us to focus on the fundamental, implementation-independent issues, rather than on the intricate performance-mandated design points. Indeed, the ability to separate correctness from performance concerns pervades our work; the formalization of MSSP reinforced our conviction in this respect.

We found the process of mechanizing our proofs in Maude to be easy and intuitive. Deriving the Maude modules from a manual (pencil-and-paper) effort [9] was completed in well under a week, mostly by a novice Maude user. The mechanization did force an even more rigorous approach, which, in turn, exposed even more fundamental assumptions we were making. For example, our discovery that commit order is not important is a good example of how Maude assisted us — having to be explicit about associativity and commutativity of operators brought this issue to the fore. That said, we were on occasion frustrated by the system's inability to reduce certain terms as required, which forced us to sometimes organize the modules in a non-ideal fashion. In mitigation, this problem eased as our experience grew, but certainly a proof assistant tool, which permits its user to specify explicitly which rewriting rules — be they equational or transitional — should be applied, would have been a boon.

In summary, our efforts in the formal verification of MSSP have been enormously fruitful. In fact, our positive experiences have motivated further work. We have recently started reasoning about MSSP operation on machine state, such as memory-mapped I/O addresses, where we cannot rely on accesses being *idempotent*. Speculative execution is precluded in such regions, demanding that we impose task boundaries and proceed, non-speculatively, as per SEQ.

References

1. Arvind and X. Shen. Using term rewriting systems to design and verify processors. *IEEE Micro*, 9(3):36–46, May/June 1999.
2. J.R. Burch and D.L. Dill. Automatic verification of pipelined microprocessor control. In *Proc. International Conference on Computer Aided Verification*, volume 818 of LNCS, pages 68–80, June 1994.
3. M. Clavel, F. Durán, S. Eker, P. Lincoln, N. Martí-Oliet, J. Meseguer, and C. Talcott. *Maude 2.0 Manual*, 2003. http://maude.cs.uiuc.edu/manual.
4. M. Clavel, F. Durán, S. Eker, and J. Meseguer. Building equational proving tools by reflection in rewriting logic. In *CAFE: An Industrial-Strength Algebraic Formal Method*. Elsevier, 2000.
5. D.L. Dill, A.J. Drexler, A.J. Hu, and C.H. Yang. Protocol verification as a hardware design aid. In *Proc. IEEE International Conference on Computer Design: VLSI in Computers and Processors*, pages 522–525, October 1992.
6. L. Lamport. What good is temporal logic? In *Information Processing '83: Proc. IFIP 9th World Congress*, pages 657–668, September 1983.
7. J. Meseguer. Conditional rewriting logic as a unified model of concurrency. *Theoretical Computer Science*, 96(1):73–155, April 1992.
8. P. Salverda, G. Roşu, and C. Zilles. Maude formalization of MSSP. http://fsl.cs.uiuc.edu/mssp.
9. P. Salverda and C. Zilles. Formal verification of MSSP. Technical Report UIUCDCS-R-2003-2384, University of Illinois at Urbana-Champaign, December 2003.
10. J. Sawada and W.A. Hunt. Trace table based approach for pipelined microprocessor verification. In *Proc. International Conference on Computer Aided Verification*, volume 1254 of LNCS, pages 364–375, June 1997.
11. J. Sawada and W.A. Hunt. Processor verification with precise exceptions and speculative execution. In *Proc. International Conference on Computer Aided Verification*, volume 1427 of LNCS, pages 135–146, June 1998.
12. G. Sohi, S. Breach, and T. Vijaykumar. Multiscalar processors. In *Proc. 22nd Annual International Symposium on Computer Architecture*, pages 414–425, June 1995.
13. C. Zilles. *Master/slave speculative parallelization and approximate code*. PhD thesis, University of Winsconsin - Madison, 2002.
14. C. Zilles and G. Sohi. Master/slave speculative parallelization. In *Proc. 35th Annual ACM/IEEE International Symposium on Microarchitecture*, pages 85–96, November 2002.

Systematic Implementation of Real-Time Models⋆

Martin De Wulf, Laurent Doyen⋆⋆, and Jean-François Raskin

Computer Science Department, Université Libre de Bruxelles, Belgium

Abstract. Recently we have proposed the "almost ASAP" semantics as an alternative semantics for timed automata. This semantics is useful when modeling real-time controllers : control strategies modeled with this semantics are robust and implementable (without making the synchrony hypothesis). We show in this paper how to effectively encode this semantics using timed automata along with their classical semantics. We have implemented a tool set that allows us to verify, using HyTech and Uppaal, the almost ASAP behavior of controllers and generate automatically provably correct code from verified models. To illustrate the applicability of our results, we show how we have synthesized the code for the Philips Audio Control Protocol for Lego Mindstorms™.

1 Introduction

Timed automata are an important formal model for the specification and analysis of real-time systems. Formalisms like timed automata and hybrid automata are central in the so-called *model-based development* methodology for embedded controllers. The steps underlying that methodology can be summarized as follows: (*i*) construct a (timed/hybrid automaton) model Env of the environment in which the controller will be embedded; (*ii*) make clear what is the control objective: for example, prevent the environment to enter a set of Bad states; (*iii*) design a (timed automaton) model Cont of the control strategy; (*iv*) verify that $\mathsf{Reach}([\![\mathsf{Env} \parallel \mathsf{Cont}]\!]) \cap \mathsf{Bad} = \emptyset$. When Cont has been proven correct, it would be valuable to ensure that an implementation Impl of that model can be obtained in a systematic way in order to ensure the conservation of correctness, that is to ensure that $\mathsf{Reach}([\![\mathsf{Env} \parallel \mathsf{Impl}]\!]) \cap \mathsf{Bad} = \emptyset$ is obtained by construction.

Unfortunately, this is often not possible for several *fundamental* and/or *technical* reasons. First, the notion of time used in the traditional semantics of timed automata is *continuous* and defines *perfect clocks* with *infinite precision* while implementations can only access time through *digital* and *finitely precise* clocks. Second, timed automata react *instantaneously* to events and time-outs while implementations can only react within a given, usually small but not zero, *reaction*

⋆ Supported by the FRFC project "Centre Fédéré en Vérification" funded by the Belgian National Science Fundation (FNRS) under grant nr 2.4530.02.
⋆⋆ Research fellow supported by the Belgian National Science Foundation (FNRS).

J.S. Fitzgerald, I.J. Hayes, and A. Tarlecki (Eds.): FM 2005, LNCS 3582, pp. 139–156, 2005.
© Springer-Verlag Berlin Heidelberg 2005

delay. Third, timed automata may describe control strategies that are *unrealistic*, like *zeno-strategies* or strategies that ask the controller *to act faster and faster* [CHR02]. For one of those three reasons, a model for a digital controller that has been proven correct may not be implementable (at all) or it may not be possible to turn it systematically into an implementation that is proven correct w.r.t. this model.

To overcome those problems, we recently proposed an alternative semantics to timed automata in [DDR04]. This semantics is called the Almost ASAP semantics, AASAP for short. The AASAP semantics of a timed automaton A, noted $[\![A]\!]_\Delta^{\mathsf{AAsap}}$, is a parametric semantics that leaves as a parameter Δ, which takes value $\delta \in \mathbb{Q}^{\geq 0}$, the *reaction delay* of the controller. This semantics relaxes the classical semantics of timed automata in that it does not impose on the controller to react instantaneously but imposes on the controller to react *within δ time units*. We have proven that a timed controller is implementable with a *sufficiently fast* hardware if there exists $\delta \in \mathbb{Q}^{>0}$ such that $\mathsf{Reach}([\![\mathsf{Env}]\!] \parallel [\![\mathsf{Cont}]\!]_\delta^{\mathsf{AAsap}}) \cap \mathsf{Bad} = \emptyset$.

To use the AASAP semantics in practice, we need tool support. In [DDR04], we have shown that the AASAP semantics of a controller can be encoded using a single parameter timed automaton. Unfortunately, this construction is exponential in all cases, which makes it useless for all but the toy examples. In this paper, we define a new compositional construction that avoids the exponential blow-up. The exponential behavior can still appear during the verification phase but only in the worst case. Thanks to this new construction, we have implemented a tool set in order to manipulate the AASAP semantics on top of HyTech [HHWT95] and Uppaal [PL00]. We show the practical interest of our construction by applying our tool set to a non-trivial example: the Philips Audio Control Protocol [BPV94]. We show how the AASAP semantics can be used to produce provably correct executable code for this protocol. The code that we have produced automatically can be run on Lego Mindstorms™. With this case study, we believe that we have shown that the AASAP semantics is useful when supported by computer aided verification tools and that it can be used to produce correct code for non-trivial embedded controllers without making the synchrony hypothesis. To the best of our knowledge, this is the first time that provably correct (without making the synchrony hypothesis) real-time code is produced for a non-trivial case study.

The rest of the paper is organized as follows. In Section 2, we recall some preliminary notions. In Section 3, we review the syntax and classical semantics of timed automata. In Section 4, we recall the AASAP semantics and summarize its properties. In Section 5, we present our compositional construction. In Section 6, we present our tool set. In Section 7, we show how to apply the AASAP semantics to synthesize provably correct code for a real-time protocol.

2   Preliminaries

Definition 1. [STTS] *A structured timed transition system* T *is a tuple* $\langle S, \iota, \Sigma_{\mathsf{in}}, \Sigma_{\mathsf{out}}, \Sigma_\tau, \to \rangle$, *where S is a (possibly infinite) set of states, $\iota \in S$ is the initial* state, the set of labels is structured in three disjoint components: Σ_{in} is the finite set of incoming labels, Σ_{out} is the finite set of outgoing labels, Σ_τ is the finite set of internal labels, and $\rightarrow \subseteq S \times \Sigma_{in} \cup \Sigma_{out} \cup \Sigma_\tau \cup \mathbb{R}^{\geq 0} \times S$ is the transition relation.

A state $s \in S$ of a STTS $\mathcal{T} = \langle S, \iota, \Sigma_{in}, \Sigma_{out}, \Sigma_\tau, \rightarrow \rangle$ is *reachable* if there exists a finite sequence $s_0 s_1 \ldots s_n$ of states such that $s_0 = \iota$, $s_n = s$ and for any i, $0 \leq i < n$, there exists $\sigma \in \Sigma_{in} \cup \Sigma_{out} \cup \Sigma_\tau \cup \mathbb{R}^{\geq 0}$ such that $(s_i, \sigma, s_{i+1}) \in \rightarrow$. The set of reachable states of $\mathcal{T}$ is noted $\mathsf{Reach}(\mathcal{T})$.

Some More Notions. Due to the lack of space, we only present intuitively other notions that are useful in the sequel. The reader will find formal definitions in [DDR05]. We use a natural definition of the *composition* $\mathcal{T}^1 \| \mathcal{T}^2$ of two STTS $\mathcal{T}^1$ and $\mathcal{T}^2$ with synchronizations similar to the ones in the input-output automata framework [LT87]: a common label must be an output label (sending) in one of the STTS and an input label (receiving) in the other. The composition $\mathcal{T}^1 \| \mathcal{T}^2$ is a STTS where synchronized labels are considered as internal.

Such syncronizations is a blocking communication mechanism. This may be problematic as on one hand we want to verify that the controller does not control the environment by refusing to synchronize on its output, and on the other hand, we do not want our controller to issue outputs that can not be accepted by the environment. To avoid such problems we impose *input enabledness* of the STTS that we compose, which means that input labels have the property of being enabled in every state. In this point, the presentation differs from [DDR04].

Finally, given two *input enabled* STTS $\mathcal{T}^1$ (the controller) with state space S^1, $\mathcal{T}^2$ (the environment) with state space S^2 and a set $B \subseteq S^2$ of bad states, we say that $\mathcal{T}^1$ *controls* $\mathcal{T}^2$ *to avoid* B if $\mathsf{Reach}(\mathcal{T}^1 \| \mathcal{T}^2) \cap S^1 \times B$ is empty.

3 Timed Automata and Urgency

Let X be a finite set of real-valued variables. A valuation for X is a function $v : X \rightarrow \mathbb{R}$. We write $[X \rightarrow \mathbb{R}]$ for the set of all valuations for X. Let Δ be a *parameter*. Define the set of *terms* to be $\mathsf{T} = \mathbb{Q} \cup \{+\infty\}$, and the set of *parametric terms* to be $\mathsf{PT} = \mathsf{T} \cup \{c + \Delta, c - \Delta \mid c \in \mathbb{Q}\}$. A *(parametric) rectangular constraint* over X is a formula of the form $\varphi \equiv a \sim_1 x \sim_2 b$ where $x \in X$, $\sim_1, \sim_2 \in \{<, \leq\}$ and a, b are (parametric) terms. Let $lb(\varphi) = a$ and $rb(\varphi) = b$ denote the left (resp. right) bound of φ. A *(parametric) rectangular predicate* is a finite set of (parametric) rectangular constraints interpreted as a conjunction. A *(parametric) multirectangular predicate* is a finite set of (parametric) rectangular predicates interpreted as a disjunction. Given $\delta \in \mathbb{Q}$ and a parametric term a, let $[\![a]\!]_\delta = a$ if $a \in \mathsf{T}$ and $[\![a]\!]_\delta = c + \delta$ (resp. $c - \delta$) if $a = c + \Delta$ (resp. $c - \Delta$). For a parametric rectangular predicate p, a valuation v and a rational $\delta \in \mathbb{Q}$, we write $v \models_\delta p$ iff $[\![a]\!]_\delta \sim_1 v(x) \sim_2 [\![b]\!]_\delta$ for all "$a \sim_1 x \sim_2 b$" in p. For a parametric multirectangular predicate q, we write $v \models_\delta q$ iff there exists $p \in q$ such that $v \models_\delta p$. For a parametric (multi)rectangular predicate p, let $[\![p]\!]_\delta$ denote the set $\{v \mid v \models_\delta p\}$. We sometimes write $v \models p$ instead of $v \models_0 p$.

We say that a rectangular predicate over X is in normal form if it contains at most one rectangular constraint for each variable $x \in X$, with the convention that the empty predicate p (such that $[\![p]\!] = \emptyset$) is represented by $\{x \in [+\infty, +\infty] \mid x \in X\}$; any rectangular predicate can be put in that normal form. Let g be a rectangular predicate in normal form, then $g(x)$ denotes the rectangular constraint "$a \sim_1 x \sim_2 b$" if it is the constraint over x in g and true if there is no constraint over x in g. We defined predicates as sets because it is useful in the sequel for manipulating the predicates that appear in timed automata. However, some operations are easier to represent with classical boolean operations ($\wedge$, $\vee$, $\neg$). It is easy to extend the definition of such operators to our set-predicates. For example, for two multirectangular predicates q and r, the multirectangular predicate $q \wedge r$ is the set $\bigcup_{p_1 \in q, p_2 \in r} \{p_1 \cup p_2\}$.

We note $\mathsf{PRect}(X)$ the set of parametric rectangular predicates, $\mathsf{MultPRect}(X)$ the set of parametric multirectangular predicates and $\mathsf{Rect}_c(X)$ the set of rectangular predicates containing only closed rectangular constraints ($\sim_1, \sim_2 \in \{\leq\}$).

Let $v : E_1 \to \mathbb{R}$ be a valuation, let $E_2 \subseteq E_1$, and $c \in \mathbb{R}$, then $v[E_2 := c]$ denotes the valuation v' such that $v'(e) = c$ if $e \in E_2$ and $v'(e) = v(e)$ if $e \notin E_2$. In the sequel, we sometimes write $v[e := c]$ instead of $v[\{e\} := c]$. Let $v : X \to \mathbb{R}$ be a valuation, for any $t \in \mathbb{R}^{\geq 0}$, $v - t$ is a valuation such that for any $x \in X$, $(v-t)(x) = v(x) - t$. We define $v + t$ in a similar way. We extend this definition to valuations v in $[X \to \mathbb{R}^{\geq 0} \cup \{\bot\}]$ as follows: $(v+t)(x) = v(x) + t$, if $v(x) \in \mathbb{R}^{\geq 0}$, and $(v + t)(x) = \bot$ otherwise. We are now equipped to define our flavor of timed automata [AD94] (with *one* parameter and a urgency flag Asap) and their *classical* semantics.

Definition 2. [Single parametric timed automata] A *single parametric timed automaton*[1] is a tuple $\langle \mathsf{Loc}, l_0, \mathsf{Var}, \mathsf{Inv}, \mathsf{Lab}, \mathsf{Edg}, \mathsf{Asap} \rangle$ where (i) Loc is a finite set of locations representing the discrete states of the automaton. (ii) $l_0 \in \mathsf{Loc}$ is the initial location. (iii) $\mathsf{Var} = \{x_1, \ldots, x_n\}$ is a finite set of real-valued clocks whose values continuously increase as time passes with first derivative equal to one. (iv) $\mathsf{Inv} : \mathsf{Loc} \to \mathsf{MultPRect}(\mathsf{Var})$ is the invariant condition. The automaton can stay in location l as long as the tuple of values of the variables $x_1, \ldots, x_n$ lies in $\mathsf{Inv}(l)$. To ensure the existence of an initial state, we require that the valuation v_0 such that $v_0(x) = 0$ for every $x \in \mathsf{Var}$ lies in $\mathsf{Inv}(l_0)$. (v) $\mathsf{Lab} = \mathsf{Lab}_{\mathsf{in}} \cup \mathsf{Lab}_{\mathsf{out}} \cup \mathsf{Lab}_\tau$ is a structured finite alphabet of labels, partitioned into input labels $\mathsf{Lab}_{\mathsf{in}}$, output labels $\mathsf{Lab}_{\mathsf{out}}$, and internal labels Lab_τ. (vi) $\mathsf{Edg} \subseteq \mathsf{Loc} \times \mathsf{Loc} \times \mathsf{PRect}(\mathsf{Var}) \times \mathsf{Lab} \times 2^{\mathsf{Var}}$ is a set of edges. An edge (l, l', g, σ, R) represents a discrete transition from location l to location l' with guard g, event σ and a subset $R \subseteq \mathsf{Var}$ of the variables to be reset. The guard g is a rectangular predicate. (vii) $\mathsf{Asap} : \mathsf{Edg} \to \{\top, \bot\}$ is a special flag used to model urgency.

Definition 3. [Semantics of single parametric timed automata] Let $A = \langle \mathsf{Loc}, l_0, \mathsf{Var}, \mathsf{Inv}, \mathsf{Lab}, \mathsf{Edg}, \mathsf{Asap} \rangle$ be a timed automaton and $\delta \in \mathbb{Q}^{\geq 0}$. The semantics of A is the STTS $[\![A]\!]_\delta = (S, \iota, \Sigma_{\mathsf{in}}, \Sigma_{\mathsf{out}}, \Sigma_\tau, \to)$ where: (i) $S = \{(l, v) \mid l \in \mathsf{Loc} \wedge v \in$

---

[1] In this paper, single parametric timed automata always use the parameter Δ.

$[\![\mathsf{Inv}(l)]\!]_\delta\}$. (ii) $\iota = (l_0, v_0)$ such that for any $x \in \mathsf{Var} : v_0(x) = 0$. (iii) $\Sigma_{in} = \mathsf{Lab}_{in}$, $\Sigma_{out} = \mathsf{Lab}_{out}$, and $\Sigma_\tau = \mathsf{Lab}_\tau$. (iv) the transition relation $\rightarrow$ is defined as follows:

(a) For the discrete transitions, $((l, v), \sigma, (l', v')) \in\rightarrow$ iff there exists an edge $(l, l', g, \sigma, R) \in \mathsf{Edg}$ such that $v \models_\delta g$, $v' = v[R := 0]$.

(b) For the continuous transitions $((l, v), t, (l', v')) \in\rightarrow$ iff: first $l = l'$, second for any edge $e = (l_1, l_2, g, \sigma, R) \in \mathsf{Edg}$: if $l_1 = l$ then $\mathsf{Asap}(e) = \bot$ and third $\forall x \in \mathsf{Var} : v'(x) = v(x) + t$ and $\forall t' \in [0, t] : v + t' \in [\![\mathsf{Inv}(l)]\!]_\delta$

For simplicity, we often say timed automaton instead of single parametric timed automaton. We use the classical definition of the synchronized product $A_1 \times A_2$ of two timed automata. For the urgency flag, an edge in the product is flagged Asap if one of the corresponding edges in A_1 or A_2 is flagged. This is the semantics used in the HyTech tool for the Asap flag [HHWT95]. Notice that (in the final product only), the Asap flag can be replaced by a clock which is reset on every transition, and forced by an invariant to stay nil in every location with an outgoing Asap edge, showing that Asap is a feature that does not add expressive power to timed automata, but just allows us to design timed automata in a modular way.

4   Elastic Controllers and AASAP Semantics

Controllers are specified using a subclass of timed automata, called ELASTIC[2], without invariants and with only closed guards. In general, invariants are used to express urgency but in ELASTIC urgency is implicit : a controller shall make an action (almost) as soon as it becomes possible. Formally, this almost urgency is defined in the AASAP semantics of the controller by allowing some delay (bounded by a parameter Δ) before forcing an enabled transition.

Definition 4. [ELASTIC Controllers] An ELASTIC controller A is a tuple $\langle \mathsf{Loc}, l_0, \mathsf{Var}, \mathsf{Lab}, \mathsf{Edg} \rangle$ where Loc is a finite set of locations, $l_0 \in \mathsf{Loc}$ is the initial location, $\mathsf{Var} = \{x_1, \ldots, x_n\}$ is a finite set of clocks, Lab is a finite structured alphabet of labels, partitioned into input labels Lab_{in}, output labels Lab_{out}, and internal labels Lab_τ, Edg is a set of edges of the form (l, l', g, σ, R) where $l, l' \in \mathsf{Loc}$ are locations, $\sigma \in \mathsf{Lab}$ is a label, $g \in \mathsf{Rect}_c(\mathsf{Var})$ is a guard and $R \subseteq \mathsf{Var}$ is a set of clocks to be reset.

Notations. We define the function $\mathsf{TrueSince} : [\mathsf{Var} \rightarrow \mathbb{R}^{\geq 0}] \times \mathsf{Rect}_c(\mathsf{Var}) \rightarrow \mathbb{R}^{\geq 0} \cup \{-\infty\}$, noted TS, as follows: either $v \models g$ and $\mathsf{TS}(v, g) = t$ where t is s.t. $v - t \models g \wedge \forall t' > t : v - t' \not\models g$, or $v \not\models g$ and $\mathsf{TS}(v, g) = -\infty$.

Let $p \equiv a \sim_1 x \sim_2 b$ be a rectangular constraint. Given $\Delta_1, \Delta_2 \in \mathsf{PT}$, the symbol $\langle$ standing either for $[$ or $($ and the symbol $\rangle$ standing either for $]$ or $)$, we define the notation $_{\Delta_1}\langle p \rangle_{\Delta_2}$ for the parametric rectangular constraint:

$$a - \Delta_1 \sim'_1 x \sim'_2 b + \Delta_2$$

---

[2] Event-based LAnguage for Simple TImed Controllers.

where $\sim_1'$ stands either for $\leq$ if $\langle$ is $[$, or for $<$ if $\langle$ is $($, and $\sim_2'$ is interpreted symetrically. For example, let $p \equiv 2 \leq x \leq 5$, then $-\frac{1}{3}(p)_\Delta \equiv 2 + \frac{1}{3} < x \leq 5 + \Delta$. The notation is naturally extended to rectangular predicates.

With those two additional notations we are now ready to define the AASAP semantics [DDR04].

Definition 5. [AASAP semantics] Given an ELASTIC controller $A = \langle \mathsf{Loc}, l_0, \mathsf{Var}, \mathsf{Lab_{in}}, \mathsf{Lab_{out}}, \mathsf{Lab_\tau}, \mathsf{Edg} \rangle$ and $\delta \in \mathbb{Q}^{\geq 0}$, the AASAP semantics of A is the STTS $[\![A]\!]_\delta^{\mathsf{AAsap}} = \langle S, \iota, \Sigma_{\mathsf{in}}, \Sigma_{\mathsf{out}}, \Sigma_\tau, \rightarrow \rangle$ where:

$(A1)$ S is the set of tuples (l, v, I, d) where $l \in \mathsf{Loc}$, $v \in [\mathsf{Var} \rightarrow \mathbb{R}^{\geq 0}]$, $I \in [\Sigma_{\mathsf{in}} \rightarrow \mathbb{R}^{\geq 0} \cup \{\bot\}]$ and $d \in \mathbb{R}^{\geq 0}$;

$(A2)$ $\iota = (l_0, v, I, 0)$ where v is such that for any $x \in \mathsf{Var} : v(x) = 0$, and I is such that for any $\sigma \in \Sigma_{\mathsf{in}}$, $I(\sigma) = \bot$;

$(A3)$ $\Sigma_{\mathsf{in}} = \mathsf{Lab_{in}}$, $\Sigma_{\mathsf{out}} = \mathsf{Lab_{out}}$, and $\Sigma_\tau = \mathsf{Lab_\tau} \cup \overline{\mathsf{Lab_{in}}} \cup \{\epsilon\}$;

$(A4)$ The transition relation is defined as follows:

- for the discrete transitions, we distinguish five cases:

$(A4.1)$ let $\sigma \in \mathsf{Lab_{out}}$. We have $((l, v, I, d), \sigma, (l', v', I, 0)) \in\rightarrow$ iff there exists $(l, l', g, \sigma, R) \in \mathsf{Edg}$ such that $v \models_\delta {}_\Delta[g]_\Delta$ and $v' = v[R := 0]$;

$(A4.2)$ let $\sigma \in \mathsf{Lab_{in}}$. We have $((l, v, I, d), \sigma, (l, v, I', d)) \in\rightarrow$ iff
  · either $I(\sigma) = \bot$ and $I' = I[\sigma := 0]$;
  · or $I(\sigma) \neq \bot$ and $I' = I$.

$(A4.3)$ let $\bar{\sigma} \in \overline{\mathsf{Lab_{in}}}$. We have $((l, v, I, d), \bar{\sigma}, (l', v', I', 0)) \in\rightarrow$ iff there exists $(l, l', g, \sigma, R) \in \mathsf{Edg}$, $v \models_\delta {}_\Delta[g]_\Delta$, $I(\sigma) \neq \bot$, $v' = v[R := 0]$ and $I' = I[\sigma := \bot]$;

$(A4.4)$ let $\sigma \in \mathsf{Lab_\tau}$. We have $((l, v, I, d), \sigma, (l', v', I, 0)) \in\rightarrow$ iff there exists $(l, l', g, \sigma, R) \in \mathsf{Edg}$, $v \models_\delta {}_\Delta[g]_\Delta$, and $v' = v[R := 0]$;

$(A4.5)$ let $\sigma = \epsilon$. We have for any $(l, v, I, d) \in S$: $((l, v, I, d), \epsilon, (l, v, I, d)) \in\rightarrow$.

- for the continuous transitions:

$(A4.6)$ for any $t \in \mathbb{R}^{\geq 0}$, we have $((l, v, I, d), t, (l, v+t, I+t, d+t)) \in\rightarrow$ iff the two following conditions are satisfied:
  · for any edge $(l, l', g, \sigma, R) \in \mathsf{Edg}$ with $\sigma \in \mathsf{Lab_{out}} \cup \mathsf{Lab_\tau}$, we have that: $\forall t' : 0 \leq t' \leq t : (d + t' \leq \delta \vee \mathsf{TS}(v + t', g) \leq \delta)$
  · for any edge $(l, l', g, \sigma, R) \in \mathsf{Edg}$ with $\sigma \in \mathsf{Lab_{in}}$, we have that: $\forall t' : 0 \leq t' \leq t : (d + t' \leq \delta \vee \mathsf{TS}(v + t', g) \leq \delta \vee (I + t')(\sigma) \leq \delta)$

Comments on the AASAP *Semantics.* Rule $(A1)$ defines the states that are tuples of the form $\langle l, v, I, d \rangle$. The first two components, location l and valuation v, are the same as in the classical semantics; I and d are new. The function I records, for each input event σ, the time elapsed since its oldest "untreated" occurrence. The treatment of an event σ happens when a transition labelled with $\bar{\sigma}$ is fired. Once this oldest occurence is treated, the function returns $\bot$ for σ until a new occurence of σ, forgetting about the σ's that happened between the oldest occurence and the treatment. The time elapsed since the last location change in the controller is recorded by d. Rule $(A2)$ and $(A3)$ are straightforward. Rules

($A4.1 - 6$) require more explanations. Rule ($A4.1$) defines when it is allowed for the controller to emit an output event. The only difference with the classical semantics is that we enlarge the guard by the parameter Δ. Rules ($A4.2$) defines how inputs from the environment are received by the controller. The controller maintains, through the function I, a list of events that have occurred and are not treated yet. An input event σ can be received at any time, but only the age of the oldest untreated σ is stored in the I function. Note that the rule ensures input enabledness of the controller. Rule ($A4.3$) defines when inputs are treated by the controller. An input σ is treated when a transition with an enlarged guard and labelled with $\bar{\sigma}$ is fired. Once σ has been treated, the value of $I(\sigma)$ goes back to $\perp$. Rule ($A4.4$) is similar to ($A4.1$). Rule ($A4.5$) expresses that the ϵ event can always be emitted. Rule ($A4.6$) specifies how much time can elapse. Intuitively, time can pass as long as no transition starting from the current location is *urgent*. A transition labeled with an output or an internal event is urgent in a location l when the control has been in l for more than δ time units $(d + t' \geq \delta)$ and the guard of the transition has been true for more than δ time units $(\mathsf{TS}(v + t', g) \geq \delta)$. A transition labeled with an input event σ is urgent in a location l when the control has been in l for more than δ time units $(d + t' \geq \delta)$, the guard of the transition has been true for more that δ time units $(\mathsf{TS}(v + t', g) \geq \delta)$ and the last untreated occurrence of σ event has been emitted by the environment at least δ time units ago $(I + t'(\sigma) \geq \delta)$ (we define $\perp$ to be smaller than any rational value). This notion of urgency parameterized by Δ is the main difference between the AASAP semantics and the usual ASAP semantics.

Properties. We informally recall the main properties of the AASAP semantics which have been established in [DDR04].

First, the AASAP semantics has the desirable property that "faster is better": if a controller with reaction time bounded by δ_1 safely controls an environment, then so does the same controller with a reaction time bounded by any $\delta_2 < \delta_1$.

Second, we can implement a controller that has been proven correct (that is, such that for some $\delta > 0$ its AASAP semantics safely controls the environment). The correctness of the controller is preserved by the implementation provided the hardware is sufficiently fast and has a sufficiently precise digital clock. This has been formally proven by showing that the AASAP semantics can simulate (in the formal sense) a program semantics which defines what is an implementation of an ELASTIC controller. Intuitively, it is a procedure that repeats forever *execution rounds* defined as follows: (i) first, the current time is read in the clock register of the CPU and stored in a variable, say T; (ii) the list of input events to treat is updated: the input sensors are checked for new events issued by the environment; (iii) guards of the edges of the current locations are evaluated with the value stored in T. If at least one guard evaluates to true then take nondeterministically one of the enabled transitions; (iv) the next round is started. All we require from the hardware is to respect the following two requirements: (i) the clock register of the CPU is incremented every Δ_P time units and (ii) the time spent in one loop is bounded by a fixed value Δ_L. We choose this semantics for its simplicity and also because it is obviously implementable. The condition for the preservation of the correctness is that $\delta > 3\Delta_L + 4\Delta_P$.

Third, the AASAP semantics can be encoded by a classical single parameter timed automaton, so that it can by analyzed automatically by timed automata model-checkers like HyTech or Uppaal. However, this encoding has a limited interest in practice because its size is always exponential in $|\mathsf{Lab_{in}}|$, the number of input labels of the controller. We solve this problem in the next section by giving a new translation which is compositional and at most quadratic in the size of the controller.

5   Compositional Construction for the AASAP Semantics

The main idea underlying our compositional construction is to treat the incoming events (issued by the environment) independently of the control structure of the Elastic controller, with a network of automata. This leads to technical difficulties we explain and address in this section.

Following the rule $(A4.6)$ defining *almost urgency* of the AASAP semantics, there are essentially three reasons for allowing time to pass: (i) either the controller has been in its current location for less than Δ time units, (ii) or all last untreated occurences of an event have been issued by the environment less than Δ time units ago, (iii) or finally the guard of the outgoing transitions have not been enabled for more than Δ time units. Roughly, those conditions will be checked in our compositional construction by respectively A^2, which is a transformation of the Elastic controller A, and two types of widgets: the *event-watchers* and the *guard-watchers*.

In timed automata, there is essentially one way for modeling urgency: invariants on locations. Roughly, if we have a transition guarded by a lower bound constraint g, it can be forced as soon as it is enabled by adding as invariant in its source location the closure of $\neg g$. E.g. for a guard $x \geq 3$ we can add the invariant $x \leq 3$. This way, time is blocked when the guard is satisfied and the discrete transition is forced. If we enlarge the invariant by Δ ($x \leq 3 + \Delta$), we get the *almost urgency* we need. To formalize this idea, we will need to introduce some more notations:

Additional Notations. (i) Given an Elastic controller $A = \langle \mathsf{Loc}, l_0, \mathsf{Var}, \mathsf{Lab}, \mathsf{Edg}\rangle$ and a location $l \in \mathsf{Loc}$, let $G_{\mathsf{act}}(l) = \{g \mid (l, l', g, \sigma, R) \in \mathsf{Edg} \wedge \sigma \in \mathsf{Lab_{out}} \cup \mathsf{Lab}_\tau\}$ be the set of guards labelling output transitions or internal transitions, and for $\alpha \in \mathsf{Lab^1_{in}}$, let $G_{\mathsf{evt}}(l, \alpha) = \{g \mid (l, l', g, \alpha, R) \in \mathsf{Edg}\}$ be the set of guards labelling event transitions. (ii) Then define $\bar{\varphi}_{\mathsf{act}}(l) = \bigwedge_{g \in G_{\mathsf{act}}(l)} \neg(-\Delta(g)_0)$ and $\bar{\varphi}_{\mathsf{evt}}(l, \alpha) = \bigwedge_{g \in G_{\mathsf{evt}}(l, \alpha)} \neg(-\Delta(g)_0)$. For example, let $G_{\mathsf{act}}(l) = \{2 \leq x \leq 5, 0 \leq y \leq 1\}$, then $\bar{\varphi}_{\mathsf{act}}(l) \equiv (x \leq 2 + \Delta \vee x \geq 5) \wedge (y \leq \Delta \vee y \geq 1)$.

Those constraints will be used as invariant to match the third part of rule $(A4.6)$. The constraint $\bar{\varphi}_{\mathsf{act}}(l)$ will be used as an invariant for location l in A^2 to force an output transition when it becomes possible. The constraint $\bar{\varphi}_{\mathsf{evt}}(l, \alpha)$

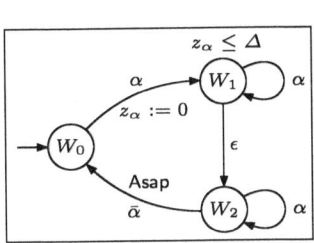

Fig. 1. Event-Watcher W_α

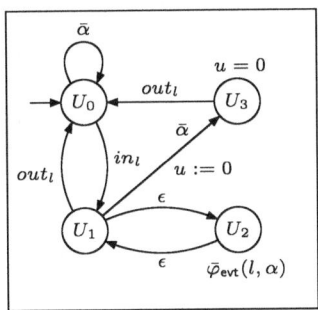

Fig. 2. Guard-Watcher $W_\alpha^l(\bar\varphi_{\mathsf{evt}}(l, \alpha))$

will be used in the *guard-watchers*, to ensure that when a guard has been true for enough time, the corresponding transition becomes urgent (as long as it is allowed by other parts of rule $(A4.6)$).

Those invariants are central to our construction, but if we want a compositional construction (a product of automata), invariants are too restrictive to express urgency since urgency also depends on the current state of the other automata offering enabled synchronizations in the product. Hence, we should not block time simply when a transition is enabled in *one* automaton but only when it is enabled in *every* automaton of the product. Therefore, some compositional mechanism is needed to model urgency in a product: we will use the Asap flag. Remember that this flag expresses the fact that a transition is urgent as soon as it is enabled in the whole product.

The formal definition of our construction is given in Definition 6. From an ELASTIC controller A and a parameter Δ we construct $\mathcal{F}(A, \Delta)$ as a product of three types of components: event-watchers, guard-watchers and A^2 directly obtained from A. We omitt the formal definitions of event-watchers and guard watchers which should be clear from the figures and anyway can be found in [DDR05].

Event-Watcher. Associated to an event $\alpha \in \Sigma_{\mathsf{in}}$, we define W_α (see Fig. 1) that records the event α. It has a clock z_α encoding the value of $I(\alpha)$ in the AASAP semantics. z_α records the time elapsed since the last untreated event α was issued by the environment. When $I(\alpha) \neq \bot$, the value of the clock z_α is equal to $I(\alpha)$.

This widget is intended to record the occurrence of the events α (as expressed by rule $(A4.2)$ in the definition of the AASAP semantics), and then to propose a synchronization on $\bar\alpha$ with an Asap flag in location W_2. Remember that the notation $\bar\alpha$ corresponds to the detection of event α by the controller. From the invariant of location W_1, this synchronization will not become urgent before Δ time units.

Guard-Watchers. We introduce *Guard-Watchers* (see Fig. 2) to monitor the truth value of a set of guards. They are associated to an event $\alpha \in \Sigma_{\mathsf{in}}$ and a

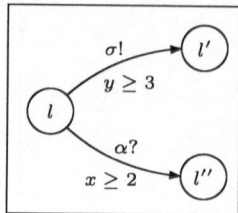

Fig. 3. An ELASTIC controller A

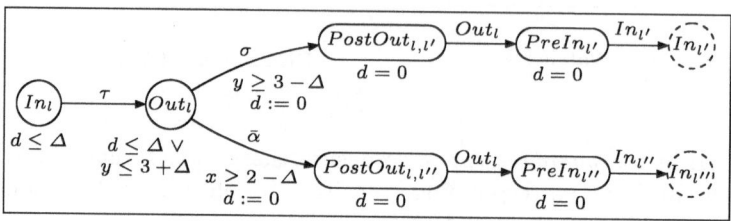

Fig. 4. The timed automaton A^2 associated to the ELASTIC controller A of Fig. 3

location $l \in \mathsf{Loc}$. When the controller is not in location l, the guard-watchers $W_\alpha^l(G)$ do not influence the execution, being in location U_0 and offering a self-loop synchronization on $\bar{\alpha}$. When location l is reached, the synchronization on in_l forces $W_\alpha^l(G)$ enter location U_1 and to become active. The watcher get back in U_0 as soon as l is exited by out_l. Thus, it is active when it is not in U_0. Its role is then to prevent the label $\bar{\alpha}$ to become urgent whenever there is no transition labeled with $\bar{\alpha}$ that has been enabled for more than Δ units of time. Hence, we use $W_\alpha^l(G)$ with the set of guards $G = \bar{\varphi}_{\mathsf{evt}}(l, \alpha)$.

Controller Transformation. We illustrate the transformation of the ELASTIC controller with an example. The timed automaton A^2 corresponding to the ELASTIC controller A of Fig. 3 is depicted on Fig. 4. The automaton A^2 has a similar structure to A. It is used to *(i)* guarantee a maximum delay of Δ when location changes (as modeled by the variable d in the AASAP semantics) *(ii)* make transitions labeled with actions $\sigma \in \mathsf{Lab}_{\mathsf{out}} \cup \mathsf{Lab}_\tau$ urgent when their guard has been satisfied for more than Δ time units (through invariant of Out_l) and *(iii)* enlarge the guards of the controller's transitions (as expressed by rules $(A4.1)$, $(A4.3)$ and $(A4.4)$).

Definition 6. [Compositional construction $\mathcal{F}$] Let $A = \langle \mathsf{Loc}^1, l_0^1, \mathsf{Var}^1, \mathsf{Lab}^1, \mathsf{Edg}^1 \rangle$ be an ELASTIC controller. The compositional construction $\mathcal{F}(A, \Delta)$ is the synchronized product of the following timed automata:

- the event-watchers W_α for every $\alpha \in \mathsf{Lab}_{\mathsf{in}}^1$,
- the guard-watchers $W_\alpha^l(G_{\mathsf{evt}}(l, \alpha))$ for every $\alpha \in \mathsf{Lab}_{\mathsf{in}}^1, l \in \mathsf{Loc}^1$,
- and the timed automaton $A^2 = \langle \mathsf{Loc}^2, l_0^2, \mathsf{Var}^2, \mathsf{Inv}^2, \mathsf{Lab}^2, \mathsf{Edg}^2, \mathsf{Asap}^2 \rangle$ where:
  (i) $\mathsf{Loc}^2 = \{PreIn_l, In_l, Out_l, PostOut_{l,l'} \mid l, l' \in Loc^1\}$; *(ii)* $l_0^2 = In_{l_0^1}$;

(iii) $\mathsf{Var}^2 = \mathsf{Var}^1 \cup \{d\}$; (iv) $\mathsf{Lab}^2_{out} = \mathsf{Lab}^1_{out}$, $\mathsf{Lab}^2_{in} = \emptyset$ and $\mathsf{Lab}^2_\tau = \mathsf{Lab}^1_\tau \cup \overline{\mathsf{Lab}^1_{in}} \cup \{\tau, in_l, out_l\}$; (v) Edg^2 contains (a) the edges $(Out_l, PostOut_{l,l'}, \Delta[g]_\Delta, \sigma, R \cup \{d\})$ such that there exists $(l, l', g, \sigma, R) \in \mathsf{Edg}^1$ with $\sigma \in \mathsf{Lab}^1_{out} \cup \mathsf{Lab}^1_\tau$ (b) the edges $(Out_l, PostOut_{l,l'}, \Delta[g]_\Delta, \bar{\alpha}, R \cup \{d\})$ such that there exists $(l, l', g, \alpha, R) \in \mathsf{Edg}^1$ with $\alpha \in \mathsf{Lab}^1_{in}$ and (c) the edges $(PostOut_{l,l'}, PreIn_{l'}, \emptyset, out_l, \emptyset)$ for each $l, l' \in Loc^1$, and the edges $(PreIn_l, In_l, \emptyset, in_l, \emptyset)$ and $(In_l, Out_l, \emptyset, \tau, \emptyset)$ for each $l' \in Loc^1$. (vi) $\mathsf{Asap}^2(e) = \bot$ for every $e \in \mathsf{Edg}^2$; (vii) The function Inv^2 is defined as follows. For each $l, l' \in Loc^1$, (a) $\mathsf{Inv}^2(In_l) = \{\{d \leq \Delta\}\}$ (b) $\mathsf{Inv}^2(Out_l) = \{\{d \leq \Delta \vee \bar{\varphi}_a(l)\}\}$ and (c) $\mathsf{Inv}^2(PreIn_l) = \mathsf{Inv}^2(PostOutl, l') = \{\{d = 0\}\}$.

In summary, $\mathcal{F}(A, \Delta) = A^2 \times \prod_{\alpha \in \mathsf{Lab}^1_{in}} W_\alpha \times \prod_{\alpha \in \mathsf{Lab}^1_{in}, l \in Loc^1} W^l_\alpha(G_{evt}(l, \alpha))$.

The correctness of our compositional construction is established by the following theorem.

Theorem 1. *For any* ELASTIC *controller A, for any environment* STTS *E and a set* Bad *of its states, for any $\delta \in \mathbb{Q}^{>0}$, $[\![A]\!]^{\mathsf{AAsap}}_\delta$ controls E to avoid* Bad *iff $[\![\mathcal{F}(A, \Delta)]\!]_\delta$ controls E to avoid* Bad.

Since the correctness of AASAP semantics of A implies its implementability, we can verify the compositional construction with an automatic tool and generate systematically the implementation code. In the second part of this paper, we show how we have applied this methodology in practice on a real-world protocol.

6   Tool Set

We briefly describe the tool set that we have implemented. The structure of the tool set is depicted in Fig. 5 and it consists of three tools: (i) ELASTIC2HYTECH, (ii) HYTECH2UPPAAL, and (iii) ELASTIC2BRICK.

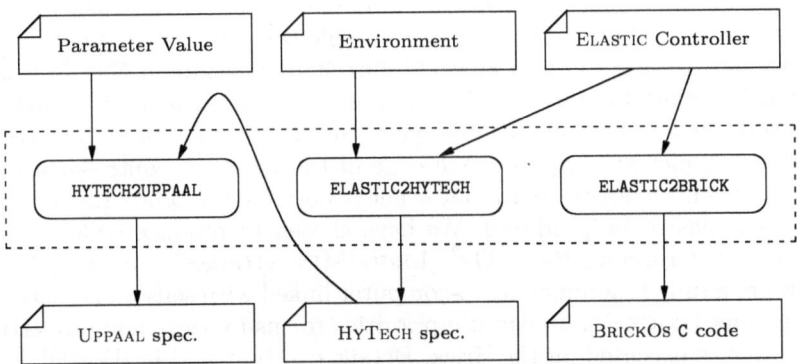

Fig. 5. Structure of our tool set

ELASTIC2HYTECH is the main component of the tool set: it implements the compositional construction of Section 5. Given an ELASTIC controller Cont (expressed in an HyTech like syntax), it produces a one-parameter HyTech specification Cont$'(\Delta)$ following the construction defined in the previous section. To obtain a model of the entire system, this specification of the controller has to be composed with a model of the environment (in which the controller is embedded). This is given as a product of rectangular automata (in HyTech syntax). The environment is noted Env in the sequel. We can then use HyTech to reason about the system. The following three correctness problems can be formulated and answered with HyTech (if the analysis terminates):

- [Fixed] Given a set of bad states Bad, a value $\delta \in \mathbb{Q}^{\geq 0}$, does the controller, when reacting within δ, control the environment to avoid Bad, that is: $\mathsf{Reach}(\llbracket \mathsf{Cont}'(\Delta)\|\mathsf{Env}\rrbracket_\Delta) \cap \mathsf{Bad} = \emptyset$
- [Existence] Given a set of bad states Bad, does there exist a value $\delta \in \mathbb{Q}$ such that when the controller reacts within δ, it controls the environment to avoid Bad, that is: $\exists \delta > 0 : \mathsf{Reach}(\llbracket \mathsf{Cont}'(\Delta)\|\mathsf{Env}\rrbracket_\delta) \cap \mathsf{Bad} = \emptyset$
- [Maximization] Given a set of Bad, what is the largest value for $\delta \in \mathbb{Q}^{\geq 0}$ such that when the controller reacts within δ, it controls the environment to avoid Bad, that is: $\max\{\delta > 0 : \mathsf{Reach}(\llbracket \mathsf{Cont}'(\Delta)\|\mathsf{Env}\rrbracket_\delta) \cap \mathsf{Bad} = \emptyset\}$

To tackle large examples, we also use UPPAAL. The tool HYTECH2UPPAAL translates HyTech specifications into UPPAAL specifications. As UPPAAL is restricted to the analysis of timed automata (and it does that very efficiently), it is only applicable if the environment can be modeled as a product of timed automata and the parameter Δ is fixed. Obviously, this allows us to answer the [fixed] version of the correctness problem. Thanks to the "faster is better" property of the AASAP semantics, by doing a binary search on the value space of the parameter δ, we can approximate the maximal value of δ for which the controller is correct up to any precision.

The main purpose of the AASAP semantics is to give a way to synthesize executable code for a controller from its model and to ensure that the properties that have been proved on the model are preserved on the code (without making the synchrony hypothesis). To obtain executable code from the ELASTIC model of a controller, we use the tool ELASTIC2BRICK that produces C-code from an annotated ELASTIC specification. The annotations assign to each transition a piece of code that has to be executed when the transition is fired. The translation is very simple: we assign to each edge of the ELASTIC controller a thread that is ran when the associated input event is perceived or when the associated output event has to be produced. We have chosen to produce code for LEGO MINDSTORMS™ running BRICKOS[3]. LEGO MINDSTORMS™ are toys but the internals are a fully functional micro-computer linked with sensor and actuators. When running BRICKOS, we can use priorities to ensure real-time properties of the code that is executed on the Brick. Details can be found in [Doy03].

---

[3] http://brickos.sourceforge.net/

7   Case Study: The "Philips Audio Control Protocol"

Introduction. Bosscher et al study in [BPV94] "a simple protocol for the physical layer of an interface bus that connects the devices of a stereo equipment". This protocol was proposed by Philips engineers. The protocol is based on Manchester encoding to transmit binary sequences on a wire between a single sender and a single receiver.

In our case study, we will use LEGO MINDSTORMS™ Bricks to implement the sender and the receiver. To connect the two Bricks, we use a wire plugged to an output gate of the sender and to an input gate of the receiver. The difficulties here to implement the protocol are similar to the ones that the engineers in Philips were facing: (*i*) although the receiver knows the length of a time slot, it does not know when it begins (the two Bricks are running asynchronously); (*ii*) a receiver does not know the length of the bit string it is receiving; (*iii*) only UP signals can be reliably detected by our sensors (this constraint is taken to fit with the case study of [BPV94]); (*iv*) the sender and the receiver have digital clocks that have finite granularity, so there will be imprecision in both sending and receiving times; (*v*) in BRICKOS sensors are polled periodically. As a consequence, the moment at which a bit is perceived can be substantially later than the moment it has been sent. The first three difficulties should be solved by the logic of the protocol. The last two difficulties are much lower level and we would like to forget them when designing a high level version of the protocol. This is exactly what the AASAP semantics allows us to do.

Next, we present the idealized version of the protocol and how we modeled it with two ELASTIC controllers: one for the sender and one for the receiver. Here, the environment is an observer that compares the sequence of bits sent by the sender with the sequence of bits decoded by the receiver. The observer reaches the location *error* whenever the two sequences do not match.

Afterwards, we explain how we can use the AASAP semantics during the verification process and verify the robustness of the protocol. The verification phase allows us to generate code that is correct by construction.

ELASTIC *Models.* An idealized version of the protocol uses evenly spaced time slots. To transmit a 1, the sender must let the signal go from low voltage to high in the middle of a slot and from high to low for a 0. To repeat a bit, the sender is thus forced between two slots to turn the signal off for a 1 or on for a 0. The receiver is not able to detect precisely moments when the signal goes down and then only relies on the UP signals to decode the messages. This implies that a message has to begin by a 1 and that messages ending in 10 or in 1 are not distinguishable without adding information bits. Rather than adding bits, the protocol restricts messages to be either odd in length or to end in 00.

Our modelisation of the protocol can be found in Fig. 6 for the sender and Fig. 7 for the receiver. There is an additional *observer automaton* playing the role of the environment on Fig. 8 that allows us to verify the correct transmission of the bits (this observer was proposed by Ho and Wong-Toi in [HWT95]). The

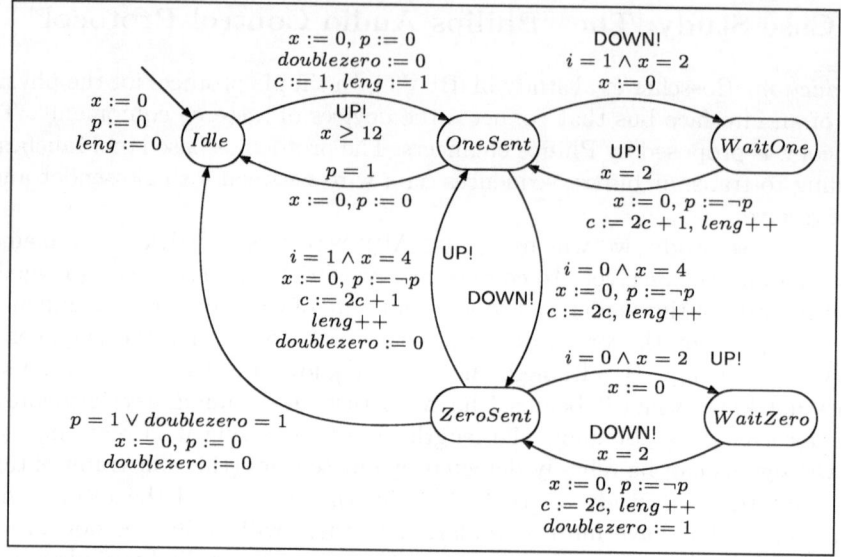

Fig. 6. The Sender automaton

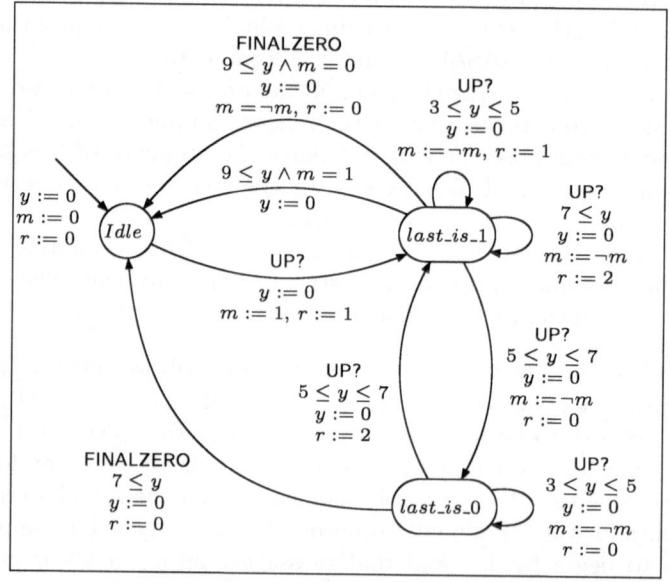

Fig. 7. The Receiver automaton

unit of time of the model, noted U, is a quarter of the time slot. This unit is not written in the constraints, to alleviate the presentation.

One can easily check that the sender automaton can send any sequence conforming to the protocol restrictions. Arrival in location *OneSent* (*ZeroSent*)

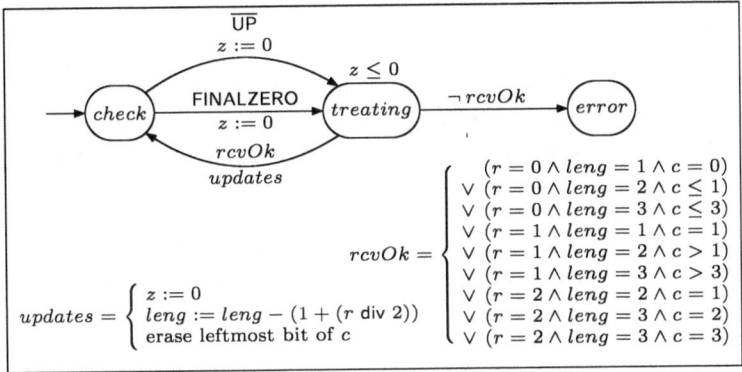

Fig. 8. The Observer automaton

means the signal for a 1 (a 0) has just been sent. The clock x is used for the timing of the sequence. The discrete variable i is non-deterministically set to 1 or 0 each time a bit is sent (not shown on the figures). Its value determines which shall be the next bit. The discrete variables p and *doublezero* encode respectively if the current sequence is odd in length and if it ends in 00. Finally, the discrete variables c and *leng* are used to encode the bits that have been sent but not decoded by the receiver yet. c simply encodes in an integer the binary word composed of the last such bits and *leng* is the number of those bits. The decrementing of c and *leng* is done by the observer automaton every time it succeeds in matching a sent bit with a received bit.

The receiver automaton decodes its incoming UP signals by rounding its local time for when it received the signal to the nearest possible time it expects a signal. This is what makes the protocol robust. If no signal is received in due time, the sequence is interpreted as being complete. The discrete variable m is used to encode parity of the received sequence. It allows the receiver to know if it has to complete a sequence with an additional 0 to conform to the protocol restrictions. The discrete variable r encodes the one or two bits that were last received. This variable is checked by the observer automaton against c and *leng* of the sender to verify if the sent bits are the same as the received ones. The label FINALZERO does not correspond to an event. It is an internal action done when the receiver understands it must add a 0 to the sequence to end it. The observer automaton then synchronizes on this label to know a new bit has been decoded. As said before, the receiver does not synchronize on DOWN signals.

This modelisation uses finite range discrete variables, which are not present in the formal definitions. This is not a problem since all those discrete variables are bounded and thus could be encoded in locations. For the sake of clarity, we did not do this. Furthermore, the tools that we are using allow the use of such finite range discrete variables.

Parametric Verification. Let us now turn to the use of the AASAP semantics during the verification phase. We take the opportunity here to present some methodological aspects too.

Using ELASTIC2HYTECH, we generate for the sender and the receiver the HYTECH specification of their AASAP semantics following Definition 6. Those two semantics are noted $[\![\mathsf{Sender}(\Delta)]\!]^{\mathsf{AAsap}}_{\delta_1}$ and $[\![\mathsf{Receiver}(\Delta)]\!]^{\mathsf{AAsap}}_{\delta_2}$.

We can first check that if the protocol executed in an idealized setting, that is for $\delta_1 = 0$ and $\delta_2 = 0$, is correct. This is formalized by the following question: $\mathsf{Reach}([\![\mathsf{Sender}(\Delta)]\!]^{\mathsf{AAsap}}_0 \| [\![\mathsf{Receiver}(\Delta)]\!]^{\mathsf{AAsap}}_0 \| [\![\mathsf{Observer}]\!]) \cap \mathsf{Bad} \neq \emptyset$, where Bad are the states in which the observer is in location $error$. With HYTECH (or UPPAAL), we can easily show that this test is passed successfully by our modelisation of the protocol. If this verification had failed then we should have concluded that the protocol was flawed in its logic.

To continue the study of the protocol and determine if it can be implemented, we should check its robustness. In our context, we must determine what are the maximum values of δ_1 and δ_2 which ensure that the system $[\![\mathsf{Sender}(\Delta)]\!]^{\mathsf{AAsap}}_{\delta_1} \|$ $[\![\mathsf{Receiver}(\Delta)]\!]^{\mathsf{AAsap}}_{\delta_2} \| [\![\mathsf{Observer}]\!] \cap \mathsf{Bad} = \emptyset$. Those maximal value will be expressed in the unit of time U of the system that we have not fixed so far. Remember U is a quarter of a timeslot. By tuning this value, we can then maximize the throughput of the protocol. We should then look for the smallest implementable U on our implementation platform. For BRICKOS, the value $\Delta_L U$ (length of the loop in the execution procedure) and $\Delta_P U$ (precision of the clocks) can be set to as low as 6 ms and 1 ms. To guarantee a correct implementation of $\mathsf{Sender}(\Delta)$ (and $\mathsf{Receiver}(\Delta)$), we need to have $\Delta > 3\Delta_L + 4\Delta_P$, and so $\Delta U > 22ms$.

So, we know that $\delta_1 U$ and $\delta_2 U$ should be srictly below 22 ms. If $\delta_1 \leq \delta_2$, the infimum for U is $\frac{22\,\text{ms}}{\delta_1}$ else it is $\frac{22\,\text{ms}}{\delta_2}$. Now if we increase the value of one of the parameters δ_i, the correct value for the other decreases. This is because increasing the parameter value for the AASAP semantics of a controller strictly increases its looseness, forcing the other to be more precise as compensation, which corresponds to a smaller value for its parameter. Using this fact, we can conclude that the best U for the system will be obtained when δ_1 and δ_2 are equal.

Guiding HYTECH with this information, by a parametric search, we found that, for ensuring correctness, the parameters must be strictly less than $\frac{1}{4}U$. In fact, we proved that a sufficient condition to avoid the $error$ state is that $\delta_1 + \delta_2 < \frac{1}{2}$. Execution times of different analysis are given in Fig. 9. Note that to make HYTECH terminate, we needed to give some initial constraints. Execution times with UPPAAL are very encouraging: the problems solved are simpler as the models are not parametric but this problems are those to be solved in practice as a precise parametric analysis is nice in theory but not required in practice (if the target platform is fixed).

Implementation. From annotated models of the sender and the receiver, we have generated, using ELASTIC2BRICK the C-code for the sender and the receiver. The C files are about 500 lines long for each controller. The annotations of the models are very natural. Here are some examples of annotations. Assume that we want to use the protocol to exchange variable length strings of bits that are stored in an array, say A in the sender and B in the receiver. Instead of assigning the bit variable i non-deterministically, we should execute the annotation {i := A[j];

Tool	Constraint	Result	Time
HyTech	$\delta_1 + \delta_2 < 1/2$	Safe	55s
	$\delta_1 = \delta_2 = 1/5$	Safe	50s
	$\delta_1 = \delta_2 = 1/4$	Unsafe	90s
Uppaal	$\delta_1 = \delta_2 = 1/5$	Safe	< 1s
	$\delta_1 = \delta_2 = 1/4$	Unsafe	< 1s

Fig. 9. Execution times for the different models

j++;}, and in the Receiver automaton, we add the code {B[k] := α; k++;} to transitions setting r to $\alpha \in \{0, 1\}$, and the code {B[k]:=0; B[k+1]:=1; k+=2;} to the transition setting r to 2.

Evaluation. The code that we have obtained is correct by construction and can safely be executed on LEGO MINDSTORMS™ Brick as an alternative communication mean with real-time guarantees. For that, it suffices to give the highest level of priority to the protocol to ensure its real-time behavior. This should not spoil the behavior of other applications running on the Brick as the resources needed by the protocol are very low. Now, let us look at the performance of the protocol in our implementation. The throughput obtained, when the length of the sequence goes to infinity, is around 2.84 bits per seconds. This may look quite low and we could think that far better throughput could be obtained by a hand-made implementation. But this is not the case. Indeed, we can show using the results of Ho and Wong-Toi [HWT95] and by taking into account only the imprecision due to reading on digital clocks every time slice, that the throughput of the protocol on LEGO MINDSTORMS™ is bounded from above by around 4.16 bits per seconds. So, the price in term of performance loss to obtain automatically generated and correct code is not too high in our opinion. Let us also note that we were only able to find error by testing when the throughput was set around 7 bits per seconds. That shows the limit of testing at least when done in a naive way.

References

[AD94]   Rajeev Alur and David L. Dill. A theory of timed automata. *Theoretical Computer Science*, 126(2):183–235, 1994.

[BPV94]   D. Bosscher, I. Polak, and F. Vaandrager. Verification of an Audio Control Protocol. In H. Langmaack, W.-P. de Roever, and J. Vytopil, editors, *Formal Techniques in Real-Time and Fault-Tolerant Systems*, volume 863, pages 170–192, Lübeck, Germany, 1994. Springer-Verlag.

[CHR02]   F. Cassez, T.A. Henzinger, and J.-F. Raskin. A comparison of control problems for timed and hybrid systems. In *HSCC 02: Hybrid Systems— Computation and Control*, Lecture Notes in Computer Science 2289, pages 134–148. Springer-Verlag, 2002.

[DDR04]   M. De Wulf, L. Doyen, and J.-F. Raskin. Almost ASAP semantics: From timed models to timed implementations. In *HSCC 04: Hybrid Systems—Computation and Control*, Lecture Notes in Computer Science 2993, pages 296–310. Springer-Verlag, 2004.

[DDR05]   M. De Wulf, L. Doyen, and J.-F. Raskin. Systematic implementation of real-time models (extended version). Technical Report 543, U.L.B., 2005. http://www.ulb.ac.be/di/publications/.

[Doy03]   Laurent Doyen. A systematic implementation of simple timed controllers. Technical Report 504, U.L.B., 2003.

[HHWT95]   Thomas A. Henzinger, Pei-Hsin Ho, and Howard Wong-Toi. Hytech: The next generation. In *16th Annual Real-Time Systems Symposium (RTSS)*, pages 56–65. IEEE Computer Society Press, 1995.

[HWT95]   P.-H. Ho and H. Wong-Toi. Automated analysis of an audio control protocol. In P. Wolper, editor, *Proceedings of the 7th International Conference On Computer Aided Verification*, volume 939, pages 381–394, Liege, Belgium, 1995. Springer Verlag.

[LT87]   N. Lynch and M. Tuttle. Hierarchical correctness proofs for distributed algorithms. In *6th ACM Symp. on Principles of Distributed Computing*, pages 137–151, 1987.

[PL00]   Paul Pettersson and Kim G. Larsen. UPPAAL2k. *Bulletin of the European Association for Theoretical Computer Science*, 70:40–44, February 2000.

Timing Tolerances in Safety-Critical Software

Alan Wassyng*, Mark Lawford*, and Xiayong Hu

Software Quality Research Laboratory, Department of Computing and Software,
McMaster University, Hamilton, Canada
{wassyng, lawford, huxy}@mcmaster.ca

Abstract. Many safety-critical software applications are hard real-time systems. They have stringent timing requirements that have to be met. We present a description of timing behaviour that includes precise definitions as well as analysis of how functional timing requirements interact with performance timing requirements, and how these concepts can be used by software designers. The definitions and analysis presented explicitly deal with tolerances in all timing durations. Preliminary work indicates that some requirements may be met at significantly reduced CPU bandwidth through reduced variation in cycle time.

Keywords: safety-critical, real-time, timing tolerances, requirements.

1 Introduction

Specifying, implementing and verifying real-time requirements for embedded software systems can be a difficult and time consuming task. Hence real-time systems have become an active area of research in the formal methods community. Practical implementations have to worry about sampling rates, schedulability, computation time, latency, and jitter, all of which involve tolerances in some form when interfacing a physical plant and a software control system. In this paper we make the case that several different types of tolerances need to be fully specified at the requirements level in order to properly deal with the timing tolerances that are inherent in the system implementation. These include tolerances on functional timing requirements, and tolerances that allow for deviation from the idealized behaviour specified by the requirements models. This work builds on analysis and definitions that were used in safety-critical software applications over many years at Ontario Power Generation in Canada [9].

The extensive survey of formal methods for the specification and verification of real-time systems in [1] contains references to over 200 publications. The overwhelming majority of the cited works are dedicated to the specification and validation of real-time requirements. Despite this intensity of research, relatively little work has been done on formally modeling timing tolerances.

Recent work has begun to address the issue of timing tolerances required to verify implementations of requirements modeled as timed automata with ASAP

---

* Partially supported by NSERC.

J.S. Fitzgerald, I.J. Hayes, and A. Tarlecki (Eds.): FM 2005, LNCS 3582, pp. 157–172, 2005.

semantics [2, 3]. Wulf, et al, consider the case of implementing a continuous-time controller with a discrete-time system, assuming that there is a delay Δ associated with the controller's reaction to the environment. Both the controller and the plant are first modeled as timed automata. Their control objective is to ensure that the closed-loop system satisfies a safety property by avoiding bad states. Provided that all control actions can be delayed by up to some fixed $\Delta > 0$ without violating the safety property, they say that the controller is "implementable". A PSPACE-complete decision procedure to test implementability is described in [3], while [2] provides a semi-decision procedure to compute the maximal reaction delay Δ allowable by the implementation that still preserves the correctness of the closed loop system. It further shows that the system is implementable by a cyclic executive with loop time upper bound Δ_L and a finite precision clock with a resolution of Δ_P, provided that $\Delta > 3\Delta_L + 4\Delta_P$. In this work response allowance ra and sample interval ts correspond most closely to Δ and Δ_L in [2] and implicitly we assume a clock resolution of 1 time unit. Based on our definitions, and using simple mathematical arguments, we are able to come to a somewhat surprising result that allows some timing requirements to be verifiably implemented at a significantly lower CPU bandwidth.

The remainder of this paper is organized as follows: Section 2 provides the notation and definitions of terms and operators, and specifically differentiates between functional and performance timing requirements. Section 3 describes the relationship between the two performance timing requirements, while Section 4 details the interaction of functional and performance timing requirements. Conclusions are provided in Section 5.

2   Definitions

2.1   The Requirements Model

The requirements model we use is a finite state machine with an arbitrarily small clock-tick. This enables us to straddle the time continuous and time discrete domains. Many other models could be used and would require minimal changes in the following definitions.

Stimuli are referred to as *monitored variables*, and responses are *controlled variables*.

The finite state machine is assumed to describe idealized behaviour, i.e. results are produced instantaneously. If $C(t)$ is the vector of values of all controlled variables at time t, $M(t)$ is the vector of values of all monitored variables at time t, $S(t)$ is the vector of values of all state variables at time t, we can define relations R (requirements) and NST (next state) as follows:

$$C(t_k) = R(M(t_k), S(t_k))$$
$$S(t_{k+1}) = NST(M(t_k), S(t_k)), \text{ for } k = 0, 1, 2, \ldots \tag{1}$$

where the time of initialization is t_0, and the time between t_k and t_{k+1} is an arbitrarily small time, δt. It is almost always necessary to decompose the construction of R and NST into a number of intermediate functions. NST in our

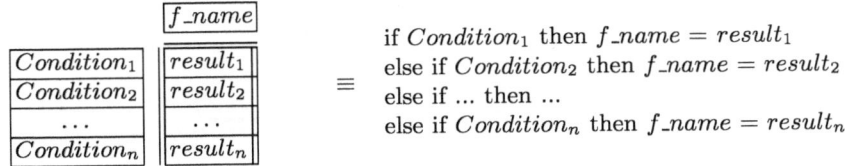

<table>
<tr><td></td><td>f_name</td></tr>
<tr><td>$Condition_1$</td><td>$result_1$</td></tr>
<tr><td>$Condition_2$</td><td>$result_2$</td></tr>
<tr><td>...</td><td>...</td></tr>
<tr><td>$Condition_n$</td><td>$result_n$</td></tr>
</table>

$\equiv$

if $Condition_1$ then $f\_name = result_1$
else if $Condition_2$ then $f\_name = result_2$
else if ... then ...
else if $Condition_n$ then $f\_name = result_n$

Disjointness: $Condition_i \wedge Condition_j \Leftrightarrow False, \forall i, j = 1..n, i \neq j$, and
Completeness: $Condition_1 \vee ... \vee Condition_n \Leftrightarrow True$.

Fig. 1. Horizontal Condition Tables

formulations is usually trivial since we strive to keep state data at the requirements level to a very simple form, namely the previous values of intermediate functions and variables.

2.2 Notation

Current time is denoted by t_{now}. We indicate elements of state data by subscripting the identifiers. $variable_{-n}$ means the value of $variable$, n clock-ticks prior to the current one.

Where possible, we use *tabular expressions* to define functions. We are convinced that tabular expressions (function tables) are a superb notation for describing software functions. Disjointness and completeness criteria help us in ensuring that the functional descriptions are unambiguous and complete [6]. There have been a number of publications on the semantics and usage of tabular expressions (e.g. [7, 8, 9]). The tabular expressions we use here are particular simple (they are called *horizontal condition tables*). Fig. 1 presents an example table together with its informal semantics.

2.3 Functional Timing Requirements

Functional timing requirements are timing requirements that are directly related to the required behaviour of the application. Some of the more common functional timing requirements are described below, and mathematical definitions are provided.

Sustained Timing Requirements: A common functional timing requirement is one that specifies that a condition must be sustained over a particular time duration. For example, to filter out the effect of a noisy signal we may specify that an event in which a sensor signal is above its setpoint should be sustained for 300 ms before it can cause a "trip". This means that the implementation must guarantee that if the sensor event is sustained for less than 300 ms, the trip must not occur. Similarly, if the sensor event is sustained for 300 ms or longer, the trip must be generated. Without tolerances on the time duration, these requirements would be impossible to meet.

Many of the concepts and analyses we present are best illustrated when applied to sustained timing requirements. For this reason we discuss this example in detail.

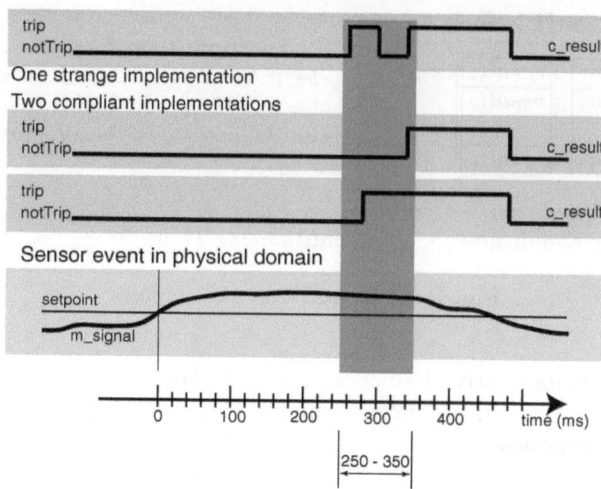

Fig. 2. Two Valid Implementations of a Sustained Timing Requirement

We can introduce tolerances on the time duration in the above example. Assume that the sensor trip condition should be sustained for 300 ±50 ms.

Fig. 2 shows an implementation of the behaviour specified above for a controlled variable c_result and sustained condition $m\_signal \geq setpoint$. The strange behaviour in the top implementation is almost certainly not what the specifier intended, but it may be compliant with its specification. How should we interpret this specification? A logical interpretation is that c_result should not equal trip until $m\_signal \geq setpoint$ has been True for at least 250 ms, and that c_result must equal trip if $m\_signal \geq setpoint$ has been True for 350 ms.

The problem is: what happens in the range 250–350 ms? Fig. 2 shows another two possible implementations that really would be compliant with this requirement. The difference here is that for each event we have effectively restricted ourselves to a single representative duration inside the specified range.

There are a number of important points to emphasize. i) The time duration is measured from when the event started in the physical application domain. It is not measured from the time it is detected. Since the requirements are (supposed to be) developed by the domain experts, and should be independent of any implementation, it does not make sense to define timing requirements with reference to when events are detected. ii) Many different implementations are valid. The behaviour in the dark shaded interval representing time in the interval [250, 350] ms is not deterministic. It is vital that everyone has the same understanding of what the requirement means. iii) Even though we have introduced tolerances into the requirement, the requirement still describes idealized behaviour understood within the constraints of the requirements model. For instance, it does not take into account that processing time is not infinitely small, and it makes no reference to how often the application samples the values of the sensor.

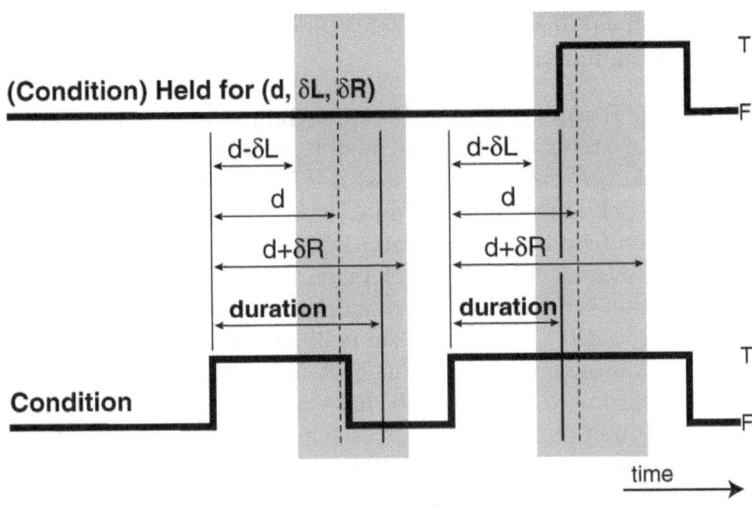

Fig. 3. "Held for" Functional Timing Requirement

(Condition :bool) **Held for** (d: $\mathbb{R}^{>0}$, δL, $\delta R : \mathbb{R}^{\geq 0}$) :bool
where duration(Condition: bool): $[d - \delta L, d + \delta R]$
  Event_start_time(Condition :bool) : $\mathbb{R}^{\geq 0}$
Initially: duration = any value in $[d - \delta L, d + \delta R]$
  Event_start_time$_{-1}$ = 0
  Condition$_{-1}$ = False

	duration	Event_start_time
(Condition = True) & (Condition$_{-1}$ = False)	Any value in $[d-\delta L, d+\delta R]$	t_{now}
(Condition = False) OR (Condition$_{-1}$ = True)	No Change	No Change

		Held for
Condition = True	$t_{now}-$ Event_start_time$\geq$ duration	True
	$t_{now}-$ Event_start_time$<$ duration	False
Condition = False		False

Fig. 4. Formal Definition of "(Condition) Held for $(d, \delta L, \delta R)$"

To model sustained events, we developed an infix operator, *(Condition) Held for (d, δL, δR)*, which uses a *duration* defined by the constant time d (> 0), with tolerances $-\delta L, +\delta R$, $0 \leq \delta L < d, 0 \leq \delta R$. "Held for" is illustrated in Fig. 3, and is defined formally using tabular expressions in Fig. 4. A critical concept is that although duration can be any value in the interval $[d - \delta L, d + \delta R]$, it must be constrained so that duration has only a single value throughout an event. An event in this case means that *Condition* changes from False to True. Without this constraint, many different bizarre behaviours are possible, all of them clearly not the intent of the function.

Periodic Timing Requirements: Periodic timing requirements are common in hard real-time systems. To help us model periodic timing requirements we developed a function, *Periodic(Condition, d, δL, δR)*. This function (*Periodic*) is True for 1 clock-tick at the instant that *Condition* changes from False to True, and, as long as *Condition* remains True, the function is True again, some time "period" after the most recent time it changed from False to True. The effective *period* of the function is defined by the constant duration d (> 0), with tolerances $-\delta L, +\delta R, 0 \leq \delta L < d, 0 \leq \delta R$. *Periodic* is illustrated in Fig. 5, and is defined formally using tabular expressions in Fig. 6. A different kind of periodic function is one that is synchronized with an external clock as illustrated in Fig. 7.

If the periodic functional requirement is synchronized with an external clock, definitions equivalent to t **mod** period = 0 are useless when the period involves tolerances. The requirement t **mod** 400±50 ms = 0 results in milli-second intervals of [350-450], [700-900], [1050-1350], [1400-1800], [1750-2250], [2100-2700], ..., and after a relatively short time period the requirement does not constrain behaviour much at all. A practical, formal specification of this periodic functional requirement can be developed from $\forall n : \mathbb{N} \cdot t_n \in [n \cdot d - \delta L, n \cdot d + \delta R]$, and is defined using tabular expressions in Fig. 8. This definition does not deal explicitly with a consistent clock drift, but this could be included by specifying d as a constrained function of time.

2.4   Performance Timing Requirements

Functional behaviour of the application is (typically) described using a model that describes the ideal behaviour of the application. It totally ignores the fact that an implementation cannot continuously monitor sensor values and requires a finite, non-zero amount of time to process its results. To complete the description of the required behaviour, a requirements document must also specify the performance tolerances that are allowed in meeting functional timing requirements. There are two different performance timing requirements, *timing resolution* and *response allowance*. These are defined and discussed in the following two sections.

Timing Resolution: Each monitored variable has a timing resolution associated with it. The definitions for this interval are different for time continuous and time discrete monitored variables.

The timing resolution (TR) for a time continuous monitored variable is the minimum time duration of an initiating event dependent on that monitored variable for which the application must guarantee that it will detect that event. Thus, the TR is also an indication of the maximum time interval that the trip computer can allow between successive sampling instances for that stimulus.

The TR for a time discrete monitored variable is the smallest time interval separating two events dependent on that monitored variable, in which the application must guarantee that it will detect both events.

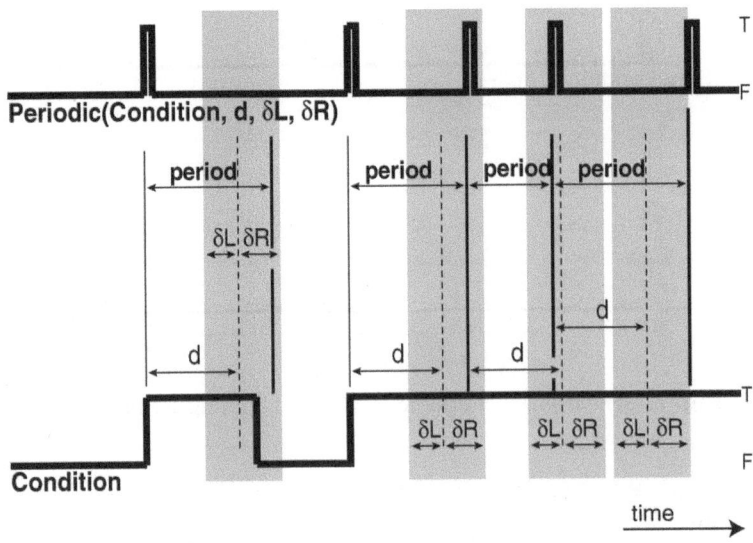

Fig. 5. A Periodic Functional Timing Requirement

Periodic(Condition :bool, d :$\mathbb{R}^{>0}$, δL, δR : $\mathbb{R}^{\geq 0}$) :bool
where period(Periodic$_{-1}$: bool): $[d - \delta L, d + \delta R]$
       previous_pulse_time(Condition :bool) : $\mathbb{R}^{\geq 0}$
Initially: period = any value in $[0, \delta R]$; previous_pulse_time$_{-1}$ = 0; Periodic$_{-1}$ = False

	period
Periodic$_{-1}$ = True	Any value in [d-δL, d+δR]
Periodic$_{-1}$ = False	No Change

			Periodic	previous_pulse_time
Condition = True		Condition$_{-1}$ = False	True	t_{now}
	Condition$_{-1}$ = True	$t_{now} \geq$ previous_pulse_time$_{-1}$ + period	True	t_{now}
		$t_{now} <$ previous_pulse_time$_{-1}$ + period	False	No Change
	Condition = False		False	No Change

Fig. 6. Formal Definition of "Periodic(Condition, d, δL, δR)"

These situations are illustrated in Fig. 9. Note that if a monitored variable is used in determining the behaviour of two (or more) controlled variables, it is probable that at least two different events (one on each controlled-monitored variable path) are dependent on that monitored variable, and that the monitored variable could have two different TRs associated with it. In general, we assign a TR for each controlled-monitored variable pair in which the controlled variable value can be affected by the value of the monitored variable.

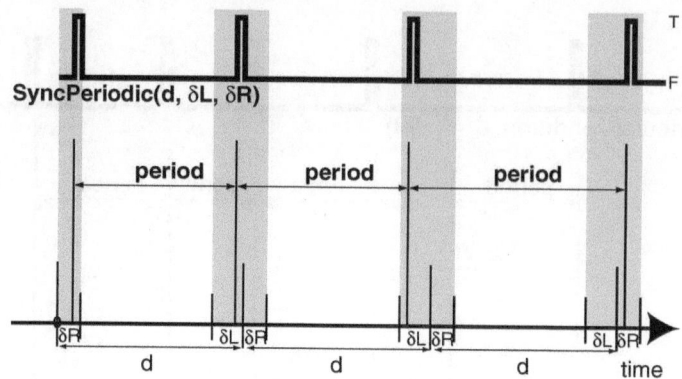

Fig. 7. Synchronized Periodic Functional Timing Requirement

SyncPeriodic$(d : \mathbb{R}^{>0}, \delta L, \delta R : \mathbb{R}^{\geq 0}) : bool$
where n: $\mathbb{N}$, and $\Delta : \mathbb{R}$
Initially: $n = 0$; $\Delta =$ any value in $[0, \delta R]$; SyncPeriodic$_{-1}$ = False

	Δ	n
SyncPeriodic$_{-1}$ = True	Any value in [-δL, δR]	n + 1
SyncPeriodic$_{-1}$ = False	No Change	No Change

	SyncPeriodic
$t_{now} \geq$ n·d + Δ	True
$t_{now} <$ n·d + Δ	False

Fig. 8. Formal Definition of "$SyncPeriodic(d, \delta L, \delta R)$"

Response Allowance: The Response Allowance (RA) for a controlled-monitored variable pair specifies an allowable processing delay. Each controlled variable must have an RA specified for it. The RA applies to the controlled variable and the particular monitored variable on which the controlled variable's behaviour depends. The RA is measured from the time the event actually occurred in the physical domain, until the time the value of the controlled variable is generated and crosses the application boundary into the physical domain.

Some important considerations:

1. The RA for the pair c-m is meaningless if c does not change its value in response to a change in the value of m (the effect must be visible externally).
2. The time sequence of externally generated values of a controlled variable c cannot be altered by consideration of the RAs for each c-m pair. For instance, we cannot allow c to change from *trip* = True (evaluated at time t) to *trip*

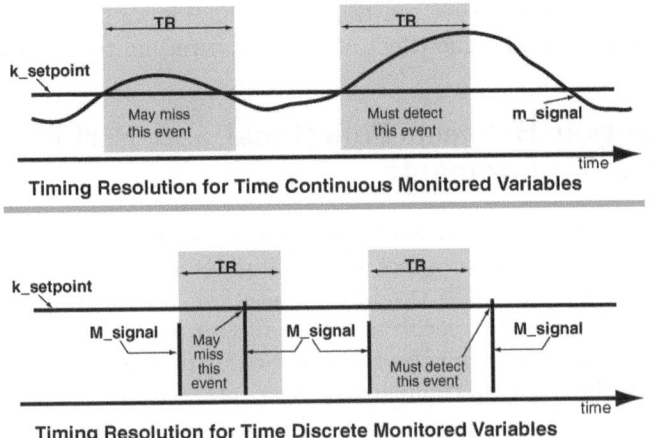

Fig. 9. Timing Resolution

= False (evaluated at time $t - \delta t$, δt is an arbitrarily small positive number) simply because the RA was large enough to allow this.

3   Relationship Between Response Allowance and Timing Resolution

Consider the case where c, a controlled variable, depends solely on m, a monitored variable. We must specify both a TR (value tr) and RA (value ra) for the c-m pair. Now, in the implementation, let ts represent the sampling interval used for m, and tp the processing time required to output c, measured from the instant that the value of m was sampled. Then, if the implementation is to comply with its timing requirements, it is clear that we must insist that $ts + tp \leq ra$. Since $tp > 0$ and $ts \leq tr$ (it is permitted to equal ra), it follows that $tr < ra$. So, unless there is a reason to use a more restrictive TR for m, we can assume a default upper limit for TR equal to the RA for the c-m pair. This is the least restrictive requirement that we can place on the software design. It leaves the designer free to choose a sampling interval anywhere in the range $[0, ra)$ as long as the RA is satisfied.

In most real applications, the TR for a monitored variable would be determined, initially, from a study of the possible transients associated with the particular monitored variable. If the physically motivated TR is larger than the associated RA then the TR would have to be constrained by the value of the RA. If the physically motivated TR is smaller than the associated RA, then that smaller value must be used as the specified TR.

The RA itself is always derived from consideration of the physical application. In safety-critical applications, absolute compliance with the RA is clearly just as important as compliance with any other requirement.

In the following section we see that both the TR and RA may need to be modified once we consider the effect of functional timing requirements.

4   Interaction Between Functional and Performance Timing Requirements

There are a number of interactions between functional and performance timing requirements. Some of them affect the timing resolution by imposing restrictions on sampling intervals in the implementation. Other interactions force us to consider exactly how to specify response allowances for controlled-monitored variable pairs that are also involved in functional timing behaviours.

We use sustained events to illustrate these interactions.

4.1   Timing Resolution for Sustained Events

Given a sustained timing requirement we need to consider whether it is possible to implement a design so that the requirement can be met. We can identify two different categories of sustained events. The first one, as discussed in Section 2.3, is where the behaviour depends on values of one or more monitored variables. In this case the event is timed from the time at which the event was initiated in the physical domain. The second kind is one in which the sustained event depends only on the values of controlled variables (or is synchronized in some way with an external clock). In this case the event is timed from the instant at which the event is initiated within the software domain. This kind of event is typically easier to deal with since the inherent uncertainty of when the event actually occurred is removed from consideration.

The following two sections present analyses of these cases.

Sample Intervals for Events That Depend on Monitored Variables: We know from earlier discussion (Section 2.3) that if we specify behaviour in the form of $(Condition)$ $Held$ for $(d, \delta L, \delta R)$, and $duration \in [d - \delta L, d + \delta R]$, then the requirement means that we cannot make the final decision as to whether "Held for" generates True or False based on values that were sampled before we are sure that $d - \delta L$ time has elapsed since the event occurred in the physical domain. We also cannot delay the decision past $d + \delta R$.

The situation is illustrated in Fig. 10. Let us assume that the sample intervals are ts_0, ts_1, ts_2, etc. Since our analysis has to hold for real industrial applications, we do not assume a constant sample interval. We do assume that we can place limits on the sample intervals. We call these limits ts_min and ts_max. Once we have these limits, we know that $ts\_min \leq ts_j \leq ts\_max$ for each $j \in \{0..n\}$. We will see later that any variation in sample intervals results in fewer feasible implementations. If the event is detected at sample time 1, then we know that the event must have occurred sometime between sample time 0 and sample time 1. We can now assume that $Condition$ remains True at sample times 2, 3, ,..., n-2. (If it does not remain True, we simply terminate the event and the "Held for" value becomes False.)

If we study the situation in Fig. 10, we see that the only way we can be certain that we base our decision on values sampled in the time interval $[d - \delta L, d + \delta R]$ is to ensure that we have at least two sample points inside that interval. It turns out this is a necessary condition, but it is not sufficient.

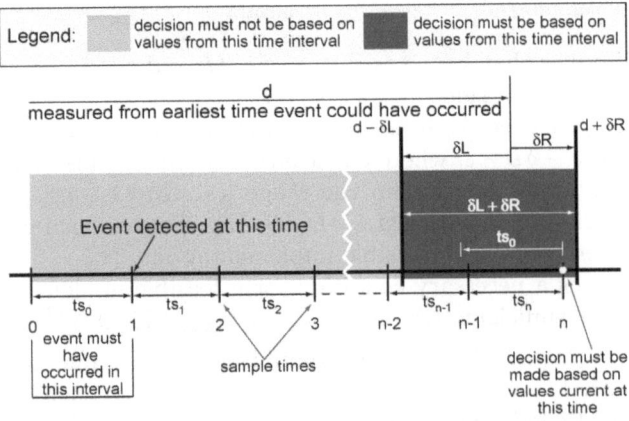

Fig. 10. Sample Intervals Required for Sustained Events

The earliest the event could have occurred is immediately after values were sampled at sample point 0. The latest the event could have occurred is immediately prior to sample point 1. We choose to measure all relevant times from sample point 0, i.e. from the earliest time it could have occurred. Now we can consider the two sample points in the interval $[d - \delta L, d + \delta R]$ (assuming we manage to get two samples in that interval). The later time in the interval (sample point n in Fig. 10) must be to the left of the $d + \delta R$ boundary because the times are measured from the earliest time the event could have occurred. So we know that decisions based on values sampled at sample point n are not too late. For it to be too early, the actual event would have had to occur immediately prior to sample point 1. In this case, we should subtract ts_0 from the time at sample point n and check to see if the resulting time is less than $d - \delta L$. If all sample intervals were equal, having two sample points in the interval would be sufficient to prove that sample point n could not be too early. However, since $ts_n \le ts\_max$, there is a chance that $(sample\ point\ n) - ts_0$ could lie outside the interval, in which case the decision would be made based on values that are too early. The following analysis copes with all the questions we have raised. Note that we could have chosen to measure times from time of detection. The analysis would have to be adjusted accordingly.

Case 1: $0 < ts\_max \le \frac{1}{2}(\delta L + \delta R)$: In this case it is easy to see that it is always possible to implement the sustained event.

Case 2: $\frac{1}{2}(\delta L + \delta R) < ts\_max \le (\delta L + \delta R)$: It may happen that the hardware platform is not fast enough for us to arrange a sample interval that always works as defined in Case 1. It is still possible to find sample intervals that allow us to implement the sustained event.

It is crucial to realize that if $ts\_max > \frac{1}{2}(\delta L + \delta R)$ then the only way we can ensure that two samples, ts_max apart, fall in the duration interval, is if the last sample point to the left of the interval is not "too close" to $d - \delta L$. Let $k_{min} = int(\frac{d-\delta L}{ts\_max})$, and $k_{max} = int(\frac{d-\delta L}{ts\_min})$, where int(r) truncates r to an integer.

$k_{min} \neq k_{max}$ implies that $k_{max} \cdot ts\_min \leq d - \delta L$ and $k_{max} \cdot ts\_max > d - \delta L$, since $k_{max} > k_{min}$.

This means that there is always some combination of sample intervals such that $\sum_{j=1}^{k} ts_j = d - \delta L - \epsilon$, where ϵ is arbitrarily small. This implies that there are always sample intervals within the range $[ts\_min, ts\_max]$ such that there is only one sample point within $[d - \delta L, d + \delta R]$. Thus we can conclude that if $k_{min} \neq k_{max}$ then there is no feasible implementation.

So, $k_{min} = k_{max}$ is a necessary condition for a feasible implementation. Unfortunately it is not sufficient. Let $k = k_{min} = k_{max}$. Then $\sum_{j=1}^{k} ts_j \leq d - \delta L$, and $\sum_{j=1}^{k+1} ts_j \geq d - \delta L$, for any combination of sample intervals within $[ts\_min, ts\_max]$. The worst case is when $ts_j = ts\_max$ for each $j \in \{1, 2, ..., k + 2\}$. So, a sufficient condition when $k_{min} = k_{max}$ is that $(k+2) \cdot ts\_max \leq d + \delta R$.

Case 3: $(\delta L + \delta R) < ts\_max$: The sustained event cannot be implemented.

Examples of Feasible Sample Interval Ranges for Sustained Events: It is instructive to examine the ranges of sample intervals that result in feasible implementations of sustained events that are dependent on monitored variables. The analysis from Case 2 was implemented in a spreadsheet and graphs showing the feasible sample intervals were generated (Fig. 11). Each graph lists [d-δL, d+δR]. It also shows the nominal sample intervals as labels along the x-axis, and lists the deviations as $(-\ell, +r)$. So, for ts=50, with deviation $(-3, +2)$ we have ts_min=47 and ts_max=52. A deviation of $(-0, +0)$ indicates a constant sample interval (pretty much impossible to achieve).

Fig. 11 shows that in the case when $duration \in [400 - 50, 400 + 60]$, rather than requiring the code to run with every $ts \leq 50ms$ (a 20Hz or faster task), it is possible to detect the event with every $ts \in [74\text{-}1, 74+2]\ ms$ (roughly a 13.5Hz task). This represents an approximately 32% reduction in CPU time required for the task! This pattern results in a positive cycle. Making execution times more precise may present the opportunity to reduce the CPU load, which in turn should make it easier to meet timing requirements. While scheduling conflicts may be more difficult to resolve with the tighter constraints on a larger ts, we note that the tolerances only restrict when the sample of input m must be taken, not when output c must be updated, which is specified by the response allowance.

Intuitively, when tolerances are allowed on the sample time (non-zero jitter), it is more difficult to detect sustained conditions of longer duration with the same precision. E.g., as the duration changes from [200-50, 200+60] to [300-50, 300+60] to [400-50, 400+60] in Fig. 11, the available sample times in [50,110] are first significantly reduced then completely eliminated.

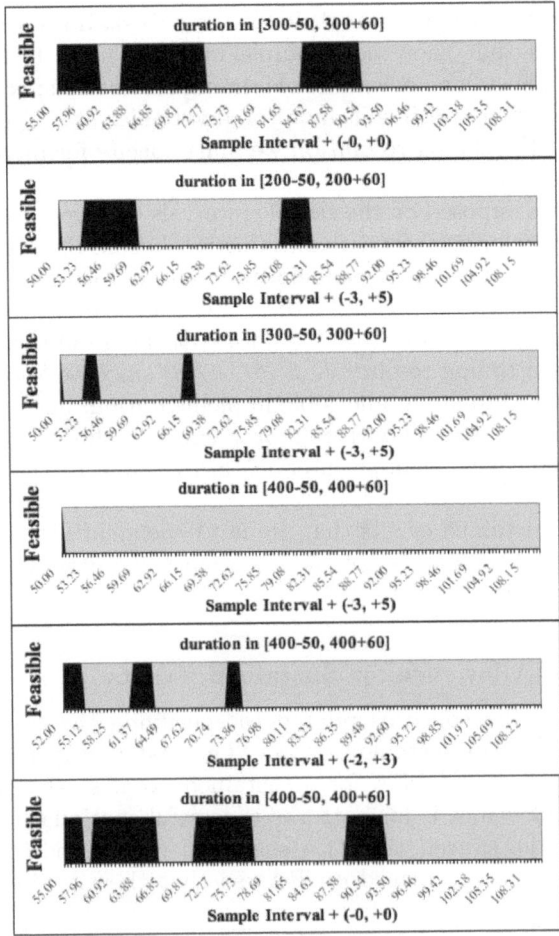

Fig. 11. Feasible Sample Intervals for Various Durations and Tolerances

Sample Intervals for Events That Depend on Controlled Variables:
In this case the uncertainty as to when the event occurred has been removed.
Thus, any sample interval less than or equal to $(\delta L + \delta R)$ suffices since we need
only a single sample point in the interval. Smaller sample intervals allow us to
define the boundaries of the interval more precisely, but any point in the interval
satisfies the requirement. However, larger sample intervals are also possible. For
instance, sample intervals in the range $d - \delta L \leq ts \leq d + \delta R$ also work, giving
us two sample points, one at the start of the event and another in the desired
interval. We have called these "sample points", however, it is more accurate
to term them "evaluation points", since no monitored variable is sampled, the
current value of a controlled variable is simply used in a function evaluation. We
can see therefore, that this kind of sustained event is affected by specified RAs
rather than TRs. This is discussed further in Section 4.2.

Specifying Timing Resolution Affected by Sustained Events: We have presented analyses that show how sample intervals must be restricted to be able to implement sustained events. Since timing resolution specifies a maximum sample interval for time continuous monitored variables, it is clear that sustained events may affect the timing resolution we must specify for monitored variables involved in those events.

The restrictions imposed on the sample intervals however, are not enforceable by specifying a more or less restrictive timing resolution. If we look at Cases 1, 2 and 3 for the sustained events dependent on monitored variables, we see that all sample intervals in Case 1 are feasible, there are disjoint ranges of feasible sample intervals for specific events for Case 2, and no feasible sample intervals for Case 3. We can specify a timing resolution of $(\delta L + \delta R)$ since we know that anything greater than that results in an infeasible implementation, but in fact, this is not sufficient. One way of dealing with this problem is to shift the responsibility of determining exactly what sample intervals are feasible to the software design phase.

In the case of sustained events that are not dependent directly on monitored variables, timing resolution is not an issue since monitored variables cannot directly affect the event.

4.2   Response Allowance for Sustained Events

There are two specific concerns related to specifying the response allowance for variables involved in sustained events. The first is a general one. How do we cope with specifying the RA for a sustained event so that it is clear what the requirement allowance is for both the successful continuation of a sustained event, as well as the cancellation of a sustained event. The second concern is what restrictions must be placed on RAs so that the sustained event can be implemented.

1. We begin by assuming that monitored variable m and controlled variable c are involved in the sustained event. If the functional requirement does not involve a sustained event the RA is based on a physical analysis of the required behaviour. We call this ra_{c-m}. This is a suitable RA to use for the case when the sustained event is canceled. In other words, given a sustained event specified by $(Condition)\ Held\ for\ (d,\ \delta L,\ \delta R)$, if $Condition$ changes from True to False, the application must generate the value of c within ra_{c-m} measured from the time the event occurred in the physical domain. Now what if the sustained event is successful? We know that we have $d + \delta R$ within which to determine that fact (measured from the initiation of the event in the physical domain). We also have some time in which to calculate the value of c. The problem is that we do not know how much of ra_{c-m} to add to $d + \delta R$. One solution is to add the entire ra_{c-m}, in spite of the fact that this "double counts" any portion of ra_{c-m} that was allocated to detecting the event. We are examining alternative strategies but this is the best we have to date. Thus, the RA for sustained events is specified in the form: $ra_{true}\ Held\ for\ (d,\ \delta L,\ \delta R)/ra_{false}$. This is interpreted as specifying a response allowance of ra_{true} when the

event continues to completion (because of that "Held for" event), and ra_{false} when the event is canceled. Example: an RA of 250 ms is specified for a c-m pair, and the event "$(f\_sentrip = e\_trip)$ $Held\ for\ (k\_delay)$" also involves that pair, where $k\_delay = 500\ ms \pm 25\ ms$. ra_{c-m} is documented as: 775 $ms\ Held\ for\ (k\_delay)$ / 250 ms. We could specify ra_{c-m} simply by 775 ms/250 ms, but the $Held\ for\ (k\_delay)$ provides useful information.

2. In the case of a sustained event that depends on controlled variables, we saw earlier that it is relatively easy to arrange that at least one evaluation point lies in the interval of interest. Since the evaluation depends on the previous value of a controlled value, the RA for that variable serves the same purpose as the timing resolution does for monitored variables. Thus, to ensure that a "fresh" value of the controlled variable is used in the evaluation, we specify that the RA for that controlled variable must be no larger than $d + \delta R$. Of course, it may already have been specified to be more restrictive than that by the domain experts. In such cases the more restrictive value is used.

5   Conclusion

We have presented precise definitions for timing requirements that include tolerances on the time durations. Our analysis, based on these definitions, shows that it is possible to specify and verify critical timing requirements using simple mathematics that is accessible to both software engineers and domain experts. These definitions and related analyses can form the basis of a comprehensive, practical approach to specifying timing requirements in high reliability real-time and embedded systems.

In many safety-critical applications, when operating at the limits of the available hardware, sampling faster is simply not an option. Thus in order to meet all system deadlines, we may be forced into a situation where $ts\_max > \frac{1}{2}(\delta L + \delta R)$ for a given requirement. We have shown that it is still possible to find implementable sampling intervals that satisfy the relevant timing requirements. Our analysis also demonstrates that even low jitter in the sampling can prevent our being able to design an implementation that satisfies its timing requirements.

Acknowledgments

The work presented in this paper is based on the efforts of many current and former employees and consultants of Ontario Power Generation Inc., and AECL, including: Glenn Archinoff, Dominic Chan, Peter Froebel, Rick Hohendorf, David Lau, Jeff McDougall, Greg Moum, Mike Viola, and Alanna Wong. We also acknowledge and thank David Parnas. This work reflects the successful application of many of his pioneering and fundamental ideas regarding software engineering.

References

1. Wang, F.: Formal verification of timed systems: A survey and perspective. Proceedings of the IEEE **92** (2004) 1283–1307
2. Wulf, M.D., Doyen, L., Raskin, J.F.: Almost asap semantics: From timed models to timed implementations. In: HSCC04. Vol. 2993 of LNCS. (2004) 296–310
3. Wulf, M.D., Doyen, L., Markey, N., Raskin, J.F.: Robustness and implementability of timed automata. In: FORMATS04,. Vol. 3253 of LNCS., Grenoble (2004) 152–166
4. Abadi, M., Lamport, L.: An old-fashioned recipe for real time. ACM Transactions on Programming Languages and Systems **16** (1994) 1543–1571
5. Shankar, N.: Verification of real-time systems using PVS. In Courcoubetis, C., ed.: CAV '93. Vol. 697 of LNCS., Elounda, Greece, Springer-Verlag (1993) 280–291
6. Parnas, D.L., Madey, J.: Functional documents for computer systems. Science of Computer Programming **25** (1995) 41–61
7. Janicki, R., Khédri, R.: On a formal semantics of tabular expressions. Science of Computer Programming **39** (2001) 189–213
8. Wassyng, A., Janicki, R.: Using tabular expressions. In: Int. Conf. on Software and Systems Engineering and their Applications. Vol. 4., Paris (2003) 1–17
9. Wassyng, A., Lawford, M.: Lessons learned from a successful implementation of formal methods in an industrial project. In Araki, K., Gnesi, S., Mandrioli, D., eds.: FME 2003. Vol. 2805 of LNCS., Springer-Verlag (2003) 133–153

Timed Testing with TorX

Henrik Bohnenkamp* and Axel Belinfante

Formal Methods and Tools,
Department of Computer Science, University of Twente,
Postbus 217, NL-7500 AE Enschede, The Netherlands
{bohnenka, belinfan}@cs.utwente.nl

Abstract. TorX is a specification-based, on-the-fly testing tool that tests for ioco conformance of implementations w.r.t. a formal specification. This paper describes an extension of TorX to not only allow testing for functional correctness, but also for correctness w.r.t. timing properties expressed in the specification. An implementation then passes a timed test if it passes according to ioco, and if *occurrence times* of outputs or of quiescence signals are legal according to the specification. The specifications are described by means of non-deterministic safety timed automata. This paper describes the basic algorithms for ioco, the necessary modifications to standard safety timed automata to make them usable as an input formalism, a test-derivation algorithm from timed automata, and the concrete algorithms implemented in TorX for timed testing. Finally, practical concerns with respect to timed testing are discussed.

Keywords: Model-based on-the-fly Testing, Timed Automata, Real-Time Testing, TORX, Tools.

1 Introduction

Testing is one of the most natural, intuitive and effective methods to increase the reliability of software. Formal methods have been employed to analyse and systematise the testing idea in general, and to define notions of correctness of implementations with respect to specifications in particular. Moreover, practical approaches to testing have been derived from testing theories [4, 15, 8, 9]. The *ioco* testing theory [14] reasons about black-box conformance testing of software components. Specifications and implementations are modeled as labelled transition systems (LTS) with inputs and outputs. An important ingredient of the theory is the notion of *quiescence, i.e.,* the absence of output, which is considered to be observable. Quiescence provides additional information on the behaviour of the implementation under test (IUT) and therefore allows to distinguish better between correct and faulty behaviour. The *ioco* theory defines a notion of correctness, the **ioco** implementation relation, and defines how to derive sound

* This work is supported by the Dutch National Senter project TANGRAM.

J.S. Fitzgerald, I.J. Hayes, and A. Tarlecki (Eds.): FM 2005, LNCS 3582, pp. 173–188, 2005.
© Springer-Verlag Berlin Heidelberg 2005

test-cases from the specification. The set of all *ioco* test-cases (which is usually of infinite size) is exhaustive, *i.e.*, in theory it is possible to distinguish all faulty from all *ioco*-correct implementations by executing all test-cases. In practice, *ioco*-test-cases can be used to test software components and to find bugs. The testing tool TORX has been developed [4, 15] to derive *ioco* test-cases automatically from a specification, and to apply them to an IUT. TORX does *on-the-fly testing*, *i.e.*, test-case derivation and execution is done simultaneously. TORX has been used successfully in several industry-relevant case-studies [2, 3].

This paper is about an extension of TORX to allow testing of real-time properties: *real-time testing*. Real-time testing means that the decisions whether an IUT has passed or failed a test is not only based on which outputs are observed, given a certain sequence of inputs, but also on *when* the outputs occur, given a certain sequence of inputs *applied at predefined times*. Our approach is influenced by, although independent of, the *tioco* theory [6], an extension of *ioco* to real-time testing. Whereas the *tioco* theory provides a formal framework for timed testing, we describe in this paper an algorithmic approach to real-time testing, inspired by the existing implementation of TORX. We use as input models non-deterministic *safety timed automata*, and describe the algorithms developed to derive test-cases for timed testing.

Related Work. Real-time testing has recently come more and more into focus of research. In [11, 12] approaches are described in which timed automata are used as specification formalism, and algorithms are described to do on-the-fly timed testing based on these specifications. These approaches are most similar to the one we describe in this paper. However, the big difference is that we take in our approach *quiescence* into account.

TORX itself has in fact already been used for timed testing [2]. Even though the approach was an ad-hoc solution to test for some timing properties in a particular case study, the approach has shown a lot of the problems that come with practical real-time testing, and has provided solutions to many of them. This early case-study has accelerated the implementation work for our TORX extensions immensely.

Structure of the Paper. In Section 2, we introduce *ioco*, describe the central algorithms of TORX, and comment on *tioco*. In Section 3, we introduce the class of models we use to describe specifications, and describe the algorithms necessary to do testing. In Section 4, we describe an abstract algorithm to derive test-cases from timed automata, and describe how we have implemented this in TORX. In Section 5, we address practical issues regarding timed testing. We conclude with Section 6.

Notational Convention. We will frequently define structures by means of tuples. If we define a tuple $T = (e_1, e_2, \ldots, e_n)$, we often will use a kind of *record* notation known from programming languages in order to address the components of the tuple, *i.e.*, we will write $T.e_i$ if we mean component e_i for T, for $i = 1, \ldots, n$.

2 Preliminaries

2.1 The *ioco* Way of Testing

In this section we give a summary of the *ioco* theory (*ioco* is an abbreviation for "*IO-conformance*"). Details can be found in [14].

The *ioco* Theory. A *labelled transition system* (LTS) is a tuple $(S, s_0, Act, \rightarrow)$, where S is a set of states, $s_0 \in S$ is the initial state, Act is a set of labels, and $\rightarrow \subseteq S \times Act \cup \{\tau\} \times S$ is the transition relation. Transitions $(s, a, s') \in \rightarrow$ are frequently written as $s \overset{a}{\rightarrow} s'$. τ is the *invisible* action. The set of all transition systems over label set Act is denoted as $\mathcal{L}(Act)$. Assume a set of input labels L_I, and a set of output labels L_U, $L_I \cap L_U = \emptyset$, $\tau \notin L_I \cup L_U$. Elements from L_I are often suffixed with a "?" and elements from L_U with an "!" to allow easier distinction. An LTS $L \in \mathcal{L}(L_I \cup L_U)$ is called an Input/Output transition system (IOTS) if L is *input-enabled*, *i.e.*, $\forall s \in S, \forall i? \in L_I : \exists s' \in L.S : s \overset{i?}{\rightarrow} s'$. Input-enabledness ensures that IOTS can never deadlock. However, it might be possible that from certain states no outputs can be produced without prior input. This behaviour is described by the notion of *quiescence*: let $L \in \mathcal{L}(L_I \cup L_U)$, and $s \in L.S$. Then s is *quiescent* (denoted $\delta(s)$), iff $\forall a \in L_U \cup \{\tau\} : \neg\exists s' \in L.S : s \overset{a}{\rightarrow} s'$. We introduce the *quiescence label*, $\delta \notin L_I \cup L_U \cup \{\tau\}$, and define the δ-*closure* $\Delta(L) = (L.S, L.s_0, L_I \cup L_U \cup \{\tau\} \cup \{\delta\}, \rightarrow')$, where $\rightarrow' = L.\rightarrow \cup \{(s, \delta, s) \mid s \in L.S \wedge \delta(s)\}$. It is this definition of quiescence which makes it necessary to postulate strongly convergent LTS, *i.e.*, which do not have infinite computations with only a finite trace. We introduce some more notation to deal with transition systems. Assume LTS L. For $a \in Act \cup \{\tau\}$, we write $s \overset{a}{\rightarrow}$, iff $\exists s' \in L.S : s \overset{a}{\rightarrow} s'$. We write $s \overset{a_1,...,a_n}{\longrightarrow} s'$ iff $\exists s_1, s_2, \ldots, s_{n-1} \in L.S : s \overset{a_1}{\rightarrow} s_1 \overset{a_2}{\rightarrow} s_2 \cdots s_{n-1} \overset{a_n}{\rightarrow} s'$. We write $s \Longrightarrow s'$ iff $s \overset{\tau,...,\tau}{\longrightarrow} s'$, and $s \overset{a}{\Longrightarrow} s'$ iff $\exists s'', s''' \in L.S : s \Longrightarrow s'' \overset{a}{\rightarrow} s''' \Longrightarrow s'$. Let $L \in \mathcal{L}(L_I \cup L_U)$. For a state $s \in L.S$, the set of *suspension traces* from s, denoted by $Straces(s)$, are defined as $Straces(s) = \{\sigma \in (L_I \cup L_U \cup \{\delta\})^* \mid s \overset{\sigma}{\Longrightarrow}\}$, where $\Longrightarrow$ is defined on top of $\Delta(L).\rightarrow$. We define $Straces(L) = Straces(L.s_0)$. For $L \in \mathcal{L}(L_I \cup L_U)$ and $s \in L.S$, we define $out(s) = \{o \in L_U \mid s \overset{o}{\rightarrow}\} \cup \{\delta \mid \delta(s)\}$, and, for $S' \subseteq L.S$, $out(S') = \bigcup_{s \in S'} out(s)$. Furthermore, for $s \in L.S$, $\underline{s \text{ after } \sigma} = \{s' \in L.S \mid s \overset{\sigma}{\Longrightarrow} s'\}$, and for $S \subseteq L.S$, $\underline{S \text{ after } \sigma} = \bigcup_{s \in S} s \text{ after } \sigma$. We define $\underline{L \text{ after } \sigma} = L.s_0 \text{ after } \sigma$.

Let $Spec, Impl \in \mathcal{L}(L_I \cup L_U)$ and let $Impl$ be an IOTS. Then we define

$$Impl \text{ ioco } Spec \Leftrightarrow \forall \sigma \in Straces(Spec) : out(\underline{Impl \text{ after } \sigma}) \subseteq out(\underline{Spec \text{ after } \sigma}).$$

Testing for *ioco* Conformance: Test-Case Derivation. To test a real system, we need a specification of it. From the specification test-cases can be derived that are sound with respect to *ioco*, *i.e.*, their execution will never lead to a test failure if the implementation is *ioco*-correct. Test cases are deterministic, finite, non-cyclic LTS with two special states **pass** and **fail**, which are supposed to be *terminating*. Test-cases are defined in a process-algebraic notation, with the following syntax: $T \longrightarrow \textbf{pass} \mid \textbf{fail} \mid a; T \mid \sum_{i=1}^{n} a_i T_i$, for

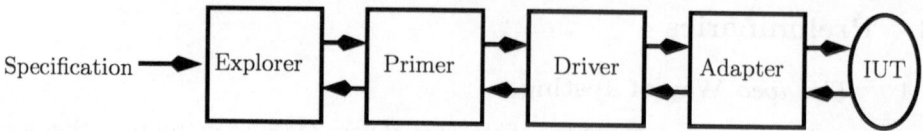

Fig. 1. The TorX tool architecture

$a, a_1, \ldots, a_n \in L_I \cup L_U \cup \{\delta\}$. Assuming an LTS $L \in \mathcal{L}(L_I \cup L_U)$ as a specification, test cases are defined recursively (with finite depth) according to the following rules. Starting with the set $S = \{L.s_0\}$,

1. $T :=$ **pass** is a test-case;
2. $T := a; T'$ is a test-case, where $a \in L_I$ and, assuming that $S' = S$ **after** a and $S' \neq \emptyset$, T' is a test-case derived from set S';
3. For $\overline{out(S)} = (L_U \cup \{\delta\}) \setminus out(S)$,

$$T := \sum_{x \in \overline{out(S)}} x; \mathbf{fail} \quad + \sum_{x \in out(S)} x; T_x$$

is a test-case, where the T_x for $x \in out(S)$ are test-cases derived from the respective sets $S_x = S$ **after** x.

2.2   On-the-Fly *ioco* Testing: TorX

In Figure 1 we see the tool structure of TorX. We can distinguish four tool components (not counting the IUT): EXPLORER, PRIMER, DRIVER and ADAPTER. The EXPLORER is the software component that takes a specification as input and provides access to an LTS representation of this specification. The PRIMER is the software component that is *ioco* specific. It implements part of the test-case derivation algorithm for the *ioco* theory. In particular, the PRIMER interacts directly with the EXPLORER, *i.e.,* the representation of the specification, in order to compute so-called *menus*. Menus are sets of transitions with input, output or δ labels, which according to the model are allowed to be applied to the IUT or allowed to be observed.

The PRIMER is triggered by the DRIVER. The DRIVER is the only active component and acts therefore as the motor of the TorX tool chain. It decides whether to apply a stimulus to the IUT, or whether to wait for an observation from the ADAPTER, and it channels information between PRIMER and ADAPTER.

The ADAPTER has several tasks: i) interface with the IUT; ii) translate abstract actions to concrete actions and and apply the latter to the IUT; iii) observe the IUT and translate observations to abstract actions; iv) detect absence of an output over a certain period of time and signal quiescence.

The recursive definition of test-cases as described in Section 2.1 allows to derive and execute test-cases simultaneously, *on-the-fly*. The core algorithm is the computation of *menus* from a set of states S. The output menu contains transitions labeled with the actions from the *out*-set $out(S)$. The input menu contains all inputs that are allowed to be applied to the IUT, according to the specification. The reason to keep transitions, rather than actions, in menus is that it is necessary to know the destination states which can be reached after applying an input or observing an output. The computation of a menu requires for each state in S the bounded exploration of a part of the state-space. Recursive descent into the state-space is stopped if a transition with an input or output label is seen.

The algorithm for the computation of menus is given in Fig. 2. We assume an LTS $Spec \in \mathcal{L}(L_I \cup L_U)$. Input to the algorithm is a set S of states. Initially, $S = \{L.s_0\}$. After trace $\sigma \in (L_I \cup L_U \cup \{\delta\})^*$ has been observed, $S = \underline{L \text{ after } \sigma}$. Note that the transitions with δ labels are implicitly added to the *out* set when appropriate. Therefore, the EXPLORER does not have to deal with the δ-closure of the LTS it represents.

Given the computed menus *in*, *out*, the DRIVER component decides how to proceed with the testing. The algorithm is given in Fig. 3. In principle, the DRIVER has to choose between the three different possibilities that have been given for the *ioco* test-case algorithm in Section 2.1: i) termination, ii) applying an input in set *in*, or iii) waiting for an output.

```
Algorithm Compute_Menu
1    input: Set of states S
2    output: Set of transitions in, out
3    in := ∅
4    out := ∅
5    already_explored := ∅
6    foreach s ∈ S
7        already_explored := already_explored ∪ {s}
8        S := S \ {s}
9        is_quiescent := true
10       foreach q →a q' ∈ Spec.→ ∩ ({s} × Act ∪ {τ} × L.S)
11           if a = τ
12               is_quiescent := false
13               if q' ∉ already_explored : S := S ∪ {q'}
14           else :
15               if a ∈ L_I : in := in ∪ {q →a q'}
16               else :
17                   out := out ∪ {q →a q'}
18                   is_quiescent := false
19       end
20       if is_quiescent : out := out ∪ {s →δ s}
21   end
22   return(in, out)
```

Fig. 2. Menu computation

With the variables *wait* and *stop* we denote a probabilistic choice: whenever one of them is references they are either **false** or **true**. The driver control loop therefore terminates with probability one. The choice between ii) and iii) is also done probabilistically: if the ADAPTER has no observation to offer to the DRIVER, the variable *wait* is consulted. To describe the algorithm of the DRIVER, we enhance the definition of $\cdot$ **after** $\cdot$ to menus. If M is a menu, then we define $\underline{M \text{ after } a} = \{q' \mid (q \xrightarrow{a} q') \in M\}$.

```
Algorithm Driver_Control_Loop
1    input: —
2    output: Verdict pass or fail
3    (in, out) = Compute_Menu({s_0})
4    while ¬stop :
5        if ADAPTER.has_output() ∨ wait:
6            if out after ADAPTER.output() = ∅: terminate(fail)
7            (in, out) = Compute_Menu(out after ADAPTER.output())
8        else:
9            choose i? ∈ {a | q →a q' ∈ in}
10           if ADAPTER.apply_input(i?) :
11               (in, out) = Compute_Menu(in after i?)
12   end
13   terminate(pass)
```

Fig. 3. Driver Control Loop

Quiescence in Practice. From the specification point-of-view, quiescence is a reachability property. In the real world, a non-quiescent implementation will produce an output after some finite amount time. If an implementation never produces an output, it is quiescent. Therefore, from an implementation point-of-view, quiescence can be seen as a timing property, and one that can not be detected in finite time. In theory, this makes quiescence detection impossible. However, in practice it is possible to work with approximations to quiescence. A system that is supposed to work at a fast pace, like in the order of milli-seconds, can certainly be considered as being quiescent, if after two days of waiting no output has appeared. Even two hours, if not two minutes of waiting might be a sufficient to conclude that the system is quiescent. It seems to be plausible to approximate quiescence by waiting for a properly chosen time interval after the occurrence of the latest event. This is the approach chosen for TORX. The responsibility to detect quiescence and to send a synthetic action, the *quiescence signal*, lies with the ADAPTER.

2.3   *tioco* Testing Theory

Even though development of the *tioco* theory and our own work described here has been mostly independent from each other, some important decisions made for *tioco* have been adapted for our own approach.

In *tioco*, the formalism used to model specification and implementation of timed systems are so-called *timed transition systems* with input and output labels (TIOTS). Timed transition systems are LTS with an explicit notion of time and delay. An implementation relation **tioco** is defined, and also a test-case derivation algorithm. *tioco* is meant as an extension of *ioco* to timed testing. Therefore, the theory has to deal with quiescence. As explained in Section 2.2, quiescence is in real life a property related to time, and the methods to approximate the occurrence of quiescence is reused from the approach chosen for TORX. However, since TIOTS have an explicit notion of time, the quiescence approximation approach has to be taken explicitly into account in the definition of test-cases. It is in principle straightforward to define quiescence on the level of TIOTS in terms of reachability, but the derived test-cases must define explicitly when a δ is allowed to be *observed*. In order to define this unambiguously, an assumption is made which must be met by an implementation in order to ensure the soundness of *tioco* testing.

Definition 1 (*tioco* Quiescence Prerequisite). *For an implementation Impl there is an $M \in \mathbb{R}$ such that*

- *Impl produces an output within M time units, counted from the last input or output, or,*
- *if it does not, then Impl is quiescent.*

It is in general the responsibility of the system designer to ensure that this assumption holds and to provide a reasonable value for M. In general, there will be systems which can never fulfil this property. Quiescence for TIOTS is (informally) defined as follows.

Definition 2 (*tioco* Quiescence). *A state in a TIOTS is quiescent iff there is no state reachable by τ-steps or by delaying, where a transition with an output label is enabled.*

Note that this definition of quiescence is more general than the one for *ioco*. A state that can make a τ-step can in *tioco* still be considered as quiescent, whereas in *ioco* not.

Related to the handling of quiescence is another property in the *tioco* theory which we adopt: the *no-forced-input* property. A system must not be forced to get inputs at a certain time in order to proceed. This basically states that if a state is quiescent, *i.e.*, if it can only proceed by accepting inputs, it must be ensured that there is no urgency requirement on the application of an input. If a state in an TIOTS specification waits for inputs, it must be allowed to wait for these inputs forever.

3   Absolute-Time Timed Automata

The input formalism chosen for our timed-testing extensions of TorX are non-deterministic safety timed automata [10]. In this section we will introduce the necessary background needed to describe our testing approach.

3.1   From Timed Automata to Zones

Our approach makes use of zone-based semantics of timed automata known from the literature. A comprehensive treatment on semantics and algorithms for timed and zone automata is given in [5]. In the following we will give a nano-tutorial on this subject.

A time domain $\mathbb{T}$ is a totally ordered, well-founded additive monoid with neutral element 0 that is also the minimum in the ordering, and with $d + d' \leq d$ iff $d' = 0$, for all $d \in \mathbb{T}$. In the following we assume a fixed time domain $\mathbb{T}$. Let $\mathcal{C}$ be a set of clock variables. An *atomic clock-constraint* is an inequality of the form $b_l \prec x - y \prec b_u$ or $b_l \prec x \prec b_u$, for $x, y \in \mathcal{C}$, $\prec \in \{<, \leq\}$, and $b_l, b_u \in \mathbb{T}$ with $b_l \leq b_u$. Clock constraints are conjunctions of atomic clock constraints. The set of all clock constraints over clock set $\mathcal{C}$ is denoted by $\mathcal{B}(\mathcal{C})$. Atomic clock constraints of the form $b_l \prec x - y \prec b_u$ are also called *clock-difference constraint*.

Definition 3 (Timed Automaton). *A timed automaton T is a tuple $(N, \mathcal{C}, Act, l_0, E, I)$, where*

- *N is a finite set of locations,*
- *$\mathcal{C}$ is a set of clock variables,*
- *Act is a set of labels,*
- *$l_0 \in N$ is the initial location,*
- *$E \subseteq N \times \mathcal{B}(\mathcal{C}) \times Act \cup \{\tau\} \times 2^{\mathcal{C}} \times N$ is the set of edges*
- *$I : N \rightarrow \mathcal{B}(\mathcal{C})$ assigns invariants to locations.*

We define $\mathcal{A}(Act)$ to be the set of timed automata over the label set Act.

The edges $(l, g, a, r, l') \in E$ are abbreviated $l \xrightarrow{g,a,r} l'$, where $g \in \mathcal{B}(\mathcal{C})$ is called *guard* of the edge, and $r \subseteq \mathcal{C}$ *clock reset*. Guards and invariants are clock constraints. Note that in the literature the set of clocks is usually not explicitly mentioned in the definition of a timed automaton, but in the following it is necessary to remember on which set of clocks the semantics of a timed automaton is defined.

A *clock valuation* is a function $u : \mathcal{C} \to \mathbb{T}$. For $d \in \mathbb{T}$, we define $(u + d)(c) = u(c) + d$. If a valuation u satisfies a clock constraint $C \in \mathcal{B}(\mathcal{C})$, *i.e.*, if the relational expression obtained by replacing all occurrences of clock names c by $u(c)$ evaluates to true, we write $u \in C$. If $r \subseteq \mathcal{C}$, then $u[r \mapsto 0](c) = 0$, if $c \in r$, and $u[r \mapsto 0](c) = u(c)$, otherwise.

The semantics of a timed automaton is a transition system where states are pairs (l, u) of locations and clock valuations. Initial state is $(l_0, \{c \mapsto 0 \mid c \in \mathcal{C}\})$. Transitions are defined as follows.

$$\frac{u \in I(l) \quad (u+d) \in I(l)}{(l,u) \xrightarrow{d} (l,u+d)} (d \in \mathbb{T}) \qquad \frac{l \xrightarrow{g,a,r} l' \quad u \in g \quad u' = u[r \mapsto 0] \quad u' \in I(l')}{(l,u) \xrightarrow{a} (l',u')} \tag{1}$$

If $\mathbb{T}$ is a continuous set, like $\mathbb{R}^+$, the transition system defined by the two rules have a continuous state-space. It is well known, however, that under certain conditions it is possible to abstract from the continuous transitions defined above, and derive a discrete representation of the timed automaton, the *region automaton* [1]. More efficient in time and space however is the construction of a *zone automaton* [5], which is an abstraction of the region automaton. A *clock zone* is the maximal set of clock valuations that satisfy a given clock constraint. In order to define the semantics of a timed automaton in terms of a zone automaton, a number of operations on clock zones are defined (in decreasing order of precedence). The time-passing operator $\Uparrow z$, which is defined as $\Uparrow z = \{u + d \mid u \in z, d \in \mathbb{T}\}$; Conjunction of clock zones $z \wedge z'$, defined as $z \wedge z' = z \cap z'$. Clock reset $z[r \mapsto 0]$ for $r \subseteq \mathcal{C}$, defined as $z[r \mapsto 0] = \{u[r \mapsto 0] \mid u \in z\}$.

We denote the set of all clock zones on clocks in $\mathcal{C}$ as $\mathcal{Z}(\mathcal{C})$, or just $\mathcal{Z}$, if $\mathcal{C}$ is clear from the context. We define $Succ(z, i, g, r, i') = (\Uparrow z \wedge i \wedge g)[r \mapsto 0] \wedge i'$ for clock zone $z \in \mathcal{Z}$, clock resets $r \subseteq \mathcal{C}$ and clock constraints i, g, i'.

The state space of a zone automaton underlying a timed automaton $T = (N, \mathcal{C}, Act, l_0, E, I)$ is a sub-set of $N \times \mathcal{Z}$, and, following [5], its elements are called *zones* (without "*clock-*"). The zone automaton $ZA(T)$ of T is a labelled transitions system $(S, s_0, Act, \twoheadrightarrow) \in \mathcal{L}(Act)$, where $S \subseteq N \times \mathcal{Z}$, $s_0 = (l_0, \{c = 0 \mid c \in \mathcal{C}\})$, and $\twoheadrightarrow$ is defined by the following rule:

$$\frac{l \xrightarrow{g,a,r} l' \quad z' = Succ(z, I(l), g, r, I(l')) \neq \emptyset}{(l, z) \xrightarrow{a} (l', z')}. \tag{2}$$

Zone automata derived by this rule are discrete, but in general still infinite. For a certain class of timed automata it is however possible to construct a finite quotient of zones by so-called normalisation (*cf.* [5]). The use of normalisation will however not be necessary for our purposes.

3.2   Absolute Time in Zone Automata

For our testing approach we have decided to measure time absolutely, *i.e.*, testing-relevant events like the application of an input to the IUT or the observation of an output from the IUT is time stamped in absolute time, measured from "system start". When "system start" is, is an arbitrary choice. Using absolute time does not have any particular advantage or disadvantage. Our approach would work equally well with relative time, *i.e.*, with measurements of the time that passes between two observable events. The choice for absolute time was the fact that some simple computations on time stamps were not necessary.

We have therefore to introduce a notion of absolute time in timed automata. We do this by introducing a special clock, denoted by ABS, a clock which is never referenced in the considered timed automaton, and which therefore is never reset. So, if $T = (N, C, Act, l_0, E, I)$ is a timed automaton, we define the absolute-time version $\text{ABS}(T)$ of T as $T = (N, C \cup \{\text{ABS}\}, Act, l_0, E, I)$. Note that clock zones are defined relative to a clock set. All clocks in the clock set are considered in order to compute successor clock zones. Adding ABS to the clock set adds therefore one more dimension to the clock zones. We define the absolute-time zone automaton of a timed automaton T with clock set $T.C$ as the zone automaton $ZA(\text{ABS}(T))$. Given a zone $q = (l, z)$ of $\text{ABS}(T)$, the valuations of the absolute time clock ABS in clock zone z describes the time interval in which it is allowed to sojourn in zone q. In the following, we will denote the projection of a clock zone $z \in \mathcal{Z}(C \cup \{\text{ABS}\})$ on the absolute times scale as $z^{\downarrow}$, *i.e.*, $z^{\downarrow} = \{u(\text{ABS}) \mid u \in z\}$.

3.3   Inputs and Outputs in Timed Automata

We distinguish again a set of input labels, L_I, and a set of output labels, L_U, and special symbol δ to denote quiescence. We consider now the set of timed automata $\mathcal{A}(L_I \cup L_U)$.

The semantics of timed automata, as defined with (1) defines a timed transition system (TTS), and assuming the label sets L_I and L_U for the timed automaton, this TTS is a TIOTS. Therefore, we can apply in principle the quiescence definition of [6] to define quiescence for Timed Automata with inputs and outputs. The definition is however not useful to detect quiescence *algorithmically*. Fortunately, it is possible to express the conditions for quiescence on the level of the timed automaton itself, by modifying and adding switches. Similar to the *ioco* case, we will call such a modified version of a timed automaton T the δ-closure of T. The definition of the δ-closure below takes the *tioco* definition of quiescence as well as the *tioco* Quiescence Prerequisite (*cf.* Definitions 1 and 2) into account. We therefore assume the existence of a real number M which is mentioned in Definition 1, and denote the δ-closure of T as $\Delta_M(T)$.

Definition 4 (δ-closure of a timed automaton). *Let $T = (N, C, Act, l_0, E, I)$ be a timed automaton with $Act = L_I \cup L_U$, and let $M \in \mathbb{R}, M > 0$. Then the δ-closure $\Delta_M(T)$ of T is a timed automaton $(N', C', Act', l'_0, E', I')$, where $N' = N$, $C' = C \cup \{\text{QC}\}$, $Act' = Act \cup \{\delta\}$, $l'_0 = l_0$, $I' = I$, and $E' = E_1 \cup E_2 \cup E_3 \cup E_4$ with $E_1 = \{(e.l, e.g \wedge (\text{QC} < M), e.a, e.r \cup \{\text{QC}\}, e.l') \mid e \in E \wedge e.a \in L_U\}$, $E_2 = \{(e.l, e.g, e.a, e.r \cup \{\text{QC}\}, e.l') \mid e \in E \wedge e.a \in L_I\}$, $E_3 = \{e \mid e \in E \wedge e.a = \tau\}$ and $E_4 = \{(l, \text{QC} > M, \delta, \emptyset, l) \mid l \in N\}$.*

The idea behind this definition is the following. The assumption is that the IUT fulfils the *tioco* Quiescence Prerequisite. Therefore, it will only produce outputs within M time units since the last input or output has been seen. This means that in the specification every location in which it is allowed to stay after M time units have passed, a δ should be accepted. Moreover, if more then M time units have passed, no output in the timed automaton needs to be enabled anymore. Therefore, we add the clock QC $\notin C$. It measures the time since the last observable behaviour of the IUT has happened. Consequently, every switch which has an input or output label resets clock QC. The δ label is added to the action set, and every location in N gets a self-loop switch with δ label, which is only enabled if QC $> M$. The set E' thus comprises the disjoint sets $E_1, \ldots, E_4$. E_1 contains all edges of E with output label, where the guards are extended with the constraint QC $< M$. QC is reset if the switch is taken. E_2 contains all edges of E with an input label, but with the clock reset extended by QC again. E_3 contains all (unmodified) switches of E with a τ label. E_4 contains only self-loops with δ label. These switches denote the occurrence of a quiescence signal. The guard for all of these switches is QC $> M$. Note that the clock QC is not reset, since otherwise switches with output labels could become enabled again.

Similar to the *tioco* theory, we postulate the *no-forced-input* property (see Section 2.3, *cf.* [6]). In the context of timed automata, we thus require that, whenever it is possible to accept quiescence in a location, it must always be possible to stay in that location forever.

4   Timed Automata Testing with TorX

The timed testing approach we have implemented in TorX is based on the absolute-time zone automata, derived from δ-closed timed automata.

4.1   Test-Cases

In order to define the test-cases we are executing with TorX, we adapt the definition of $\cdot$ **after** $\cdot$ (*cf.* Section 2.1) to work on zones.

Definition 5 ($\cdot$ after$_t$ $\cdot$). *Let $T = (N, C, L_I \cup L_U, l_0, E, I)$ be a timed automaton, and let $ZA(\mathrm{ABS}(\Delta(T))) = (S, s_0, L_I \cup L_U \cup \{\delta\}, \longrightarrow)$ the absolute-time zone automaton derived from its δ-closure. Let $S' \subseteq S$. Then, for $a \in L_I \cup L_U \cup \{\delta\}$ and $t \in \mathbb{T}$,*

$$S' \text{ after}_t\ a@t = \{(l', z'') \mid \exists (l, z) \in S' : (l, z) \xrightarrow{a} (l', z')$$
$$\text{and } z'' = (z' \wedge \mathrm{ABS} = t) \neq \emptyset\} \tag{3}$$

The set S' **after**$_t$ $a@t$ contains all those zones which can be reached by executing action a at time t from clock zones in S'. Moreover, the successor zones reflect the fact that $\mathrm{ABS} = t$ at the time of entering.

Based on this definition, we can give a semi-formal definition of the timed test-cases that are being executed with TorX. As for *ioco* (*cf.* Section 2.1), we

Table 1. Computation of menus from timed automata

```
Algorithm Compute_Menu_TA
1     input:  Set of zones S
2     output: Set of zone automata transitions in, out
3     in := ∅
4     out := ∅
5     already_explored := ∅
6     foreach s = (l, z) ∈ S
7         already_explored := already_explored ∪ {s}
8         S := S \ {s}
9         foreach e ∈ {e' ∈ E | e.l = l}
10            if z' = Succ(z, I(e.l), e.g, e.r, I(e.l')) ≠ ∅ :
11                if e.a = τ: S := S ∪ {(e.l', z')}
12                else :
13                    if e.a ∈ L_I : in := in ∪ {s ─ᵃ→ (e.l', z')}
14                    else : out := out ∪ {s ─ᵃ→ (e.l', z')}
15            end
16        end
17    return(in, out)
```

express the test-cases in a process-algebra-like notation[1]. We distinguish again three steps.

1. $T :=$ **pass** is a test-case;
2. Application of input:

$$T := i@t; T' \quad + \sum_{\substack{t' < t \land o \in L_U \\ S \ \mathbf{after_t} \ o@t' = \emptyset}} o@t'; \mathbf{fail} \quad + \sum_{\substack{t' < t \land o \in L_U \\ S \ \mathbf{after_t} \ o@t' \neq \emptyset}} o@t'; T_{o@t'}$$

for $i \in L_I$ and for $t \in \mathbb{T}$ chosen such that $S' = \underline{S \ \mathbf{after_t} \ i@t} \neq \emptyset$, and for T' being a test-case derived from S', and the $T_{o@t'}$ test-cases derived from $\underline{S \ \mathbf{after_t} \ o@t'}$. Note that it is necessary to take outputs into account which do arrive at the time $t' < t$.

3. Waiting for outputs or signalling of quiescence:

$$T := \sum_{\substack{o \in L_U \cup \{\delta\} \\ S \ \mathbf{after_t} \ o@t = \emptyset}} o@t; \mathbf{fail} \quad + \sum_{\substack{o \in L_U \cup \{\delta\} \\ S \ \mathbf{after_t} \ o@t \neq \emptyset}} o@t; T_{o@t}.$$

Here, all outputs including δ are considered. The outputs $o@t$ which yield an empty successor set $\underline{S \ \mathbf{after} \ o@t}$ result in a test failure. All other outputs lead to a test-case $T_{o@t}$, where $T_{o@t}$ is derived from $\underline{S \ \mathbf{after} \ o@t} \neq \emptyset$.

---

[1] semi-formal: we do abuse the Σ sign to denote non-deterministic choice over a potentially continuous set of possibilities, which is not well-defined.

Table 2. DRIVER control loop for timed systems

```
Algorithm Driver_Control_Loop_TA
1    input: —
2    output: Verdict pass or fail
3    (in, out) = Compute_Menu_TA({(l₀, {x = 0 | x ∈ C})})
4    while ¬ stop:
5      if ADAPTER.has_output() ∨ wait:
6        o@t := ADAPTER.output()
7        if out afterₜ o@t = ∅: terminate(fail)
8        (in, out) := Compute_Menu_TA(out afterₜ o@t, t)
9      else:
10       choose i@t ∈ {a@t' | (l, z) —ᵃ→ (l, z') ∈ in ∧ t' ∈ z'↓}
11       if ADAPTER.apply_input(i@t):
12         (in, out) = Compute_Menu_TA(in afterₜ i@t, t)
13     end
14   terminate(pass)
```

4.2   Menu Computation

In Table 1 the algorithm for menu computation **Compute_Menu_TA** is given. We assume a timed automaton $Spec \in \mathcal{A}(L_I \cup L_U)$ and consider its δ-closure $\Delta_M(Spec)$ for an appropriately chosen value M. The input of the algorithm is a set of zones S derived from $(ZA(\text{ABS}(\Delta_M(Spec))))$ (line 1). The output comprises two sets, the *in* menu and the *out* menu. (lines 3, 4, 17). The set *already_explored* is used to keep track of zones already explored (line 5). We have an outer loop over all states (*i.e.*, zones (l, z)) in the set S (lines 6–16). The contents of S varies during the computation. All states considered inside the loop are added to *already_explored* and removed from S (lines 7, 8). The inner loop (line 9 – 15) considers every switch e with source location l. First, the successor clock zone z' of z according to switch e is computed (line 10). If z' is not empty, transitions of the zone automaton are added to the sets *in* or *out*, depending on the labels of switch e (lines 11–14). Note that transitions with label δ are added to the *out* menu. In case of a τ label, the resulting zone is added to set S (line 11). In essence, the menu computation is a bounded state-space exploration of the zone automaton with sorting of the generated transitions according to their labels.

4.3   Driver Control Loop

We enhance the definition of $\cdot$ **after**$_t$ $\cdot$ to menus.

Definition 6 ($\cdot$ **after**$_t$ $\cdot$). *Let $T = (N, C, Act, l_0, E, I)$ be a timed automaton, and let $ZA(\text{ABS}(T)) = (S, s_0, Act, \longrightarrow)$ be its absolute-time zone automaton. Let $M \subseteq \longrightarrow$. Then, for $a \in Act$ and $t \in \mathbb{T}$,*

$$M \textbf{ after}_t \, a@t = \{(l', z'') \mid (l, z) \xrightarrow{a} (l', z') \in M$$
$$and \ z'' = (z' \wedge \text{ABS} = t) \neq \emptyset\} \qquad (4)$$

If the set M is a menu computed by **Compute_Menu_TA**, each transition $(l, z) \xrightarrow{a} (l', z')$ contains the interval of all times at which a us allowed to happen: the interval $z'^{\downarrow}$. The set M **after$_t$** $a@t$ then computes a set of successor zones from M which can be reached by executing a at exactly time t. For a zone $(l, z) \in M$ **after$_t$** $a@t$, $z^{\downarrow} = [t, t]$ holds.

In Table 2, we see the algorithm for the DRIVER control loop of TORX, enhanced to deal with time. Menus are computed with **Compute_Menu_TA**, and the successor states are computed with $\cdot$ **after$_t$** $\cdot$. When an input is applied, not only an input $i? \in in$ is chosen, but also a time instance $t \in z'^{\downarrow}$ (line 10), at which time to apply the input.

The variables *wait* and *stop* have the same meaning as in the *ioco* algorithm (*cf.* Section 2.2).

4.4   *ioco*, *tioco*, and TorX

The algorithms for menu computation and test execution are very similar to the ones implemented for untimed TORX. However, there are some slight differences, which we will comment here.

The most important difference is that the δ-closure of the timed automaton can not be computed anymore by the PRIMER. Rather, the δ-closure is done beforehand, and the primer does not need to distinguish anymore between a δ label and arbitrary outputs. The reason for this is that quiescence is a timing property that has to be dealt with on zone-automaton level. These computations are however in the responsibility of the EXPLORER. As a consequence, contrary to our initial hopes, the algorithms that existed for untimed TORX can not be reused. However, the changes are simple and the principle remains the same.

Another big difference is that we allow for the more general definition of quiescence from the *tioco* theory. Attempts to use the more restricted *ioco* definition turned out to be not successful, since unsound test-cases could be produced.

5   Timed Testing in Practice

5.1   Notes on the Testing Hypothesis

The *Testing Hypothesis* is an important ingredient in the testing theory of Tretmans [14]. The hypothesis is that the IUT can be modelled by means of the model class which forms the basis of the testing theory. In case of *ioco* the assumption is that the IUT can be modelled as an input-enabled IOTS. Under this assumption, the results on soundness and completeness of *ioco*-testing do apply to the practical testing approach. In this paper, we have not defined a formalism that we consider as model for an implementation, so we can not really speak of a *testing hypothesis*. Still, it is important to give some hints on what properties a real IUT should have in order to make timed testing feasible. We mention four points.

First, we require input enabledness, as for the untimed case. That means, whenever it is decided to apply an input to the IUT, it is accepted, regardless of whether this input really does cause a non-trivial state-change of the IUT or not.

Second, it is plausible to postulate that all time measurements are done relative to the same clock that the IUT refers to. In practice this means that the TORX ADAPTER should run on the same host as the IUT and reference the same hardware clock. If measurements would be done by different clocks, measurement errors caused by clock skew and drifts might spoil the measurement, and thus the test run.

Third, as has been pointed out in Section 2.3, the *system designer* has to ensure that the implementation behaves such that quiescence can be detected according to Section 2.3, Def. 1.

Fourth, up to now we left open which time domain $\mathbb{T}$ to choose for our approach. The standard time domain used for timed automata are real numbers, however, in practice only floating-point numbers, rather than real numbers can be used. Early experiments have however shown that floats and doubles quite quickly cause numerical problems. Comparisons of time stamps turn out to be to inexact due to rounding and truncation errors. In the TORX implementation we use thus fixed-precision numbers, *i.e.,* 64 bit integers, counting micro-seconds. This happens to be the time representation used for the UNIX operating system family.

5.2   Limitations of Timed Testing

Even though the timed testing approach described in this paper seems to be easy enough, timed testing is not easy at all. Time is a complicated natural phenomenon. It can't be stopped. It can not be created artificially in a lab environment. Time runs forward, it runs everywhere, and, leaving Einstein aside, everywhere at the same pace. For timed testing this means that there is no time to waste. The testing apparatus, TORX, in this case, must not influence the outcome of the testing approach. However, the execution of TORX does consume time, and the question is when the execution time of TORX does influence the testing.

- Assume that input $i?$ is allowed to be applied at time $0 \leq t \leq b$. Assume that the testing tool needs $b/2$ to prepare to apply the input. Then the input can never be applied between time 0 and $b/2$. If there is an error hiding in this time interval, it will not be detected.
- Assume that the tester is too slow to apply $i?$ before b. Then this input can not be applied, and some behaviour of the IUT might never be exercised.

This basically means that the speed of the testing tool and the speed of communication between tester and IUT determine the maximal speed of the IUT that can be reliably tested.

Springintveld et al. [13] define an algorithm to derive test-cases for testing timed automata. They prove that their approach to test timed automata is possible and even complete, but in practice infeasible, due to the enormous number of test-cases to be run. This is likely also the case for our approach and thus limits the extend to which timed testing can be useful. Automatic selection of meaningful test-cases might be an important ingredient in future extensions of our approach. For the time being, our goal is to find out how far we can get with timed testing *as is* in practice. This will be subject of our further research.

6   Conclusions and Further Work

In this paper we have presented Timed TorX, a tool for on-the-fly real-time testing. We use non-deterministic safety timed automata as input formalism to describe system specifications, and we demonstrate how to use standard algorithms for zone-computations in order to make our approach work. It turns out that the existing TorX algorithms, especially in the PRIMER and DRIVER can in principle be reused in order to deal with time. The major difference is that the δ-closure of the specification is now an explicit step, and cab not be done implicitly in the PRIMER anymore.

Our approach is strongly related to the *tioco* testing theory [6]. Esp. the notion of quiescence we have defined in Section 3.3 is strongly motivated by the *tioco* definition. We have much confidence that the δ-closure we have defined for timed automata ensures that the test-cases and the on-the-fly testing algorithm as presented in this paper are indeed an instantiation of the *tioco* theory. However, a formal proof of this assertion has still to be provided.

Timed testing relies on precise measurement of time stamps, but measurement errors can never be avoided. Timed automata live in an ideal world. It is perfectly normal to specify that a particular output should occur exactly two seconds after a certain input. But what if the output comes after 2.001 seconds? Should this considered to be a failure or not? One approach would be to allow for slack, *i.e.*, don't allow for discrete values but for intervals in the specification of occurrence times. However, this defers the problem only to the boundary of the intervals. An approach that is currently considered is to go away from hard pass/fail verdicts, but to define continuous metrics which allow to express quantitatively how far an implementation deviates from the specification. Work on this is based on [7].

Acknowledgements. We thank Conrado Daws, Ed Brinksma and Laura Brandán Briones for discussions on timed automata, *tioco* theory and timed testing in general. Furthermore we thank Jan Tretmans for helpful comments on quiescence. Tim Willemse pointed out a mistake in an earlier approach to implement quiescence.

References

1. R. Alur and D. L. Dill. A theory of timed automata. *Theor. Comp. Science*, 126(2):183–235, 1994.
2. A. Belinfante. Timed testing with TorX: The Oosterschelde storm surge barrier. In M. Gijsen, editor, *Handout 8e Nederlandse Testdag*, Rotterdam, 2002. CMG.

3. A. Belinfante, J. Feenstra, L. Heerink, and R. G. de Vries. Specification based formal testing: The easylink case study. In *2nd Workshop Emb. Systems (PROGRESS '01)*, pages 73–82, 2001.
4. A. Belinfante, J. Feenstra, R.G. de Vries, J. Tretmans, N. Goga, L. Feijs, S. Mauw, and L. Heerink. Formal test automation: A simple experiment. In G. Csopaki, S. Dibuz, and K. Tarnay, editors, 12th *Int. Workshop on Testing of Communicating Systems*, pages 179–196. Kluwer, 1999.
5. Johan Bengtsson and Wang Yi. Timed automata: Semantics, algorithms and tools. In J. Desel, W. Reisig, and G. Rozenberg, editors, *Lectures on Concurrency and Petri Nets:*, volume 3098 of *LNCS*, pages 87–124. Springer–Verlag, 2004.
6. Laura Brandán Briones and Ed Brinksma. A test generation framework for quiescent real-time systems. In J. Grabowski and B. Nielsen, editors, *Formal Approaches to Testing of Software (FATES '04)*, volume 3395 of *LNCS*, pages 64–78, 2005.
7. L. de Alfaro, M. Faella, and M. Stoelinga. Linear and branching metrics for quantatative transition systems. In *Proc. ICALP'04*, volume 3142 of *LNCS*, pages 97–109. Springer–Verlag, 2004.
8. J-C. Fernandez, C. Jard, T. Jeron, and C. Viho. Using on-the-fly verification techniques for the generation of test suites. In R. Alur and T.A. Henzinger, editors, *Computer Aided Verification (CAV '96)*, volume 1102 of *LNCS*, pages 348–359. Springer-Verlag, 1996.
9. J-C. Fernandez, C. Jard, T. Jeron, and C. Viho. An experiment in automatic generation of test suites for protocols with verification technology. *Science of Computer Programming*, 29(1–2):123–146, 1997. Special Issue on COST 247, Verification and Validation Methods for Formal Descriptions.
10. T. A. Henzinger, X. Nicollin, J. Sifakis, and S. Yovine. Symbolic model checking for real-time systems. *Journal Inf. and Comp.*, 111(2):193–244, 1994.
11. M. Krichen and S. Tripakis. Black-box conformance testing for real-time systems. In S. Graf and L. Mounier, editors, *Proc. 11th Int. SPIN Workshop (SPIN 2004)*, volume 2989 of *LNCS*, pages 109–126. Springer-Verlag, 2004.
12. M. Mikucionis, B. Nielsen, and K. G. Larsen. Real-time system testing on-the-fly. In K. Sere and M. Waldén, editors, *15th Nordic Workshop on Programming Theory*, number 34, pages 36–38. Abo Akademi, Department of Computer Science, Finland, 2003.
13. J.G. Springintveld, F.W. Vaandrager, and P.R. D'Argenio. Testing timed automata. *Theoretical Computer Science*, 254(1–2):225–257, 2001.
14. J. Tretmans. Test Generation with Inputs, Outputs and Repetitive Quiescence. *Software—Concepts and Tools*, 17(3):103–120, 1996.
15. J. Tretmans and H. Brinksma. Torx: Automated model based testing. In A. Hartman and K. Dussa-Ziegler, editors, *Proc. 1st European Conf. on Model-Driven Software Engineering*, Nürnberg, 2003.

Automatic Verification and Conformance Testing for Validating Safety Properties of Reactive Systems*

Vlad Rusu, Hervé Marchand, and Thierry Jéron

IRISA/INRIA, Campus de Beaulieu, Rennes, France
First.Last@irisa.fr

Abstract. This paper presents a combination of verification and conformance testing techniques for the formal validation of reactive systems. A formal specification of a system, which may be infinite-state, and a set of safety properties are assumed. Each property is verified on the specification using automatic techniques based on abstract interpretation, which are sound, but, as a price to pay for automation, are not necessarily complete. Next, for each property, a test case is automatically generated from the specification and the property, and is executed on a black-box implementation of the system to detect violations of the property by the implementation and non-conformances between implementation and specification. If the verification step did not conclude, the test execution may also detect violations of the property by the specification.

Keywords: verification, conformance testing, symbolic test generation

1 Introduction

Formal verification and conformance testing are two well-established approaches for validating reactive systems. Both approaches consist in checking the consistency between two representations of a system:

- formal verification typically compares a formal *specification* of the system with respect to some higher-level required *properties*;
- conformance testing [1, 5] compares the observable behaviour of a black-box *implementation* of the system with that described by the specification.

A formal validation chain for reactive systems, combining verification and conformance testing, may naturally consist of the following steps:

1. the properties are automatically verified on the specification;
2. test cases are automatically derived from the specification and the properties;
3. the test cases are executed on the black-box implementation of the system, to check the satisfaction of the properties by the implementation and the conformance between implementation and specification.

---

* The full version of this paper is available as IRISA report [17].

J.S. Fitzgerald, I.J. Hayes, and A. Tarlecki (Eds.): FM 2005, LNCS 3582, pp. 189–204, 2005.

In this paper we formally define and study such a validation chain. We consider a general class of specifications which may be infinite-state (automata extended with variables, which communicate with the environment by means of inputs and outputs carrying parameters). In this setting, the verification step (in particular, for safety properties) is undecidable. In order to keep it automatic and ensure that it always terminates, we adopt approximate, conservative verification techniques based on abstract interpretation [7], which may either prove the property, or terminate with a "don't know" answer.

The main contribution of the paper lies in the second step of the proposed validation chain. It is a test generation algorithm that takes into account the infinite-state nature of the specifications and the incompleteness of the verification step. The algorithm takes as inputs a specification and a safety property, and produces a test case for checking the conformance between a given implementation and the specification, and the satisfaction of the safety property by the implementation. To deal with infinite-state specifications and properties, the algorithm is *symbolic*: it does not attempt to enumerate the (potentially infinite) domain of the specification's variables, but deals with the variables by means of symbolic computations. As a consequence of the incompleteness of the verification step, the test cases generated by our algorithm may also detect violations of the property by the *specification* when executed on the *implementation*. Hence, test execution may detect one or several of the following inconsistencies:

– violation of the property by the specification,
– violation of the property by the implementation,
– violation of conformance between implementation and specification.

These results are returned to the user in the form of test verdicts, and may be employed to fix errors in the implementation, specification, or the properties.

The rest of the paper is organised as follows. Section 2 presents the model of Input-Output Symbolic Transition Systems (IOSTS) and, in Section 3 we set the framework for verification and testing using IOSTS as the underlying model.

Section 4 defines our symbolic test generation algorithm. The algorithm is proved correct, in the sense that the verdicts returned by test execution correctly characterise the relations between implementation, specification, and property. Moreover, the (infinite) set of all test cases generated in this manner may, in principle, discover all implementations that do not conform to a given specification according to the standard **ioco** relation [19]. As a by-product of the correctness proofs, we show that **ioco**-conformance with respect to a given specification is a safety property. We also provide a symbolic construction of the canonical tester [4] for **ioco**-conformance with respect to a given specification.

Section 5 outlines a technique for optimising test cases towards detecting the violation of the property. We show that this optimisation preserves the correctness of the test verdicts. The overall approach is illustrated on a simple example. The full version of this paper [17] contains a larger example (the Bounded Retransmission Protocol [11]) and provides proofs of the results.

2   The IOSTS Model

The model of Input-Output Symbolic Transition Systems (IOSTS) is inspired from I/O automata [15]. Unlike I/O automata, IOSTS do not require *input-completeness* (i.e., all input actions do not need to be enabled all the time).

Definition 1 (IOSTS). *An IOSTS is a tuple* $\langle D, \Theta, Q, q^0, \Sigma, T \rangle$ *where*

- *D is a finite set of typed* Data, *partitioned into a set V of variables and a set P of parameters. For $d \in D$, type(d) denotes the type of d.*
- *Θ is the initial condition, a Boolean expression on V,*
- *Q is a nonempty, finite set of locations and $q^0 \in Q$ is the initial location.*
- *Σ is a nonempty, finite alphabet, which is the disjoint union of a set $\Sigma^?$ of input actions and a set $\Sigma^!$ of output actions[1]. For each action $a \in \Sigma$, its signature $sig(a) = \langle p_1, \ldots, p_k \rangle \in P^k$ ($k \in \mathbb{N}$) is a tuple of parameters.*
- *T is a set of transitions. Each transition is a tuple $\langle q, a, G, A, q' \rangle$ made of:*
  - *a location $q \in Q$, called the origin of the transition.*
  - *an action $a \in \Sigma$ called the action of the transition.*
  - *a Boolean expression G on $V \cup sig(a)$, called the guard.*
  - *an assignment A, which is a set of expressions of the form $(x := A^x)_{x \in V}$ such that, for each $x \in V$, the right-hand side A^x of the assignment $x := A^x$ is an expression on $V \cup sig(a)$.*
  - *a location $q' \in Q$ called the destination of the transition.*

A simple example of IOSTS is depicted in Figure 1. This system expects a *START* input carrying an integer parameter p, and saves the value of p into the variable x. Then, as long as x is strictly positive, its value is emitted to the environment via the output *MSG* carrying the parameter m. The variable x is decreased by 1, and when it reaches 0, the *STOP* output is emitted.

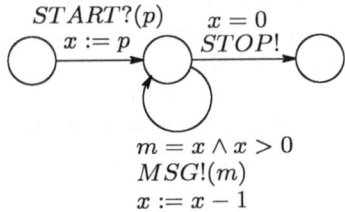

Fig. 1. Sample IOSTS S

Semantics. The semantics of IOSTS is described in terms of input-output labelled transitions systems (IOLTS).

---

[1] For simplicity, only input and output actions are considered here. A more detailed model, which also contains internal actions, is defined in the full paper.

Definition 2. *An IOLTS is a tuple* $\langle S, S^0, \Lambda, \rightarrow \rangle$ *where* S *is a set of* states, *which may be infinite,* $S^0 \subseteq S$ *is the set of* initial states, $\Lambda = \Lambda^? \cup \Lambda^!$ *is a set of (input or output)* actions, *and* $\rightarrow \subseteq S \times \Lambda \times S$ *is the* transition relation.

Intuitively, the IOLTS semantics of an IOSTS $\langle D = V \cup P, \Theta, Q, q^0, \Sigma, \mathcal{T} \rangle$ enumerates of the possible tuples of values (hereafter called *valuations*) of parameters P and variables V. Let $\mathcal{V}$ denote the set of valuations of the variables V, and Π denote the set of valuations of the parameters P. Then, for an expression E involving (a subset of) $V \cup P$, and for $\nu \in \mathcal{V}$, $\pi \in \Pi$, we denote by $E(\nu, \pi)$ the value obtained by substituting in E each variable by its value according to ν, and each parameter by its value according to π. For $P' \subseteq P$, we denote by $\Pi_{P'}$ the restriction of the set Π of valuations to the set P' of parameters.

Definition 3. *The semantics of an IOSTS* $\mathcal{S} = \langle D, \Theta, Q, q^0, \Sigma, \mathcal{T} \rangle$ *is an IOLTS* $[\![\mathcal{S}]\!] = \langle S, S^0, \Lambda, \rightarrow \rangle$, *defined as follows:*

- *the set of states is* $S = Q \times \mathcal{V}$,
- *the set of initial states is* $S^0 = q^0 \times \mathcal{V}^0$, *with* $\mathcal{V}^0 = \{\nu \in \mathcal{V} | \Theta(\nu) = true\}$
- *the set of actions* $\Lambda = \{\langle a, \pi \rangle | a \in \Sigma, \pi \in \Pi_{sig(a)}\}$, *also called the set of valued actions, is partitioned into the sets* $\Lambda^?$ *of valued inputs and* $\Lambda^!$ *of valued outputs, such that for* $\# \in \{?, !\}$, $\Lambda^{\#} = \{\langle a, \pi \rangle | a \in \Sigma^{\#}, \pi \in \Pi_{sig(a)}\}$.
- $\rightarrow$ *is the smallest relation in* $S \times \Lambda \times S$ *defined by the following rule:*

$$\frac{\langle q, \nu \rangle, \langle q', \nu' \rangle \in S \quad \langle a, \pi \rangle \in \Lambda \quad t = \langle q, a, G, A, q' \rangle \in \mathcal{T} \quad G(\nu, \pi) = true \quad \nu' = A(\nu, \pi)}{\langle q, \nu \rangle \xrightarrow{\langle a, \pi \rangle} \langle q', \nu' \rangle}$$

The rule says that the valued action $\langle a, \pi \rangle$ takes the system from a state $\langle q, \nu \rangle$ to a state $\langle q', \nu' \rangle$ if there exists a transition $t = \langle q, a, G, A, q' \rangle$ whose guard G evaluates to *true* when the variables evaluate according to ν and the parameters carried by the action a evaluate according to π. Then, the assignment A of the transition maps the pair (ν, π) to ν'.

Definition 4 (run). *A* run fragment *is a sequence of alternating states and valued actions* $s_1 \xrightarrow{\alpha_1} s_2 \xrightarrow{\alpha_2} \cdots s_{n-1} \xrightarrow{\alpha_{n-1}} s_n$. *A* run *is a run fragment that starts in an initial state.*

A state is *reachable* if it is the last state of a run. For a sequence $\sigma = \alpha_1 \alpha_2 \cdots \alpha_n$ of valued actions, we sometimes write $s \xrightarrow{\sigma} s'$ for $\exists s_1, \ldots s_{n+1} \in S$. $s = s_1 \xrightarrow{\alpha_1} s_2 \xrightarrow{\alpha_2} \cdots s_n \xrightarrow{\alpha_n} s_{n+1} = s'$. For a set of states $S' \subseteq S$ of the IOSTS we write $s \xrightarrow{\sigma} S'$ if there exists a state $s' \in S'$ such that $s \xrightarrow{\sigma} s'$.

Definition 5 (trace). *The* trace *of a run* ρ *is the projection of* ρ *on* $\Lambda^! \cup \Lambda^?$. *The set of traces of an IOSTS* $\mathcal{S}$ *is denoted by* Traces($\mathcal{S}$).

Let $F \subseteq Q$ be a set of locations of an IOSTS S. A run ρ is *recognised by* F if it ends in a state in $F \times V$. A trace is *recognised by* F if it is the projection on $\Lambda^! \cup \Lambda^?$ of a recognised run. The set of recognised traces is denoted by $RTraces(S, F)$.

An IOSTS is *deterministic* if in each location, the guards of the transitions labelled by the same action are mutually exclusive. All the IOSTS considered in this paper are deterministic. In the full version [17], more general IOSTS are also considered (nondeterministic IOSTS with internal actions). A symbolic *determinisation* operation, which consists in transforming a nondeterministic IOSTS into a deterministic one having the same set of traces, is also presented. The operation is proved correct and terminates for a subclass of IOSTS [20].

3   Verification and Conformance Testing with IOSTS

This section sets the framework for verification and conformance testing with IOSTS. First, we present a few operations on IOSTS, and then the satisfaction relation and the conformance relation between IOSTS are formally defined.

3.1   Parallel Product

The *parallel product* of two IOSTS is an IOSTS whose set of traces (resp. recognised traces) are the intersection of the set of traces (resp. recognised traces) of the operands. This operation imposes that the IOSTS have no shared variables, but are defined on the same alphabets of actions and same parameters.

Definition 6 (Compatible IOSTS). *For $j = 1, 2$, the two IOSTS $S_j = \langle D_j = V_j \cup P_j, \Theta_j, Q_j, q_j^0, \Sigma_j, T_j \rangle$ with data D_j and alphabet $\Sigma_j = \Sigma_j^? \cup \Sigma_j^!$ are compatible if $V_1 \cap V_2 = \emptyset$, $P_1 = P_2$, $\Sigma_1^! = \Sigma_2^!$, $\Sigma_1^? = \Sigma_2^?$.*

Definition 7 (Parallel Product). *The parallel product $S = S_1 \| S_2$ of two compatible IOSTS S_1, S_2 is the IOSTS $\langle D, P, \Theta, Q, q^0, \Sigma, T \rangle$ that consists of the following elements: $V = V_1 \cup V_2$, $P = P_1 = P_2$, $\Theta = \Theta_1 \wedge \Theta_2$, $Q = Q_1 \times Q_2$, $q^0 = \langle q_1^0, q_2^0 \rangle$, $\Sigma^? = \Sigma_1^? = \Sigma_2^?$, $\Sigma^! = \Sigma_1^! = \Sigma_2^!$ The set T of transitions of the composed system is the smallest set defined by the rule:*

$$\frac{\langle q_1, a, G_1, A_1, q_1' \rangle \in T_1 \quad \langle q_2, a, G_2, A_2, q_2' \rangle \in T_2}{\langle \langle q_1, q_2 \rangle, a, G_1 \wedge G_2, A_1 \cup A_2, \langle q_1', q_2' \rangle \rangle \in T}$$

Lemma 1 (traces of the parallel product).
   $Traces(S_1 \| S_2) = Traces(S_1) \cap Traces(S_2)$.
   $RTraces(S_1 \| S_2, F_1 \times F_2) = RTraces(S_1, F_1) \cap RTraces(S_2, F2)$.

3.2   Quiescence and Suspension IOSTS

In conformance testing it is assumed that the environment may observe not only outputs, but also *absence of outputs* (i.e., in a given state, the system does not emit any output for the environment to observe). This is called *quiescence* in conformance testing [19]. On a black-box implementation, quiescence is observed using timers: a timer is reset whenever the environment sends a stimulus to the implementation; when the timer expires, the environment observes quiescence.

In order to distinguish a quiescence that is also present in a specification from one that is not, quiescence can be made explicit on a specification by a symbolic operation called *suspension*. This operation transforms an IOSTS S into an IOSTS S^δ, also called the *suspension IOSTS* of S. Each location q of S^δ contains a new self-looping transition, labelled with a new output action δ, which may be fired if and only if no other output action may be fired in q. Formally,

Definition 8 (Suspension). *Given* $S = \langle D = V \cup P, \Theta, Q, q^0, \Sigma = \Sigma^! \cup \Sigma^?, \mathcal{T} \rangle$ *an IOSTS, the suspension IOSTS* S^δ *is the tuple* $\langle D = V \cup P, \Theta, Q, q^0, (\Sigma^! \cup \{\delta\}) \cup \Sigma^?, \mathcal{T} \cup \bigcup_{q \in Q} \langle q, \delta, G_{\delta,q}, (v := v)_{v \in V}, q \rangle \rangle$ *where*

$$G_{\delta,q} : \bigwedge_{a \in \Sigma^!} \neg G_{a,q} \text{ where } G_{a,q} : \bigvee_{t = \langle q, a, G, A, q' \rangle \in \mathcal{T}} \exists sig(a).G. \tag{1}$$

For the IOSTS S depicted in Figure 1, the IOSTS S^δ is depicted in Figure 2. The guard $x < 0$ of the transition labeled δ is obtained by simplifying the expression $\neg(x = 0 \vee \exists m, m = x \wedge x > 0)$, which corresponds to Formula (1) above.

In this system, a *START* input with a negative parameter ($p < 0$) does not allow for *MSG* or *STOP* outputs, i.e., the system is quiescent after *START*. This is made explicit by the special output $\delta!$ after *START*.

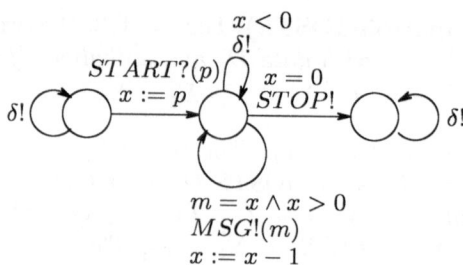

$$x < 0$$
$$\delta!$$
$$START?(p) \qquad x = 0$$
$$x := p \qquad STOP!$$
$$\delta! \qquad \qquad \delta!$$

$$m = x \wedge x > 0$$
$$MSG!(m)$$
$$x := x - 1$$

Fig. 2. Suspension IOSTS S^δ

3.3   Verification of Safety Properties

The problem considered here is: given a reactive system modelled by an IOSTS S, and a safety property ψ defined on its traces, does S satisfy ψ? We model safety properties using *observers*, which are deterministic IOSTS equipped with a set of "bad" locations; the property is violated when a "bad" location is reached.

Definition 9 (Observer). *An observer is a deterministic IOSTS* ω *together with a set of dedicated locations* $Violate_\omega \subseteq Q_\omega$, *which are deadlocks (no outgoing transitions). An observer* (ω, $Violate_\omega$) *is compatible with an IOSTS* M *if* ω *is compatible with* M. *The set of observers compatible with* M *is denoted* $\Omega(M)$.

An observer $\omega \in \Omega(M)$ defines a safety property on $(\Lambda_M^! \cup \Lambda_M^?)^*$, namely, the property that is satisfied by all sequences in $(\Lambda_M^! \cup \Lambda_M^?)^* \setminus RTraces(\omega, Violate_\omega)$ (and those sequences only). In particular, if M is the suspension IOSTS $\mathcal{S}^\delta$ of a given IOSTS $\mathcal{S}$, then the property is satisfied by a subset of $(\Lambda_S^! \cup \{\delta\} \cup \Lambda_S^?)^*$.

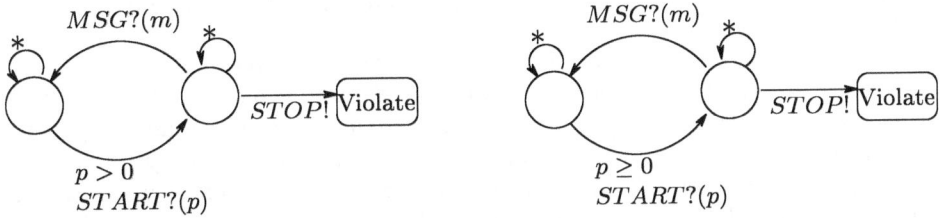

Fig. 3. Sample observers : ω_1 (left), ω_2 (right)

For example the observer ω_1 depicted in Figure 3 describes the safety property which says that between $START$ input carrying a parameter $p > 0$, and a $STOP$ output, the system must exhibit at least one MSG output. The set of "bad" locations is $\{Violate\}$. The self-loops "*" denote all actions (including the quiescence δ) that do not label other outgoing transitions. The observer ω_2 depicted on the right-hand side of Figure 3 describes almost the same property (except for the fact that $START$ input carries a parameter $p \geq 0$). An IOSTS satisfies an observer if no trace of the IOSTS is recognised by the observer:

Definition 10 (IOSTS Satisfies Observer). *For an IOSTS $\mathcal{S}$ and an observer $(\omega, Violate_\omega) \in \Omega(\mathcal{S})$, we say that $\mathcal{S}$ satisfies $(\omega, Violate_\omega)$, denoted by $\mathcal{S} \models (\omega, Violate_\omega)$, if $Traces(\mathcal{S}) \cap RTraces(\omega, Violate_\omega) = \emptyset$.*

Let Q denote the set of locations of $\mathcal{S}$. Then, $Traces(\mathcal{S}) = RTraces(\mathcal{S}, Q)$ and $RTraces(\mathcal{S}\|\omega, Q \times Violate_\omega) = RTraces(\mathcal{S}, Q) \cap RTraces(\omega, Violate_\omega)$ (cf. Lemma 1). Hence, checking $\mathcal{S} \models (\omega, Violate_\omega)$ amounts to checking the emptyness of the set $RTraces(\mathcal{S}\|\omega, Q \times Violate_\omega)$. This can be done checking that the intersection between the set of *reachable states* of $\mathcal{S}\|\omega$, and the set of states whose locations lie in $Q \times Violate_\omega$, is empty. Alternatively, the intersection between the set of states from which $Q \times Violate_\omega$ is reachable (also called the *coreachable set* of $Q \times Violate_\omega$), and the set of initial states, can be checked for emptyness.

However, reachable and coreachable sets are not computable in general because of undecidability problems. Approximate analysis techniques such as abstract interpretation [7], can be used to compute over-approximations of them.

Our tool STG (Symbolic Test Generation) [6] is interfaced with a tool called NBac [13] for this purpose. First, STG automatically computes the product $\omega\|\mathcal{S}$, and then, NBac automatically performs an approximate reachability analysis (from the initial states) and approximate coreachability analysis (to the violating locations) of the product. These tools can be employed to prove, e.g., that the IOSTS $\mathcal{S}^\delta$ depicted in Figure 2 does satisfy the observer ω_1 depicted in Figure 3. (The violating locations are found unreachable, hence, the property holds).

On the other hand, it is impossible *in general* to prove automatically that an IOSTS does *not* satisfy an observer. Such a situation occurs with the IOSTS S^δ in Figure 2 and the observer ω_2 depicted in the right-hand side of Figure 3: S^δ does not satisfy ω_2, because a *START* input carrying the parameter $p = 0$ allows for a *STOP* output to be emitted (without any *MSG* inputs in between), which violates the property of interest (the *Violate* location is reached).

Combining observers. The parallel product of two observers $(\omega, Violate_\omega)$ and $(\varphi, Violate_\varphi)$ can be also interpreted in terms of safety properties. We use these properties in Section 4. A natural choice is to equip the product $\omega \| \varphi$ with the set of locations $Violate_\omega \times Violate_\varphi$; by Lemma 1, $RTraces(\omega \| \varphi, Violate_\omega \times Violate_\varphi) = RTraces(\omega, Violate_\omega) \cap RTraces(\varphi, Violate_\varphi)$; hence, we obtain a safety property which is violated whenever both safety properties described by $(\omega, Violate_\omega)$ and $(\varphi, Violate_\varphi)$ are violated. Alternative choices for the violating locations are, e.g., $Violate_\omega \times (Q_\varphi \setminus Violate_\varphi)$, which indicates the violation of the former property, but not that of the latter; and, $(Q_\omega \setminus Violate_\omega) \times Violate_\varphi$, which indicates the violation of the latter, but not of the former property.

3.4   Conformance Testing

A *conformance relation* formalises the set of implementations that behave consistently with a specification. An implementation $\mathcal{I}$ is not a formal object (it is a physical system) but, in order to reason about conformance, it is necessary to assume that the semantics of $\mathcal{I}$ can be modelled by a formal object. We assume here that it is modelled by an IOLTS (cf. Definition 2). The notions of trace and quiescence are defined for IOLTS just as for IOSTS. The implementation is assumed to be *input-complete*, i.e., all its inputs are enabled in all states.

These assumptions are called *test hypothesis* in conformance testing. The central notion in conformance testing is that of *conformance relation*; the standard **ioco** relation defined by Tretmans [19] can be rephrased as

Definition 11 (ioco). *An inplementation $\mathcal{I}$ **ioco**-conforms to a specification S, denoted by $\mathcal{I}$ **ioco** S, if $Traces(S^\delta) \cdot (\Lambda^! \cup \{\delta\}) \cap Traces(\mathcal{I}^\delta) \subseteq Traces(S^\delta)$.*

Intuitively, an implementation $\mathcal{I}$ **ioco**-conforms to its specification S, if, after each trace of the suspension IOSTS S^δ, the implementation only exhibits outputs and quiescences allowed by S^δ. Hence, in this framework, the specification is *partial* with respect to inputs, i.e., after an input that is not described by the specification, the implementation may have any behaviour, without violating conformance to the specification. This corresponds to the intuition that a specification models a given set of services that must be provided by a system; a particular implementation of the system may implement more services than specified, but these additional features should not influence its conformance.

Example. An implementation that exhibits the trace $START?(1) \cdot STOP!$ does not conform to the specification S depicted in Figure 1 - this trace is not present in the IOSTS S^δ (Figure 2). For the same reason, the trace $START?(1) \cdot \delta!$

reveals a non-conformance to S. On the other hand, a trace such as $START?(1) \cdot$ $START?(1) \cdot STOP!$ does not pose problems for conformance, as S^{δ} does not constrain the traces of the system after the second $START?$ in any way.

4   Test Generation for Safety and Conformance

This section shows how to generate a test case from a specification using a safety property as a guide. The test case attempts to detect violations of the property by an implementation of the system and violations of the conformance between the implementation and the specification. Moreover, if the verification step (Section 3.3) could not establish the fact that the specification satisfies the property, the generated test cases may also detect violations of the property by the specification when executed on the implementation.

We show that the test cases generated by our method always return correct verdicts. In this sense, the test generation method itself is correct.

Outline. We first define the *output-completion* $\Sigma^!(M)$ of an IOSTS M. We then show that the output-completion of the IOSTS of S^{δ} is a *canonical tester* [4] for S and the **ioco** relation defined in Section 3.4 (a canonical tester for a specification with respect to a given relation allows, in principle, to detect every implementation that disagrees with the specification according to the relation). This derives from the fact, stated in Lemma 2 below, that **ioco**-conformance to a specification S is equivalent to satisfying (a safety property described by) an observer obtained from $\Sigma^!(S^{\delta})$. By composing this observer with another observer $(\omega, \mathit{Violate}_\omega)$ we obtain test cases for checking the conformance to S and the satisfaction of $(\omega, \mathit{Violate}_\omega)$.

Definition 12 (output-completion). *Given* $M = \langle D, \Theta, Q, q^0, \Sigma, \mathcal{T} \rangle$ *a deterministic IOSTS, the output completion of* M *is the IOSTS* $\Sigma^!(M) = \langle D, \Theta, Q \cup \{\mathit{Fail}_M\}, q^0, \Sigma, \mathcal{T} \cup \bigcup_{q \in Q, a \in \Sigma^!} \langle q, a, \bigwedge_{t=\langle q,a,G_t,A_t,q_t' \rangle \in \mathcal{T}} \neg G_t, (x := x)_{x \in V}, \mathit{Fail}_M \rangle \rangle.$

Interpretation: $\Sigma^!(M)$ is obtained from M by adding a new location $\mathit{Fail}_M \notin Q$, and for each $q \in Q$ and $a \in \Sigma^!$, a transition with origin q, destination Fail_M, action a, identity assignments and guard $\bigwedge_{t=\langle q,a,G_t,A_t,q_t' \rangle \in \mathcal{T}} \neg G_t$. Hence, any output not fireable in M becomes fireable in $\Sigma^!(M)$ and leads to the new (deadlock) location Fail_M. The output-completion of an IOSTS M can be seen as an observer, by choosing $\{\mathit{Fail}_M\}$ as the set of violating locations. The following lemma says that conformance to a specification S is a safety property, namely, the property whose negation is represented by the observer $(\Sigma^!(S^{\delta}), \{\mathit{Fail}_{s^{\delta}}\})$.

Lemma 2. $\mathcal{I}$ **ioco** S *iff* $\mathcal{I}^{\delta} \models (\Sigma^!(S^{\delta}), \{\mathit{Fail}_{s^{\delta}}\}))$.

The lemma also says that the IOSTS $\Sigma^!(S^{\delta})$ is a canonical tester for **ioco**-conformance to S. Indeed, $\mathcal{I}^{\delta} \models (\Sigma^!(S^{\delta}), \{\mathit{Fail}_{s^{\delta}}\})$ can be interpreted as the fact that execution of $\Sigma^!(S^{\delta})$ on the implementation $\mathcal{I}$ never leads to a "Fail" verdict; the fact that this is equivalent to $\mathcal{I}$ **ioco** $\mathcal{S}$ (as stated by Lemma 2) amounts to having a canonical tester [4].

A canonical tester is, in principle, enough for detecting all implementations that do not conform to a given specification. However, our goal in this paper is to detect, in addition to such non-conformances, other potential violations of other (additional) safety properties coming from, e.g., the system's requirements.

The observers (cf. Definition 9) employed for expressing such properties also serve as a test selection mechanism; by Lemma 1, the product between an observer and the canonical tester can be used to define a subset of traces of interest among the many possible traces of the canonical tester.

We first note that for an IOSTS M and an observer $(\omega, Violate_\omega) \in \Omega(M)$, the IOSTS $\omega \| \Sigma^!(M)$ can be interpreted as an observer of M by choosing its set of violating locations. Let for now this set be $Violate_\omega \times \{Fail_M\}$, denoted by $ViolateFail_{\omega\|\Sigma^!(M)}$. The subscript is omitted whenever it is clear from the context.

Definition 13. *For* $(\omega, Violate_\omega) \in \Omega(\mathcal{S}^\delta)$, $test(\mathcal{S}, \omega) \triangleq \omega \| \Sigma^!(\mathcal{S}^\delta)$.

In the rest of the section we show that every $test(\mathcal{S}, \omega)$ can be seen as a test case that refines the canonical tester, as violations of $(\omega, Violate_\omega)$ are also checked.

Proposition 1. $\mathcal{I}$ **ioco** $\mathcal{S}$ *iff*
$$\forall(\omega, Violate_\omega) \in \Omega(\mathcal{S}^\delta).\ \mathcal{I}^\delta \models (test(\mathcal{S}, \omega), ViolateFail_{test(\mathcal{S}, \omega)}).$$

Interpretation. The IOSTS $test(\mathcal{S}, \omega)$ can be seen as a test case to be executed in parallel with an implementation $\mathcal{I}$. Proposition 1 says that if this execution enters a location in $ViolateFail_{test(\mathcal{S}, \omega)}$ $(= Violate_\omega \times \{Fail_{\mathcal{S}^\delta}\})$, then the implementation violates both the property defined by $(\omega, Violate_\omega)$ and the conformance to specification $\mathcal{S}$. In this situation, the **ViolateFail** verdict is given:

ViolateFail: the implementation violates the property *and* the conformance

The proposition also says that the (infinite) set $\{test(\mathcal{S}, \omega)|(\omega, Violate_\omega) \in \Omega(\mathcal{S}^\delta)\}$ of test cases is "exhaustive" for checking **ioco**-conformance to a given specification $\mathcal{S}$, meaning that all non-conformances may, in principle, be detected.

We now consider another interpretation of the IOSTS $\omega\|\Sigma^!(M)$, which leads to another test verdict. Choosing the violating locations to be $(Q_\omega \setminus Violate_\omega) \times \{Fail_M\}$ results in a different observer. We denote by $Fail_{\omega\|\Sigma^!(M)}$ the set $(Q_\omega \setminus Violate_\omega) \times \{Fail_M\}$. The subscript is omitted whenever the context is clear.

Proposition 2. *For an IOSTS* $\mathcal{S}$ *and* $(\omega, Violate_\omega) \in \Omega(\mathcal{S}^\delta)$,
$$\mathcal{I}^\delta \not\models (test(\mathcal{S}, \omega), Fail_{test(\mathcal{S}, \omega)}) \Rightarrow \neg(\mathcal{I}\ \textbf{ioco}\ \mathcal{S})$$

Proposition 2 says that when $test(\mathcal{S}, \omega)$ enters a location in the set $Fail_{test(\mathcal{S}, \omega)}$ $(= (Q_\omega \setminus Violate_\omega) \times \{Fail_{\mathcal{S}^\delta}\})$ when executed on an implementation $\mathcal{I}$, then $\mathcal{I}$ violates conformance to $\mathcal{S}$. The property ω is not violated (the $Violate_\omega$ set is not entered). In this case, the **Fail** verdict is given:

> **Fail**: the implementation violates the conformance, but not the property

A third interpretation of the IOSTS $\omega || \Sigma^!(M)$ as an observer can be given, by choosing the set of violating locations to be $Violate_\omega \times Q_M$. We denote this set by $Violate_{\omega||\Sigma^!(M)}$, and omit the subscript whenever it is clear from the context.

Proposition 3. *For an IOSTS S and observer $(\omega, Violate_\omega) \in \Omega(S^\delta)$, $\mathcal{I}^\delta \not\models (test(S, \omega), Violate_{test(S,\omega)}) \Rightarrow \mathcal{I}^\delta \not\models (\omega, Violate_\omega) \wedge S^\delta \not\models (\omega, Violate_\omega)$.*

Proposition 3 says that when $test(S, \omega)$ enters a location in $Violate_{test(S,\omega)}$ when executed on an implementation $\mathcal{I}$, then a violation of the property by both specification and implementation is detected. Hence, the **Violate** verdict is given:

> **Violate**: the specification and the implementation violate the property

Discussion. Propositions 1, 2, and 3 show that the test generation algorithm, i.e., the construction of the IOSTS $test(S, \omega)$ and of its three verdicts, are *correct*, in the sense that verdicts correctly describe the relations between specification, implementation, and property. The verdict **ViolateFail** (resp. **Fail**) detects the violation of the property and of the conformance (resp. of the conformance only) by the implementation. This holds independently of whether the specification satisfies the property or not; indeed, the execution of the test case on the implementation may detect violations of the property by the specification using the **Violate** verdict. The ability to generate test cases from a property and a specification which may or may not satisfy the property is important, because verification is undecidable for the infinite-state systems considered in this paper.

A natural question that arises is why a violation of the property by the implementation is always detected simultaneously with either (1) a violation of the property by the specification or (2) a violation of the conformance between implementation and specification. The reason is that our test cases are extracted from the specification, i.e., they only contain traces of the specification. An implementation may only violate a property without (1) or (2) occurring when it executes a trace that diverges at some point from the specification by an *input*; indeed, as seen in Section 3.4, this does not compromise conformance and, of course, the specification cannot violate the property on a trace that it does not contain. Such traces are excluded from the generated test cases by construction.

Alternatively, these traces could be included in the test cases, but this implies to perform an *input-completion* of the specification (similar to Definition 12) first, and could lead to test cases that are typically too large for use in practice.

Building an actual test case. To build an actual test case from $test(S, \omega)$, all inputs are transformed into outputs and reciprocally (this operation is called *mirror* ; in the test execution process, the actions of the implementation and those of the test case must complement each other). For the IOSTS S depicted in Figure 1 and the observer ω_2 depicted in Figure 3, the corresponding test case (before simplification) is depicted in Figure 4. Finally, the result is automatically analysed and simplified using the NBac tool [13] for statically eliminating transitions that cannot lead to the violation of the property any more (cf. Section 5).

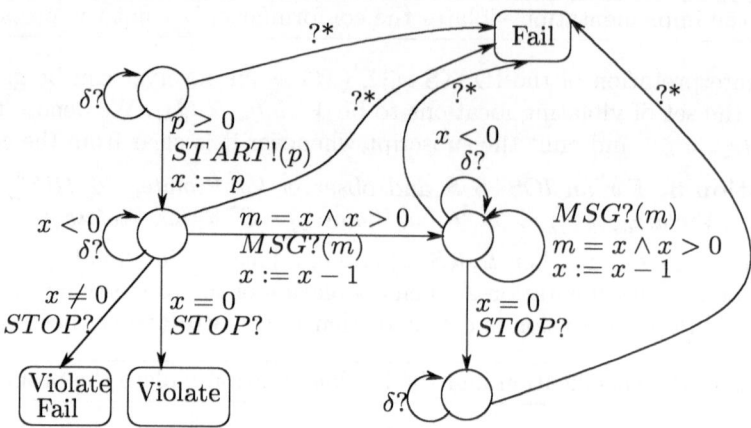

Fig. 4. Before selection: test case obtained from S (Figure 1) and ω_2 (Figure 3)

5   Test Selection

The main goal of the testing process is to detect violations of the system's required properties by the system's implementation. In this section we outline a technique for statically detecting and eliminating locations and transitions of a test case (generated from a specification and a property as described in Section 4) from which this goal cannot be achieved any more; the resulting test case attempts to keep the implementation in states where it may still violate the property. We show that this optimisation preserves correctness of test verdicts.

The violation of a property - described as an observer (ω, $Violate_\omega$) - by an implementation is materialised by reaching the *ViolateFail* and *Violate* sets of locations in the IOSTS $test(S, \omega)$(cf. Section 4). For a state s of an IOSTS and a location q of the IOSTS, we say that s is *coreachable* for the location q if there exists a valuation v of the variables such that $s \xrightarrow{\sigma} \langle q, v \rangle$. Then, the test selection process consists (ideally) in selecting, from a given test case, the subset of states that are coreachable for the locations in *Violate* $\cup$ *ViolateFail*.

It should be quite clear that an exact computation of this set of states is impossible in general. However, there exist techniques that allow to compute an over-approximation of it. We here use one such technique based on abstract interpretation and implemented in the NBac tool [13]. Given a location q of an IOSTS, the tool computes, for each location l, a *symbolic coreachable state* for q:

Definition 14 (symbolic coreachable state). *For l, q two locations of an IOSTS S, we say $\langle l, \varphi_{l \to q} \rangle$ is a symbolic coreachable state for q if $\varphi_{l \to q}$ is a formula on the variables of the IOSTS such that, if a state of the form $\langle l, v \rangle$ is coreachable for q, then $v \models \varphi_{l \to q}$ holds.*

I.e., $\langle l, \varphi_{l \to q} \rangle$ over-approximates the states with location l that are coreachable for q. The following algorithm uses this information for *pruning* a test case.

Definition 15 (pruning). *For an IOSTS S and an observer $(\omega, \text{Violate}_\omega)$ from the set $\Omega(S^\delta)$, let $prune(S, \omega)$ be the IOSTS computed as follows.*

- *first, the IOSTS $mirror(test(S, \omega))$ is computed as in Section 4. Let L be its set of locations, T its set of transitions, and $\Sigma = \Sigma^! \cup \Sigma^?$ its alphabet, where $\Sigma^! = \Sigma_S^?$ and $\Sigma^? = \Sigma_S^! \cup \{\delta\}$. Let also $Inconc \notin L$ be a new location.*
- *then, for each location $l \in L$, a symbolic coreachable state $\langle l, \varphi_{l \to q}\rangle$, for each location $q \in \text{Violate} \cup \text{ViolateFail}$ is computed. Let φ_l denote the formula $\bigvee_{q \in \text{Violate} \cup \text{ViolateFail}} \varphi_{l \to q}$*
- *next, for each location $l \in L$ of the IOSTS, and each transition $t \in T$ of the IOSTS with origin l, guard G, and label a,*
  - *if $a \in \Sigma^!$ then*
    - *if $G \wedge \varphi_l$ is unsatisfiable, then t is eliminated from T,*
    - *otherwise, the guard of t becomes $G \wedge \varphi_l$*
  - *if $a \in \Sigma^?$, then*
    - *the guard of t becomes $G \wedge \varphi_l$*
    - *a new transition is added to T, with origin l, destination $Inconc$, action a, guard $G \wedge \neg\varphi_l$, and identity assignments.*

The *pruning* operation consists in detecting transitions whose firing leads to states where the *Violate* and *ViolateFail* sets of locations are unreachable. This is done by performing a coreachability analysis to these locations using the NBac tool [13]. If such a "useless" transition is labelled by an *output*, then it may be removed from the test case (a test case controls its outputs, hence, it may decide not to perform an output if violations of the property cannot be detected afterwards). On the other hand, *inputs* cannot be prevented from occurring, hence, the transitions labelled by *inputs*, by which the *Violate* and *ViolateFail* sets of locations cannot be reached any more, are reoriented to a new location, called *Inconc*. Reaching *Inconc* during test execution is interpreted as a verdict:

Inconc: violations of the property cannot be detected any more

Proposition 4. *The test case obtained by after pruning is correct, i.e., Propositions 1, 2 and 3 still hold when $test(S, \omega)$ is replaced with $prune(S, \omega)$.*

The test case obtained after pruning $test(S, \omega_2)$ is depicted in Figure 5. It starts by sending a $START$ with a positive parameter p to the implementation, and then waits for inputs. If the implementation replies with $STOP$, the test execution terminates with a verdict, which depends on whether the parameter p was strictly positive or was equal to zero:

- If $p > 0$, the sequence $START(p) \cdot STOP$ exhibits a non-conformance between implementation (which accepts this sequence) and specification (which does not accept it). This sequence is also a witness for the violation of the property by the implementation: the verdict is *ViolateFail*;
- If $p = 0$, $START(p) \cdot STOP$ is a witness for violation of the property defined by ω_2 by both implementation and specification: the verdict is *Violate*.

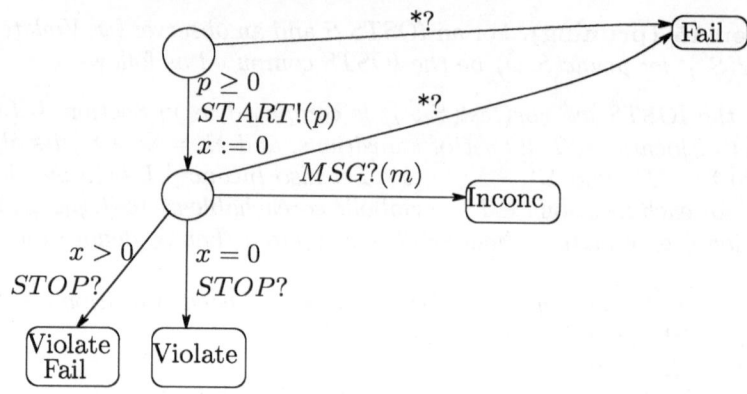

Fig. 5. After selection: test case obtained from $\mathcal{S}$ (Figure 1) and ω_2 (Figure 3)

Finally, if the implementation replies with *MSG* after *START*, the current test case cannot detect violations of the property any more, and the verdict is *Inconc*.

6   Conclusion and Related Work

A system may be viewed at several levels of abstraction: high-level *properties*, operational *specification*, and black-box *implementation*. In our framework properties and specifications are described using Input-Output Symbolic Transition Systems (IOSTS), which are extended automata that operate on symbolic variables and communicate with the environment through input and output actions carrying parameters. IOSTS are given a formal semantics in terms of input-output labelled transition systems (IOLTS). The implementation is a black box, but it is assumed that its semantics can be described by an unknown IOLTS. This allows to formally link the implementation and the specification by a conformance relation. A satisfaction relation links them both to higher-level properties.

A validation methodology is proposed for checking these relations, i.e., for detecting inconsistencies between the different views of the system: First, the properties are automatically verified on the specification using abstract interpretation techniques. Then, test cases are automatically generated from the specification and the properties, and are executed on the implementation of the system. If the verification step was successful, that is, it has established that the specification satisfies a property, the test execution may detect the violation of the property by the implementation and the violation of the conformance relation between implementation and specification. On the other hand, if the verification did not allow to prove a property, the test execution may additionally detect a violation of the property by the specification. Any inconsistencies obtained in this manner are reported to the user in the form of test verdicts. The approach is proved correct and is illustrated on a simple example. The full version of this paper [17] illustrates the approach on a larger example (the BRP protocol [11]).

Related Work. In [8] an approach for generating tests from a specification and from observers describing linear-time temporal logic requirements is described. The generated test cases do not check for conformance, they only check the fact that the implementation does not violate the requirements.

The approach described in [2] considers a specification S and an invariant P assumed to hold on S. Then, mutants S' of S are built using standard mutation operators, and a combined machine is generated, which extends sequences of S with sequences of S'. Next, a model checker is used to generate sequences that violate P, which prove that S' is a mutant of S violating P. Finally, the obtained sequences are interpreted as test cases to be executed on the implementation.

The authors of [9] start from a specification S and a temporal-logic property P assumed to hold on S, and use the ability of model checkers to construct counter-examples for $\neg P$ on S. These counter-examples can be interpreted as *witnesses* (i.e., test cases) for P on S. The papers [3, 12] extend this idea by formalising standard coverage criteria (all-definitions, all-uses, *etc*) using observers (resp. in temporal logic). Again, test cases are generated by model checking the observers (or the temporal-logic formulas) on the specification.

The approaches described in all these papers rely on model checking, hence, they only work for finite-state systems; moreover, they do not formally relate satisfaction of properties to conformance testing, and, except for [8], they do not formally define a conformance relation.

In [18] we present an approach for combining model checking and conformance testing for finite-state systems, which can be seen as a first step of the approach presented here, which deals with infinite-state systems. In the finite-state framework of [18] verification is decidable, which heavily influences the whole approach: for example the test generation algorithm (based on enumerative model checking) does not need to take into account the possibility that the property might be violated by the specification.

A different approach for combining model checking and black-box testing is black-box checking [16]. Under some assumptions on the implementation (the implementation is deterministic; an upper bound n on its number of states is known), the black-box checking approach constructs a complete test suite of size exponential in n for checking properties expressed by Büchi automata.

Our approach can also be related to the combination of verification, testing and monitoring proposed in [10]. In their approach, monitoring is passive (pure observation), whereas ours is reactive and adaptive, guided by the choice of inputs to deliver to the system as pre-computed in a test case.

Finally, in [14] we propose a symbolic algorithm for selecting test cases from a specification be means of so-called *test purposes*. The difference with the present paper lies mainly in methodology. Test purposes in [14] are essentially a pragmatic means for test selection - they have to be provided by the user. In contrast, test selection in the present paper consists in automatically attempting to violate a safety property that was automatically verified (succesfully or not) on the specification. Moreover, test purposes can be classified as *reachability* properties, which have an exactly opposite semantics to the safety properties considered here (reachability properties are negations of safety properties).

References

1. ISO/IEC 9646. Conformance Testing Methodology and Framework, 1992.
2. P. Ammann, W. Ding, and D. Xu. Using a model checker to test safety properties. In *International Conference on Engineering of Complex Computer Systems*. IEEE Computer Society, 2001.
3. J. Blom, A. Hessel, B. Jonnson, and P. Pettersson. Specifying and generating test cases using observer automata. In *Workshop on Formal Approaches to Software Testing (Fates'04)*, pages 137–152, 2004.
4. E. Brinskma. A theory for the derivation of tests. In *Protocol Specification, Testing and Verification (PSTV'88)*, pages 63–74, 1988.
5. E. Brinskma, A. Alderen, R. Langerak, J. van de Laagemat, and J. Tretmans. A formal approach to conformance testing. In *Protocol Secification, Testing and Verification (PSTV'90)*, pages 349–363, 1990.
6. D. Clarke, T. Jéron, V. Rusu, and E. Zinovieva. STG: a symbolic test generation tool. In *Tools and Algorithms for the Construction and Analysis of Systems (TACAS'02)*, number 2280 in LNCS, pages 470–475, 2002.
7. P. Cousot and R. Cousot. Abstract intrepretation: a unified lattice model for static analysis of programs by construction or approximation of fixpoints. In *4th ACM Symposium on Principles of Programming Languages*, pages 238–252, 1977.
8. J.C. Fernandez, L. Mounier, and C. Pachon. Property-oriented test generation. In *Formal Aspects of Software Testing Workshop*, number 2931 in LNCS, 2003.
9. A. Gargantini and C.L. Heitmeyer. Using model checking to generate tests from requirements specifications. In *ESEC/SIGSOFT FSE*, pages 146–162, 1999.
10. K. Havelund and G. Rosu. Synthesizing monitors for safety properties. In *Int. Conference on Tools and Algorithms for Construction and Analysis of Systems (TACAS'02), Grenoble, France*, number 2280 in LNCS, pages 342–356, 2002.
11. L. Helmink, M. P. A. Sellink, and F. Vaandrager. Proof-checking a data link protocol. In *Types for Proofs and Programs (TYPES'94)*, number 806 in LNCS, pages 127–165, 1994.
12. H. Hong, I. Lee, O. Sokolsky, and H. Ural. A temporal logic based theory of test coverage and generation. In *Tools and Algorithms for Construction and Analysis of Systems (TACAS'02)*, number 2280 in LNCS, pages 327–341, 2002.
13. B. Jeannet. Dynamic partitioning in linear relation analysis. *Formal Methods in System Design*, 23(1):5–37, 2003.
14. B. Jeannet, T. Jéron, V. Rusu, and E. Zinovieva. Symbolic test selection based on approximate analysis. In *Int. Conference on Tools and Algorithms for Construction and Analysis of Systems (TACAS'05), Grenoble, France (to appear)*, 2005.
15. N. Lynch and M. Tuttle. Introduction to IO automata. *CWI Quarterly*, 3(2), 1999.
16. D. Peled, M. Vardi, and M. Yannakakis. Black-box checking. *Journal of Automata, Languages and Combinatorics*, 7(2):225 – 246, 2001 2001.
17. V. Rusu, H. Marchand, and T. Jéron. Verification and symbolic test generation for safety properties. Technical Report 1640, IRISA, august 2004. Available at http://www.irisa.fr/vertecs/Publis/Ps/PI-1640.pdf.
18. V. Rusu, H. Marchand, V. Tschaen, T. Jéron, and B. Jeannet. From safety verifcation to safety testing. In *Intl. Conf. on Testing of Communicating Systems (TestCom04)*, number 2978 in LNCS, 2004.
19. J. Tretmans. Testing concurrent systems: A formal approach. In *CONCUR'99*, number 1664 in LNCS, pages 46–65, 1999.
20. E. Zinovieva. *Symbolic Test Generation for Reactive Systems*. PhD thesis, University of Rennes I, November 2004.

Adding Conflict and Confusion to CSP

Christie Bolton

Department of Computer Science
University of Warwick
Coventry CV4 7AL
christie@dcs.warwick.ac.uk

Abstract. In the development of concurrent systems two differing approaches have arisen: those with *truly concurrent* semantics and those with *interleaving* semantics. The difference between these two approaches is that in the coarser interleaving interpretation parallelism can be captured in terms of non-determinism whereas in the finer truly concurrent interpretation it cannot. Thus processes $a \parallel b$ and $a.b + b.a$ are identified within the interleaving approach but distinguished within the truly concurrent approach.

In this paper we explore the truly concurrent notions of *conflict*, whereby transitions can occur individually but not together from a given state, and *confusion*, whereby the conflict set of a given transition is altered by the occurence of another transition with which it does not interfere. Having provided a translation from Petri nets, a truly concurrent formalism, to CSP, an interleaving formalism, we demonstate how the CSP model-checker FDR can be used to detect the presence of both conflict and confusion in Petri nets.

This work is of interest for two reasons. Firstly, from a practical point of view: to the author's knowledge, no existing tool for modelling Petri nets can perform these checks and we address that issue. Secondly, and perhaps more significantly, we bridge the gap between truly concurrent and interleaving formalisms, demonstrating that true concurrency can be captured in what is typically considered to be an interleaving language.

Keywords: True Concurrency; Interleaving Concurrency; Petri Nets; CSP; Conflict; Confusion; Automatic Verification.

1 Introduction

In the development of critical systems standards dictate that it is necessary to first design and analyse abstract models of the system. For such systems, testing alone is inadequate as it can only *detect* errors not *verify their absence*. Rather, we must formally, and preferably automatically, *prove* that the system satisfies the required properties. Formal verification is especially important when modelling concurrent, distributed and communicating systems; their high complexity level makes them especially vulnerable to errors.

Within concurrency theory two distinct approaches can be identified: those with *truly concurrent* semantics and those with *interleaving* semantics. The dif-

J.S. Fitzgerald, I.J. Hayes, and A. Tarlecki (Eds.): FM 2005, LNCS 3582, pp. 205–220, 2005.

ference between these two approaches is that in the coarser interleaving interpretation parallelism can be captured in terms of non-determinism whereas in
the finer truly concurrent interpretation it cannot; only in true concurrency
can we distinguish between the concurrent execution of actions and the non-
deterministic choice between the possible orders of their executions. Thus processes $a \parallel b$ and $a.b + b.a$ as illustrated in Figure 1 are identified within the
interleaving approach but distinguished within the truly concurrent approach.
Examples of truly concurrent formalisms include trace theory [9], Petri net
theory [13], prime event structures [19], pomsets [14], and others (cf. e.g., [12, 3]).
Examples of interleaving formalisms include CSP [8], CCS [10, 11] and ACP [2].
Motivations for the need for the finer truly concurrent model are given in e.g. [14].

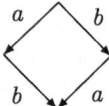

Fig. 1. A labelled transition system modelling both $a \parallel b$ and $a.b + b.a$

Three notions central to true concurrency are *causal dependency, conflict,*
and *confusion*: the first is when one action is enabled only after another has
occured; the second is when two or more actions can occur individually but
not together from a given state; and the third is when the conflict set of a given
action, that is the set of actions with which the given action conflicts from a given
state, is altered by the occurence of another action with which the first action
does not interfere. Confusion can arise when there is a mixture of concurrency
and conflict.

In this paper we use the truly concurrent formalism of *Petri nets* [13, 16], a
formalism that has both graphical and mathematical representations and hence
is both formal and intuitive, to explore the above notions. There are many different types of net (cf. [15]) but here we restrict ourselves to safe Petri nets in
which each place contains at most one token.

Having provided a translation from Petri nets to process algebra CSP [8, 17],
an interleaving formalism, we demonstate how the CSP model-checker FDR [7]
can be used to detect the presence of both conflict and confusion in Petri nets.
The increasing importance of model-checking as a technique for verifying and
validating the correctness of systems is fully discussed by Clarke et al. in [6].
It should be noted that neither the translation from Petri nets to CSP nor the
structure of the CSP tests for conflict and confusion are unique up to isomorphism: the definitions presented here have been chosen for ease of understanding
for those not familiar with CSP rather than for speed of verification.

The contribution of this paper is two-fold. Firstly, and from a practical perspective, we demonstrate how conflict and confusion, ideas central to true concurrency, can be automatically detected in Petri nets: to the author's knowledge,
no existing tool for modelling Petri nets can perform these checks [18, 1]. Sec-

ondly, and perhaps more significantly, from a theoretical perspective, we demonstrate how the gap between truly concurrent and interleaving formalisms can be bridged. Moreover, true concurrency can be captured, and truly concurrent properties reasoned about, in what is traditionally considered to be an interleaving language.

The paper begins with a brief introduction to Petri net theory followed by a discussion of the concepts of concurrency, causal dependency, conflict and confusion. After a brief introduction to the subset of the language of CSP that is needed for the rest of the paper we present a translation from Petri nets to CSP. This is followed by tests for using the CSP model-checker to automatically detect conflict and both conflict-increasing and conflict-decreasing confusion in Petri nets. We conclude with a discussion of this and related work.

2   Petri Nets

Petri net theory was first proposed by Carl Petri in the early 1960s [13]. His intention was to develop a technique for modelling distributed systems and in particular notions of concurrency and non-determinism, that was at the same time both graphical and intuitive, and formal and mathematical.

2.1   Graphical Representation

Petri's nets comprise of: a set of circles or *places* denoting local state; a set of boxes or *transitions* denoting actions; and a set of arrows from places to transitions and transitions to places denoting flow. Thus a net is an ordered bipartite directed graph.

In addition, a set of *marked* places, that is places containing tokens and from which transitions are enabled, may be identified. Marked places are indicated by a filled circle within the circle representing the place. By way of an example, Figure 2 illustrates the Petri nets corresponding to $a \parallel b$, the parallel composition of a and b, and $a.b + b.a$, the non-deterministic choice between their possible orderings. This example will be of particular interest throughout the paper: it is the simplest example of two processes that are distinguished in true concurrency

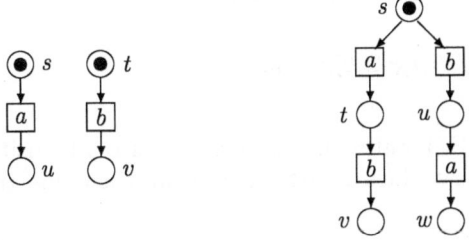

Fig. 2. Petri nets modelling $a \parallel b$ and $a.b + b.a$

but not in the interleaving approach. Places may or may not be named within the graphical representation of a Petri net.

A transition is enabled only if there is a token in each of its preconditions and no token in any of its postconditions. If this is the case and the transition occurs then each such token is removed and a token is added to each place in the transition's post-conditions. For instance, if transition a fires in the nets illustrated in Figure 2 then they will be transformed to the nets illustrated in Figure 3.

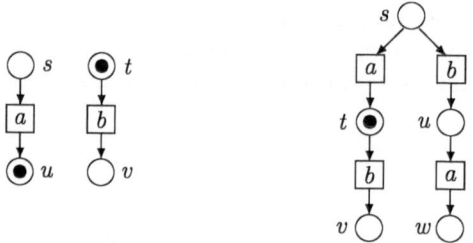

Fig. 3. Petri nets modelling $a \parallel b$ and $a.b + b.a$ after transition a occurs

Provided they do not interfere, that is they share no common preconditions or postconditions, a set of transitions all of which are enabled may fire together in a single atomic step. Tokens are removed from all places in the disjoint union of their preconditions and put in all places in the disjoint union of their post-conditions.

2.2   Formal Representation

As well as the intuitive graphical form illustrated in Figure 2, Petri nets can be captured formally and mathematically.[1] Net $\mathcal{N}$ is the quadruple $(P_{\mathcal{N}}, T_{\mathcal{N}}, F_{\mathcal{N}}, L_{\mathcal{N}})$ where $P_{\mathcal{N}}$ is the set of places, $T_{\mathcal{N}}$ is the set of transitions, and the flow relation $F_{\mathcal{N}} \subseteq (P_{\mathcal{N}} \times T_{\mathcal{N}}) \cup (T_{\mathcal{N}} \times P_{\mathcal{N}})$ links places and transitions. The total function $L_{\mathcal{N}} : T_{\mathcal{N}} \rightarrow Action$ identifies, or labels, transitions with their associated actions. This enables one set of behaviours to follow a certain occurrence of an action and another set of behaviours to follow another occurrence of the same action. Where the function $L_{\mathcal{N}}$ is injective we represent it as the identity function.

The healthiness conditions are as follows:

- $P_{\mathcal{N}} \cap T_{\mathcal{N}} = \emptyset$;   (P1)
- $\mathrm{dom}\, F_{\mathcal{N}} \cup \mathrm{ran}\, F_{\mathcal{N}} = P_{\mathcal{N}} \cup T_{\mathcal{N}}$; and   (P2)
- $\mathrm{dom}\, L_{\mathcal{N}} = T_{\mathcal{N}}$.   (P3)

The first condition (P1) states that no place is also a transition, and the second (P2) states that every place is attached to at least one transition and every

---

[1] A variety of different models have been used for formally capturing Petri nets (cf. [15]). Throughout this paper we will use that described in this section.

transition is attached to at least one place. The third condition (P3) states that every transition has an associated action.

A *marked net* is a pair $(\mathcal{N}, M_{\mathcal{N}})$ where $\mathcal{N}$ is a net and $M_{\mathcal{N}}$ records the number of tokens in each place. Typically $M_{\mathcal{N}}$ is represented as a total function from places to integers, however, since we are concerned in this paper only with *safe nets*, nets in which places can contain at most one token, we simply take $M_{\mathcal{N}} \subseteq P_{\mathcal{N}}$ to be the set of all marked places.

The marked nets modelling $a \parallel b$ and $a.b + b.a$, as illustrated in Figure 2 can therefore respectively be captured as $(\mathcal{N}, \{s, t\})$ and $(\mathcal{N}', \{s\})$ where

$$\mathcal{N} = (\{s, t, u, v\}, \{a, b\}, \{(s, a), (a, u), (t, b), (b, v)\}, \mathrm{id}[\{a, b\}])$$
$$\mathcal{N}' = (\{s, t, u, v, w\}, \{a_1, a_2, b_1, b_2\},$$
$$\{(s, a_1), (a_1, t), (t, b_1), (b_1, v), (s, b_2), (b_2, u), (u, a_2), (a_2, w)\},$$
$$\{(a_1, a), (a_2, a), (b_1, b), (b_2, b)\}).$$

The definition of $\mathcal{N}'$ illustrates how the labelling function is used to capture varying behaviour after different occurences of the same transition. In particular, although transitions a_1 and a_2 both correspond to action a in $a.b + b.a$, no transition can occur after a_2 whilst transition b_1 can occur after transition a_1.

3   Concurrency, Conflict and Confusion

In this section we formally define the notions such as conflict and confusion in concurrent systems that we will be using throughout the rest of the paper.

3.1   Presets, Postsets, Purity and the Availability of Transitions

Given transition $t \in T_{\mathcal{N}}$, we write ${}^{\bullet}_{\mathcal{N}}t$ to represent the *preset* or *preconditions* of t in $\mathcal{N}$, and $t^{\bullet}_{\mathcal{N}}$ to represent the *postset* or *postconditions* of t in $\mathcal{N}$. More formally, given net $\mathcal{N}$ and transition $t \in T_{\mathcal{N}}$, ${}^{\bullet}_{\mathcal{N}}t = \{p : P_{\mathcal{N}} \mid (p, t) \in F_{\mathcal{N}}\}$ and $t^{\bullet}_{\mathcal{N}} = \{p : P_{\mathcal{N}} \mid (t, p) \in F_{\mathcal{N}}\}$. A Petri net N is *pure* provided no place lies in the preset and the postset of the same transition, that is $(\forall t)_{T_{\mathcal{N}}}[{}^{\bullet}_{\mathcal{N}}t \cap t^{\bullet}_{\mathcal{N}} = \emptyset]$.[2] In this paper we are concerned only with *pure* Petri nets.

A transition $t \in T_{\mathcal{N}}$ is enabled in marked net $(\mathcal{N}, M_{\mathcal{N}})$ precisely when all of its preset and none of its postset is marked, or equivalently ${}^{\bullet}_{\mathcal{N}}t \subseteq M_{\mathcal{N}}$ and $t^{\bullet}_{\mathcal{N}} \cap M_{\mathcal{N}} = \emptyset$. If t occurs then the net is transformed to $(\mathcal{N}, M'_{\mathcal{N}})$ where $M'_{\mathcal{N}} = (M_{\mathcal{N}} \setminus {}^{\bullet}_{\mathcal{N}}t) \cup t^{\bullet}_{\mathcal{N}}$. Given pure net $\mathcal{N}$, transition $t \in T_{\mathcal{N}}$ and set of markings $C \subseteq P_{\mathcal{N}}$, we write $C[t\rangle_{\mathcal{N}}$ to indicate that t is enabled from state C in $\mathcal{N}$. Further, we write $C[t\rangle_{\mathcal{N}} C'$ to indicate not only that t is enabled from state C but also that $\mathcal{N}$ will be transformed from state C to state C' if t occurs. The above notation can be used in Boolean expressions. For instance $\neg\, C[t\rangle_{\mathcal{N}}$ states that transition t is not enabled if the only marked places are those in C.

---

[2] We use $(\forall x)_X[bool]$ to denote that Boolean *bool* holds for all x in X.

3.2   Interference and Concurrency

Two transitions $t_1, t_2 \in T_\mathcal{N}$ *interphere* with one another in net $\mathcal{N}$ when a member of the preset or postset of one lies in the preset or postset of the other: thus *Interfere*$(\mathcal{N}, t_1, t_2)$ is the predicate $t_1 \neq t_2 \wedge (\overset{\bullet}{_\mathcal{N}}t_1 \cup t_1 \overset{\bullet}{_\mathcal{N}}) \cap (\overset{\bullet}{_\mathcal{N}}t_2 \cup t_2 \overset{\bullet}{_\mathcal{N}}) \neq \emptyset$. For later use we define the function *IntFree* for net $\mathcal{N}$ and set of transitions $ts \subseteq T_\mathcal{N}$ that returns true precisely when there is no interference between members of ts.

$$IntFree(\mathcal{N}, ts) = (\forall\, t_1, t_2)_{T_\mathcal{N}} [(t_1 \neq t_2) \Rightarrow \neg\, Interfere(\mathcal{N}, t_1, t_2)]$$

The set of transitions $U \subseteq T_\mathcal{N}$ can occur individually and without interference at $C \subseteq P_\mathcal{N}$ in N, written $C[U\rangle_\mathcal{N}$, precisely when predicates $(\forall\, t)_U [C[t\rangle_\mathcal{N}]$ and *IntFree*$(\mathcal{N}, U)$ both hold. Thus $C[U\rangle_\mathcal{N}$ indicates that the transitions in set U can all occur *concurrently* at C in $\mathcal{N}$.

3.3   Causal Dependency, Conflict and Confusion

We say that transitions $t_1, t_2 \in T_\mathcal{N}$ are *causally dependent* or in *sequence* at $C \subseteq P_\mathcal{N}$ in net $\mathcal{N}$ if t_1 is enabled at C but t_2 is not although it is then enabled after t_1 has occured. More formally, predicates $C[t_1\rangle_\mathcal{N}$, $\neg\, C[t_2\rangle_\mathcal{N}$ and $C'[t_2\rangle_\mathcal{N}$ all hold where $C[t_1\rangle_\mathcal{N} C'$.

Conversely, transitions $t_1, t_2 \in T_\mathcal{N}$ are in *conflict* at $C \subseteq P_\mathcal{N}$ in $\mathcal{N}$ if they can occur individually but not together at C. In particular, predicates $C[t_1\rangle_\mathcal{N}$ and $C[t_2\rangle_\mathcal{N}$ both hold but $\neg\, C[\{t_1, t_2\}\rangle_\mathcal{N}$: equivalently,

$$t_1 \neq t_2 \wedge (\overset{\bullet}{_\mathcal{N}}t_1 \cup \overset{\bullet}{_\mathcal{N}}t_2) \subseteq C \wedge (t_1 \overset{\bullet}{_\mathcal{N}} \cup t_2 \overset{\bullet}{_\mathcal{N}}) \cap C = \emptyset \wedge Interfere(\mathcal{N}, t_1, t_2).$$

Given net $\mathcal{N}$, transition $t \in T_\mathcal{N}$ and state $C \subseteq P_\mathcal{N}$ such that $C[t\rangle_\mathcal{N}$, we define *Conflicts*$(\mathcal{N}, C, t)$ to be the set of transitions that are in conflict with t at C. More formally, *Conflicts*$(\mathcal{N}, C, t) = \{t' \in T_\mathcal{N} : C[t'\rangle_\mathcal{N} \wedge \neg\, C[\{t, t'\}\rangle_\mathcal{N}\}$.

A mixture of concurrency and conflict may result in a situation called *confusion* whereby the conflict set of one transition is altered by the occurence of another apparently unrelated transition. In particular, transition t is confused at state C from which it is enabled if there is another transition t' also enabled at C and with which it does not interfere such that the conflict set of t before the occurence of t' is not equal to the conflict set of t after the occurence of t'. More formally, transition $t \in T_\mathcal{N}$ is confused at state $C \subseteq P_\mathcal{N}$ in $\mathcal{N}$ precisely when there exists $t' \in T_\mathcal{N}$ such that $C[\{t, t'\}\rangle_\mathcal{N}$ and *Conflicts*$(\mathcal{N}, C, t) \neq$ *Conflicts*$(\mathcal{N}, C', t)$ where $C[t'\rangle_\mathcal{N} C'$.

There are two types of confusion: conflict-increasing (asymmetric) confusion and conflict-decreasing (symmetric) confusion. The former occurs when additional conflict is introduced, or *Conflicts*$(\mathcal{N}, C, t) \subset$ *Conflicts*$(\mathcal{N}, C't)$, and the latter occurs when some of the conflict is eliminated, or *Conflicts*$(\mathcal{N}, C, t) \supset$ *Conflicts*$(\mathcal{N}, C', t)$. Examples of these are respectively illustrated in Figures 4 and 5.

Conflict-Increasing
Confusion

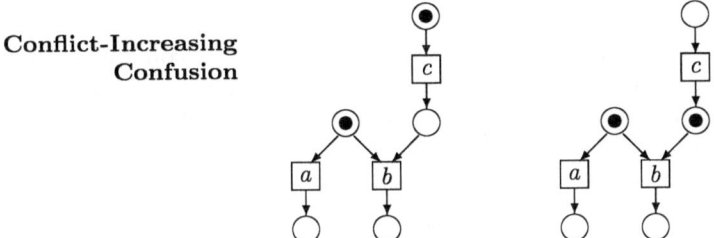

Fig. 4. Initially, transitions a and b are not in conflict. However after the occurrence of c, b becomes enabled and conflict between a and b is introduced

Conflict-Decreasing
Confusion

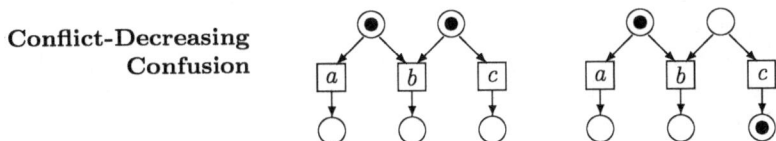

Fig. 5. Transitions a and b are initially in conflict. After the occurrence of c they are no longer in conflict since b is no longer enabled

A single net can contain instances of both conflict-increasing and conflict-decreasing confusion.

4   CSP

The process algebra Communicating Sequential Processes (CSP) [8, 17] is a mathematical language for capturing the behaviour of systems by the recording the occurrence of events. Analysis of the system can then be performed by using the model-checker FDR to *compare* a formal specification *SPEC*, a simple process capturing specific desired properties of the system, with the process describing the model itself.

4.1   Syntax

In this section we give a brief introduction to the subset of the CSP syntax that we will be using throughout the rest of the paper, as well as the traces semantic model for the language [17].

A *process*, as defined in [8], is a pattern of communication that describes the behaviour of a system. Behaviour is described in terms of *events* or synchronous atomic communications, marking points in the evolution of the system. Compound events can be constructed using '.' the dot operator, and a family of compound events is called a *channel*. Channels can be used to represent the passing of values between components. Simple processes may be combined to create more complex composite processes. Moreover processes can be defined in terms of mutually-recursive equations.

The simplest process is *Stop*, the process that denotes deadlock. No events can be performed and this process marks the end of a pattern of communication. For any event a and process P, the process $a \to P$ is willing to communicate event a and, if that event occurs, will subsequently behave as P.

The *choice operator*[3] comes in two forms: the binary operator, and the choice over an indexed set of processes. Given processes P and Q, a set of processes $R(i)$ indexed over some set I, and a predicate $p(i)$ for $i \in I$, the following processes are as described:

$P \square Q$ a choice between P and Q;

$\square \, i : I \mid p(i) \bullet R(i)$ a choice over the set of processes $R(i)$ such that $p(i)$.

There are various representations of the parallel operator in CSP. Throughout the paper we will use the following: given processes P and Q and set of events X, the process $P \parallel_X Q$ denotes the *parallel* combination of P and Q synchronised on set X. Events in the alphabet of P but not in X can be performed without the cooperation of Q and similarly events in the alphabet of Q but not in X can be performed without the cooperation of P. No event in X can occur without the cooperation of both P and Q. We write $\parallel i : I \bullet [A(i)] P(i)$ to denote an *indexed parallel* combination of processes in which each process $P(i)$ can evolve independently but must synchronise upon every event from the set $A(i)$. In an *interleaving* parallel combination no synchronisation is required; therefore in the combination $P \parallel\!\parallel Q$, processes P and Q evolve independently.

Renaming is a useful technique. The process $P[[a'/a]]$ behaves exactly as process P except that every occurrence of the event a is replaced by the event a'. Multiple renamings are performed in the natural way.

4.2 Semantics

There are various ways of describing the behaviour of CSP processes: we may give them an *algebraic semantics* defined by a set of algebraic laws; we may give them an *operational semantics* describing programs using transition diagrams; or we may give them a *denotational semantics* mapping the language into an abstract model based on sets of behaviours.

Various denotational semantic models have been proposed for CSP. Three established models are the *traces* model, the *stable failures* model and the *failures-divergences* model as defined by Roscoe [17]. In addition the *singleton failures* model was introduced in [4] and a further family of failures-based models was discussed in [5]. In this paper we are concerned only with the traces model, $\mathcal{T}$.

---

[3] There are in fact two choice operators in CSP: one denoting internal choice and the other denoting external choice. An *internal choice* is resolved between the processes involved without reference to the environment, whereas an *external choice* may be influenced by the environment and is resolved by the first event to occur. These operators are indistinguishable within the traces semantic model with which we are concerned here and which we will formally introduce in Section 4.2. Hence we consider only external choice throughout this paper.

The Traces Model. A *trace* records a history of behaviour. It is expressed as a sequence of events in which the process has engaged with the head of the sequence being the first event that was communicated. Given a process P, the set $\mathcal{T}[\![P]\!]$ is the set of all possible finite traces of P. Thus the semantic domain of the traces model is the set $\mathbb{P}(\Sigma^*)$ where Σ is the set of all events.

Healthiness Conditions The healthiness conditions of $\mathcal{T}$ are given below:

- $\langle\rangle \in \mathcal{T}[\![P]\!]$,   (T1)
- $tr \frown tr' \in \mathcal{T}[\![P]\!] \Rightarrow tr \in \mathcal{T}[\![P]\!]$.   (T2)

Condition (T1) states that the empty trace is a possible trace of every process and condition (T2) states that the set of traces of any process is prefix-closed.

Semantic Laws The semantic laws for the traces model are then as follows:

$$\mathcal{T}[\![Stop]\!] = \{\langle\rangle\}$$
$$\mathcal{T}[\![a \rightarrow P]\!] = \{tr : \mathcal{T}[\![P]\!] \bullet \langle a\rangle \frown tr\} \cup \langle\rangle$$
$$\mathcal{T}[\![P \,\square\, Q]\!] = \mathcal{T}[\![P]\!] \cup \mathcal{T}[\![Q]\!]$$
$$\mathcal{T}[\![P \,\|_X\, Q]\!] = \{tr : \Sigma^* \mid \operatorname{ran} tr \subseteq \alpha(P) \cup \alpha(Q) \;\wedge \\ tr \upharpoonright (\alpha(P) \cup X) \in \mathcal{T}[\![P]\!] \;\wedge \\ tr \upharpoonright (\alpha(Q) \cup X) \in \mathcal{T}[\![Q]\!]\}$$

where $\alpha(P)$ is the alphabet of process P and where sequence $tr \upharpoonright X$ is the longest subsequence of tr containing only elements from the set X.

4.3   Refinement

The refinement ordering induced by the traces model is based upon reverse containment. One process is traces-refined by another if every trace of the second is also a trace of the first. Given processes P and Q we write

$$P \sqsubseteq_T Q \Leftrightarrow \mathcal{T}[\![Q]\!] \subseteq \mathcal{T}[\![P]\!].$$

The model-checker FDR [7] is used for automatically analysing large or complex systems in CSP. Typically a process *IMPL* modelling the system in question is compared with a more abstract model *SPEC*: thus $SPEC \sqsubseteq_T IMPL$. Model-checker FDR will perform an exhaustive breadth-first search identifying any trace of *IMPL* that is not also a trace of *SPEC*.

5   Capturing Marked Petri Nets as CSP Processes

Used in the conventional manner, the process algebra CSP which adopts an interleaving approach to concurrency cannot model truly concurrent systems. However, in this section we demonstrate that this restriction, the inability to distinguish between the concurrent execution of actions and the non-deterministic choice between the possible orders of their executions, can be overcome if presets and postsets are taken into consideration.

We model a net as the parallel combination of a collection of simple processes, one for each place. Each such process permits the execution of an event corresponding to a transition it lies in the preset of only if it contains a token; similarly, it permits the execution of a transition it lies in the postset of only if it does not contain a token. In fact, to fully mirror the truly concurrent behaviour of Petri nets, we permit the atomic execution of *sets* of transitions provided there is no interference. Thus the process corresponding to each place $p \in P_\mathcal{N}$ in a safe net can be captured by the following pair of mutually recursive processes.

$$FullPlace(\mathcal{N}, p) = \Box\, ts : \mathbb{P}\, T_\mathcal{N} \mid p \in \bigcup_{t \in ts} {}^\bullet_\mathcal{N} t \bullet trans.ts \rightarrow EmptyPlace(\mathcal{N}, p)$$

$$EmptyPlace(\mathcal{N}, p) = \Box\, ts : \mathbb{P}\, T_\mathcal{N} \mid p \in \bigcup_{t \in ts} t^\bullet_\mathcal{N} \bullet trans.ts \rightarrow FullPlace(\mathcal{N}, p)$$

Initially all marked places $p \in M_\mathcal{N}$ behave as $FullPlace(\mathcal{N}, p)$ and all unmarked places $p \in P_\mathcal{N} \setminus M_\mathcal{N}$ behave as $EmptyPlace(\mathcal{N}, p)$. Thus

$$Place(\mathcal{N}, M_\mathcal{N}, p) = \text{if } p \in M_\mathcal{N} \text{ then } FullPlace(\mathcal{N}, p) \text{ else } EmptyPlace(\mathcal{N}, p).$$

To ensure the choice of $ts \in \mathbb{P}\, T_\mathcal{N}$ is restricted to interference-free sets we define

$$NoInterfere(\mathcal{N}) = \Box\, ts : \mathbb{P}\, T_\mathcal{N} \mid IntFree(\mathcal{N}, ts) \bullet trans.ts \rightarrow NoInterfere(\mathcal{N})$$

where *IntFree* is as defined in Section 3.2. Thus process $N_{(\mathcal{N}, M_\mathcal{N})}$ corresponding to marked safe net $(\mathcal{N}, M_\mathcal{N})$ is given by the alphabetized parallel combination

$$N_{(\mathcal{N}, M_\mathcal{N})} = (\, \|_{p \in P_\mathcal{N}} [\alpha(\mathcal{N}, p)] Place(\mathcal{N}, M_\mathcal{N}, p)\,) \,\|_{\Sigma_\mathcal{N}} NoInterfere(\mathcal{N})$$

for $\Sigma_\mathcal{N} = \{trans.ts \mid ts \in \mathbb{P}\, T_\mathcal{N}\}$ where the set $\alpha(\mathcal{N}, p)$ contains the *trans* event for all sets of transitions and where p lies in the preset or the postset of at least one transition: $\alpha(\mathcal{N}, p) = \{trans.(\{t\} \cup ts) \mid t \in T_\mathcal{N}, ts \in \mathbb{P}\, T_\mathcal{N}, p \in ({}^\bullet_\mathcal{N} t \cup t^\bullet_\mathcal{N})\}$.

Experienced CSP users will observe that the above definition is an efficient model: parallel processes will not spawn other parallel processes. Moreover, recursive nets are no more complex than non-recursive nets.

6   Testing for Conflict

We observed in Section 3.3 that conflict occurs in a net when a pair of transitions that are both enabled from a reachable state interfere: thus we have conflict in marked net $(\mathcal{N}, M_\mathcal{N})$ modelled by process $N_{(\mathcal{N}, M_\mathcal{N})}$ if we can find a sequence of place and transition events, $tr \in \Sigma_\mathcal{N}{}^*$ and a pair of transitions $t_1, t_2 \in T_\mathcal{N}$ such that $tr \,^\frown \langle trans.\{t_1\}\rangle \in \mathcal{T}[\![\, N_{(\mathcal{N}, M_\mathcal{N})}\,]\!]$ and $tr \,^\frown \langle trans.\{t_2\}\rangle \in \mathcal{T}[\![\, N_{(\mathcal{N}, M_\mathcal{N})}\,]\!]$ and $Interfere(\mathcal{N}, t_1, t_2)$.

6.1   Using CSP to Capture Conflict

Recall that the model-checker FDR compares two processes, the "SPEC" and the "IMPL", or "LHS" and "RHS" as we will find it more convenient to call them for the rest of this paper. FDR identifies any traces in process RHS that are not present in process LHS. Therefore, if we construct LHS and RHS to be almost identical processes that differ precisely when conflict is present, we can guarantee that FDR will flag all such instances. We achieve this by interleaving two copies of the process corresponding to the net, one primed and one unprimed, and putting them in parallel with a *control* process. The reason for having two copies is that FDR cannot perform backtracking; thus we keep the two copies in step and then demonstate that from the same state they can separately perform distinct conflicting transitions.

Until the occurence of a special event *check*, the control processes on both sides keeps the two copies in step: every unprimed event *trans.ts* is followed directly by the corresponding primed event *trans'.ts*. After the *check* event the behaviour of *RHS* and *LHS* may differ. In particular the right-hand control process allows the unprimed copy to perform an event corresponding to a singleton transition, say $trans.\{t1\}$ for $t1 \in T_\mathcal{N}$. Then, if such a conflicting transition $t_2 \in T_\mathcal{N}$ where $Interfere(\mathcal{N}, t_1, t_2)$ exists, this is followed by event $trans'.\{t2\}$. Conversely, after the *check* event the left-hand control process permits only a single transition event $trans.\{t1\}$ for $t1 \in T_\mathcal{N}$ before deadlocking. Thus, if conflict is present, process *RHS* will be able to perform a final event that process *LHS* cannot perform, and FDR will flag the error.

Before formally defining *LHS* and *RHS* we introduce the primed variant of $N_{(\mathcal{N}, M_\mathcal{N})}$, that is $N'_{(\mathcal{N}, M_\mathcal{N})} = N_{(\mathcal{N}, M_\mathcal{N})}[[trans'.ts/trans.ts \mid ts \in \mathbb{P}\, T_\mathcal{N}]]$, with alphabet $\Sigma'_\mathcal{N} = \{trans'.ts \mid ts \in \mathbb{P}\, T_\mathcal{N}\}$.[4] The left-hand and right-hand processes for detecting conflict are then expressed as the parallel combination of their respective control processes with an interleaving of primed and unprimed copies of the process corresponding to the given net.

$$LHS_{conflict}(\mathcal{N}, M_\mathcal{N}) = (N \, ||| \, N') \, \|_{\Sigma_\mathcal{N} \cup \Sigma'_\mathcal{N}} \, ControlL_c(\mathcal{N})$$

$$RHS_{conflict}(\mathcal{N}, M_\mathcal{N}) = (N \, ||| \, N') \, \|_{\Sigma_\mathcal{N} \cup \Sigma'_\mathcal{N}} \, ControlR_c(\mathcal{N})$$

Before the *check* event occurs both control processes simply keep in step the unprimed and primed copies of the process corresponding to the net.

$$ControlL_c(\mathcal{N}) = \Box\, ts : \mathbb{P}\, T_\mathcal{N} \bullet trans.ts \to trans'.ts \to ControlL_c(\mathcal{N})$$
$$\Box$$
$$check \to AfterCheckL_c(\mathcal{N}).$$

$$ControlR_c(\mathcal{N}) = \Box\, ts : \mathbb{P}\, T_\mathcal{N} \bullet trans.ts \to trans'.ts \to ControlR_c(\mathcal{N})$$
$$\Box$$
$$check \to AfterCheckR_c(\mathcal{N}).$$

---

[4] In Sections 7 and 8 we will use a double primed variant of process $N_{(\mathcal{N}, M_\mathcal{N})}$, that is $N''_{(\mathcal{N}, M_\mathcal{N})} = N_{(\mathcal{N}, M_\mathcal{N})}[[trans''.ts/trans.ts \mid ts \in \mathbb{P}\, T_\mathcal{N}]]$ with alphabet $\Sigma''_\mathcal{N} = \{trans''.ts \mid ts \in \mathbb{P}\, T_\mathcal{N}\}$, as well as set $\Sigma'''_\mathcal{N} = \{trans'''.ts \mid ts \in \mathbb{P}\, T_\mathcal{N}\}$.

After the *check* event, the controling process on the left-hand side, $ControlL_c$ permits one *trans* event, $trans.\{t_1\}$ for some $t_1 \in T_{\mathcal{N}}$, before deadlocking. Conversely, the controling process on the right-hand side, $ControlR_c$ permits one *trans* event, $trans.\{t_1\}$ and then, *if there exists a transition $t_2 \in T_{\mathcal{N}}$ that conflicts with t_1*, allows a further event $trans'.\{t_2\}$.

$$AfterCheckL_c(\mathcal{N}) = \Box\, t_1 : T_{\mathcal{N}} \bullet trans.\{t_1\} \rightarrow Stop$$
$$AfterCheckR_c(\mathcal{N}) = \Box\, t_1 : T_{\mathcal{N}} \bullet trans.\{t_1\} \rightarrow$$
$$\Box\, t_2 : T_{\mathcal{N}} \mid Interfere(\mathcal{N}, t_1, t_2) \bullet trans'.\{t_2\} \rightarrow Stop$$

Thus, if conflict is present, the right-hand side will be able to execute a trace that the left-hand side can not. Model-checker FDR will detect this discrepancy and the following refinement check will fail.

$$LHS_{conflict}(\mathcal{N}, M_{\mathcal{N}}) \sqsubseteq_{\mathcal{T}} RHS_{conflict}(\mathcal{N}, M_{\mathcal{N}})$$

7   Testing for Conflict-Decreasing Confusion

As observed in Section 3.3, conflict-decreasing confusion can arise when there is a mixture of concurrency and conflict. We need to demonstrate that the conflict set of a given transition is reduced by the occurence of another transition with which it does not interfere. Equivalently, we have conflict-decreasing confusion in net $\mathcal{N}$ modelled by process $N_{(\mathcal{N}, M_{\mathcal{N}})}$ after sequence of transitions $tr \in \mathcal{T} [\![\, N_{(\mathcal{N}, M_{\mathcal{N}})}\,]\!]$ if we can find transitions $t_1, t_2, t_3 \in T_{\mathcal{N}}$ where t_1 and t_3 do not interfere such that t_1, t_2 and t_3 are all enabled after tr and such that t_1 and t_2 conflict after trace tr but not after trace $tr \frown \langle trans.\{t_3\}\rangle$.

Recall that in Section 6 we needed two copies, one primed and one unprimed, of the process corresponding to the given net in order to detect conflict: processes $N_{(\mathcal{N}, M_{\mathcal{N}})}$ and $N_{(\mathcal{N}, M_{\mathcal{N}})}{}'$ are needed to demonstrate that there is conflict between t_1 and t_2 after trace $tr \in \mathcal{T} [\![\, N_{(\mathcal{N}, M_{\mathcal{N}})}\,]\!]$. It follows that we need a third copy, $N_{(\mathcal{N}, M_{\mathcal{N}})}{}''$, to demonstrate that t_2 is no longer enabled after transition t_3 and hence that some of the conflict has been eliminated: observe that t_1 is still enabled after t_3 since it was enabled before t_3 and they do not interfere.

When detecting conflict in Section 6 we constructed processes *LHS* and *RHS* that differed only if conflict was present. Each was built from the parallel combination of a control process and interleaved copies of the process corresponding to the given net. Similarly, here we construct processes *LHS* and *RHS* that differ only if conflict-decreasing confusion is present and build them from the parallel combination of a control process and (this time three) interleaved copies of the process corresponding to the given net.

$$LHS_d(\mathcal{N}, M_{\mathcal{N}}) = (N \,|\!|\!|\, N' \,|\!|\!|\, N'') \,\|_{\Sigma_{\mathcal{N}} \cup \Sigma'_{\mathcal{N}} \cup \Sigma''_{\mathcal{N}}}\, ControlL_d(\mathcal{N})$$
$$RHS_d(\mathcal{N}, M_{\mathcal{N}}) = (N \,|\!|\!|\, N' \,|\!|\!|\, N'') \,\|_{\Sigma_{\mathcal{N}} \cup \Sigma'_{\mathcal{N}} \cup \Sigma''_{\mathcal{N}}}\, ControlR_d(\mathcal{N})$$

Before the occurence of the *check* event, both control processes keep in step the three copies of the process corresponding to the net.

$ControlL_d(\mathcal{N}) = \Box\, ts : \mathbb{P}\,T_{\mathcal{N}} \bullet trans.ts \rightarrow trans'.ts \rightarrow trans''.ts \rightarrow ControlL_d(\mathcal{N})$
$\qquad\qquad\quad \Box$
$\qquad\qquad\quad check \rightarrow AfterCheckL_d(\mathcal{N})$

$ControlR_d(\mathcal{N}) = \Box\, ts : \mathbb{P}\,T_{\mathcal{N}} \bullet trans.ts \rightarrow trans'.ts \rightarrow trans''.ts \rightarrow ControlR_d(\mathcal{N})$
$\qquad\qquad\quad \Box$
$\qquad\qquad\quad check \rightarrow AfterCheckR_d(\mathcal{N})$

After the *check* event, the controling processes on both sides permit one *trans* event, $trans.\{t_1\}$ for some $t_1 \in T_{\mathcal{N}}$, followed by a *trans'* event, $trans.\{t_2\}$ for some $t_2 \in T_{\mathcal{N}}$ such that t_1 and t_2 conflict, followed in turn by a *trans''* event, $trans''.\{t_3\}$ for some $t_3 \in T_{\mathcal{N}}$ that does not interfere with t_1. Only after this point might the behaviour of the two sides differ. The control process on the left-hand side permits the event $trans''.\{t_2\}$, although this will be blocked by process $N_{(\mathcal{N},M_{\mathcal{N}})}''$ if t_2 is not enabled after t_3. Conversely, the process on the right-hand side always permits without obstruction from $N_{(\mathcal{N},M_{\mathcal{N}})}''$ the event $trans'''.\{t_2\}$ which will subsequently be renamed to $trans''.\{t_2\}$.[5]

$AfterCheckL_d(\mathcal{N}) =$
$\quad \Box\, t_1 : T_{\mathcal{N}} \bullet trans.\{t_1\} \rightarrow$
$\qquad \Box\, t_2 : T_{\mathcal{N}} \mid Interfere(\mathcal{N}, t_1, t_2) \bullet trans'.\{t_2\} \rightarrow$
$\qquad\quad \Box\, t_3 : T_{\mathcal{N}} \mid IntFree(\mathcal{N}, \{t_1, t_3\}) \bullet trans''.\{t_3\} \rightarrow trans''.\{t_2\} \rightarrow Stop$
$AfterCheckR_d(\mathcal{N}) =$
$\quad \Box\, t_1 : T_{\mathcal{N}} \bullet trans.\{t_1\} \rightarrow$
$\qquad \Box\, t_2 : T_{\mathcal{N}} \mid Interfere(\mathcal{N}, t_1, t_2) \bullet trans'.\{t_2\} \rightarrow$
$\qquad\quad \Box\, t_3 : T_{\mathcal{N}} \mid IntFree(\mathcal{N}, \{t_1, t_3\}) \bullet trans''.\{t_3\} \rightarrow trans'''.\{t_2\} \rightarrow Stop$

Thus, if one side can perform trace $tr^\frown\langle check, trans.\{t_1\}, trans'.\{t_2\}, trans''.\{t_3\}\rangle$ then so can the other. However, the right-hand side can always extend this trace with the event $trans'''.\{t_2\}$, to be renamed to $trans''.\{t_2\}$ but the left-hand side can it extend it with $trans''.\{t_2\}$ only if t_2 is still enabled after t_3, that is if conflict-decreasing confusion is *not* present.

Hence, whenever conflict-decreasing confusion *is* present, the right-hand side will be able to execute a trace that the left-hand side can not. Model-checker FDR will detect this discrepancy and the following refinement check, incorporating the necessary renaming, will fail.

$$LHS_d(\mathcal{N}, M_{\mathcal{N}}) \sqsubseteq_\mathcal{T} (\, RHS_d(\mathcal{N}, M_{\mathcal{N}})\,)[[trans''.ts/trans'''.ts \mid ts \in \mathbb{P}\,T_{\mathcal{N}}]]$$

8   Testing for Conflict-Increasing Confusion

Conflict-increasing confusion, like conflict-decreasing confusion, can arise when there is a mixture of concurrency and conflict. This time the conflict set of a

---

[5] The purpose of the renaming is to avoid synchronisation with $N_{(\mathcal{N},M_{\mathcal{N}})}''$.

given transition is *augmented* by the occurence of another transition with which it does not interfere. Equivalently, we have conflict-increasing confusion in net $\mathcal{N}$ modelled by process $N_{(\mathcal{N},M_{\mathcal{N}})}$ after sequence of transitions $tr \in \mathcal{T}[\![\ N_{(\mathcal{N},M_{\mathcal{N}})}\ ]\!]$ if we can find transitions $t_1, t_2, t_3 \in T_{\mathcal{N}}$ where t_1 and t_3 do not interfere but t_1 and t_2 do, such that t_1 and t_3 are all enabled after tr and such that t_2 is enabled after trace $tr \frown \langle trans.\{t_3\}\rangle$ but not after trace tr.

The techniques for demonstrating the presence of conflict-increasing confusion are similar to those for demonstrating the presence of conflict-decreasing confusion. Once more both the left-hand side and the right hand side are built from the parallel combination of a control process and an interleaving of the unprimed, primed and double-primed variants of the process corresponding to the given net. This time the unprimed process is used to demonstrate the availability of t_1, the double-primed process is used to demonstrate the availability of t_2 after t_3 whilst the primed process concerns the possible availability of t_2 before t_3: the right-hand side will guarantee the execution of $trans'.\{t_3\}$ through renaming whilst this event will be unavailable on the left-hand side when conflict-increasing confusion is present.

The identical behaviour of the left-hand side and the right-hand side before the *check* event can therefore be captured by

$$LHS_i(\mathcal{N}, M_{\mathcal{N}}) = (N\ |\!|\!|\ N'\ |\!|\!|\ N'')\ \|_{\Sigma_{\mathcal{N}} \cup \Sigma'_{\mathcal{N}} \cup \Sigma''_{\mathcal{N}}}\ ControlL_i(\mathcal{N})$$

$$RHS_i(\mathcal{N}, M_{\mathcal{N}}) = (N\ |\!|\!|\ N'\ |\!|\!|\ N'')\ \|_{\Sigma_{\mathcal{N}} \cup \Sigma'_{\mathcal{N}} \cup \Sigma''_{\mathcal{N}}}\ ControlR_i(\mathcal{N})$$

where

$$ControlL_i(\mathcal{N}) = \square\, ts : \mathbb{P}T_{\mathcal{N}} \bullet trans.ts \rightarrow trans'.ts \rightarrow trans''.ts \rightarrow ControlL_i(\mathcal{N})$$
$$\square$$
$$check \rightarrow AfterCheckL_i(\mathcal{N})$$

$$ControlR_i(\mathcal{N}) = \square\, ts : \mathbb{P}T_{\mathcal{N}} \bullet trans.ts \rightarrow trans'.ts \rightarrow trans''.ts \rightarrow ControlR_i(\mathcal{N})$$
$$\square$$
$$check \rightarrow AfterCheckR_i(\mathcal{N}).$$

After the *check* event the behaviour may vary. Having shown that t_1 is enabled and that t_3 and t_2 are enabled in sequence, the processes may differ if t_2 is not enabled before t_3 since the right-hand side is constrained to synchronise with $N_{(\mathcal{N},M_{\mathcal{N}})}'$ whilst the left-hand side is not.

$$AfterCheckL_i(\mathcal{N}) =$$
$$\square\, t_1 : T_{\mathcal{N}} \bullet trans.\{t_1\} \rightarrow$$
$$\square\, t_2, t_3 : T_{\mathcal{N}} \mid Interfere(\mathcal{N}, t_1, t_2) \wedge IntFree(\mathcal{N}, \{t_1, t_3\}) \bullet$$
$$trans''.\{t_3\} \rightarrow trans''.\{t_2\} \rightarrow trans'.\{t_2\} \rightarrow Stop$$
$$AfterCheckR_i(\mathcal{N}) =$$
$$\square\, t_1 : T_{\mathcal{N}} \bullet trans.\{t_1\} \rightarrow$$
$$\square\, t_2, t_3 : T_{\mathcal{N}} \mid Interfere(\mathcal{N}, t_1, t_2) \wedge IntFree(\mathcal{N}, \{t_1, t_3\}) \bullet$$
$$trans''.\{t_3\} \rightarrow trans''.\{t_2\} \rightarrow trans'''.\{t_2\} \rightarrow Stop$$

If one side can perform trace $tr \frown \langle check, trans.\{t_1\}, trans''.\{t_3\}, trans''.\{t_2\}\rangle$ then so can the other. However, the right-hand side can always extend this trace with the event $trans'''.\{t_2\}$, to be renamed to $trans'.\{t_2\}$, but the left-hand side can it extend it with $trans'.\{t_2\}$ only if t_2 is enabled before t_3, that is if conflict-increasing confusion is *not* present.

Hence, whenever conflict-decreasing confusion *is* present, the right-hand side will be able to execute a trace that the left-hand side can not. Model-checker FDR will detect this discrepancy and the following refinement check, incorporating the necessary renaming, will fail.

$$LHS_i(\mathcal{N}, M_\mathcal{N}) \sqsubseteq_T (\, RHS_i(\mathcal{N}, M_\mathcal{N}) \,)[[trans'.ts/trans'''.ts \mid ts \in \mathbb{P}\, T_\mathcal{N}]]$$

9   Discussion

In this paper we have presented a translation from Petri nets to CSP and shown how this translation might be used to automatically detect instances of conflict and confusion in CSP. This is a slightly surprising result since the interleaving semantic models of CSP cannot distinguish between the concurrent execution of actions and the non-deterministic choice between the possible orders of their executions. It is only because we include flow information, or presets and postsets of transitions, that these notions can be captured and hence detected.

Why Confusion is of Concern. As observed in Section 1, motivations for truly concurrent models over their interleaving counterparts are given in many papers on Petri nets, trace theory and pomsets e.g. [14]. Here we consider a simple example, an unfortunate model of a control system that might have been developed from a component concerning safety and another concerning maintenance, that illustrates why the presence of confusion might be of concern. The parallel com-

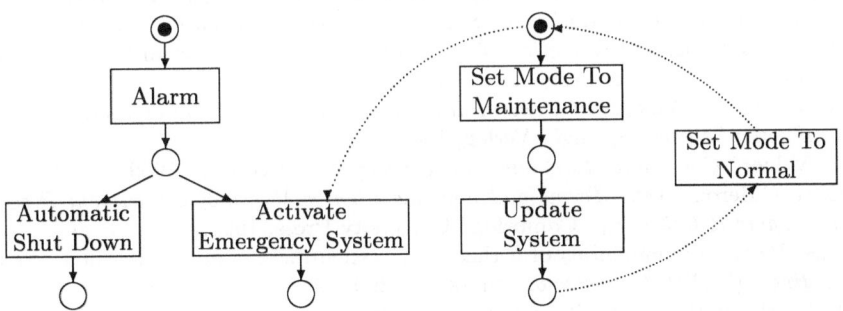

Fig. 6. A simplified model of a control system

bination of these components lead to confusion: the emergency system cannot always be activated whenever the system might be automatically shut down.

Tractability of Verification. State space explosion is always of paramount concern when model-checking. Even though, as we have observed, clarity has been chosen over efficiency in our CSP models as presented here, the state space will grow at a reasonable rate as we only have three interleaved copies of the net.

Conclusions. As systems get more and more complex there is a move towards building separate components for managing distinct parts of a system. Whilst factorisation is a useful technique, our simple example in Figure 6 illustrates the increasing importance this will place on the detection of confusion.

Acknowledgements. The author like to thank Bill Roscoe, Michael Goldsmith and Gavin Lowe for helpful comments leading to cleaner and more efficient CSP definitions. In addition thanks go to Doron Peled who initially suggested that this might be an interesting avenue to explore.

References

1. Petri nets tool database. Available via URL.
   http://www.daimi.au.dk/PetriNets/tools/.
2. J. A. Bergstra and J. W. Klop. Algebra of communicating processes with abstraction. *Theoretical Computer Science*, 37(1), 1985.
3. E. Best, F.S. de Boer, and C. Palamidessi. Partial order and sos semantics for linear constraint programs. In *Proceedings of Coordination 97*, volume 1282 of *LNCS*. Springer-Verlag, 1997.
4. C. Bolton. *On the Refinement of State-Based and Event-Based Models*. D.Phil., University of Oxford, 2002.
5. C. Bolton and G. Lowe. A hierarchy of failures-based models. In *Proceedings of the 10th International Workshop on Expressiveness in Concurrency: EXPRESS'03*, 2003.
6. E. Clarke, O. Grumberg, and D. Peled. *Model-Checking*. The MIT Press, 1999.
7. Formal Systems (Europe) Ltd. *Failures-Divergence Refinement FDR 2 User Manual*, 1999. Available via URL http://www.fsel.com/fdr2_manual.html.
8. C. A. R. Hoare. *Communicating Sequential Processes*. Prentice Hall, 1985.
9. A. Mazurkiewicz. Introduction to trace theory. In V. Diekert and G. Rozenberg, editors, *The book of traces*. World Scientific, 1995.
10. R. Milner. *A Calculus of Communicating Systems*, volume 92 of *Lecture Notes in Computer Science*. Springer-Verlag, 1980.
11. R. Milner. *Communications and concurrency*. Prentice Hall, 1989.
12. E.-R. Olderog. *Nets, Terms and Formulas: Three Views of Concurrent Processes and Their Relationship*. Cambridge University Press, 1991.
13. C.A. Petri. Fundamentals of a theory of asynchronous information flow. In *Proceedings of IFIP, Congress'62*, pages 386–390, 1962.
14. V. Pratt. On the composition of processes. In *Proceedings of 1982 ACM Symposium on Principles of Programming Languages (POPL)*, 1982.
15. W. Reisig. *Petri Nets*. Springer, 1982.
16. W. Reisig and G. Rozenberg. Informal introduction to petri nets. *Lecture Notes in Computer Science*, 1491, 1998.
17. A. W. Roscoe. *The Theory and Practice of Concurrency*. Prentice Hall, 1997.
18. H. Störrle. An evaluation of high-end tools for petri-nets. Technical Report 9802, Ludwig-Maximilians-Universität München, 1997.
19. G. Winskel. *Events in Computation*. D.Phil, University of Edinburgh, 1980.

Combining CSP and B for Specification and Property Verification*

Michael Butler[1] and Michael Leuschel[1,2]

[1] School of Electronics and Computer Science,
University of Southampton,
Highfield, Southampton, SO17 1BJ, UK
{mjb,mal}@ecs.soton.ac.uk
[2] Institut für Informatik, Heinrich-Heine Universität Düsseldorf,
Universitätsstr. 1, D-40225 Düsseldorf
leuschel@cs.uni-duesseldorf.de

Abstract. PROB is a model checking tool for the B Method. In this paper we present an extension of PROB that supports checking of specifications written in a combination of CSP and B. We explain how the notations are combined semantically and give an overview of the implementation of the combination. We illustrate the benefit that appropriate use of CSP, in conjunction with our tool, gives to B developments both for specification and for verification purposes.

Keywords: B-Method, Tool Support, Model Checking, Animation, Logic Programming, Constraints.

1 Introduction

The B-method, originally devised by J.-R. Abrial [1], is a theory and methodology for formal development of computer systems. It is used by industries in a range of critical domains, most notably railway control. B is based on the notion of *abstract machine* and the notion of *refinement*. The variables of an abstract machine are typed using set theoretic constructs such as sets, relations and functions. Typically these are constructed from basic types such as integers and given types from the problem domain (e.g., *Name, User, Session*, etc). The invariant of a machine is specified using predicate logic. Operations of a machine are specified as *generalised substitutions*, which allow deterministic and nondeterministic state transitions to be specified. There are two main proof activities in B: *consistency checking*, which is used to show that the operations of a machine preserve the invariant, and *refinement checking*, which is used to show

---

* This research is being carried out as part of the EU funded research projects: IST 511599 RODIN (Rigorous Open Development Environment for Complex Systems) and IST-2001-38059 ASAP (Advanced Specialization and Analysis for Pervasive Systems).

J.S. Fitzgerald, I.J. Hayes, and A. Tarlecki (Eds.): FM 2005, LNCS 3582, pp. 221–236, 2005.

that one machine is a valid refinement of another. These activities are supported by industrial strength tools, such as Atelier-B [19] and the B-toolkit [3]. In this paper, we focus on consistency checking.

In previous work [11], we have presented the PROB animator and model checker. Based on Prolog, the PROB tool supports automated consistency checking of B machines via *model checking* [5]. For exhaustive model checking, the given sets must be restricted to small finite sets, and integer variables must be restricted to small numeric ranges. This allows the checking to traverse all the reachable states of the machine. PROB can also be used to explore the state space non-exhaustively and find potential problems. The user can set an upper bound on the number of states to be traversed or can interrupt the checking at any stage. PROB will generate and graphically display counter-examples when it discovers a violation of the invariant. PROB can also be used as an animator of a B specification. So, the model checking facilities are still useful for infinite state machines, not as a verification tool, but as a sophisticated debugging and testing tool.

In the Event B approach [2], a B machine is viewed as a reactive system that continually executes enabled operations in an interleaved fashion. This allows parallel activity to be easily modelled as an interleaving of operation executions. However, while B machines are good at modelling parallel activity, they can be less convenient at modelling sequential activity. Typically one has to introduce an abstract 'program counter' to order the execution of actions. This can be a lot less transparent than the way in which one orders action execution in process algebras such as CSP [9]. CSP provides operators such as sequential composition, choice and parallel composition of processes, as well as synchronous communication between parallel processes.

Our motivation is to use CSP and B together in a complementary way. B can be used to specify abstract state and can be used to specify operations of a system in terms of their enabling conditions and effect on the abstract state. CSP can be used to give an overall specification of the coordination of operations. To marry the two approaches, we take the view that the execution of an operation in a B machine corresponds to an event in CSP terms. Semantically we view a B machine as a process that can engage in events in the same way that a CSP process can. The meaning of a combined CSP and B specification is the parallel composition of both specifications. The B machine and the CSP process must synchronise on common events, that is, an operation can only happen in the combined system when it is allowed both by the B and the CSP. There is much existing work on combining state based approaches such as B with process algebras such as CSP and we review some of that in a later section.

In [10] we presented the CIA (CSP Interpreter and Animator) tool, a Prolog implementation of CSP. As both ProB and CIA are implemented in Prolog, we were provided with a unique opportunity to combine these two to form a tool that supports animation and model checking of specifications written in a combination of CSP and B. This paper reports on the combined tool. In Section 2 we provide an overview of the PROB and CIA tools. In Section 3 we describe how the tools are combined and what the effect of the combination is.

We envisage two main uses of the combined tool. Firstly it can be used to animate and model check specifications which are a combination of B and CSP. We illustrate this in Section 4. The second use of the tool, described in Section 5, is to analyse trace properties of a B machine. In this case the behaviour is fully specified in B, but we use CSP to specify some desirable or undesirable behaviours and use PROB to find traces of the B machine that exhibit those behaviours.

2   Background

ProB. PROB [11] is an animation and model checking tool for the B method. PROB 's animation facilities allow users to gain confidence in their specifications, and unlike the animator provided by the B-Toolkit, the user does not have to guess the right values for the operation arguments or choice variables. The undecidability of animating B is overcome by restricting animation to finite sets and integer ranges, while efficiency is achieved by delaying the enumeration of variables as long as possible. PROB also contains a model checker [5] and a constraint-based checker, both of which can be used to detect various errors in B specifications.

The PROB system has been developed mainly in SICStus Prolog, with graphical user interfaces implemented in Tcl/Tk and also Java. PROB uses the JBTools package to translate abstract machine notation (AMN) [1] specifications into XML, while the Pillow package allows the conversion of XML files into a Prolog term representation. The PROB front end then postprocesses the general Prolog term tree representation of the Pillow library output into a more structured representation that serves as the input to the PROB interpreter. The PROB *interpreter* recurses through this structured representation of B machines and makes calls to the PROB *kernel*, which implements support for the basic datatypes and operations of the B-language. The PROB kernel itself is written in SICStus Prolog with co-routining (i.e., **when** declarations) and constraints (finite domain constraints using CLP(FD)). The PROB animator, and the various checking tools described below all make use of the PROB interpreter in various ways.

PROB provides two ways of systematically checking a B machine: 1. a *temporal* model checking [5] which tries to find a sequence of operations that, starting from an initial state, leads to a state which violates the invariant (or exhibits some other error, such as deadlocking, assertion violations, or abort conditions); and 2. a *constraint-based* checking, which finds a state of the machine that satisfies the invariant, but where we can apply a single operation to reach a state that violates the invariant (or again exhibits some other error). More details can be found in [11]. Recently *refinement checking* has also been added, which can be used to check refinement between two B specifications. In case refinement is violated, PROB displays a sequence of operations that can be performed by the "refinement" machine but not by the specification machine.

The CSP Interpreter and Animator. CSP is a process algebra defined by Hoare [9]. The first semantics associated with CSP was a denotational seman- tics in terms of traces, failures and (failure and) divergences. An operational semantics has later been developed [15], which forms the basis of the interpreter and animator presented in [10]. This interpreter was also developed in SICStus Prolog. No CLP (Constraint Logic Programming) primitives were used but co- routining (i.e., `when` declarations) were used to ensure that channel constraints are delayed until they are sufficiently instantiated to evaluate them. The imple- mentation presented in [10] covers a large part of CSP, see Figure 1. In the light of integration with PROB we have improved the parser (which uses Prolog's Def- inite Clause Grammars) and we have moved much closer to the CSP-M syntax as employed by FDR [16, 7].[1]

As the CSP interpreter is also written also in SICStus Prolog, at least from a technical point of view, it is now feasible to integrate CSP and B. In the following section we describe how this was done, starting out from the theoretical underpinnings and then leading on to the practical aspects.

Operator	Syntax	Ascii Syntax
stop	$STOP$	`STOP`
skip	$SKIP$	`SKIP`
prefix	$a \rightarrow Q$	`a->P`
conditional prefix	$a?x : C \rightarrow P$	`a?x:C->P`
external choice	$P \square Q$	`P [] Q`
internal choice	$P \sqcap Q$	`P |~| Q`
interleaving	$P|||Q$	`P ||| Q`
parallel composition	$P \, [A] \, Q$	`P [| A |] Q`
sequential composition	$P; Q$	`P ; Q`
hiding	$P \backslash A$	`P \ A`
renaming	$P[R]$	`P [[ R ]]`
timeout	$P \triangleright Q$	`P [> Q`
interrupt	$P \triangle_i Q$	`P /\ Q`
if then else	$if \; C \; then \; P \; else \; Q$	`if C then P else Q`
let expressions	$let \; v = e \; in \; P$	`let V=E in P`
agent definition	$A = P$	`A = P;`

Fig. 1. Summary of syntax of CSP

3   Combining B and CSP

In our work we have adopted and developed the approach of integration depicted in Figure 2. (How this compares to earlier work is discussed later in the paper.) In

---

[1] But there are still a few differences and extra features. For example, multiple process definitions are allowed and treated like an external choice and process definitions can be terminated by a double semicolon to ease error recovery during parsing. However, variable names still have to start with an uppercase letter or an underscore and channel declarations are ignored.

essence, the B and CSP specifications are composed in parallel. The B operations must synchronize with channel events of the CSP specification having the same name as the B operation. Channel events of the CSP which have no counterpart in the B (such as channel D in Figure 2) can occur independently, while B operations that have no CSP counterpart are prevented from being executed. Below we present more formally how this synchronization is achieved, starting out from the state information of a combined B/CSP specification and then progressing on to how to formally perform the synchronization.

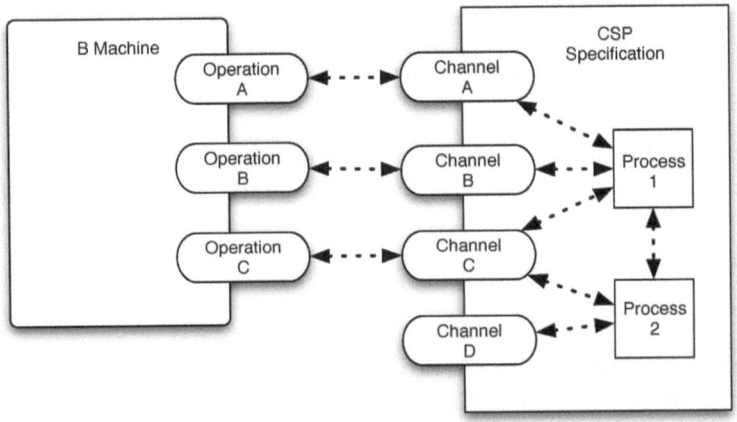

Fig. 2. Illustrating the synchronisation of B and CSP specifications

Combining State Information. The state of a B machine is a mapping from variables to values, while the state of a CSP process is a syntactic process expression. So, for example, the state of the simple B machine in Figure 3 immediately after executing $Set(cc)$ would be represented as $\{xx \mapsto cc\}$, while the state of the simple CSP specification in Figure 4 would be $Get.cc \to MAIN$. A state of a combined B/CSP specification is thus simply a pair, whose first component is a B state and second component a CSP process expression. For example, the state of the combination of Figures 3 and 4 immediately after executing $Set(cc)$ would be $(\{xx \mapsto cc\}, Get.cc \to MAIN)$.

Mapping Operations to Channels. The approach we have chosen is to translate every argument and return value of a B operation into a separate data value of a CSP channel. To ease the writing of succinct CSP specifications, we do not require the CSP to provide all channel values. If channel values are missing any B value is allowed for synchronization on that argument.

For a B operation of the form $X \longleftarrow op(Y) \hat{=} S$, we refer to $a \longleftarrow op(b)$ as an operation call. We first define a function *channel* which maps B operation calls

MACHINE *Simple*   OPERATIONS
SETS
$\quad AA = \{aa, bb, cc\}$ *Set(newval)*$\hat{=}$
VARIABLES $\quad$ PRE $\;$ *newval* $\in AA$
$\quad xx$ $\quad$ THEN $\;$ *xx := newval*
INVARIANT $\quad$ END;
$\quad xx \in AA$ *res* $\longleftarrow$ *Get* =
INITIALISATION $\quad$ BEGIN $\qquad$ *res := xx*
$\quad xx := aa$ $\quad$ END

Fig. 3. Simple B machine

$$Set?\,Val \rightarrow Get!\,Val \rightarrow MAIN$$

Fig. 4. Simple CSP Specification

to possible CSP channel events. Let *op* be an operation of a B machine taking $n \geq 0$ arguments and returning $m \geq 0$ values, and let $a_1, \ldots, a_n$ be arguments to that operation and let $r_1, \ldots, r_m$ be return values. We then define

$$channel(r_1, \ldots, r_m \leftarrow op(a_1, \ldots, a_n)) = \{\; op.a_1.\ldots.a_k \mid 0 \leq k \leq n \} \;\cup$$
$$\{\; op.a_1.\ldots.a_n.r_1.\ldots.r_k \mid 1 \leq k \leq m \}$$

(If m is 0 we take the liberty of not writing the result arrow "$\leftarrow$".)

For example for the B machine in Figure 3, we have

$$channel(Set(aa)) \;=\; \{Set, Set.aa\}$$
$$channel(aa \leftarrow Get) \;=\; \{Get, Get.aa\}$$

Intuitively, this means that a channel event *Set* will synchronise with all possible executions of the B operation *Set*, whereas *Set.aa* will synchronise only with the execution of *Set* for the particular argument *aa*.

Deriving an Operational Semantics. We suppose that the B operational semantics is given by a ternary relation $\rightarrow$ (in practice computed by PROB), where $\sigma \rightarrow_o \sigma'$ with $o = r_1, \ldots, r_m \leftarrow op(a_1, \ldots, a_n)$ means that in the state σ of a B machine we can execute the operation *op* with arguments $a_1, \ldots, a_k$ giving the return values $r_1, \ldots, r_m$ and producing the new state σ'.

The CSP operational semantics is given by a similar relation $\rightarrow$, where $P \rightarrow_{ch.a_1.\ldots.a_n} P'$ denotes the fact that the process expression P can produce the channel event $ch.a_1.\ldots.a_n$ and evolve into the new process expression P'.

We can now define our new operational semantics of a combined B and CSP specification by $(\sigma, P) \rightarrow_A (\sigma', P')$ iff $\sigma \rightarrow_o \sigma'$ and $P \rightarrow_A P'$ and $A \in channel(O)$.

Computing the Operational Semantics. The question now is: how can we compute $(\sigma, P) \rightarrow_A (\sigma', P')$ in practice? The first part, $\sigma \rightarrow_o \sigma'$, is computed by PROB, while $P \rightarrow_A P'$ is computed by the CSP interpreter. The remaining final part, checking $A \in channel(O)$ has been implemented by unifying the B operation arguments with the CSP channel values (those provided). So, synchronisation is achieved by Prolog unification. This means we have a very flexible way of combining CSP and B as information can flow in both directions. In other words, the CSP can drive the B or vice-versa or a combination thereof. The use of co-routining in both PROB and the CSP interpreter not only makes this kind of synchronization possible but also efficient. Indeed, both the B and CSP parts can provide concrete data values, and as soon as those are available the co-routining mechanism will trigger the relevant tests in either the B or the CSP part (or both). If any of those tests fail the search space is immediately pruned, resulting in a (possibly considerable) efficiency gain, when compared to computing the B and CSP operational semantics in isolation.[2]

Observe that in this translation, no distinction is made between arguments and return values. Indeed, PROB itself makes little distinction between arguments and return values (the only difference is that it is easier to extract typing for arguments). This allows for a very flexible way of synchronising, e.g., giving the CSP the option of imposing return values or just retrieving them.

The Implementation. The above described combination of B and CSP has been integrated into the latest release of PROB. Many of PROB's features specific to B continue to work for combined B/CSP specifications: backtrackable automatic animation, graphical visualization possibly with optional state space reduction [12], temporal model checking with detection of invariant, assertion violations or deadlocks, refinement checking, and many more.

Figure 5 shows the state space, as visualized by the new version of PROB, for the combination of the B machine from Figure 3 and the CSP specification from Figure 4. The figure clearly shows how the CSP has imposed that every Set operation is followed by a Get operation. The CSP also imposes that the Get operation must return the same value as was given to the Set operation. Hence, the absence of deadlocks in Figure 5 (formally verified by PROB) can be viewed as proving a temporal property of the B machine: whenever one does a Set operation with argument x one can perform a Get operation and the result is equal to x.[3] We will return to this usage of combining CSP and B in Section 5.

To conclude this section, let us use the same B machine from Figure 3 but use the following CSP specification:

$$MAIN = Set \rightarrow Cst \qquad Cst = Get \rightarrow Cst$$

Here, we have used the CSP to restrict the B machine so that its variable can only be assigned once, and that the variable value can only be read after it has

---

[2] In the worst case if both B and CSP wait for each other to provide concrete data values the PROB enumeration of the B datatypes will be triggered and drive the interpreter.

[3] In CTL one could write $\forall x.(AG\ Set(x) \Rightarrow X(x \leftarrow Get))$.

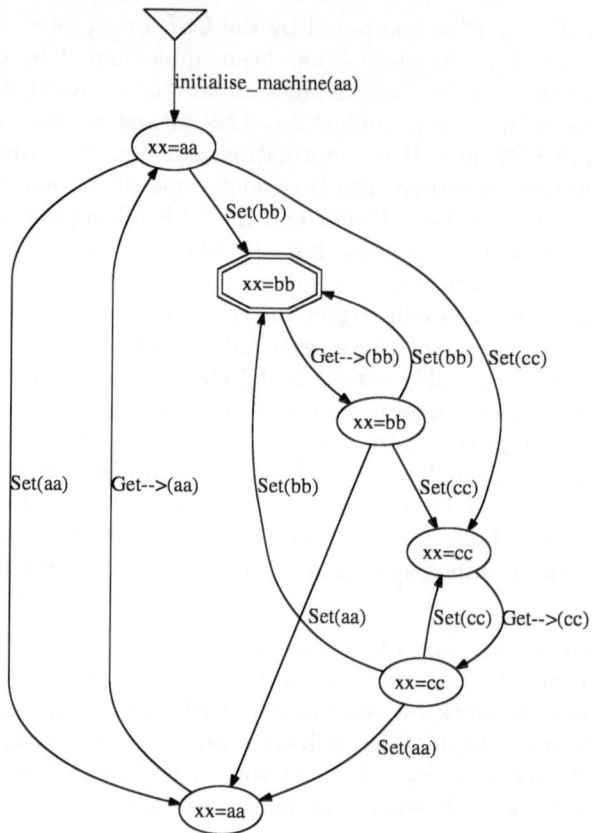

Fig. 5. The state space of combination of the two simple B and CSP specifications

been assigned. This is a simple illustration of how one can use the combination of B and CSP for specification purposes, and the state space computed by PROB can be found in Figure 6. In the next section we will illustrate this usage on a more interesting example.

4   Specifying Using B and CSP

In this section we illustrate the use of a combination of B and CSP to specify a system. The example we use to illustrate this concerns a service for distributing tokens to customers via offices and is based on [8]. The B part of our specification models a database mapping customers to the number of available tokens (Figure 7). It provides operations for creating and deleting customers which add or remove mappings for a customer to or from the database. There are operations for allocating a token to a customer as well as operations for requesting tokens and collecting tokens. Requesting tokens has no effect on the database. If there is more than one token available for a customer, the number of tokens collected

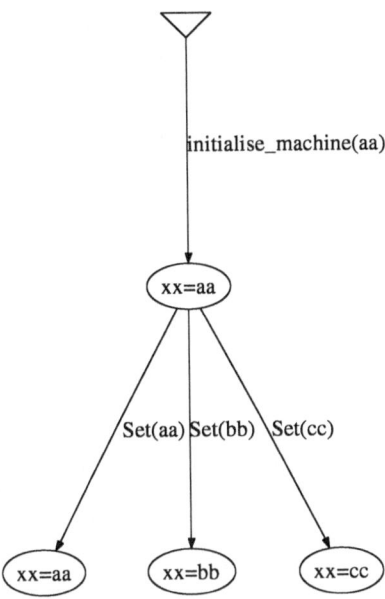

Fig. 6. The state space of *Simple* when using another CSP specification

is nondeterministically chosen to be less than or equal to the number of tokens available for that customer.

The finiteness of the sets *OFFICE* and *CUST* in Figure 7 is required for exhaustive model checking. Finiteness is also imposed by restricting the maximum number of tokens allocated to a customer using the constant mx. The *AllocToken* operation is guarded to ensure that this allocation is never exceeded.

We wish to impose a certain coordination protocol on the operations of the system in Figure 7. Operations such as *CollectToken* and *AllocToken* should only be available after a customer has been added to the system. Furthermore, before a customer can collect tokens, they must first request those tokens at an office. This coordination is described by the CSP process *MAIN* of Figure 8. This process consists of three parallel instances of the *Cust* process, one for each customer. In a *Cust* process, *AddCust* is the only operation available initially. Once *AddCust* has been performed, allocation and collection of tokens can proceed in parallel, modelled by the process $(Collection(C)[|RemCust|]Allocation(C))$. Collection and allocation synchronise on the *RemCust* event because both are terminated by this event. Collection of tokens by a customer is intended to take place at offices to which customers have access. Before customers can collect tokens from an office, they must first request tokens at that office via a *ReqToken* operation. Only then can they collect some (or all) of the tokens available for them. The definition of *Collection* also ensures that a customer cannot be removed in between requesting some tokens and collecting those tokens.

The overall behaviour of the service is determined by the parallel composition of the B and CSP parts. In this case, the CSP specification ensures that

MACHINE *Tokens*
SETS
   $OFFICE = \{o1, o2\}$;
   $CUST = \{c1, c2, c3\}$
CONSTANTS *mx*
PROPERTIES $mx \in \mathbb{N} \wedge mx = 3$
VARIABLES *tokens*
INVARIANT $tokens \in CUST \nrightarrow (0..mx)$

INITIALISATION $tokens := \{\}$

OPERATIONS

$AddCust(cc)\hat{=}$
   PRE $cc \in CUST \wedge cc \notin dom(tokens)$
   THEN $tokens := tokens \cup \{cc \mapsto 0\}$
   END;

$RemCust(cc) =$
   PRE $cc \in CUST$
   THEN $tokens := \{cc\} \lhd tokens$
   END;

$AllocToken(cc) =$
   PRE $cc \in CUST \wedge cc \in dom(tokens)$
   SELECT $tokens(cc) < mx$ THEN
     $tokens(cc) := tokens(cc) + 1$ END
   END;

$ReqToken(cc, pp) =$
   PRE $cc \in CUST \wedge pp \in OFFICE$
   THEN *skip*
   END;

$toks \longleftarrow CollectToken(cc, pp) =$
   PRE $cc \in CUST \wedge pp \in OFFICE \wedge$
     $cc \in dom(tokens)$
   THEN
     IF $tokens(cc) = 0$
     THEN $toks := 0$
     ELSE
       ANY *nn* WHERE $nn : \mathbb{N} \wedge$
        $1 \leq nn \wedge nn \leq tokens(cc)$
       THEN $toks := nn \|$
        $tokens(cc) := tokens(cc) - nn$
     END END END

Fig. 7. Tokens B machine

the *AddCust* operation must be invoked before any of the other operations are allowed, and that tokens must be requested before they can be collected. The PROB tool allows the combined specification to be animated so that the overall behaviour can be explored interactively.

Now consider the preconditions of the operations of Figure 7. The *AddCust* operation has $cc \notin dom(tokens)$ as a precondition, while the *AllocToken* and *CollectToken* operations have $cc \in dom(tokens)$ as a precondition. The preconditions represent assumptions about the conditions under which these operations will be invoked but are not enforced by the B machine on its own. Normally, when checking the consistency of a B machine using PROB, operation preconditions are used to restrict the reachable states by treating them in exactly the same way as operation guards. This form of checking detects no errors in the machine of Figure 7. An alternative form of checking can be applied in PROB which treats a violation of a precondition as an error. That is, an error is raised if a machine can reach a state which violates an operation precondition. With this second form of model checking, when the machine of Figure 7 is checked, an error is detected straightaway because the initial state violates the preconditions of *AllocToken* and *CollectToken*. However, when this form of checking is applied to the combined B and CSP specification, no violation of preconditions is detected by PROB. This is because the CSP enforces an order on the invocation of the operations which guarantees that the preconditions are always satisfied.

$$MAIN \quad = \quad Cust(c1) \ ||| \ Cust(c2) \ ||| \ Cust(c3)$$

$$Cust(C) \quad = \quad AddCust.C \rightarrow (Collection(C) [\![RemCust]\!] Allocation(C)) \ ; \ Cust(C)$$

$$Collection(C) \quad = \quad (\ ReqToken.C?O \rightarrow CollectToken.C.O \rightarrow Collection(C)$$
$$\square \ RemCust.C \rightarrow SKIP)$$

$$Allocation(C) \quad = \quad (\ AllocToken.C \rightarrow Allocation(C)$$
$$\square \ RemCust.C \rightarrow SKIP)$$

Fig. 8. Tokens CSP equations

5 Verifying Properties of B Machines Using CSP

In the previous section, we illustrated how a system could be specified as a combination of CSP and B. In this section we illustrate how CSP specifications can be used to analyse trace properties of specifications written purely in B. With this approach we use CSP to specify some desirable or undesirable behaviours and use PROB to find traces of the B machine that exhibit those behaviours. To specify a desirable property, we use a special CSP process called *GOAL*. A desirable trace is one that leads to the *GOAL* process. An undesirable trace is one that leads to the *ERROR* process.

To illustrate the use of *GOAL* and *ERROR*, we consider a simple mobile agent system. Once agents have been created they can have a location or be in transit between locations. When an agent is at some location, it can send and receive messages to and from other agents. Messages can be sent to agents even if they are in transit in which case the messages can be received when the receiving agent reaches a location. The simple agent system is specified by the B machine of Figure 9. In this specification, *agents* represents the set of created agents, $msgs(a)$ represents the set of messages waiting to be received by agent a, and $loc(a)$ represents the location of agent a. If a is in *agents* but not in the domain of *loc*, then a is in transit.

A desirable property of the agent system is that it is possible for an agent to receive a message since this is an important service for agents. Clearly some sequence of operations must happen before an agent can receive a message. There is a danger that our specification of the operations is too restrictive so that a trace leading to receipt of a message would not be possible. Figure 10 contains a CSP process which leads to the *GOAL* process when a *Receive* event is executed.

We do not want the CSP process to place any constraints on the *Create*, *Send*, *Arrive* or *Depart* operations. To achieve this we use the special *RUN* process. *RUN* takes a list of events and continually iterates over the choice of those events. For example, we have

MACHINE *MobileAgents*
SETS $MSG = \{m1, m2\}$;
  $AGENT = \{a1, a2\}$;
  $LOC = \{l1, l2\}$
VARIABLES *agents, loc, msgs*
INVARIANT
  $agents \in \mathbb{P}(AGENT) \wedge$
  $msgs \in agents \rightarrow \mathbb{P}(MSG) \wedge$
  $loc \in agents \nrightarrow LOC$
INITIALISATION
  $agents := \{\} \parallel msgs := \{\} \parallel loc := \{\}$
OPERATIONS

$Create(aa) \hat{=}$
  PRE
    $aa \in AGENT \setminus agents$
  THEN
    $agents := agents \cup \{aa\} \parallel$
    $msgs := msgs \cup \{aa \mapsto \{\}\}$
  END;

$Arrive(aa, ll) \hat{=}$
  PRE
    $aa \in agents \setminus dom(loc) \wedge$
    $ll \in LOC$
  THEN
    $loc(aa) := ll$
  END;

$Depart(aa, ll) \hat{=}$
  PRE
    $aa : agents \wedge ll : LOC \wedge$
    $(aa| \mapsto ll) \in loc$
  THEN
    $loc := \{aa\} \lhd loc$
  END;

$Send(aa, bb, ll, mm) \hat{=}$
  PRE
    $aa \in agents \wedge bb \in agents \wedge$
    $mm \in MSG \wedge ll \in LOC \wedge$
    $aa \neq bb \wedge (aa \mapsto ll) \in loc$
  THEN
    $msgs(bb) := msgs(bb) \cup \{mm\}$
  END;

$mm \longleftarrow Receive(bb, ll) \hat{=}$
  PRE
    $bb \in agents \wedge ll \in LOC \wedge (bb \mapsto ll) \in loc$
  THEN
    ANY $m1$ WHERE
      $m1 \in MSG \wedge m1 \in msgs(bb)$
    THEN
      $msgs(bb) := msgs(bb) - m1 \parallel$
      $mm := m1$
    END
  END

Fig. 9. Mobile agents B machine

$$MAIN \;=\; Test1 \;\mid\mid\mid\; RUN[Create, Send, Arrive, Depart]$$
$$Test1 \;=\; Receive \rightarrow GOAL$$

Fig. 10. Goal test for agents

$$MAIN \;=\; TEST2 \;\mid\mid\mid\; RUN[Create, Arrive, Depart, Send?A?B?L.m2, Receive]$$
$$TEST2 \;=\; Receive?A?L.m1 \rightarrow ERROR$$

Fig. 11. Error test for agents

$$RUN[A, B] \;=\; (\; A \rightarrow RUN[A, B] \;\;\square\;\; B \rightarrow RUN[A, B] \;)$$

We interleave the *Test1* process with *RUN*[*Create, Send, Arrive, Depart*]. If *RUN* was not interleaved with the test process, then the *Create, Send, Arrive* and *Depart* operations could never take place in the combined system.

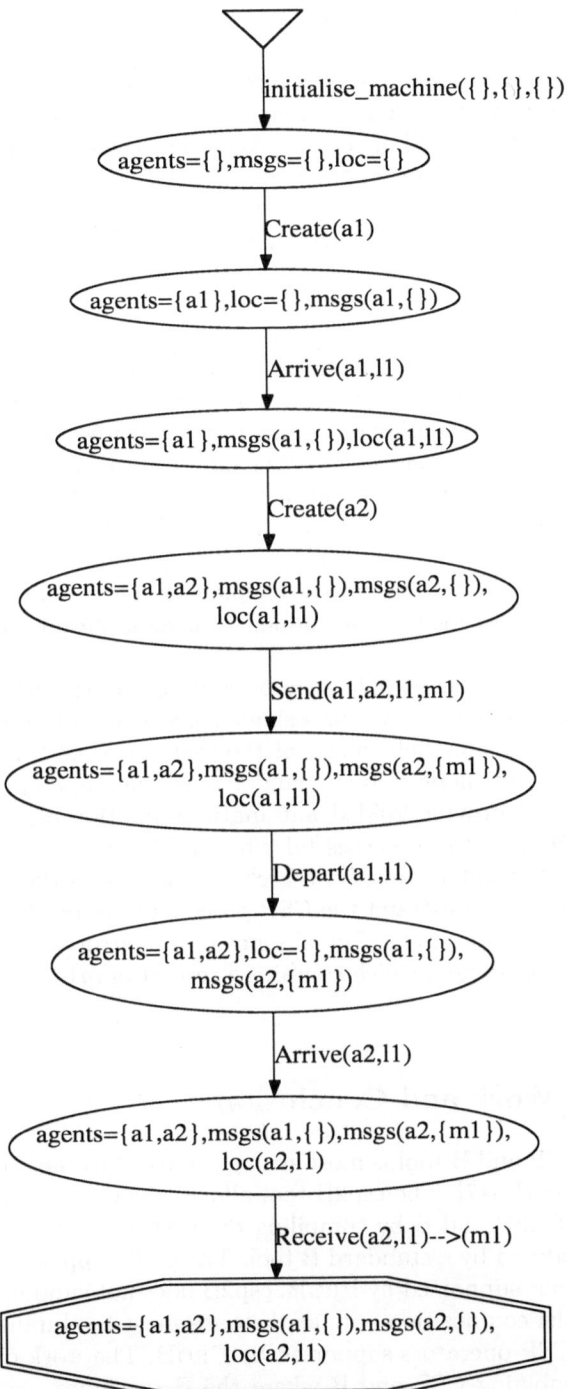

Fig. 12. Trace leading to *GOAL* process as displayed by PROB

Figure 12 is generated by PROB and it illustrates a trace of events and corresponding machine states which lead to a message being received by an agent. All of the events leading to the receipt are required because both agents need to exist before one can send a message to the other and an agent needs to be at a location in order to send or receive. As well as the event trace, the diagram allows us to see the evolution of the state of the B machine. This is useful for helping to validate the specification. To find the desirable trace, PROB checks the parallel composition of the B machine and the CSP process, attempting to find a trace leading to the *GOAL* process. In this case it finds the trace illustrated in Figure 12.

An undesirable behaviour of agent system would be that an agent receives a message without the message having been sent to the agent. This behaviour is encoded in the CSP process of Figure 11. The main constraint imposed by this CSP process is that the *Send* operation is prevented from sending message $m1$. An error arises when message $m1$ is received by an agent. Receipt of message $m1$ represents an error since it could not have been preceded by a send of $m1$ because of the constraint on sending. In this case, PROB performs an exhaustive search but fails to find a trace leading to the *ERROR* process. This is as expected since the *Receive* operation requires a recipient to have some message in their message set, and messages only get added to a message set through the *Send* operation.

There is a very significant difference between a *GOAL* test and an *ERROR* test. Success of a *GOAL* test gives us a single trace leading to the goal. It tells us nothing about all possible behaviours of the system. Nonetheless the existence of the goal trace can increase our confidence in the validity of the B model and can be used to provide guided automatic animation of a B machine. We deem an *ERROR* test to be successful when PROB finds no trace leading to the error process through exhaustive search. In the case of the error test for the agent system, the only constraint the CSP process places on the B machine is to prevent sending of message $m1$. The absence of any error traces means there is no trace of the agent system which contains a receipt of $m1$ but does not contain a send of $m1$.

6   Related Work and Conclusion

Our combined CSP and B tool is most strongly related to the csp2B tool [4] and the CSP∥B approach [17]. The csp2B tool allows specifications to be written in a combination of CSP and B by compiling the CSP to a pure B representation which can be analysed by a standard B tool. The CSP support by csp2B is more restricted than that supported by PROB: csp2B does not support internal choice and allows parallel composition only at the outermost level unlike the arbitrary combination of CSP operators supported by PROB. The work of [17] is focused on a style of combining CSP and B where the B machines are passive and all the coordination is provided by the CSP. This means the operations of their B machines cannot be guarded though they can have preconditions. They have developed compositional rules for proving that CSP controllers do not lead to violation of operation preconditions. Also, we now have a all-in-one animation and model checking tool; a considerable practical advantage.

There has been much work on combining CSP with Z and Object-Z, including [6], [18] and [13]. Like our approach, these treat Z specifications as CSP processes and model the composition of the CSP and Z parts as parallel composition. The work described in [14] describes an approach to translating Z to CSP so that CSP-Z specifications can be model checked. This translation is not automated though. The Circus language is a rich combination of Z and CSP allowing Z to be easily embedded in CSP specifications and providing refinement rules for development [20]. We are not aware of any tools that allow for model checking of Z and CSP specifications directly.

The combined model checker for CSP and B is an enhancement of the existing PROB checker allowing for automated consistency checking of specifications written in a combination of CSP and B. We have shown how PROB can now be used to automatically check consistency between B and CSP specifications (i.e., checking that no B preconditions are ever violated). We have also shown how PROB can be used to check whether a pure B specification satisfies trace properties expressed in CSP. This form of checking serves to increase our confidence in the validity of B models.

PROB also supports refinement checking between B models and between combinations of CSP and B. Further work is required to enhance the scalability of the model checking approach, especially for refinement checking (although some quite large, realistic specifications have already been successfully verified). Our view is that PROB is a valuable complement to the usual theorem prover based development in B. Wherever possible there is value in applying model checking to a size-restricted version of a B model before attempting semi-automatic deductive proof.

Acknowledgements

We would like to thank anonymous referees for their helpful feedback.

References

1. J.-R. Abrial. *The B-Book*. Cambridge University Press, 1996.
2. J.-R. Abrial and L. Mussat. Introducing dynamic constraints in B. In D. Bert, editor, *Second International B Conference*, April 1998.
3. U. B-Core (UK) Limited, Oxon. *B-Toolkit, On-line manual*, 1999. Available at http://www.b-core.com/ONLINEDOC/Contents.html.
4. M. J. Butler. csp2B: A Practical Approach to Combining CSP and B. *Formal Asp. Comput.*, 12(3):182–198, 2000.
5. E. M. Clarke, O. Grumberg, and D. Peled. *Model Checking*. MIT Press, 1999.
6. C. Fischer. CSP-OZ: A combination of Object-Z and CSP. In H. Bowmann and J. Derrick, editors, *Formal Methods for Open Object-Based Distributed Systems (FMOODS'97)*, pages 423–438. Chapman & Hall, 1997.

7. Formal Systems (Europe) Ltd. *Failures-Divergence Refinement — FDR2 User Manual.*
8. P. Hartel, M. Butler, A. Currie, P. Henderson, M. Leuschel, A. Martin, A. Smith, U. Ultes-Nitsche, and B. Walters. Questions and answers about ten formal methods. In *Proc. 4th Int. Workshop on Formal Methods for Industrial Critical Systems*, Trento, Italy, Jul 1999.
9. C. Hoare. *Communicating Sequential Processes.* Prentice–Hall, 1985.
10. M. Leuschel. Design and implementation of the high-level specification language CSP(LP) in Prolog. In I. V. Ramakrishnan, editor, *Proceedings of PADL'01*, LNCS 1990, pages 14–28. Springer-Verlag, March 2001.
11. M. Leuschel and M. Butler. ProB: A Model Checker for B. In K. Araki, S. Gnesi, and D. Mandrioli, editors, *Proceedings FME 2003, Pisa, Italy*, LNCS 2805, pages 855–874. Springer, 2003.
12. M. Leuschel and E. Turner. Visualizing larger states spaces in ProB. In *Proceedings ZB'2005*, LNCS. Springer-Verlag, April 2005. To appear.
13. B. P. Mahony and S. Dong. Blending Object-Z and Timed CSP: An introduction to TCOZ. In *20th International Conference on Software Engineering (ICSE'98)*, pages 95–104, 1998.
14. A. Mota and A. Sampaio. Model-checking CSP-Z: strategy, tool support and industrial application. *Sci. Comput. Program.*, 40(1):59–96, 2001.
15. A. Roscoe. *The Theory and Practice of Concurrency.* Prentice–Hall, 1998.
16. J. B. Scattergood. *Tools for CSP and Timed-CSP.* PhD thesis, Oxford University, 1997.
17. S. Schneider and H. Treharne. Verifying controlled components. In E. A. Boiten, J. Derrick, and G. Smith, editors, *Proceedings Integrated Formal Methods, IFM 2004, Canterbury, UK*, LNCS 2999, pages 87–107. Springer, 2004.
18. G. Smith. A semantic integration of Object-Z and CSP for the specification of concurrent systems. In J. S. Fitzgerald, C. B. Jones, and P. Lucas, editors, *Proceedings FME '97*, LNCS 1313, pages 62–81. Springer, 1997.
19. F. Steria, Aix-en-Provence. *Atelier B, User and Reference Manuals*, 1996. Available at `Available at http://www.atelierb.societe.com/index_uk.html`.
20. J. Woodcock and A. Cavalcanti. The semantics of Circus. In D. Bert, J. P. Bowen, M. C. Henson, and K. Robinson, editors, *Proceedings ZB 2002, Grenoble, France*, LNCS 2272, pages 184–203. Springer, 2002.

Operational Semantics for
Model Checking **Circus**

Jim Woodcock, Ana Cavalcanti, and Leonardo Freitas

Department of Computer Science,
University of York, UK
{jim, alcc, leo}@cs.york.ac.uk

Abstract. *Circus* is a combination of Z, CSP, and the refinement calculus, and is based on Hoare & He's *Unifying Theories of Programming*. A model checker is being constructed for the language to conduct refinement checking in the style of FDR, but supported by theorem proving for reasoning about the complex states and data types that arise from the use of Z. FDR deals with bounded labelled transition systems (LTSs), but the *Circus* model checker manipulates LTSs with possibly infinite inscriptions on arcs and in nodes, and so, in general, the success or failure of a refinement check depends on interaction with a theorem prover. An LTS is generated from a source text using an operational interpretation of *Circus*; we present a Structured Operational Semantics for *Circus*, including both its process-algebraic and state-rich features.

1   Introduction

Circus [31, 32, 1, 23, 2, 3] is a state-rich process algebra based on Z [11, 33] and CSP [21], with a refinement calculus for deriving implementations from their specifications. Current work involves constructing a tool-set for supporting the language, including a theorem prover and a model checker. The development of the model checker is inspired by FDR, the model checker for CSP [19, 5]; however, a significant and novel aspect of the *Circus* model checker is the need to address the state-rich aspects of the language. The resulting procedure is refinement checking supported by theorem proving.

In its internal computations, FDR uses finite, labelled transition systems that are derived from source texts using the operational semantics of CSP. In order to construct the *Circus* model checker, we first need to explore the operational semantics of the language, including those state-based features not found in CSP. This leads to transition systems where the diagram is finite, but where the arcs and nodes may carry inscriptions involving infinite data types. This operational semantics must be proved congruent to the denotational semantics of *Circus*, which is different from the set-based presentation of the failures-divergences model used for CSP: it uses the unifying theories of programming (UTP) [10].

We present a Plotkin-style Structured Operational Semantics [17] for *Circus*, also based on UTP and using Z as a metalanguage [33], hence knowledge of

J.S. Fitzgerald, I.J. Hayes, and A. Tarlecki (Eds.): FM 2005, LNCS 3582, pp. 237–252, 2005.

Z is assumed. The operational semantics is inspired by the implementation of CSP_M [24] in FDR [5], but has been adapted and extended to accommodate the state-rich features of *Circus*. The underlying automata theory and its properties have been formalised using the Z/Eves theorem prover [14].

In the next section, we give a brief overview of *Circus* and the UTP. Following this, we present the operational semantics for basic actions, declarations, synchronisation, schema expression, external choice, and interleaving; other operators are omitted for lack of space. In our final section, we discuss our results, put them in context, and look forward to future work.

2   Circus and the UTP

Circus is a forum for exploring the combination of process algebra and model-based abstract data types, and it is distinguished from similar combinations [4, 26] by being based firmly on the notion of refinement. Thus, the process algebra used is CSP and data types are specified in Z, since failure-divergences refinement and schema structuring have both proved their usefulness in describing industrial-scale development. Current experience is showing that when the refinement calculus is extended to include the operators of the process algebra, then its use also scales up to address large-scale architectural issues.

Unifying Theories of Programming [10] provides a single theoretical framework, based on an alphabetised relational calculus, that can be used for unification of many programming language paradigms. A theory in UTP is composed of an alphabet of names, a signature of language constructs, and a set of healthiness conditions. Programs, designs, and specifications are all interpreted as relations between an initial and an intermediate or final observation of behaviour. The following programming theories have all been modelled in the UTP: imperative, reactive, parallel, higher-order, and declarative [10, 30]; object oriented [6, 7, 8]; real-time [27]; and mobility [28, 29].

The semantics of *Circus* is defined in the UTP, where Z and the refinement calculus inhabit the theory of designs (pre-post specifications), and where CSP is the embedding of designs in the theory of reactive processes. Thus, everything that one might write in Z, CSP, or the refinement calculus may be freely mixed in a *Circus* specification. This is in contrast with other approaches, where the appropriate Z, VDM, or B specification is interpreted as a communicating abstract data type [4, 26]. The result is a rigid system architecture, which has its advantages: the abstract data type and the process algebra remain orthogonal throughout development, and so can be analysed separately using existing tools. It also has its disadvantages: every program that can be developed will have to adopt this architecture, and clearly many desirable programs do not.

A *Circus* program consists of a network of processes, each with encapsulated data and channels for communication and synchronisation. Within a process, there is a rich state with its attendant operations and process-algebraic behaviours, called *actions*; a distinguished main action defines the behaviour of the process. An action has no encapsulated data: it operates on a data space shared with other actions inside the same process. Parallel composition defines partitions to avoid the usual problems of reasoning about shared data.

In the UTP denotational semantics, four kinds of observations may be made of *Circus* actions: (i) the *wait* variable distinguishes intermediate states from final ones; (ii) the *okay* variable distinguishes terminating states from non-terminating ones; (iii) the *tr* variables records the trace of past events; and (iv) the *ref* variable describes a set of events that are being refused by the process while it waits. For example, if a process has been started in a state where the events a and b have already occurred (in that order), and the process is waiting to perform the event c (but not a or b), then the following observations will hold: $okay \land \neg \ wait \land okay' \land wait' \land tr' = tr = \langle a, b \rangle \land ref' \subseteq \{a, b\}$. The components of the process state also appear in the alphabet.

Circus programs satisfy all the healthiness conditions for CSP processes found in [10], many of which are familiar from the failures-divergences semantics of CSP [9, 21, 25], and they form a complete lattice ordered by reverse implication. Thus, a process S is refined by another process I with the same alphabet $S \sqsubseteq I$, providing that $[S \Leftarrow I]$, where the brackets denote universal closure. In this paper, we provide an operational semantics for *Circus* actions.

3   Transition Relation

We define a transition relation capturing the operational semantics of *Circus*. An earlier abstract version has been formally mechanised in detail using the Z/Eves theorem prover [22]. All definitions and proof scripts that have guided our implementations are available from [34]. We introduce names, and well-formed Z expressions and predicates: *Name*, *ZExpr*, *ZPred*. Values and types are made from Z expressions: $Value == ZExpr$, and $Type == \mathbb{P} \, ZExpr$.

As usual, our transition relation connects one node to another using an arc; so it is a tertiary relation: $\mathbb{P}(Node \times Arc \times Node)$. The arcs in our relation are labelled with sets of events, and correspond to a communication permitted by a channel type definition; events range over the set Σ, and are channel-name/value pairs: $\Sigma == Name \times Value$ and $Arc \ == \ \mathbb{P} \, \Sigma$. These sets may be infinite. An empty arc represents a silent transition: either successful termination or internal progress. This is in contrast to the operational semantics of CSP_M, where two special events are used for silent transitions: $\checkmark$ (tick) and τ (tau). The former represents successful termination, whereas the latter represents internal progress. Deadlock in CSP_M is represented by lack of available events, and divergence is represented by an infinite sequence of τ's (a τ-loop in the automaton).

Nodes are configuration/environment pairs. The former contains the process's state and the action yet to be executed; the latter contains various declarations. The state $St \triangleq ASt \land USt$ contains both observational of the UTP ASt and the process state USt. In the following definition, $Boolean ::= t \mid f$.

$ASt \ \triangleq \ [\, okay, wait : Boolean; \ tr : \text{seq } \Sigma \,]$

Refusals are not explicitly recorded; instead, they may be deduced from the outgoing arcs from each node. The schema $Obs \ \triangleq \ [\, \Delta St \mid tr \textsf{ prefix } tr' \,]$ defines all allowed observations between before and after states during the evaluation of the semantics; its invariant requires that no process can change the history of past events (a healthiness condition).

As said above, a configuration comprises a state and an action that remains to be executed: $Config == St \times Action$, where

$$
\begin{aligned}
Action \ ::= \ & \Omega \mid \textsf{Skip} \mid \textsf{Stop} \mid \textsf{Chaos} \mid \textsf{N} \mid \mu \, \textsf{X} \bullet \textsf{A} \mid \textbf{let} \ \textsf{LocalEnv} \bullet \textsf{A} \\
& \mid \ \textbf{var} \ \textsf{x} : \textsf{T} \bullet \textsf{A} \mid \textsf{c} \to \textsf{A} \mid \textsf{c!v} \to \textsf{A} \mid \textsf{c?x} : \textsf{P} \to \textsf{A} \mid \textsf{c?x} : \textsf{P!e} \to \textsf{A} \\
& \mid \ \textsf{A} \, ; \, \textsf{B} \mid \textsf{SExpr} \mid \textsf{g} \, \& \, \textsf{A} \mid \textsf{A} \sqcap \textsf{B} \mid \textsf{A} \, \square \, \textsf{B} \mid \textsf{A} \setminus \textsf{hs} \mid \textsf{A} \, \|[\, \textsf{ns}_0 \mid \textsf{ns}_1 \,]\| \, \textsf{B} \\
& \mid \ \textsf{A} \, [\, \textsf{ns}_0 \mid \textsf{cs} \mid \textsf{ns}_1 \,] \, \textsf{B}
\end{aligned}
$$

Following ideas from CSP_M tools [18, 5], we have included an action Ω to denote a final configuration; it is not part of the user's syntax.

The declaration environment contains the names of channels, variables, actions, and unused names, which partition the given set of names.

Env

$chs, vars, acts, fresh : \mathbb{P} \, Name$
$cType, vType : Name \nrightarrow Type$
$aCtx : Name \nrightarrow Action$

$\langle chs, vars, acts, fresh \rangle$ partition $Name$
$\mathrm{dom}\, cType = chs \wedge \mathrm{dom}\, vType = vars \wedge \mathrm{dom}\, aCtx = acts$

Now we can define a node as a pair: $Node == Config \times Env$.

The declared type of a channel or variable name is determined by the functions $cType$ and $vType$, respectively. The function $aCtx$ records the syntax that is associated with an action name. Environments are updated to include new declarations; we give only the function for adding new channel declarations.

$cDecl : Env \times Name \times Type \nrightarrow Env$

$\mathrm{dom}\, cDecl =$
$\quad = \{ \, Env; \ N : Name; \ T : Type \mid N \in fresh \bullet (\theta Env, N, T) \, \}$

$\forall \, Env; \ N : Name; \ T : Type; \ A : Action \mid N \in fresh \bullet$
$\quad cDecl(\theta Env, N, T)$
$\quad\quad = \theta Env[cType := (cType \oplus \{ \, N \mapsto T \, \}), fresh := (fresh \setminus \{ \, N \, \})]$

In Z/Eves' syntax, substitution of expressions for variables is denoted by ":=", so the function updates exactly two components: $cType$ and $fresh$. More generally, we give the semantics of a theta expression $\theta S[x := e]$ within a predicate P using existential quantification and standard renaming, provided y is fresh and e has the same type as x.

$$
P(\theta S[x := e]) \equiv \exists \, y : \{ \, e \, \} \bullet P(\theta S[y/x])
$$

We define a transition system only for certain configurations: stable states are those in which $okay$ is true ($Stable \mathrel{\widehat{=}} [\, St \mid okay = t \,]$); and normal states are stable states in which $wait$ is false ($Normal \mathrel{\widehat{=}} [\, Stable \mid wait = f \,]$).

Two key functions in the definition of the operational semantics are *enabled*, which gives the set of enabled arcs for a node, and *arcStep*, which returns the set of nodes that can be reached from a given node by following a given arc. These functions are defined piecewise over the syntax of *Circus* actions. Their domains are defined as the nodes where the states are in normal configurations; the domain of *arcStep* insists that we are interested in stepping only through arcs that are enabled.

$$enabled : Node \nrightarrow \mathbb{P}\, Arc$$
$$arcStep : Node \times Arc \nrightarrow \mathbb{P}\, Node$$

$$\text{dom}\, enabled = \{\, \mathsf{A} : Action;\ Normal;\ Env \bullet ((\theta St, \mathsf{A}), \theta Env)\,\}$$

$$\text{dom}\, arcStep = \{\, \mathsf{A} : Action;\ a : Arc;\ Normal;\ Env \mid$$
$$a \in enabled((\theta St, \mathsf{A}), \theta Env) \bullet (((\theta St, \mathsf{A}), \theta Env), a)\,\}$$

These functions abstractly define a general theory of automata, where the edges are sets of events (arcs) and the configurations are nodes. Therefore, the operational semantics of *Circus* is given in terms of these semantic functions for each available operator in the BNF syntax. As mentioned before, this is close to the operational semantics of CSP_M in FDR, where similar semantic functions named *inits* and *after* are defined.

There is a relationship between these two functions. The domain of *arcStep* is a relation (a set of pairs), which may be lifted to a set-valued function using relational image. This function is almost exactly *enabled*: we have to remove all pairs that *arcStep* would have mapped to the empty set, since these pairs can have no enabled arcs.

$$\forall n : Node \bullet enabled(n) = (\text{dom}(arcStep \rhd \{\emptyset\}))(\!|\,\{n\}\,|\!)$$

The following well-formedness theorem is proved as a consequence of this relationship, and each definition below is proved to respect it.

Theorem 1 (Well-formedness). *An arc a is enabled in node n formed by an action A in a stable before state ($\theta St[okay := t]$) and an environment (θEnv) exactly when it is possible to reach at least one target node through n via a.*

$$\forall St;\ Env;\ A : Action;\ a : Arc;\ n : Node \bullet$$
$$n = ((\theta St, \mathsf{A}), \theta Env) \land okay = t \Rightarrow a \in enabled\ n \Leftrightarrow arcStep(n, a) \neq \emptyset$$

If the process diverges, the well-formedness theorem is no longer guaranteed.

We have proved this theorem for our underlying abstract automata theory, which is important for the implicit relationship between refusals sets and *enabled*.

An observation is stable whenever it has started (*okay*), and has not diverged (*okay'*). Valid observations are those where the trace history has been preserved (*tr* prefix *tr'*), as well as the state invariant. An observation is normal whenever its before state is normal and the after state is stable.

$$StableObs \,\widehat{=}\, Obs \land \Delta Stable$$
$$NormalObs \,\widehat{=}\, StableObs \land Normal$$

A stable observation can make progress initially ($okay \wedge \neg\, wait$), reach a stable valid observation in an after state ($okay' \wedge wait' \wedge tr$ prefix tr'), but nothing is known about its termination yet ($wait'$ is unconstrained).

In the following sections, we define $enabled$ and $arcStep$ for a representative subset of *Circus* actions.

4   Basic Actions

Skip has only one possible behaviour—termination—so it has exactly one transition.

$$\forall Normal;\ Env \bullet enabled((\theta St, \mathsf{Skip}), \theta Env) = \{\,\emptyset\,\}$$

A *Terminating* observation is normal with $wait'$ false. Silent termination does not change tr. Read-only observations are normal.

$$
\begin{aligned}
Terminating &\;\widehat{=}\; [\, NormalObs \mid wait' = f \,] \\
SilentlyTerminating &\;\widehat{=}\; [\, Terminating \mid tr' = tr \,] \\
ReadOnly &\;\widehat{=}\; [\, NormalObs \mid \Xi\, USt \,]
\end{aligned}
$$

Since the initial state in the semantics of Skip is normal, the empty arc leads to a final configuration with action Ω in an after state that silently terminates.

$$
\begin{aligned}
&\forall Normal;\ Env \bullet \\
&\quad arcStep(((\theta St, \mathsf{Skip}), \theta Env), \emptyset) \\
&\qquad = \{\, SilentlyTerminating;\ ReadOnly \bullet ((\theta St', \Omega), \theta Env) \,\}
\end{aligned}
$$

For the final configuration $(\theta St, \Omega)$ from a normal before state we have that

$$\forall Normal;\ Env \bullet enabled((\theta St, \Omega), \theta Env) = \emptyset$$

and since $enabled$ gives the empty set of arcs, so the domain of $arcStep$ for Ω is also empty. Finally, we observe the difference between an empty set being $enabled$, and $enabled$ returning a singleton set containing just the empty set. The former is related to termination or internal progress; the latter is a final configuration with no outgoing arcs.

Stop represents a final action (Ω) in a waiting after state, where neither communication nor user state updates have happened. *Waiting* defines read-only observations where the after state is waiting for interaction ($wait'$). *SilentlyWaiting* defines waiting observations where no communication has taken place.

$$
\begin{aligned}
Waiting &\;\widehat{=}\; [\, ReadOnly \mid wait' = t \,] \\
SilentlyWaiting &\;\widehat{=}\; [\, Waiting \mid tr' = tr \,]
\end{aligned}
$$

Like Skip, the definition of Stop also uses a silent transition through an empty arc; the final state is given by *SilentlyWaiting* with the original environment.

$$
\begin{aligned}
&\forall Normal;\ Env \bullet enabled((\theta St, \mathsf{Stop}), \theta Env) = \{\emptyset\} \\
&\forall Normal;\ Env \bullet \\
&\quad arcStep(((\theta St, \mathsf{Stop}), \theta Env), \emptyset) = \{\, SilentlyWaiting \bullet ((\theta St', \Omega), \theta Env) \,\}
\end{aligned}
$$

A deadlocked configuration accepts nothing, whereas a waiting configuration can progress whenever some arc becomes *enabled*. FDR has a similar representation.

Chaos has every possible behaviour, and this is represented as the power set of Σ.

$$\forall\, Normal;\ Env \bullet enabled((\theta St, \mathsf{Chaos}), \theta Env) = \mathbb{P}\ \Sigma$$

An observation is unpredictable whenever we move from a normal before state to an after state where only the minimal constraints hold. Leaving the value of $okay'$ unconstrained allows the possibility of divergence.

$$UnpredictableObs \ \widehat{=}\ Normal \wedge Obs$$

The behaviour after any transition is not entirely arbitrary, even in the presence of divergence: the state invariant will continue to hold and the trace will not be corrupted (the minimal constraints). In the semantics of Chaos, each arc leads back to Chaos in an after state with these two constraints.

$$\forall\, Normal;\ Env;\ a : Arc \bullet$$
$$arcStep(((\theta St, \mathsf{Chaos}), \theta Env), a)$$
$$= \{\, UnpredictableObs \bullet ((\theta St', \mathsf{Chaos}), \theta Env) \,\}$$

Thus, divergence is characterised by an unstable after state ($okay'$ false) that *might* occur after an unpredictable observation. This is different from FDR, where divergence is recorded as a τ-loop in the transition system. These loops are detected by restricting the transition system to τ events, and then calculating the transitive closure [19], where the standard implementation is depth-first search (DFS). Research on a parallel version of FDR using graph pruning to detect divergence is under development [13].

An interesting side-effect of using the UTP characterisation of divergence might give an important performance improvement for the implementation of divergence detection, because no DFS is needed. Instead, a more efficient search such as parallel variations of breadth-first search (BFS) are being analysed. The outcome of this investigation and the parallel implementation of other model-checking algorithms are left as future work.

5   Channel Declarations

Channel declarations are not permitted in *Circus* actions, but instead, they are evaluated during the contextual analysis that builds the initial environment. We define the syntax for declaration of channels and actions using a free-type *Decl*.

$$Decl ::= \mathbf{channel}\ \mathsf{N} : \mathsf{T}\ |\ \mathbf{channel}\ \mathsf{N}\ |\ \mathsf{N}\ \widehat{=}\ \mathsf{A}$$

Next, the function *declare* is defined; it updates an original environment with a given declaration of a channel.

$$declare : Env \times Decl \nrightarrow Env$$

$$\mathrm{dom}\, declare = \{\, Env;\ D : Decl;\ N : Name \mid N \in fresh \bullet (\theta Env, D)\,\}$$

This function is partial, since some declarations might not be well-formed. Unlike in CSP, *Circus* channels are strongly typed; thus, a channel declaration includes the new channel name with its declared type in the given environment; it is defined using the function *cDecl* defined in Section 3.

$$\forall \Delta Env;\ N : Name;\ T : Type \bullet$$
$$declare(\theta Env, \textbf{channel } N : T) = cDecl(\theta Env, N, T)$$

Events are formed from a channel name and a communicated value; but for synchronisation events, where no value is communicated, we define a special value *Synch*: it cannot be referred to by the user. Synchronisation channels are included in environments with the given name and the singleton type $\{\, Synch\,\}$.

$$\forall \Delta Env;\ N : Name \bullet declare(\theta Env, \textbf{channel } N) = cDecl(\theta Env, N, \{Synch\})$$

This allows a homogeneous declaration of channel types in the environment.

6   Input Prefixing: c?x : P → A

The enabled arcs of input prefixing contains events formed by the channel name and all values allowed by the declared channel type filtered by predicate P.

$$\forall Normal;\ Env \bullet$$
$$enabled((\theta St, \textsf{c?x} : \textsf{P} \to \textsf{A}), \theta Env) = \{\,\{\, v : cType\ c \mid \textsf{P} = t \bullet (c, v)\,\}\,\}$$

The transition for a synchronisation is defined using the schema *Communicating*, which requires that: (i) the before and after states are normal; (ii) the state invariant and the trace history are maintained; (iii) no modifications happen in the user state; (iv) the set of possible synchronisations includes the one in question; and (v) the after state trace is extended with the synchronisation event. *Progressing* $\widehat{=} [\,ReadOnly \mid wait' = f\,]$ specifies (i)–(iii). The declaration of available events on input variable *given?*, and the selection of an event using output variable *e!* from *given?* specify (iv). The extension of *tr* specifies (v).

$$Communicating\ \widehat{=}$$
$$[\,Progressing;\ given? : Arc;\ e! : \Sigma \mid e! \in given? \land tr' = tr \frown \langle e!\rangle\,]$$

These two definitions can now be used in the clause for *arcStep*.

$$\forall Normal;\ Env \bullet$$
$$\textbf{let}\ allowed == \{\, v : cType\ c \mid \textsf{P} = t \bullet (c, v)\,\} \bullet$$
$$arcStep(((\theta St, \textsf{c?x} : \textsf{P} \to \textsf{A}), \theta Env), allowed)$$
$$= \{\, Communicating[given? := allowed] \bullet$$
$$\textbf{let}\ lEnv == ((\textsf{x}, \mathrm{ran}\ allowed), second\ e!) \bullet$$
$$((\theta St', (\textbf{let}\ lEnv \bullet \textsf{A})), \theta Env)\,\}$$

The state is updated according to the *Communicating* schema where the given events are those allowed; however, the communicated value must be available for the evaluation of the following action A. This is achieved by introducing a new local variable x implicitly declared through the special syntax (**let** *lEnv* • A), where the type is just that of *c*. Its value is that communicated: *second e!*.

The evaluation of the local environment for input communication is similar to that for variable declarations. The only difference is that the implicitly declared variable x must have a value from the communication that just took place.

$$\forall \, Normal; \; Env \bullet$$
$$\quad enabled(\, (\, \theta St, (\textbf{let } lEnv == ((x, T), v) \bullet A)\,), \theta Env\,)$$
$$\quad = enabled((\theta St, A), vDecl(\theta Env, x, T))$$

The function *vDecl* extends the environment to include x; its definition is omitted for lack of space. For *arcStep*, we do something similar. We enrich the state in order to evaluate the action; removing the local variable from the environment afterwards ensures that the scope is indeed local. This is achieved using *vRemove*.

$$\forall \, Normal; \; Env; \; a : Arc \bullet$$
$$\quad arcStep(((\theta St, (\textbf{let } lEnv == ((x, T), v) \bullet A)), \theta Env), a)$$
$$\quad = \textbf{let } ExtSt \; \widehat{=} \; [\, x, x' : T \mid x' = x = v\,] \bullet$$
$$\qquad \{\, A' : Action; \; UnpredictableObs; \; Env' \mid$$
$$\qquad \quad ((\theta St', A'), \theta Env') \in$$
$$\qquad \qquad arcStep(((\theta(St \wedge ExtSt), A), vDecl(\theta Env, x, T)), a) \bullet$$
$$\qquad \qquad ((\theta(St' \setminus (x, x')), (\textbf{let } lEnv == ((x, T), x') \bullet A'),$$
$$\qquad \qquad \quad vRemove(\theta Env', x))\, \}$$

Schemas cannot be written in **let** clauses as shown above. For clarity, we have used this notation, but in Z/Eves *ExtSt* has to be defined separately. In calculating the semantics of a *Circus* program, this results in a proliferation of small schemas that need to be introduced, and nested scope has to be eliminated in advance. This does not lead to problems when reasoning about the semantics.

7   Schema Expression: SExpr

Successful evaluation of schema expressions is represented with a silent transition via an empty arc *enabled*; however, as schema expressions can diverge if executed outside their preconditions, we allow any arc to be enabled.

$$\forall \, Normal; \; Env \bullet$$
$$\quad enabled((\theta St, \mathsf{SExpr}), \theta Env) = \mathbb{P} \, \Sigma$$

Provided the precondition holds, a schema expression successfully terminates silently performing the operation in the user state. This leads to a final configuration that is terminating on the same environment.

$$\forall \, Normal; \; Env \mid \text{pre } \mathsf{SExpr} \bullet$$
$$\quad arcStep(((\theta St, \mathsf{SExpr}), \theta Env), \emptyset)$$
$$\qquad = \{\, Silently\,Terminating \mid \mathsf{SExpr} \bullet ((\theta St', \Omega), \theta Env)\, \}$$

When the precondition does not hold, evaluation of schema expressions leads to an after state with unpredictable observations, where the only guarantees are that the state invariant holds, and the trace history is not forgotten.

$$\forall \mathit{Normal};\ \mathit{Env};\ a : \mathit{Arc} \mid \neg\ \mathsf{pre}\ \mathsf{SExpr} \bullet$$
$$\quad arcStep(((\theta St, \mathsf{SExpr}), \theta \mathit{Env}), a)$$
$$\quad\quad = \{\, \mathit{UnpredictableObs} \bullet ((\theta St', \mathsf{SExpr}), \theta \mathit{Env}) \,\}$$

There is an implicit contextual analysis assumed on the unpredictable case. In order to calculate pre SExpr, both input (?) and output (!) variables on the schema expression must be in context in the given environment.

8   External Choice: **A □ B**

External choice has the arcs of both actions initially enabled. This includes empty arcs meaning either internal progress or termination, and visible communication on nonempty arcs.

$$\forall \mathit{Normal};\ \mathit{Env};\ \mathsf{A}, \mathsf{B} : \mathit{Action} \bullet$$
$$\quad enabled((\theta St, \mathsf{A}\ \square\ \mathsf{B}), \theta \mathit{Env})$$
$$\quad\quad = enabled((\theta St, \mathsf{A}), \theta \mathit{Env}) \cup enabled((\theta St, \mathsf{B}), \theta \mathit{Env})$$

External choice is rather complex with respect to progress on the transition system. Intuitively, there are many cases to consider: visible communication, silent termination, internal progress, and the possibility of deadlock or divergence on either action, and deadlock on both actions. We analyse the cases separately.

Firstly, visible communication ($tr' \neq tr$) happens only when a prefixing is communicating. This communication represents the choice being resolved; it is formally defined by the schema *Choosing* as a normal observation that changes the trace. That is, from a normal before state ($okay \wedge \neg\ wait$) it reaches a stable after state ($okay'$) with valid observations (tr prefix tr'), where the trace has been extended ($tr' \neq tr$).

$$Choosing\ \hat{=}\ [\, NormalObs \mid tr' \neq tr \,]$$

Whenever a visible communication happens, the choice is resolved to the following action that arises from either A or B. A first definition for *arcStep*, considering the case in which A is chosen, is as follows.

$$\forall \mathit{Normal};\ \mathit{Env};\ a : \mathit{Arc} \bullet$$
$$\quad arcStep(((\theta St, \mathsf{A}\ \square\ \mathsf{B}), \theta \mathit{Env}), a)$$
$$\quad\quad = \{\, C : \mathit{Action};\ Choosing \mid$$
$$\quad\quad\quad\quad ((\theta St', C), \theta \mathit{Env}) \in arcStep(((\theta St, \mathsf{A}), \theta \mathit{Env}), a) \bullet$$
$$\quad\quad\quad\quad ((\theta St', C), \theta \mathit{Env}) \,\} \cup$$

That is, from a normal before state, A leads to C on a stable after state according to the schema *Choosing* on the same environment.

Silent termination on either action also resolves the choice. The difference is that silent termination always leads to the final action Ω.

$\{$ *Terminating* $\mid ((\theta St', \Omega), \theta Env) \in arcStep(((\theta St, \mathsf{A}), \theta Env), a) \bullet$
$\quad ((\theta St', \Omega), \theta Env) \} \cup$

This models the fact that termination cannot be refused. It is a direct consequence of the denotational semantics of *Circus*. This approach is also taken in Roscoe's CSP [21] and FDR [24,5]. Alternatively, Hoare's CSP [9] forbids the choice of termination in an external choice, and Schneider's CSP [25] requires cooperation with the external environment when termination is offered in an external choice.

Now we consider internal progress in either action, say A again. Action $(\mathsf{A} \,\square\, \mathsf{B})$ leads to $(\mathsf{A}' \,\square\, \mathsf{B})$ in an after state that is ready for further progress $(\mathsf{A}' \neq \Omega)$, provided that A leads to A' in an after state as defined by the schema *SilentlyProgressing* $\widehat{=} [\, Progressing \mid tr' = tr \,]$.

$\{$ A' : *Action*; *SilentlyProgressing* $\mid$
$\quad A' \neq \Omega \wedge ((\theta St', A'), \theta Env) \in arcStep(((\theta St, \mathsf{A}), \theta Env), a) \bullet$
$\quad ((\theta St', A' \,\square\, \mathsf{B}), \theta Env) \} \cup$

Internal (silent) progress happens on the resolution of internal choice, evaluation of variable declaration, action call, and so forth. Additionally, although after states observed due to internal progress are the same as those observed due to successful termination, the ambiguity is cleared because we insist that A' is different from final action Ω.

The possibility of deadlock in either action is defined next. Whenever action A leads to action A' in an after state that is silently waiting, deadlock might occur if the *enabled* arcs of A' is the empty set because A' is refusing every possible event.

$\{$ A' : *Action*; *SilentlyWaiting* $\mid$
$\quad ((\theta St', A'), \theta Env) \in arcStep(((\theta St, \mathsf{A}), \theta Env), a) \bullet$
$\quad ((\theta St', A' \,\square\, \mathsf{B}), \theta Env) \} \cup$

Whenever either action is already deadlocked ($\mathsf{Stop} \,\square\, \mathsf{B}$), the choice is resolved to the remaining action, since the deadlocked action will have no arcs *enabled* (*arcStep* on the right-hand side is empty, and so the result is also empty). Of course, when both actions of the choice are deadlocked, so is the external choice.

Next, we need to consider divergence in either action, say A once more. If A leads to A' on an unpredictable after state, the external choice might be divergent; the result is A' in a possibly divergent state.

$\{$ A' : *Action*; *UnpredictableObs* $\mid$
$\quad ((\theta St', A'), \theta Env) \in arcStep(((\theta St, \mathsf{A}), \theta Env), a) \bullet$
$\quad ((\theta St', \mathsf{A}'), \theta Env) \}$

Putting all these cases together for both actions of the choice, we get the complete definition for *arcStep* of external choice.

9   Interleaving: $A \,\|[\, \mathsf{ns_0} \mid \mathsf{ns_1} \,]\|\, B$

Interleaving synchronises only on successful termination. In our semantics, successful termination happens whenever we reach a final configuration with Ω in an after state according to the observations of *Terminating*. An empty arc represents termination. Therefore, this is the only place where the original refusals (or acceptances) sets need to be readjusted. An empty arc can be allowed initially only if both actions are willing to terminate successfully. One possibility for the semantics is similar to that used in CSP_M [24].

$$\forall\, Normal;\ Env \bullet$$
$$\quad enabled((\theta St, A \,\|[\, \mathsf{ns_0} \mid \mathsf{ns_1} \,]\|\, B), \theta Env)$$
$$\quad = (enabled((\theta St, A), \theta Env) \cup enabled((\theta St, B), \theta Env)) \setminus \{\emptyset\}$$
$$\qquad \cup\ enabled((\theta St, A), \theta Env) \cap enabled((\theta St, B), \theta Env) \cap \{\emptyset\}$$

However, since an *enabled* empty arc also represents other transitions such as internal progress, this would wrongly enforce synchronisation in this case as well.

We cannot exploit the observational variables, as we do not yet know the possible after states of the enabling configuration for either action. Instead, the differentiation of these cases must be in the *arcStep* function. Soundness is guaranteed by the well-formedness theorem.

$$a \in enabled((\theta St, A), \theta Env) \Leftrightarrow arcStep(((\theta St, A), \theta Env), a) \neq \emptyset$$

Therefore, the enabled arcs of interleaving are those enabled on either action, and the distinction on distributed termination is left to *arcStep*.

$$\forall\, Normal;\ Env;\ A, B : Action \bullet$$
$$\quad enabled((\theta St, A \,\|[\, \mathsf{ns_0} \mid \mathsf{ns_1} \,]\|\, B), \theta Env) =$$
$$\qquad enabled((\theta St, A), \theta Env) \cup enabled((\theta St, B), \theta Env)$$

In the case of distributed termination, both A and B reach Ω through an empty arc in a final configuration with *Terminating* observations.

$$\forall\, Normal;\ Env;\ a : Arc \bullet$$
$$\quad arcStep(((\theta St, A \,\|[\, \mathsf{ns_0} \mid \mathsf{ns_1} \,]\|\, B), \theta Env), a)$$
$$\quad = \{\ Terminating \mid$$
$$\qquad ((\theta St', \Omega), \theta Env) \in (arcStep(((\theta St, A), \theta Env), \emptyset)$$
$$\qquad\qquad\qquad\qquad \cap arcStep(((\theta St, B), \theta Env), \emptyset))\ \bullet$$
$$\qquad ((\theta St', \Omega), \theta Env)\ \}$$

In the absence of divergence, an enabled event is accepted by $(A \,\|[\, \mathsf{ns_0} \mid \mathsf{ns_1} \,]\|\, B)$ whenever it is accepted by either A or B. We define the schema *Interleaving0*, which describes the observations allowed when A makes its independent progress; the schema *Interleaving1* is defined similarly. We need three versions of the state: (i) the before state shared by both actions and the resulting interleaving; (ii) the after state of the action being evaluated independently; and (iii) the after state of the interleaving.

$$\boxed{\begin{array}{l}
\textit{Interleaving0} \\[4pt]
\hline
\textit{UnpredictableObs} \\
\textit{UnpredictableObs}[okay_0/okay', wait_0/wait', tr_0/tr', userVars_0/userVars'] \\
ns? : \mathbb{P}\,Name \\[4pt]
\hline
okay' = okay_0 \wedge wait' = wait_0 \wedge tr' = tr_0 \\
\theta\,USt' = \theta\,USt
\end{array}}$$

UnpredictableObs describes valid observations (tr prefix tr') from a normal before state ($okay \wedge \neg\, wait$), where either divergence ($\neg\, okay'$), visible communication ($tr' \neq tr$), internal progress ($\neg\, wait' \wedge tr' = tr \wedge \Xi\, USt$), or waiting ($wait' \wedge tr' = tr \wedge \Xi\, USt$) are possible on the after sate.

After state variables of A are 0-subscripted to distinguish them from the after state variables of the interleaving. In *Interleaving1*, we use 1 as a subscript to distinguish the after state.

We have the case where independent progress is made on one action (say A). Action (A $\|[\,ns_0 \mid ns_1\,]\|$ B) reaches (A' $\|[\,ns_0 \mid ns_1\,]\|$ B) whenever A leads to A' through the arc a.

$$\begin{array}{l}
\forall\, Normal;\ Env;\ a : Arc\ \bullet \\
\quad arcStep(((\theta St, \mathsf{A}\,\|[\,\mathsf{ns_0} \mid \mathsf{ns_1}\,]\|\,\mathsf{B}), \theta Env), a) \\
\quad = \{\ A' : Action;\ Interleaving0[\mathsf{ns_0}/ns?]\ | \\
\qquad\quad ((\theta St_0, A'), \theta Env) \in arcStep(((\theta St, \mathsf{A}), \theta Env), a)\ \bullet \\
\qquad\quad ((\theta St', A'\,\|[\,\mathsf{ns_0} \mid \mathsf{ns_1}\,]\|\,\mathsf{B}\,), \theta Env)\ \}
\end{array}$$

The effect on the after state of the interleaving is defined according to observations allowed by the *Interleaving* schema with appropriate substitution for the input name set.

10   Discussion

Our *Circus* model checker will permit the checking of certain kinds of infinite state processes using an algorithm inspired by FDR. We require the LTS to have a finite diagram bounded in size, but inscriptions on the nodes and arcs can involve infinite states and transitions. To see how our operational semantics compresses the graph of an LTS, consider the following two examples.

The process $c?x : \mathbb{N} \to SKIP$ communicates a natural number and then terminates: the CSP_M LTS branches infinitely; the *Circus* LTS has just a single arc to a node that is followed by termination.

The CSP_M process $P(i) = a!i \to P(i{+}1)$ outputs the natural numbers, starting at i. The parametrised process $P(0)$ has an infinite number of nodes, each indexed with a natural number, and a long thin LTS with transitions between successor nodes. The state-based process $\mathbf{var}\ i := 0 \bullet (\mu X \bullet a!i \to i := i + 1;\ X)$ has the same behaviour, but without the infinite graph. ¿From its start node, the declaration enriches the environment with the variable i. From this node, there is a single transition labelled with the set of events $\{\ i : \mathbb{N} \bullet a.i\ \}$, followed by two transitions in sequence representing the assignment and recursive call. This makes a total of four nodes and four transitions. Both processes can be written in *Circus*, but the state-based style encourages the second.

The *Circus* model-checking algorithm tries to establish similarity between two LTSs: an implementation and its putative specification. It can confirm refinement or generate counterexamples for systems with modest data types, but in general it requires the proof of verification conditions to distinguish the outcome of model checking attempts and to compute counterexamples.

The verification conditions may be easily decidable, as would be the case when the programs involved are data independent in the sense of Lazić and Roscoe [21]. Other programs give rise to infinite state machines, but with bounded arcs, like the data flow example in [9]. In such cases, certain checks can be made with economical effort. For example, freedom from deadlock can be checked using the LTS, with the possibly infinite nodes giving rise to verification conditions that all partial functions have been applied within their domains (Z/Eves' *domain checks* [22]), which can be made automatic when appropriate preconditions are present in the Z specification.

Most model checking attempts fail, as a user debugs both the specification and the implementation, and we envisage a similar pattern with our tool. At first, many verification conditions are generated, which the user must scrutinise and judge. As the cycle of attempts continues, a pattern emerges, and similar verification conditions are generated in individual attempts. It is now worthwhile developing an appropriate theory and tuning its automation so that the stable set of verification conditions are discharged mechanically. New verification conditions appear in subsequent attempts, and most are dealt with by the theory. In this way, as the debugging converges to a correct refinement, the level of automation converges with it.

One of our guiding principles is to take our own medicine in building the tool, and so to develop crucial parts of the program using formal specification and refinement. Indeed, the formal model in UTP makes precise the connection between model checking and theorem proving, and this use of formalism is important for credibility as well as for soundness. The operational semantics presented in this paper is one of the departure points for the formal derivation of the algorithms used in the tool. Publication gives an opportunity for public scrutiny of the tool's development, as well as making its specification and algorithms available for other tool builders.

Our operational semantics is inspired by that for CSP_M used in FDR. Our most important contribution is the treatment of infinite constructions such as schema expressions and other state-related features of *Circus*. Our operational and denotational semantics are presented in a uniform theoretical framework, making their proof of congruence much easier. Finally, the two operational semantics differ in various details, particularly to do with silent transitions, distributed termination, and divergence.

The two functions *enabled* and *arcStep* are used to define a transition relation between configurations (states and action pairs) $(s, P) \rightarrow (t, Q)$. As described in [10], this may be interpreted as saying that an implementation that is required to execute P in state s is permitted to execute the shorter action Q in state t. This gives us an independent correctness criterion for the operational semantics: $(s \; ; \; P)$ must be refined by $(t \; ; \; Q)$, where $(s \; ; \; P)$ is the program P started in state s. In this context, the state is represented by an assignemnt.

We have used the Z/Eves theorem prover to analyse the soundness of our description by proving refinement using the denotational semantics. This check for soundness is not yet complete, since there is no mature version of UTP embedded in a theorem prover yet. Nevertheless, research on this front is well advanced: the works in [15, 16] describe deep embeddings of the UTP in the theorem provers Z/Eves [14] and ProofPowerZ [12]. Eventually, this will enable us to mechanise the proof of the correctness of all of our operational semantics with respect to *Circus*'s denotational semantics.

Acknowledgements

We are grateful to QinetiQ Malvern for their long-term support of the *Circus* project, to the Royal Society for an Industry Fellowship, and jointly to the Universities of Kent and York for a *Circus* studentship. We are thankful to Peter Mosses for several illuminating discussions.

References

1. A.L.C. Cavalcanti, A.C.A. Sampaio, and J.C.P. Woodcock. Refinement of actions in *Circus*. *REFINE 2002. Electronic Notes in Theor. Comp. Sci.* **70**(3) 2002.
2. A.L.C. Cavalcanti, A.C.A. Sampaio, and J.C.P. Woodcock. A refinement strategy for *Circus*. *Formal Aspects of Computing* **15**(2–3):146–181 2003.
3. A.L.C. Cavalcanti and J.C.P. Woodcock. Predicate transformers in the semantics of *Circus*. *IEE Proceedings Software* **150**(2):85–94 2003.
4. C. Fischer. Combining CSP and Z. *Technical Report*. Univ. Oldenburg. 1996.
5. Michael Goldsmith. *FDR2 User's Manual version 2.67.* FSEL. May 2000.
6. He Jifeng, Zhiming Liu, and Xiaoshan Li. A Relational Model for Object-Oriented Programming. *Tech. Rep. 231*. UNU/IIST, P. O. Box 3058, Macau, May 2001.
7. He Jifeng, Zhiming Liu, and Xiaoshan Li. Towards a Refinement Calculus for Object Systems. *Procs ICCI2002* pp.69–77. IEEE Computer Society Press 2002.
8. He Jifeng, Zhiming Liu, and Xiaoshan Li. Modelling Object-oriented Programming with Reference Type and Dynamic Binding. *Tech. Rep.* **280**. UNU/IIST. 2003.
9. C.A.R. Hoare. *Communicating Sequential Processes*. Prentice Hall 1985.
10. C.A.R. Hoare and He J. *Unifying Theories of Programming*. Prentice Hall 1998.
11. *Information Technology — Z Formal Specification Notation — Syntax, Type System and Semantics*. ISO/IEC 13568:2002.
12. Lemma-One. *ProofPower Tutorial,* 2003.
13. Jeremy M. R. Martin and Yvonne Huddart. Parallel Algorithms for Deadlock and Livelock Analysis of Concurrent Systems. *Commun. Proc. Archs*. IOS Press 2000.
14. Irwin Meisels and Mark Saaltink. *Z/Eves 1.5 Reference Manual. Technical Report TR-97-5493-03d*. ORA Canada, September 1997.
15. Gift Nuka and Jim Woodcock. Mechanising the alphabetised relational calculus. *WMF2003. Electronic Notes in Theoretical Computer Science* **95** 2004.

16. Marcel Oliveira, Ana Cavalcanti, and Jim Woodcock. Unifying theories in Proof-PowerZ. *Draft*. University of York. January 2005.
17. G. D. Plotkin. A Structural approach to Operational Semantics. *Journal of Logic and Algebraic Programming* **60–61**:19–140 2004.
18. *ProBE User's Manual version 1.28*. Formal Systems (Europe) Ltd. May 2000.
19. A. W. Roscoe. Model Checking CSP. In [20] chapter 21 pp.353–378 1994.
20. A.W. Roscoe. *A Classsical Mind: Essays for C.A.R. Hoare*. Prentice Hall 1994.
21. A. W. Roscoe. *Theory and Practice of Concurrency*. Prentice Hall 1997.
22. Mark Saaltink. Z/Eves 2.0 User's Guide. *Technical Report TR-99-5493-06a*. ORA Canada 1999.
23. A.C.A. Sampaio, J.C.P. Woodcock, and A.L.C. Cavalcanti. Refinement in *Circus*. *FME 2002 Lecture Notes in Computer Science* **2391**:451–470 2002.
24. B. Scattergood. *The Semantics and Implementation of Machine Readable CSP*. PhD thesis. Oxford University 1998.
25. S. Schneider. *Concurrent and Real-Time Systems: The CSP Approach*. Wiley 2000.
26. S. Schneider and H. Treharne. Communicating B Machines. *ZB2002. Lecture Notes in Computer Science* **2272**:415–435. 2002.
27. Adnan Sherif and He Jifeng. Toward a Time Model for *Circus*. *ICFEM 2002. Lecture Notes in Computer Science* **2495** pp.613–624. Springer-Verlag.
28. Xinbei Tang and Jim Woodcock. Towards mobile processes in unifying theories. *SEFM 2004*. IEEE Computer Society 2004.
29. Xinbei Tang and Jim Woodcock. Travelling processes. *Mathematics of Program Construction. Lecture Notes in Computer Science* **3125**:381–399 2004.
30. J. C. P. Woodcock. Unifying Theories of Parallel Programming. In *Logic and Algebra for Engineering Software*. IOS Press, 2002.
31. Jim Woodcock and Ana Cavalcanti. A Concurrent Language for Refinement. *5th Irish Workshop on Formal Methods*, 2001.
32. Jim Woodcock and Ana Cavalcanti. The Semantics of *Circus*. *ZB 2002. Lecture Notes in Computer Science*:184–203 Springer-Verlag 2002.
33. Jim Woodcock and Jim Davies. *Using Z: Specification, Refinement, and Proof*. Prentice Hall 1996.
34. www-users.cs.york.ac.uk/~leo.

Control Law Diagrams in *Circus*

Ana Cavalcanti[1], Phil Clayton[2], and Colin O'Halloran[2]

[1] Department of Computer Science, University of York
York, England
[2] Systems Assurance Group, QinetiQ
Malvern, England

Abstract. Control diagrams are routinely used by engineers in the design of control systems. Yet, currently the formal verification of programs that implement the diagrams is a challenge. We present a strategy to translate block diagrams to *Circus*, a notation that combines Z, CSP, and a refinement calculus. This work is based on existing tools that produce Z and CSP specifications from discrete-time block diagrams. By using a combined notation, we provide a specification that considers both functional and behavioural aspects of these diagrams, and can cover a wider range of blocks. Moreover, the *Circus* refinement calculus can be used to verify implementations, and reason about the block diagrams.

Keywords: Z, CSP, Simulink, refinement.

1 Introduction

A popular and intuitive representation for expressing control system specifications is that of block diagrams. In this notation, a system is modelled by a, possibly cyclic, directed graph of blocks interconnected by wires. This graph includes inputs and outputs to the system, which are signals carried by the wires. Roughly speaking, the blocks represent functions that determine how the outputs are calculated from the inputs. In a continuous-time model, signals continuously vary with time. In a discrete-time model, signals are sampled at discrete time intervals; input and output take place in cycles.

Due to the criticality of many control systems, analysis has been a major concern; numerical modelling and simulation are the established techniques. Recently, there have been efforts to use logic to capture the meaning of control diagrams and to support reasoning [4, 3, 10]. Our work has a different focus: derivation and verification of implementations, as opposed to validation of systems.

Discrete-time diagrams written using Simulink are considered in [2]. Simulink is a popular tool that is part of the Matlab environment [1]; its use in the avionics and automotive sectors is standard. In [2] we find the description a tool, ClawZ, that translates control law diagrams to Z. The translation is based on an extensive Z library that formalises the meaning of many of the blocks. The version of Z used is that implemented in the theorem prover ProofPower [11].

ClawZ has been extensively and successfully used at the Systems Assurance Group at QinetiQ in the proof of correctness of Ada programs with respect to

J.S. Fitzgerald, I.J. Hayes, and A. Tarlecki (Eds.): FM 2005, LNCS 3582, pp. 253–268, 2005.

Simulink specifications. As described in [14], the output of ClawZ is used to construct a refinement conjecture (called a compliance argument) that can be formally verified using tools integrated with ProofPower.

In Z, reactivity and concurrency cannot be modelled directly; ClawZ captures only the functional behaviour of one cycle of a control system. Basically, the Z specification that it generates defines how the outputs of a cycle can be determined in terms of the inputs (and possibly, state information).

QinetiQ developed another tool, called ClaSP, to support the definition of a CSP [16] specification that captures the parallelism inherent in a control law diagram. In principle, the computation embedded in the blocks can be performed in parallel; order is imposed only by the wiring. ClaSP is used in the verification by model checking of distributed cyclic scheduling.

Circus [19, 6] is a combination of Z and CSP with a refinement calculus; it aims at the specification and design of state-rich reactive systems. *Circus* includes a theory and a technique of refinement that support the calculation of concurrent implementations from centralised specifications. The semantics is based on Hoare and He's unifying theories of programming [9].

In this work, we give a semantics to control diagrams using *Circus*, so that we can capture functionality and concurrency. We reuse ClawZ and ClaSP, which capture a partial semantics of these diagrams. Our semantics is a strategy to translate the outputs of extended versions ClawZ and ClaSP to a *Circus* specification: extensions are needed to enlarge the subset of the diagrammatic notation that is covered. Even so, the existing experience with ClawZ and ClaSP improves our confidence in the suitability of the *Circus* semantics.

Using *Circus*, we can model blocks whose output can be disabled or depends on the order of arrival of input signals. Moreover, the *Circus* specification can capture the behaviour of the system over any number of cycles; our model of a diagram is a process that proceeds recursively executing cycle after cycle.

With a *Circus* model, we are able to use refinement to reason about diagrams and their implementations. Separate analyses that consider functionality and concurrency independently are not needed. Properties that are based on both the functionality and the scheduling policies of an implementation can be handled.

In the next section, we present a brief introduction to Simulink control law diagrams. In Section 3 we describe ClawZ, ClaSP, and *Circus*; the extensions of ClawZ and ClaSP are described in Sections 4 and 5. Our translation strategy is presented in Section 6; refinement is discussed and exemplified in Section 7. In Section 8 we summarise our results, and discuss future and related work.

2   Control Law Diagrams

Our work is based on the Simulink notation; an example is presented in Figure 1. That diagram specifies a PID (Proportional Integral Derivative) controller that is being used to control a fuel metering valve of an aircraft. Each box in a diagram is called a block; the wires carry signals. The inputs and outputs of a

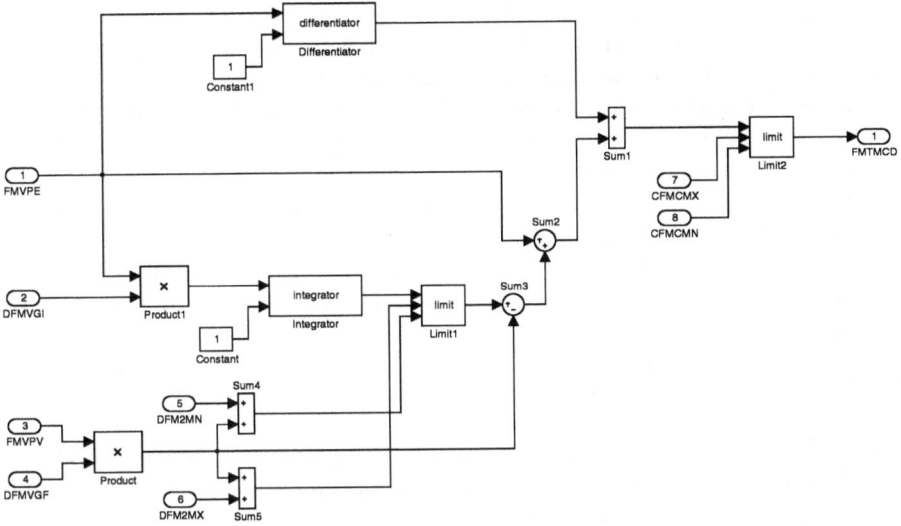

Fig. 1. PID (Proportional Integral Derivative) controller

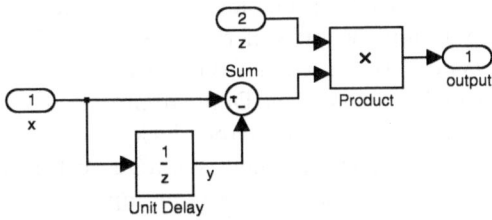

Fig. 2. PID Differentiator

system are represented by rounded boxes containing numbers. In our example, there are eight inputs and one output.

Typically, a block takes some input signals and produces some outputs according to a function determined by the kind of block in question. There are libraries of blocks in Simulink, and they can also be user-defined.

The rectangular boxes without inputs output the constant value they display. The circles are sum blocks. Boxes enclosing names are subsystems; they denote control systems defined in other diagrams. For example, the diagram that corresponds to the Differentiator block is presented in Figure 2.

Blocks can have state. For instance, blocks labelled $1/z$ are unit delay blocks. They store the value of the input signal, and output the value stored in the previous cycle. In each cycle, the output depends on the values of the inputs and of the state that may be held in the blocks, but other factors may be relevant.

For example, subsystems may be conditionally executed: an action subsystem has an activate input and is executed when it is true; an enabled subsystem has an enabling input and is executed when its value is greater than zero. When a subsystem is not executed, its outputs can either be held at their previous value or reset to an initial value. Any state contained in blocks within the subsystem is held until the subsystem is about to be executed again, at which point the state can be held or reset to an initial value. Merge blocks take a number of inputs and produce one output: the most recently calculated input.

In the next section, we present two models for control diagrams provided by two tools. ClawZ uses Z to provide a relational model for blocks, which covers state, but not concurrency and the behaviour of conditionally executed subsystems and merge blocks. ClaSP, on the other hand, cannot capture functionality.

3   ClawZ, ClaSP, and *Circus*

ClawZ characterises each block of a Simulink diagram, including constants, as a set of bindings, typically defined as a schema. In the Z specification of a diagram, there is a set of bindings for each block, and a set of bindings corresponding to the whole diagram. Part of the output of ClawZ for the PID diagram in Figure 1 is presented in Figure 3; the Z notation is that adopted by ProofPower.

The schema *pidspec* declares the inputs and the outputs of the diagram, and includes (the schemas that specify) the blocks. The predicate of *pidspec* (omitted) specifies how the inputs and outputs of the diagram and of each of the blocks are connected. The type $\mathbb{U}$ is a universal type in ProofPower.

We present only the definition of the Differentiator; it is a schema that declares the inputs and outputs of the Differentiator block, and each of the blocks in its diagram (Figure 2). The predicate, which is similar to that of *pidspec*, equates, for instance, the inputs of the Product block to an input of the whole Differentiator and the output of the Sum block.

ClawZ includes a library of block definitions. The Product block of the Differentiator is defined in terms of the library block *Product_M2*. The Unit Delay block specification uses *UnitDelay_g*; it is a function that takes a binding that defines the initial value of the unit delay state, and gives a set of bindings. In ProofPower, there is support for real numbers: 0 *e* 0 is the real number 0.

ClaSP provides a simple characterisation of the wiring in a diagram; it ignores the calculations performed by the blocks. The output of ClaSP is not really a CSP specification, but a set of pairs that is used as argument for a CSP process that defines the concurrent behaviour of the diagram. The set includes one pair for each block in the diagram: the first element of the pair is the set of input signals of the block, and the second element is a sequence of output signals.

The output of ClaSP for the PID is shown in Figure 4. To make model checking practical, the CSP process that uses this set of pair determines an order of execution for the blocks; this is why the outputs are identified by sequences. The massive parallelism intrinsic in a block diagram leads to processes that have a large number of states and are difficult to model check.

Circus is a language for refinement; it includes specification constructs from Z and Morgan's refinement calculus [13], CSP constructs to model communica-

Z
| $pidspec\_Differentiator\_Product \mathrel{\widehat{=}} Product\_M_2$

Z
| $pidspec\_Differentiator\_UnitDelay \mathrel{\widehat{=}} UnitDelay\_g \ (X_0 \mathrel{\widehat{=}} o \ e \ o)$

Z

_pidspec_Differentiator_
| $In_1? : U; \ In_2? : \ U;$
| $Product : pidspec\_Differentiator\_Product;$
| $Sum : pidspec\_Differentiator\_Sum;$
| $UnitDelay : pidspec\_Differentiator\_UnitDelay;$
| $Out_1! : U$
|___
| $Out_1! = Product.Out_1!;$
| $Product.In_1? = In_2? \wedge Product.In_2? = Sum.Out_1!;$
| $Sum.In_2? = UnitDelay.Out_1!;$
| $UnitDelay.In_1? = Sum.In_1? = In_1?$

Z

pidspec
| $In_1? : U; \ In_2? : U; \ In_3? : U; \ In_4? : U; \ In_5? : U; \ In_6? : U; \ In_7? : U; \ In_8? : U;$
| $Constant : pidspec\_Constant; \ Constant_1 : pidspec\_Constant_1;$
| $Differentiator : pidspec\_Differentiator;$
| ...
| $Out_1! : U$
|___
| ...

Fig. 3. ClawZ output for the PID (ProofPower notation)

tion and concurrency, and Dijkstra's language of guarded commands. A *Circus* program is a sequence of paragraphs, just like in Z, but they also include channel and process declarations. Section 6 gives examples.

A process encapsulates state and exhibits behaviour. Like a *Circus* program, an explicit definition of a process is a sequence of paragraphs; Figure 6 has an example. A distinguished paragraph introduces the state schema. At the end, a main action specifies the behaviour of the process. Actions are (composed of) Z operations, CSP processes, and guarded commands. Typically, a process includes several paragraphs to define actions that are combined in the main action to specify the behaviour of the process. Processes can be combined using CSP operators: choice, parallelism, hiding, and others.

Communications are events, just like in CSP; if their occurrence entails a state change, a state operation needs to be used. If a Z operation is used outside its precondition, it diverges, just like in Z. Guards can be explicitly defined.

Parallelism is alphabetised; we can either define a synchronisation set or the alphabet of the parallel processes. A synchronisation set determines the channels for which communication requires synchronisation. The alphabet of a process is

$\{ (\, \{ \, FMVPE \, \}, \langle \, Differentiator\_out \, \rangle \,), (\, \{ \, FMVPE, DFMVGI \, \}, \langle \, Product1\_out \, \rangle \,),$
$(\, \{ \, FMVPE, Sum3\_out \, \}, \langle \, Sum2\_out \, \rangle \,), (\, \{ \, FMVPV, DFMVGF \, \}, \langle \, Product\_out \, \rangle \,),$
$(\, \{ \, Product1\_out \, \}, \langle \, Integrator\_out \, \rangle \,), (\, \{ \, DFM2MN, Product\_out \, \}, \langle \, Sum4\_out \, \rangle \,),$
$(\, \{ \, DFM2MX, Product\_out \, \}, \langle \, Sum5\_out \, \rangle \,),$
$(\, \{ \, CFMCMX, CFMCMN, Sum1\_out \, \}, \langle \, FMTMCD \, \rangle \,),$
$(\, \{ \, differentiator\_out, Sum2\_out \, \}, \langle \, Sum1\_out \, \rangle \,),$
$(\, \{ \, integrator\_out, Sum5\_out, Sum4\_out \, \}, \langle \, Limit1\_out \, \rangle \,),$
$(\, \{ \, Limit1\_out, Product1\_out \, \}, \langle \, Sum3\_out \, \rangle \,) \, \}$

Fig. 4. ClaSP output for the PID

the set of channels that it can use; synchronisation is required for the channels in the intersection of alphabetised parallel processes. In the case of actions, there is a concern about conflicting access to the state. The parallel composition of actions A_1 and A_2 with a synchronisation set cs is written $A_1 [\![\, ns_1 \mid cs \mid ns_2]\!] A_2$, where ns_1 and ns_2 are disjoint sets of names of state components. Both A_1 and A_2 have access to the initial value of all state components; however, A_1 can only modify the components named in ns_1, and A_2 can only modify those in ns_2. The same concerns apply for interleaving of actions.

A refinement calculus and strategy is available for *Circus* [6]. The strategy aims at calculating concurrent implementations from centralised specifications. Using the *Circus* refinement theory, we can implement and reason about the *Circus* model of a diagram. Examples are considered in Section 7.

4   Extensions to ClawZ

The translation of diagrams to *Circus* is based on the output of extended versions of ClawZ and ClaSP. ClawZ is extended to include action and enabled subsystems, and merge blocks; they are representative in the treatment of conditional execution and order of arrival of inputs. In the translation of an action subsystem, we need a record of the enabling condition and the value of its outputs separately. The schema that records the enabling condition is named after the block with the suffix *_Enabling*. Schemas with suffix *_Enabled* and *_Disabled* define the values of the outputs in the case the system is enabled and in the case the system is disabled. The schema that defines the subsystem combines these schemas. For enabled subsystems, the strategy is similar.

The definition of a merge block requires information about whether the inputs have been computed or not, and their order of arrival. Below, we present the definition of a merge block with two inputs $In1?$ and $In2?$. Two extra inputs $In1\,Computed?$ and $In2\,Computed?$ determine whether the values input have been freshly calculated or are just default or held values. The boolean type $BOOL$ is available in ProofPower, although it is not part of Standard Z. The component $arrOrder$ is a sequence of input indexes that defines the order of arrival of the inputs. The single output is $Out1!$.

If a block has a state, its Z specification would typically involve three schemas to define the state, the initial state, and the calculation of outputs. The ClawZ library, however, includes many block definitions, and, for clarity and simplicity, it groups the definition of each block in a single schema. Components *state*, *state'*, and *initial_state* record the value of the state at the beginning of each cycle, and its initial value. This is the approach we adopt in *Merge2*.

Merge2

$In1?, In2? : \mathbb{U}$
$In1\,Computed?, In2\,Computed? : BOOL$
$arrOrder : \text{seq}\,1\ldots2$
$state, state', initial\_state : \mathbb{U}$
$Out1! : \mathbb{U}$

$initial\_state = (0\ e\ 0)$
$In1\,Computed? \wedge \neg\, In2\,Computed? \Rightarrow Out1! = In2? = state'$
$In2\,Computed? \wedge \neg\, In1\,Computed? \Rightarrow Out1! = In1? = state'$
$\neg\, In1\,Computed? \wedge \neg\, In2\,Computed? \Rightarrow Out1! = state = state'$
$In1\,Computed? \wedge In2\,Computed? \Rightarrow$
$\quad last\ arrOrder = 1 \Rightarrow Out1! = In1? = state' \wedge$
$\quad last\ arrOrder = 2 \Rightarrow Out1! = In2? = state'$

The extra information (*In1 Computed?*, *In2 Computed?*, and *arrOrder*) required by *Merge2* is determined in the *Circus* specification.

5   Extensions to ClaSP

ClaSP is extended to incorporate a more elaborate view of blocks, since it considers that a block produces all its outputs once it receives all its inputs. There are, however, even basic blocks, like the unit delay, which can produce its output before it receives its input. (This is currently handled by assuming some arbitrary input.) Although ClaSP models all the possible flows of execution, it cannot show the relationship between the order of input signals and an output value. This means that some information about parallelism in a Simulink diagram can be lost making automated verification impossible in some circumstances.

We use Z to characterise the form of the output of the extended version of ClaSP. Again, it is not actually a CSP process, but information about the structure of the diagram that is used to define the *Circus* specification.

We use given sets *NAME*, *Signal*, and *Block* to represent the valid specification names, and the sets of signal and block names used in the diagram. For a given diagram, the output produced by ClaSP gives the name of the diagram, its inputs and outputs, and a characterisation of each of its blocks.

ClaSPOutput

$spec : NAME$
$inputs, outputs : \mathbb{P}\,Signal$
$blocks : Block \rightarrow BlockWiring$

The wiring of a block defines its inputs, outputs, and the dependencies between them; these determine the independent flows of execution that can arise to calculate different outputs.

Values of a free type *Enabled* are used to record whether a flow of execution is *always* enabled or enabling depends on the values of some special input signals: *Enabled* ::= *always* | *esigs* << $\mathbb{P}$ *Signal* >>. In a flow, the order in which the signals are received may be relevant. We also need to know the signals that a flow requires (*rinps*), and the outputs that it produces (*pouts*).

$$Flow \mathrel{\widehat{=}} [\, enabled : Enabled;\; ordered : BOOL;\; rinps, pouts : \mathbb{P}\, Signal\,]$$

The block wiring information includes the order of the inputs and outputs to establish a correspondence between the inputs and outputs of the ClawZ schema that defines the functionality of the block and the signals in the diagram.

```
┌─ BlockWiring ─────────────────────────────────────────────
│ inps, outs : seq Signal
│ flows : ℙ Flow
├───────────────────────────────────────────────────────────
│ ∀ f : flows | f.enabled ∈ ran esigs • (esigs~ f.enabled) ⊆ ran inps
│ (∀ f : flows • f.rinps ⊆ ran inps) ∧ ⋃{ f : flows • f.pouts } = ran outs
│ ∀ f₁, f₂ : flows • f₁ ≠ f₂ ⇒ f₁.pouts ∩ f₂.pouts = ∅
└───────────────────────────────────────────────────────────
```

The invariant establishes that the enabling signals and the required inputs of a flow are inputs of the block, and every output of the diagram is an output of a flow. For inputs, we do not have the same restriction, as there may be inputs that are not required to produce outputs; a unit delay block is a simple example. Finally, different flows should produce distinct outputs.

Part of the extended ClaSP output for the PID diagram is in Figure 5. The blocks are very simple: they have one flow, which is always enabled, and whose output does not depend on the input order. The constants are also blocks, with no inputs, and just one output. Even though blocks like the Differentiator represent a diagram, from the point of view of the PID, it is just a block. The internal communications that take place inside the Differentiator are ignored.

This does not mean, however, that ClaSP does not need to inspect the subsystems to determine the model of a diagram. A subsystem can, for example, have several flows of execution, or have a behaviour that depends on the order of the inputs are received. This information can only be determined by analysing the blocks of the subsystem.

6 Translation Strategy

The starting points for the translation are a *ClaSPOutput* which we call clasp, and a Z specification, called clawz, produced by the extended version of ClawZ. We refer to a definition D in clawz as clawz.D.

The *Circus* specification of a diagram first declares all signals as channels. It also declares a synchronisation channel *end_cycle*; after taking all its inputs

⟨ *spec* ↦ *pidspec*,
  inputs ↦ { *FMVPE*, *DFMVGI*, *FMVPV*, *DFMVGF*,
              DFM2MN, *DFM2MX*, *CFMCMX*, *CFMCMN* },
  output ↦ { *FMTMCD* },
  blocks ↦ { *Differentiator* ↦ ⟨ *inps* ↦ ⟨ *FMVPE*, *Constant1_out* ⟩,
                                    outs ↦ ⟨ *Differentiator_out* ⟩
                                    flows ↦ { ⟨ *enabled* ↦ *always*, *ordered* ↦ *false*
                                                rinps ↦ { *FMVPE*, *Constant1_out* },
                                                pouts ↦ { *Differentiator_out* } ⟩ } ⟩,
              Constant1 ↦ ⟨ *inps* ↦ ⟨ ⟩, *outs* ↦ ⟨ *Constant1_out* ⟩
                              flows ↦ { ⟨ *enabled* ↦ *always*, *ordered* ↦ *false*
                                          rinps ↦ { },
                                          pouts ↦ { *Constant1_out* } ⟩ } ⟩,
              Sum1 ↦ ⟨ *inps* ↦ ⟨ *Differentiator_out*, *Sum2_out* ⟩, *outs* ↦ ⟨ *Sum1_out* ⟩
                        flows ↦ { ⟨ *enabled* ↦ *always*, *ordered* ↦ *false*
                                    rinps ↦ { *Differentiator_out*, *Sum2_out* },
                                    pouts ↦ { *Sum1_out* } ⟩ } ⟩, ... } ⟩

Fig. 5. Extended ClaSP output for the PID

and producing all its outputs, each block of a diagram waits to synchronise on *end_cycle* before proceeding to the next cycle. In this way, all blocks are kept in phase. The *Circus* specification corresponding to the PID starts as follows.

> **channel** *FMVPE*, *Differentiator_out*, ..., *CFMCMX*, *CFMCMN*, ... : $\mathbb{U}$
> **channel** *end_cycle*;

Next, the *Circus* specification includes the ClawZ library, which is used in clawz.

6.1   The Diagram

Blocks and diagrams are defined as processes. The whole diagram is a process called clasp.spec, which is defined as the parallel execution of all the blocks.

> **process** clasp.spec $\widehat{=}$
>   (‖ B : Block • B) \ (Signal \ (clasp.inputs ∪ clasp.outputs))

The alphabet of each block includes its inputs and outputs, and *end_cycle*. For conciseness, we use sets and sequences of signals to define channel sets in *Circus*.

> αB = ran(clasp.blocks B).inps ∪ ran(clasp.blocks B).outs ∪ { *end_cycle* }

The synchronisation required by the parallelism determines the possible flows of execution for the diagram. For the *PID*, we have the process sketched below.

> **process** *pidspec* $\widehat{=}$
>   (*Differentiator* ⟦*FMVPE*, *Constant1_out*, *Differentiator_out*, *end_cycle*⟧
>   ‖
>   *Sum1* ⟦ *Differentiator_out*, *Sum2_out*, *Sum1_out*, *end_cycle* ⟧ ...)
>   \ ⟦ *Constant1_out*, *Differentiator_out*, *Sum2_out*, ..., *end_cycle* ⟧

The processes that represent the Differentiator and the Sum1 blocks are required to synchronise on the channels *Differentiator_out* and *end_cycle* (the intersection of their alphabets); the processes for Sum1 and Limit2 are required to synchronise on *Sum1_out* and *end_cycle*; and so on. Because the internal channels are hidden, in an implementation, we do not need to have a separate process for each block; refinement can lead to combination and splitting of blocks.

6.2   The Blocks

The process that corresponds to a block B is defined explicitly, independently of whether the block is simple, like Sum1, or a subsystem, like Differentiator. In clasp we have a record of the outputs of a subsystem that may be produced independently and in parallel, but not of internal communications. For example, to model the interaction between the blocks of the Differentiator in Figure 2, we need to translate that diagram; the translation of the PID diagram in Figure 1 does not include them. In the next section we discuss the relation between the *Circus* process that models the Differentiator in the translation of the PID and the *Circus* process obtained by translating the Differentiator diagram itself.

We first consider the translation of a block whose flows are always enabled and do not depend on the order of the inputs. The state of the B process includes a component for each component named *state* used in the definition of B in clawz.

process B $\widehat{=}$ **begin**

___state B_State_____
    $def1\_state$: T1; $\ldots$$defn_state$: Tn
_____

Each defi is a definition in clawz such that clawz.B involves defi, and defi is a set of bindings with a component of type Ti called *state*. We define formally what it means for clawz.B to involve defi.

Definition 1. *A type T_1 involves a type T_2 if and only if (i) $T_1 = T_2$; or (ii) exits a type T_3 such that $T_1 = \mathbb{P}\, T_3$, and T_3 involves T_2; or (iii) there are types $T_3, \ldots, T_n$, such that $T_1 = T_3 \times \ldots T_n$, and any of the T_i involves T_2; or (iv) T_1 is a schema with a component whose type involves T_2.*

For example, the schema *pidspec_Differentiator* characterises the PID Differentiator; it has a component *UnitDelay* of type *pidspec_Differentiator_UnitDelay*, which is a set of bindings with a component called *state* defined by *UnitDelay_g*. So, the process *pidspec_Differentiator*, which is defined in Figure 6, has a state component called *pidspec_Differentiator_UnitDelay_state*.

After the state declaration, we include clawz.B and all the definitions in clawz that it uses. The initialisation of the state is based on the clawz specification.

___Init_____
    B_State'
    _____
    $\exists\, b$: defi $\bullet$ defi$\_state' = b.initial\_state$
_____

A component defi_*state*, corresponding to a *state* component of a definition defi

process *pidspec_Differentiator* $\widehat{=}$ **begin**

state
   pidspec_Differentiator_State $\widehat{=}$ [*pidspec_Differentiator_UnitDelay_state* : $\mathbb{U}$]

   pidspec_Differentiator_UnitDelay from Figure 3 and other definitions it uses.

Init
pidspec_Differentiator_State'

$\exists\, b : pidspec\_Differentiator\_UnitDelay \bullet$
   $pidspec\_Differentiator\_UnitDelay\_state' = b.initial\_state$

Calculate_pidspec_Differentiator
$\Delta pidspec\_Differentiator\_State;\ In1?, In2?, Out1! : \mathbb{U}$

$\exists\, b : pidspec\_Differentiator \bullet$
   $b.In1? = In1? \wedge b.In2? = In2? \wedge$
   $b.UnitDelay.state = pidspec\_Differentiator\_UnitDelay\_state \wedge$
   $b.UnitDelay.state' = pidspec\_Differentiator\_UnitDelay\_state' \wedge$
   $b.Out1! = Out1!$

Calculate_pidspec_Differentiator_out $\widehat{=}$
   Calculate_pidspec_Differentiator \ (*pidspec_Differentiator_UnitDelay_state'*) $\wedge$
   $\Xi pidspec\_Differentiator\_State$

Execute_Differentiator_out $\widehat{=}$
   var $In1, In2 : \mathbb{U} \bullet$
      $(\ FMVPE?x \rightarrow In1 := x\ )\ [\![\, \{In1\} \mid \{In2\} \,]\!]\ (\ Constant1\_out?x \rightarrow In2 := x\ );$
      var $Out1 : \mathbb{U} \bullet$
         $Calculate\_pidspec\_Differentiator\_out;\ Differentiator\_out!\,Out1 \rightarrow Skip$

Calculate_pidspec_Differentiator_State $\widehat{=}$
   Calculate_pidspec_Differentiator \ (*Out1!*)

StateUpdate $\widehat{=}$
   var $In1, In2 : \mathbb{U} \bullet$
      $(\ FMVPE?x \rightarrow In1 := x\ )\ [\![\, \{In1\} \mid \{In2\} \,]\!]\ (\ Constant1\_out?x \rightarrow In2 := x\ );$
      Calculate_pidspec_Differentiator_State;

$\bullet$ *Init*;
   $\mu X \bullet (\ Execute\_Differentiator\_out\ [\![\ \{\,\}$
            $\mid\ \{\!|\ FMVPE, Constant1\_out\ |\!\}\ \mid$
            $\{\ pidspec\_Differentiator\_UnitDelay\_state\ \}\ ]\!]\ StateUpdate\ );$
         $end\_cycle \rightarrow X$
end

Fig. 6. *Circus* process for the block Differentiator

in clawz, is initialised with the value of the component *initial_state* of that definition. We identify a binding b of type defi, whose value for *initial_state* defines the initial value of defi_*state*. For example, if defi is a unit delay, defi is a set whose bindings all have the same value for *initial_state*: that in the diagram.

The main action starts with the initialisation, and recursively proceeds in parallel to execute each of the flows and update the state, before synchronising on *end_cycle*. The flows proceed independently, but a block can only start a new cycle when all the flows, (and all the blocks of the diagram) have finished.

- *Init*;
  $\mu X \bullet (\ Flows\ [\![\ \{\ \}\ |\ \mathsf{rlnps}\ |\ \{\![\alpha\mathsf{B\_State}]\!\}\ ]\!]\ StateUpdate\ );\ end\_cycle \to X$
  end

The flows do not update the state, and so the action *Flows* is associated with the empty set of state component names; on the other hand, *StateUpdate* is associated with the set B_*State* including all state components. When an input is received, it needs to be made available to the flows and to the action that updates the state, and so they synchronise. The set rlnps contains all the inputs required by at least one flow of B.

$$\mathsf{rlnps} \mathrel{\widehat{=}} \bigcup\{\ \mathsf{f} : (\mathsf{clasp.blocks\ B}).\mathsf{flows} \bullet \mathsf{f.rinps}\ \}$$

As already observed, not all inputs are required by a flow; the input of a unit delay block is a simple example.

The action *Flows* executes the flows in (clasp.blocks B).flows in parallel.

$$Flows \mathrel{\widehat{=}} \mathop{|\!|\!|} \mathsf{f} : (\mathsf{clasp.blocks\ B}).\mathsf{flows}\ \{\ \}\ |\ \mathsf{f.rinps} \cup \mathsf{f.pouts} \bullet Execute\_f$$

They do not change any of the state components; they only produce outputs. Their alphabets are the required inputs and the produced outputs.

In the Differentiator, there is only one flow, so the interleaving in *Flows* is reduced to a single process *Execute_Differentiator_out* (Figure 6). It synchronises with the action *StateUpdate* on the inputs *FMVPE* and *Constant1_out*.

For each flow f, the action *Execute_f* takes the required inputs, and then calculates and produces the outputs.

$$\begin{aligned} Execute\_f \mathrel{\widehat{=}}\ &\textbf{var}\ \mathsf{Ini} : \mathbb{U} \bullet \\ &\quad \mathop{|\!|\!|} \mathsf{inp} : \mathsf{f.rinps}\ \{\ \mathsf{Ini}\ \} \bullet \mathsf{inp}?x \to \mathsf{Ini} := x; \\ &\quad \textbf{var}\ \mathsf{Outj} : \mathbb{U} \bullet \\ &\quad CalculateOutputs;\ \mathop{|\!|\!|} \mathsf{out} : \mathsf{f.pouts} \bullet \mathsf{out}!\mathsf{Outj} \to Skip \end{aligned}$$

First, *Execute_f* declares variables to record the values of the inputs; we declare Ini when the i-th input is required by the flow: (clasp.blocks B).inps i $\in$ f.rinps. Similarly, to calculate the outputs, *Execute_f* declares variables Outj for each output produced by f: those in f.pouts. In *Execute_Differentiator_out* there are two input variables *In*1 and *In*2, and one output variable *Out*1.

The inputs are received in any order, through each of the channels inp in f.rinps. The value x of the input is recorded in the corresponding variable Ini.

Similarly, outputs are sent in any order through the channels in f.pouts. In our example, since there is only one output, the interleaving is reduced to one action.

The definition clawz.B specifies the state changes and the outputs of B, but it is not an operation over the state B_*State*. We define a schema *Calculate*_B that lifts clawz.B to B_*State*. It includes the input and output variables; Z decorations are used, since *Circus* allows us to keep the Z style and refer to local variables as inputs or outputs. In *Calculate*_B, we identify a binding b of type clawz.B using the input values in Ini to determine the value of the Ini? components of b, and the _*state* components to determine the value of the corresponding components of b. The new value of the state and the outputs are defined by b.

__ *Calculate*_B _____

ΔB_*State*; Ini?, Outj! : $\mathbb{U}$

$\exists\, b :$ clawz.B $\bullet$ b.Ini? $=$ Ini? $\wedge$ b.defi.*state* $=$ defi_*state* $\wedge$
$\qquad\qquad$ b.defi.*state'* $=$ defi_*state'* $\wedge$ b.Outj! $=$ Outj!

If B has a state component defi_*state*, it is because clawz.B includes a component defi with a *state* component. To define the schema CalculateOutputs, we hide the final value of the state in *Calculate*_B, and conjoin the result with Ξ B_*State* so that the state is not modified (see *Calculate_pidspec_Differentiator_out*).

The action that updates the state takes all the inputs.

$StateUpdate \,\widehat{=}\, \mathbf{var}\ \mathsf{Ini} : \mathbb{U}\ \bullet$
$\qquad\qquad\qquad |\!|\!| \ \mathsf{inp} : (\mathsf{clasp.blocks\,B}).\mathsf{inps}\{\,\mathsf{Ini}\,\} \bullet \mathsf{inp}?x \to \mathsf{Ini} := x;$
$\qquad\qquad\qquad \mathsf{CalculateState};$

In principle, all the inputs in (clasp.blocks B).inps are needed. The definition of CalculateState uses *Calculate*_B; it simply hides the output variables. An example is presented in Figure 6: *Calculate_pidspec_Differentiator_State*.

6.3   Enabling Conditions and Order of Inputs

For flows that have enabling conditions or depend on the order of the inputs, *Execute*_f needs to be changed. For lack of space, we do not present the definitions in detail. To capture the order of the inputs, the interleaving in *Execute*_f needs to be replaced with a recursive action that takes any of the outstanding inputs at each step and records its value and index in a sequence. It terminates once all inputs have been received. The resulting sequence of indexes is used as an extra parameter for the calculation of outputs and state updates.

The presence of action and enabled subsystems leads to the possibility that some outputs are not computed. In this case, for every output signal o, we need two channels: o, as explained before, and oComputed of type *BOOL*. The communication of outputs in *Execute*_f needs to be defined as follows.

$\qquad |\!|\!|\ \mathsf{o} : \mathsf{f.pouts} \bullet \mathsf{o}!\mathsf{Outj} \to \mathsf{oComputed}!true \to Skip$

If o is an internal channel, so should be oComputed. If f is a flow that is not always enabled, it needs to use the _Enabling schema produced by ClawZ to determine whether an output should be computed or not. Blocks that need that information should declare oComputed in its alphabet.

7   Refinement

In the translation of a diagram, a block that corresponds to a subsystem is regarded mostly as a black box. As already said, even though we consider flows of execution and requirements to record the order of arrival of the inputs of a subsystem, we do not model its internal communications. We can, however, translate the diagram that corresponds to the subsystem. For example, in the PID diagram, Differentiator is a block; in the translation of the PID, it is defined as a single process (Figure 6). If, on the other hand, we consider the diagram that specifies this block (Figure 2), we get the following *Circus* output.

process *Differentiator* $\mathrel{\widehat=}$
  (*Sum* ⟦ *a*, *b*, *Sum_out*, *end_cycle* ⟧
    ‖
  Product ⟦ *c*, *Sum_out*, *output*, *end_cycle* ⟧
    ‖
  UnitDelay ⟦ *a*, *b*, *end_cycle* ⟧) \ ⟦ *Sum_out*, *b* ⟧

For lack of space, we have to omit the processes *Sum*, *Product*, and *UnitDelay* that model the blocks in Figure 2. This new process refines *pidspec_Differentiator* in Figure 6, given that the channels are renamed properly.

  pidspec_Differentiator
$\sqsubseteq$
  Differentiator[*a*, *output* := *FMVPE*, *Differentiator_out*]

The renaming is needed because the diagram of a block does not keep the original names of inputs and outputs. The *Circus* refinement calculus can be used to prove this refinement; it is a typical derivation of a distributed implementation from a centralised specification. The state does not require refinement; the major effort is in expressing the recursive main action of *pidspec_Differentiator* as a parallelism. In [15] we tackle a similar problem in an industrial case study.

A refinement relationship should hold every time we translate a diagram and a subsystem corresponding to one of its blocks. The implementation obtained for the subsystem follows the architecture of the diagram, with a process for each of the blocks. As already said, however, this is not the only possible implementation.

Refinement can also be used to reason about diagrams. For example, an action subsystem that takes its input from a block whose output always satisfies the condition of the action subsystem can become a simple subsystem. To prove that, we can calculate the *Circus* model, refine it to simplify the process that defines the action subsystem, and translate it back to a diagram. We can use the same approach to eliminate unnecessary blocks. To make this approach appealing to engineers, however, we need to provide a lot of automation. The algebraic approach of a refinement calculus is, therefore, very appropriate.

8   Conclusions

We have presented a semantics for discrete-time Simulink diagrams using a combination of Z and CSP called *Circus*. Our model captures the functionality of a diagram over any number of cycles, and the inherent parallelism between blocks. Cyclic diagrams involving feedback loops are also covered. There are several combinations of Z with a process algebra [8]; *Circus* is distinctive in its refinement theory. Our semantics opens the possibility of reasoning about control law diagrams using refinement. We discussed some examples, based on a PID controller.

PID controllers are considered in [3], where weakest preconditions are used for reasoning about control systems; the technique can be extended to handle static analysis of programs and concurrency. In [12], Mahony used Isabelle/HOL tools to mechanise an assertion reasoning technique based on predicate transformers for dataflow networks with feedback loops. This is a graphical notation like control law diagrams; however, parallelism needs to be indicated explicitly.

The technique proposed in [4] is a Hoare logic to reason about the frequency response of continuous-time control systems. Continuous systems are also studied in [10], with a focus on timing analysis, as opposed to functionality and concurrency. Our interest is on program verification, rather than system analysis; extension of our model to include multirate diagrams is in our plans.

We are working on the implementation of CliC, a tool to automate the translation strategy presented here. We are also working on a theorem prover and a model checker for *Circus*, all based on ProofPower. These tools will be a powerful resource in the analysis of control diagrams and their implementation.

In [5], a translation from discrete-time Simulink diagrams to Lustre is presented. It formalises the typing system of Simulink and type-checks diagrams before the translation; it also handles multirate diagrams. The results seem to be complementary to those obtained with ClawZ, which assumes that all signals have type double, and can only cope with single rate diagrams, but with a larger number of block types. Lustre is a functional programming language, and ClawZ aims at supporting verification by refinement of Ada programs.

Additional experience with refinement of *Circus* models for control law diagrams will lead to a suite of refinement laws that are adequate to this domain of application. For example, powerful laws should be available to prove the refinement of *pidspec_Differentiator* discussed in the previous section. The proposal, proof, and tool support for the application of these laws is in our agenda of work.

A Simulink model can include a stateflow block, which is defined by a diagram that has local data and includes finite state machines, flow-diagram notations, and state-transition diagrams. The finite state machine reacts to events triggered in the Simulink model; the reactions lead to state changes that affect the behavior of the Simulink model. Stateflow diagrams are studied in [18, 17]. We will investigate the use of *Circus* to model stateflow diagrams; it seems promising as *Circus* can cope with both the data and reactive aspects of the problem. Ultimately, we want to cover the whole of the Simulink notation in a uniform framework for program verification based on *Circus*.

Acknowledgements

This work is funded by the Royal Society. We discussed it with Mark Adams, Alfred Smith, Ian Toyn, Karen Stephenson, Gaius Wilson, and Jim Woodcock. We are also grateful to anonymous referees for useful suggestions.

References

1. *The MathWorks. Simulink.* http: //www.mathworks.com/products/simulink.
2. R. Arthan, P. Caseley, C. O'Halloran, and A. Smith. ClawZ: Control laws in Z. In *ICFEM 2000*, pages 169 – 176. IEEE Press, 2000.
3. J. Blow and A. Galloway. Generalised Substitution Language and Differentials. In *ZB 2002*, volume 2272 of *LNCS*, pages 396 – 415. Springer-Verlag, 2002.
4. R. J. Boulton, R. Hardy, and U. Martin. 6th International Workshop on Hybrid Systems. In *A Hoare-Logic for Single-Input Single-Output Continuous-Time Control Systems*, volume 2623 of *LNCS*, pages 113 – 125. Springer-Verlag, 2003.
5. P. Caspi, A. Curic, A. Maignan, C. Sofronis, and S. Tripakis. Translating Discrete-Time Simulink to Lustre. In *EMSOFT 2003*, volume 2855 of *LNCS*, pages 84 – 99. Springer-Verlag, 2003.
6. A. L. C. Cavalcanti, A. C. A. Sampaio, and J. C. P. Woodcock. A Refinement Strategy for *Circus. Formal Aspects of Computing*, 15(2 - 3):146 — 181, 2003.
7. A. L. C. Cavalcanti and J. C. P. Woodcock. ZRC—A Refinement Calculus for Z. *Formal Aspects of Computing*, 10(3):267—289, 1999.
8. C. Fischer. How to Combine Z with a Process Algebra. In *ZUM'98*. Springer-Verlag, 1998.
9. C. A. R. Hoare and He Jifeng. *Unifying Theories of Programming.* Prentice-Hall, 1998.
10. M. Jersak, D. Ziegenbein, F. Wolf, K. Richter, and R. Ernst. Embedded System Design using the SPI Workbench. In *3rd International Forum on Design Languages*, 2000.
11. D. J. King, R. D. Arthan, and I. C. L. Winnersh. Development of Practical Verification Tools. *ICL Systems Journal*, 11(1), 1996.
12. B. Mahony. Workshop on Formalising Continuous Mathematics. In *The DOVE Approach to the Design of Complex Dynamic Processes*, pages 167 – 187, 2002.
13. C. C. Morgan. *Programming from Specifications.* Prentice-Hall, 2nd edition, 1994.
14. C. O'Halloran and A. Smith. Verification of Picture Generated Code. In *ASE 1999*, pages 127 – 136. IEEE Press, 1999.
15. M. V. M. Oliveira, A. L. C. Cavalcanti, and J. C. P. Woodcock. Refining Industrial Scale Systems in Circus. In *CPA 2004*, pages 281–309. IOS Press, September 2004.
16. A. W. Roscoe. *The Theory and Practice of Concurrency.* Prentice-Hall Series in Computer Science. Prentice-Hall, 1998.
17. C. Spencer. Model Checking for Stateflow Diagram with Floating Point Variables and Complex Expressions. Master's thesis, Carnegie Mellon University, 2002.
18. A. Tiwari. Formal Semantics and Analysis Methods for Simulink Stateflow Models. Technical report, SRI International, 2002. http://www.csl.sri.com/∼tiwari/-stateflow.html.
19. J. C. P. Woodcock and A. L. C. Cavalcanti. The Semantics of *Circus*. In *ZB 2002*, volume 2272 of *LNCS*, pages 184—203. Springer-Verlag, 2002.
20. J. C. P. Woodcock and J. Davies. *Using Z—Specification, Refinement, and Proof.* Prentice-Hall, 1996.

Verification of a Signature Architecture with HOL-Z

David Basin[1], Hironobu Kuruma[2], Kazuo Takaragi[2], and Burkhart Wolff[1]

[1] ETH Zurich, CH-8092 Zurich, Switzerland
{basin,bwolff}@inf.ethz.ch
[2] Hitachi Systems Development Laboratory, Yokohama Japan
{kuruma,takara}@sdl.hitachi.co.jp

Abstract. We report on a case study in using HOL-Z, an embedding of Z in higher-order logic, to specify and verify a security architecture for administering digital signatures. We have used HOL-Z to formalize and combine both data-oriented and process-oriented architectural views. Afterwards, we formalized temporal requirements in Z and carried out verification in higher-order logic.

The same architecture has been previously verified using the SPIN model checker. Based on this, we provide a detailed comparison of these two different approaches to formalization (infinite state with rich data types versus finite state) and verification (theorem proving versus model checking). Contrary to common belief, our case study suggests that Z is well suited for temporal reasoning about process models with rich data. Moreover, our comparison highlights the advantages of this approach and provides evidence that, in the hands of experienced users, theorem proving is neither substantially more time-consuming nor more complex than model checking.

1   Introduction

While there is increasing consensus about the usefulness of formal methods for developing and validating critical systems, there are many options and schools of thought on how best to do this. Formal methods can be loosely characterized along different dimensions in terms of what views of the system they emphasize, the proof techniques used, etc. When most of the complexity of the system stems from the way that processes interact, and the data manipulations are comparatively simple, then the use of a process-oriented modeling language, like a process algebra or some kind of communicating automata, is typically favored and model checking is the preferred means of verification. On the other hand, when data is structured into rich data types (e.g., formalizing problem domains, interface requirements, and the like) that are subject to complex manipulations, then data-oriented modeling languages are considered superior and verification is carried out by theorem proving. But what about systems whose design encompasses both complex data and nontrivial interaction and whose requirements speak about both the operations on data and their temporal sequencing? Here

J.S. Fitzgerald, I.J. Hayes, and A. Tarlecki (Eds.): FM 2005, LNCS 3582, pp. 269–285, 2005.
© Springer-Verlag Berlin Heidelberg 2005

there is less consensus and the options available include using abstraction to simplify the data model to enable model checking, theorem proving, and even combining formal methods.

In this paper, we look at an example of one such system: a security architecture used for a digital signature application. The architecture is based on the secure operating system DARMA (Hitachi's platform for Dependable Autonomous hard Realtime MAnagement) [2], which is used to control the interaction between different subsystems, running on different operating platforms. In particular, DARMA is used to ensure data integrity by separating user API functions, which run on a potentially open system (e.g., connected to the Internet), from those that actually manipulate signature-relevant data, which run on a separate, protected system. Any model of this architecture must formalize both the processes that run on the different platforms and the data that the processes manipulate to produce signatures. Moreover, the modeling formalism must be capable of formalizing data-integrity requirements, expressed as temporal properties about how the different data stores can change.

Here we present a model of the signature architecture that combines data-oriented and process-oriented aspects. We describe the system's state and its state transitions in the specification language Z [14]. As Z is a very rich specification language, we also use it to formalize a simple process model describing the system's semantics in terms of the set of its traces, i.e., those state sequences possible. This provides a basis for naturally formalizing the system's integrity requirements as trace requirements and carrying out verification by induction over the set of traces. Our first contribution in this paper is to show how the use of a sufficiently expressive data-modeling language provides a foundation for formalizing a trace-based model of process interaction. Thus, there is no need to resort to different formal methods to formalize and combine the different system views since this can all be done within Z itself. Moreover, via the embedding of Z in higher-order logic (HOL-Z), we can prove system correctness by theorem proving within the Isabelle/HOL system [6, 12].

In a previous case study [5], the same architecture was formalized and verified using the SPIN model checker [10]. Our second contribution is to provide a detailed comparison of these two different approaches to formalization (infinite state with rich data types versus finite state) and verification (theorem proving versus model checking). Perhaps surprisingly, our experience shows that in the hands of an experienced user, theorem proving is neither substantially more time-consuming nor more complex, and in some regards it is considerably simpler, than working with a process-oriented view alone using a model checker. Moreover we document a number of tradeoffs where the additional complexity is counterbalanced by additional benefits, for example, a more general architecture, stronger theorems, and an increased confidence in the system gained by formalizing and proving system invariants.

Overall, our modeling and verification of signature architecture is one of the largest case studies made using HOL-Z. Previous case studies also include a security architecture (for controlling access to a repository) [7], but there the emphasis was on data refinement, rather than the verification of temporal properties of system runs. The studies are complementary in that together they illustrate how HOL-Z can be used to formalize, verify, and refine architectures at different levels of abstractions, covering both data and process-oriented aspects.

Organization. In Section 2, we provide an informal overview of both the signature architecture and its security requirements. We describe our formalization of the architecture in Section 3 and its properties and correctness proofs in Section 4. In Section 5, we conclude with an in-depth comparison with a previous case study based on model checking. Note that all definitions and complete proof scripts for this case study are given in [4].

2   The Signature Architecture

2.1   Overview

The signature architecture is based on two ideas. The first is that of a *hysteresis signature* [15], which is a cryptographic approach designed to overcome the problem that, for some applications, digital signatures should be valid for very long time periods. Hysteresis signatures address this problem by chaining signatures together so that the signature for each document signed depends on hash values computed from all previously signed documents. These chained signatures constitute a signature log and to forge even one signature in the log an attacker must forge (breaking the cryptographic functions behind) a chain of signatures.

The signature system reads the private keys of users from key stores, and reads and updates signature logs. Hence, the system's security relies on the confidentiality and integrity of this data. The second idea is to protect these using a secure operating platform. For this purpose, Hitachi's DARMA system [2] is used to separate the user's operating system (in practice, Windows) from a second operating system used to manage system data (e.g., Linux). This compartmentalization plays a role analogous to network firewalls, but here the two systems are protected by controlling how functions in one system can call functions in the other. In this way, one can precisely limit how users access the functions and data for hysteresis signatures that reside in the Linux operating system space.

Our model is based on a 13 page Hitachi document, which describes the signature architecture using diagrams (like Figures 1 and 2) and text, as well as discussions with Hitachi engineers.

2.2   Functional Units and Dataflow

The signature architecture is organized into five modules, whose high-level structure is depicted in Figure 1. The thick-lined boxes represent modules and the thin-lined boxes represent individual functions.

The first module contains three functions, which execute in the user operating system space. We call this the "Windows-side module" to reflect the

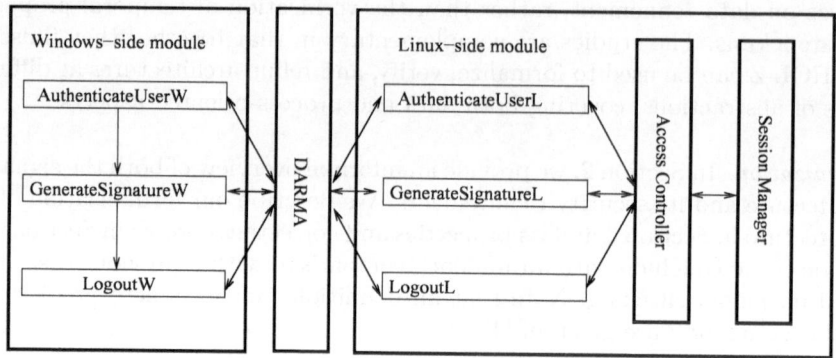

Fig. 1. The Signature Architecture

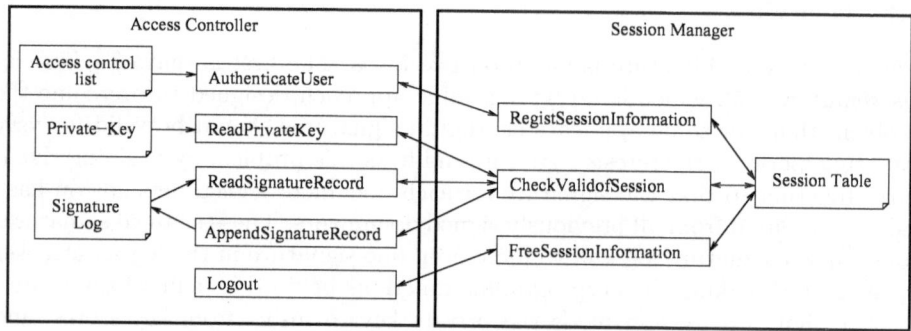

Fig. 2. The Access Controller and Session Manger Modules

(likely) scenario that they are part of an API available to programs running under the Windows operating system. These functions are essentially proxies. When called, they forward their parameters over the DARMA module to the corresponding functions in the second, protected system, which is here called the "Linux-side module", again reflecting a likely implementation. There are two additional (sub)modules, each also executing on the second system, which package data and functions for managing access control and sessions.

To create a hysteresis signature, a user takes the following steps on the Windows side:

1. The user application calls *AuthenticateUserW* to authenticate the user and generate a session identifier.
2. The application calls *GenerateSignatureW* to generate a hysteresis signature.
3. The application calls *LogoutW* to logout, ending the session.

As explained above, each of these functions uses DARMA to call the corresponding function on the Linux side and DARMA serves to restrict access from the

Parameters

Input:

username: Name of the user who generates the hysteresis signature.

password: The *password* for *username*

Output:

SessionID: If the user authentication is successful, *SessionID* > 0,
otherwise *SessionID* ≤ 0.

Details

1. Sends *username, password* and *command* to Linux side using *Communicate W*. The *command* is information used by the Linux-side module to distinguish the type of data that it receives.
2. Outputs *SessionID* returned by *Communicate W*.

Fig. 3. Interface Description for *Authenticate User W*

Parameters

Input:

username: Sent by *Authenticate User W* through *Darma*.

password: Sent by *Authenticate User W* through *Darma*.

Output:

SessionID: If the user authentication is successful, then *SessionID* > 0,
otherwise *SessionID* ≤ 0.

Details

1. Calculate the hash value of *password* using the Keymate/Crypto API. If successful, go to step 2, otherwise set *SessionID* to *CrypotErr* (≤0) and return.
2. Authenticate the user using the function *Authenticate User* of *Access Controller*.
3. Output *SessionID* returned by *Authenticate User*.

Fig. 4. Interface Description for *Authenticate UserL*

Windows side to only these three functions. The Linux functions themselves may call any other Linux functions, including those of the *Access Controller*, which controls access to data (private keys, signature logs, and access control lists). The *Access Controller* in turn uses functions provided by the *Session Manager*, which manages session information (*SessionID*, etc.), as depicted in Figure 2.

The Hitachi documentation provides an interface description for each of these functions. Two representative examples are presented in Figures 3 and 4. These are the descriptions of the functions *Authenticate User W* and *Authenticate UserL*. The former calls DARMA and returns a session identifier while the latter does the actual work of checking the password and communicating with the access controller.

2.3 Properties

The Hitachi documentation also states three requirements that the signature architecture should fulfill. These state that authenticated users are limited to generating one signature (with their private key) per authentication.

R1. The signature architecture must authenticate a user before the user generates a hysteresis signature.

R2. The signature architecture shall generate a hysteresis signature using the private key of an authenticated user.

R3. The signature architecture must generate only one hysteresis signature per authentication.

3 Formal Model

3.1 Formal Method Used

For our work, we have used Z as our modeling language and the environment Isabelle/HOL-Z for theorem proving. As Z is well established and extensively documented, e.g., [11, 14, 16], we will assume the reader's familiarity with it. HOL-Z [6] is a system built upon Isabelle/HOL [12]. It provides a front end for creating "literate specifications", where specifications are mixed with informal explanations and are constructed as LATEX documents, typeset using standard Z macros and idioms. These specifications are processed by HOL-Z and translated into a conservative shallow embedding of Z in HOL. HOL-Z also provides tactic support tailored to reasoning about Z specifications and implements various verification and refinement techniques.

3.2 The Data Model

Our formalization of the system state and operations is basically standard and closely follows Hitachi's informal specification: we formalize a state schema for each of the different modules and an operation schema for each function.

State Schemas. As examples, we present two state schemas: the session manager and DARMA. The session manager maintains a session table, which associates user names and session identifiers to information on access permissions for keys and the signature log.

$$
\begin{aligned}
&SESSION\_TABLE == \\
&\quad (USER\_ID \setminus \{NO\_USER\}) \nrightarrow \\
&\qquad (SESSION\_ID \setminus AUTH\_ERRORS) \nrightarrow \\
&\qquad\quad [pkra : PRI\_KEY\_READ\_ACCESS \,; \\
&\qquad\quad slwa : SIG\_LOG\_WRITE\_ACCESS]
\end{aligned}
$$

In this definition, $USER\_ID$, $SESSION\_ID$, $PRI\_KEY\_READ\_ACCESS$, and $SIG\_LOG\_WRITE\_ACCESS$ are the types of user identifiers, session identifiers, and permissions on private keys and signature log access, respectively. NO_USER and $AUTH\_ERRORS$ are constants representing error elements. The session manager also stores the set of session identifiers currently in use.

SessionManager

$session\_table : SESSION\_TABLE$
$session\_IDs : \mathbb{F}\, SESSION\_ID$
___
$\forall x, y : \mathrm{dom}(session\_table) \bullet$
$\qquad (\exists s : SESSION\_ID \bullet s \in \mathrm{dom}(session\_table(x))$
$\qquad\qquad \wedge\, s \in \mathrm{dom}(session\_table(y))) \Rightarrow\ x = y$
$\forall x : \mathrm{dom}(session\_table) \bullet$
$\qquad \forall s : \mathrm{dom}(session\_table(x)) \bullet \mathrm{dom}(session\_table(x)) = \{s\}$

The predicate part of this schema states that a session identifier is associated with at most one user identifier and, conversely, that each user identifier is associated with at most one session identifier. From this predicate, it follows that each authenticated user has exactly one, unique session identifier.

The DARMA module serves as a communication medium. Its state records which of the three Windows-side functions are called along with its arguments and the return value from the Linux side. Part of this schema is given below, where we have elided declarations for the arguments and return values for the signature generation and logout functions.

DARMA

$Command : COMMAND$
$User\_authentication\_uid : USER\_ID \setminus \{NO\_USER\}$
$User\_authentication\_pw : \mathrm{seq}\, CHAR$
$Authentication : SESSION\_ID \setminus \{x : SESSION\_ERROR \bullet Inr(x)\}$
$\qquad \vdots$

Operation Schemas. Each of the module functions is associated with an operation schema. The association is mostly straightforward, although one aspect that requires explanation is the way that we model DARMA's use as a communication medium. To formalize this, each operation schema includes a copy of the DARMA state and explicitly relates the schema's local input/output variables (respectively postfixed by "?" and "!", following the standard Z convention) with their DARMA counterparts.[1] We illustrate this below, for the module functions *AuthenticateUserW* and *AuthenticateUserL*, which were described in Section 2.2.

The schema *AuthenticateUserW* models the identically named function, given in Figure 3. This function is quite simple and essentially acts as a proxy, forwarding values over DARMA. Hence the only thing to model is this communication.

AuthenticateUserW _____

$userid? : USER\_ID$
$password? : \operatorname{seq} CHAR$
$session\_id! : SESSION\_ID$
$DARMA$

$User\_authentication\_uid = userid?$
$User\_authentication\_pw = password?$
$Command = authenticate\_user$
$session\_id! = Authentication$

Here the variables $User\_authenticate\_uid$, $User\_authenticate\_pw$, $Command$, and $Authentication$ are state variables from the DARMA state schema. The first two are assigned the input values $userid?$ and $password?$, coming from the user. $Command$ represents the name of the function called, named here by the constant $authenticate\_user$. Finally the output of the schema, $session\_id!$, is assigned $Authentication$, representing communication from DARMA (as we will see below, this represents the output of *AuthenticateUserL*).

The actual work in authenticating users and registering session information is carried out on the Linux side by *AuthenticateUserL*. Our operation schema here formalizes the description given in Figure 4. Step 1 of the informal description is reflected in the test of the hash value. Step 2 is modeled in the first *else* branch, using an auxiliary function for user authentication, which returns either a new session identifier or an error value. The remainder of the specification formalizes how to proceed, depending on whether the hash calculation and authentication succeeded or failed. In the former case ($Authentication \notin AUTH\_ERRORS$), the session manager's state is updated: the session table records, for this user identifier and session identifier, the right to read the user's private key and to update the signature log, and the set of session identifiers is updated with the new session identifier. In the latter case ($Authentication \in AUTH\_ERRORS$), the session manager's state is unchanged. Note that the result of *AuthenticateUserL* is stored both in the output $SessionID!$ and in the DARMA variable $Authentication$.

---

[1] Logically, the input and output variables are determined by the DARMA state and could be eliminated. However, not only do they clarify the information flow, they also help to maintain the correspondence between our formal specification and Hitachi's informal interface descriptions (see Figures 3 and 4) with their explicit inputs and outputs. Note too that, as it is standard for Z, reference to input and output, as well as other imperative notions like assignment, is just a conceptual convenience; the semantics of Z schemas is, of course, the standard declarative one, given by sets of bindings.

```
┌─ AuthenticateUserL ──────────────────────────────────
  ΔSessionManager
  ΞHysteresisSignature
  ΞAccessController
  username? : USER_ID
  password? : seq CHAR
  SessionID! : SESSION_ID
  DARMA
├───────────────────────────────────────────────────────
  Command = authenticate_user
  Authentication = if hashFailure(User_authentication_pw)
       then CRYPT_ERR
       else AuthenticateUser(User_authentication_uid,
           hash(User_authentication_pw), access_control_list,
           session_table, session_IDs)
  session_table' = if Authentication ∉ AUTH_ERRORS
       then session_table ∪
           {User_authentication_uid ↦ {Authentication ↦
               ⦇pkra == accept_read_prikey, slwa == accept_write_siglog⦈}}
       else session_table
  session_IDs' = if Authentication ∉ AUTH_ERRORS
       then session_IDs ∪ {Authentication} else session_IDs
  username? = User_authentication_uid
  password? = User_authentication_pw
  SessionID! = Authentication
└───────────────────────────────────────────────────────
```

In this schema, the functions *hashFailure* and *AuthenticateUser* are defined separately by axiomatic definitions. For example, *AuthenticateUser* checks the user identifier and the hashed password against an access control list. In the case of a successful authentication, a new session identifier is generated.

3.3   The Process Model

In general, there are many possible ways of enriching a data model with process-oriented aspects, ranging from the use of combined (data/process-oriented) formal methods, e.g., [8, 13], to working with a fixed notion of abstract machine and execution semantics, e.g., [1]. In our case, we proceed by formalizing the system traces within Z.

Architecture as Transition System. We use Z's schema calculus to "wire together" the parts of our data model into an architectural description by specifying how the Windows-side operations interact with the Linux-side operations over DARMA. First, we separately collect all the client-side and server-side operations. We use schema disjunction here to model nondeterministic choice: This transition relation models a system where the Windows-side functions may be called in any order and with any values, valid or invalid. Afterwards, we use schema conjunction to model the parallel composition of the client-side operations with the server-side operations and we use existential quantification (again in Z's schema calculus) to hide the shared DARMA state. This models synchronous internal communication between the sides. (Internal communication within each side is not modeled here.) The resulting architectural description defines a global transition relation.

$$ClientOperation ==$$
$$\quad AuthenticateUserW \lor GenerateSignatureW \lor LogoutW$$

$$ServerOperation ==$$
$$\quad AuthenticateUserL \lor GenerateSignatureL \lor$$
$$\quad LogoutL \lor NopOperationL$$

$$System == \exists DARMA \bullet ClientOperation \land ServerOperation$$

Note that $NopOperationL$ models a "no-op" operation on the Linux side by simply stuttering the Linux-side state. It results when DARMA is called from the client side, but a client-side error occurs and the step is aborted.

Afterwards, we specify the global state of the system by composing the states of the system components ($HysteresisSignature$ formalizes the part of the Linux-side module's state that manages the signature logs). Similarly, we specify the initial state, given schemas (not shown here) specifying the initial states of the different modules.

$$GlobalState ==$$
$$\quad SessionManager \land HysteresisSignature \land AccessController$$

$$Init ==$$
$$\quad SessionManagerInit \land HysteresisSignatureInit \land AccessControllerInit$$

System Traces. The schema $System$ formalizes a transition relation, whose state variables range over the input/output variables of all operation schemas (e.g., variables like $username?$ and $SessionID!$ from $AuthenticateUserW$). To reason about the system behavior, what we actually need is a transition relation expressed in terms of just those variables in $GlobalState$ (e.g., state variables such as $session\_table$ and $session\_IDs$ from the state schema $SessionManager$). Hence, to proceed, we project the transition relation $System$ to those state variables in $GlobalState$ by existentially quantifying over the remaining variables. This construction can be elegantly formalized using Z's schema comprehension:

$$Next == \{System \bullet (\theta GlobalState, \theta GlobalState')\} .$$

This builds the relation that consists of pairs $(\theta GlobalState, \theta GlobalState')$, whose components formalize the variable tuples (so-called *characteristic bindings* in Z) in the pre-state and post-state.

Afterwards, we define the set of traces. Each trace is represented by a function that describes how the global state of the system can evolve over time.

$$Traces ==$$
$$\{f : \mathbb{N} \rightarrow GlobalState \mid f(0) \in Init \wedge (\forall i : \mathbb{N} \bullet (f(i), f(i+1)) \in Next)\}$$

4   Properties and Proofs

4.1   Formalizing the Security Requirements

The architecture's informal requirements, given in Section 2.3, are phrased in terms of temporal relationships between *events*. For example, (R1) states that "the signature architecture must authenticate a user before the user generates a hysteresis signature." This, and the other two requirements, can be formalized as a set of traces that constitutes a safety property over a set of events and we can formalize the correctness of the architecture by stating that each such property holds for every system trace.

First we must formalize the relevant events. In model checking, it is common to associate events with different states in a transition system, which correspond to execution events like calls to particular functions. Unfortunately, this leaves open the question of where these events are actually generated. Moreover, it is not well suited to a more abstract, declarative approach to modeling where there are no program points, only sequences of program states. Here we will take an alternate, less operational approach. We introduce abstract *event predicates* that characterize the *state changes* associated with events, i.e., they specify the effect of events rather than their cause. An event predicate, therefore, is a (possibly parameterized) relation over pairs of states that characterizes when a relevant state change occurs.

Let us now turn to (R1), our first requirement. The formalizations of the other two requirements are similar. (R1) can be formalized in terms of three event predicates: the session table changes due to a user authenticating himself by logging in; the session table changes due to a user logging out; and the signature log changes (due to a generated hysteresis signature), for some user. Below is an axiomatic definition formalizing the first of these predicates.

$$userDoesLogin : USER\_ID \rightarrow (GlobalState \leftrightarrow GlobalState)$$

$$\forall uid : USER\_ID ; s1, s2 : GlobalState \bullet$$
$$(s1, s2) \in userDoesLogin(uid)$$
$$\Longleftrightarrow$$
$$uid \notin \mathsf{dom}(s1.session\_table) \wedge uid \in \mathsf{dom}(s2.session\_table)$$

We can now directly formalize (R1) in terms of the relative positions (reflecting the relative time) where these predicates hold in the system traces. Our requirement states that at every point where a user changes the signature log, there exists a previous time point where the user logged in, and moreover he has not logged out since then. In other words, there must be a login for the user before the associated signature log entry is changed and his session must still be valid.

$$\vdash \forall t : Traces \ ; \ n : \mathbb{N} \ ; \ uid : USER\_ID \ \bullet$$
$$(t(n), t(n+1)) \in siglogChanges(uid)$$
$$\Rightarrow$$
$$(\exists k : 0 \dots (n-1) \ \bullet \ (t(k), t(k+1)) \in userDoesLogin(uid)$$
$$\land \ (\forall j : (k+1) \dots (n-1) \ \bullet$$
$$(t(j), t(j+1)) \notin userDoesLogout(uid)))$$

Note that we have formalized our requirement in terms of consecutive pairs of time points and relationships between time points. An alternative, also possible in Z, would be to embed the operators of a temporal logic like LTL over our traces in order to express these dependencies using temporal modalities.

4.2   Proofs

All three requirements were proved using the proof environment for HOL-Z. In Section 5, we provide statistics on our verification effort. Here we restrict ourselves to a few comments on its overall structure.

The verification required proving 173 theorems. Many of these were simple lemmas, for example, for simplifying expressions, which were then incorporated into Isabelle's automatic proof procedures. The bulk of the preparatory work centered around formalizing and proving (1) properties of operation schemas, (2) architecture decomposition theorems, and (3) global invariants.

With respect to (1), for each operation schema we stated and proved lemmas that characterize its preconditions, postconditions, and invariants in terms of its inputs, outputs, pre-state, and post-state. The theorems proven were of the form

$$OP(in, out, \sigma, \sigma') \Rightarrow COND(in, out, \sigma, \sigma') \Rightarrow \Phi(\sigma, \sigma'),$$

where OP is an operation schema, $COND$ a side-condition and Φ is one of:

$INV(\sigma, \sigma')$, expressed in terms of (state variables from) the pre-state σ and the post-state σ';

$PRE(\sigma)$, expressing a condition on the pre-state σ; or

$POST(\sigma')$, expressing a condition on the post-state σ'.

An example of such a lemma is the invariant

$$\vdash \ AuthenticateUserL \Rightarrow uid : \mathrm{dom}(session\_table)$$
$$\Rightarrow session\_table'(uid) = session\_table(uid),$$

stating that when a user identifier is in the session table, its entries remain unchanged after another user is authenticated. Note that, as this example illustrates, HOL-Z is syntactically more liberal than Z. This invariant is a HOL-Z formula, but strictly speaking not a Z formula, since it combines Z schema expressions and predicate calculus expressions and it is not closed.

In general, the complexity of proving these lemmas ranged from easy (as in this case) to very high, both in terms of the conceptual work required to understand why they hold and in terms of the proof effort required in Isabelle.

With respect to (2), one of the main lemmas proved was an *architecture decomposition theorem*, which states that the signature architecture can make progress in exactly four ways:

1. an *AuthenticateUserW* step occurs in parallel with an *AuthenticateUserL* step;

2. a *GenerateSignatureW* step starts and aborts due to an internal error while running in parallel with *NopOperationL* (a stuttering step on the Linux side);

3. a *GenerateSignatureW* step occurs in parallel with a *GenerateSignatureL* step; or

4. a *LogoutW* step occurs in parallel with a *LogoutL* step.

By using the Z schema calculus, this theorem can be compactly expressed as:

$$
\begin{aligned}
\vdash \quad &(\exists\, DARMA \bullet AuthenticateUserW \wedge AuthenticateUserL) \vee \\
&(\exists\, DARMA \bullet GenerateSignatureW \wedge NopOperationL) \vee \\
&(\exists\, DARMA \bullet GenerateSignatureW \wedge GenerateSignatureL) \vee \\
&(\exists\, DARMA \bullet LogoutW \wedge LogoutL) \\
\Leftrightarrow \quad &System\,.
\end{aligned}
$$

This theorem explains in which ways synchronous communication over DARMA is possible. We use it in the right-to-left direction as a kind of "elimination rule" that decomposes assumption over steps in traces by case-splitting: if we have a trace t and a system transition $(s, s') = (t(n), t(n+1))$, a property $P(s, s')$ holds if it holds for the four possible system transitions.

With respect to (3), we proved a large number of global invariants, i.e., formulas of the form $\forall t : traces \bullet INV(t(n), t(n+1))$. Examples of such invariants are that the signature log monotonically increases, and that the domain of the session table and signature log are always bounded by the domain of the table of private keys. These lemmas, as well as the proofs of the three requirements, were proven by induction over the positions in a trace. In the inductive case, the architecture decomposition theorem was applied to decompose the step into possible cases. In each case, either other global invariants or relevant lemmas about properties of operation schemas were used to reason about the consecutive states. Hence, induction and decomposition served as the primary mechanism to reduce the reasoning about global invariants to standard reasoning about local preconditions, postconditions and invariants of operations.

5   Theorem Prove or Model Check?

In previous work [5], we used the SPIN model checker [10] to verify a PROMELA model of the signature architecture. There, we formulated an executable model in terms of synchronously communicating processes, one for each of the different system modules. The requirements were formalized either in linear temporal logic or by augmenting the model (e.g., adding monitor processes) and SPIN was used to verify the result. While there have been other general comparisons of theorem proving versus model checking, e.g., [9], and considerable work on their integration, there appear to be few studies that examine their relationship concretely on an in-depth case study. We take up this challenge here and make both quantitative and qualitative comparisons between our two formalizations. The results, we believe, help shed light on the relative strengths and weaknesses of the different approaches.

Note that any such comparison must be made and interpreted with care. The conclusions can differ considerably depending, for example, on the expertise of those carrying out the verification, the specific formalisms and tools used, and what is actually measured (see [3] for a discussion of these points). To ensure an accurate comparison, we have kept statistics on both efforts (times spent are estimates) and also ensured that each verification was made on an equal footing: Both verifications were carried out by a team consisting of an expert in the formal method and an engineer with limited initial knowledge in the formal method.

Figure 5 provides a quantitative comparison of two approaches. We explain the differences below.

Measurement	PROMELA/SPIN	HOL-Z/Isabelle
Model Variants	4	1
Model Size	647 lines (average)	550 lines
Model Bounds	2 users, 2 sessions	unbounded
Property Size	184 lines	50 lines
Proof Size	none	3662 lines
Property Specification Time	6 days	2 days
System Modeling Time	17 days	12 days
Verification Time	(included above)	19 days
Proof Checking Time	14 hours	12 minutes
Total Time	23 days	33 days
Expert Input Required	10%	60%

Fig. 5. Statistics on the Two Verifications

Size. In PROMELA, we built an initial model of the system, which we adapted afterwards for each of the three properties that we verified. The 647 lines of specification is the average size of the four models created. Despite the fact that the HOL-Z model differs substantially from the PROMELA models, they are all of roughly similar size. This stems from the fact that the HOL-Z model is more detailed than the PROMELA models in some respects and more abstract in others. For example, HOL-Z state schemas are more detailed since they define not only data types, but also invariants. On the other hand, HOL-Z operation schemas are typically smaller as they abstractly specify the relationship between states, rather than the sequence of operations used to change states.

In contrast, the HOL-Z property specifications are considerably more concise, due to their greater generality. In the PROMELA models, all of the relevant data domains (messages, keys, users, etc.) were bounded to support finite-state model checking. Hence all statements quantifying over these sets must be translated into finite, but large, conjunctions or disjunctions. Moreover, rather than using event predicates as in HOL-Z, we had to formulate state changes in terms of explicit statements about program points as well as manipulated data. This too results in a more voluminous specification. So here we see one of the advantages of working with a general, behavioral model as opposed to a programing language-based (PROMELA) model.

Time. More time was spent in the theorem-proving approach than in the model-checking approach.[2] The main difference is due to the fact that model checking is automatic as opposed to interactive (the 19 days reflects the time spent interacting with the theorem prover). Folk wisdom is that, because of automation, model checking is much less time consuming than theorem proving. While this is indeed the case for the verification time itself, the *overall* time reduction, about 30%, is not so significant. Moreover, this difference is even less significant when one accounts for the fact that, in the HOL-Z verification, 5 of these days were spent proving stronger formalizations of the properties (see below).

However, the numbers point only indirectly to what is probably the most interesting difference: *how* the time was spent. With SPIN, once a model and a property are specified, the verification effort is focused on simplifying the problem so that the model checker terminates. This involves tuning constants as well as introducing abstractions and other simplifications. In some cases, the complexity of the model may even increase, due to the addition of auxiliary variables, assertions, and new (monitor) processes. All of these additions were necessary during our verification and hence the need to create three additional model variants, one for each property verified. The time spent with these activities was substantial and is reflected both in the increased time taken for system modeling and for property specification.

Note that these efforts are quite different from those required for verification in HOL-Z. Our HOL-Z verification was based on only one model, the general system model. We neither had to work out any abstractions or restrictions in advance nor to make subsequent changes during verification. Hence the specification time was shorter. In return, substantially more time was required for verification. Although some of this time was spent pushing low-level proof details

---

[2] Proof checking times, measuring the times taken by the SPIN and Isabelle systems, are on a 3 gigaherz Pentium IV computer with 1 gigabyte of RAM.

through the Isabelle system, as explained in Section 4.2, much of it concerned discovering, formalizing, and proving auxiliary system invariants, which were required to prove the properties of interest.

Although discovering and proving invariants is a more time-consuming activity than (PROMELA) model simplification, it is certainly also a more insightful one. Many of the invariants are interesting in their own right as they lead to a better understanding of why the architecture actually works. Moreover, in our work, they also led to our discovering problems in our formalization of Hitachi's requirements. For example, a direct formalization of the first requirement (that signature generation requires a prior login) overlooks the fact that the login session must still be valid, in other words, there cannot be a logout between these events. This weaker statement (i.e., omitting the last conjunct in the theorem statement in Section 4.1) is what we formalized and verified in SPIN. In HOL-Z, working through the necessary invariants led us to realize that the stronger theorem was actually intended and held.

Expertise needed. In both case studies, expert input was needed, albeit to a different degree and in different places. In both approaches, it was possible for an engineer with limited initial knowledge of the formal method to build the first model after receiving some training for the task. In the SPIN case study, most of the expert help required was in formulating properties (which turned out to be surprisingly tricky) and simplifying the PROMELA models so that SPIN would terminate. For the HOL-Z model, an expert review and restructuring of the model was needed. Finding suitably abstract formulations in Z appears to require more expertise than finding "natural" formulations in PROMELA, which was perceived as a kind of programming language. While formulating the security properties in Z was possible without expert advice, this was not so with theorem proving, where considerable hands-on work by the expert was necessary. This is reflected by the 60% expert contribution reported in Table 5.

What was modeled and verified. Finally, the numbers given do not reflect that there were substantial differences in what was modeled and verified. A standard benefit of using a rich logic, like HOL-Z, is that one can directly model infinite data domains in their full generality, rather than settling for some finite approximation. This was also the case here, where PROMELA modeling required bounding all of the relevant data domains. Hence, the HOL-Z model is both more general and the theorems proven are significantly stronger.

A more subtle difference stems from the use of a declarative versus an operational approach. In HOL-Z we did not need to commit to either particular data types or concrete procedures for data manipulation. This leaves us considerably more flexibility in how the architecture can be refined and for exploring changes. As an example, in the Hitachi architecture, a user may only log in once before logging out again, i.e., a user may be associated with only one session. However, an alternative architecture is one that supports multiple sessions per user. Modeling these kinds of changes in our architecture is trivial. Here, we can specify this alternative simply by deleting the second constraint in the predicate part of the session manger schema (Section 3.2), which requires that each user identifier is associated with at most one session identifier. In this case, almost all of the system invariants proven go through, unchanged.

References

1. J.-R. Abrial. *The B-book: assigning programs to meanings.* Cambridge University Press, 1996.
2. T. Arai, T. Sekiguchi, M. Satoh, T. Inoue, T. Nakamura, and H. Iwao. Darma: Using different OSs concurrently based on nano-kernel technology. In *Proc. 59th-Annual Convention of Information Processing Society of Japan*, volume 1, pages 139–140. Information Processing Society of Japan, 1999. In Japanese.
3. D. Basin and M. Kaufmann. The Boyer-Moore Prover and Nuprl: An experimental comparison. In G. Huet and G. Plotkin, editors, *Logical Frameworks*, pages 90 – 119. Cambridge University Press, 1991.
4. D. Basin, H. Kuruma, K. Takaragi, and B. Wolff. Specifying and verifying hysteresis signature system with HOL-Z. Technical Report 471, ETH Zürich, January 2004. Available at the URL http://kisogawa.inf.ethz.ch/WebBIB/publications/papers/2005/HSD.pdf.
5. D. Basin, K. Miyazaki, and K. Takaragi. A formal analysis of a digital signature architecture. In S. Jajodia and L. Strous, editors, *Integrity and Internal Control in Information Systems, IV*, pages 31–48. Kluwer Academic Publishers, 2004.
6. A. D. Brucker, F. Rittinger, and B. Wolff. HOL-Z 2.0: A proof environment for Z-specifications. *Journal of Universal Computer Science*, 9(2):152–172, Feb. 2003.
7. A. D. Brucker and B. Wolff. A case study of a formalized security architecture. In *Electronic Notes in Theoretical Computer Science*, volume 80. Elsevier Science Publishers, 2003.
8. C. Fischer. CSP-OZ: A combination of Object-Z and CSP. In *Proceedings of FMOODS'97: Formal Methods for Open Object-Based Distributed Systems*, volume 2, pages 423–438. Chapman & Hall, 1997.
9. A. Gupta. Formal hardware verification methods: A survey. *Journal of Formal Methods in System Design*, 1:151–238, 1992.
10. G. J. Holzmann. The model checker SPIN. *Software Engineering*, 23(5):279–295, 1997.
11. International Standard ISO/IEC 13568:2002. Information technology — Z formal specification notation — syntax, type system and semantics.
12. T. Nipkow, L. C. Paulson, and M. Wenzel. *Isabelle/HOL — A Proof Assistant for Higher-Order Logic*, volume 2283 of *Lecture Notes in Computer Science*. Springer, 2002.
13. G. Smith and J. Derrick. Refinement and verification of concurrent systems specified in Object-Z and CSP. In *Proceedings of the International Conference of Formal Engineering Methods*, pages 293–302. IEEE Computer Society Press, 1997.
14. J. M. Spivey. *The Z Notation: A Reference Manual.* Prentice-Hall International, New Jersey, second edition, 1992.
15. S. Susaki and T. Matsumoto. Alibi establishment for electronic signatures. *Information Processing Society of Japan*, 43(8):2381–2393, 2002. In Japanese.
16. J. Woodcock and J. Davies. *Using Z.* Prentice-Hall International, New Jersey, 1996.

End-to-End Integrated Security and Performance Analysis on the DEGAS Choreographer Platform

Mikael Buchholtz [1], Stephen Gilmore [2], Valentin Haenel [2],
and Carlo Montangero [3]

[1] Informatics and Mathematical Modelling, The Technical
University of Denmark, Lyngby, Denmark
mib@imm.dtu.dk
[2] Laboratory for Foundations of Computer Science,
The University of Edinburgh, Scotland
stg@inf.ed.ac.uk, valentin.haenel@gmx.de
[3] Dipartimento di Informatica, Università di Pisa, Pisa, Italy
carlo.montangero@di.unipi.it

Abstract. We present a software tool platform which facilitates security and performance analysis of systems which starts and ends with UML model descriptions. A UML project is presented to the platform for analysis, formal content is *extracted* in the form of process calculi descriptions, analysed with the analysers of the calculi, and the results of the analysis are *reflected* back into a modified version of the input UML model. The design platform supporting the methodology, *Choreographer*, interoperates with state-of-the-art UML modelling tools. We illustrate the approach with a well known protocol and report on the experience of industrial users who have applied Choreographer in their development work.

Keywords: security analysis, performance analysis, process calculi, UML.

1 Introduction

The safety and reliability of networked software applications becomes a highly significant matter as such systems play an ever-increasing role in society and public life. Software systems win the trust of users by being secure against attack and by remaining available and responsive under increasing workload. Security and quality-of-service valuations such as these give rise to subtle and complex questions about these complex systems. Determining the answers to these questions necessitates careful modelling and analysis of these systems in well-founded formal calculi. Such reasoning is both too detailed and too arduous to be undertaken by hand and so modelling and design tools play a crucial role in designing and evaluating the computing applications of today and tomorrow.

Choreographer is an integrated design platform for qualitative and quantitative modelling of software systems. The main idea is to cater for formal veri-

J.S. Fitzgerald, I.J. Hayes, and A. Tarlecki (Eds.): FM 2005, LNCS 3582, pp. 286–301, 2005.

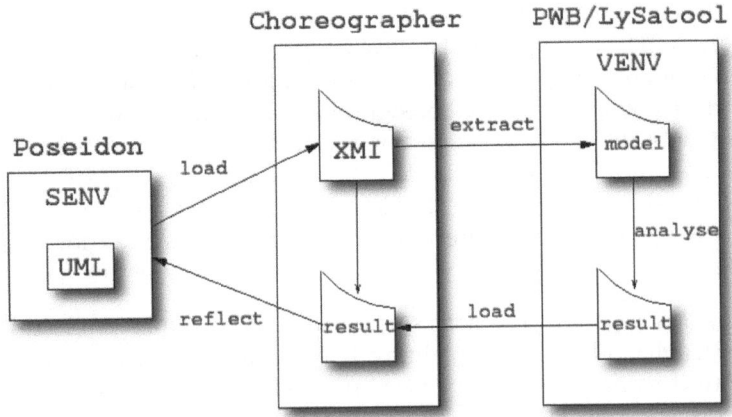

Fig. 1. Software architecture of the tool chain used by Choreographer

fication of properties of system models through application of existing analysis tools and techniques. However, these analysis tools will largely be hidden from the developer, who only needs to relate to the analysis at the level of a model of the system, which is already familiar. To this end, the Choreographer processes UML models as its input, and writes modified versions of these as its output. The many stages of model manipulation and transformation which take place between input and output will be performed fully automatic and, consequently, are of no concern for the developer.

The architecture of the Choreographer tool as illustrated in Figure 1 is to consider the interface to a specification environment (SENV) and a processing interface to a verification environment (VENV). Models which are input for analysis are channelled from the SENV to the VENV via software connectors known as *extractors*. The extracted formal content is passed to the VENV for analysis. The results of the analysis are recombined with the input model and channelled from the VENV back to the SENV via software connectors known as *reflectors*. The extraction, the verification, and the reflection are all automated and can therefore run without input from the user of Choreographer.

In this paper we discuss a specific configuration of the architecture in which the SENV is the Poseidon UML platform from Gentleware [1] and both the LySatool [2] and the PEPA Workbench [3, 4] are VENVs. The software tool chain which is formed when these are connected is also depicted in Figure 1.

The qualititative analysis is deployed to investigate the security of the communication protocols used in the application. The analysis guarantees there are no successful attacks on the authentication of the communicated messages provided that there are no attacks on the underlying crypto-system used to protect messages. In the case where authentication may be breached the analysis reports where the breach may occur.

The quantitative analysis which is provided is a performance analysis of the system model. This identifies components which are under-utilised or overutilised indicating poor deployment of computational resources. The identification of these problems prompts the developer to revisit the design in order to improve its score on the performance metrics of greatest importance.

In the development of the Choreographer platform we were concerned to support not only the UML notation but the UML design process in order that UML developers would be comfortable with working with the platform. That is, we devoted considerable effort in the design of the extractors to ensuring that the UML was being used as more than just a graphical syntax for the process calculi beneath.

Structure of this paper: In the next section we discuss the methodology behind the Choreographer platform, explaining how it has been used in practice. In Section 3 we describe the security properties which Choreographer can verify, and how this is achieved. In Section 4 we progress to a description of using Choreographer for performance evaluation based on the generation and solution of continuous-time Markov chains. Section 5 details the extraction and reflection operations which connect the UML input and output to the analysis routines beneath. Section 6 is a small example, making the foregoing descriptions concrete. Section 7 relates our experience of building the Choreographer platform. Section 8 reports on the experiences of our industrial users. A description of related work and conclusions follow.

2   Methodology

The methodology which we follow is to first attempt a security analysis and then, if this is successful, progress to a performance analysis. The reasoning behind this methodology is that the security analysis rests on static analysis procedures which have a lower asymptotic complexity than the state-space generation and iterative numerical procedures which are needed for the performance analysis. Thus, ordering them in this way potentially gives a significant saving in the overall computation time by avoiding the performance analysis of an erroneous protocol.

To use the Choreographer platform a modeller first composes a UML model in the Poseidon modelling tool. A UML model is represented by a collection of diagrams describing parts of the system from different points of view; there are seven main diagram types. For example, there will typically be a static structure diagram (or *class diagram*) describing the classes and interfaces in the system and their static relationships (inheritance, dependency, etc.). State diagrams, a variant of Harel state charts, can be used to record dynamic behaviour. Interaction diagrams, such as sequence diagrams, are used to illustrate the way objects of different classes interact in a particular scenario.

Having described a security protocol using a UML sequence diagram we apply the For-LySa extractor to generate a LySa model which we analyse with the LySatool. If the LySatool detects errors in the protocol, indicating that it is insecure, the results are reflected back to the UML level, so that we can view the results in the Poseidon tool. Having identified these flaws we can repair the protocol and continue with performance analysis. Here, we extract a PEPA process algebra model from the UML input. We solve this for its equilibrium probability distribution using successive over-relaxation (SOR), then reflect. The information returned from the analysis quantifies the percentage of time that the principals and the server spend in their local states, pointing to performance-related problems such as under- or over-utilisation, starvation, bottlenecks, or hotspots in the system. We can investigate the potential benefits to be obtained by improving the implementation of the activities in the system, thereby identifying the place or places where it will be most profitable to spend developer effort.

Evidently, it is possible to discover at this stage that the required improvements in the execution of the activities of the system might be infeasible to achieve, especially in the setting of weak computing devices such as smartcards or low-end PDAs or in a thin client context with intermittent or very narrow bandwidth connections between devices. If this is the case, then a developer working at the early modelling stage of the system development process would need to revisit the initial protocol design and perhaps re-design this to involve fewer message exchanges or reduce the amount of asymmetric cryptography used. This will initiate another cycle of security analysis and performance analysis in pursuit of the levels of security and performance demanded of the system.

3   Security Analysis

For our security analysis we rely on techniques from data and control flow analysis. These are analysis techniques that automatically compute information about the entire behaviour of a software system including its behaviour when the systems is under attack. A trademark of these techniques is that they are automatic and complexity-wise efficient, which makes them well-suited as back-end analysis tools for Choreographer.

In more detail, the analysis techniques work by finding conservative over-approximations to system behaviour. That is, the analysis computes an over-approximation of the behaviour of a system under attack from any arbitrary attacker. With regards to security, this means that the analysis can *guarantee the absence* of attacks because they provide information about the entire behaviour of a system. However, because the analysis techniques are approximative they cannot guarantee the presence of attacks and may report warnings about possible attacks that in fact do not exist. In the following, we discuss a control flow analysis that guarantees authentication properties for encrypted network communication.

3.1   Protocols and Authentication

The usual remedy to protect network protocols from intervention by malicious attackers is to apply cryptography so that parts of the messages may be kept outside the control of the attacker. Cryptography may be applied to attain many different security properties such as confidentiality, authenticity, non-repudiation, etc. Here, we focus on checking an authentication property, namely that "messages protected by encryption should only be decrypted at the right places".

The verification technique we use builds on the modelling of protocols in LySa, which is a process calculus in the π-calculus tradition. LySa is specifically tailored to model central aspects of security protocols [5] such as (perfect) cryptography, nonces, network communication, etc. A protocol modelled in LySa will be analysed in a scenario with several kinds of principals: an *initiator* of the protocol, a *responder*, and a *server*, referred to as a trusted third party, a key distribution centre, a certificate authority, etc. Additionally, there can be many principals acting as initiators and as responders.

To specify the authentication property that encrypted messages end up at the right places, the LySa process is annotated: each encryption and decryption point is named ℓ, ℓ', etc., and is furthermore annotated with its intended destinations and origins.

Our verification relies on a control flow analysis [5] of LySa, which is implemented in the LySatool [2]. The analysis tells whether the authentication properties are satisfied for all executions of the LySa process executed in parallel with an arbitrary attacker process. The analysis reports all possible breaches of the authentication properties in an error component ψ: a pair (ℓ, ℓ') in ψ means that something encrypted at ℓ was decrypted at ℓ' breaking the specified authentication property. The analysis computes over-approximations of ψ, i.e. it may report an error that is not actually there. However, [5] illustrates that this is not a big problem in practice.

3.2   Modelling Protocols in UML

To model security protocols in UML consistently, we have defined a specific profile [6]. The profile introduces stereotypes for core concepts like principals, keys, and messages, and for the concepts needed for the analysis.

To specify a protocol in UML so that the ForLySa extractor [6] can feed the LySatool analyser [2], the designer exploits the stereotypes in a class diagram to present the structure of the protocol. This involves first of all specifying the intended communications and the involved messages. The structure of each message type is specified in a distinct diagram that includes the decorations needed to specify the authentication property. Then, the local information of each principal must be introduced, like session keys or temporary storage, and their operations to build and dissect messages.

Then, the designer presents the dynamics of the protocol in a sequence diagram, which formally specifies a canonical run of the protocol (see 3 for an example). Each message exchange in the protocol is divided into three steps: 1. the sender packages the message, 2. the message is communicated, and 3. the recipient processes the incoming message. Each step is described by one or more UML stimuli in the sequence diagram, each associated to an operation of their target. Each operation is specified by pre- and post-conditions, for instance to specify how to decrypt part of a message, what to check in an incoming message, or what to store for later usage in the principal. The language [6] used in these conditions is presented to the designer with a semantics in term of the UML modelling concepts. This semantics reflects the precise one given by the translation in LySa.

Finally, the places mentioned by the authentication properties are specified as notes associated with the stimuli in steps 1 and 3 above, to provide the necessary hooks for the feedback from the LySatool. These notes are placeholders which will support the notification of eventual errors resulting from the analysis. If the analysis reports an error being the pair (ℓ, ℓ') in ψ, the note introducing ℓ will be modified by the reflector to list ℓ', thereby signalling the error reported by the analysis.

4 Performance Evaluation

Well-engineered, safe systems need to deliver reliable services in a timely fashion with good availability. For this reason, we view quantitative analysis techniques as being as important as qualitative ones. The quantitative analysis of computer systems through construction and solution of descriptive models is a hugely profitable activity: brief analysis of a model can provide as much insight as hours of simulation and measurement [7]. Jane Hillston's Performance Evaluation Process Algebra (PEPA) [8] is an expressive formal language for modelling distributed systems. PEPA models are constructed by the composition of components which perform individual activities or cooperate on shared ones. To each activity is attached an estimate of the rate at which it may be performed.

Using such a model, a system designer can determine whether a candidate design meets both the behavioural and the temporal requirements demanded of it. That is: the protocol may be secure, but can it be executed quickly enough to complete the message exchange within a specified time bound, with a given probability of success?

Rather than composing process calculus models directly—although Choreographer also supports this mode of operation—we extract these from UML class, state and collaboration diagrams. For the purposes of performance analysis we extract a process calculus model in PEPA. The extractor for PEPA is documented in [9].

4.1 Analysis Process

We automatically generate a Continuous-Time Markov Chain (CTMC) from the PEPA model and solve it for its equilibrium probability distribution using procedures of numerical linear algebra such as the pre-conditioned biconjugate gradient method or successive over-relaxation implemented in the PEPA Workbench. The relationship between the process algebra model and the CTMC representation is the following. The process terms (P_i) reachable from the initial state of the PEPA model by applying the operational semantics of the language form the states of the CTMC (X_i). For every set of labelled transitions between states P_i and P_j of the model $\{(\alpha_1, r_1), \ldots, (\alpha_n, r_n)\}$ add a transition with rate r between X_i and X_j where r is the sum of $r_1, \ldots, r_n$. The activity labels (α_i) are necessary at the process algebra in order to enforce synchronisation points, but are no longer needed at the Markov chain level.

Under conditions on the form of the model where every state is positive-recurrent, every such CTMC has a stationary probability distribution over the states of the chain. Knowing the rates associated with the activities of the system this stationary probability distribution can be obtained using procedures of numerical linear algebra such as Gaussian elimination, conjugate gradient methods, or over-relaxation methods such as Jacobian over-relaxation or successive over-relaxation.

Such a stationary probability distribution is rarely the desired end result of the performance analysis process but meaningful performance measures such as throughput and utilisation can be directly calculated from the stationary distribution. State-space generation and numerical solution is the computationally expensive part of performance analysis. The size of the state-space of the system is bounded by the product of the sizes of the sequential components in the model and thus modelling with continuous-time Markov chains is subject to the familiar *state-space explosion* problem, requiring the modeller to abstract in order to reduce model complexity.

4.2   Representing Model Components in UML

Markov chain modelling is based on finite-state representations of systems. The requirement to generate a finite state-space for the CTMC leads PEPA models to be structured as a concurrent composition of finite-state sequential processes. This led to a natural representation of the sequential process part of these models within the UML via the use of *state diagrams*, a variant of Harel's statecharts [10], together with a class diagram for each category of component. To represent a concurrent composition of those we used a *collaboration diagram* to specify an operational configuration of the system with some numbers of instances of each class of component synchronising over the activity names which they had in common. This diagram type provided the concurrent composition of the sequential components.

Class diagrams are used for other purposes in the model. A class with the reserved name *Rates* is used to store the values of the rate variables used in the model to quantify the time cost of performing any activity in the model. All activities are timed, and quantified by a rate variable which governs a negative exponential distribution, as used throughout Markovian modelling.

5   Extraction and Reflection

Process calculus content is automatically extracted from input UML models and analysis results are automatically re-integrated into UML models. The categories of software tools which perform these operations are *extractors* and *reflectors*, which we describe briefly here.

The transport format for UML content is XML in the XML Metadata Interchange format (XMI) used for exchanging UML models between UML tools. Our extractors and reflectors are implemented in the Java programming language using its native API for XML parsing. Before the XMI format of the model can be processed, it must first be retrieved from the archive format of the UML tools which we support (primarily the Poseidon [1] tool from Gentleware). We have written data loaders for the NetBeans platform which open these archive files to find the XMI content inside, and correspondingly close such archives.

The extractors traverse the object instance graph of the XML document following the UML metamodel structure to retrieve the diagram content of relevant type. This graph traversal involves following cross-references within the XMI content to find class diagrams referenced by a collaboration diagram, or state diagrams associated with a class, or the local states within a state diagram.

The tree traversal performed by the extractors inspects the tree only, without modifying it. In contrast, the tree traversal performed by the reflectors modifies the tree to update states with additional analysis results, adding or modifying child elements of the model as necessary. Finally, this passes the modified XML tree to the output routines of Choreographer for serialisation and archival.

6   Example: Checking a Simple Authentication Protocol

As a simple example, we apply Choreographer to analyse variations on the Wide-Mouthed-Frog protocol, originally presented in [11].

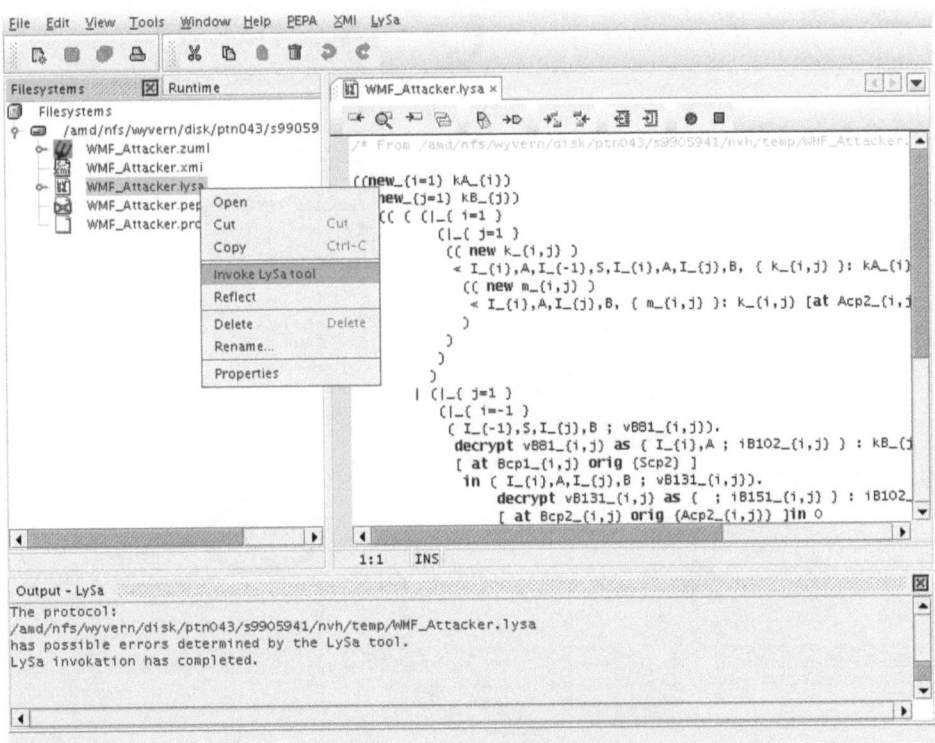

Fig. 2. Invoking the LySatool on a security model in Choreographer

The protocol describes key exchange between two principals A and B through a trusted server. The principals A and B have no prior communication history with each other but both have previously contacted the server and have retained keys K_{AS} and K_{BS} respectively. The protocol has three steps.

1. Principal A sends a message to the server including the name of B and the new session key K_{AB}, encrypted under K_{AS}.
2. The server decrypts this and sends the name of A and the new key K_{AB} to B, encrypted under K_{BS}.
3. Principal A sends a message to B encrypted under K_{AB}.

The first step in checking such a protocol with Choreographer is to formalise the protocol in a UML model, using primarily a sequence diagram to express the protocol as shown in Figure 3. The UML model includes annotations of the

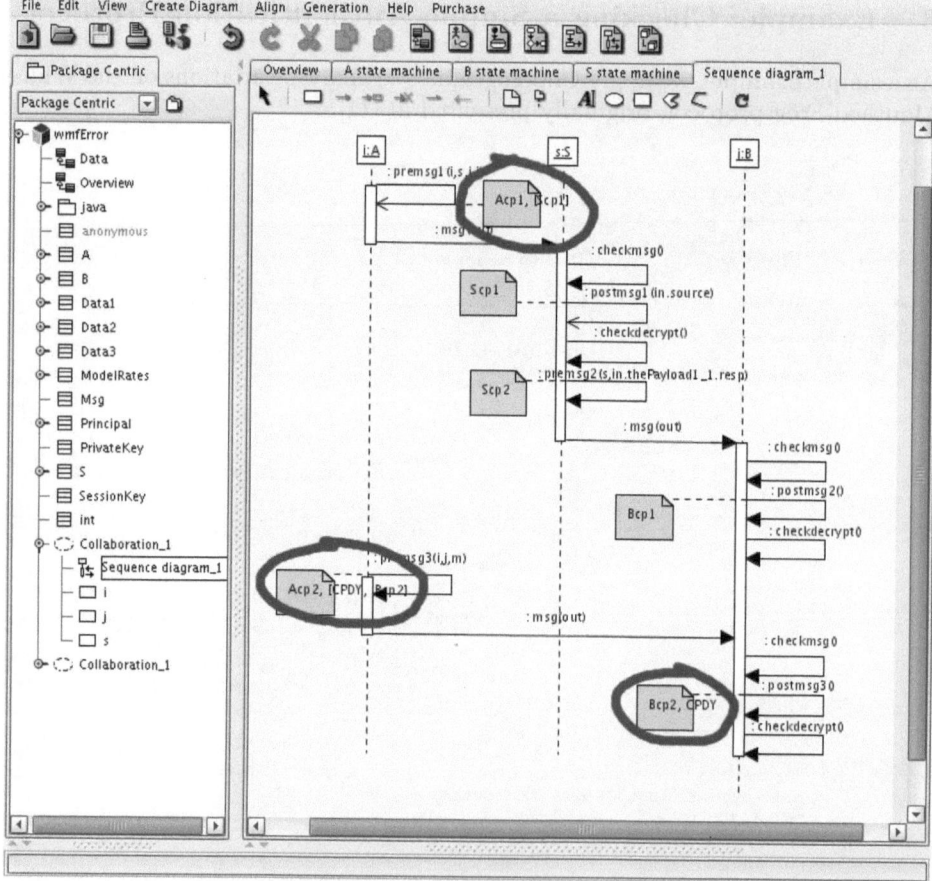

Fig. 3. Viewing the sequence diagram describing the protocol in Poseidon with the result from the LySatool reflected into the UML model (changes circled)

authentication properties that the protocol is intended to have. These annotations take the form of notes attached at points of encryption and decryption along with information on where encryptions and decryptions are intended to take place. For example, the content of the third message will be encrypted at a point called Acp2 and is intended to be decrypted at Bcp3.

We open this UML model in Choreographer and extract a LySa process calculus representation of the protocol, and apply the LySatool to check the authentication properties as shown in Figure 2. The LySatool finds that the properties may be violated and, consequently, the reflector modifies the sequence diagram, reporting the errors, as circled on Figure 3. For example, the decryption at Bcp3 may decrypt messages coming from the attacker (denoted CPDY) instead of coming only from Acp2 as intended. Based on these errors the modeller may pin-point the problem, modify the protocol description in UML, and re-run the analysis until the analyser guarantees that there are no errors in the protocol.

At this point the user is able to continue with a performance analysis of the model. Again, the process calculus representation is extracted by Choreographer from the UML model and processed by the analysis tool — in this case, the PEPA Workbench. The Workbench derives the reachability graph underlying

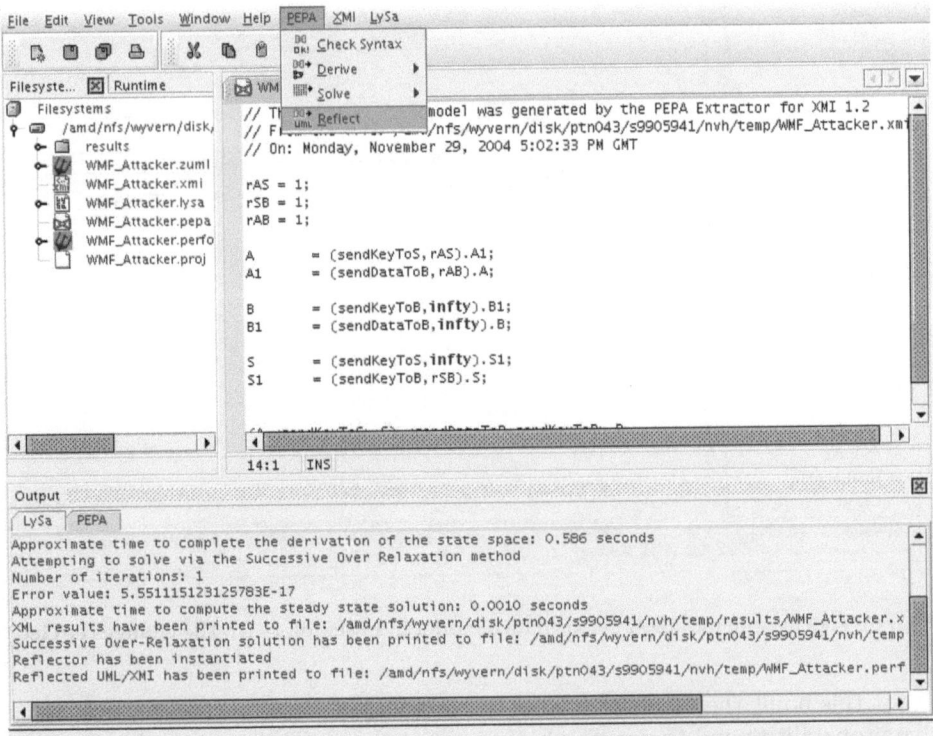

Fig. 4. Reflecting the results of performance analysis back to UML using Choreographer

the process algebra model, interprets this as a continuous-time Markov chain and computes the stationary probability distribution for this chain. The commentary from the Workbench on this calculation can be seen in the tabbed pane at the bottom of the screenshot in Figure 4. These results can again be reflected back to the UML level.

Viewed in the Poseidon modelling tool, the performance model is described by a UML state diagram as the one shown in Figure 5 where rate(rAB) and rate(rBA) describes transition rates of moving between the states. Furthermore, a UML collaboration diagram (not shown) describes the parallel composition of a number of instances of these sequential components. The results of the analysis tell the user the probability of being in each of the local states. This information is reflected back into the UML model as circled on Figure 5. Each state now is tagged with a record of the probability of being in this state in the long run.

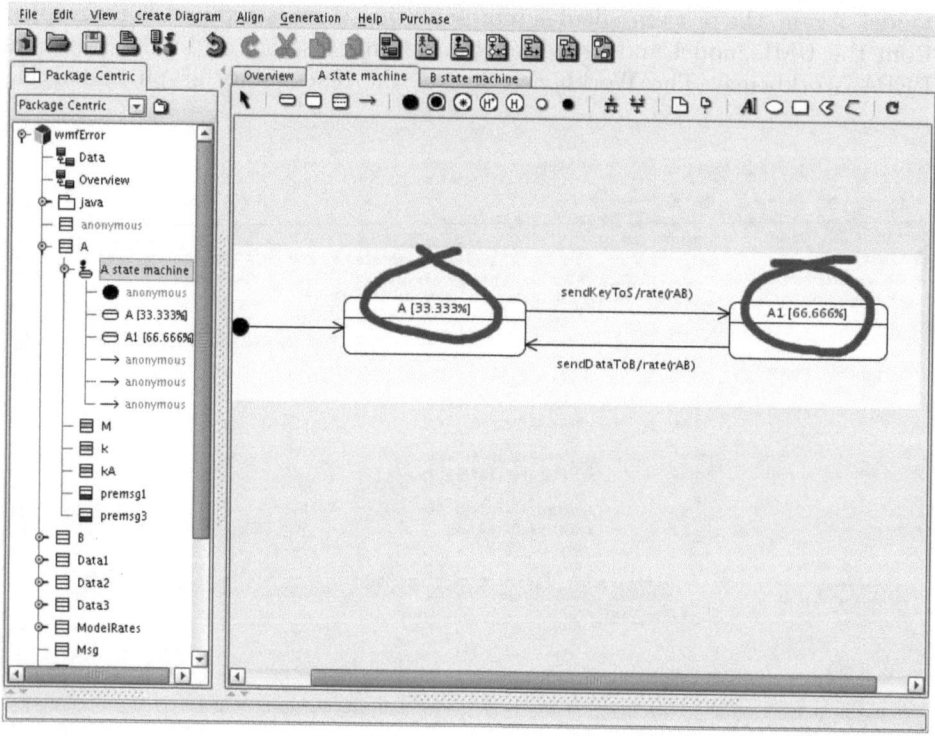

Fig. 5. Viewing the modified performance model in Poseidon (with the changes circled)

At this point the modeller is able to consider the consequences of these relative probabilities and to decide whether or not they indicate acceptable levels of performance with respect to these rates of performance of the activities of the model.

7 Engineering Issues

Our functional requirements for the Choreographer design platform were that it should provide access to the analysis procedures of the PEPA performance analysis tool (the PEPA Workbench in both its ML and Java editions [3, 4]) and the LySa security analysis tool (the LySatool [2]). In addition, it needs to interoperate with a fully-featured UML tool.

Our non-functional requirements on the platform were that we wanted to develop a professional quality tool in a constrained time, with a modest budget for developer effort. We also had the requirement that the tool should be available across platforms (in our case, Windows and Linux). We evaluated the generic IDEs of Eclipse and NetBeans and the Argo/UML, XDE, MagicDraw and Poseidon UML tools. We took the decision to build the Choreographer platform on top of NetBeans on the Java platform and have it interoperate with Poseidon. This decision was a complex engineering compromise between a number of conflicting tensions. Our choice went a considerable way towards addressing portability concerns but the portability issue was impacted also by the availability of the analysers and UML drawing tools we wanted to integrate with.

We wanted Choreographer to have two dimensions of portability. The first is the most obvious one, that it should run successfully on both Windows and Linux. This requirement for code portability has been successfully addressed. The second dimension of portability was that we wanted the Choreographer platform to interoperate with many UML tools via the standard XML Interchange format (XMI) for UML diagrams. Choreographer needs to deal with these because it reads from and writes into this import/export format. This data portability requirement was the more difficult problem, and one which we have not been able to solve perfectly. There are many versions of the XMI standard for UML, and different UML tools implement their chosen version to a more or less satisfactory extent. Some releases of the UML tools which we tried wrote non-well-formed XMI output, even according to their own criteria. Such inconsistency makes interoperation essentially a matter of writing a custom reader/writer pair for every version of every UML tool with which one wants to interoperate, which is the trap which standards such as XMI were intended to prevent developers falling into.

A configuration which we considered for Choreographer was XDE and Eclipse together. The XDE UML tool is provided as an Eclipse plug-in, so this is a natural coupling. We rejected this combination because the XDE tool is not available in a Linux release. We chose not to interoperate with MagicDraw because it is not freely available. We could not work with Argo/UML because it did not represent some aspects of the UML diagrams in the XMI format, thus crippling its use as an import/export model exchange format.

A potential source of non-portability might have been the formal analysis tools which we used. These had been implemented in Java or the functional programming language Standard ML. However, we discovered that the Standard ML of New Jersey compiler which we used had very closely conforming versions for Linux and Windows, making the portability of these formal analysis tools essentially only a matter of working around small differences in the versions of the standard library for the two platforms. This level of minor tuning is also required for application development in the Java language, which has given more effort to ensuring cross-platform portability than perhaps any other programming language.

8   Experiences of the Industrial Users

The Choreographer design platform has been used by the industrial partners in our project on two separate developments. In the first, the partner was a large multi-national company designing a web-based micro-business portal. In the second, the partner was a small developer targeting telecommunications services designing a multi-player on-line role-playing game for mobile applications. Both used the Choreographer platform independently, consulting us when they had problems but otherwise operating without an expert on formal specification or verification on-hand.

The industrial partners had no previous experience of using the LySatool and the PEPA Workbench and their use of them was solely via the Choreographer extraction/reflection discipline. The most significant potential sources of error along the tool chain are i) in the UML constructs used in the input model; ii) communication of the UML model from the UML tool to the extractor; iii) model exchange between the extractor and the process calculus analyser; iv) in the use of the analyser; and v) from the analyser to the reflector. Almost all of the problems reported by our industrial users were of type i), ii) or iii).

Errors of the first kind included choosing the wrong type of connections between class instances in the collaboration diagrams, or omitting to include collaborations between instances of classes which needed to collaborate. Errors of the second kind included the UML tools writing non-well-formed archive files with missing or corrupt XMI content. Errors of the third kind are found because the process calculus analysis tools check the well-formedness of the model before continuing with the analysis. This is to ensure that as many problems as possible with the model are caught before a potentially expensive analysis process begins.

8.1   Reflections on the Experience

Our anticipation of the difficulties for the industrial users was quite far removed from the actual difficulties encountered. The fact that many of the errors were related to UML processing surprised us. We had assumed that the asymptotic complexity of the analysis procedures used in performance analysis would be a problem for models of industrial scale. The PEPA Workbench uses sparse matrices to store CTMCs internally but other representations such as multi-terminal binary decision diagrams (MTBDDs) allow the representation of much larger state spaces. Thinking that this would be a problem, we had previously developed a compiler from PEPA into the input language of the MTBDD-based model-checker Prism [12]. We developed a custom reflector for this tool which we tested with the PEPA extractors and reflectors to analyse our own UML models [13].

In fact, the state-space explosion proved not to be a problem for the use of Choreographer by our industrial partners. The models which they built were much smaller than we had anticipated. So much so, that using sparse matrices is perhaps not even necessary and dense matrices and direct solution methods might even have been applicable.

9   Related Work

Tool support for the automated analysis of security requirements in the UMLsec framework [14] is described and accessible at [15]. The relevant elements of the UML specification are translated in the input language of the model-checker SPIN and the dynamic property to be verified is translated in Linear Temporal Logic. The UML models are stored in a MDR library, and accessed via the generated JMI interface.

Work which is similar in spirit to our own approach is that of Petriu and Shen [16] where a layered queueing network model is automatically extracted from an input UML model with performance annotations in the format specified by a special-purpose UML profile [17]. We do not follow the same UML profile because it is not supported by our modelling tool. Additionally, the performance evaluation technology which we deploy (process algebras and CTMC-based solution) is quite different from layered queueing networks.

Another performance engineering method which is similar to ours is that of López-Grao, Merseguer and Campos [18] where UML diagrams are mapped into GSPNs which can be solved by GreatSPN. We use different UML diagram types from these authors and, again, a different performance evaluation technology. Stochastic Petri nets and stochastic process algebras have different, but complementary, modelling strengths [19].

One feature of our work which is distinctive from both of the above is the role of a *reflector* in the system to present the results of the performance evaluation back to the UML modeller in terms of their input model. We consider this to be a strength of our approach. We do not only compile a UML model into a model amenable for analysis, we also present the results back to the modeller in the UML idiom.

10   Conclusions

Strong and justified belief in the networked software applications is engendered via formal analysis using well-founded calculi and tools. Such apparatus for formal reasoning is often daunting to those who most need to make use of, and benefit from, formal analysis techniques, namely systems designers and software developers working on state-of-the-art systems. To this community, and their colleagues in project management and product development, a graphical notation such as the UML has much greater appeal than the blunt, cold formality of process calculi. By establishing a two-way connection between the UML and calculi such as LySa and PEPA, the Design Environments for Global ApplicationS (DEGAS) project has elevated the analysis process to the UML level, thereby bringing the benefits of the analysis without exposing the unfamiliar languages used.

It is not the case that an inexperienced modeller can use the Choreographer platform to verify any security property of interest or to compute any performance measure that they wish without needing any understanding of the abstraction, modelling and mathematical analysis beneath. However, we hope that we have gone some way to providing automated support for useful security and performance properties and to circumventing an unnecessary notational hurdle if this was acting as an impediment to the understanding and uptake of modern static and dynamic analysis technology.

Acknowledgements. The authors are supported by the DEGAS (Design Environments for Global ApplicationS) project IST-2001-32072 funded by the FET Proactive Initiative on Global Computing. We thank Matthew Prowse for helpful discussions on his extraction algorithm for PEPA. The work reported here builds on a number of prior works by the members of the DEGAS project. It is a pleasure to thank the other members of the project for their contributions and comments on the work reported here.

References

1. Gentleware AG systems.   Poseidon for UML web site, November 2004. http://www.gentleware.com/.
2. Mikael Buchholtz. LySa — a process calculus. Web site hosted by Informatics and Mathematical Modelling at the Technical University of Denmark, April 2004. http://www.imm.dtu.dk/cs_LySa/.
3. S. Gilmore and J. Hillston. The PEPA Workbench: A Tool to Support a Process Algebra-based Approach to Performance Modelling. In *Proceedings of the Seventh International Conference on Modelling Techniques and Tools for Computer Performance Evaluation*, number 794 in Lecture Notes in Computer Science, pages 353–368, Vienna, May 1994. Springer-Verlag.
4. N.V. Haenel. *User Guide for the Java Edition of the PEPA Workbench—Tabasco release*. LFCS, Edinburgh, October 2003.
5. C. Bodei, M. Buchholtz, P. Degano, F. Nielson, and H.R. Nielson. Automatic validation of protocol narration. In *Proc. of the 16th Computer Security Foundations Workshop (CSFW 2003)*, pages 126–140. IEEE Computer Security Press, 2003.
6. M. Buchholtz, C. Montangero, L. Perrone, and S. Semprini. For-LySa: UML for authentication analysis. In C. Priami and P. Quaglia, editors, *Proceedings of the second workshop on Global Computing*, volume 3267 of *Lecture Notes in Computer Science*, pages 92–105. Springer Verlag, 2004.
7. Isi Mitrani. *Probabilistic Modelling*. Cambridge University Press, 1998.
8. J. Hillston. *A Compositional Approach to Performance Modelling*. Cambridge University Press, 1996.

9. C. Canevet, S. Gilmore, J. Hillston, M. Prowse, and P. Stevens. Performance modelling with UML and stochastic process algebras. *IEE Proceedings: Computers and Digital Techniques*, 150(2):107–120, March 2003.

10. D. Harel. Statecharts: A visual formalism for complex systems. *Sci. Comput. Programming*, 8:231–274, 1987.

11. M. Burrows, M. Abadi, and R.M. Needham. A logic of authentication. *ACM Transactions on Computing Systems*, 8(1):18–36, February 1990.

12. D. Parker. *PRISM 1.3 User's Guide*. University of Birmingham, February 2003. http://www.cs.bham.ac.uk/~dxp/prism.

13. S. Gilmore and L. Kloul. A unified tool for performance modelling and prediction. In B. Littlewood S. Anderson and M. Felici, editors, *Proceedings of the 22nd International Conference on Computer Safety, Reliability and Security (SAFECOMP 2003)*, volume 2788 of *LNCS*, pages 179–192. Springer-Verlag, 2003.

14. Jan Jürjens. *Secure Systems Development with UML*. Springer, 2004.

15. Jan Jürjens. Umlsec webpage. Accessible at http://www.umlsec.org, 2002–04.

16. D.C. Petriu and H. Shen. Applying the UML performance profile: Graph grammar-based derivation of LQN models from UML specifications. In A.J. Field and P.G. Harrison, editors, *Proceedings of the 12th International Conference on Modelling Tools and Techniques for Computer and Communication System Performance Evaluation*, number 2324 in Lecture Notes in Computer Science, pages 159–177, London, UK, April 2002. Springer-Verlag.

17. B. Selic, A. Moore, M. Woodside, B. Watson, M. Bjorkander, M. Gerhardt, and D. Petriu. Response to the OMG RFP for Schedulability, Performance, and Time, revised, June 2001. OMG document number: ad/2001-06-14.

18. J.P. López-Grao, J. Merseguer, and J. Campos. From UML activity diagrams to stochastic Petri nets: Application to software performance analysis. In *Proceedings of the Seventeenth International Symposium on Computer and Information Sciences*, pages 405–409, Orlando, Florida, October 2002. CRC Press.

19. S. Donatelli, J. Hillston, and M. Ribaudo. A comparison of Performance Evaluation Process Algebra and Generalized Stochastic Petri Nets. In *Proc. 6th International Workshop on Petri Nets and Performance Models*, Durham, North Carolina, 1995.

Formal Verification of Security Properties of Smart Card Embedded Source Code

June Andronick[1], Boutheina Chetali[1], and Christine Paulin-Mohring[2]

[1] Axalto, Smart Cards Research
{jandronick, bchetali}@axalto.com
36-38, rue de la Princesse, BP45, 78431 Louveciennes Cedex, France
[2] Université Paris-Sud,
Laboratoire de Recherche en Informatique, UMR 8623 CNRS,
Bâtiment 490, F-91405 Orsay Cedex, France
paulin@lri.fr

Abstract. This paper reports on a method to handle the verification of various security properties of imperative source code embedded on smart cards. The idea is to combine two program verification approaches: the functional verification at the source code level and the verification of high level properties on a formal model built from the program and its specification. The method presented uses the Caduceus tool, built on top of the Why tool. Caduceus enables the verification of an annotated C program and provides a validation process that we used to generate a high level formal model of the C source code. This method is illustrated by an example extracted from the verification of a smart card embedded operating system.

Keywords: Theorem Proving, Smart Card, Security, Source code verification, Formal Methods.

Introduction

In domains where security is a major issue, as in the smart card world, the need of confidence in the programs developed is increasing dramatically. This leads to a strong development of methodologies and tools which aim at strengthening this confidence. In particular, formal methods are proposed to provide formal verification of the correctness of crucial and sensitive programs.

Several approaches have been studied for the formal verification of systems. A first approach consists in building a model of the target system in a formal framework and in reasoning about the model in the same framework. The weakness of this approach lies in the confidence in that the model actually represents the system. However, some methods, like the automatic generation of source code, enable to strengthen this link between the model of the system and the code implementing it.

Another approach consists in verifying directly the source code of the system implementation. Functional properties of the system are defined by inserting

J.S. Fitzgerald, I.J. Hayes, and A. Tarlecki (Eds.): FM 2005, LNCS 3582, pp. 302–317, 2005.

annotations in the code and a proof obligation generator is used to verify these properties.

The idea presented in this paper is to combine the two approaches, in order to prove *global security properties* on a *verified* model. In other words, the model consists in the code *specification*, that is the set of annotations, and the source code verification method is used to prove that the specification, i.e. the model, is verified by the implementation. This proof constitutes a *formal* link between the model and its implementation. Hence, the high level verification can be done on the *verified* model.

Our approach is somehow similar to the one proposed by the JCVM tool (see [7]) generating a formal model from a Java Card source code. The main difference, besides the fact that we are here interested in the C language, is that we use only the formal specification, whereas the JCVM tool build a model of the program itself, which may make the proofs heavier.

We use the Caduceus tool ([21, 22]), built on top of the Why tool ([19, 20]), which provides a *multi-prover* formal framework for the verification of C programs. Its architecture enables the definition of an *automatic* generation of a high level model in a formal environment (the proof assistant Coq [32]) where the verification of security properties is possible.

We use this method for the formal verification of an operating system module embedded on a smart card. Due to its central position in the architecture of smart cards, its validation is crucial for the confidence in the whole system. For intelligibility reasons, only a simplified case study will be presented in this paper, though a real embedded operating system module has been verified.

The paper is organised as follows. Section 1 points out the different formal verification approaches, their limitations and the approach proposed in this paper. Section 2 presents the case study used in this paper in order to illustrate our approach. Section 3 starts with a presentation of the Caduceus tool and then describes in detail our validation method.

1   Formal Verification

1.1   Model Verification Approach

A classical approach of formal verification consists in building a model of the system in a formal framework, for instance a theorem prover language, and target properties are proved to be satisfied by this model. This approach can be found for instance in industrial domains, when formal methods are used to increase the security level of products. A model of a given sensitive system is usually built from the system requirements specification. Security policies can then be translated into security properties and proved in the same formal framework.

In this approach, the implementation is generally developed in parallel with the verification process. Therefore the main problem is to justify the link between the verified model and the implementation. This correctness of the model with respect to the source code is mandatory to claim that the code verifies the target properties. An usual way to strengthen this link is to refine the high level model in lower level models, until a low level model whose link with the code is as straightforward as possible, in terms of data structures and functions. The link between two levels is proved using an abstraction property.

Such a "top-down" refinement approach has been used to prove the correctness of the *Java Card Virtual Machine* embedded into smart cards (see [16]). A high level formal model of the JCVM has been developed in the Formavie Project and security properties such as the confidentiality and the integrity of the embedded applets have been proved on this model (see [3, 2]).

A first weakness of the verification at the model level, using refinement, is in terms of optimisation, maintenance, and reusability. Indeed, any modification of the source code needs an update of all the models and formal links. Another weakness is that the last step between the lowest level and the implementation is *informal*. This missing link can be provided by the automatic generation of source code from the formal models, when it is possible. It enables to derive code from the specification after having verified properties on this specification. Such method has been investigated in [8, 29, 23] with the B tool to generate Java Card or C programs. Also, [14] and [10] proposes an embedded Java Card bytecode verifier, generated from formal models. But this method is not well suited for low level programs, close to the hardware layer, such as operating system programs. These programs are usually written by smart card experienced developers, since some very technical optimisations are usually needed, for instance when managing the memory.

A way to avoid those weaknesses is to consider the source code as the starting point of the verification.

1.2   Source Code Verification Approach

Several tools for the verification at the source code level exist. One possible approach, taken for instance in the BALI project (see [4] and e.g. [33]), consists in modelling the syntax and semantics of the source code in a proof assistant, using a so-called *deep embedding*, and in proving general theorems on the language. This approach is well suited for meta-theoretical studies but is less practical for actual development of verified code by developers.

An alternative approach consists in inserting annotations into source code and in using a proof tool to verify, automatically or interactively, that the code implements the properties defined by the annotations. Annotations are usually special comments inserted in the source file which can be ignored by the compiler but recognised by the verification tool. They may usually express preconditions and postconditions of functions, variables modified by functions, loop invariants, global invariants, etc. Annotations may be defined by the programmer, or generated, entirely or partially, from the code. For instance, properties specific to the language, such as out-of-bounds array access, can be statically deduced from the code.

Following this idea, several tools have been developed, in particular for programs written in Java. The Java Modeling Language JML ([25]) is a formal annotation language, that can be analysed by different tools in order to produce documentation, perform dynamic tests and handle properties verification. It is used for the verification of Java programs in the tools ESC/Java ([17, 18]), LOOP ([26]), Jack ([12, 11]) or Krakatoa ([27]). On the other hand, the Key tool ([1]) proposes an UML based specification for the verification of Java Card applications, while the Jass tool ([5]) is a Design by Contract extension for Java, enabling run-time checks of specification violation, with a possible specification of global properties using traces.

We are interested in a similar approach for C programs. A lot of tools allow to do static analysis of C code (see [31]) but few of them handle explicit preconditions and postconditions. However, the Caveat tool ([15]) provides semi-automatic verification of C programs, where the annotations are built separately from the code. In this paper, we shall use the Caduceus tool which is a direct adaptation of the Java/JML technology for C programs.

All these tools offer the guarantee that given properties are verified *at the source code level*. But the fact that these properties have to be expressed in the annotation language gives rise to several limitations:

- the annotation language is a first-order predicate logic. Therefore the definition of some properties, such as reachability in data structures, becomes heavy whereas it would be immediate in a higher order language. However, some tools allow to use predicates in the annotations that may be instantiated only in the higher order theorem prover used;
- if the proof of several properties is needed, each function annotation will contain the conjunction of all these properties. Thus the code is more "polluted" and the verification process can be heavier;
- properties expressed using annotations are *local* to the function considered. This is well suited for the verification of *functional* properties, such as "the result of a function must be null". But it is often necessary to prove *global* properties over combination of several functions or high level temporal properties, such as the absence of dead-lock. However, existing methods propose a way to express such global properties in a local way, either within the annotation language, using some variables to represent a global state of the program (see [6, 24]), or by introducing new annotated code to be proved, representing the global properties.

1.3   Our Approach

This paper presents a combination of the previous approaches. We use the annotations in order to define a model of the system and we *prove* that the given implementation of this system corresponds to its model. Then the expected security properties can be checked directly on the verified model, which provides a certain level of abstraction with respect to the code.

This method is used to model and verify an operating system module by annotating each function by the description of its behaviour. The case study is described in the following section.

2   Case Study

2.1   Context

Smart cards are devices where the confidence in the embedded software is crucial. Besides, a smart card needs to be inserted into a reader to obtain power. So if the card is suddenly removed from the reader, the program that was running on card is interrupted. Such a *tearing*, or *power off*, must give rise to coherence verification, stability checks, recovery properties proof, etc. For all these reasons, formal verification is becoming an essential step.

A tearing may have no consequence for some operations. But other operations must be processed *atomically*, i.e., either all instructions of the operation are executed, or none are. This is the case of a *transaction*: if a tearing occurs during the processing of a transaction, all the operations done from the beginning of the transaction must be aborted. Other operations, such as the erasing of a memory segment, need to be *complete* in the sense that they must be resumed or processed again if a power off occurred.

In order to ensure this kind of properties of the "tearing sensitive" operations, variables are usually used to store the current state of the operations. A variable indicates either that the operation has started and is currently *ongoing*, or that it has been *committed*. The variables may also be *unused* if no such operation has yet occurred. In order to model this, we could introduce a set of possible states $state = \{\,ongoing - committed - unused\,\}$ and different variables, such as *transaction_state* or *erase_state*, keeping track of the status of the corresponding operations. Then when the card is reset, all states are checked and if some are ongoing, specific measures are taken.

2.2   The Source Code

In our case study, an array `all_states` is used to store the states of all the "tearing sensitive" operations:

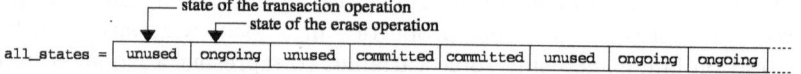

For capacity and optimisation reasons, only the smallest space needed to store this information is used. For instance, two bits are sufficient to represent a state:

```
#define STATE_UNUSED      0    /* 00b */
#define STATE_ONGOING     1    /* 01b */
#define STATE_COMMITTED   2    /* 10b */
```

Therefore, an unsigned char which contains eight bits may represent four states. The array `all_states` can thus be defined as follows:

```
unsigned char all_states[DIM];
```

where 4*DIM is large enough to contain states of all tearing sensitive operations.

This optimisation implies that to access a given state in the array, a *byte number* and a *slot number* must be given:

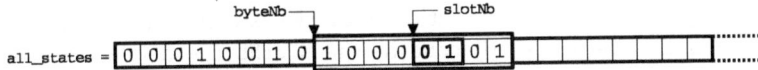

The access functions are defined as follows:

```
unsigned char getState(int byteNb, int slotNb)
        { return GETBITS(all_states[byteNb], 2*slotNb, 2);}
void setState(int byteNb, int slotNb, unsigned char newst)
        { all_states[byteNb] =
                SETBITS(all_states[byteNb], 2*slotNb, 2, newst);}
```

The macros `GETBITS` and `SETBITS` used are defined with bit operations:

```
#define GETBITS(X,P,N)    (X>>(8-N-P)&~(~0<<N))
#define SETBITS(X,P,N,Y)
                ((X|(Y<<(8-N-P)))&(~((~Y&~(~0<<N))<<(8-N-P))))
```

Actually, the macro `GETBITS(X,P,N)` gives the `N` bits from position `P` in the byte `X`. The macro `SETBITS(X,P,N,Y)` returns the byte `X` with the `N` bits that begin at position `P`, set to the rightmost `N` bits of `Y`, leaving the other bits unchanged. More precisely, the leftmost bits of `X` are unchanged *if* `Y` has at most `N` significant bits, i.e. if the integer `Y` is less than 2^N.

$$X = \boxed{x7\;x6\;x5\;x4\;x3\;x2\;x1\;x0} \quad \text{GETBITS(X,P,N)} = \boxed{0\;0\;0\;0\;0\;x4\;x3\;x2}$$

$$Y = \boxed{0\;0\;0\;0\;0\;y2\;y1\;y0} \quad \text{SETBITS(X,P,N,Y)} = \boxed{x7\;x6\;x5\;y2\;y1\;y0\;x1\;x0}$$

$$\text{in fact}\quad (x7|y5)\;(x6|y4)\;(x5|y3)$$

2.3   Verification Using Existing Approaches

Let us illustrate the approaches presented in Section 1, and more specially their limitations, on the case study presented in the previous section.

Model verification approach. Let us show here that the missing formal link between the model and the code allows to verify properties on the model that are not verified by the code. Usually, for easiness reason, a high level model is used, since it allows to verify high level properties without taking into account low level aspects such as memory allocation. But making this choice increases the risk of an incorrect abstraction. For instance, in our example, an intuitive way to build a model is to define `all_states` as an array of states, where a `state` is an union set of three values: `ongoing`, `committed` and `unused`. The low level aspects of bit manipulation used to retrieve or modify some bits of a byte are abstracted. Therefore some source code bugs may not be detected by any verification on the model. For instance, in the source code, the `SETBITS` macro has the following comment :

```
/* return X with the N bits that begin at position P set to
    the rightmost N bits of Y, leaving the other bits unchanged */
```

This comment is not correct since it does not mention the condition that `Y` must be less than 2^N. If this condition is not satisfied, the leftmost bits of `X` are modified. In particular, if the function `setState` is called with a `newst` greater or equal than 2^2, the slots adjacent to the `slotNb` are also modified. In our operating system module, the function `setState` is actually called only with one of the three defined states that are less than 2^2. But if the program is reused, one could define:

```
#define STATE_ABORT_STARTED  3    /* 11b */
#define STATE_ABORT_DONE     4    /* 100b */
```

and use `setState(byteNb,slotNb,STATE_ABORT_DONE)`. This would overwrite the adjacent slots in `all_states`:

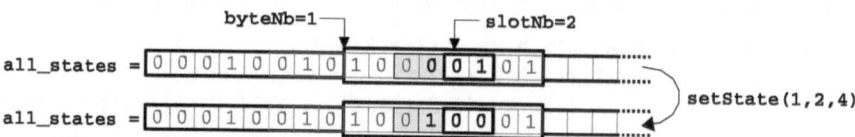

This undesirable behaviour would not be detected with a verification on the high level model since the bit operations are not represented after the abstraction:

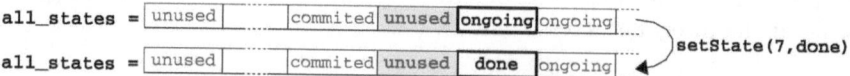

Actually the model is even incorrect since the adjacent state in the array remains `unused` in the model whereas it becomes `ongoing` in the source code.

Source Code Verification Approach. As already mentioned, the difficulty in handling the verification using inserted annotations consists in the definition of *global properties*. To illustrate this in our case study, here is an example of global property that may not be easily proved using only annotations:

> *"if* `getState(byteNb,slotNb)` *is called just after a call to* `setState(byteNb,slotNb,newst)`, *then the result is* `newst`"

Another example of temporal property is the following: let `commit_next_ongoing` be a function which sets to `committed` the first occurrence of `ongoing` in the array `all_states`. This function would be called at reset and we would like to prove properties such as: *"for any initial configuration of* `all_states`, *there exists a finite sequence of calls to* `commit_next_ongoing` *ending with* `all_states` *containing no* `ongoing` *state"*.

3   Source Code Verification of Global Properties

As already mentioned, the idea presented in this paper is to combine the two approaches presented in Section 1 in order to prove that the *source code* verifies some *high level* and *global* security properties. Our method is based on four steps:

1. a specification step: the program is annotated by the specification of its functions. This specification becomes the *local* model of the program.
2. a validation step: the soundness of the local model with respect to the source code is proved using a source code verification tool.

3. a high level modelling step: a memory state transition model, or *global* model, is formally generated from the local model of the code.
4. a security verification step: high level and global security properties are defined and proved to be satisfied by the global model.

We use the Caduceus tool since it offers an architecture which enables such a verification method and meets the requirements needed for our verification of embedded operating system. Indeed it handles C programs and generates explicitly the local model. Caduceus is built on top of the back-end verification tool Why. However, in this paper, we will not do the distinction between the two levels of analysis and refer only to *Caduceus* for actually the combination of both systems. In the following, we present the main aspects of Caduceus (for more details see [21, 22, 19, 20]) and then detail each step of our approach, illustrated on the case study.

3.1   The Caduceus Tool

Annotations. Caduceus is a verification tool at the source code level. It is based on Hoare logic with preconditions and postconditions, but with an additional explicit interpretation of both the specification and the code as state functions. The programs handled are ANSI C source code, annotated with a specification language inspired by the Java Modelling Language (JML, see [25]). Annotations are used to define functional properties of each function. Formulae are expressed in a first-order language where C expressions without side-effects can be used as well as predicate variables (to be interpreted later) and specific keywords. They may express functions preconditions (with the keyword **requires**), side-effects (with **assigns**), postconditions (with **ensures**), global invariants, loop invariants, loop variants and loop side-effects, logical functions (**logic**) or predicate (**predicate**), etc. Moreover, in the postcondition, the construction \result may be used for the result returned by the function and \old for the initial state of the function. Finally, the keyword \nothing can be found in the assign clause to state that the function has no side-effect.

Translation. Caduceus interprets a C program using a memory model. Instead of modelling the memory as a big array, Caduceus follows Burstall and Bornat's approach (see [9, 13]) where a spatial separation divides the memory into disjoint memory locations whenever it is possible: for instance, two different fields of a structure will be in separated memory locations. This separation ensures "for free" that changes made in one memory location do not affect the other locations. Within a single memory location, the separation of variables is also ensured, in the sense that a *proof obligation* is generated whenever the separation is not clearly established.

The model identifies the notions of pointer and array. Hence, the *basic values* are either direct values in numeric types (integers or reals) or pointers. A value p of type **pointer** is either the **null** pointer or a pair (**base_addr(p)**,**offset(p)**) made of the address of the memory block containing p and the offset of p within this block. Then, the memory state of the C program is represented by a set of global variables corresponding to statically separated memory spaces. Each memory space maps pointers to values. For instance, a variable intP may be used to represent the part of memory where arrays of integers are allocated. We can visualise intP as a function which associates each base address corresponding to an allocated array of size n to a piece of memory of size n containing the integer values in the array.

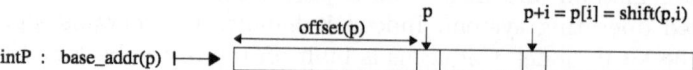

Caduceus provides an access function acc(intP,p) retrieving the value pointed by p in the state intP and a modification function upd(intP,p,3) whose result is a new memory state intP' where the value pointed by p becomes 3. Moreover, as shown in the figure, a pointer arithmetic function shift(p,i) allows to represent the C expression p+i or p[i]. Finally an additional variable alloc represents an *allocation store* which tells which addresses are allocated and the size of the block it points to. This allows annotations such as (valid alloc p), or (valid_range p i j), etc.

Another aspect that must be taken into account by Caduceus is the *effects inference*. Caduceus computes for each C function the set of memory variables and global variables which are read and/or modified.

To conclude, Caduceus interprets each C construction as a functional transformation of values of memory states, using a monadic interpretation.

Verification. The Caduceus tool generates *verification conditions*. These are the missing parts of the verification process that must be proved in order to ensure the soundness of the program with respect to the specification given in the annotations. A specific aspect of Caduceus is its independence with respect to the prover. Therefore the verification conditions may be checked in any of the theorem provers proposed (PVS [28], Simplify [30], Coq [32], ...)

Due to its interactive and higher order aspects, the Coq theorem prover (see [32]) has been chosen for our verification method. Moreover, when used with Coq, Caduceus provides a *validation term* ensuring the correctness of each function in the program, which is useful for our method, as explained Section 3.4. The validation term is a proof of $\forall \mathbf{x}. \; Pre(\mathbf{x}) \rightarrow \exists \mathbf{x}'. \; Post(\mathbf{x}, \mathbf{x}')$ where $\mathbf{x}$ and $\mathbf{x}'$ represents the values of memory variables modified by the function before and after the function call. Assuming the input memories $\mathbf{x}$ satisfies the precondition, an output state can be reached which satisfies the postcondition. In the Coq system, which is based on Type Theory, the validation term corresponds to an executable functional term which represents our semantics of the given C program. Type checking this validation term therefore ensures the correctness of the program with respect to its specification[1]. See [20] for a more detailed analysis of this technology.

---

[1] This is of course under the condition of the correctness of Caduceus functional interpretation of C programs.

3.2   Specification Step

The annotations are used in order to describe the function behaviour, i.e., its specification. In our case study, the postcondition of `getState` must indicate that the result of the function contains the two bits at position `2*slotNb` in the byte `all_states[byteNb]`. Talking about a given bit of an integer in the annotation language is quite impossible. Moreover, a Coq library provides support for binary representation of integers. Therefore, we define a logical function `GetBits`, which is declared in the annotations, and will be instantiated in the Coq language:

```
/*@ logic int GetBits(int b,int p,int n) */
```

This function represents the same operation as the `GETBITS` macro, i.e., it gives the n bits from position p in the byte b. Once declared, this function can be used in any annotation. On the other hand, the precondition of `getState` indicates that the indexes `byteNb` and `slotNb` are valid in the array `all_states`. Finally, `getState` does not modify any global variable. The specification of `getState` can thus be expressed as follows:

```
/*@ requires (0<=byteNb<DIM) && (0<=slotNb<8/2)
 @ assigns \nothing
 @ ensures \result == GetBits(all_states[byteNb],2*slotNb,2)*/
unsigned char getState(int byteNb, int slotNb)
   { return GETBITS(all_states[byteNb], 2*slotNb, 2);}
```

For the `setState` function, an additional precondition must be added mentioning that the new state must be less than 2^2. Concerning what is modified by `setState`, it consists of two bits of `all_states[byteNb]`. However, the assign clause may not represent the bits of an integer. Therefore the assigns clause will contain the whole byte `all_states[byteNb]` and the postcondition is used to indicate that the two bits at position `2*slotNb` become equal to the `newst` given and that the other bits are unchanged:

```
/*@ requires (0<=byteNb<DIM) && (0<=slotNb<8/2)
 @        && (0<=newst<2^2)
 @ assigns all_states[byteNb]
 @ ensures (GetBits(all_states[byteNb],2*slotNb,2)==newst)
 @    && ( \forall int j;  0<=j<8/2 && (j!=slotNb) =>
 @          GetBits(all_states[byteNb],2*j,2) ==
 @          GetBits(\old(all_states[byteNb]),2*j,2) )  */
void setState(int byteNb, int slotNb, unsigned char newst)
   { all_states[byteNb] =
        SETBITS(all_states[byteNb], 2*slotNb, 2, newst);}
```

3.3   Validation Step

The validation step consists in proving the verification conditions generated by Caduceus. When used with Coq, the verification conditions are lemma statements that may be proved interactively. In our example, the main goals to be established concern the postconditions of the two functions. For the `getState` function, the following goal has to be proved:

> `| \result == GetBits(all_states[byteNb],2*slotNb,2)`

where `\result` is built by the macro `GETBITS`, i.e., it consists in a combination of binary operations. Concerning `setState`, two goals have to be proved:

> 1. `(GetBits(all_states[byteNb],2*slotNb,2)  ==  newst)`
> 2. `\forall int j;  0<=j<8/2 && (j!=slotNb) =>`
>   `   GetBits(all_states[byteNb],2*j,2) ==`
>   `   GetBits(\old(all_states[byteNb]),2*j,2) )`

All these goals are equality statements between two bytes. The idea is to do the analysis at a bit level, using Coq libraries defining binary representation of integers and binary operations. In other words the goals are proved using an auxiliary lemma stating that two bytes are equal if all their bits are pairwise equal. This needs the definition of a function computing the *ith* bit of a given byte. Moreover, lemmas are needed to compute the *ith* bit for all binary operations, in order to obtain the *ith* bits of `\result`.

Finally, the function `GetBits` that has been only declared is defined using the Coq library. Then we need to know the *ith* bits of the byte resulting from the `GetBits` operation: `(ith (GetBits x p n) i) = (ith x (i+(8-n-p)))` for any `x, p, n` and `i` such that $(0{\leq}p{\mid}8)$, $(0{\leq}n{\mid}8{-}p)$, and $(0{\leq}i{\mid}n)$.

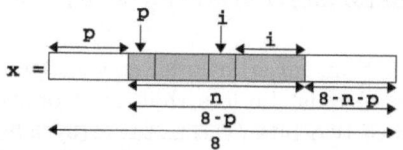

3.4   High Level Modelling Step

Our goal is to be able to express high level global properties. Such properties are defined in terms of states at function call and states resulting from the function execution. Examples of higher order properties are:

- *"if the state before the call to the function f satisfies P, then there exists a state resulting from a finite sequence of calls to f which satisfies Q"*

- *"if the state s before the call to the function f satisfies P and s' is the state resulting from the execution of f from s, then the call to the function g from the state s' results in a state satisfying Q".*

Therefore we would like to model a function as a *transition* relation between two memory states. In other words, we would like to define, for each given function f, a binary relation $f\_transition$ such that **x** is in relation with **x'** by this relation (denoted by ($f\_transition$ **x x'**)) if **x'** is the state resulting from the execution of f from the state **x**.

The identification of the memory states **x** and **x'** depends on the memory model. The memory model chosen here is the one defined in Caduceus, described in Section 3.1. A memory state is made of the global variables of the program (numeric values or references), the global variables corresponding to the memory segments (e.g. $intP$) and a variable $alloc$ storing the allocated addresses.

More precisely, for each function f with a list $\overrightarrow{a}$ of parameters, Caduceus computes the set $\overrightarrow{z}$ of "read-only" variables (variables of the program and variables representing memory segments) and the set $\overrightarrow{t}$ of "read-written" variables. Caduceus also computes the precondition $Pre_f(\overrightarrow{a}, \overrightarrow{z}, \overrightarrow{t})$ from the *requires* clause of the annotation and the memory states computed. In the same way, the postcondition $Post_f(result, \overrightarrow{a}, \overrightarrow{z}, \overrightarrow{t@}, \overrightarrow{t})$ is computed, where $\overrightarrow{t}$ corresponds to the values after the function call and $\overrightarrow{t@}$ to the values at function call. The postcondition also includes the *assign* clause of the function.

For instance, for the function $\texttt{setState}$, a single state variable $intP$ is introduced, corresponding to the memory segment where all_states is allocated. The list of parameters $\overrightarrow{a}$ is $(byteNb, slotNb, newst)$, the list of read-only variables $\overrightarrow{z}$ is $(all\_states, alloc)$ and the list of read-written variables $\overrightarrow{t}$ is $(intP)$. The precondition contains the *requires* clause, together with a validity condition of the variable all_states in the allocation table $alloc$:

$(0 \leq byteNb < DIM)$ *and* $(0 \leq slotNb < 8/2)$ *and* $(0 \leq newst < 2^2)$ *and*
$(valid\_states\ all\_states\ alloc)$

Finally the postcondition combines the *assigns* and the *ensures* clauses:

$(GetBits(acc(intP, shift(all\_states, byteNb)), 2 * slotNb, 2) = newst)$ *and*
$(\forall\, j : int.\ (0 \leq j < 8/2\ \text{ and }\ j \neq slotNb)\ \rightarrow$
$(GetBits(acc(intP, shift(all\_states, byteNb)), 2 * j, 2) =$
$GetBits(acc(intP@, shift(all\_states, byteNb)), 2 * j, 2))\ )$ *and*
$assigns(alloc, intP@, intP, pointer\_loc(shift(all\_states, byteNb)))$

Using the memory states computed by Caduceus, there are two approaches for the *transitional definition* of a function f: we may use the *code* of the function or only its *specification*. Using the code means defining the resulting state **x'** as the translation of the *code*: $\mathbf{x'} = \bar{f}(\mathbf{x})$, where $\bar{f}$ represents the functional translation of the C program. This approach may be useful if some computational aspects of the function are needed to prove a specific property and are not represented in the specification of the function. However this needs an explicit functional interpretation $\bar{f}$ of the code, which may be huge, giving rise to heavy proofs. Let us note that, in addition, this model of the code is provided by Caduceus only when used with the Coq prover (see Remark below).

We choose a more abstract approach following the idea that since we proved that the specification represents the program, the function can be modelled only by its specification. In other words, **x** and **x'** are in relation by $f\_transition$ if **x** verifies the precondition of f and **x'** verifies its postcondition:

$(f\_transition\ \mathbf{x}\ \mathbf{x'})\ \equiv\ Pre_f(\mathbf{x}) \wedge Post_f(\mathbf{x}, \mathbf{x'})$

More precisely, using the work performed by Caduceus in order to identify **x** and **x'**, $f\_transition$ has the following form:

$(f\_transition\ result\ \overrightarrow{a}\ \overrightarrow{z}\ \overrightarrow{t@}\ \overrightarrow{t}\ )\ \equiv\ Pre_f(\overrightarrow{a}, \overrightarrow{z}, \overrightarrow{t@}) \wedge Post_f(result, \overrightarrow{a}, \overrightarrow{z}, \overrightarrow{t@}, \overrightarrow{t})$

Of particular note is the prover independence of the method itself, since annotations are first order formulae. However, targeted properties will have to be expressed in the chosen prover. Therefore, in the case of complex temporal properties, such as properties on transitive closures, higher order provers will be more suited.

Going further into technical aspects, Caduceus does not actually give access to the functional translation of the precondition and the postcondition directly, but only to the *validation term*, and *only* when used with the Coq theorem prover. The validation term has the following type:

$$f\_valid : \forall \mathbf{x}.\ Pre_f(\mathbf{x}) \rightarrow \exists \mathbf{x}'.\ Post_f(\mathbf{x}, \mathbf{x}')$$

However, a trick of the Coq language using type inference allows to express the property $Pre_f(\mathbf{x}) \wedge Post_f(\mathbf{x}, \mathbf{x}')$ as a simple expression only using f_valid.

Remark: in the first approach mentioned, using the functional interpretation of the *code*, the memory state **x'** is actually the witness built by the validation term. Therefore, this approach is also possible only when Caduceus is used with the Coq prover.

The fact that the validation term is only provided with the Coq prover is a major argument in our choice of Coq. Another argument being an easier definition of global or temporal properties.

3.5   Security Verification Step

In this final section, we show that the global properties mentioned in Section 2.3 can be expressed and proved using our global model.

The first property was: "*if* getState(byteNb,slotNb) *is called just after a call to* setState(byteNb,slotNb,newst), *then the result is* newst". This property has the following statement in Coq:

```
Lemma get_set :
    forall (byteNb slotNb newst:Z)(all_states:pointer)
           (alloc:alloc_table)(intP:memory Z)(intP0:memory Z),
    (setState_transition byteNb slotNb newst all_states alloc
                    intP intP0)
 -> (getState_transition byteNb slotNb all_states alloc
                    intP0 newst).
```

The proof is straightforward after unfolding the transition definition.

The second property was: "*for any initial configuration of* all_states, *there exists a finite sequence of calls to* commit_next_ongoing *ending with* all_states *containing no* ongoing *state*". The specification of commit_first_ongoing states that either there was already no ongoing state in all_states and then nothing is done, or the first ongoing state of all_states before the call is changed into a committed state. In Coq, a finite sequence of calls to such a function can be defined inductively using the transitional formal model of the function. Then the Coq statement of the property states that for any array all_states and initial state intP, there exists a memory state intP0 such that this state results from the successive calls to commit_first_ongoing from intP and that there is no `ongoing` state in `all_states` in the state `intP0`. The memory state `intP0` given in the proof is the witness of the validation term and the proof is done inductively on the size of the sequence of calls: one step of the function makes the number of `ongoing` states decrease by one, therefore, after a finite number of calls, this number reaches zero.

We presented here simple global properties since the case study has been shortened for the illustration. Thus only few functions were presented. But once the whole system is specified and its model is generated, other global security properties concerning the behaviour of the entire system may be proved.

4   Conclusion

In the smart cards world where *security* and *performance* are the main business criteria, formal verification activity becomes a mandatory step. Building high level models of the system being developed to prove correctness properties is useful but is still expensive, as it requires experts. Moreover, a formal link between the models and the actual system implementation is lacking. The goal is then to build tools generating secure code from verified high level models. But those tools have to be improved to take into account the scarce resources of smart cards. Another immediate solution is to reason directly on the source code. This method could be handled by the developer, but reasoning at this low level limits the expressiveness of the properties to prove.

The method we proposed here allows to combine the two approaches and to take benefits from both. A functional verification is performed at the source code level by the insertion of annotations describing the expected behaviour of the program. This step strengthen the confidence in the code by providing a proof that its execution will have the expected behaviour. The originality of our method is to use the program specification already defined in the annotations, to derive a high level model allowing the definition and verification of high level security properties. The model is thus *automatically* generated from an *existing* formal specification. Moreover, the missing formal link between the model and the code is provided by the formal derivation of the model from a formal specification, together with the formal proof that this specification is verified by the code. Therefore global security properties concerning the behaviour of the whole system can be proved on the model, in a independent way.

Our future work will consist in generalising the method in order to handle a wider class of embedded programs and to be able to express a wider range of smart card security properties. For instance, casts of pointer or structure are used in our embedded source code, but this is the main unsupported feature of Caduceus. This is due to the memory separation model used in Caduceus, that becomes incorrect in the presence of such casts. The memory model must therefore be adapted to handle any embedded source code. Another extension would be to represent the tearing in the annotation language. This would allow to define the conditions that must hold even if a tearing occurs. Since the high level model is derived from the annotations, global properties could then be proved concerning the global behaviour of the system in the case of a power off. An interesting direction would also be to investigate an automatic transformation of temporal security properties into properties expressed on our high level model. In this context, a comparison with model checking based methods, which is missing in this paper, should be made.

Finally, our method allows a faster transfer of the tools to the developers, giving them the possibility to define properties directly on their source code. This will help us to achieve our main goal of a wide deployment of formal verification tools to the developers to produce automatically a secure embedded code.

Acknowledgements. We would like to thank Jean Christophe Filliâtre, Thierry Hubert and Claude Marché for their useful help and support in using Caduceus.

References

1. W. Ahrendt, T. Baar, B. Beckert, R. Bubel, M. Giese, R. Hähnle, W. Menzel, W. Mostowski, A. Roth, S. Schlager, and P. H. Schmitt. The KeY tool. *Software and System Modeling*, 2004. Online First issue, to appear in print. http://www.key-project.org/.
2. J. Andronick, B. Chetali, and O. Ly. Formal Verification of the Integrity Property in Java Card Technology. In *International Conference on Research in Smart Cards (Esmart'03)*, September 2003.
3. J. Andronick, B. Chetali, and O. Ly. Using Coq to Verify Java Card Applet Isolation Properties. In *International Conference on Theorem Proving in Higher Order Logics (TPHOLs'03)*, volume 2758 of *LNCS*, pages 335–351. Springer-Verlag, September 2003.
4. The Bali project. http://isabelle.in.tum.de/bali/.
5. D. Bartetzko, C. Fischer, M. Möller, and H. Wehrheim. Jass - Java with Assertions. In K. Havelund and G. Rosu, editors, *Workshop on Runtime Verification 2001*, volume 55 of *Electronic Notes in Theoretical Computer Science*. Elsevier Science, July 2001. http://csd.informatik.uni-oldenburg.de/~jass/.
6. G. Barthe, L. Burdy, M. Huisman, J.-L. Lanet, and M. Pavlova. Enforcing High-Level Security Properties For Applets. In *Sixth Smart Card Research and Advanced Application IFIP Conference (CARDIS'04)*, August 2004.
7. G. Barthe, G. Dufay, L. Jakubiec, B. P. Serpette, and S. Melo de Sousa. A Formal Executable Semantics of the JavaCard Platform. In D. Sands, editor, *Proceedings of the 10th European Symposium on Programming Languages and Systems (ESOP'01)*, volume 2028 of *LNCS*, pages 302–319. Springer-Verlag, 2001.
8. D. Bert, S. Boulmé, M.-L. Potet, A. Requet, and L. Voisin. Adaptable Translator of B Specifications to Embedded C Programs. In K. Araki, S. Gnesi, and D. Mandrioli, editors, *FME 2003: Formal Methods*, volume 2805 of *LNCS*, pages 94–113. Springer-Verlag Heidelberg, October 2005.
9. R. Bornat. Proving Pointer Programs in Hoare Logic. In *Proceedings of the 5th International Conference on Mathematics of Program Construction (MPC'00)*, pages 102–126. Springer-Verlag, 2000.
10. L. Burdy, L. Casset, and A. Requet. Formal Development of an Embedded Verifier for Java Card Byte Code. In *Proceedings of the 2002 International Conference on Dependable Systems and Networks (DSN'02)*, pages 51–58. IEEE Computer Society, 2002.

11. L. Burdy, J.-L. Lanet, and A. Requet. Java Applet Correctness: A Developer-Oriented Approach. In K. Araki, S. Gnesi, and D. Mandrioli, editors, *International Symposium of Formal Methods Europe (FME'03)*, volume 2805 of *LNCS*, pages 422–439. Springer-Verlag, September 2003.
12. L. Burdy and A. Requet. Jack : Java Applet Correctness Kit, November 2002.
13. R. Burstall. Some Techniques for Proving Correctness of Programs which Alter Data Structures. *Machine Intelligence*, 7:23–50, 1972.
14. L. Casset. Development of an Embedded Verifier for Java Card Byte Code Using Formal Methods. In L.-H. Eriksson and P. Lindsay, editor, *Proceedings of the International Symposium of Formal Methods Europe (FME'02)*, volume 2391 of *LNCS*, pages 290–309. Springer-Verlag, 2002.
15. The Caveat Project. `http://www-drt.cea.fr/Pages/List/lse/LSL/Caveat/index.html/`.
16. B. Chetali, C. Loiseaux, E. Gimenez, and O. Ly. An Interpretation of the Common Criteria EAL7 level : Formal Modeling of the Java Card Virtual Machine. In *3rd International Common Criteria Conference (ICCC'02)*, May 2002.
17. ESC/Java. `http://research.compaq.com/SRC/esc/`.
18. ESC/Java2. `http://www.sos.cs.ru.nl/research/escjava`.
19. J.-C. Filliâtre. The Why Verification Tool. `http://why.lri.fr/`.
20. J.-C. Filliâtre. Verification of Non-Functional Programs using Interpretations in Type Theory. *Journal of Functional Programming*, 13(4):709–745, July 2003.
21. J.-C. Filliâtre and C. Marché. The Caduceus tool for the Verification of C Programs. `http://why.lri.fr/caduceus/`.
22. J.-C. Filliâtre and C. Marché. Multi-Prover Verification of C Programs. In *Sixth International Conference on Formal Engineering Methods (ICFEM)*, volume 3308 of *LNCS*, pages 15–29, Seattle, November 2004. Springer-Verlag.
23. A. Hammad, A. Requet, B. Tatibouët, and J.-C. Voisinet. Java Card Code Generation from B Specifications. In J. S. Dong and J. Woodcock, editors, *5th International Conference on Formal Engineering Methods (ICFEM'03)*, volume 2885 of *LNCS*, pages 306–318. Springer-Verlag Heidelberg, November 2003.
24. M. Huisman and K. Trentelman. Extending JML Specifications with Temporal Logic. In *Algebraic Methodology And Software Technology (AMAST'02)*, volume 2422 of *LNCS*, pages 334–348. Springer-Verlag, 2002.
25. G. T. Leavens, K. Rustan M. Leino, E. Poll, C. Ruby, and B. Jacobs. JML: Notations and Tools Supporting Detailed Design in Java. In *OOPSLA 2000 Companion*, pages 105–106. ACM, October 2000.
26. Loop. `http://www.sos.cs.ru.nl/research/loop`.
27. C. Marché, C. Paulin-Mohring, and X. Urbain. The Krakatoa Tool for Java Program Verification, 2002. `http://krakatoa.lri.fr/`.
28. The PVS system. `http://pvs.csl.sri.com/`.
29. A. Requet and G. Bossu. Embedding Formally Proved Code in a Smart Card: Converting B to C. In *Third International Conference on Formal Engineering Methods (ICFEM'00)*, pages 15–24. IEEE Press, 2000.
30. The Simplify decision procedure (part of ESC/Java). `http://research.compaq.com/SRC/esc/simplify/Simplify.1.html`.
31. Static Source Code Analysis Tools for C. `http://www.spinroot.com/static/`.
32. The Coq Development Team LogiCal Project. *The Coq Proof Assistant Reference Manual.* `http://pauillac.inria.fr/coq/doc/main.html`.
33. D. von Oheimb and T. Nipkow. Machine-checking the Java Specification: Proving Type-Safety. In J. Alves-Foss, editor, *Formal Syntax and Semantics of Java*, volume 1523 of *LNCS*, pages 119–156. Springer-Verlag, 1999.

A Formal Model of Addressing for Interoperating Networks

Pamela Zave

AT&T Laboratories—Research, Florham Park, NJ 07932, USA
pamela@research.att.com

Abstract. Designing network address spaces for interoperation among domains is a challenging task. A formal model in Alloy is used to clarify the problems and explore solutions. Basic connectivity requirements are proposed, and two different sets of constraints are shown to satisfy them.

Keywords: networks, network design, network requirements, Alloy.

1   Introduction

Universal connectivity is an important goal of networking. Today the world-wide network is divided into a vast and diverse collection of administrative domains. These domains include topologically distinct networks such as cellular networks, WiFi networks, and private IP subnetworks. They also include overlay networks such as virtual private networks and protocol-specific voice-over-IP networks.

To achieve the goal of universal connectivity, administrative domains must interoperate. By definition, an administrative domain controls its own address space. Yet interoperation requires that a client attached to one domain be able to produce and use an address identifying a client attached to another domain.

This paper concerns the problem of designing address spaces and interoperation mechanisms that satisfy basic connectivity requirements. This is more difficult than it sounds at first hearing. Addresses[1] can be non-unique, syntactically constrained, scarce, transient, and used for many purposes at many levels of abstraction. There is no established notion of "good addressing" [4].

Equally important, interoperation is an inherently confusing subject. This work was motivated by my experience designing an overlay voice-over-IP network [1]. Our team had seemingly endless discussions about interoperation, which never led to any clarity or comfort with the subject. I built the formal model described here in the hope of dispelling that confusion. Unfortunately, now that the confusion is gone, it is impossible to recreate what was so confusing. Fortunately, now that the model exists, no one need experience that particular confusion again.

---

[1] The identifiers used in networking are known as as *names, addresses,* and *locators,* among other things. This paper uses the term *addresses,* because it is most general and fits well with an emphasis on routing.

J.S. Fitzgerald, I.J. Hayes, and A. Tarlecki (Eds.): FM 2005, LNCS 3582, pp. 318–333, 2005.
© Springer-Verlag Berlin Heidelberg 2005

Another difficulty is that very little is known about the user-level requirements on connection networks. Networking has always been and still is, to an
overwhelming extent, a bottom-up engineering activity. Researchers are just beginning to look at the global properties they might try to satisfy with better
network designs, which makes any contribution in this area especially timely.

The formal model is written in the Alloy language, which offers a powerful
combination of relational and predicate logic [8]. The language is also attractive
because of the Alloy Analyzer [7], which was used extensively in this study.

The model shown here is both simplified and abbreviated. The full model is
available on the Web [3].

2   Connections

The model is concerned with networks that form persistent connections between
agents. Agents represent either hardware devices, particularly I/O devices, or
software systems. Most of the concepts in this section are illustrated in Figure 1.

The set of agents is partitioned into *clients*, which are the users of networking,
and *servers*, which are part of the network infrastructure. The signatures of these
object types in Alloy are:

```
abstract sig Agent { attachments: set Domain }
sig Server extends Agent { }
sig Client extends Agent { knownAt: Address -> Domain }
```

Each agent has a set *attachments* of domains to which it is attached so it can
use their facilities. If an *address, domain* pair appears in the *knownAt* field of
a client, then *address* is published as a way of reaching the client from *domain*.
An extra fact (Alloy constraint) says that each such pair can be published by at
most one client.

Addresses are primitive objects. Each *domain* has an address *space* (set of
usable addresses) and a *map* from its address space to agents:

```
sig Domain { space: set Address, map: space -> Agent }
```

An additional fact says that if an agent is in the range of a domain's map, it
is attached to the domain. At this stage of modeling there is no relationship
between *knownAt* and *map*, because *map* is in the network infrastructure and
knownAt is in the user environment.

The persistent connections created by domains are called *hops*. A hop has
fields containing the *domain* that created it, its initiating agent *initiator*, its
accepting agent *acceptor*, and its *source* and *target* addresses. If a field declaration
in an object does not have an explicit set or relation marking, the value of the
field is always a single object.

```
sig Hop { domain: Domain,
          initiator, acceptor: Agent, source, target: Address }
```

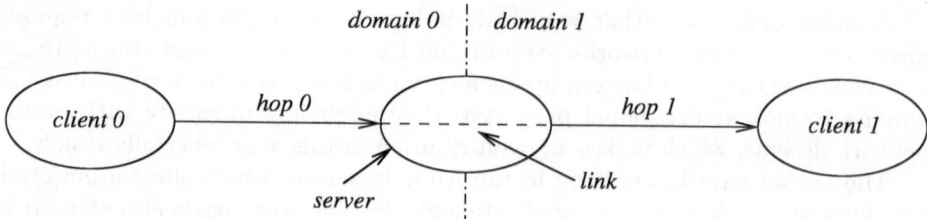

Fig. 1. A connection through two domains. The server is attached to both domains

Additional facts say that both agents are attached to hop's domain, and that both addresses are in the *space* of the hop's domain. In Figure 1, the arrow representing *hop 0* shows that its initiator is *client 0* and its acceptor is the *server*.

Most important of all, a fact says that the hop domain's *map* relation maps the hop's target address to the hop's acceptor agent. A domain's map models routing in the domain.

Servers can form multi-hop connections by creating internal *links* between hops they are participating in. Like a hop, a link is expected to transmit data more or less transparently.[2] A *link* has fields representing the server creating it and the two distinct hops *oneHop* and *anotherHop* it connects:

```
sig Link { server: Server, oneHop, anotherHop: Hop }
```

Additional facts say that the server of a link is a participant (initiator or acceptor) in both of its hops. Also, a hop belongs to at most one link in each server. This ensures that each connection between clients will be a linear chain of alternating hops and links, without forks or joins.

Because hops and links work together to form connections, it is convenient to have a direct representation of their closure. This is contained in two fields of a *connections* object. A pair of hops is in the binary relation *atomConnected* if and only if they are linked together. The binary relation *connected* on hops is the transitive closure of *atomConnected*.

```
one sig Connections { atomConnected, connected: Hop -> Hop }
```

The modifier *one* indicates that there is exactly one *connections* object.

This basic model is extremely simple for something as complex as networking, but it is sufficient to study many questions, particularly those related to routing and addressing. It allows servers to be gateways between domains, as in Figure 1, or to link hops within domains.

For simplicity, it completely eliminates the temporal dimension of network protocols. It ignores the possibility that an agent might refuse a connection, or be unable to accept one because it is busy. It also ignores multipoint connections,

---

[2] Part of the function of a server might be to filter or transform the data in some way, in which case it will be less than fully transparent.

because these are formed using point-to-point connections as building blocks, and are not directly relevant to routing.

An instance of this model is a snapshot of network state. Thus agent mobility is not represented directly, but is reflected by changes in agents' attachments and domains' maps.

3   Interoperation

In this model, interoperation between domains is viewed as a *feature* that can be added to networks, along with many other types of feature not discussed in this paper. Any feature is installed in a domain'and has some set of servers that implement it:

```
abstract sig Feature { domain: Domain, servers: set Server }
```

An additional fact says that every feature has at least one server, and every server implements exactly one feature.

A server of an interoperation feature is a gateway from its *domain* to a second domain called its *toDomain*. When the server accepts a hop in its *domain*, it initiates a corresponding hop in its *toDomain*, and links the two hops together. The source and target addresses of the initiated hop are obtained by applying an interoperation translation relation *interTrans* to the source and target addresses of the accepted hop.

If a client wishes to connect to a client attached to a different domain, it must have a target address it can use in its own domain to request the connection. Conversely, a client must have an address in every domain from which it is reachable. The presence of *interTrans* reflects the fact that a client's addresses in foreign domains may look very different from its native addresses in domains to which it is attached. These differences can arise because of syntactic restrictions, overlapping native address spaces, and historical factors.

The relationships among address spaces are illustrated by interoperation of the PSTN and two Internet overlay networks for telecommunications, the ones defined by SIP [10] and BoxOS [1].

The PSTN was the first domain to be designed. Its address space allows only digit strings of limited length, so a typical native address is 12223334444.

SIP was the second domain to be designed (history is often important because newer domains usually bear the burden of interoperating with older domains). The SIP address space is based on URI syntax. A typical native address is sip:alice@host1. In SIP *all* addresses have the prefix sip, so a foreign PSTN address has the form sip:12223334444?user=phone.

BoxOS was the third domain to be designed. Its address space is also based on URI syntax, and a typical native address is boxos:bob@host2. A foreign PSTN address has the form pstn:12223334444. A foreign SIP address has the form sip:alice@host1.

Note that native addresses of a domain can be *contained* in the address space of another domain, as SIP addresses are contained in the BoxOS address space, or

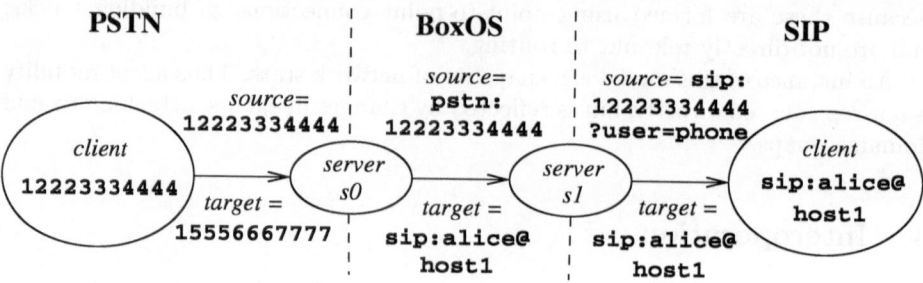

Fig. 2. Interoperation of two domains through a third domain

encoded in the address space of another domain, as PSTN addresses are encoded in the BoxOS address space. This distinction determines whether translation is an identity or not.

Figure 2 shows how the PSTN and SIP domains would interoperate if they were attached to each other only through a BoxOS domain. The three source addresses are addresses of the initiating client in three different domains. The target addresses are addresses of the accepting client in different domains. Note that server *s1* must know how to translate the address of a PSTN client, even though the PSTN is neither its *domain* nor its *toDomain*.

The PSTN address space has no encoding of SIP addresses. There are two ways that a PSTN client can request a connection to a SIP client. The first possibility is to dedicate a PSTN address to each reachable SIP client, so that interoperation translation of addresses is one-to-one. This is the method illustrated by Figure 2, where PSTN `15556667777` corresponds to `sip:alice@host1` in both BoxOS and SIP.

A more common method is to dedicate a single PSTN address to an interoperation server. The interoperation server prompts the user for a foreign address; because it has full use of the voice channel, it can use speech recognition or digit codes to get the alphabetic characters and punctuation of a URI. The server then translates its target PSTN address to the entered foreign address, so it is performing a one-to-many translation. This situation is discussed further in Section 5.3.

An example of a many-to-one translator is a dynamic, single-address Network Address Translator (NAT). This is an interoperation server that translates many private, unregistered IP addresses to a single public, registered IP address representing the entire subnetwork served by the NAT (see also Section 6).

The signature of an interoperation feature is as follows. The constraints within the signature apply separately to each interoperation feature.

```
sig InteropFeature extends Feature { toDomain: Domain,
    exported, imported, remote, local: set Address,
    interTrans: exported some -> some imported } {
    domain != toDomain
```

```
exported in domain.space    && remote in exported
imported in toDomain.space && local  in imported
remote.interTrans = local                                    }
```

Four address sets play a role in interoperation. The sets *exported* and *imported* are in the address spaces of the *domain* and *toDomain,* respectively. They are the true domain and range of the feature's *interTrans* relation. This is indicated by the declaration of *interTrans,* whose keywords say that each element of *exported* corresponds to *some* element of *imported,* and each element of *imported* corresponds to *some* element of *exported,*

The subset *remote* of *exported* contains those addresses that trigger the feature because they point to agents in domains other than the *domain* of the feature. The set *local* is the relational image of *remote* under *interTrans.* Note that "local" is a relative term; for example, in Figure 2, server *s0* translates remote 15556667777 to `sip:alice@host1`, which is more local to BoxOS than to the PSTN, but only truly local to SIP.

An address is defined as *foreign* in a domain if it triggers some interoperation feature in that domain. An address is defined as *native* in a domain if it maps to a client in that domain. An unused address is neither foreign nor native.

A fact in the model says that if an address is foreign in a domain, it maps to some agent in that domain, and every agent it maps to is a server of an interoperation feature triggered by it. The constraint allows a domain to have more than one interoperation feature triggered by the same address.

The primary function of an interoperation server is described by this fact:

```
fact { all f: InteropFeature, g: Agent, h1: Hop |
   g in f.servers && h1.acceptor = g &&
   h1.domain = f.domain && h1.target in f.remote
=> (some l: Link, h2: Hop |
      l.agent = g && l.oneHop = h1 && l.anotherHop = h2 &&
      h2.domain = f.toDomain && h2.initiator = g &&
      h2.target in (h1.target).(f.interTrans) &&
      (h1.source in f.exported =>
         h2.source in (h1.source).(f.interTrans)) )          }
```

Note that the relational composition operator (dot) is also used for field selection in Alloy, because a field in a signature is really a function from objects of the signature type to field values. Note also that there is no distinction between an individual and a singleton set, nor between a set and a unary relation, so individuals can participate in relational composition.

The fact determines what an interoperation server must do if it is the acceptor of a triggering hop, meaning a hop in its feature's domain and with a target address in its feature's *remote* set. The server must initiate a corresponding hop in its *toDomain,* and link the two hops together. Note that if the source of the triggering hop is not in *exported,* it cannot be translated by *interTrans,* and the source of the initiated hop is unconstrained.

4   Requirements on Interoperation

Now we come to the most interesting question: What requirements should inter-operation satisfy? As mentioned in Section 1, this territory is largely unexplored.

One complication in formulating requirements is that a connection network can be modified by a wide variety of features, as mentioned in Section 3. Because the purpose of many features is to alter network behavior in ways that are observable by users (and presumably serve the needs of users), it seems almost impossible to find properties that should be satisfied regardless of which features are present.

For one example, many addresses used to request connections represent, not particular clients, but more abstract concepts [12]. An abstract address might represent a *group* of interchangeable clients, or it might represent a *person* who might be located near, and thus able to use, different devices (clients) at different times. A request for a connection to an abstract address is routed to a feature server that chooses a target client appropriate to the time or other circumstances, and does whatever else is necessary to redirect the request to that target. Thus features that support abstract addresses can make routing nondeterministic.

To understand interoperation, it seems necessary to isolate it from the effects of features that might interact with it, such as those supporting abstract addresses. Its requirements can then be based on the assumption that an address should point to at most one client.

In the absence of a classification of other network features that would tell us which ones can interact with interoperation, we simply eliminate them all with a fact stating that all features are interoperation features.

Other constraints on the model (not shown here) say that an interoperation server cannot do anything but perform its primary function as described in Section 3. A hop with an unused target address can be routed to an interoperation server, but the server cannot link it to any other hop.

As an incidental result of these restrictions, in any connection between two clients, one client is the initiator of its hop and the other client is the acceptor of its hop. This incidental result is employed to facilitate formalization of interoperation requirements.

The most obvious requirement is that an *address, domain* pair published as a way of reaching a client always reaches that client. The formalization of the *reachability requirement* says that if a client is requesting a connection to an address in a domain in another client's *knownAt* set, then the first client is connected to the second client through that request. As explained above, we can assume that the second client is the acceptor of its hop:

```
assert Reachability { all c: Connections,
    g1, g2: Client, h: Hop, a: Address, d: Domain |
      g1 = h.initiator && d = h.domain && a = h.target &&
      (a->d) in g2.knownAt
   => (some h2: Hop | g2 = h2.acceptor && (h->h2) in c.connected) }
```

The second requirement concerns the *returnability* of connections. It is desirable that a client accepting a connection should be able to take the source address it has received, request a second connection to it, and get a connection to the same client that initiated the first connection. Many telecommunication features for automatic callback rely on an assumption of returnability. Naturally, real callback features operate in a temporal context, so the second connection exists at a later time than the first connection.

The formalization of the *returnability requirement* postulates a connection between two clients, and identifies a return-request hop *h3* with the necessary relation to a hop *h2* from which it is derived. It then asserts that a complete return connection exists.

```
assert Returnability { all c: Connections,
    g1, g2: Client, h1, h2, h3: Hop |
    h1.initiator = g1 && h2.acceptor = g2 &&
    (h1->h2) in c.connected &&
    h3.initiator = g2 &&
    h3.domain = h2.domain && h3.target = h2.source
=> (some h4: Hop | h4.acceptor = g1 && (h3->h4) in c.connected) }
```

The third requirement considered in this paper is motivated by the fact that many real address spaces overlap. The *non-uniqueness requirement* means that an address for a client need not be globally unique. Formally, the requirement is satisfied if the following predicate can be instantiated in a model that satisfies the other requirements.

```
pred NonUniqueness (g1, g2: Client, d1, d2: Domain, a: Address) {
    (a->d1) in g1.knownAt && (a->d2) in g2.knownAt          }
```

5   Satisfying the Requirements

5.1   Methods of Reasoning

Satisfying the requirements entails adding constraints to the model, checking that the model with the additional constraints is still consistent and allows the expected useful instances, and proving that the model with the additional constraints satisfies the requirements.

The Alloy Analyzer finds instances of predicates, for example the non-uniqueness predicate above. Such instances show that a model is consistent, and that it does, indeed, allow the expected configurations and behavior.

The Alloy Analyzer also searches for counterexamples of assertions. Although the search is limited to instances of a bounded size, within those limits it is exhaustive. Every theorem and lemma was checked in this way by the Alloy Analyzer, and no counterexamples to them were found. With respect to the thoroughness of the search, there are two cases.

If an assertion refers to no recursive concepts, then the searchable instance set is satisfactorily large. A typical search space would allow up to 3 domains,

6 features, 10 agents, 6 addresses, 4 hops, and 3 links, which is large enough to include all conceivable counterexamples with three domains. For these assertions, Alloy analysis is more convincing than a manual proof (see Section 7).

If an assertion includes recursive concepts, on the other hand, the search bounds must be smaller. Also, Alloy analysis of this model has a fundamental limitation associated with recursive concepts (see Section 7). For these assertions analysis is less convincing, and is supplemented by manual inductive proofs.

5.2   Satisfying the Requirements with Generic Constraints

This section shows how to satisfy the requirements with a set of general-purpose constraints. While the constraints are plausible, they may be too stringent in some circumstances. Section 5.3 show a special case might be handled with looser constraints.

In Section 2, *connections* was introduced as a signature for a unique object containing only derived fields. A previously unmentioned field of *connections* is a ternary relation *reachedBy*, defined so that a *client, address, domain* triple is present if and only if the address in the domain can reach the client, either directly or through interoperation:

```
one sig Connections {... reachedBy: Client -> Address -> Domain } {
   ...
   all g: Client, a: Address, d: Domain | (a->d) in g.reachedBy iff
   ( g in a.(d.map) ||
     some f: InteropFeature |
       f.domain = d && a in f.remote &&
       some ( (a.(f.interTrans) -> f.toDomain) & g.reachedBy )
   )
                                                                      }
```

An address in a domain reaches the client directly if the address maps to the client in the domain. An address in a domain reaches the client indirectly if it triggers an interoperation feature in the domain, and if the feature can map it to an *address, domain* pair that reaches the client. An arrow is a Cartesian product operator, so *(a.(f.interTrans) → f.toDomain)* is the set of all pairs that can be produced by *f* from *a*. The last expression intersects this with *g.reachedBy*, and evaluates to *true* if the intersection is nonempty.[3]

The general-purpose strategy for guaranteeing reachability is straightforward. First, constraints ensure that if an *address, domain* pair can be used to reach a client, then routing to that pair is deterministic, and *always* reaches the client. The constraints for deterministic routing are:

```
fact Constraint1 { all a: Address, d: Domain |
   some ( a.(d.map) & Client ) => one a.(d.map) }
fact Constraint2 {
```

---

[3] The actual Alloy code for *reachedBy* has an additional constraint to guarantee that the value is a least fixed point.

```
    all f: InteropFeature, a: Address | lone a.(f.interTrans) }
fact Constraint3 { all a: Address, d: Domain |
    lone f: InteropFeature | f.domain = d && a in f.remote }
```

Constraint 1 says that if the agents that a domain maps an address to, intersected with the set of all clients, is nonempty (*some*), then the domain maps that address to exactly one agent. In other words, if an address maps to a client in a domain, it maps only to that client in that domain. Constraint 2 says that the address translation performed by an interoperation feature is a partial function (the quantifier *lone* means one or zero). Constraint 3 says that an address triggers at most one interoperation feature in a domain.

The second part of the strategy is to constrain a client's *reachedBy* set to contain its *knownAt* set:

```
fact Constraint4 {
    all c: Connections, g: Client | g.knownAt in g.(c.reachedBy) }
```

This relates its published addresses to network routing.

Constraints 1 through 3 are easy to apply, because they constrain individual domains. Constraint 4 is not localized, because of the recursive definition of *reachedBy*. This is not surprising, as reachability demands a routing path from any domain in which in which a client has a known address to a domain where the client is directly accessible.

The *reachedBy* set of a client is often larger than its *knownAt* set. For one example, a mobile device might be attached temporarily to a domain where its address is not published. For another example, a domain might provide connections among other domains without having any clients of its own, in which case there is no need to publish any of its addresses. When resource allocation changes, interoperation routes can change without any change observable to clients.

Returnability is much more difficult to satisfy. It depends on every previous constraint except Constraint 4. In addition, to begin with the obvious, the return address of a hop is its source address, so we need constraints to guarantee that the information in the source address is accurate and complete:

```
fact Constraint5 { all h: Hop | h.initiator in Client =>
    h.source in ((h.domain).map).(h.initiator) }
fact Constraint6 {
    all f: InteropFeature | f.domain.space in f.exported }
```

Constraint 5 says that if a hop is initiated by a client, its source must be an address of the client in the domain. Constraint 6 says that every interoperation feature's *exported* set must include the address space of its domain. This prevents the loss of source information during interoperation.

The core constraints for returnability require that each interoperation feature have a partner feature that provides its return path. The constraints are obvious, while the definition of an adequate partner feature is not:

```
pred PartnerTo (f1, f2: InteropFeature) {
    f1.domain = f2.toDomain && f1.toDomain = f2.domain &&
    (f1.imported - f1.local) in f2.remote                    }
fact Constraint7 { all f1: InteropFeature |
    some f2: InteropFeature | PartnerTo(f1,f2)               }
fact Constraint8 { all f1, f2: InteropFeature |
    PartnerTo(f1,f2) => (f1.interTrans).(f2.interTrans) in iden }
```

Constraints 7 and 8 say that each interoperation feature has a partner, and that
the *interTrans* relations of partners invert each other.

Figure 3 provides the intuition to understand the definition of partnership,
and how it supports returnability. This figure describes a network in which the
domains could be pictured in a horizontal line, with each domain interoperating
only with the domains on its immediate left and right.

The figure shows the address spaces of two neighboring domains, except for
unused addresses. Each address space is divided into native addresses of the
domain, addresses that encode native addresses of domains to the left (*Lnative*),
and addresses that encode native addresses of domains to the right (*Rnative*).
These two domains have interoperation features *f1* and *f2* that are partners of
each other.

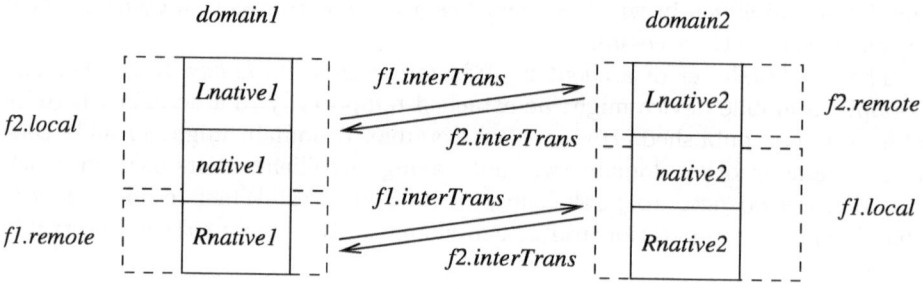

Fig. 3. Partner interoperation features

If a hop in *domain1* is routed to a server of *f1*, its target will be in *Rnative1*.
Its source will be in *Lnative1* or *native1*. Its source cannot be in *Rnative1* because
if it were, *the connection path would have passed through the native domain of the
target on its way to domain1*. Because routing is deterministic, the path would
have ended in the native domain of the target.

Because of Constraint 8, the partition of the address space of *domain1* corresponds to a partition of the address space of *domain2*. The hop target translates
to an address in *f1.local*. The hop source translates to an address in *f1.imported
- f1.local*. If *f2* satisfies *(f1.imported - f1.local) in f2.remote* then any hop in *do-
main2* targeting the translated source address will trigger *f2*, and will be linked
by *f2* to a continuing hop in *domain1*.

The actual proof of returnability encompasses all connection topologies, including rings and grids. Its essence is a generalization of the above argument,

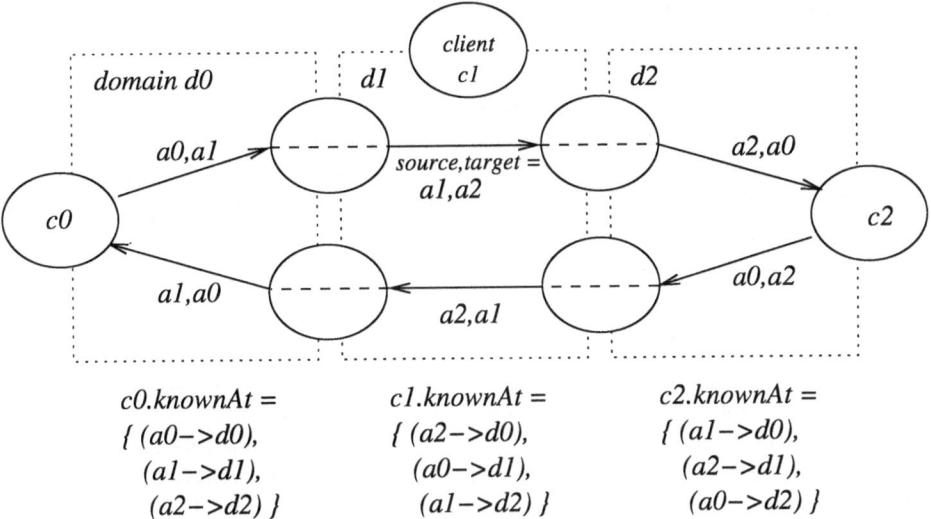

Fig. 4. The requirements do not depend on global uniqueness of addresses

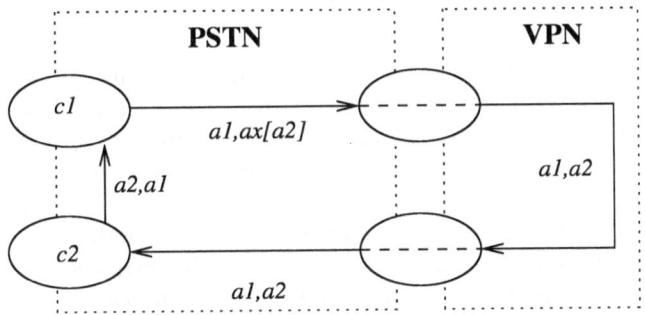

Fig. 5. Interoperation of a VPN with the PSTN

which can be summarized as follows: From any *address, domain* pair reaching a client, there is a unique path (sequence of domains) to the client. If an address *source* is the source of a hop in a *domain* then the path of the connection from its originating client to the hop is the reverse of the unique path from *source, domain* to the client. If the hop's *target* triggers a feature *f* in *domain*, and if *source* is in *f.remote*, then the unique path to the client of *target, domain* retraces at least one step of the path routing so far. This contradicts the assumption of deterministic routing, so *source* cannot be in *f.remote*.

The model instance in Figure 4, generated by the analyzer with all constraints in force, shows that the non-uniqueness requirement is satisfied. Each of the three clients is attached to one domain and has address *a0* in that domain. Yet each client is known in every domain. In the figure, a hop is labeled with a *source, target* pair of addresses. Either path could be the return path of the other.

Because returnability does not require Constraint 4, it can be satisfied even when reachability is not. A real-world example of this is a dual-mode cellphone[4] at a WiFi hotspot, placing voice-over-IP calls. If the WiFi domain has no cooperative agreement with the device's home cellular domain, then it does not inform the home cellular domain of the device's presence at the WiFi hotspot. In this case there is no forwarding from its known address in the home cellular domain to its temporary WiFi address, and the device is not reachable. At the same time, if the constraints for returnability are satisfied, the device's outgoing calls will be returnable at the temporary address until it leaves the WiFi hotspot.

5.3   A Special Case

Figure 5 shows a Virtual Private Network (VPN) interoperating with the PSTN. The picture is not geographically accurate, as the two clients are on opposite coasts of the U.S. The VPN belongs to a corporation which provides it so employees can make long-distance business calls at low cost. PSTN hops to and from the interoperation servers are local, while VPN hops are long-distance.

In the figure, client $c1$ at PSTN address $a1$ is using access address ax to reach the VPN gateway, then entering address $a2$ using touch tones on the voice channel. The gateway translates ax to $a2$ and makes the long-distance connection to client $c2$ at PSTN address $a2$. The figure also shows the connection when $c2$ (not an employee of the VPN owner) returns the call to $c1$.

We wish to know if this network satisfies the requirements, and the results in the previous section are not suitable. As in an example in Section 3, address translation from the PSTN to the VPN is one-to-many, violating Constraint 1.

We can create a formal model that is closer to the truth by extending the PSTN address space to include pairs of numbers, where the first number is dialed, and the optional second number is entered through touch tones. Then interoperation translation from the PSTN to the VPN projects a pair of numbers $ax[an]$ onto its second number an, and is a function. But now Constraint 8 is violated, because interoperation translation applied to number pairs is not invertible.

Fortunately, there is additional information that can be brought to bear: number pairs are never used as source addresses. Because the basic Alloy model is already available, it is quick work to try a version in which the *targetOnly* addresses of a domain are never used as source addresses in the domain, and Constraint 8 does not apply to them.

This version does not satisfy returnability, and examination of a counterexample shows why. The interoperation feature $f1$ from the PSTN to the VPN translates both $a2$ and the *targetOnly* address $ax[a2]$ to $a2$. The address $a2$ must be in the $f2.remote$ set of its partner $f2$, but it is not, because $ax[a2]$ is in $f1.remote$, and therefore $a2$ is in $f1.local$. The solution is to remove the influence of the *targetOnly* address $ax[a2]$ from the computation of the partnership constraint on $f2.remote$.

---

[4] A dual-mode cellphone is a WiFi device as well as a cellphone.

With the definition of partnership modified appropriately, analysis shows quickly and convincingly that returnability is satisfied for this network. The *reachedBy* set of client *c2* consists of *(a2→PSTN)*, *(a2→VPN)*, and *(ax[a2]→PSTN)*.

6   Related Work

The most prominent address-related networking problem is understanding reachability at the level of Internet routing, which is "staggeringly complex" [6]. At this level of abstraction, routing information is distributed dynamically by the policy-driven Border Gateway Protocol (BGP) and other local protocols. A path from one point to another includes multiple hops within the same domain. There are packet filters to block packets, and packet transformers to modify them.

While it does not seem feasible to capture all of this in an Alloy model, important aspects of it do seem approachable. For example, Feamster and Balakrishnan study routing only in steady BGP states, taking the position that important requirements can be violated by steady states as well as transient states [6].

The model presented here is valid for packet routing in the sense that only connection requests are really manipulated, and a connection request is equivalent to a packet. In [11] reachability is defined directly for packet routing: for any pair of points, there is a reachable set containing the packets that can travel from the first to the second point. It would be interesting to see how an Alloy model based on this definition compares to the present one. The goal of [11] is polynomial computation of reachable sets in a stable configuration of a specific network, taking into account routing information, packet filters, and packet transformations.

It seems clear that logic-based modeling and analysis has something to contribute to these efforts. The proofs in [6] are informal, yet my experience suggests that network routing has subtleties that only the precision of a completely formal model is likely to expose. The algorithm in [11] might be made even more useful if it were possible to explore invariant relationships among various architectural constraints. Certainly Feamster argues for continuing, broad-spectrum research on correctness and verification of network routing [5].

It is well-known that NATs cause problems in the Internet by allowing addresses that are not globally unique. Currently the worst problems are dynamic and protocol-specific [2]: How does a NAT know that a protocol is finished using an address, so that it can re-use the address while maintaining a one-to-one interoperation translation? How does a NAT find and apply interoperation translation to addresses embedded in the payloads of packets? Nevertheless, general principles of addressing and interoperation should be a sanity check on all specific proposals.

7   Evaluation and Future Work

As a modeling language, Alloy is very pleasant to use. The combination of relational logic and predicate logic is a powerful one. Although Alloy is first-order, quantification over objects with relation-valued fields provides many of the benefits of a second-order language. Typing is strong but avoids unnecessary distinctions. The syntax is highly streamlined, with a few operators applied uniformly in many contexts to do many jobs. The extended quantifier vocabulary *no, lone, one, some* and *all* provides major shortcuts in writing logical and relational expressions. The complete model is 190 lines of Alloy code.

Analysis by model enumeration is often exhilarating and illuminating, and equally often tedious and frustrating. The Alloy team is working on features and capabilities in the Analyzer that will reduce tedium and frustration. Many of them are already installed, but because they are not yet documented, they are not really available to most users.

Recursion in the definition of *reachedBy* corresponds, in a network, to extending a connection path with additional hops. If the routing data contains a closed loop, the effect on routing will be a path that is extended indefinitely (until terminated by some external mechanism).

Alloy analysis of this model cannot reveal a problem of this kind. Any analysis will impose a maximum length on paths. If a model instance contained a request for a connection to an address that caused such a problem, the connection could not be completed according to the model's constraints within the maximum path length. Thus there cannot be a model instance containing such a request, and its absence tells us nothing about whether there is a routing problem of this kind.

Despite this limitation, the research was undertaken in an analyze-first-prove-last style, which worked fairly well. Alloy's push-button analysis was extremely helpful in building intuition, encouraging experimentation, and finding errors at all levels. It was also a huge reassurance that a continually evolving model was improving as well as changing. The entire experience causes me to trust bounded model enumeration more than manual proof, when enumeration is known to be reasonably comprehensive or at least representative.

All the discoveries were made using analysis alone—proofs served only to confirm and explain. Considering the most difficult result in this paper, which is the satisfaction of returnability, this had good and bad sides. On the good side, experimentation gave me a hypothesis and the confidence to try to prove it. On the bad side, I did not really understand why the hypothesis worked until I proved it, although I believed that I understood it before.

Of course, this is not a controlled experiment. It is likely that a practitioner of a prove-first-analyze-last style would find that proof attempts detect most errors. And a person who was able to find an optimal interleaving of the two techniques, particularly with the help of an automated proof checker, would have the best results of all. Above all, it is important to remember that all of these tools are aids to thought, and none of them is a substitute for it.

Experience suggests that Alloy models with many more object types and facts could be written and read easily. As model enumeration became less convincing, proof could take a larger role. This is fortunate, because there is an unlimited supply of unanswered questions about networking. Section 6 hints at the richness of packet routing at the resource level. At the level of features and services, [12] shows how to manage interactions among features that manipulate abstract addresses. The results are limited, however, by the assumption that every address is globally unique. It would be valuable to have a single model combining interoperation features, which remove the limitation, with abstract-address features.

Other areas of networking in which addresses have semantics and are manipulated include directory lookup (including DNS and a growing number of protocol-specific Internet name spaces), security (including uses of self-authenticating names and trusted domains), and mobility [9]. Experience shows that almost any two functions that translate addresses can interact, so the likelihood of address-related problems in these areas is high.

References

1. G. W. Bond, E. Cheung, K. H. Purdy, P. Zave, and J. C. Ramming. An open architecture for next-generation telecommunication services. *ACM Transactions on Internet Technology*, 4(1):83–123, February 2004.
2. R. Bush and K. Moore. NATs are evil—Well, maybe just bad for you. https:// rip.psg.com/ ~randy/ 040226.apnic-nats.pdf, 2004.
3. The Distributed Feature Composition (DFC) Web site. http:// www.research. att.com/projects/dfc.
4. P. Faltstrom and G. Huston. A survey of Internet identities. Internet Architecture Board, draft-iab-identities-00.txt, 2004.
5. N. Feamster. Practical verification techniques for wide-area routing. In *Proceedings of the ACM SIGCOMM Workshop on Hot Topics in Networks*, 2003.
6. N. Feamster and H. Balakrishnan. Towards a logic for wide-area internet routing. In *Proceedings of the ACM SIGCOMM Workshop on Future Directions in Network Architecture*, 2003.
7. D. Jackson. Automating first-order relational logic. In *Proceedings of the Eighth ACM SIGSOFT International Symposium on the Foundations of Software Engineering*, pages 130–139. ACM, 2000.
8. D. Jackson, I. Shlyakhter, and M. Sridharan. A micromodularity mechanism. In *Proceedings of the Ninth ACM SIGSOFT International Symposium on the Foundations of Software Engineering*, pages 62–73. ACM, 2001.
9. G.-C. Roman, G. P. Picco, and A. L. Murphy. Software engineering for mobility: A roadmap. In *Proceedings of the Twenty-second International Conference on Software Engineering*, pages 241–258. IEEE Computer Society, June 2000.
10. J. Rosenberg, H. Schulzrinne, G. Camarillo, A. Johnston, J. Peterson, R. Sparks, M. Handley, and E. Schooler. SIP: Session Initiation Protocol. IETF Network Working Group Request for Comments 3261, 2002.
11. G. Xie, J. Zhan, D. A. Maltz, H. Zhang, A. Greenberg, G. Hjalmtysson, and J. Rexford. On static reachability analysis of IP networks. Technical report, AT&T Research, 2004.
12. P. Zave. Address translation in telecommunication features. *ACM Transactions on Software Engineering and Methodology*, 13(1):1–36, January 2004.

An Approach to Unfolding Asynchronous Communication Protocols

Yu Lei[1] and S. Purushothaman Iyer[2]

[1] Department of Computer Science and Engineering,
University of Texas at Arlington, Arlington, TX 76019
ylei@cse.uta.edu
[2] Department of Computer Science,
North Carolina State University, Raleigh, NC 27695
purush@csc.ncsu.edu

Abstract. We present an approach to directly unfold asynchronous communication protocols that are modeled as a group of Extended Finite State Machines (EFSMs) communicating through shared message queues. A novel aspect of our approach is that we reduce the redundancy in representing the states of message queues by storing individual messages separately in our unfolding representation. Our approach can also take advantage of the compositional nature of these protocols to minimize the size of a complete finite prefix of their potentially infinite unfoldings. Our empirical results indicate that our approach can produce very compact state space representations.

Keywords: Software Verification, State Space Search, Unfolding, EFSM.

1 Introduction

One common strategy to analyze the behavior of communication protocols is to search through their state space. This strategy can be easily automated. However, it suffers from the state explosion problem, i.e., the number of states to be searched can be enormous for many protocols. One approach to dealing with this problem is unfolding, which involves transforming a protocol modeled as a Petri net to an acyclic net that preserves the behavior of the original net. Since the acyclic net is simpler in structure, it is amenable to protocol analysis. In addition, the acyclic net preserves the partial order semantics, i.e., allowing independent events to be left unordered. This avoids a major source of state explosion due to interleaving of independent events. As a result, unfolding can produce a very compact state space representation.

A major challenge with unfolding is that a naive unfolding process will produce an infinite representation for protocols that have a finite state space but exhibit infinite behaviors. McMillan [1] described an algorithm to construct a complete finite prefix of a potentially infinite unfolding of a Petri net by identifying nodes of the acyclic net, called *cut-off points*, where unfolding can be

J.S. Fitzgerald, I.J. Hayes, and A. Tarlecki (Eds.): FM 2005, LNCS 3582, pp. 334–349, 2005.

terminated while still representing all the reachable states of the original net. McMillan's algorithm was later improved by Esparza et al. [2], where a new condition to determine cut-off points was defined. The new condition allows unfolding to be terminated earlier, which results in a smaller complete finite prefix. In [3], Esparza and Romer provided another new condition for determining cut-off points for unfolding synchronous transition systems. The new condition takes advantage of the compositional nature of these systems to further reduce the size of their complete finite prefixes.

In this paper we describe an approach to unfolding asynchronous communication protocols. These protocols consist of processes that interact with each other by sending and receiving messages through shared queues. Existing approaches can be applied by first modeling these protocols as a Petri net and then unfold the net. However, protocols are typically described at a higher level of abstraction than Petri net. In our approach, we model these protocols as a group of communicating Extended Finite State Machines (EFSMs), and then directly unfold them, i.e., without any intermediate transformation to a Petri net. Directly working with EFSMs allows us to exploit the full power of variables and arithmetic/logic expressions at the specification level. A novel aspect of our approach is that in our unfolding representation, we store individual messages separately while still preserving the FIFO semantics of shared queues. This implicit encoding of message queues reduces the redundancy in representing the states of these queues. Moreover, our approach can take advantage of the compositional nature of these protocols to minimize the size of their complete finite prefix. As a proof-of-concept, we have developed a prototype tool and conducted several case studies. The empirical results indicate that our approach can produce very compact state space representations.

Road map: Section 2 introduces the EFSM model. Section 3 defines our unfolding representation, namely, labeled occurrence net. Section 4 presents our unfolding algorithm. Section 5 discusses how to construct a complete finite prefix. Section 6 reports our case studies. Section 7 provides the concluding remarks.

2   The EFSM Model

The EFSM model is a widely used notation for describing the behavior of protocols. Informally, an EFSM is a finite state machine extended with the use of a set V of (local) variables. The extension allows us to add a guard and a computation block to each transition. We will interpret V over a finite set of integers I to simplify the formalism.

Definition 1. *An extended finite state machine W over V and I is a 5-tuple $(S, Q, s_0, \gamma_0, \delta)$, where*

- *S is a finite set of control states.*
- *Q is a finite set of bounded queues.*
- *$s_0 \in S$ is the initial control state.*
- *$\gamma_0 : V \to I$ is the initial assignment of values to variables.*

- δ *is a set of transitions such that for each transition* t, *the source control state* $head(t) \in S$ *and target control state* $tail(t) \in S$ *are defined. Additionally, every transition* t *should have at least one of the following components:*
  - *a boolean expression (i.e., a guard)* $pred(t)$ *over* V *and* I.
  - *a computational block* $comp(t)$ *consisting of a sequence of assignment statements, which involves boolean and/or arithmetic expressions over* V *and* I.
  - *a send operation* $(q!e)$ *or a receive operation* $(q?x)$, *where* $q \in Q$, e *is a boolean and/or arithmetic expression over* V *and* I, *and* $x \in V$. *We will refer to* q *as* $que(t)$.

A transition t is called a silent transition if t does not contain a send or receive operation, a send transition if t contains a send operation, and a receive transition if t contains a receive operation. In the following, we will abbreviate a transition t as $s \xrightarrow{p,A,c} s'$ where $s = head(t)$, $s' = tail(t)$, $p = pred(t)$, $A = comp(t)$, and c is a send or receive operation. Furthermore, we will treat $p : (V \to I) \to bool$ and $A : (V \to I) \to (V \to I)$ as functions that denote the semantics of the predicate and the computational block. That is, p maps an assignment of V to a boolean value, and A maps one assignment of V to another. Since the valuation function $\gamma : V \to I$ is a finite function, we will write $\gamma[x \mapsto v]$ as a function which equals γ on all variables other than x, where it equals v.

We model an asynchronous communication protocol as an EFSM system consisting of a group of EFSMs $W_1, W_2, \ldots,$ and W_n. These EFSMs communicate by sending and receiving messages through shared queues. We assume that a queue is unidirectional and can be accessed by one sender and one receiver. To simplify the notations, we also assume that these EFSMs are fully connected, i.e., given two EFSMs W_i and W_j, there exists a queue q_{ij} that has W_i as its sender and W_j as its receiver and a queue q_{ji} which has W_j as its sender and W_i as its receiver.

Let $\mathcal{W} = (W_1, W_2, \ldots, W_n)$ be an EFSM system. We will explain the semantics of $\mathcal{W}$ in terms of its global states and transitions. We first define a local state of a EFSM $W = (S, Q, s_0, \gamma_0, \delta)$ as a pair $l = (s, \gamma)$, where $s \in S$ is a control state of W and $\gamma : V \to I$ is a valuation function. A global state of $\mathcal{W}$ is a tuple $g = (l_1, \ldots, l_n; w_{12}, w_{13}, \ldots, w_{n(n-1)})$, where l_i is the local state of W_i, $1 \le i \le n$, and w_{ij} denotes the content of the message queue q_{ij}, where $1 \le i, j \le n$, $i \ne j$. The initial global state g_0 of $\mathcal{W}$ contains the initial local state $l_{i0} = (s_{i0}, \gamma_{i0})$ for each EFSM W_i and $w_{ij} = \varepsilon$ for all $1 \le i, j \le n$, $i \ne j$, where ε represents an empty queue.

Let $t = head(t) \xrightarrow{p,A,c} tail(t)$ be a transition of a participating EFSM W. Define t to be *open* at a local state $l = (s, \gamma)$ of W provided that (1) $s = head(t)$; and (2) $p(\gamma) = true$. Furthermore, let g be a global state of $\mathcal{W}$ and l be the local state of W at g. Then, a send or silent transition t of W is *enabled* at g if t is open at l. A receive transition t of W is *enabled* at g if t is open at l, and $que(t)$ is not empty at g.

Let t be a transition of an EFSM W_i that is enabled at a global state $g = (l_1, \ldots, l_n; w_{12}, \ldots, w_{n(n-1)})$ of $\mathcal{W}$. Let $l_i = (s, \gamma)$ be the local state of W_i at *g*. Let · be the normal concatenation operator. We define a global transition, $g \overset{t}{\Rightarrow} g'$, where $g' = (l_1, \ldots, l_{i-1}, l'_i, l_{i+1}, \ldots, l_n; w'_{12}, \ldots, w'_{n(n-1)})$, as follows:

- if $t = s \xrightarrow{p,A} s'$ is a silent transition, then $l'_i = (s', A(\gamma))$, and $\forall 1 \leq u, v \leq n, u \neq v, w'_{uv} = w_{uv}$.
- if $t = s \xrightarrow{p,A,q_{ij}!e} s'$ is a send transition, then $l'_i = (s', A(\gamma))$, and $\forall 1 \leq u, v \leq n, u \neq v, w'_{uv} = w_{uv}$, except that $w'_{ij} = w_{ij} \cdot \gamma(e)$, where $\gamma(e)$ is the result of evaluating e in the environment of γ.
- if $t = s \xrightarrow{g,A,q_{ji}?x} s'$ is a receive transition, and m is the message at the front of q_{ji}, then $l'_i = (s', \gamma')$, where $\gamma' = A(\gamma[x \mapsto m])$, i.e., m is bound to x before the evaluation of A, and $\forall 1 \leq u, v \leq n, u \neq v, w'_{uv} = w_{uv}$, except that $m \cdot w'_{ji} = w_{ji}$, i.e., v is removed from q_{ji}.

Let $\omega = t_1 t_2 \ldots t_m$ be a sequence of transitions. ω is an enabled transition sequence at a global state g if there exists a sequence of states $g = g_0, g_1, \ldots,$ and $g_m = g'$ such that t_i is enabled at g_{i-1} and $g_{i-1} \overset{t_i}{\Rightarrow} g_i$, where $1 \leq i \leq m$. Furthermore, we will use , $g \overset{\omega}{\Rightarrow} * g'$ to denote that ω is enabled at g and that its execution results in g'. A global state g is a reachable state of an EFSM system $\mathcal{W}$ if there exists a transition sequence ω such that $g_0 \overset{\omega}{\Rightarrow} * g$, where g_0 is the initial global state of $\mathcal{W}$.

Figure 1 shows an example EFSM system that models a simplified version of the alternating bit protocol, where W_1 is the sender process and W_2 the receiver process. Between W_1 and W_2 are two message queues q_{12} (from W_1 to W_2) and q_{21} (from W_2 to W_1). The initial states of W_1 and W_2 are $s_{1,1}$ and $s_{2,1}$. The two variables s and r, whose initial values are 0, represent the sequence and acknowledgment number, respectively. The two numbers must match before W_1 (or W_2) sends (or receives) the next message. Note that $t_{1,2}$ is used to simulate data corruption, and $t_{2,3}$ sends a negative acknowledgment.

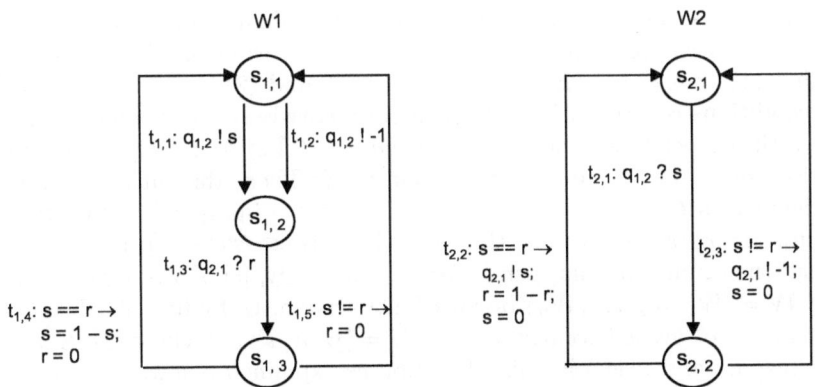

Fig. 1. An example EFSM system

3   Labeled Occurrence Net

Our unfolding representation is a restricted form of Petri net called an occurrence net. A Petri net, or simply a net, is a tuple (P, T, F), where P is a set of places and T is a set of transitions such that $P \cap T = \emptyset$, and $F \subseteq (P \times T) \cup (T \times P)$ is the flow relation. Places and transitions are also generically called nodes. The preset of a node x, denoted as $^\bullet x$, is $\{y \in P \cup T | (y, x) \in F\}$. The postset of x, denoted as $x^\bullet$, is $\{y \in P \cup T | (x, y) \in F\}$. The notions of preset and postset can be naturally extended to a set of nodes.

Let (P, T, F) be a net and x_1 and x_2 be two nodes in $P \cup T$. Let F^* be the reflexive and transitive closure of F. The nodes x_1 and x_2 are said to be in conflict, denoted as $x_1 \# x_2$, if there exist distinct transitions t'_1 and t'_2 such that $^\bullet t'_1 \cap {}^\bullet t'_2 \neq \emptyset$, $(t'_1, x_1) \in F^*$ and $(t'_2, x_2) \in F^*$. Informally, x_1 and x_2 are in conflict if there exist two paths leading to x_1 and x_2 which start at the same place and immediately branch off. If x is in conflict with itself, then x is said to be in self-conflict.

An occurrence net is a Petri net $N = (B, E, F)$ that satisfies the following constraints:

- Every place has at most one input transition, i.e., for every $b \in B$, $|^\bullet b| \leq 1$;
- F has no cycles, i.e., the transitive closure of F is a partial order;
- No element in E is in self-conflict.

The elements of B and E are called *conditions* and *events*, respectively. We will refer to the partial order induced by the transitive closure of F as the causal order of N, denoted as $<$. Two nodes x_1 and x_2 are said to be concurrent, written $x_1 \| x_2$, provided neither $x_1 < x_2$ nor $x_2 < x_1$ nor $x_1 \# x_2$.

Occurrence nets can be infinite. We will restrict ourselves to those that are well-founded, i.e., every node is finitely preceded, and in which every event has at least one input condition. Note that this restriction implies the existence of *minimal* conditions, i.e., conditions with no input events.

Let $N = (B, E, F)$ be an occurrence net. A configuration C of N is a set of events that are causally closed and conflict free. Formally, C is a subset of E such that (1) $\forall e \in C, e' \in E : e' < e \implies e' \in C$; and (2) $\forall e, e' \in C : \neg(e \# e')$. A set of conditions is a *co-set* if its elements are pairwisely concurrent. A maximal co-set with respect to set inclusion is called a *cut*. Let $Min(N)$ be the minimal conditions of N. Let C be a configuration of N. Then, the cut associated with C is defined as $Cut(C) = (Min(N) \cup C^\bullet) \setminus {}^\bullet C$. Finally, we define the local configuration $[e]$ of event e such that $[e] = \{e\} \cup \{e' \in E | e' < e\}$, i.e., $[e]$ includes e and all the events that happen before e. Obviously, $[e]$ is a configuration.

Let $\mathcal{W} = (W_1, W_2, \ldots, W_n)$ be an EFSM system. Unfolding of $\mathcal{W}$ consists of building a set of *labeled occurrence nets* $\Sigma = (B, E, F; L)$, where (B, E, F) is an occurrence net and L is a labeling function as explained below:

- A condition c of Σ is labeled by a local state l of an EFSM W_i, i.e., $L(c) = l$, or a message m sent by W_i, i.e., $L(c) = m$. In the former case, c is called a control condition. In the latter case, c is called a message condition. In both

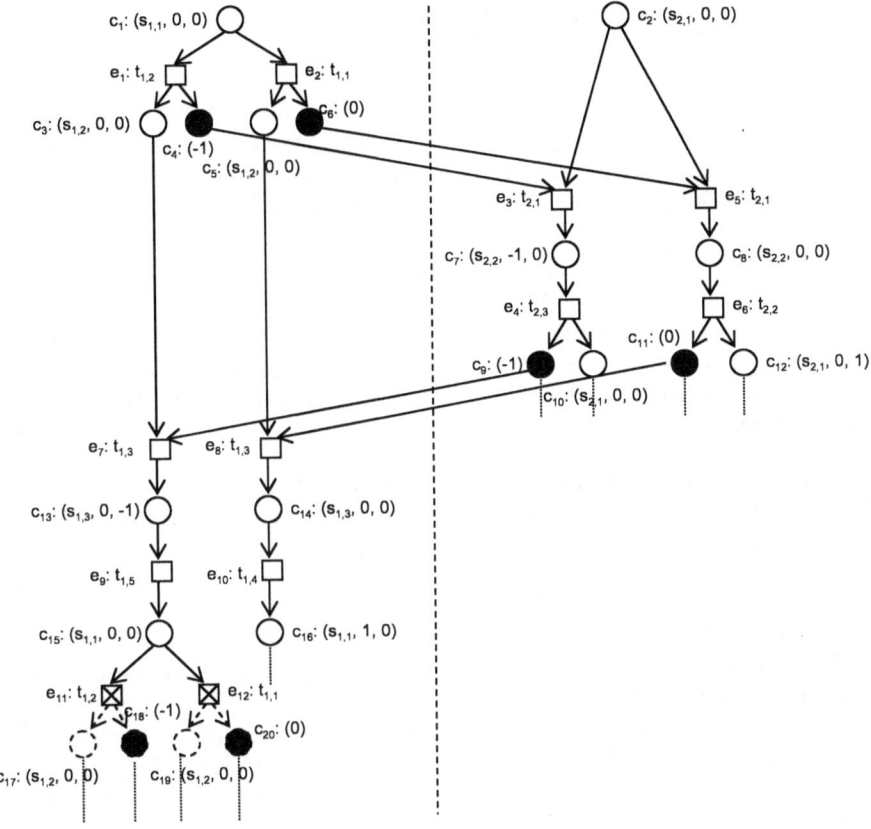

Fig. 2. An example labeled occurrence net

cases, we refer to W_i as $owner(c)$. Also, for a message condition c, we use $que(c)$ to denote the queue to which m is sent.

- An event e of Σ is labeled by a transition t of an EFSM W_i, i.e., $L(e) = t$. If t is a silent/send/receive transition, e is called a silent/send/receive event. We also refer to W_i as $owner(e)$ and $que(t)$ as $que(e)$.

Figure 2 shows a labeled occurrence net of the EFSM system in Figure 1. Each circle represents a condition; each box represents an event. A control condition (empty circle) is labeled with a local state of W_1 or W_2, which is in the form of $(control\_state, s, r)$. A message condition (solid circle) is labeled with its message value. Note that on the left side of the dashed line are conditions/events of W_1, and on the right side are those of W_2.

To illustrate some concepts introduced earlier, consider events e_1 and e_7, which are in conflict because $^\bullet e_1 \cap {}^\bullet e_2 = \{c_1\}$, and $(e_1, e_1) \in F^*$ and $(e_2, e_7) \in F^*$. Also $\{e_1, e_3, e_4\}$ is a configuration, say C, with $Cut(C) = \{c_3, c_9, c_{10}\}$. Note that C is also the local configuration of e_4, i.e., $[e_4] = C$.

4   Unfolding an EFSM System

In this section we describe an approach to directly unfolding an EFSM system. Our approach is iterative: it builds a sequence of labeled occurrence nets that preserve the semantics of a given EFSM system. We call those occurrence nets as branching processes of the given system. In the following, we first define the notion of branching process, and then present our unfolding algorithm.

We start with the notion of a *synchronizable pair*. Intuitively a synchronizable pair consists of a control condition cc and a message condition mc such that there exists at least one receive transition that is open at the local state labeling cc and can receive the message labeling mc. We wish to stress that the notion of a synchronizable pair is the key to enforce the FIFO semantics of shared queues. Note that these queues are not explicitly represented in our unfolding representation.

Definition 2. *Let $\mathcal{W}$ be an EFSM system and Σ a labeled occurrence net of $\mathcal{W}$. Let cc be a control condition and mc be a message condition of Σ. Let e_c and e_m be the input event of cc and mc, respectively. Then $p = (cc, mc)$ is a synchronizable pair in Σ provided that the following conditions are satisfied:*

- *cc and mc are concurrent, i.e., $cc \parallel mc$;*
- *There exists a receive transition t that is open at local state $L(cc)$ and $que(t) = que(mc)$; and*
- *Let mc' be a message condition such that $owner(mc') = owner(mc)$ and $que(mc') = que(mc)$. Let e'_m be the input event of mc'. If $e'_m < e_m$, there must exist a (receive) event e'_c with $owner(e'_c) = owner(e_c)$ such that $mc' \in {}^\bullet e'_c$ and $e'_c = e_c$ or $e'_c < e_c$.*

The third condition in the definition deserves some explanation. Informally, mc' represents a message condition whose message would have been placed before the message of mc in the same queue if the queue were explicitly represented, and e'_c represents the event that consumes the message of mc'. The condition demands that all the messages sent before mc must have already been consumed before cc is reached, which enforces the FIFO semantics of message queues.

Now we are able to make the following observations about evaluating a transition t that is open at the local state l labeling a control condition cc.

- If t is a send or silent transition, then t can be evaluated at l locally, i.e., its execution only requires the information encoded at l.
- If t is a receive transition, then for each message condition mc with $que(mc) = que(t)$ such that (cc, mc) forms a synchronizable pair, we can evaluate t at l with t receiving the message of mc.

Now we are ready to define the notion of branching process. We will encode a condition c as (α, e), where α is the local state or message labeling c and e the input event of c if exists or a special symbol $\perp$ otherwise . Similarly, we will encode an event e as (t, β), where t is the transition labeling e and β

the preset of e. Note that these notations encode the flow relation F and the labeling function L implicitly. Therefore, we can encode a labeled occurrence net $(B, E, F; L)$ simply as a pair (B, E).

Definition 3. *Let $\mathcal{W} = (W_1, \ldots, W_n)$ be an EFSM system. Let $g_0 = (l_{01}, \ldots, l_{0n};$ $\epsilon, \ldots, \epsilon)$ be the initial global state of $\mathcal{W}$. Then, the set of branching processes of $\mathcal{W}$ are a set of labeled occurrence nets that are inductively defined as follows:*

- *$(\{(l_{01}, \perp), \ldots, (l_{0n}, \perp)\}, \emptyset)$ is a branching process of $\mathcal{W}$;*
- *Let (B, E) be a branching process of $\mathcal{W}$. Let t be a transition with $owner(t) = W_i$. We consider three cases: (1) t is an internal transition; (2) t is a send transition; (3) t is a receive transition.*
  - *Case (1): If there exists a control condition $cc = (l, e) \in B$ such that t is open at l, $(B \cup \{(l', e')\}, E \cup \{e'\})$ is a branching process of $\mathcal{W}$, where l' is the local state reached by W_i after evaluating t at l and $e' = (t, \{cc\})$.*
  - *Case (2): If there exists a control condition $cc = (l, e) \in B$ such that t is open at l, $(B \cup \{(l', e'), (m, e')\}, E \cup \{e'\})$ is a branching process of $\mathcal{W}$, where l' is the local state reached by W_i after evaluating t at l, m is the message sent by t and $e' = (t, \{cc\})$, .*
  - *Case (3): If there exists a control condition $cc = (l, e_c) \in B$ and a message condition $mc = (m, e_m) \in B$ such that t is open at l and (cc, mc) is a synchronizable pair, $(B \cup \{(l', e')\}, E \cup \{e'\})$ is a branching process of $\mathcal{W}$, where l' is the local state reached by W_i after evaluating t at l with m and $e' = (t, \{cc, mc\})$.*

If we define union of branching processes component-wise on conditions and events, then branching processes of $\mathcal{W}$ are closed under union. Therefore, there exists a unique maximal branching process of $\mathcal{W}$, which is called the unfolding of $\mathcal{W}$. Note that the labeled occurrence net in Figure 2 is a branching process of the example EFSM system in Figure 1.

Next we show that a branching process of an EFSM system preserves the semantics of the system.

Proposition 1. *Let $\Sigma = (B, E, F; L)$ be a branching process of an EFSM system $\mathcal{W}$. Let e_1 and e_2 be any two events such that $owner(e_1) = owner(e_2)$. Then, e_1 and e_2 cannot be concurrent.*

Intuitively, the above proposition means that there is no parallelism within a single EFSM.

Proposition 2. *Let $\mathcal{W} = (W_1, W_2, \ldots, W_n)$ be an EFSM system. Let Σ be a branching process of $\mathcal{W}$. Let C be a configuration of Σ. Then, $\forall 1 \leq i \leq n$, there is exactly one (control) condition $c_i \in Cut(C)$ such that $L(c_i)$ is a local state of W_i.*

Intuitively, the above proposition means that every cut contains exactly one control condition from each EFSM.

Definition 4. *Let* $\mathcal{W} = (W_1, W_2, \ldots, W_n)$ *be an EFSM system. Let* Σ *be a branching process of* $\mathcal{W}$*. For any configuration* C *of* Σ*, define* $GState(C) = (l_1, \ldots, l_n; w_{12}, \ldots w_{n(n-1)})$*, where*

- l_i *is the label of a control condition* cc_i *in* $Cut(C)$*.*
- w_{ij}*, for* $1 \le i, j \le n$ *and* $i \ne j$*, is a sequence of messages* $m_1 \cdot \ldots \cdot m_{n_{ij}}$ *such that there are exactly* n_{ij} *message conditions* $mc_1, \ldots mc_{n_{ij}}$ *in* $Cut(C)$*, where* $mc_k = (m_k, e_k)$*,* $1 \le k \le n_{ij}$*, such that (a) for* $1 \le k \le n_{ij}$*,* $que(m_k) = q_{ij}$*; and (b)* $1 \le k_1 < k_2 \le n_{ij}$*,* $e_{k_1} < e_{k_2}$*.*

The above definition, which is well-defined due to Propositions 1 and 2, indicates that every configuration of a branching process defines a global state. For example, as mentioned earlier, $C = \{e_1, e_3, e_4\}$ is a configuration with $Cut(C) = \{c_3, c_9, c_{10}\}$ in Figure 2. Then, $GState(C) = ((s_{1,2}, 0, 0), (s_{2,1}, 0, 0); \epsilon, -1)$.

Theorem 1. *let* $\mathcal{W}$ *be an EFSM system.*

- *Let* $\Sigma = (B, E, F; L)$ *be a branching process of* $\mathcal{W}$*. For every configuration* C *of* Σ *there exists a reachable global state* g *of* $\mathcal{W}$ *so that* $GState(C) = g$*.*
- *Let* $\Sigma = (B, E, F; L)$ *be the unfolding of* $\mathcal{W}$*. For every reachable global state* g *of* $\mathcal{W}$ *there exists a configuration* C *of* Σ *so that* $GState(C) = g$*.*

Proof. Part I: This part follows from the fact that events and conditions are added into a branching process by evaluating transitions and each transition is evaluated in a way that preserves the semantics of $\mathcal{W}$.

Part II: This part can be easily proved by induction on the length of a transition sequence that reaches g from the initial state of $\mathcal{W}$, considering that any enabled transition can be evaluated to create a new branching process.

Algorithm 1 shows our unfolding algorithm, which takes as input an EFSM system $\mathcal{W}$ and produces the unfolding Σ of $\mathcal{W}$. The algorithm is iterative: It starts with the initial branching process and creates a new branching process at each iteration by adding new events into the branching process created at the previous iteration. In the algorithm, V is a queue used to keep the conditions that are yet to be expanded. In each iteration, we pull off a condition c from V. If $c = (l, e)$ is a control condition, we evaluate all the transitions that are open at l, as indicated in Definition 3. If $c = (m, e)$ is a message condition, we find control conditions (l, e') that can form a synchronizable pair with c and then evaluate all the transitions that are open at l.

The labeled occurrence net in Figure 2 is a branching process of $\mathcal{W}$ constructed by algorithm *Unfold*. We use the first few steps to illustrate the procedure. The initial branching process consists of conditions c_1 and c_2, which are kept in V. Then, we pull off c_1 from V. There are two transitions, namely, $t_{1,1}$ and $t_{1,2}$, that are open at $s_{1,1}$. Evaluating $t_{1,1}$ adds event e_2 and conditions c_5 and c_6. Evaluating $t_{1,2}$ adds events e_1 and conditions c_3 and c_4. This process can be continued to construct the unfolding of $\mathcal{W}$.

Algorithm 1 Algorithm *Unfold*

---

input: a system $\mathcal{W}$ consisting of EFSMs $W_1, W_2, \ldots, W_n$;
output: the unfolding $\Sigma = (B, E, F; L)$ of $\mathcal{W}$;
let V be an empty queue;
let $g_0 = (l_{01}, \ldots, l_{0n}; \epsilon, \ldots, \epsilon)$ be the initial global state;
add $(l_{0i}, \perp)$ for all $1 \leq i \leq n$ into B and V;
while $V \neq \emptyset$ **do**
  $c = deque(V)$;
  if c is a control condition **then**
    let $c = (l, e)$, where l is a local state of EFSM W_i;
    for each silent or send transition t of W_i open at l **do**
      let l' be the local state of W_i resulted by evaluating t at l;
      add an event $e_1 = (t, c)$ to E;
      add a control condition $c_1 = (l', e_1)$ to B and V;
      if t is a send transition **then**
        let m be the message sent by t;
        add a message condition (m, e_1) to B and V,
      end if
    end for
    for each synchronizable pair (c, c') that has not been processed **do**
      for each open receive transition r at l with $que(r) = que(c')$ **do**
        let l' be the local state of W_i resulted by evaluating t at l;
        add an event $e_1 = (r, \{c, c'\})$ to E;
        add a control condition $c_1 = (l', e_1)$ to B and V;
      end for
    end for
  else
    /*c is a message condition*/
    let $c = (m, e)$;
    for each synchronizable pair (c', c) that has not been processed **do**
      let $c' = (l', e')$, where l' is a local state of EFSM W_i;
      for each open receive transition r at l' with $que(r) = que(c)$ **do**
        let l' be the local state of W_i resulted by evaluating t at l;
        add an event $e_1 = (r, \{c', c\})$ to E;
        add a control condition $c_1 = (l', e_1)$ to B and V;
      end for
    end for
  end if
end while

---

5   Constructing a Complete Finite Prefix

Algorithm *Unfold* does not terminate for systems that have finite state space but infinite behaviors. This situation has been dealt with by the notion of *cut-off* event in [1] [2] [3]. In this section, we summarize the main results on *cut-off* events, and show that the conditions identified in [3] can also be used to identify cut-off events in our context.

Let $\mathcal{W}$ be an EFSM system and Σ the unfolding of $\mathcal{W}$. A finite prefix of Σ is *complete* if for every reachable global state g of $\mathcal{W}$, there exists a configuration C in the prefix so that (1) $GState(C) = g$ and (2) for every transition t enabled at g there is a configuration $C \cup \{e\}$ such that $e \notin C$ and e is labeled by t.

To construct a complete finite prefix, we need to identify places where unfolding can be safely terminated without loss of information. Intuitively, if two configurations C_1 and C_2 of Σ lead to the same global state of $\mathcal{W}$, i.e., $GState(C_1) = GState(C_2)$, then the continuations from $Cut(C_1)$ and $Cut(C_2)$ in Σ, i.e., the portions of Σ that lie below the two cuts, are isomorphic, i.e., they differ only in the identities of conditions and events. The motivation for identifying cut-off events is to avoid computing isomorphic continuations, since it suffices to only explore one of them.

Before we formally define a cut-off event, we first introduce the notion of an *adequate* order. Let C be a configuration. An extension of C, denoted by $C \oplus E$, is another configuration $C \cup E$, where $C \cap E = \emptyset$. A well-founded partial order $\prec$ on the configurations of Σ is *adequate* if it satisfies the following conditions:

- it refines the inclusion order, i.e., $C_1 \subset C_2$ implies $C_1 \prec C_2$;
- it is preserved by isomorphic extensions, i.e., if $C_1 \prec C_2$ and $GState(C_1) = GState(C_2)$, then $C_1 \oplus E \prec C_2 \oplus E'$, where E and E' are isomorphic extensions of C_1 and C_2, respectively.

Now we are ready to present the definition of a cut-off event.

Definition 5. *Let $\mathcal{W}$ be an EFSM system and Σ the unfolding of $\mathcal{W}$. Let $\prec$ be an adequate order on the configurations of Σ. An event e is a cut-off event if Σ contains another event e' such that $GState([e']) = GState([e])$ and $[e'] \prec [e]$.*

Note that the condition $[e'] \prec [e]$ is important to guarantee the completeness of a finite prefix, as shown in [2]. Also note that the identification of a cut-off event depends on a chosen adequate order. In the following, we present two adequate orders that were originally proposed for synchronous transition systems [3]. The two orders take into account the compositional nature of these systems in order to minimize their complete prefixes. We formally show that the two orders can also be applied to our EFSM model.

Let $\mathcal{W} = (W_1, \ldots, W_n)$ be an EFSM system and Σ the unfolding of $\mathcal{W}$. Let C be a configuration of $\mathcal{W}$. The projection of C onto W_i, denoted as $C{\downarrow}i$, is the set of events e such that $owner(e) = W_i$. It is easy to see that the events in $C{\downarrow}i$ can be put into a sequence based on the causal order $<$. Let $C{\downarrow}i = e_1 e_2 \ldots e_{k_i}$. Then, the local view of C seen by W_i, denoted by $V_i(C)$, is the sequence $t_1 t_2 \ldots t_{k_i}$, where $t_j = L(e_j)$, $1 \leq j \leq k_i$. We use $V(C) = (V_1(C), \ldots, V_n(C))$ to denote the n-tuple of local views of C.

Theorem 2 shows that a configuration can be characterized by its local views.

Theorem 2. *Let $\mathcal{W} = (W_1, \ldots, W_n)$ be an EFSM system and Σ the unfolding of $\mathcal{W}$. Let C_1 and C_2 be two configurations of Σ. If $V(C_1) = V(C_2)$, then $C_1 = C_2$.*

Proof. Let $C = C_1 \cap C_2$. We will prove that $C_1 = C_2$ by showing that $C_1 = C$ and $C_2 = C$. By symmetry, it suffices to prove $C_1 = C$. We proceed by contradiction.

Assume that $C \neq C_1$. Then C can be extended by an event $e_1 \in C_1 \backslash C$. We prove that $e_1 \in C_2$, a contradiction to $C = C_1 \cap C_2$. Let $t = L(e_1)$ be a transition of EFSM W_i. Then, $V_i(C) \cdot t$ is a prefix of $V_i(C_1)$, and since $V(C_1) = V(C_2)$ by assumption, also a prefix of $V_i(C_2)$. So C can also be extended by an event $e_2 \in C_2$ such that $t = L(e_2)$.

Next we show $e_1 = e_2$ and thus $e_1 \in C_2$. Let $c = (l, e)$ be the control condition of W_i after executing the events in $C \downarrow i$. Consider the following two cases:

- If t is a send or internal transition, the execution of t at l solely depends on l. In other words, there can only be a single execution instance of t at l. Therefore, $e_1 = e_2$.
- If t is a receive transition, the execution of t at l also depends on the message in the front of $que(t)$. In other words, e_1 and e_2 could be different execution instances of t at l which receive different messages. We show that this is impossible. Assume that e_1 and e_2 receive the message sent by events s_1 and s_2, respectively. Since a message queue has a single sender, s_1 and s_2 must belong to the same EFSM, say W_j. This means that s_1 and s_2 cannot be concurrent. Also note that s_1 and s_2 cannot be in conflict; otherwise, $V_j(C_1)$ must be different from $V_j(C_2)$. Therefore, $s_1 < s_2$ or $s_2 < s_1$. Let $c_1 = (m_1, s_1)$ and $c_2 = (m_2, s_2)$ be the message condition in the postset of s_1 and s_2, respectively. Then, either (c, c_1) or (c, c_2) is a synchronizable pair, but not both, leading to a contradiction. Therefore, $e_1 = e_2$.

Next we will introduce an auxiliary order between two transition sequences, called the *silex* order, which is used to define the two adequate orders we will present. Let σ and τ be two transition sequences. σ is smaller than τ with respect to the silex order if $|\sigma| < |\tau|$ or $|\sigma| = |\tau|$ and σ is lexicographically smaller than τ w.r.t. an arbitrary total order among the transitions. Now we are ready to present the two adequate orders:

Definition 6. *Let $\mathcal{W} = (W_1, \ldots, W_n)$ be an EFSM system and Σ the unfolding of $\mathcal{W}$. A (total) order $\prec_1$ on the configurations of Σ is defined such that given two configurations C_1 and C_2, $C_1 \prec_1 C_2$ if there exists an index i, $1 \leq i \leq n$, such that $V_j(C_1) = V_j(C_2)$ for all $1 \leq j < i$, and $V_i(C_1)$ is smaller than $V_i(C_2)$ w.r.t. the silex order.*

Definition 7. *Let $\mathcal{W} = (W_1, \ldots, W_n)$ be an EFSM system and Σ the unfolding of $\mathcal{W}$. A (total) order $\prec_2$ on the configurations of Σ is defined such that given two configurations C_1 and C_2, $C_1 \prec_2 C_2$ if one of the following conditions is satisfied:*

- *there exists an index i, $1 \leq i \leq n$, such that $|V_j(C_1)| = |V_j(C_2)|$ for all $1 \leq j < i$, and $|V_i(C_1)| < |V_i(C_2)|$; or*
- *for all $1 \leq k \leq n$, $|V_k(C_1)| = |V_k(C_2)|$, and there is an index i, $1 \leq i \leq n$, such that $V_j(C_1) = V_j(C_2)$ for all $1 \leq j < i$, and $V_i(C_1)$ is lexicographically smaller than $V_j(C_2)$ w.r.t. an arbitrary total order among the transitions.*

Theorem 3 allows us to use the two orders to determine cut-off events.

Theorem 3. *The two orders $\prec_1$ and $\prec_2$ are adequate orders.*

Proof. The adequacy proof in [3] only depends on the property that a configuration can be characterized by its local views. By Theorem 2, the same proof can apply here without modification.

As an example, consider e_{10} in Figure 2. Note that $[e_{10}] = \{e_1, e_3, e_4, e_7, e_9, e_{11}\}$. Therefore, $GState([e_{11}]) = ((s_{12}, 0, 0), (s_{21}, 0, 0); -1, \epsilon)$, and $V_1([e_{11}]) = t_{1,2} \cdot t_{1,3} \cdot t_{1,5} \cdot t_{1,2}$, and $V_2([e_{11}]) = t_{2,1} \cdot t_{2,3}$. Also note that $[e_1] = \{e_1\}$, and thus $GState([e_1]) = ((s_{12}, 0, 0), (s_{21}, 0, 0); -1, \epsilon)$, $V_1([e_1]) = t_{1,2}$ and $V_2([e_1]) = \epsilon$. Therefore, $GState([e_{11}]) = GState([e_1])$. In addition, since $|V_1([e_1])| < |V_1([e_{11}])|$, $[e_1] \prec [e_{11}]$, where $\prec$ can be $\prec_1$ or $\prec_2$. Hence, e_{11} is a cut-off event. We note that in Figure 2, e_{12} is also a cut-off event because (1) $GState([e_{12}]) = GState([e_2])$; and (2) $[e_2] \prec [e_{12}]$.

We comment that the choice between the two adequate orders is an issue of efficiency. The experiments in [3] seem to suggest that $\prec_2$ is more efficient than $\prec_1$, in the sense that the former is likely to result in smaller prefixes.

Algorithm *Unfold* can be modified to construct a complete finite prefix as follows. When we expand a condition in V, we create a new event and one or two successor conditions. In the original algorithm, we always add the successor conditions into both Σ and V. Now we modify the algorithm so that the successor conditions are added into both Σ and V if and only if the new event is not a cut-off event. Otherwise, we will only add those condition(s) into the Σ. For example, conditions c_{17}, c_{18}, c_{19}, and c_{20} will not be added to V. Since we assume that we are analyzing finite state systems, this modification guarantees termination of our unfolding algorithm.

6   Case Studies

As a proof-of-concept, we implemented our unfolding algorithm in a prototype tool. We analyzed several commonly used protocols using our prototype tool and Spin: (1) A leader election (LE) protocol, which determines the leader among a set of processes on a unidirectional ring; (2) A sliding window (SW) protocol, which exercises flow control to ensure reliable data transfer between two processes; (3) A readers and writers (RW) protocol, which implements the *concurrent-read-exclusive-write* policy to ensure the consistency of shared data; (4) A distributed mutual exclusion (ME) protocol, which ensures that at most one process can enter its critical section at any given time.

For each protocol, we analyzed several instances with a varying number of processes, except with a varying window size for the SW protocol. All the analyses are conducted on a PC running Windows XP with 1.2G HZ CPU and 512MB RAM. The Spin tool used in our studies is the standard distribution (version 4.1.2). The partial order reduction option as well as the option for checking xr/xs assertions in Spin are enabled for all the test runs.

Table 1. Results for the LE protocol

Num of Procs	Unfolding				SPIN			
	NoC	NoE	MEM	Time	NoS	NoT	MEM	Time
5	95	70	0.020	0.02	97	97	0.102	0.031
10	190	140	0.078	0.1	187	187	0.205	0.037
15	285	210	0.177	0.27	277	277	0.351	0.047
20	380	280	0.315	0.38	367	367	0.782	0.064
25	470	350	0.493	0.5	457	457	1.47	0.094

Table 2. Results for the SW protocol

Window Size	Unfolding				SPIN			
	NoC	NoE	MEM	Time	NoS	NoT	MEM	Time
1	64	50	0.006	0.01	74	79	0.102	0.121
2	1206	988	0.12	0.29	1151	1454	0.102	0.131
3	12081	9939	1.51	8.191	14694	20742	1.099	0.24

The results of our studies are reported in Tables 1, 2, 3, and 4. The first column shows the size of each protocol instance, in terms of the number of processes (for LE, RW, DME) or the window size (for SW). Note that NoR and NoW stand for the number of readers and writers, respectively. The other columns report two groups of data: one from our prototype tool, and the other from Spin. The size of unfoldings (i.e., LONs) generated by our tool is reported in terms of the number of conditions (NoC) and the number of events (NoE), and the size of state graphs generated by Spin is reported in terms of the number of states (NoS) and the number of transitions (NoT). The memory usage (MEM) is measured in Megabytes. The execution time (Time) is measured in seconds.

The memory usages reported are the total amount of memory, including the memory used for the actual state space representation and for auxiliary data structures, e.g., the working list in our tool or the search stack and hashtable in Spin. Note that Spin pre-allocates memory for the search stack and hashtable based on user-provided estimates. To accurately measure the actual memory usage, each protocol instance is analyzed twice in Spin. We intentionally over-estimate the memory needed in the first run, which reports the actual search depth and the number of states searched, and then adjust the estimates in the second run.

In Tables 1, the results from our tool and Spin are both optimal, in the sense that the memory requirements grow linearly with the problem size. In Table 2, the results from our tool and Spin are similar. Our tool uses slightly more memory than Spin. In Table 3, we reported two scenarios. In the first scenario, the number of readers is fixed as 1 and the number of writers is increased from 1 to 4. In the second scenario, the number of writers is fixed as 1 and the number of readers is increased from 1 to 4. In both scenarios, the sizes of the unfoldings increase significantly slower than the sizes of the state graphs, and our tool uses

Table 3. Results for the RW protocol

NoR + NoW	Unfolding				SPIN			
	NoC	NoE	MEM	Time	NoS	NoT	MEM	Time
1 + 1	164	132	0.023	0.04	135	192	0.102	0.213
1 + 2	997	861	0.187	0.32	1526	2301	0.512	0.269
1 + 3	4978	4450	1.154	1.60	18750	28673	6.275	0.698
1 + 4	21231	19377	5.83	16.32	263482	399682	99.521	5.143
2 + 1	1132	935	0.21	0.42	1434	2296	0.410	0.258
3 + 1	7715	6432	1.77	11.57	14276	26520	4.813	0.818
4 + 1	22940	19063	6.27	78.80	149042	312401	57.337	3.918

Table 4. Results for the ME protocol

Num of Procs	Unfolding				SPIN			
	NoC	NoE	MEM	Time	NoS	NoT	MEM	Time
3	147	133	0.032	0.02	638	126	0.307	0.17
4	3806	3690	1.192	0.63	38710	47863	18.899	0.915

significantly less memory than Spin. In Table 4, we reported two instances of the ME protocol. When we increase the number of processes to 5, neither our tool nor Spin can complete the search on the same computer. For ME with 4 processes, the unfolding is significantly smaller than the state graph.

The above results suggest that when there is a high degree of parallelism, the unfolding representations generated by our tool are much more compact than the state graphs generated by Spin. However, we note that this space reduction comes at the expense of time. We comment that the most time-consuming tasks in our tool are determining the cutoff events and computing the SC set. To obtain some empirical evidence, we profiled the longest execution in our experiments, i.e., the one that analyzes the RW protocol instance for 4 readers and 1 writer. The results indicate that 37% of the execution time are spent on determining the cutoff events, and 35% of the execution time spent on computing the SC set.

7   Conclusion

In this paper we have presented an approach to unfolding asynchronous communication protocols. We have been able to directly work with EFSMs, which allows us to exploit the full power of variables and arithmetic/logic expressions at the specification level. We have demonstrated that in our unfolding representation, we can store individual messages separately while still preserving the FIFO semantics of the message queues. This implicit representation of message queues reduces the size of our unfolding representation. We have also shown that two adequate orders, which were originally proposed for synchronous transition systems, can also be used to determine cut-off events in our context. These two orders help to minimize the size of a complete finite prefix of a potentially infinite unfolding. Our empirical results indicate that our algorithm can produce very compact state space representations.

The ultimate goal of unfolding is to analyze protocol properties. Deadlock freedom can be checked using techniques reported in [1] [4] [5]. Algorithms for model checking, which can be used to check general properties specified in some logic formalism, based on unfoldings can be found in [6] [7]. Since there exists a trade-off between the compactness of a state space representation and the time complexity of subsequent analysis based on the representation, we plan to conduct a study on the effectiveness of these algorithms based on our unfolding representation.

References

1. McMillan, K.L.: A technique of state space search based on unfolding. Formal Methods in System Design **6** (1995) 45–65
2. Esparza, J., Romer, S., Vogler, W.: An improvement of McMillan's unfolding algorithm. In: Proc. TACAS '96 Vol. 1055 of Lecture Notes in Computer Science. (1997) 87–106
3. Esparza, J., Romer, S.: An unfolding algorithm for synchronous products of transition systems. In: International Conference on Concurrency Theory. (1999) 2–20
4. Melzer, S., Romer, S.: Deadlock checking using net unfoldings. In: Int. Conf. on Computer Aided Verification. (1997) 352–363
5. Heljanko, K.: Using logic programs with stable model semantics to solve deadlock and reachability problems for 1-safe petri nets. In: Int. Conf. on Tools and Algorithms for Construction and Analysis of Systems TACAS. (1999) 240–254
6. Esparza, J.: Model checking using net unfoldings. Science of Computer Programming **23** (1994) 151–195
7. Esparza, J., Heljanko, K.: A new unfolding approach to LTL model checking. In: Intl. Conf. on Automata, Languages, and Programming. Volume 1853. (2000) 475–486

Semantics of BPEL4WS-Like Fault and Compensation Handling*

Zongyan Qiu, Shuling Wang, Geguang Pu, and Xiangpeng Zhao

LMAM and Department of Informatics, School of Math.,
Peking University, Beijing 100871, China
zyqiu@pku.edu.cn
{joycy, ggpu, zxp}@math.pku.edu.cn

Abstract. BPEL4WS is one of the most important business process modelling languages. One distinct feature of it is the fully programmable fault and compensation handling mechanism, which allows the user to specify the compensation behaviors of processes in application-specific manners. In this paper, we present a formal operational semantics to a simplified version of BPEL4WS, with some important concepts related to fault and compensation handling proposed and discussed, especially, the compensation closure and the compensation context. We also discuss some insights into the BPEL4WS language and its implementation obtained from this study.

Keywords: Business Process, Language, Semantics, BPEL4WS, Compensation handling, Fault handling.

1 Introduction

In recent years, many business process modelling languages (also known as *choreography* languages) have been introduced and used in the business application fields, such as XLANG [3], WSFL [4], BPEL4WS [5], and StAC [7]. These languages are used to define the services composed by a set of processes across networks, especially over the Internet. The complex services are defined in term of the interaction among simpler services, which might be still a composition in the same manner. Now, BPEL4WS is the most accredited candidate for becoming a standard of this field.

Some of these languages are aimed to describe services with long duration, based on communication of distributed processes, and manipulate sensitive business data in back-end databases, to support the concept of Long-Running (Business) Transactions (LRTs). Here, the ordinary assumptions about primitive operations (Atomicity, Consistency, Isolation, Durability, ACID) are not applicable in general, because that locks and isolation cannot be maintained for the long periods, and technical and business errors and fault conditions can occur in

---

* Supported by National Natural Science Foundation of China (No. 60173003).

J.S. Fitzgerald, I.J. Hayes, and A. Tarlecki (Eds.): FM 2005, LNCS 3582, pp. 350–365, 2005.

any business process instance, propagate to other processes via interactions, and cause them to go into troubles. In [5], the authors wrote:

> As a result, the overall business transaction can fail or be cancelled after many ACID transactions have been committed, and the partial work done must be undone as best as possible. Error handling in business processes therefore relies heavily on the well-known concept of compensation, that is, application-specific activities that attempt to reverse the effects of a previous activity that was carried out as part of a larger unit of work that is being abandoned.

The concept *compensation* has, of course, become one of the most important elements of the languages of this category.

Although the compensation can be regarded as a kind of exception handling mechanism, however, it has the distinct feature that compensation handlers are installed dynamically during the execution. There is still no standard definition for the compensation mechanism. [9] defined the compensation as the action taken to recover from error or cope with a change of plan, while [6] proposed a formal framework for the automatic invocation of compensation handlers in the reverse order with respect to the order of their installation.

Aimed to be a language for web services and the LRTs, BPEL4WS provides a special form of compensation mechanism. In combination with its fault handling mechanism, it offers the full ability to define fault and compensation handling in application-specific manners. The characters of the compensation mechanism in BPEL4WS include:

Scope-based (not activity-based). The compensation handlers can only be attached to the scopes;

Fault trigged. A compensation handler can only be invoked directly or indirectly by some fault handler, which is triggered by a fault in the execution;

Fully programmable. The compensation handlers are named. The installed handlers can be invoked in any order, interweaved with any other activities.

Although some works have been done on the semantics of BPEL4WS, e.g. [12], or on the compensation mechanisms, e.g. [7] and [6], there have not been formal studies on the BPEL4WS-like compensation mechanisms. As an industrial language aimed to be a standard language with seminal features, formal studies may clear the opaque points in the languages, and even uncover inadequate combinations or inconsistencies there. This is the aim of our work.

In this paper, we defined a simple language *BPEL* in Section 2, which is a simplification of BPEL4WS, and covers the most important features related to the fault and compensation handling mechanisms of the language. We presented a formal semantics for *BPEL* in Section 3, and developed the concepts of *compensation closure* and *compensation context*, which form a clear framework to the BPEL4WS-like fault and compensation handling mechanisms. We also proved two theorems to validate the semantics defined, and presented some examples for the demonstration. In Section 4, some issues related to the compensation features of BPEL4WS were discussed, including some unclear points in the language specification. We also proposed a possible dynamic resource optimization technique for the implementation of BPEL4WS compensation and fault handling mechanisms. We discussed some issues related to the extensions of our framework, with respect to the features omitted in *BPEL*. In the last two sections, some relative works were discussed, and then the conclusion.

2   The *BPEL* Language

BPEL is a subset of BPEL4WS. It includes the most important features related to the fault and compensation handling mechanism of BPEL4WS. We omit all details of BPEL4WS on the data handling level. A complete program written in *BPEL* is called a *Business Process*, or *BP* for the abbreviation. The syntax of *BP* and its components are defined as follows:

$$
\begin{array}{llll}
P & ::= & A & \text{(basic activities)} \\
  & | & \text{skip} & \text{(do nothing)} \\
  & | & \text{\textafill} & \text{(throw)} \\
  & | & P; P & \text{(sequence)} \\
  & | & P \triangleleft b \triangleright P & \text{(conditional)} \\
  & | & P \parallel P & \text{(flow, parallel composition)} \\
  & | & n : \{P ? C : F\} & \text{(scope)} \\
C, F & ::= & \text{\textcomp}\, n & \text{(compensation invocation with name)} \\
  & | & \text{\textcomp} & \text{(compensation all)} \\
  & | & \dots & \text{(similar to } P) \\
BP & ::= & \{\!| P : F |\!\} & \text{(business process)}
\end{array}
$$

Here n stands for names, b for boolean expressions. Their definitions are omitted. P stands for the process. A scope $n : \{P ? C : F\}$ has the name n and the primary activity P. F and C stand for the fault handler and compensation handler of the scope, respectively, that have the same structures as processes, except that they may include basic activities $\text{\textcomp}n$ and $\text{\textcomp}$ additionally. We ask that the $\text{\textcomp}$ appearing in a fault handler F is not in a branch of a parallel composition in F. The reason of this requirement will be discussed in Section 4.

The basic activities in BPEL4WS include assignment, various communication activities, and some others. These activities have effects on the data state or the environment. The details here are out of the concentration of this paper. We use A to represent them. The basic activity $\text{\textafill}$ throws a fault explicitly. We assume that any fault will be caught by the fault handler of the immediately enclosing scope. We will not consider the named fault until Section 4.

In BPEL4WS, the compensation or fault handler of a scope can be omitted. In these cases, the language specification assumes that the scope has the default fault and/or compensation handler with the behaviors as follows:

$$
\begin{array}{ll}
C_0 \stackrel{\text{def}}{=} \text{\textcomp} & \text{the default compensation handler} \\
F_0 \stackrel{\text{def}}{=} \text{\textcomp} ; \text{\textafill} & \text{the default fault handler}
\end{array}
$$

The handler C_0 runs all compensation handlers for immediately enclosed scopes in the reverse order of completion of those scopes. The handler F_0 runs all available compensation handlers for immediately enclosed scopes in the reverse order of completion of the corresponding scopes, and rethrows the fault to the next enclosing scope. Here we simply assume that every scope has the two handlers defined, perhaps some of them are C_0 or F_0.

The compensation handling mechanism in *BPEL* (as in BPEL4WS) is scope-based, fault triggered and programmable. The compensation handlers become active only when they are invoked, directly or indirectly, by a fault handler after a fault occurs during the execution. A compensation handler C, when installed by the normal completion of the primary activity of its scope, has the same name as the scope. The name of a handler is visible only in the immediately enclosing scope, thus, C can be invoked only in the fault handler or compensation handler of the scope. Furthermore, a set of compensation handlers installed can be selected as desired, invoked in any order. That is why we say that the compensation is fully programmable.

3   Semantics

Now we present the semantics of *BPEL*, with the focus on the fault and compensation handling. We adopt the big-step operational semantics here.

Some standard sequence operators are used in the definitions:

$$a_0 \cdot \langle a_1, \ldots, a_n \rangle = \langle a_0, a_1, \ldots, a_n \rangle$$
$$hd(\langle a_1, a_2, \ldots, a_n \rangle) = a_1$$
$$tl(\langle a_1, a_2, \ldots, a_n \rangle) = \langle a_2, \ldots, a_n \rangle$$
$$\langle a_1, , \ldots, a_n \rangle \widehat{\ } \langle b_1, \ldots, b_m \rangle = \langle a_1, \ldots, a_n, b_1, \ldots, b_m \rangle$$

Here we consider only the interactive activities that communicate with other services or clients, assuming that all basic activities are different from each other, while they may contain unique identities. The execution of a basic activity might complete (terminate successfully) or fail (terminate with a fault). We use

$$A \mapsto \boxdot \qquad A \text{ completes}$$
$$A \mapsto \boxtimes \qquad A \text{ fails}$$

respectively, to denote the two cases. We call $\boxdot$ and $\boxtimes$ the termination marks, and will use $\square$ to represent either of them, $\square \in \{\boxdot, \boxtimes\}$. Note that the termination status of an activity is determined by the environment of the *BP*. We will use Γ, possibly with subscript, to represent the environment under consideration. An environment Γ is of the form $A_1 \mapsto \square, \ldots, A_n \mapsto \square$. We assume that in any valid environment, $A_i \neq A_j$ when $i \neq j$, and use $\Gamma_1 \cup \Gamma_2$ to represent the combination of environments, assuming there is no confliction between Γ_1 and Γ_2.

The configuration of the transition system includes a process or a mark to denote the termination status, and a compensation context α:

$$P, \alpha \qquad \text{or} \qquad \square, \alpha$$

We call configurations of the form $\square, \alpha$ the terminated configurations. A compensation context is a sequence (possibly empty) of compensation closures of the form $(n : C : \alpha_1)$, where n is a name, which is actually the same as that of the scope where compensation handler C is defined, and α_1 is a compensation context. When compensation handler C is invoked, it will run in company with the context α_1. When $c = (n : C : \alpha)$, we use $c.1$, $c.2$ and $c.3$ to obtain the name, the compensation handler, and the context, respectively.

The semantics of a process is given by the relation $\Gamma \vdash cfg_1 \rightarrow cfg_2$, where cfg_2 is a terminated configuration. Now we list the rules that define the semantics with brief explanation.

3.1   Sequential Process

We consider the sequential part of *BPEL* in this section.

The activity skip always completes, in any environment:

$$\Gamma \vdash \mathsf{skip}, \alpha \rightarrow \boxdot, \alpha \tag{SKIP}$$

The basic activity Υ (throw) fails in any environment,

$$\Gamma \vdash \Upsilon, \alpha \rightarrow \boxtimes, \alpha \tag{THRW}$$

In BPEL4WS, the throw activity carries a globally defined name, to transfer the control to a specific fault handler. We omit this facility and suppose that a fault is always caught by the fault handler of its immediately enclosing scope. It is not hard to extend the definitions here to deal with named faults.

An interactive activity will complete or fail depending on the environment. It has no effects on the compensation context:

$$A \mapsto \square \vdash A, \alpha \rightarrow \square, \alpha \tag{BASIC}$$

Here we use $\square$ to represent those two different cases, $\square \in \{\boxdot, \boxtimes\}$.

We introduce following rule for the environment extension:

$$\frac{\Gamma_1 \vdash P, \alpha \rightarrow \square, \beta}{\Gamma_1 \cup \Gamma_2 \vdash P, \alpha \rightarrow \square, \beta} \tag{EXTD}$$

From now on, whenever we write $\Gamma \vdash cfg_1 \rightarrow cfg_2$, we will always assume that the environment Γ provides enough information for all basic activities in cfg_1, to determine their termination status.

The semantics of the sequential composition $P_1; P_2$ is defined by two rules, depending on the completion or failure of P_1:

$$\frac{\Gamma_1 \vdash P_1, \alpha \rightarrow \boxdot, \gamma \quad \Gamma_2 \vdash P_2, \gamma \rightarrow \square, \beta}{\Gamma_1 \cup \Gamma_2 \vdash P_1; P_2, \alpha \rightarrow \square, \beta} \qquad \frac{\Gamma \vdash P_1, \alpha \rightarrow \boxtimes, \beta}{\Gamma \vdash P_1; P_2, \alpha \rightarrow \boxtimes, \beta} \tag{SEQ-S}$$

When P_1 completes, the termination status is determined by P_2. If P_1 fails, P_2 will not be taken into the execution. The execution of P_1 (and P_2, in the first case) may extend the compensation context α to another compensation context β, by adding some compensation closure(s) in the front of α.

For the conditional, we suppose that the boolean expression b gives a value of true or false, and determines which branch is chosen. In a more detailed semantics, we will need a data state to support the evaluation of b.

$$\frac{b = \text{true} \quad \Gamma \vdash P_1, \alpha \to \Box, \beta}{\Gamma \vdash P_1 \vartriangleleft b \vartriangleright P_2, \alpha \to \Box, \beta} \qquad \frac{b = \text{false} \quad \Gamma \vdash P_2, \alpha \to \Box, \beta}{\Gamma \vdash P_1 \vartriangleleft b \vartriangleright P_2, \alpha \to \Box, \beta} \qquad \text{(COND-S)}$$

The compensation handler and fault handler are defined in a scope s, in addition to the primary activity P of s. When the execution comes to s, the primary activity P is executed with an empty context initially. When P completes, the compensation handler is installed with its context accumulated during the execution of P, which forms a compensation closure, and put in the front of α. A sequence of compensation closures will accumulate in this way:

$$\frac{\Gamma \vdash P, \langle\rangle \to \Box, \beta}{\Gamma \vdash n : \{P\,?\,C\,:\,F\}, \alpha \to \Box, (n : C : \beta) \cdot \alpha} \qquad \text{(SC-SUC)}$$

When P fails, the execution switches to the fault handler, and the termination status of the fault handler F is the termination status of the scope:

$$\frac{\Gamma_1 \vdash P, \langle\rangle \to \boxtimes, \beta \quad \Gamma_2 \vdash F, \beta \to \Box, \gamma}{\Gamma_1 \cup \Gamma_2 \vdash n : \{P\,?\,C\,:\,F\}, \alpha \to \Box, \alpha} \qquad \text{(SC-FLT)}$$

Please note that, when P fails, compensation handler C will never be installed.

The operations $\curlywedge$ and $\curlywedge n$ can appear only in the body of the fault and compensation handlers. The operation $\curlywedge$ invokes each handler in the related compensation context sequentially. There are two rules for the cases that α is not empty, and one for $\alpha = \langle\rangle$:

$$\Gamma \vdash \curlywedge, \langle\rangle \to \Box, \langle\rangle \qquad \text{(CP-ALL0)}$$

$$\frac{\Gamma \vdash C, \beta \to \Box, \gamma \quad \Gamma \vdash \curlywedge, \alpha \to \Box, \langle\rangle}{\Gamma \vdash \curlywedge, (n : C : \beta) \cdot \alpha \to \Box, \langle\rangle} \qquad \text{(CP-ALL1)}$$

$$\frac{\Gamma \vdash C, \beta \to \boxtimes, \gamma}{\Gamma \vdash \curlywedge, (n : C : \beta) \cdot \alpha \to \boxtimes, \langle\rangle} \qquad \text{(CP-ALL2)}$$

Because the compensation closures are accumulated in the front of the context, $\curlywedge$ will invoke them in the reverse order of their installation.

The execution of a series of compensation closures is not the same as the execution of a sequential composition process. There is no accumulated compensation context, and the context need to switch each time. A compensation handler is always invoked directly or indirectly as part of the processing of some fault handler. If the behavior of a compensation handler C' invoked by F' causes a fault, and the fault is uncaught by scopes within the chain of compensation handlers invoked by F', it is treated as being a fault within F'. Above semantic rules reflect this situation, as the definition of BPEL4WS specification.

Operation $\curlywedge n$ looks up the compensation closure with the name n in current compensation context. If no closure with the name is found, it acts like a skip, otherwise, the handler in the closure is executed in company with its context:

$$\frac{\Gamma \vdash gp(n,\alpha), ge(n,\alpha) \to \Box, \beta}{\Gamma \vdash \curlywedge n, \alpha \to \Box, \alpha} \qquad \text{(CP-NM)}$$

where $gp(n,\alpha)$ and $ge(n,\alpha)$ extract the process and the context of the compensation closure with name n from α, respectively:

$$\begin{aligned}
gp(n, \langle\rangle) &= \text{skip} & ge(n, \langle\rangle) &= \langle\rangle \\
gp(n, (n\!:\!C\!:\!\beta)\cdot\alpha') &= C & ge(n, (n\!:\!C\!:\!\beta)\cdot\alpha') &= \beta \\
gp(n, (m\!:\!C\!:\!\beta)\cdot\alpha') &= gp(n, \alpha') & ge(n, (m\!:\!C\!:\!\beta)\cdot\alpha') &= ge(n, \alpha') \\
\text{when } n \neq m & & \text{when } n \neq m
\end{aligned}$$

The compensation context accumulated in the invocation is abandoned.

Here are the rules for the complete business process:

$$\frac{\Gamma \vdash P, \langle\rangle \to \Box, \alpha}{\Gamma \vdash \{\!| P\!:\!F |\!\}, \langle\rangle \to \Box, \langle\rangle} \qquad \frac{\Gamma_1 \vdash P, \langle\rangle \to \boxtimes, \alpha \quad \Gamma_2 \vdash F, \alpha \to \Box, \beta}{\Gamma_1 \cup \Gamma_2 \vdash \{\!| P\!:\!F |\!\}, \langle\rangle \to \Box, \langle\rangle} \qquad \text{(BP)}$$

3.2   Parallel Process

The parallel operator $\|$ allows more than one activities to be executed concurrently. This brings new problems into the semantics. If we have $P_0; (P_1 \| P_2); P_3$, two branches P_1 and P_2 start simultaneously after P_0 completes, and only when both of them complete, can P_3 start its execution. In fact, BPEL4WS offers further mechanism to control the execution order of the parallel activities—the link dependencies. We omit this feature and put it into the further study.

From the BPEL4WS specification, when one of the branches fails, the fault handler of the innermost surrounding scope begins its behavior by implicitly terminating all other (concurrent) activities enclosed in the scope, and then starts the execution of its body. This mechanism is called the *forced termination* (by a fault occurring in another activity). To define the forced termination, a new termination mark $\boxtimes$ is introduced to describe that a process is forced to terminate. We should modify some rules defined before for the sequential processes, to take the forced termination into account.

Firstly, all basic activities will be allowed to complete their work as before[1]. But the completion can be thought as a forced termination:

$$\frac{\Gamma \vdash A, \alpha \to \Box, \alpha}{\Gamma \vdash A, \alpha \to \overline{\boxtimes}, \alpha} \qquad \text{(FORCE)}$$

The rules for the sequential composition are modified as follows:

$$\frac{\Gamma_1 \vdash P_1, \alpha \to \Box, \gamma \quad \Gamma_2 \vdash P_2, \gamma \to \tau, \beta}{\Gamma_1 \cup \Gamma_2 \vdash P_1; P_2, \alpha \to \tau, \beta} \quad \text{where } \tau \in \{\Box, \boxtimes, \overline{\boxtimes}\} \quad \text{(SEQ-SUC)}$$

---

[1] In BPEL4WS, simple basic activities, e.g., assignment, are allowed to complete their work, but the activities involving communication are interrupted and terminate prematurely. We can have other choices, and will discuss the issues in Sec. 4.

and

$$\frac{\Gamma \vdash P_1, \alpha \to \tau, \beta}{\Gamma \vdash P_1; P_2, \alpha \to \tau, \beta} \qquad \text{where } \tau \in \{\boxtimes, \overline{\boxtimes}\} \qquad \text{(SEQ-FLT)}$$

The rules for conditionals are modified to (where $\tau \in \{\boxdot, \boxtimes, \overline{\boxtimes}\}$):

$$\frac{b = \text{true} \quad \Gamma \vdash P_1, \alpha \to \tau, \beta}{\Gamma \vdash P_1 \triangleleft b \triangleright P_2, \alpha \to \tau, \beta} \qquad \frac{b = \text{false} \quad \Gamma \vdash P_2, \alpha \to \tau, \beta}{\Gamma \vdash P_1 \triangleleft b \triangleright P_2, \alpha \to \tau, \beta} \qquad \text{(COND)}$$

The original rules for the scope are kept. One new rule is added:

$$\frac{\Gamma_1 \vdash P, \langle\rangle \to \overline{\boxtimes}, \beta \quad \Gamma_2 \vdash F, \beta \to \boxdot, \gamma}{\Gamma_1 \cup \Gamma_2 \vdash n : \{P ? C : F\}, \alpha \to \overline{\boxtimes}, \alpha} \qquad \text{(SC-FORCE)}$$

When a scope is forced to terminate, its primary activity P is forced to terminate, and the control transfers to the fault handler. The language forbids the fault handler to re-throw a fault. In the other word, in this case, the fault occurring during the execution of F will not be propagated out of F. With above rule, a fault handler F will terminate with either $\boxdot$ or $\boxtimes$, but never with $\overline{\boxtimes}$. Thus, it can always finish its work, whatever it is invoked by a fault occurring in the normal execution, or invoked by the forced termination.

Now we can have a rule for parallel composition:

$$\frac{\Gamma_1 \vdash P, \alpha \to \tau_1, \alpha'^\frown\alpha \quad \Gamma_2 \vdash Q, \alpha \to \tau_2, \alpha''^\frown\alpha}{\Gamma_1 \cup \Gamma_2 \vdash P \parallel Q, \alpha \to \tau_1 \otimes \tau_2, (\alpha' \parallel \alpha'') \cdot \alpha} \quad \text{where } \tau_1, \tau_2 \in \{\boxdot, \boxtimes, \overline{\boxtimes}\} \quad \text{(PAR)}$$

The operator $\otimes$ is defined in the following table:

$\otimes$	$\boxdot$	$\boxtimes$	$\overline{\boxtimes}$
$\boxdot$	$\boxdot$	$\overline{\boxtimes}$	$\boxtimes$
$\overline{\boxtimes}$	$\overline{\boxtimes}$	$\overline{\boxtimes}$	$\boxtimes$
$\boxtimes$	$\boxtimes$	$\boxtimes$	$\boxtimes$

It is similar to the corresponding operator defined in [6].

A new form of elements is introduced into the compensation context to support parallel compensation. In this case, we should add two rules for $\barwedge$:

$$\frac{\Gamma_1 \vdash\!\barwedge, \alpha' \to \boxdot, \beta' \quad \Gamma_2 \vdash\!\barwedge, \alpha'' \to \boxdot, \beta'' \quad \Gamma_3 \vdash\!\barwedge, \alpha \to \boxdot, \beta}{\Gamma_1 \cup \Gamma_2 \cup \Gamma_3 \vdash \barwedge, (\alpha' \parallel \alpha'') \cdot \alpha \to \boxdot, \langle\rangle} \qquad \text{(CP-PAR1)}$$

and

$$\frac{\Gamma_1 \vdash\!\barwedge, \alpha' \to \tau_1, \beta' \quad \Gamma_2 \vdash\!\barwedge, \alpha'' \to \tau_2, \beta''}{\Gamma_1 \cup \Gamma_2 \vdash \barwedge, (\alpha' \parallel \alpha'') \cdot \alpha \to \boxtimes, \langle\rangle} \quad \text{either } \tau_1 = \boxtimes \text{ or } \tau_2 = \boxtimes \quad \text{(CP-PAR2)}$$

The rule for $\barwedge n$ remains the same, but the functions used in it should be revised by adding two rules as follows:

$$gp(n, (\alpha' \parallel \alpha'') \cdot \alpha) = gp(n, \alpha'^\frown\alpha''^\frown\alpha)$$
$$ge(n, (\alpha' \parallel \alpha'') \cdot \alpha) = ge(n, \alpha'^\frown\alpha''^\frown\alpha)$$

In a scope, the names for the immediately enclosed sub-scopes must not be the same. Thus, we can simply concatenate the compensation contexts.

The technique for the forced termination here is enlightened by the work in [6], and modified according to our needs. Please note that, in the execution of $P \parallel Q$, if P fails, Q should be forced to terminate. BPEL4WS has a detailed definition of forced termination on each type of activities. All activities other than the simplest ones are immediately interrupted and finished prematurely. The exact termination points depend on the relative speed of the processes. The semantics defined here, and also what in [6], is at an abstract level, which guarantees that the active activities in Q will turn to the forced termination at some points. This brings a form of non-determinism.

3.3   Two Theorems

Theorem 1 (Completeness). *The big-step semantics for the BPEL language defined above is complete, i.e., for each well-formed process $\{\!| P\!:\!F |\!\}$, there exists a finite deduction (with a suitable environment Γ):*

$$\Gamma_1 \vdash p_1, \alpha_1 \rightarrow \tau_1, \beta_1$$
$$\ldots\ldots$$
$$\Gamma_n \vdash p_n, \alpha_n \rightarrow \square_1, \beta_n$$
$$\Gamma_{n+1} \vdash q_1, \gamma_1 \rightarrow \tau_{n+1}, \beta_{n+1}$$
$$\ldots$$
$$\Gamma_{n+m} \vdash q_m, \gamma_m \rightarrow \square_2, \beta_{n+m}$$
$$\Gamma \vdash \{\!| P\!:\!F |\!\}, \langle\rangle \rightarrow \square_3, \langle\rangle$$

for some n and m, where $\Gamma_i \subseteq \Gamma$, $\tau_j \in \{\boxdot, \boxtimes, \overline{\boxtimes}\}, \square_k \in \{\boxdot, \boxtimes\}$, $p_n = P$, $q_m = F$, and each formula in the sequence is deduced from some formula(e) before it in the sequence using the operational rules defined above.

Here p_i and q_j are some texts. We use the different names for them to emphasis that there is a deduction sequence for the primary activity P and a deduction sequence for the fault handler F. The second sub-sequence can be empty.

Proof. Suppose we can construct a deduction sequence ds_1 for P with the initial compensation context $\langle\rangle$. If the termination mark of the last formula in ds_1 is $\boxdot$, then from the rule (BP), the deduction sequence of $\{\!| P\!:\!F |\!\}$ is

$$ds_1 \quad \Gamma \vdash \{\!| P\!:\!F |\!\}, \langle\rangle \rightarrow \boxdot, \langle\rangle \qquad \text{(written horizontally to save space)}$$

If the termination configuration of the last formula in ds_1 is $\boxtimes, \alpha$, and suppose we can construct a deduction sequence ds_2 for F with the initial compensation context α, and the termination mark of the last formula in ds_2 is $\square$, then the deduction sequence of $\{\!| P\!:\!F |\!\}$ is

$$ds_1 \quad ds_2 \quad \Gamma \vdash \{\!| P\!:\!F |\!\}, \langle\rangle \rightarrow \square, \langle\rangle$$

Thus, what we really need to prove is that the deduction sequences for P and F can be constructed. We will prove this by induction on the structure of P

and F. Because the only difference between P and F is that there can be some compensation invocations in F, additionally, thus, we can prove the most of cases of them together. In the following, when we say P (possibly with subscription), it always means P or F. And we will suppose the current compensation context is α all the while.

- Case $P = A$, $P = \mathsf{skip}$, or $P = \mathsf{I}$. The proof is trivial.
- Case $P = P_1; P_2$. By induction hypothesis, P_1 has a deduction sequence ds_1, with the termination status of P_1. If P_1 completes, by the hypothesis, we can construct a deduction sequence for P_2 and denote it by ds_2. Thus, from rule (SEQ-S), the complete deduction sequence for P will be:

$$ds_1 \quad ds_2 \quad \Gamma \vdash P_1; P_2, \alpha \to \Box, \beta$$

where $\Box$ and β are the same as in the last formula of ds_2. In the case when P_1 fails, the construction of the deduction for P is simpler.
- Case $P = P_1 \lhd b \rhd P_2$. The deduction sequence for P depends on the value of b. If b is true, we can have a deduction sequence for P_1, and denote it as ds_1. According to rule (COND-S), the deduction sequence for P is:

$$ds_1 \quad \Gamma \vdash P, \alpha \to \Box, \beta$$

where $\Box$ and β are the same as in the last formula of ds_1. The construction is similar when b is false.
- Case $P_1 \parallel P_2$. By hypothesis, we can construct a deduction sequence for P_1 where the termination status has two possibilities: $\boxdot$ or $\boxtimes$ till now. Here we must notice that from rule (PAR), P_1 may be forced to terminate. So we must consider the construction of a deduction sequence with the forced termination at end. We will not list them here. In fact, the construction is the same as above except that in some places, $\Box$ should be extended to include $\boxtimes$ and the corresponding rules for parallel processes are used instead. We should also note that, the forced termination can only be triggered ultimately by a real fault. In general, each real fault may cause a forced termination "tree" down and backwards. Suppose the deduction sequences for P_1 and P_2 are ds_1 and ds_2 respectively, then the deduction sequence for $P_1 \parallel P_2$ is:

$$ds_1 \quad ds_2 \quad \Gamma \vdash P_1 \parallel P_2, \alpha \to \Box_1 \otimes \Box_2, \beta$$

where $\Box_1$ and $\Box_2$ are the termination marks of the last formulae in ds_1 and ds_2, respectively. And β can also be formed from them too. When the parallel operator is the outmost one in P, $\Box_i$ equals $\boxtimes$ iff another $\Box_j$ equals $\boxtimes$, so P can has only two possibly termination states: $\boxdot$ or $\boxtimes$.
- In order to construct the deduction sequence for $n : \{P' ? C' : F'\}$, We must first consider the compensation invocations that can appear in fault handlers. Also, here we can solve the problem when P fails in the cases above.
  - Case $F = \mathsf{I} n$. Suppose the process and compensation context of the closure with name n are c and γ respectively. By hypothesis, we suppose

a deduction sequence for c in context γ is ds. From rule (CP-NM), we can get a deduction sequence for P:

$$ds \quad \Gamma \vdash P, \alpha \to \Box, \alpha$$

where $\Box$ is the termination mark of the last formula in ds.

- Case $F = \text{ꟷ}$. The deduction sequence of ꟷ is a series of deduction sequences corresponding to the compensation handlers, constructed by the rules (CP-ALL1), (CP-ALL2), (CP-PAR1), and (CP-PAR2).

The construction of the deduction sequence for a fault handler F is the same as for a normal process P, and this statement is applicable to the compensation handlers as well. We omit the details here. In the following, we will prove that the deduction sequence for a scope can be constructed.

- Case $P = n : \{P' ? C' : F'\}$. By hypothesis, we can get a deduction sequence for P', and denote it by ds_1. If P' completes, according to rule (SC-SUC), we get the deduction sequence for P:

$$ds_1 \quad \Gamma \vdash P, \alpha \to \boxdot, \beta$$

Otherwise, the fault is caught by F'. By hypothesis, we denote the deduction sequence for F' by ds_2. Then the deduction sequence for P is:

$$ds_1 \quad ds_2 \quad \Gamma \vdash P, \alpha \to \Box, \beta$$

where $\Box$ is the termination mark of the last formula in ds_2.

At the outmost level, the forced termination can appear only in the parallel composition. At the inner levels, we need to consider it for other cases. This will not make real trouble to us, thus, we will not restate that here. $\qquad\Box$

BPEL4WS asks that "the fault handler for scope C begins by implicitly terminating all activities directly enclosed within C that are currently active". With our semantics, we have a theorem as follows. We omit the details of the proof here.

Theorem 2 (Forced Termination). *The behavior of any fault handler F for scope $n : \{P ? C : F\}$ begins by terminating all activities directly enclosed within the scope that are currently active.*

3.4   Examples

Example 1: A Sequential Process. Consider process $b_1 = \{n : \{A_1; m : \{A_2 ? C_2 : F_2\}; A_3 ? C' : \text{ꟷ} m; A_4\} : F\}$, where all basic activities but A_3 complete, i.e., the environment Γ is: $A_1 \mapsto \Box, A_2 \mapsto \Box, C_2 \mapsto \Box, A_3 \mapsto \boxtimes, A_4 \mapsto \Box$. For simplicity, let $P \overset{\text{def}}{=} n : \{A_1; m : \{A_2 ? C_2 : F_2\}; A_3 ? C' : \text{ꟷ} m; A_4\}$, $P' \overset{\text{def}}{=} A_1; m : \{A_2 ? C_2 : F_2\}; A_3$, and $F' \overset{\text{def}}{=} \text{ꟷ} m; A_4$. In the following, we use the semantic rules for *BPEL* above to reason about the execution of b_1.

$$
\begin{array}{lll}
(1) & A_1 \mapsto \Box \vdash A_1, \langle\rangle \to \Box, \langle\rangle & \text{(BASIC)} \\
(2) & A_2 \mapsto \Box \vdash A_2, \langle\rangle \to \Box, \langle\rangle & \text{(BASIC)} \\
(3) & A_2 \mapsto \Box \vdash m : \{A_2 ? C_2 : F_2\}, \langle\rangle \to \Box, (m : C_2 : \langle\rangle) & \text{(SC-SUC, (2))}
\end{array}
$$

(4) $A_3 \mapsto \boxtimes \vdash A_3, (m:C_2:\langle\rangle) \to \boxtimes, (m:C_2:\langle\rangle)$ (BASIC)

(5) $A_1 \mapsto \boxdot, A_2 \mapsto \boxdot, A_3 \mapsto \boxtimes \vdash P', \langle\rangle \to \boxtimes, (m:C_2:\langle\rangle)$ (SEQ-S, (1), (3), (4))

(6) $C_2 \mapsto \boxdot \vdash C_2, \langle\rangle \to \boxdot, \langle\rangle$ (BASIC)

(7) $C_2 \mapsto \boxdot \vdash \urcorner m, (m:C_2:\langle\rangle) \to \boxdot, (m:C_2:\langle\rangle)$ (CP-NM, (6))

(8) $A_4 \mapsto \boxdot \vdash A_4, (m:C_2:\langle\rangle) \to \boxdot, (m:C_2:\langle\rangle)$ (BASIC)

(9) $C_2 \mapsto \boxdot, A_4 \mapsto \boxdot \vdash F', (m:C_2:\langle\rangle) \to \boxdot, (m:C_2:\langle\rangle)$ (SEQ-S, (7), (8))

(10) $\Gamma \vdash P, \langle\rangle \to \boxdot, \langle\rangle$ (SC-FLT, (5), (9))

(11) $\Gamma \vdash b_1, \langle\rangle \to \boxdot, \langle\rangle$ (BP, (10))

Although some activity fails in the execution of b_1, the whole business process completes because of proper compensation.

Example 2: A Parallel Process. We add an activity $B_1; B_2$ to Example 1, that is parallel with the activity A_3, then have a process $b_2 = \{\!| n : \{A_1; m : \{A_2 ? C_2 : F_2\}; (B_1; B_2) \parallel A_3 ? C' : F'\} : F |\!\}$. P, P' are defined as before except that all appearances of A_3 are replaced by $(B_1; B_2) \parallel A_3$, and Γ is extended to include $B_1 \mapsto \boxdot, B_2 \mapsto \boxdot$. However, we may also modify F'. Here we omit the details and suppose that $\Gamma \vdash F', (m:C_2:\langle\rangle) \to \boxdot, \beta$. According to rule (PAR), activity $B_1; B_2$ is forced to terminate because of the fault occurring in A_3. With the semantics, we can build two derivations shown below, where the branch $B_1; B_2$ is forced to terminate before or after the start of B_2. The execution of b_2 is based on the results of Example 1. In the first case, we have

(1) $B_1 \mapsto \boxdot \vdash B_1, (m:C_2:\langle\rangle) \to \boxdot, (m:C_2:\langle\rangle)$ (BASIC)

(2) $B_1 \mapsto \boxdot \vdash B_1, (m:C_2:\langle\rangle) \to \overline{\boxtimes}, (m:C_2:\langle\rangle)$ (FORCE, (1))

(3) $B_1 \mapsto \boxdot \vdash B_1; B_2, (m:C_2:\langle\rangle) \to \overline{\boxtimes}, (m:C_2:\langle\rangle)$ (SEQ-FLT, (2))

In the second case,

(1) $B_1 \mapsto \boxdot \vdash B_1, (m:C_2:\langle\rangle) \to \boxdot, (m:C_2:\langle\rangle)$ (BASIC)

(2) $B_2 \mapsto \boxdot \vdash B_2, (m:C_2:\langle\rangle) \to \boxdot, (m:C_2:\langle\rangle)$ (BASIC)

(3) $B_2 \mapsto \boxdot \vdash B_2, (m:C_2:\langle\rangle) \to \overline{\boxtimes}, (m:C_2:\langle\rangle)$ (FORCE, (2))

(4) $B_1 \mapsto \boxdot; B_2 \mapsto \boxdot \vdash B_1; B_2, (m:C_2:\langle\rangle) \to \overline{\boxtimes}, (m:C_2:\langle\rangle)$ (SEQ-SUC, (1), (3))

Both of them have the fact below:

$$B_1 \mapsto \boxdot, B_2 \mapsto \boxdot, A_3 \mapsto \boxtimes \vdash (B_1; B_2) \parallel A_3, (m:C_2:\langle\rangle) \to \overline{\boxtimes} \otimes \boxtimes, (m:C_2:\langle\rangle)$$
$$B_1 \mapsto \boxdot, B_2 \mapsto \boxdot, A_3 \mapsto \boxtimes \vdash (B_1; B_2) \parallel A_3, (m:C_2:\langle\rangle) \to \boxtimes, (m:C_2:\langle\rangle)$$ (PAR)

From the example, we can see that when a branch in parallel process fails, the time when the other activities that are currently active are forced to terminate is non-determinate.

4   Discussion

4.1   Language Issues

The intention of this work is to make our language *BPEL* as close as possible to what of BPEL4WS [5], within the issues considered here. With this idea, we meet many problems, with the language specification, and with how to formally define it. We discuss some problems related to the language in this subsection.

Within this work, we uncovered some problems which are not clearly defined in the BPEL4WS specification, or probably defined not adequately. We list some of them here with brief discussions:

- The BPEL4WS specification says that, the operator $\curlywedge$ (operator compensate in [5]) runs "all available compensation handlers for immediately enclosed scopes in the reverse order". It says nothing about the handlers installed parallelly. In our definition, we assume that these handlers will execute parallelly. Another choice is to linearize them arbitrarily.
- The operator $\curlywedge$ goes not very well with parallel structures. For example, could we write a fault handler of the form $P_1; (Q_1 \parallel (Q_2; \curlywedge; Q_3)); P_2$? What happens when Q_1 fails, or a handler called by $\curlywedge$ fails? Beware that a sequence of handler invocations is not the same as a sequential composition, because the compensation context should be switched for each of the handlers. When one of the parallel branches fails, should the other branches be forced to terminate? The language specification does not define this. In fact, any definition will bring some problems. Under this consideration, we simply forbid that $\curlywedge$ runs in parallel with other processes.
- BPEL4WS is announced to become a language to specify business processes and protocols, and support LRTs. We are ready to think about a business process that needs to run over days, or even over months or years. As shown very clearly in our semantics, the longer the process runs, the bigger the compensation contexts accumulate. This accumulation will consume much resource. What we think is that, when a transaction in a process comes to its real end, the programmers need a means to clear the compensation context related to it, for example, the *accept* operator of StAC [7].

The last point above raises some implementation issues as well. When a subtask P in a business process comes to its real end, we could enclose it in a scope $n : \{P\,?\,\mathsf{skip} : \ldots\}$, i.e., with an empty compensation handler. In this form, all the compensation handlers in the enclosed scopes (including those in the even nested scopes) will never be invoked. Thus, the implementation can clear the compensation context accumulated in the execution of P. We hope that the implementation is smart enough to recognize this situation.

Furthermore, if a compensation handler is not invoked directly or indirectly by a fault handler, it will never have a chance to run. Then, when a scope completes, we might have a chance to abandon some compensation handlers and their companion contexts. For example, if for the scope $n : \{P\,?\,C : F\}$, P completes and produces a context $\langle c_1, c_2, c_3 \rangle$, and C calls only c_2, then we can make a closure of the form $(n : C : \langle c_2 \rangle)$, and release all resources occupied by c_1 and c_3. This is a kind of dynamic resource optimization. We can also think it as a kind of garbage collection.

4.2   Other Problems

If a fault occurs in a scope, the fault handler terminates all activities in the scope that are currently active. The rule (FORCE) allows basic activities to complete their work. In BPEL4WS, with the same situation, the activities involving communication are interrupted and terminate prematurely. We can use the rule below to replace rule (FORCE), to simulate the premature termination:

$$A \mapsto \boxdot \vdash A, \alpha \to \overline{\boxtimes}, \alpha$$

This means that, even if A can complete, it might be forced to terminate in some situation. Furthermore, we can divide the basic activities into two categories, in which one is interruptable, while the other is not.

There are some other structures in BPEL4WS, including the choice, iteration, wait operation, etc. Dealing with the choice and wait operation asks us to include data state into the framework described here.

We can include the iteration by extending the syntax with a form $b * P$. If there are scopes in an iteration, and the scopes complete, more than one compensation closures with the same name may be installed into the corresponding context. This brings no problem to operator $\barwedge$. However, what is the meaning when we invoke such handlers by $\barwedge n$? BPEL4WS specification does not make it clear. If what we want is to call all the closures with name n in the reverse order of the installation, we can modify the rule (CP-NM) to implement that. In fact, as we think, the iteration goes not very well with the named compensation in BPEL4WS. For example, if we have $b * (\dots; (n_1 : \{P_1 ? C_1 : F_1\}); (n_2 : \{P_2 ? C_2 : F_2\}); \dots)$ and the body of it is executed a number of times, a series of compensation closures named n_1 and n_2 alternately will be installed. In this case, could we write $\barwedge n_1$ afterward? And what is the meaning of it? Any answer will not be very satisfactory.

It seems that the fully programmable compensation handling is a good idea, and indispensable in some cases. The authors of BPEL4WS give an example in the [5], Section 13.2. On the other hand, the allowance of any structures and combinations in the fault and compensation handlers might bring troubles to the semantics, the implementation and the use of the language. A bundle of mechanisms to provide enough powerful, safe and easy-use programmable compensation is still a topic to investigate.

5   Relative Works

The concept *compensation* has its root to the seminal work of *Saga* [8] and open nested transactions [11], and has been studied for a long time in the transaction processing world. In recent years, some works have been done towards the formal definition of the concept. M. Mazzara *et al.* suggested to merge the fault and compensation handling into a general framework of event handling [10], and presented an operational semantics for their language. They also explained how to program manually the processes of exception handling and nested transactions with compensation handlers in their language.

In the recent paper [6], R. Bruni, *et al.* presented the operational semantics for a series of languages, and some additional features. The compensation in these languages is basic-activity-oriented (each basic activity is in company with a compensation) with no name. The compensation is triggered by a special command, and always executed in the reverse order with respect to the installation. Although there is a simple discussion about programmable compensation, that is not really programmable—at least not as what in BPEL4WS.

The paper [7] showed the recent work of M. Butler *et al.* on their language StAC (Structured Activity Compensation), where the language and its formal operational semantics were presented. The semantics of StAC was defined on its semantic language $StAC_i$, which had a complex operational semantics based on the indexed compensation tasks. The authors suggested to use their indexed compensation to model the compensation of BPEL4WS.

L. Bocchi, *et al.* presented in their paper [2] an extension of the asynchronous π-calculus with long-running transactions. The language has a structure called *failure bag*, which plays the similar role as the compensation context in our semantics, but presents at another level.

On the other hand, paper [1] proposed a general framework to systematically evaluate the capabilities and limitations of the language, and presented a detailed, but informal analysis of the language BPEL4WS. The author of [12] developed a process algebra to derive the interactive behavior of a business process out from a BPEL4WS specification. However, the paper focus on the detailed semantics of BPEL4WS, and intentionally neglects a number of aspects, including timeouts, fault handlers, compensation handlers, and so on.

6   Conclusion

BPEL4WS is one of the most important business process modelling languages, aimed to specify the business services which are formed by distributed, interoperational and heterogeneous components (processes) over networks. One distinct feature of BPEL4WS is the fully programmable fault and compensation handling mechanism, which allows the user to specify the compensation behaviors of processes in application-specific manners. The compensation is scope-based, fault-triggered. Each compensation handler belongs to a scope, and can be active only when it is invoked directly or indirectly by a fault handler.

In this paper, we studied the semantics of the fault and compensation handling in the BPEL4WS vein. A simple language *BPEL* is defined, which covers the features of BPEL4WS related to fault and compensation handling. Then a formal operational semantics for the language is presented. In this semantics, we proposed the concepts *compensation closure* and *compensation context*, which capture the execution structure and the process of the programmable compensation, and form a good framework to the semantics, and perhaps, to the structures of implementation of BPEL4WS.

We defined first a set of rules for the semantics of the sequential part of the language, and then extended it to deal with the parallel parts, with an additional concept of *forced termination*. Then we proved that the semantics is complete, and it follows the requirement that before a fault handler starts its work, the activities of the same scope which are active will all terminate (as defined by the BPEL4WS specification). At last, some examples are given to show how this semantics works. From this study, we obtain good insights into something of the BPEL4WS-like compensation, which are related to the language design and the implementation. We proposed a dynamic resource optimization technique for the implementation, and discussed some subtleties of the language.

As the further work, we are going to integrate the link mechanism into this framework, which is an important way supporting the synchronous of parallel structures in BPEL4WS specification. This will help us to capture and understand all the control flow of the BPEL4WS-like languages. We have already started the work on the semantics of the detailed level of BPEL4WS, and plan to integrate these works together, to form a complete semantics of the language.

References

1. W. Aalst, M. Dumas, and A. Hofstede, and P. Wohed, Analysis of web services composition languages: the case of BPEL4WS. *LNCS 2813*, pp. 200-215. Springer, 2003.
2. L. Bocchi, C. Laneve, and G. Zavattaro. A calculus for long-running transactions. *Proc. of FMOODS'03, LNCS 2884*, pp. 124-138. Springer, 2003.
3. S. Thatte. XLANG: Web Service for Business Process Design, http:www.gotdotnt. com/team/xmlwsspecs/xlang-c/default.html.
4. F. Leymann. WSFL: Web Serices Flow Languag, http://www-3.ibm.com/ software/solutions/webservices/pdf/WSDL.pdf.
5. BPEL4WS, *Business Process Execution Language for Web Service*, http://www. siebel.com/bpel, 2003.
6. Roberto Bruni, Hernán Melgratti, and Ugo Montanari, Theoritical foundations for compensation in flow composition languages, *POPL'05*, ACM, 2005.
7. M. Butler and C. Ferreira. An operational semantics for StAC, a language for modelling long-running business transactions. *LNCS 2949*, pp. 87-104. Springer, 2004.
8. H. Garcia-Molina and K. Salem. Sagas, *Proc. of ACM SIGMOD'87*, pp. 249-259. ACM Press, 1987.
9. J. Gay and A. Reuter. *Transaction Processing: Concepts and techniques*, Morgan Kaufmann, 1993.
10. M. Mazzara and R. Lucchi. A framework for generic error handling in business processes. *Proc. WS-FM'04, ENTCS* Vol. 105, pp. 133-145, Elsevier, 2004.
11. J. Moss. *Nested Transactions: An Approach to Reliable Distributed Computing*. PhD thesis, Dept. of Electrical Eng. and Computer Sci., MIT, 1981.
12. M. Viroli. Towards a formal foundation to orchestration languages. Proc. of WS-FM'04, ENTCS Vol. 105, pp. 51-71, Elsevier, 2004.

On Some Galois Connection Based Abstractions for the Mu-Calculus

Dragan Bošnački

Eindhoven University of Technology,
Den Dolech 2, P.O. Box 513, 5612 MB Eindhoven, The Netherlands
d.bosnacki@tue.nl

Abstract. In this paper we give some abstractions that preserve sublanguages of the universal part of the branching-time μ-calculus L_μ. We first extend some results by Loiseaux et al. by using a different abstraction for the universal fragments of L_μ which are treated in their work. We show that this leads to a more elegant theoretical treatment and more practical verification methodology. After that, we define an abstraction for a universal fragment of L_μ in which the formulas can contain the $\Box$-operator only under an even number of negations. The abstraction we propose is inspired by the work of Loiseaux et al., and Kesten and Pnueli. From the former we use the approach based on Galois connections, while from the latter we borrow the idea of "rewriting" the original formula using contracting/expanding abstractions. We argue that, besides removing some unnecessary syntactic restrictions, our approach leads to more compact and practical solutions to the abstraction problems.

Keywords: abstraction, property preservation, mu-calculus, model checking.

1 Introduction

Probably the main obstacle in the practical applications of the automated formal verification methods, like model checking, is the state-explosion problem, i.e., the excessive memory and time requirements caused by the size of the analyzed systems. Property preserving abstractions (c.f. [3, 10, 7]) are among the most successful techniques for tackling this problem. The idea behind these techniques is to construct, based on the original system model and the checked property, a smaller finite model by abstracting from the non-essential features of the system. Usually, the abstraction is designed such that the property is preserved in at least one direction: if the property holds for the obtained abstract model, than it also holds in the original (concrete) one.

An approach that addresses such a preservation is the Abstract Interpretation framework. Originally introduced for sequential programs [4], it was later extended to concurrent systems (e.g. [10, 5, 7]). Our paper can be seen as an extension of the work by Loiseaux et al. from [10]. Inspired by the ideas from

J.S. Fitzgerald, I.J. Hayes, and A. Tarlecki (Eds.): FM 2005, LNCS 3582, pp. 366–381, 2005.

Abstract Interpretation [4], in [10] a framework is developed to treat abstractions on the level of transition systems, which is based on the formal machinery of Galois connections between the concrete and abstract state spaces.

In this paper we give abstractions that preserve some universal fragments of the branching-time μ-calculus L_μ. Although the specifications in the μ-calculus are probably less comprehensible compared to other temporal logics, like LTL or CTL^*, the advantage of the μ-calculus is that it is strictly more expressive than those logics. Thus, all results about the μ-calculus automatically transfer to those logics.

We first improve on the results of [10] by introducing an abstraction for the two universal fragments of L_μ, $\Box L_\mu$ and $\Box L_\mu^+$, which differs from the one from [10]. ($\Box L_\mu$ allows negations only in front of atomic propositions, i.e., the formulas are in the so called positive normal form, while $\Box L_\mu^+$ does not allow negations at all.) Such an abstraction results with a verification methodology which is simpler and more direct than the one presented in [10]. For example, the obtained results were implemented successfully in practice for timer abstractions in [2].

In technical terms, our abstraction is expressed by means of $\widetilde{\alpha}$, the dual of the abstraction function α as defined in [10]. We show that the natural assumption that each state of the abstract state space must be related to a state of the concrete state space simplifies the proofs as well as the formulation of the results.

The second contribution of this paper is an abstraction for a universal fragment of the μ-calculus, which we denote with $\Box^e L_\mu$ and which is syntactically more general then the above mentioned fragments. In $\Box^e L_\mu$ the formulas may contain the $\Box$-operator only under even number of negations. The abstraction we propose for $\Box^e L_\mu$ is a combination of [10] and the work of Kesten and Pnueli [8]. From the former we reuse the basic methodology based on Galois connections, while from the latter we borrow the idea of "rewriting" the original formula using contracting/expanding abstractions. In fact, the "rewriting" amounts to just determining whether the atomic propositions are under an even or odd number of negations.

The abstraction of [10] cannot handle the fragment $\Box^e L_\mu$, because the latter allows negations. As $\Box^e L_\mu$ is a proper superset of $\Box L_\mu^+$ and $\Box L_\mu$, which can be handled by the abstraction of [10], our abstraction is obviously more general. But even if restricted to $\Box L_\mu^+$ and $\Box L_\mu$ our approach has advantages compared to [10], because it is more direct/automated and imposes less strict conditions on the abstraction. More liberal conditions often imply smaller abstract state spaces and therefore, more efficient verification. With regard to [8] our approach is an improvement because $\Box^e L_\mu$ is strictly more expressive than LTL which is used there. For example, the property "proposition p holds for all even execution steps along all executions of some process" can be expressed in $\Box^e L_\mu$, but not in LTL. We postpone the more detailed discussion about the contributions and the comparison with these references and other related work until the end of Section 4.

Paper layout. The next section provides the necessary background about transition systems, predicate transformers, and Galois connections, as well as definitions and results about the μ-calculus and abstractions. The main contributions of the paper are in Sections 3 and 4. Section 3 contains the first set of results as anticipated above, i.e., some preservation results about the universal fragments $\Box L_\mu$ and $\Box L_\mu^+$. In Section 4 we describe the abstraction that preserves the more general fragment $\Box L_\mu^e$. The last section concludes and discusses some possibilities for future work.

2 Preliminaries

In the first part of this section we recall some definitions and results from [10] about transition systems, predicate transformers and Galois connections.

2.1 Transition Systems, Predicate Transformers

Definition 1 (Transition Systems). *A transition system is a pair $S = (Q, R)$, where Q is a set of states and $R \subseteq Q \times Q$ is a transition relation.*

As we deal with μ-calculus in the rest of the paper we consider all properties to be state properties, i.e., interpreted as sets of states.

Definition 2 (Predicate Transformers pre and post). *Given a relation $\rho \subseteq Q_1 \times Q_2$, we define $pre[\rho] : 2^{Q_2} \to 2^{Q_1}$ and $post[\rho] : 2^{Q_1} \to 2^{Q_2}$ as*

$$- pre[\rho] \stackrel{def}{=} \lambda X.\{q_1 \in Q_1 : \exists q_2 \in X.q_1 \rho q_2\}$$
$$- post[\rho] \stackrel{def}{=} \lambda X.\{q_2 \in Q_2 : \exists q_1 \in X.q_1 \rho q_2\}$$

Thus, for $Q_2' \subseteq Q_2$, $pre[\rho](Q_2')$ gives the set of "predecessors" of the states of Q_2' with regard to the relation ρ and, similarly, for $Q_1' \subseteq Q_1$, $post[\rho](Q_2')$ is the set of "successors" of the states of Q_1' via ρ.

Definition 3 ((De Morgan) Dual Function).

Given a function $\alpha : 2^{Q_1} \to 2^{Q_2}$ we define its dual $\tilde{\alpha} \stackrel{def}{=} \lambda X.\overline{\alpha(\overline{X})}$, where $\overline{Q}$ denotes the complement of Q.

2.2 Galois Connections

Here we give some standard definitions and properties about Galois connections. See [10] for the proofs and more properties.

Note 4. We denote with Id_Q the identity function on 2^Q. Given two functions $f : Q \to Q'$ and $g : Q' \to Q''$, and $q \in Q$ we denote their composition $g(f(q))$ as $g \circ f$.

Definition 5 (Galois connection and Galois preinsertion). *Given two sets of states Q_1 and Q_2, a Galois connection from 2^{Q_1} to 2^{Q_2} is a pair of monotonic* *functions* (α, γ), *where* $\alpha : 2^{Q_1} \to 2^{Q_2}$ *and* $\gamma : 2^{Q_2} \to 2^{Q_1}$, *such that* $Id_{Q_1} \subseteq \gamma \circ \alpha$ *and* $\alpha \circ \gamma \subseteq Id_{Q_2}$. *(Here we assume that* $\subseteq$ *is a pointwise extension of the standard* $\subseteq$ *to functions.) A Galois connection* (α, γ) *is a Galois preinsertion iff* $\alpha(Q_1) = Q_2$ *and* $\widetilde{\gamma}(Q_2) = Q_1$.

Proposition 6 (Some Basic Galois Connection Properties). *For any Galois connection* (α, γ) *from* 2^{Q_1} *to* 2^{Q_2} *the following properties hold:*

- $\alpha(\emptyset) = \emptyset$,
- α *distributes over* $\cup$ *and* γ *distributes over* $\cap$.
- $(\widetilde{\gamma}, \widetilde{\alpha})$ *is a Galois connection from* 2^{Q_2} *to* 2^{Q_1},

The following propositions show the links between the binary relation ρ from Q_1 to Q_2 and the (functions of the) Galois connections from 2^{Q_1} to 2^{Q_2}.

Proposition 7 (Galois connections generated by relations). *Given a relation* $\rho \subseteq Q_1 \times Q_2$, *the pair* $(post[\rho], \widetilde{pre}[\rho])$ *is a Galois connection from* 2^{Q_1} *to* 2^{Q_2} *and* $(pre[\rho], \widetilde{post}[\rho])$ *is a Galois connection from* 2^{Q_2} *to* 2^{Q_1}.

Proposition 8 (Relations induced by Galois connections). *If* (α, γ) *is a Galois connection from* 2^{Q_1} *to* 2^{Q_2}, *then there exists a unique relation* $\rho \subseteq Q_1 \times Q_2$ *such that* $\alpha = post[\rho]$ *and* $\gamma = \widetilde{pre}[\rho]$.

Notice that if (α, γ) is a Galois preinsertion, because of $\alpha(Q_1) = Q_2$, each q_2 in Q_2 is an image under ρ of some q_1 from Q_1 and also, because of $\widetilde{\gamma}(Q_2) = Q_1$, each q_1 from Q_1 has an image q_2 in Q_2, i.e. ρ is total both on its domain and range.

2.3 Abstractions

We define the notion of abstraction as a simulation based on Galois connections. The whole approach is inspired by the notion of *abstract interpretation* originated by Cousot [4]. We first give an intuition behind the definition (see [1, 10] for more detail).

Let us consider a (concrete) system $S_1 = (Q_1, R_1)$. Designing an abstraction boils down to choosing an abstract state space Q_2 and a *description* relation $\rho \subseteq Q_1 \times Q_2$. Since we want that each concrete state has at least one abstract counterpart and there is no much sense having abstract states that are not related to any concrete state, we require that ρ is total on both Q_1 and Q_2. Intuitively, as we want to preserve the dynamic aspects of the system, we have to define the abstract transition relation R_2 in accord with ρ, such that the latter induces a simulation relation between S_1 and S_2 (c.f. [10]).[1] Then, because of easier formal treatment, we substitute ρ with a pair of (monotonic) functions α and γ, where $\alpha : 2^{Q_1} \to 2^{Q_2}$ is the point-wise lifting of ρ to the sets of states,

---

[1] The way of choosing/computing the above mentioned sets and relations is beyond the scope of this paper. We refer the reader for more detail to, for instance, 4.4.1 from [5] or 4.2 from [10].

i.e. $\alpha = post[\rho]$, and $\gamma : 2^{Q_2} \to 2^{Q_1}$ is the dual of the inverse image of ρ, i.e. $\gamma = \widetilde{pre}[\rho]$. (See Propositions 7 and 8.) Thus, in the following definition the simulation requirement is given in terms of α, γ, R_1 and R_2:

Definition 9 (Abstraction). *Let $S_1 = (Q_1, R_1)$ and $S_2 = (Q_2, R_2)$ be two transition systems and let (α, γ) be a Galois preinsertion from 2^{Q_1} to 2^{Q_2}. We define*

$$S_1 \sqsubseteq_{(\alpha,\gamma)} S_2 \text{ iff } \alpha \circ pre[R_1] \circ \gamma \subseteq pre[R_2].$$

We say that S_2 is an abstraction *of S_1.*

The abstraction definition from [10] allows a more general Galois connection instead of a Galois preinsertion. However from a practical point of view using a Galois preinsertion, i.e., requiring that each state in the abstract state space Q_2 is an image of some concrete state from Q_1, is natural because we always try to work with an abstraction which is as "small" as possible. Having abstract states which are not related to some concrete state does not make much sense, because such states would introduce an extra behavior which has no counterpart in the concrete system. This could lead to spurious counterexamples (false negatives) which is one of the main problems in the practical application of abstractions.

Intuitively, as a consequence of the simulation and with properly chosen interpretations I_1, I_2, a given formula f of some logic holds on S_1 if it holds on S_2, under the condition that $\widetilde{\gamma}(I_2(f)) \subseteq I_1(f)$. In other words, the concretization of each interpretation which satisfies f in the abstract system "falls" in the set of interpretations that satisfy f in the concrete system. The preservation result holds for formulas of temporal logics without existential quantification over paths, e.g. the universal fragments of the μ-calculus or LTL [10, 6]. We give later a more formal treatment of these issues.

2.4   The Propositional μ-Calculus

We briefly recall the syntax and the semantics of the propositional μ-calculus L_μ and we define the fragments that we are going to consider in the sequel.

Definition 10 (L_μ syntax). *Let $\mathcal{P}$ be a set of atomic propositions, $\mathcal{X}$ a set of variables, and let $p \in \mathcal{P}$ and $X \in \mathcal{X}$. The set of the formulas of the propositional μ-calculus L_μ is defined by the following grammar:*

$$f ::= \top \mid p \mid X \mid \Diamond f \mid f \vee f \mid \neg f \mid \mu X.f$$

where in the last clause ($\mu X.f$) f is syntactically monotonic on X, i.e., each occurrence of X in f is under an even number of negations.

We extend L_μ in a standard way with the formulas $\bot, f \wedge g, f \Rightarrow g, \nu X.f(X)$ and $\Box f$ which are defined as abbreviations for $\neg\top, \neg(\neg f \vee \neg g), \neg f \vee g, \neg\mu X.\neg f(\neg X)$, and $\neg\Diamond\neg f$, respectively.

Intuitively, the meaning of a formula $\Diamond f$ is that f is true for some immediate successor of a given state, while $\Box f$ means that f is true in all immediate successors. Variables can be considered as formulas that have to be interpreted depending on some environment that maps variables to sets of states. In a sense they are auxiliaries in the context of the fix point operators. The meaning of $\mu X.f$ (resp. $\nu X.f$) the least (resp. the greatest) fix point, is the smallest (resp. greatest) set X of states for which f holds, where f usually depends on X. For instance, assuming transition systems in which every state has a successor, the claim "proposition p is true in all states that are reachable from a given state" is expressed by the formula $\nu X.(p \wedge \Box X)$, while $\mu X.(p \vee \Diamond X)$ expresses "there exists a path along which p eventually holds".

Formally, the semantics of the formulae is defined for a given transition system $S = (Q, R)$ and an interpretation function for the atomic propositions $I_{\mathcal{P}} : \mathcal{P} \to 2^Q$. A formula f with n free variables is interpreted via a function $I : L_\mu \times (2^Q)^n \to 2^Q$. In particular, a closed formula is interpreted as a subset of Q.

Definition 11 (Semantics of the μ-Calculus).
For a valuation $V = (V1, \ldots, V_n) \in (2^Q)^n$ of the variables, the interpretation function I is defined by induction on the formula structure as follows:

- $I(\top) = Q$,
- $I(p) = I_{\mathcal{P}}(p)$,
- $I(X_j)(V) = V_j$,
- $I(f_1 \vee f_2)(V) = I(f_1)(V) \cup I(f_2)(V)$,
- $I(\neg f)(V) = \overline{I(f)(V)}$,
- $I(\Diamond f)(V) = pre[R](I(f)(V))$,
- $I(\mu X.f)(V) = \bigcap \{Q' \subseteq Q : I(f)[Q'/X](V) \subset Q'\}$.

where $I(f)[Q/X](V)$ means that each occurrence of X in $I(f)$ is replaced by Q. (For brevity, in the first two clauses we omit the valuation V.)

We say that a formula of the (extended) language L_μ is in *positive normal form* iff all the negations occur only applied to atomic propositions. Often one needs to consider fragments of L_μ that involve only universal (resp. existential) computation over the computation sequences. The former are achieved by allowing only the usage of the $\Box$ (resp. $\Diamond$) operator in the formulas. More formally, the universal and existential fragments of L_μ, $\Box L_\mu$ and $\Diamond L_\mu$, are defined respectively with the following grammars:

$$g ::= \top \mid \bot \mid p \mid \neg p \mid X \mid \Box g \mid g \vee g \mid g \wedge g \mid \mu X.g \mid \nu X.g$$

$$h ::= \top \mid \bot \mid p \mid \neg p \mid X \mid \Diamond h \mid h \vee h \mid h \wedge h \mid \mu X.h \mid \nu X.h$$

Notice that both $\Box L_\mu$ and $\Diamond L_\mu$ allow only formulas in positive normal form. So called *positive* fragments of $\Box L_\mu$ and $\Diamond L_\mu$, denoted by $\Box^+ L_\mu$ and $\Diamond^+ L_\mu$, respectively, are obtained by totally forbidding the usage of $\neg$ – even in front of atomic propositions.

Note 12. One can consider the interpretation I as being parameterized by the transition system S, the set of atomic propositions $\mathcal{P}$, and their interpretation $I_{\mathcal{P}}$. When we need to emphasize this we write $I[S, \mathcal{P}, I_{\mathcal{P}}]$ for the interpretation function.

Definition 13 (Satisfaction and Preservation of Formulas). *Given a for-mula* $f \in L_\mu$ *and a transition system* $S = (Q, R)$ *with an interpretation function* I *as in Def. 11 we say that* S *satisfies* f *(denoted as* $S \models f$*) iff* $I(f) = Q$, *i.e., the formula holds in each state of* S.

Lemma 14 (Satisfaction and Preservation of Formulas).
Let $S_1 = (Q_1, R_1)$ *and* $S_2 = (Q_2, R_2)$ *be two transition systems such that* $S_1 \sqsubseteq_{(\alpha, \gamma)} S_2$. *Then, for all formulas* $f, g \in L_\mu$ *and corresponding interpretation functions* I_1, I_2:

- $\widetilde{\gamma}(I_2(f)) \subseteq I_1(g)$ *implies* $S_2 \models f \Rightarrow S_1 \models g$, *and*
- $\alpha(I_1(g)) \subseteq I_2(f)$ *implies* $S_1 \models g \Rightarrow S_2 \models f$.

Proof. Suppose $S_2 \models f$. According to Def. 13 this means that $I_2(f) = Q_2$. Since (α, γ) is a preinsertion $\widetilde{\gamma}(I_2(f)) = Q_1$. Using the condition of the lemma this gives $Q_1 \subseteq I_1(g)$. On the other hand, it is easy to see from the interpretation definition (Def. 11) that $I_1(g) \subseteq Q_1$. Thus, $I_1(g) = Q_1$, which is equivalent to $S_1 \models g$.

The second implication can be proved in an analogous way.   □

3   Some Preservation Results About $\Box L_\mu$ and $\Box L_\mu^+$

This section and the next contain the main contributions of this paper. In this section we give some results related to the preservation of the sublanguages $\Box L_\mu$ and $\Box L_\mu^+$ which expand the material from [10]. We show that, for our abstraction definition based on Galois preinsertion instead of Galois connection, $\widetilde{\alpha}$ coincides with what is known in the literature as contracting abstraction. This significantly simplifies the theory and leads to its more efficient application, which is discussed at the end of the section.

As the interpretation function I in Def. 11, which defines the μ-calculus semantics, is parameterized by the interpretation of the atomic propositions, the latter is in the core of the preservation results.

Definition 15 (Consistency). *Let* Q_1 *and* Q_2 *be two sets of states and* $I_\mathcal{P} : \mathcal{P} \rightarrow 2^{Q_1}$ *an interpretation of the atomic propositions. A given function* $\alpha : 2^{Q_1} \rightarrow 2^{Q_2}$ *is consistent with* $I_\mathcal{P}$ *iff*

$$\forall p \in \mathcal{P}.\alpha(\overline{I_\mathcal{P}(p)}) \cap \alpha(I_\mathcal{P}(p)) = \emptyset.$$

The definition of consistency can be lifted in an obvious way for an interpretation function I of a μ-calculus formula over Q_1 which is parameterized with a given interpretation of propositions $I_\mathcal{P}$ according to Def. 11. In that case we also write $I(p)$ instead of $I_\mathcal{P}(p)$.

Intuitively, α is consistent with $I_\mathcal{P}$ if for all atomic propositions the images under α of the interpretations of p and $\neg p$ are not contradictory. Note that, in this case, for all $s_1 \in Q_1, s_2 \in Q_2$ such that $s_2 \in \alpha(\{s_1\})$, $s_1 \in I_1(p)$ iff $s_2 \in I_2(p)$, where $I_1(p) = I_\mathcal{P}(p)$ and $I_2(p) = \alpha(I_1(p))$. Or, intuitively, s_2 satisfies p iff each image s_1 satisfies p. The notion of consistency coincides with the notion of *precise* abstraction from [8].

Besides the consistent (precise) interpretation of the atomic proposition in the abstract domain, we use also *contracting* (also called *universal, underapproximation*) and *expanding* (*existential, overapproximation*) interpretations of the atomic propositions defined by $I_2(p) = \alpha(I_1(p)) - \alpha(\overline{I_1(p)})$ and $I_2(p) = \alpha(I_1(p))$, respectively. For all $s_1 \in Q_1, s_2 \in Q_2$ such that $s_2 \in \alpha(\{s_1\})$, $s_1 \in I_1(p)$ if $s_2 \in I_2(p)$ in case of the contracting abstraction, and $s_2 \in I_2(p)$ if $s_1 \in I_1(p)$, for the expanding one.

Intuitively, in a contracting abstraction, if p holds in s_2, all the states which are concretizations of s_2 have to satisfy p too, while in case of expanding abstraction one requires that at least one concretization satisfies p. Notice the duality of the contracting and expanding abstractions with respect to the negation, which is one of the key aspects of the abstraction we define later in Section 4.

Proposition 16 (Contracting Abstraction via $\widetilde{\alpha}$). *Let (α, γ) be a Galois preinsertion from 2^{Q_1} to 2^{Q_2}. Then for all $Q \subseteq Q_1$, $\alpha(Q) - \alpha(\overline{Q}) = \widetilde{\alpha}(Q)$.*

Proof. By the definition of Galois preinsertion (Def. 5) $\alpha(Q_1) = Q_2$. Since $Q \cup \overline{Q} = Q_1$ and by the distributivity of α over $\cup$ (Prop. 6) we have that $\alpha(Q) \cup \alpha(\overline{Q}) = Q_2$, which is equivalent to $\overline{\alpha(\overline{Q})} \subseteq \alpha(Q)$. Using this further we get $\alpha(Q) - \alpha(\overline{Q}) = \alpha(Q) \cap \overline{\alpha(\overline{Q})} = \overline{\alpha(\overline{Q})} = \widetilde{\alpha}(Q)$. $\square$

Note 17. In view of the above proposition, we can also state the condition for the contracting abstraction as $I_2(p) = \widetilde{\alpha}(I_1(p))$. This seemingly trivial observation leads to much more elegant proofs and many properties of the abstraction become direct consequences of the basic properties of Galois connections.

Proposition 18 (Consistency of $\widetilde{\gamma}$). *Let S_1 and S_2 be transition systems such that $S_1 \sqsubseteq_{(\alpha, \gamma)} S_2$, I_1 and I_2 their corresponding interpretation functions, $\mathcal{P}$ a set of propositions. And let us assume a contracting abstraction for the atomic propositions, i.e., for all $p \in \mathcal{P}$, $I_2(p) = \widetilde{\alpha}(I_1(p))$. Then, if α is consistent with I_1, then $\widetilde{\gamma}$ is consistent with I_2.*

Proof. Using the definition of I_2 we obtain $\widetilde{\gamma}(I_2(p)) \cap \widetilde{\gamma}(\overline{I_2(p)}) = \widetilde{\gamma}(\widetilde{\alpha}(I_1(p))) \cap \widetilde{\gamma}(\overline{\widetilde{\alpha}(I_1(p))}) = \widetilde{\gamma}(\widetilde{\alpha}(I_1(p))) \cap \widetilde{\gamma}(\alpha(\overline{I_1(p)}))$.

By $\alpha(Q_1) = Q_2$ (because (α, γ) is a Galois preinsertion) we have $\alpha(I_1(p)) \cup \alpha(\overline{I_1(p)}) = Q_2$. Together with the fact that $\alpha(I_1(p)) \cap \alpha(\overline{I_1(p)}) = \emptyset$, (which follows from the consistency of α (Def. 15)) and the definition of $\widetilde{\alpha}$ this gives $\alpha(\overline{I_1(p)}) = \overline{\alpha(I_1(p))} = \widetilde{\alpha}(\overline{I_1(p)})$.

Thus, $\widetilde{\gamma}(\widetilde{\alpha}(I_1(p))) \cap \widetilde{\gamma}(\alpha(\overline{I_1(p)})) = \widetilde{\gamma}(\widetilde{\alpha}(I_1(p))) \cap \widetilde{\gamma}(\widetilde{\alpha}(\overline{I_1(p)})) \subseteq I_1(p) \cap \overline{I_1(p)} = \emptyset$ which establishes the claim. $\square$

As sometimes the proofs of consistency of the abstraction α are more intuitive than the proofs of consistency of the concretization $\widetilde{\gamma}$, the last property could be quite important in practice.

The following theorem from [10] is a basis for the preservation results in this subsection.

Theorem 19 (Preservation of $\Box L_\mu^+$ and $\Box L_\mu$). *Let $S_1 = (Q_1, R_1)$ and $S_2 = (Q_2, R_2)$ be two transition systems such that $S_1 \sqsubseteq_{(\alpha,\gamma)} S_2$, $\mathcal{P}$ a set of atomic propositions, and $I_\mathcal{P} : \mathcal{P} \to Q_2$ an interpretation function for the atomic propositions in S_2. Further, let $I_1 = I[S_1, \mathcal{P}, \tilde\gamma \circ I_\mathcal{P}]$ and $I_2 = I[S_2, \mathcal{P}, I_\mathcal{P}]$, where I is as in Def. 11. Then*

$$\tilde\gamma(I_2(f)) \subseteq I_1(f)$$

- *for any formula f of $\Box L_\mu^+$, and*
- *if α is consistent with $I_\mathcal{P}$, also for any formula f of $\Box L_\mu$.*

Proof. The theorem is Theorem 2, item 1B, from [10] rephrased with our denotations and terminology. □

Thus, the interpretation function of the atomic propositions of the concrete system is $\tilde\gamma \circ I_\mathcal{P}$ – a concretization of its counterpart from the abstract system. Using Theorem 19 we can formulate the following preservation result:

Theorem 20 (Preservation of $\Box L_\mu^+$ and $\Box L_\mu$ under $\tilde\alpha$). *Let $S_1 = (Q_1, R_1)$ and $S_2 = (Q_2, R_2)$ be two transition systems such that $S_1 \sqsubseteq_{(\alpha,\gamma)} S_2$, $\mathcal{P}$ a set of atomic propositions, and $I_\mathcal{P} : \mathcal{P} \to Q_1$ an interpretation function for the atomic propositions in S_1. Further, let $I_1 = I[S_1, \mathcal{P}, I_\mathcal{P}]$ and $I_2 = I[S_1, \mathcal{P}, \tilde\alpha \circ I_\mathcal{P})]$ be the interpretation functions for S_1 and S_2, respectively. Then,*

$$S_2 \models f \Rightarrow S_1 \models f,$$

- *for any formula f of $\Box L_\mu^+$*
- *and, if α is consistent with $I_\mathcal{P}$, also for any formula f of $\Box L_\mu$.*

Proof. By Theorem 19 $\tilde\gamma(I_2(f)) \subseteq I_1'(f)$, where $I_1' = I[S_1, \mathcal{P}, \tilde\gamma \circ \tilde\alpha \circ I_\mathcal{P}]$ and $I_2 = I[S_2, \mathcal{P}, \tilde\alpha \circ I_\mathcal{P}]$, for I as in Def. 11. As f (of $\Box L_\mu^+$) is syntactically monotonic (no negations) also the interpretation function I_1' is monotonic (on the interpretation of the atomic propositions). Thus, as because of the Galois connection $(\tilde\gamma, \tilde\alpha)$, $\tilde\gamma \circ \tilde\alpha(I_\mathcal{P}) \subseteq I_\mathcal{P}$, we obtain $I_1'(f) = I[S_2, \mathcal{P}, \tilde\gamma \circ \tilde\alpha(I_\mathcal{P})](f) \subseteq I[S_2, \mathcal{P}, I_\mathcal{P}](f) = I_1(f)$. The preservation claim in the theorem follows by transitivity and Lemma 14.

Like in the proof of Prop. 18, one can show that for a consistent α: $\alpha \circ I_\mathcal{P} = \tilde\alpha \circ I_\mathcal{P}$. Also by Prop. 18 if α is consistent with $I_\mathcal{P}$, then $\tilde\gamma$ is consistent with $\tilde\alpha \circ I_\mathcal{P}$. The definition of consistency implies that α is defined on the whole set 2^{Q_1}. As a consequence, the relation ρ implied by Prop. 8 is defined for each element of Q_1, which further implies that $\tilde\alpha(Q_2) = Q_1$. Using a reasoning dual to the one we used in the proof of Prop. 18 to show that $\alpha = \tilde\alpha$ we obtain that $\tilde\gamma \circ \tilde\alpha \circ I_\mathcal{P} = \gamma \circ \tilde\alpha \circ I_\mathcal{P}$. Now taking into account the above and by the basic Galois properties that $\tilde\gamma \circ \tilde\alpha = \gamma \circ \alpha \supseteq Id_{Q_1}$ and $\tilde\gamma \circ \tilde\alpha \subseteq Id_{Q_1}$ we conclude $\tilde\gamma \circ \tilde\alpha \circ I_\mathcal{P} = I_\mathcal{P}$. By substituting the last equality in I_1' above one can show that $I_1'(f) = I_1(f)$ which implies the preservation of the formulas of $\Box L_\mu$. □

Application. Based on Theorem 20 one can develop a straightforward verification method. Given a system $S_1 = (Q_1, R_1)$, a set of atomic propositions $\mathcal{P}$ occurring in a formula $f \in \Box L_\mu^+(\Box L_\mu)$ and an interpretation function for the propositions $I_\mathcal{P}$, we first give an abstraction relation ρ which is total on Q_1 and Q_2, and compute the abstract system S_2. Then we verify if S_2 satisfies f with interpretation (of the atomic propositions) $\tilde{\alpha} \circ I_\mathcal{P}$. If f holds for S_2, then it holds for S_1 too (with the original interpretation $I_\mathcal{P}$).

This method has an advantage over the one suggested in [10] (Section 6.3) in the sense that with their method, in general, one only shows that f holds for S_1 with the interpretation function $\tilde{\gamma} \circ \alpha \circ I_\mathcal{P}$. This is a disadvantage compared to the method described above, because if one wants to further show also the correctness under $I_\mathcal{P}$, one has to use an additional arguments, which is often not obvious.

4   Contracting-Expanding Abstraction for the μ-Calculus

In this section we give an abstraction which preserves formulas from the language $\Box^e L_\mu$ which is a superset of $\Box L_\mu$. In $\Box^e L_\mu$ negation operators are not applied only to atomic propositions. As we want to stay within the universal fragment, the only constraint (besides the standard syntactic monotonicity on variables) is that the $\Box$ operator is under an even number of negations. (Otherwise, one gets implicit existential fragments, i.e., the $\Diamond$ operator which is dual to $\Box$.)

Definition 21 ($\Box^e L_\mu$ syntax). *Let $\mathcal{P}$ be a set of atomic propositions, $\mathcal{X}$ a set of variables, and let $p \in \mathcal{P}$ and $X \in \mathcal{X}$. The set of the formulas of $\Box^e L_\mu$ is defined by the following grammar:*

$$f ::= \top \mid p \mid X \mid \Box f \mid f \vee f \mid \neg f \mid \mu X.f$$

where in the last case each occurrence of X is under an even number of negations. Also, each f of $\Box^e L_\mu$ is syntactically monotonic on the $\Box$ operator, i.e., each occurrence of the latter is under an even number of negations.

In order to obtain preservation abstraction for the formulas of $\Box^e L_\mu$, we take the approach from [8] in the sense that the original formula f is first "rewritten" into its contraction f^-, and the interpretation in the abstract state space is defined on the latter. In that regard, we slightly depart from [10] where the same formula f is interpreted by means of two different interpretation functions (actually, one function parameterized by the atomic proposition interpretation) in the abstract and concrete state spaces.[2] Given a formula $f \in \Box^e L_\mu$ interpreted via an interpretation I_1 on the concrete system S_1, we want to define a corresponding formula f^- with interpretation I_2 on the abstraction S_2 such that if f^- holds on S_2 then f holds on S_1.

The contracting and expanding operators, $(\cdot)^-$ and $(\cdot)^+$, respectively, which map f into its contraction f^- and expansion f^+, resp., are defined as below.

---

[2] An equivalent alternative approach which is more in the spirit of [10] is also possible: One can give only a new interpretation function defined inductively via two functions I_2^- and I_2^+ for the abstract domain. We decided to take the approach in the paper mainly because of the sake of clarity - the denotation is more compact.

The new formulas f^- and f^+ are defined over the same set of variables $\mathcal{X}$, but with a new set of propositions $\mathcal{P}^{\mp} = \{p^- \mid p \in \mathcal{P}\} \cup \{p^+ \mid p \in \mathcal{P}\}$. In other words, $\mathcal{P}^{\mp}$ is obtained by replacing in $\mathcal{P}$ each proposition p with its two superscripted versions p^- and p^+.

Definition 22 (Contracting/expanding abstraction of formulas). *Given a formula f of $\square^e L_\mu$ we define inductively its contraction f^- and expansion f^+ as follows:*

- $(\top)^- = (\top)^+ = \top,$
- $(p)^- = p^-, (p)^+ = p^+,$
- $(X)^- = (X)^+ = X,$
- $(\neg f)^- = \neg f^+, (\neg f)^+ = \neg f^-,$
- $(\square f)^- = \square f^-, (\square f)^+ = \square f^+,$
- $(f_1 \vee f_2)^- = f_1^- \vee f_2^-, (f_1 \vee f_2)^+ = f_1^+ \vee f_2^+,$
- $(\mu X.f)^- = \mu X.f^-, (\mu X.f)^+ = \mu X.f^+.$

where $p^-, p^+ \in \mathcal{P}^{\mp}$ are as defined above.

Note that structure remains preserved and only the atomic propositions of the original formula f are replaced with their contractions or expansions p^- and p^+. Intuitively, the latter represent the contracting and expanding abstractions of the original proposition p. Thus, assuming a proposition interpretation function $I_{\mathcal{P}} : \mathcal{P} \to 2^{Q_1}$ for the concrete system S_1, we define the proposition interpretation function $I_{\mathcal{P}^{\mp}} : \mathcal{P}^{\mp} \to 2^{Q_2}$ for the abstract system S_2 for a given $p \in \mathcal{P}$ as $I_{\mathcal{P}^{\mp}}(p^-) = \widetilde{\alpha}(I_{\mathcal{P}}(p))$ and $I_{\mathcal{P}^{\mp}}(p^+) = \alpha(I_{\mathcal{P}}(p))$.

Now we can define the interpretation function of the formulas as $I_2 = I[S_2, \mathcal{P}^{\mp}, I_{\mathcal{P}^{\mp}}]$ where I is defined as in Def. 11, or in an unfolded form:

Definition 23 (Interpretation in the abstract domain). *For a valuation $V = (V1, \ldots, V_n) \in (2^{Q_2})^n$ of the variables, the interpretation function I_2 is defined by induction on the formula structure as follows:*

1. $I_2(\top) = Q_2;$
2. $I_2(p^-) = \widetilde{\alpha}(I_1(p)), I_2(p^+) = \alpha(I_1(p));$
3. $I_2(X_j)(V) = V_j;$
4. $I_2(g_1 \vee g_2)(V) = I_2(g_1)(V) \cup I_2(g_2)(V);$
5. $I_2(\neg g)(V) = \overline{I_2(g)(V)};$
6. $I_2(\square g)(V) = \square I_2(g)(V) = \widetilde{pre}[R](I_2(g)(V));$
7. $I_2(\mu X.g)(V) = \bigcap\{Q' \subseteq Q_2 : I_2(g)[Q'/X](V) \subseteq Q'\}$

where I_1 is the interpretation function defined on the concrete system as in Def. 11.

The fact that interpretation I_2 differs from the standard interpretation only in the interpretation of the atomic propositions is important from a practical point of view because it means that we can apply standard methods (designed for non-abstracted systems) for the verification of abstract systems.

The main property that we want to show is

Theorem 24. *Given two transition systems $S_1 = (Q_1, R_1)$ and $S_2 = (Q_2, R_2)$, such that $S_1 \sqsubseteq_{(\alpha, \gamma)} S_2$, and a formula f of $\square^e L_\mu$,*

- *$S_2 \models f^- \Rightarrow S_1 \models f$ and*
- *$S_1 \models f \Rightarrow S_2 \models f^+$.*

This follows, via Lemma 14, from the following result:

Lemma 25 (Preservation of $\square^e L_\mu$).

   Let $S_1 = (Q_1, R_1)$ and $S_2 = (Q_2, R_2)$ be two transition systems such that $S_1 \sqsubseteq_{(\alpha, \gamma)} S_2$, and I_1 and I_2 their corresponding interpretation functions, as they are defined in Def. 11 and 23, respectively. Then, for a given formula f in $\square^e L_\mu$ and a valuation (vector) V we have

- *$\widetilde{\gamma}(I_2(f^-)(\widetilde{\alpha}(V))) \subseteq I_1(f)(V)$ and*
- *$\alpha(I_1(f)(V)) \subseteq I_2(f^+)(\alpha(V))$*

Proof. The proof is by mutual induction on the formula structure for the properties $\widetilde{\gamma}(I_2(f^-)) \subseteq I_1(f)$ and $\alpha(I_1(f)) \subseteq I_2(f^+)$. For simplicity, we omit the valuation V in the cases in which it is not relevant.

1. $\widetilde{\gamma}(I_2(\top)) = \widetilde{\gamma}(Q_2) = Q_1 = I_1(\top)$, because (α, γ) is a Galois preinsertion. Similarly, $\alpha(I_1(\top)) = \alpha(Q_1) = Q_2 = I_2(\top)$.
2. $\widetilde{\gamma}(I_2(p^-)) = \widetilde{\gamma}(\widetilde{\alpha}(I_1(p))) \subseteq I_1(p)$, because by Prop. 6 $(\widetilde{\gamma}, \widetilde{\alpha})$ is a Galois connection and using the basic properties of Galois connections from Def. 5. The second property (co-property) holds trivially: $\alpha(I_1(p)) = I_2(p^+)$.
3. $\widetilde{\gamma}(I_2(X_j)(\widetilde{\alpha}(V))) = \widetilde{\gamma}(\widetilde{\alpha}(V_j)) \subseteq V_j = I_1(X_j)(V)$, by a similar reasoning like for the atomic propositions case. Also, immediately by the interpretation definitions, $\alpha(I_1(X_j)(V)) = \alpha(V_j) = I_2(X_j)(\alpha(V))$.
4. $\widetilde{\gamma}(I_2((f_1 \vee f_2)^-)) = \widetilde{\gamma}(I_2((f_1)^-) \cup I_2((f_2)^-))$ by the definition of the contracting/expanding operators and interpretation function. As $\widetilde{\gamma}$ distributes over $\cup$ (Prop. 6), we have $\widetilde{\gamma}(I_2((f_1 \vee f_2)^-)) = \widetilde{\gamma}(I_2((f_1)^-)) \cup \widetilde{\gamma}(I_2((f_2)^-))$. By the induction hypothesis $\widetilde{\gamma}(I_2((f_1 \vee f_2)^-)) \subseteq I_1(f_1) \cup I_1(f_2) = I_1(f_1 \vee f_2)$. As α too distributes over $\cup$ (Prop. 6), the co-property can be shown in an analogous way.
5. By applying the definition of the contracting/expanding operators as well as the definition of I_2 one gets: $\widetilde{\gamma}(I_2((\neg f)^-)(\widetilde{\alpha}(V))) = \widetilde{\gamma}(I_2(\neg f^+)(\widetilde{\alpha}(V)))$.
   For the next step we need the observation that $\neg f^+$ is syntactically monotonic on the occurrences of the variables from $\mathcal{X}$, i.e. each variable in f^+ is under an odd number of negations. This is because on the top level we begin with the formula f^- which by definition is syntactically monotonic on the variables of $\mathcal{X}$. Each time a negation occurs also the superscript of the subformulae toggles which implies that a subformula of the form f_1^- always contains an even number of negations (i.e. it is always syntactically monotonic), while formulas of the form f_2^+ contain an odd number of negations. Similarly, knowing that we start with a formula which is syntactically

monotonic on the $\square$ operator, we can conclude that each occurrence of the $\square$ operator in formulas of the form f_1^- is under an even number of negations and in those of the form f_2^+ under an odd number of negations. Thus in a formula of the form $\neg f$ the subformula f cannot be of the form $\square f_1$. This is important to note because, as we will see below, one cannot show the co-property $\alpha(I_1(\neg f)) \subseteq I_2(f^+)$ (see below) for the case $\square f$, and on the other hand the co-property is used in the proof of the current case $(\neg f)$.

The syntactic monotonicity of $\neg f^+$ on the variables of $\mathcal{X}$ implies the monotonicity of $I_2(\neg f^+)$. Therefore, by the monotonicity of $\widetilde{\gamma}$ and $\widetilde{\alpha}(Q) \subseteq \alpha(Q)$, we have further $\widetilde{\gamma}(I_2(\neg f^+)(\widetilde{\alpha}(V))) \subseteq \widetilde{\gamma}(I_2(\neg f^+)(\alpha(V))) = \widetilde{\gamma}(\overline{I_2(f^+)(\alpha(V))})$, where the last equality follows by the definition of I_2. By negating both sides of the co-property from the induction hypothesis we get $\alpha(I_1(f)) \supseteq \overline{I_2(f^+)(\alpha(V))}$. Thus, using the monotonicity of $\widetilde{\gamma}$ one obtains $\widetilde{\gamma}(\overline{I_2(f^+)(\alpha(V))}) \subseteq \widetilde{\gamma}(\alpha(I_1(f))(V)) = \widetilde{\gamma}(\widetilde{\alpha}(\overline{I_1(f)(V)})) \subseteq \overline{I_1(f)(V)} = I_1(\neg f)(V)$.

The second set inequality is implied by the Galois connection $(\widetilde{\gamma}, \widetilde{\alpha})$.

The proof of $\alpha(I_1(\neg f)(V)) \subseteq I_2((\neg f)^+)(\widetilde{\alpha}(V))$ goes analogously by starting with the first part of the induction hypothesis $\widetilde{\gamma}(I_2(f^-)(\widetilde{\alpha}(V))) \subseteq I_1(f)(V)$, with the roles of α and $\widetilde{\gamma}$ swapped.

6. By the definition of $S_1 \sqsubseteq_{\langle \alpha, \gamma \rangle} S_2$ (Def. 9) we have

$$\alpha \circ pre[R_1] \circ \gamma \subseteq pre[R_2]$$

or, equivalently, by applying complement on both sides,

$$\overline{pre[R_2]} \subseteq \overline{\alpha \circ pre[R_1] \circ \gamma}.$$

Using the last set inclusion we get
$$I_2((\square f)^-) = \widetilde{pre}[R_2](I_2(f^-)) = \overline{pre[R_2](\overline{I_2(f^-)})} \subseteq$$
$$\overline{\alpha(pre[R1](\gamma(\overline{I_2(f^-)})))} =$$
$$\widetilde{\alpha}(\overline{pre[R_1](\gamma(\overline{I_2(f^-)}))}) = \widetilde{\alpha}(\widetilde{pre}[R_1](\overline{\gamma(\overline{I_2(f^-)})})) = \widetilde{\alpha}(\widetilde{pre}[R_1](\widetilde{\gamma}(I_2(f^-))))$$
$$\subseteq \widetilde{\alpha}(\widetilde{pre}[R_1](I_1(f))).$$
The last set inclusion follows by the induction hypothesis and the monotonicity of $\widetilde{\alpha}$ and $\widetilde{pre}$. Further, continuing from the property we have shown above, i.e., $I_2((\square f)^-) \subseteq \widetilde{\alpha}(\widetilde{pre}[R_1](I_1(f)))$, by the monotonicity of $\widetilde{\gamma}$ and the basic properties of the connection $(\widetilde{\gamma}, \widetilde{\alpha})$ we get
$$\widetilde{\gamma}(I_2((\square f)^-)) \subseteq \widetilde{\gamma}(\widetilde{\alpha}(\widetilde{pre}[R_1](I_1(f)))) \subseteq \widetilde{pre}[R_1](I_1(f)) = I_1(\square f).$$
Note that for this case the co-property $\alpha(I_1(\square f)) \supseteq I_2((\square f)^+)$ does not hold. However, we can prove that $\alpha(I_1(\lozenge f)) \supseteq I_2((\lozenge f)^+)$, by using a reasoning dual to the one for the $\square$ operator.

7. As $\widetilde{\gamma}$ does not distribute over $\cap$, which occurs in the definition of the fixed point operator, in this case we use the fact that $\widetilde{\gamma}(I_2(f^-) \subseteq I_1(f)$ is equivalent to $I_2(f^-) \subseteq \widetilde{\alpha}(I_1(f))$ (an easy check using the basic Galois connection properties). Thus, we effectively replace $\widetilde{\gamma}$ with $\widetilde{\alpha}$ which does distribute over $\cap$ (Prop. 6).

By the interpretation definition we have

$$I_1(\mu X.f(V)) = \bigcap \{P_1 \subseteq Q_1 : I_1(f)[P_1/X](V) \subseteq P_1\}.$$

By the monotonicity of $\widetilde{\alpha}$ and the syntactic monotonicity of f

$$I_1(f)[P_1/X](V) \subseteq P_1(*)$$

implies

$$\widetilde{\alpha}(I_1(f)[P_1/X](V)) \subseteq \widetilde{\alpha}(P_1).$$

Applying the induction hypothesis

$$I_2(f^-)[\widetilde{\alpha}(P_1)/X](\widetilde{\alpha}(V)) \subseteq \widetilde{\alpha}(I_1(f)[P_1/X](V))$$

which by transitivity gives

$$I_2(f^-)[\widetilde{\alpha}(P_1)/X](\widetilde{\alpha}(V)) \subseteq \widetilde{\alpha}(P_1)(**).$$

Thus, every P_1 that satisfies (*) satisfies also (**), which means that that for the corresponding sets of sets it holds $\{P_1 : (*)\} \subseteq \{P_1 : (**)\}$. This implies $\cap\{P_1 : (**)\} \subseteq \cap\{P_1 : (*)\}$, or in an unfolded form
$\bigcap\{P_1 : I_2(f^-)[\widetilde{\alpha}(P_1)/X](\widetilde{\alpha}(V)) \subseteq \widetilde{\alpha}(P_1)\} \subseteq \{P_1 : I_1(f^-)[P_1/X](V) \subseteq P_1\}$
$= I_1(\mu X.f^-(V))$.
By distributivity of $\widetilde{\alpha}$ over $\cap$ we get

$$\bigcap\{\widetilde{\alpha}(P_1) : I_2(f^-)[\widetilde{\alpha}(P_1)/X](\widetilde{\alpha}(V)) \subseteq \widetilde{\alpha}(P_1)\} \subseteq \widetilde{\alpha}(I_1(\mu X.f^-(V))$$

It remains to show that

$$\bigcap\{\widetilde{\alpha}(P_1) : I_2(f^-)[\widetilde{\alpha}(P_1)/X](\widetilde{\alpha}(V)) \subseteq \widetilde{\alpha}(P_1)\} \supseteq I_2(\mu X.f^-(\widetilde{\alpha}(V))).$$

This follows from the observation that

$$\{\widetilde{\alpha}(P_1) : I_2(f^-)[\widetilde{\alpha}(P_1)/X](\widetilde{\alpha}(V)) \subseteq \widetilde{\alpha}(P_1)\} \subseteq \{P_2 : I_2(f^-)[P_2/X](\widetilde{\alpha}(V)) \subseteq P_2\}.$$

Similarly as above, we have for the corresponding intersections defined over these two set families:
$\bigcap\{\widetilde{\alpha}(P_1) : I_2(f^-)[\widetilde{\alpha}(P_1)/X](\widetilde{\alpha}(V)) \subseteq \widetilde{\alpha}(P_1)\} \supseteq$
$\bigcap\{P_2 : I_2(f^-)[P_2/X](\widetilde{\alpha}(V)) \subseteq P_2\} = I_2(\mu X.f^-(\widetilde{\alpha}(V)))$,
which finally gives the wanted result $I_2(\mu X.f^-(\widetilde{\alpha}(V))) \subseteq \widetilde{\alpha}(I_1(\mu X.f(V)))$.
The co-property can be shown in an analogous way, by replacing it with its equivalent $I_1(f) \subseteq \gamma(I_2(f^+))$, because γ distributes over $\cap$.

In a straightforward way one can define a verification method based on the results of this section (we omit the details for the sake of brevity).

4.1   Comparison with Related Work

Obviously, we impose less syntactic restrictions on the fragment of the universal μ-calculus that we deal with than [10]. Since any $\Box L_\mu$ formula can be rewritten into an equivalent $\Box L_\mu^+$ formula, and any formula of the universal unrestricted μ-calculus has a semantically equivalent formula in $\Box L_\mu$ (see e.g. [10]), this might seem to have only a syntactical significance. However, our approach is also easier from practical point of view because it is more general and more automated.

For instance, in order to preserve the fragment $\Box L_\mu$ in [10] one is obliged to find a consistent abstraction, which could be a difficult task. Besides, the additional requirement on the abstraction function can result in bigger abstract state spaces than in our case. We also improve the verification method given in 6.3 of [10] with regard to formulas of $\Box^+ L_\mu$ – at the end of Section 3 we already discussed the benefits of using the contracting abstraction $\widetilde{\alpha}$ instead of the expanding α for that purpose.

With regard to [8] we are also semantically more general because they deal only with propositional LTL which is a proper subset of the universal fragment $\Box^e L_\mu$. For instance, the property "proposition p holds for all even execution steps along all executions of the system" can be expressed in $\Box^e L_\mu$ as $\nu X.p \wedge \Box\Box X$. However, the same property is impossible to express in LTL. (See, for instance, [9] for more such examples).

Once the methodology based on the Galois connection is well developed, with the same effort – sometimes even easier – one can prove more general results. The proofs become more symbolic and less operational in the sense of being more independent from the logic models (execution sequences, in the case of LTL). The arguments often boil down to symbolic (algebraic) manipulations of the abstraction/concretization functions using basic Galois connection properties.

Besides the works discussed above, another relevant reference is [7]. The main similarity with our work is that they also deal with abstraction of the μ-calculus, using Galois connections between concrete and abstract state spaces. However, their connections are defined between 2^{Q_1} and Q_2, where Q_1 and Q_2 are the concrete and the abstract state spaces, respectively, while we use the more general approach of having connections from 2^{Q_1} and 2^{Q_2}. They also assume a structure (ordering) on the abstract state space Q_2. In [7] there is also a similar approach of contracting/expanding abstractions, but they are applied to the transition relations instead of the atomic propositions. In this way mixed abstract transition systems are obtained that preserve the formulas in positive normal form of both the universal and the existential parts of L_μ. However, the drawback of this generality is that there are many formulas such that neither they nor their negations hold in the mixed abstract systems.

In temporal algebras (e.g. [11]) algebraic tools, among them Galois connections, are used to characterize temporal logics. It could be an interesting avenue for future work to relate our results to such a framework.

5   Conclusions and Future Work

In this paper we presented some abstractions for universal fragments of the branching time μ-calculus L_μ. We first gave some results by reusing the formal machinery developed in [10]. After that we combined [10] with the ideas of [8] in order to define an abstraction for a fragment of L_μ, denoted as $\Box^e L_\mu$, that allows the universal operator $\Box$ only under an even number of negations. We showed that such an abstraction preserves the formulas of this fragment.

It would be interesting to see how our framework fits in the compositionally topics of [10]. We conjecture a seamless transfer of the concepts, but this still remains to be checked. Also, one can try to improve the abstraction of $\Box^e L_\mu$ along the lines of [8] where actually one uses as a basis for (a contracted/expanded) interpretation not the atomic propositions, but instead state formulas. The latter approach can give better reductions.

References

1. K. Baukus, Y. Lakhnech, and K. Stahl. Verifying universal properties of parameterized networks. In *Proceedings of FTRTFT 2000, Puna, India*, 2000.
2. D. Bošnački, N. Ioustinova, and N. Sidorova. Using fairness to make abstractions work. In *11th Spin Workshop on Model Checking of Software SPIN 2004*, volume 2989 of *Lecture Notes in Computer Science*. Springer-Verlag, 2004.
3. E. Clarke, O. Grumberg, and D. Long. Model checking and abstraction. *ACM Trans. Prog. Lang. Sys.*, 5(16):1512–1542, 1994.
4. P. Cousot and R. Cousot. Abstract interpretaion: A unified lattice model for static analysis of programs by construction or approximation of fixpoints. In *Proceedings of POPL '73*. ACM, January 1973.
5. D. Dams. *Abstract Interpretation and Partition Refinement for Model Checking*. PhD dissertation, Eindhoven University of Thechnology, July 1996.
6. D. Dams, R. Gerth, and O. Grumberg. Abstract interpretation of reactive systems: Abstraction preserving $\forall$CTL*,$\exists$CTL*, and CTL*. In E.-R. Olderog, editor, *Proceedings of PROCOMET '94*. IFIP, North-Holland, June 1994.
7. D. Dams, R. Gerth, and O. Grumberg. Abstract interpretation of reactive systems. *ACM Transactions on Programming Languages and Systems (TOPLAS)*, 19(2), 1997.
8. Y. Kesten and A. Pnueli. Control and data abstraction: The cornerstones of practical formal verification. *International Journal on Software Tools for Technology Transfer*, 2(4):328–342, 2000.
9. O. Kupferman. Augmenting branching temporal logics with existential quantification over atomic propositions. *Journal of Logic and Computation*, 7:1–14, 1997.
10. C. Loiseaux, S. Graf, J. Sifakis, A. Bouajjani, and S. Bensalem. Property preserving abstractions for the verification of concurrent systems. *Formal Methods in System Design*, 6(1):11–44, 1995.
11. B. von Karger. Temporal algebra. In *Algebraic and Coalgebraic Methods in the Mathematics of Program Construction*, volume 2297 of *Lecture Notes in Computer Science*, pages 309–385, 2002.

Retrenching the Purse: Finite Sequence Numbers, and the Tower Pattern

Richard Banach[1], Michael Poppleton[2], Czeslaw Jeske[1], and Susan Stepney[3]

[1] School of Computer Science, University of Manchester,
Manchester M13 9PL, UK
{banach, cj}@cs.man.ac.uk

[2] Department of Electronics and Computer Science,
University of Southampton, Highfield,
Southampton SO17 1BJ, UK
mrp@ecs.soton.ac.uk

[3] Department of Computer Science, University of York,
Heslington, York YO10 5DD, UK
susan.stepney@cs.york.ac.uk

Abstract. The Mondex Electronic Purse system [18] is an outstanding example of formal refinement techniques applied to a genuine industrial scale application, and notably, was the first verification to achieve ITSEC level E6 certification. A formal abstract model including security properties, and a formal concrete model of the system design were developed, and a formal refinement was hand-proved between them in Z. Despite this success, certain requirements issues were set beyond the scope of the formal development, or handled in an unnatural manner.

Retrenchment is reviewed in a form suitable for integration with Z refinement, and is used to address one such issue in detail: the finiteness of the transaction sequence number in the purse funds transfer protocol. A retrenchment is constructed from the lowest level model of the purse system to a model in which sequence numbers are finite, using a suitable elaboration of the Z promotion [21] technique. We overview the lifting of that retrenchment to the abstraction level of the higher models of the purse system. The concessions of the various retrenchments generated, formally capture the dissonance between the unbounded sequence number idealisation and the bounded reality. Reasoning about when the concession can become valid influences the actual choice of sequence number bound. The retrenchment-enhanced formal development is proposed as an example of a widely applicable methodological pattern for formal developments of this kind: the *Tower Pattern*.

1 Introduction

The Mondex Electronic Purse [18], produced by the NatWest Development Team, is a system of Smartcard-based electronic purses carrying currency for electronic commerce applications. Clearly, this is a security-critical application. For this reason, the developers of Mondex (formerly a part of NatWest Bank), employed state of the art methods to ensure the implementation was as robust as possible. At the time of its creation (in the late 1990s), the Mondex Purse achieved an ITSEC [14] rating of E6. This

J.S. Fitzgerald, I.J. Hayes, and A. Tarlecki (Eds.): FM 2005, LNCS 3582, pp. 382–398, 2005.

requires a formal abstract model, a formal concrete model, and a proof of correspondence between them. (In the case of Mondex, the correspondence proof was a proof of refinement.) This is the the highest possible ITSEC level (corresponding these days to a Common Criteria EAL7 rating), and the development was a trailblazer for showing that fully formal techniques could be applied within realistic time and cost limitations to industrial scale applications.

The abstract model of the Mondex Purse system describes a world of purses which exchange value through atomic transactions, and specifies the security properties: purse authentication, preservation of overall system value, and correct processing of both transferred and lost value. The concrete model describes a distributed system of purses, transferring value via an insecure and lossy medium using an n-step protocol. Security features are implemented locally on each purse. In the field the purse is self-sufficient, logging any lost value from failed transactions locally, for intermittent central archiving.

The Mondex Purse verification of the security properties remains an impressive achievement, both as a landmark industrial development, and as a contribution to the theory of refinement. The separation between the abstract and concrete levels is significant, in a logical as well as a functional sense. The refinement is a composition of two simpler refinements, a "backward" refinement to, and a "forward" refinement from, an intermediate "between" model. [17] gives a readable account of how the then existing forward refinement rules in Z were insufficient to prove refinement, and how certain backward rules from the more general theory of refinement, e.g. [9], had to be implemented in Z, in order to deliver the two-stage proof. The clue to the need for this was the fact that the concrete, n-step value transfer protocol resolved certain non-determinism later than the abstract system; this is an instance of a classical counterexample by Milner [9] showing the incompleteness of the forward rules as a proof method for refinement.

Nevertheless, the necessity of having a refinement, meant that a number of requirements issues, legitimately the concern of the formal development, had to be passed over in silence, since they would strictly speaking have broken the validity of the refinement had they been incorporated in the models that were used. One can argue that curtailing the ideal scope of the refinement to some extent *always* happens: for example, it is never practical to prove refinement all the way to the physical hardware. The refinement might be pushed to source code level, then to machine code (if the compiler is not trusted); if that were insufficient one could try to refine down to the hardware design and even to the physics of the constituent devices.

Retrenchment [3, 4] has been proposed as a theory that generalizes refinement, essentially in allowing the refinement relation (classically, an invariant) to be weakened in the postcondition by a defined *concession* clause. This is inevitably a more intricate theory, offering less than the simulation property of refinement, unless extra application-specific assumptions are made. It was motivated originally by the impossibility of refining infinite to finite types, or the continuous variables of real-world physical models to discrete ones. Further work has revealed the utility of retrenchment both as anticipated [15], and as a vehicle for the flexible layering in of contrasting, even conflicting requirements in a formal development [5].

We regard the requirements issues identified in the Mondex verification – those set beyond the scope of the formal development, or handled in an unnatural manner – as "retrenchment opportunities". The aim of this paper is to show that by incorporating retrenchment as a formal transformation of models, one can broaden the scope and accuracy of the formal modelling in a manner sympathetic to the existing refinement-based development. This yields a way of getting the best of both worlds: the clarity and rigour of the original refinement-based development, without an artificial denial of the existence of the attendant other issues.

The rest of the paper is structured as follows. In section 2 we give an overview of the Mondex development, and identify the requirements issues that motivate the application of retrenchment. Section 3 reviews the proof rules for refinement and retrenchment in a Z setting. Section 4 focuses on one of these aspects, the finiteness of the sequence number. A retrenchment is defined between the concrete purse and a new purse model, identical to the former in all but making the sequence number finite. This retrenchment is then extended to the world of purses by a suitable adaptation of the Z promotion used in [18]. Section 5 overviews how this retrenchment of the concrete model of the Purse system can be lifted to the abstract model of the system. Section 6 gives a probabilistic validation of the lifted retrenchment, assessing the risk of the purse sequence number breaching its bound, deriving an acceptable value for the bound thereby. Section 7 concludes and recapitulates. It is observed that the structure of refinements and retrenchments derived in the present paper is more widely applicable than just the present work, and we elevate it to status of a generally applicable methodological pattern for widening the remit of formal developments using retrenchments: the *Tower Pattern*.

2   The Mondex Purse: From Refinement to Retrenchment

The Mondex Electronic Purse described in [18] consists of three models: A(abstract), B(between), and C(concrete). The A model is a highly abstract expression of atomic value transfer between purses, allowing an atomic notion of loss in transit. It is a model targetted purely at the security properties of the system; it does not capture all the many other system requirements. Model B captures the elements of the value transfer protocol, and is thus nonatomic; it is also enhanced with extra structure and constraints needed to achieve a backward refinement from model A. Model C is model B without the extra structure and constraints. These can be established by an induction on the length of the execution, leading to a forward refinement between models B and C. It is thus shown that model C is a refinement of model A.

We have indicated that [18] is a development of the security properties of the Mondex Purse, not a full specification of the system. Even within these limitations, some requirements aspects, in principle deserving to be included within the formal development, were omitted or handled unnaturally in modelling, in order to establish the refinement between models. One of the aims of this paper is to show that by incorporating retrenchment into the formal development armoury, the tension that arises about whether some feature should be included or not in the refinement-based development is eased. This is because versions with and without the feature may be formally related via a retrenchment and the development paths with and without the feature may be drawn together, in part automatically. Here then is a brief summary of the Mondex "retrenchment opportunities":

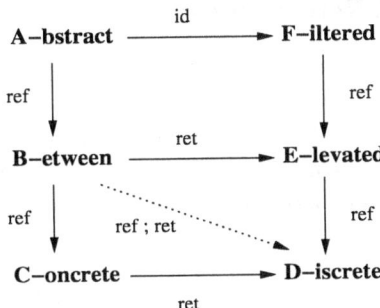

Fig. 1. A development pattern for refinement with retrenchment

- Sequence Number: The integrity of the protocol depends partly on the sequence number of the transaction in progress. Sequence numbers occur in the B, C models where they are naturals; in reality they are bounded numbers.
- Log Full: Transfers completing abnormally are logged by purses. The concrete model implements the abstract "lost value" component in terms of an off-card exception archive into which purses' log contents are saved. A purse needs to be assured that the data is safely in the archive before it can clear it from its own, highly constrained, log memory. Logs occur in the B, C models where they are unbounded; in reality they are finite.
- Hash Function: Clearing a purse's log after its contents are centrally archived is done via a message containing a "clear" code. The purse log contents are assumed to be in total injective correspondence with the clear codes, as that property is required in the proof. In reality of course a cryptographic hash function is used, which is neither total, nor injective, but is informally argued to be "sufficiently injective".
- Balance Enquiry: Each purse has a balance enquiry operation. If this is invoked at a particular point in the middle of a B model value transfer, a discrepancy can occur between the model A and model B balances due to differences in where nondeterminism is resolved in the two models. This is handled formally by a modelling trick, using finalisation instead of the enquiry operation to observe the state.

In this paper we focus on the sequence number in detail, leaving the others to be explored elsewhere. Our strategy is to build a tower of models D, E, F which retrench C, B, A respectively, and so that the obvious refinement/retrenchment squares commute. See Fig. 1 which shows the models, the epithets that accompany them, and their interrelationships. Since the variables involved in the sequence number retrenchment do not appear in the A model, if we take a sufficiently "noninvasive" approach to the construction of model D, it turns out that models A and F can subsequently be identified, though this is a fragile property.

Briefly, model D retrenches model C to take into account the boundedness of actual sequence numbers. Model D is then lifted to the abstraction level of model B, yielding model E; this is essentially model D but with the additional invariants. Noting that model E is refinable from model A, yields model F (the top of the tower) as a copy of model A.

3   Refinements and Retrenchments

In this section we briefly review the notions of refinement and retrenchment used in this paper. For refinement, we adopt the formulation in [8] as used in the Mondex development. We give only the forward rules for refinement, since these formed the basis for the definition of retrenchment [3]; we do not need to consider the backward rules further here. The nomenclature in our definitions will be in line with that needed for the various models in our discussion of the Mondex development below.

The A to B refinement is a backward refinement. The B to C refinement is a forward refinement. We call the between model B "abstract" in this context; it is given by the ADT $(B, BInit, \{BOp \mid BOp \in \mathsf{Ops}\})$, and the concrete model C is given by the ADT $(C, CInit, \{COp \mid COp \in \mathsf{Ops}\})$. So schemas B, C give the abstract and concrete state spaces, and the corresponding per-operation I/O spaces are given by schemas BI_{Op}, BO_{Op} and CI_{Op}, CO_{Op}. We assume a retrieve relation $R_{BC} : [B ; C]$ between the two state spaces, and for each operation Op, input and output mapping relations $RI_{BC,Op} : [BI_{Op} ; CI_{Op}]$ and $RO_{BC,Op} : [BO_{Op} ; CO_{Op}]$. Forward refinement is given by three proof obligations (POs), *initialization, applicability* and *correctness*:

$$\forall C' \bullet CInit \Rightarrow \exists B' \bullet BInit \wedge R'_{BC} \tag{1}$$

$$\forall B; BI_{Op}; C; CI_{Op} \bullet R_{BC} \wedge RI_{BC,Op} \wedge \mathrm{pre}\, BOp \Rightarrow \mathrm{pre}\, COp \tag{2}$$

$$\forall B; BI_{Op}; C; CI_{Op}; C'; CO_{Op} \bullet R_{BC} \wedge RI_{BC,Op} \wedge \mathrm{pre}\, BOp \wedge COp$$
$$\Rightarrow \exists B'; BO_{Op} \bullet BOp \wedge R'_{BC} \wedge RO_{BC,Op} \tag{3}$$

Note that (1)-(3) do not mention finalisation. We deal with the issue of observation, and specifically of relating the outputs of the abstract and concrete models (normally handled via finalisation) "on the fly", in line with the tack taken in retrenchment.

The C to D development step is a forward retrenchment. For this, the abstract model is the C ADT, and the concrete model is given by ADT $(D, DInit, \{(DOp, DI_{Op}, DO_{Op}) \mid Op \in \mathsf{Ops}\})$. Similar notational conventions apply. The retrenchment is given by firstly a *retrieve* relation $R_{CD} : [C ; D]$ between the state spaces; and secondly we have the within, output and concedes relations on a per-operation basis. The *within* relation is between the input-state spaces $W_{CD,Op} : [CI_{Op} ; C ; DI_{Op} ; D]$. The *output* and *concedes* relations are normally defined over both full input-state-output frames with types $O_{CD,Op} ; C_{CD,Op} : [CI_{Op} ; C ; C' ; CO_{Op} ; DI_{Op} ; D ; D' ; DO_{Op}]$, though in practice, we often omit such parts of these signatures as are not needed. We call these three relations the *retrenchment data*.

Two POs define a retrenchment between two models: *initialisation* as for refinement (1), and *correctness* which is analogous to refinement correctness (3); note that applicability issues are understood to be subsumed in (5) via the within relation:

$$\forall D' \bullet DInit \Rightarrow \exists C' \bullet CInit \wedge R'_{CD} \tag{4}$$

$$\forall C; CI_{Op}; D; DI_{Op}; D'; DO_{Op} \bullet R_{CD} \wedge W_{CD,Op} \wedge DOp$$
$$\Rightarrow \exists C'; CO_{Op} \bullet COp \wedge ((R'_{CD} \wedge O_{CD,Op}) \vee C_{CD,Op}) \tag{5}$$

4   The Sequence Number Retrenchment

The starting point for the sequence number retrenchment is the C model of the world of purses. We concentrate on just the simplest operation of [18] that is nontrivially affected, the single purse *CConPurse* operation *CIncreasePurseOkay*. This is an abstraction (for an individual purse and at C level) of a number of lower level operations that do or do not need to increment the purse transaction sequence number. It is implicit that sequence number *CnextSeqNo* is a natural, thus unbounded.

We retrench *CIncreasePurseOkay* to operation *DIncreasePurseOkay* of new D model purse *DConPurse*[1], where *DConPurse* 'is as' *CConPurse* apart from *DnextSeqNo*, which is of finite type $BN == 0..BIGNUM$. We assume the usual arithmetic operations for *BN* defined by restriction, where we liberally coerce when necessary, and where *BIGNUM* is a matter of implementation choice. *CConPurseIncrease* hides the C purse sequence number *CnextSeqNo*, thus $\Xi CConPurseIncrease$ denotes skip, i.e. no change on all state apart from *CnextSeqNo*. *DConPurseIncrease* 'is as' *CConPurseIncrease*.

CConPurseIncrease ==
   CConPurse $\setminus$ (*CnextSeqNo*)

___*CIncreasePurseOkay*___
$\Delta CConPurse$
Cm?, *Cm*! : *CMESSAGE*
___
$\Xi CConPurseIncrease$
$CnextSeqNo' \geq CnextSeqNo$
$Cm! = \perp$

___*DIncreasePurseOkay*___
$\Delta DConPurse$
Dm?, *Dm*! : *DMESSAGE*
___
$\Xi DConPurseIncrease$
$(DnextSeqNo < BIGNUM \Rightarrow$
  $DnextSeqNo' \geq DnextSeqNo \wedge$
$Dm! = \perp)$
$(DnextSeqNo = BIGNUM \Rightarrow$
  $DnextSeqNo' = DnextSeqNo \wedge$
$Dm! = DpurseBlocked\ Dname)$

$\perp$ is a general purpose message used in Mondex which is of-no-concern here, and *DpurseBlocked Dname* is a special message emitted when *BIGNUM* is reached, identifying the purse in question, *Dname*.

The above constitutes a minimally invasive retrenchment of *CIncreasePurseOkay*, in that not only is it the case that inside a guard the C model behaviour is preserved, but even outside the guard there are no new purse states to threaten the validity of the reasoning about the refinements in [18]. Far more aggressive D model designs are obviously possible.

We come to the retrenchment data itself. *CDConPurseIncreaseEquality* is shorthand for equalities between corresponding C and D variables in *CConPurseIncrease* and *DConPurseIncrease* respectively. Under the vacuous *within* $W_{CD,IncreasePurseOkay}$ constraint on before states and inputs, the pair of operation instances *CIncreasePurseOkay*,

---

[1] We augment the common convention of pre-capitalizing the names of Z types (schema and other) by prefixing a single character $A, B, \ldots$ to a name as required, to denote the model in question. Thus *CThing* is a schema or other type in the C model, whereas *Dthing* is a variable, usually a schema component, in the D model. A further lexical schema convention we employ, to save space, is to say *DSchema* 'is as' *CSchema* to indicate that the text of *DSchema* can be generated from that of *CSchema* by replacing all *Cthings* by *Dthings*.

DIncreasePurseOkay establishes either $R'_{CD} \land O_{CD,IncreasePurseOkay}$ (*retrieve* and *output* relations), or $C_{CD,IncreasePurseOkay}$ (*concedes* relation). This concession states the possible inequality between C, D sequence numbers and uses the D level error message.

```
┌─ R_CD ─────────────────────────
│  CConPurse;  DConPurse
│  CDConPurseIncreaseEquality
│ ─────────────────────────────
│  CnextSeqNo = DnextSeqNo
```

```
┌─ W_CD,IncreasePurseOkay ───────
│  CConPurse;  DConPurse
│  Cm? : CMESSAGE
│  Dm? : DMESSAGE
```

```
┌─ O_CD,IncreasePurseOkay ───────
│  Cm! : CMESSAGE
│  Dm! : DMESSAGE
│ ─────────────────────────────
│  Cm! = Dm!
```

```
┌─ C_CD,IncreasePurseOkay ───────
│  CConPurse ';  DConPurse '
│  CDConPurseIncreaseEquality '
│  Cm! : CMESSAGE
│  Dm! : DMESSAGE
│ ─────────────────────────────
│  CnextSeqNo' ≥ DnextSeqNo'
│  Cm! = ⊥
│  Dm! = DpurseBlocked Dname
```

4.1   Promotion of the Purse Retrenchment

We review the Z technique of promotion [21, 10] of a local-state (purse) to a global-state (world) operation. The global state schema, say *World*, is defined as an indexing function from some index set *Ind* to the space of all possible local state elements, these being given by schema *LS*. To enable concise world-level description of an operation working on only a single copy of the local state, the promotion framing schema $\Phi LSOp$ is defined. $\Phi LSOp$ contains both a global state schema *World* and a local state schema *LS*, and also an input parameter $i?$ of type *Ind*, identifying the required local state element for access or update. An equality identifies the target *LS* element $f(i?)$ through the index function f with the local state binding θLS. The final predicate ensures that all elements other than $f(i?)$ remain unchanged.

$\Phi LSOp$ is generic insofar as it allows the mechanical definition of a world-level operation *WorldOp* corresponding to a local operation *LSOp* without constraining the behaviour of that local operation in any way:

```
┌─ World ────────────────────────
│  f : Ind ⇸ LS
```

$WorldOp ==$
$\qquad \exists\, \Delta LS \bullet \Phi LSOp \land LSOp$

```
┌─ ΦLSOp ────────────────────────
│  ΔWorld
│  ΔLS
│  i? : Ind
│ ─────────────────────────────
│  i? ∈ dom f
│  θLS = f(i?)
│  f' = f ⊕ {i? ↦ θLS '}
```

The above is the classical, index-function-based form of promotion. Recently certain promotion *patterns* [19, 20] have been proposed for various forms of local-to-global structuring, some having been based on promotion use in Mondex.

As in the C world, individual D model purses are promoted to the D world of purses, as given in the schemas that follow. *DConWorld* 'is as' *CConWorld*. Beyond the (purse-NAME-)indexed map of purses, the world contains the *Dether* of all messages ever sent between purses, and the *Darchive* of all transaction exception logs uploaded from purses. There are two *DConWorld* constraints: we equate each internal purse name to its corresponding index, and we ensure each archive entry identifies its originating purse.

Promotion of the D model 'is as' that of the C model of [18]: *ΦDOp* 'is as' *ΦCOp*, where *Dm?, Dm!* are the input and output messages to and from *DIncreasePurseOkay*. *DIncrease*, the promoted and wrapped operation, 'is as' *CIncrease*. N.B. *DIgnore* 'is as' *CIgnore*, and just skips at world level.

$\quad$*DConWorld* _____

DconAuthPurse : *NAME* $\rightarrowtail$ *DConPurse*
Dether : $\mathbb{P}$ *DMESSAGE*
Darchive : $\mathbb{P}$ *DLogbook*

$\forall n$: dom *DconAuthPurse* • (*DconAuthPurse n*).*Dname* = n
$\forall nld$: *Darchive* • *first nld* ∈ dom *DconAuthPurse*

$\quad$*ΦDOp* _____

Δ*DConWorld*; Δ*DConPurse*
Dm?, Dm! : *DMESSAGE*
Dname? : *NAME*

Dm? ∈ *Dether*
Dname? ∈ dom *DconAuthPurse*
θ*DConPurse* = *DconAuthPurse Dname?*
DconAuthPurse' = *DconAuthPurse* ⊕ {*Dname?* ↦ θ*DConPurse '*}
Darchive' = *Darchive*
Dether' ⊆ *Dether* ∪ {*Dm!*}

$$DIncrease == DIgnore \lor (\exists \Delta DConPurse \bullet \Phi DOp \land DIncreasePurseOkay)$$

Having defined the D model, the next job is to promote the retrenchment of individual purse operations such as *CIncreasePurseOkay* to a retrenchment at the *CConWorld*-to-*DConWorld* level, between *CIncrease*, (not quoted but with the same syntax as) *DIncrease*. Any theory of promotion of retrenchments must be grounded in the promotion of refinements. A good treatment is given by [10], including presentation of a simple world-level retrieve relation resulting from the distribution of the local retrieve relation through promotion. We base our approach on this form. Given a retrieve relation R between local states *Abs* and *Conc*, the promoted retrieve relation R^P [10] between *AbsWorld* and *ConcWorld* (with index functions *Absf*, *Conf* respectively) simply asserts the local one for all local state elements:

$$\underline{\quad R^P \quad}$$

> $AbsWorld;\ ConcWorld$
>
> ---
>
> $\mathrm{dom}\ Concf = \mathrm{dom}\ Absf$
> $\forall n : \mathrm{dom}\ Concf \bullet \exists R \bullet \theta Abs = Absf(n) \wedge \theta Conc = Concf(n)$

The promotion of retrenchments offers a choice of approaches, depending on what one wishes to emphasise. In [6] we explore this in some detail, but space limitations here do not permit us to show the full variety of possibilities on the present example. Instead, we apply just one of the approaches, perhaps the most interesting one: *precise promotion*.

The essential point is this. Let us imagine the system has been running for some time and that some or many elements have already engaged in operations. In terms of the retrenchment, some elements will be in the local state element retrieve relation R, while others may have already conceded (and so may no longer be in R). Assuming all elements are in R (as for refinement) thus gives an unduly restricted syntactic picture of the correspondence between the dynamics of the abstract and concrete worlds. In precise promotion, we introduce an extra world variable *good* to keep track of which elements are doing what, regarding the retrenchment.

Since there are two worlds, there are two obvious places in which to put the extra variable, the abstract or the concrete world. For most retrenchments the concrete world is the most natural place to put the extra information, and we do so here; so the extra variable is *Dgood*. Moreover, for this to work effectively, we require a separability axiom (6) to hold for all common operations Op. Given a concrete D model step, $DEstRet^{PP}_{DOp}/DNotEstRet^{PP}_{DOp}$ assert the existence/non-existence respectively of an abstract C world step that witnesses the refinement. Given a D step, $DEstCon^{PP}_{DOp}$ asserts the existence of a C step that witnesses the concession. The separability axiom is:

$$DEstRet^{PP}_{DOp} \wedge DEstCon^{PP}_{DOp} \Leftrightarrow \mathsf{false} \tag{6}$$

where

$$DEstRet^{PP}_{DOp} == D;\ DI_{Op};\ D';\ DO_{Op} \mid DOp\ \wedge$$
$$(\exists C;\ CI_{Op};\ C';\ CO_{Op} \bullet R_{CD} \wedge W_{CD,Op} \wedge COp \wedge (R'_{CD} \wedge O_{CD,Op}))$$
$$DEstCon^{PP}_{DOp} == D;\ DI_{Op};\ D';\ DO_{Op} \mid DOp\ \wedge$$
$$(\exists C;\ CI_{Op};\ C';\ CO_{Op} \bullet R_{CD} \wedge W_{CD,Op} \wedge COp \wedge C_{CD,Op})$$
$$DNotEstRet^{PP}_{DOp} == D;\ DI_{Op};\ D';\ DO_{Op} \mid DOp\ \wedge$$
$$\neg(\exists C;\ CI_{Op};\ C';\ CO_{Op} \bullet R_{CD} \wedge W_{CD,Op} \wedge COp \wedge (R'_{CD} \wedge O_{CD,Op}))$$

Given a C-to-D retrenchment (5), and axiom (6), it can be deduced from a given concrete step alone, whether R_{CD} is reestablished or $C_{CD,Op}$ holds. This allows the concrete promotion to accurately maintain the *Dgood* variable as follows.

We need suitable enhancements to: the promoted operations (which become DOp^{PP}), to the promoted world construction itself (which becomes $DConWorld^{PP}$), and to the framing schema (which becomes ΦDOp^{PP}). The latter differs from ΦDOp only in the replacment of $DConWorld$ by $DConWorld^{PP}$, so we do not reproduce it in full.[2]

$$
\begin{array}{l}
\underline{\quad DConWorld^{PP} \quad\rule{5cm}{0pt}} \\
\quad DConWorld \\
\quad Dgood : \mathbb{P}\,NAME \\
\underline{\rule{0pt}{1.5ex}} \\
\quad Dgood \subseteq \mathrm{dom}\, DconAuthPurse \\
\end{array}
$$

$$
\begin{aligned}
DIncrease^{PP} == DIgnore \vee (\,&\exists\,\Delta DConPurse \bullet \Phi DOp^{PP} \wedge DIncreasePurseOkay \\
&\wedge (DEstRet^{PP}_{DIncrease} \Rightarrow Dgood' = Dgood) \\
&\wedge (DNotEstRet^{PP}_{DIncrease} \Rightarrow Dgood' = Dgood \setminus \{Dname?\}))
\end{aligned}
$$

It is clear that $DIncrease^{PP}$ is a refinement of $DIncrease$ via a retrieve relation that simply projects away $Dgood$, as $DIncrease^{PP}$ arises from $DIncrease$ by the addition of $Dgood$, whose value is never used in the update of any $DIncrease$ variable.

With these details in place, we can write down the precisely promoted retrenchment between the $CConWorld$ and $DConWorld^{PP}$ $Increase$ operations. For this, it is easy to see that (6) holds, in particular, by examining whether the output of $DIncrease$ is $\perp$ or $DpurseBlocked\ Dname?$. For $\perp$, $R'_{CD} \wedge O_{CD,IncreasePurseOkay}$ is established by the identity of outputs, and the 'is as' identity of the seqence number predicates. For $DpurseBlocked\ Dname?$, $C_{CD,IncreasePurseOkay}$ is established by definition of the outputs and by the skip on $DnextSeqNo$.

The retrenchment below employs a *focused* pattern of precise promotion, in that the within, output, concedes relations only refer to the named local state element $Dname?$. Since the promoted operation acts on only one element, implicitly all other elements in $Dgood$ maintain the local retrieve relation R'_{CD}. An *inclusive* pattern is also available which covers all $Dgood$ elements, explicitly claiming R'_{CD} in the concession for the elements in $Dgood \setminus \{Dname?\}$; for brevity we present the focused pattern here. Since archive entries are tagged with the originating purse's name, we can identify those C/D archive subsets corresponding to purses in $Dgood?$, and we assume for simplicity that all messages in the ether are tagged with originator's and addressee's names as the first two fields of the message.[3] " CDnamedConPurseIncreaseEquality *name* " is (not legal Z, for brevity, but) shorthand for equalities of named other purses' of-no-concern data in the following:

---

[2] Note that there is a somewhat philosophical question regarding the nature of the $Dgood$ variable: should it be viewed as a genuine system variable or not? In this paper we do not go beyond saying that the viability of the precise promotion's using $Dgood$, attests to the ability of the concrete model's being able to keep track of the retrieving elements should it so choose.

[3] Note that this is a considerable simplification compared to [18]. In [18] it is the case that: (i) the models do not concern themeselves with details of physical message transmission, (ii) the relevant data can nevertheless be inferred indirectly from the contents of the message body.

R_{CD}^{PP} ─────────────────────────────
$\quad$ CConWorld; DConWorld^{PP}
─────────────────────────────
dom CconAuthPurse = dom DconAuthPurse
∀ Dnm : Dgood •
$\quad$ (CconAuthPurse Dnm).CnextSeqNo = (DconAuthPurse Dnm).DnextSeqNo
$\quad$ ∧ " CDnamedConPurseIncreaseEquality Dnm "
Dgood ◁ Carchive = Dgood ◁ Darchive
(Dgood × Dgood) ◁ Cether = (Dgood × Dgood) ◁ Dether

$W_{CD,Increase}^{PP}$ ──────────────────
$\quad$ CConWorld; DConWorld^{PP}
$\quad$ Cm? : CMESSAGE
$\quad$ Dm? : DMESSAGE
$\quad$ Cname?, Dname? : NAME
──────────────────
$\quad$ Cname? = Dname?
$\quad$ Cname? ∈ Dgood

$O_{CD,Increase}^{PP}$ ──────────────────
$\quad$ ΔDConWorld^{PP}
$\quad$ Cm! : CMESSAGE
$\quad$ Dm! : DMESSAGE
$\quad$ Dname? : NAME
──────────────────
$\quad$ Dgood' = Dgood
$\quad$ Cm! = Dm!

$C_{CD,Increase}^{PP}$ ──────────────────────────────
$\quad$ CConWorld '; ΔDConWorld^{PP}
$\quad$ CDConPurseIncreaseEquality'
$\quad$ Cm! : CMESSAGE
$\quad$ Dm! : DMESSAGE
$\quad$ Dname? : NAME
──────────────────────────────
Dgood' = Dgood − {Dname?}
" CDnamedConPurseIncreaseEquality Dname? "
(CconAuthPurse' Cname?).CnextSeqNo ≥ (DconAuthPurse' Dname?).DnextSeqNo
Cm! = ⊥
Dm! = (DpurseBlocked Dname?)
Dgood' ◁ Carchive' = Dgood' ◁ Darchive'
(Dgood' × Dgood') ◁ Cether' = (Dgood' × Dgood') ◁ Dether'

5 Lifting the Retrenchment

The previous section described in fair detail how, despite its awkwardness, the real world finiteness of the sequence number can be taken account of, in a model that could be appended to the preexisting development. In this section we sketch rather briefly how this new D model can be related to the other models in the Mondex development, clarifying the relationship between sequence number finiteness and the concerns of these higher level models.

Essentially, the level of abstraction of the D model is first lifted to the level of the B model (this giving the E model) and then it is observed that there is a refinement from the A model to the E model, due to the nonintrusiveness of the D model. So the construction of the F model becomes just a rebadging of the A model. See Fig. 1.

The lifting of the D model to the E model makes use of a generic construction [1] for lifting the concrete model of a retrenchment to the level of abstraction of the retrenchment's abstract system; the model generated, typically called U, then refines to the retrenchment's concrete system. This generic construction builds U out of the two original systems in the retrenchment. The required level of abstraction is defined indirectly via a collection of properties specific to the construction, and U captures this level by being refinable to any system that also enjoys these properties. Thus U is the most abstract such system. As far as the construction goes, any suitable system interrefinable with U is just as good as U, so we have the option of replacing U with something more convenient if we wish.

In the Mondex case we build the E model, which matches the level of abstraction of the B model. The retrenchment that we are lifting is the composition of the B to C forward refinement and the C to D retrenchment, such compositions themselves being a matter for careful definition; see [2] for details.

For clarity and simplicity let us examine how this works for the individual purse operation *IncreasePurseOkay*. Essentially, for the *IncreasePurseOkay* operation of the generated U system we have:

$$
\begin{array}{|l}
\hline
\_\_\text{protoEIncreasePurseOkay}_____ \\
\text{BIncreasePurseOkay};\ \ \Delta DConPurse \\
\text{Dm?, Dm!} : DMESSAGE \\
\hline
(R_{BD} \wedge R'_{BD} \wedge O_{BD,IncreasePurseOkay}) \vee (R_{BD} \wedge C_{BD,IncreasePurseOkay}) \\
\hline
\end{array}
$$

In the above, *BIncreasePurseOkay* 'is as' *CIncreasePurseOkay*, and R_{BD} 'is as' R_{CD}. Similarly $O_{BD,IncreasePurseOkay}$ 'is as' $O_{CD,IncreasePurseOkay}$, and $C_{BD,IncreasePurseOkay}$ 'is as' $C_{CD,IncreasePurseOkay}$. In *protoEIncreasePurseOkay*, *BIncreasePurseOkay* contributes the steps of the B model and $\Delta DConPurse$ contributes all legal D changes of state. The B-to-D retrenchment tells us that any *DIncreasePurseOkay* step satisfies the retrenchment correctness PO in terms of some witnessing B-step. In *protoEIncreasePurseOkay* it is clear that precisely the same witness establishes the E-to-D refinement correctness PO.

We note that there is considerable duplication of state and other information in *protoEIncreasePurseOkay*; the B and D parts of the state say practically the same thing via the *BDConPurseIncreaseEquality* in R_{BD} and R'_{BD}, and the I/O is similarly either irrelevant or discernable from the D element alone.

Since, as noted above, it is sufficient to fix on a system that is interrefinable with what the construction routinely generates, it is worth reflecting on the details of the U system, to see if the duplication can be avoided. Examining the details reveals that we can replace *protoEIncreasePurseOkay* with the simpler:

EIncreasePurseOkay 'is as' *DIncreasePurseOkay*

a welcome simplification, attributable to the nonintrusive nature of our D construction.

Of course our real focus of interest is on *DIncrease* and its lifting to *EIncrease*. The single purse operation just treated provides an indication of what to expect, in that the *IncreasePurseOkay* lifting should be discernable within the *Increase* one.

The B world *Increase* operation has the same shape as the D world one:

$$BIncrease == BIgnore \lor (\exists\, \Delta BConPurse \bullet \Phi BOp \land BIncreasePurseOkay)$$

The subtlety here is that in *BIgnore* and ΦBOp, instead of $\Delta BConWorld$ (as would be expected) we have $\Delta BetweenWorld$, where *BetweenWorld* features additional structure and constraints imposed on *BConWorld* in order to enable the A-to-B backward refinement to cary through. Aside from this, the constituents of *BIncrease* 'are as' their corresponding *CIncrease* ones.

   For lack of space, the reader will have to take our word for it that the constraints in *BetweenWorld* do not materially affect our discussion; they express the consistency between the cryptographically protected messages in the ether and the purses' states; doubters can refer to [18]. We now retrace the earlier lifting construction and obtain:

---
protoEIncrease

$BIncrease;\ \Delta DConWorld^{PP}$
$Dm?, Dm! : DMESSAGE$

$(R_{BD}^{PP} \land R\,'^{PP}_{BD} \land O_{BD,Increase}^{PP}) \lor (R_{BD}^{PP} \land C_{BD,Increase}^{PP})$

It turns out that we can argue as before and replace *protoEIncrease* by *EIncrease* where:

$$EIncrease\ \text{'is as'}\ DIncrease^{PP}$$

except that *DetweenWorld* (which now 'is as' *BetweenWorld*) replaces occurences of *DConWorld* in *DIgnore* and ΦDOp in *DIncrease*^{PP}. Thus *DIncrease*^{PP} is at the right level of abstraction after all, again due to the minimalist nature of the D construction.

   Having dealt with the E model, the final step consists of observing that there is a (backward) refinement from the A model to the E model. The D level purse blocking behaviour when the sequence number overflows is simulated at A-level by the purse skipping; the A world has no sequence numbers. Aside from the fact that the details of this are beyond the scope of this paper, some points are worth making. Firstly, this is *not* a further instance of the lifting construction just used to build the E model. Secondly, the truth of it depends rather delicately on a suitable choice of retrieve and output relations, not to mention the precise notion of refinement employed and of course the minimalist nature of the D construction. Thus it is not a robust property, though it is a very pleasing one.

6   Validating the Retrenchment

In the preceding sections, we have designed the D model to do nothing useful once the limit on the sequence number has been reached. Since doing nothing is unlikely to satisfy users, it is incumbent on us to validate this design in the light of wider system requirements, which we do in this section. The argument now swings to showing that the limit in fact never arises. This can be crystallised as saying the concession of the relevant retrenchment does not become true within the lifetime of the use of the product.[4]

The validation of the concession of the C to D retrenchment depends on the value of BIGNUM, a quantity we have hitherto left unspecified. Our analysis will generate a value for BIGNUM leading to acceptable overall system properties. Note that the lifted E model's dependence on BIGNUM is like that of the D model's so we can focus on just the C to D retrenchment. Roughly speaking, we want to know how long it will take before BIGNUM is reached, which we analyse as follows.

First of all, the increments of the sequence number are not deterministic, to prevent the values of the sequence number being exploited as a covert channel in any potential cryptographic attack. Thus the increments are random variables drawn from a probability distribution Θ. Let us say that Θ has a mean μ and variance σ both about 10. From here there are two approaches, the naive and the sophisticated.

In a naive approach, we expect the accumulated total sequence number after n trials to be approximately $n\mu$. Now consider the determined shopper, making the order of 100 transations per day using the purse, resulting in a daily sequence number increment of about 10^3. Taking a year to be about 10^3 days, leads to an approximate annual sequence number increment of about 10^6. On this basis, we can estimate how different choices of BIGNUM fare against the requirement that the BIGNUM limit is never in fact reached.

Suppose BIGNUM is about 2^{16} which is about 64×10^3. The limit is encountered within a couple of months, so this value of BIGNUM is clearly unsatisfactory. Similarly, choosing 2^{64} for BIGNUM gives a limit of about 16×10^{12} years, which is a *little* more conservative than necessary.

Suppose then that BIGNUM is about 2^{32} which is about 4×10^9. Dividing by 10^6 shows that the limit is reached in about 4000 years. Putting aside considerations of whether the purse will physically withstand that much use, it is certainly the case that the financial system underpinning the purse will have collapsed by that time. So a 32 bit BIGNUM provides plenty of room for even determined use, while safeguarding against overflow, and while still not being ridiculously overconservative.

Of course one can take a more cautious approach than the above, supposing that a determined attacker will go all out to breach the sequence number limit by subjecting the purse to as many transactions as it is possible to invoke, potentially leading to different estimates. Then again, it is hard to see what such an attacker stands to gain by disabling the purse in this way, locking in the value he has managed to put into it, since the system's security properties ensure that every purse operation leaves the whole system in a state that is at best equitable, at worst in the bank's favour.

Let us now turn to a more sophisticated treatment of the same situation. We note that the individual increments of the sequence number are the "arrivals" of a renewal process [11, 16, 13]. Thus if δSN_n is the n'th increment, then as n varies, we are interested in the behaviour of the random variables:

---

[4] Note how the retrenchment framework has produced specific objects within the formal models, namely the concessions, that carry the information pertaining to the undesired state of affairs. A purely refinement based approach to the development could say nothing about such matters, disconnecting the formal world from the requirements level validation needed beyond.

$$nextSeqNo_n = \delta SN_0 + \delta SN_1 + \ldots + \delta SN_n$$

In particular, we are interested in the random variable $N(t)$ given by:

$$N(t) = \max\{n \mid nextSeqNo_n \leq t\}$$

whose distribution describes how many increments of the sequence number are needed to reach the value t. Fortunately this is all standard material that can be found in loc. cit. The first order theory of $N(t)$ says that as t tends to infinity, $N(t)$ tends to the constant distribution t/μ almost surely. Furthermore the mean of $N(t)$ tends to the number t/μ. This agrees with the values obtained naively, and in particular, for a 32 bit BIGNUM, we again derive an overflow time of four thousand years.

To ensure the random characteristics of the situation do not lead to gambler's ruin type outcomes, we check out also the second order theory of renewals. This says that as t tends to infinity,

$$\frac{N(t) - t/\mu}{\sqrt{t\sigma^2/\mu^3}}$$

converges in distibution to $N(0, 1)$, the standard normal distribution. This in turn means that the variance of $N(t)$ itself scales to $(t\sigma^2/\mu^3)^{\frac{1}{2}}$. When the numbers are substituted, this is of the order of a week or two. So in the end, the sophisticated story fully supports the naive one.

7   Conclusions, and the Tower Pattern

Above, we briefly reviewed the Mondex development and its "retrenchment opportunities." We then took the purse sequence number and showed how a more faithful treatment could be integrated with the existing refinement based development. The result was the collection of models related by refinements and retrenchments shown in Fig. 1.

One of the advantages of the retrenchment approach in dealing with model evolution situations, which the sequence number case study can be viewed as, is that it fits naturally with the idea that such evolutions often tend to be focused on judicious changes to one or more operations. In the limit, we can consider the change in each operation as a separate evolution step, expressed using a separate retrenchment, and compose them, e.g. as per [2]. For lack of space, we have not pursued this aspect here.

Note that Fig. 1 is a commutative diagram. Therefore it can be navigated in different ways with equivalent effect. For example, one can (as we did) start at the bottom of the tower, build the bottommost retrenchment, and build towards the top (it turned out that with a judicious choice of bottommost model, the top level blended seamlessly with the existing development). Alternatively one can start with the topmost retrenchment (an identity in our case), and proceed downwards, utilising different but compatible algebraic results on the combination of refinements and retrenchments [12]. This raises the general structure embodied in Fig. 1 to the level of a broadly applicable *pattern* for the deployment of retrenchment as a means of, (on the one hand) reconciling real world detail with an idealised but more transparent refinement development, or (on the other) propagating a top level requirements change down through a refinement stack, towards implementation. Of course, middle out deployments are also compatible with Fig. 1. Note that the structure in Fig. 1 remains equally useful *regardless of the specific requirements issue(s) handled by the retrenchments that comprise it*, which lie buried in the details of the various retrenchment data. Its elevation to a methodological generality, the *Tower Pattern*, is therefore eminently justified.

References

[1] R. Banach. Maximally abstract retrenchments. In *Proc. IEEE ICFEM2000*, pages 133–142, York, August 2000. IEEE Computer Society Press.

[2] R. Banach, C. Jeske, and M. Poppleton. Composition mechanisms for retrenchment. 2004. submitted, http://www.cs.man.ac.uk/~banach/some.pubs/Retrench.Composition.pdf.

[3] R. Banach and M. Poppleton. Retrenchment: An engineering variation on refinement. In D. Bert, editor, *2nd International B Conference*, volume 1393 of *LNCS*, pages 129–147, Montpellier, France, April 1998. Springer.

[4] R. Banach and M. Poppleton. Sharp retrenchment, modulated refinement and simulation. *Formal Aspects of Computing*, 11:498–540, 1999.

[5] R. Banach and M. Poppleton. Retrenching partial requirements into system definitions: A simple feature interaction case study. *Requirements Engineering Journal*, 8(2), 2003. 22pp.

[6] R. Banach, M. Poppleton, and C. Jeske. Retrenchment and promotion in Z. submitted for publication, 2004.

[7] D. Bert, J.P. Bowen, S. King, and M. Waldén, editors. *Proc. ZB2003: Formal Specification and Development in Z and B*, volume 2651 of *LNCS*, Turku, Finland, June 2000. Springer.

[8] D. Cooper, S. Stepney, and J. Woodcock. Derivation of Z refinement proof rules. Technical Report YCS-2002-347, University of York, 2002.

[9] W.-P. de Roever and K. Engelhardt. *Data Refinement: Model-Oriented Proof Methods and their Comparison*. Cambridge University Press, 1998.

[10] J. Derrick and E. Boiten. *Refinement in Z and Object-Z*. FACIT. Springer, 2001.

[11] G. Grimmett and Stirzaker D. *Probability and Random Processes*. O.U.P., 3 edition, 2001.

[12] C. Jeske. *Algebraic Integration of Retrenchment and Refinement*. PhD thesis, University of Manchester, 2005.

[13] S. Karlin and H.M. Taylor. *A First Course in Stochastic Processes*. Academic, 1975.

[14] Department of Trade and Industry. Information Technology Security Evaluation Criteria, 1991. http://www.cesg.gov.uk/site/iacs/itsec/media/formal-docs/Itsec.pdf.

[15] M. Poppleton and R. Banach. Controlling control systems: An application of evolving retrenchment. In D. Bert, J.P. Bowen, M.C. Henson, and K. Robinson, editors, *Second International Conference of B and Z Users*, volume 2272 of *LNCS*, pages 42–61, Grenoble, France, January 2002. Springer.

[16] S.L. Resnick. *Adventures in Stochastic Processes*. Birkhauser, 1992.

[17] S. Stepney, D. Cooper, and J. Woodcock. More powerful Z data refinement: Pushing the state of the art in industrial refinement. In J.P. Bowen, A. Fett, and M.G. Hinchey, editors, *11th International Conference of Z Users*, volume 1493 of *LNCS*, pages 284–307, Berlin, Germany, September 1998. Springer.

[18] S. Stepney, D. Cooper, and J. Woodcock. An electronic purse: Specification, refinement and proof. Technical Report PRG-126, Oxford University Computing Laboratory, 2000.

[19] S. Stepney, F. Polack, and I. Toyn. An outline pattern language for Z. In Bert et al. [7], pages 2–19.

[20] S. Stepney, F. Polack, and I. Toyn. Patterns to guide practical refactoring. In Bert et al. [7], pages 20–39.

[21] J. Woodcock and J. Davies. *Using Z: Specification, Refinement and Proof*. Prentice-Hall, 1996.

Strategic Term Rewriting and Its Application to a VDM-SL to SQL Conversion

T.L. Alves, P.F. Silva, J. Visser, and J.N. Oliveira

Dep. Informática, Universidade do Minho,
Campus de Gualtar, 4700-320 Braga, Portugal

Abstract. We constructed a tool, called VooDooM, which converts datatypes in VDM-SL into SQL relational data models. The conversion involves transformation of algebraic types to maps and products, and pointer introduction.

The conversion is specified as a theory of refinement by calculation. The implementation technology is strategic term rewriting in Haskell, as supported by the Strafunski bundle. Due to these choices of theory and technology, the road from theory to practise is straightforward.

Keywords: Strategic term rewriting, program calculation, VDM, SQL.

1   Introduction

The information system community is indebted to Codd for his pioneering work on the foundations of the relational data model [9]. Since then, relational database theory has been thoroughly studied [24, 34, 12]. At the heart of this we find *normalization*, a theory whereby efficient collections of (relational) files are derived from the original design, which can be encoded in a data-processing language such as SQL [16].

Functional dependency theory and normalization deviate from standard model-oriented formal specification and reification techniques [17, 10]. In the latter, designs start from abstract models which are abstract enough to dispense with normalization. Does one arrive at similar database designs by using data reification techniques?

References [29, 30, 31, 32] address a formal calculus which has been put forward as an alternative to standard normalization theory, by framing database design into the wider area of data refinement [17]. Data models, such as described by E-R diagrams, for instance, are turned into systems of equations involving set-theoretic notions such as finite mappings, sets, and sequences. Integrity constraints and business rules are identified with abstraction invariants [25] and datatype invariants [17], respectively, whose structural synthesis (analysis) by calculation is at the core of the calculus.

The main purpose of this paper is to describe the design of a *database schema calculator* which, inspired by [32], infers SQL relational meta-data from abstract data models specified in the ISO standard VDM-SL formal modelling notation [10]. The calculus is implemented using Haskell-based strategic term rewriting [23], and embedded in a full fledged source code processing tool following a grammar-centered approach to language tool development [18]. This database calculator, named VooDooM, is being used in the *Information Knowledge Fusion* (Σ!2235) project, to generate the database of a knowledge representation management system.

J.S. Fitzgerald, I.J. Hayes, and A. Tarlecki (Eds.): FM 2005, LNCS 3582, pp. 399–414, 2005.

1.1   Related Work

Most work on formal methods in relational database design is concerned with formal models of relational data. This interest dates back to (at least) [6], where a formalization of a relational data model is given using the VDM notation.

The formal specification and design of a program implementing simple update operations on a binary relational database called NDB is described in [38]. This single level description of NDB is the starting point of [11], where a case study in the modular structuring of this "flat" specification is presented. The authors present a second specification which makes use of an n-ary relation module, and a third one which uses an n-ary relation module with type and normalization constraints. They demonstrate the reusability of their modules, and also outline specifications of an n-ary relational database with normalization constraints, and an n-ary relational database with a two-level type hierarchy and no normalization constraints. However, their emphasis is on the modularization techniques adopted to organize VDM specifications into modules.

Samson and Wakelin [33] present a comprehensive survey about the use of algebraic methods to specify databases. They compare a number of approaches according to the features covered and enumerate some features not normally covered by such methods.

Barros [5] describes an extension to the traditional database design aimed at formalizing the development of (relational) database applications. A general method for the specification of relational database applications using Z is presented. A prototype is built to support the method. It provides for editing facilities and is targeted at the DBPL database management system.

The purpose of Baluta [4] is to rigorously specify the basic features of the relational data model version 2 (RM/V2) as defined by Codd [8], using the Z language.

More recently, Necco [26] exploits aspects of *data processing* which are functional in nature and can take advantage of recent developments in the area of *generic functional programming* and calculi. Generic Haskell is used to animate a generic model of a subset of the standard relational database calculus, written in the style of model-oriented formal specification.

2   Strategic Term Rewriting

In traditional term rewriting, one can distinguish the rewriting *equations* of a particular term rewriting system (TRS) from the *strategy* that is used to apply these equations to an input term. Most commonly, term rewriting environments have a fixed rewriting strategy, such as the leftmost-innermost strategy. In some rewriting environments, for instance those where the equations may be governed by conditions and may be stratified into default and regular equations, more sophisticated strategies may be employed. But in any case, these strategies are fixed, i.e. hard-wired into the environment.

By contrast, strategic term rewriting generalizes the traditional term rewriting paradigm by making rewriting strategies programmable, just as the equations are. Among the first rewriting environments to offer such programmable rewriting strategies are Stratego [35] and the Rewriting Calculus [7]. Such environments offer a small set of basic strategy combinators, which can be combined with each other and with rewriting equations to construct term rewriting systems with arbitrarily complex strategies.

Combinators		**Notation**	
$s ::=$ id	Identity strategy	d	... data
$\mid$ fail	Failure strategy	c	... data constructors
$\mid$ seq(s, s)	Sequential composition	$\overline{d}$	... data with failure "$\uparrow$"
$\mid$ choice(s, s)	Left-biased choice	a	... type-specific actions
$\mid$ all(s)	All immediate components	s	... strategies
$\mid$ one(s)	One immediate component	$a@d$	... application of a to d
$\mid$ adhoc(s, a)	Type-based dispatch	$s@d$	... application of s to d
		$d \Rightarrow \overline{d}$	... big-step semantics
		$a : t$	... type handled by a
		$d : t$	... type of a datum d
		$[d]$	... indivisible data
		$c(d_1 \cdots d_n)$	... compound data

Meaning

$$
\begin{aligned}
&\text{id}@d &&\Rightarrow d \\
&\text{fail}@d &&\Rightarrow \uparrow \\
&\text{seq}(s, s')@d &&\Rightarrow \overline{d} \quad \text{if } s@d \Rightarrow d' \wedge s'@d' \Rightarrow \overline{d} \\
&\text{seq}(s, s')@d &&\Rightarrow \uparrow \quad \text{if } s@d \Rightarrow \uparrow \\
&\text{choice}(s_1, s_2)@d &&\Rightarrow d' \quad \text{if } s_1@d \Rightarrow d' \\
&\text{choice}(s_1, s_2)@d &&\Rightarrow \overline{d} \quad \text{if } s_1@d \Rightarrow \uparrow \wedge s_2@d \Rightarrow \overline{d} \\
&\text{all}(s)@[d] &&\Rightarrow [d] \\
&\text{all}(s)@c(d_1 \cdots d_n) &&\Rightarrow c(d'_1 \cdots d'_n) \quad \text{if } s@d_1 \Rightarrow d'_1,\ldots,s@d_n \Rightarrow d'_n \\
&\text{all}(s)@c(d_1 \cdots d_n) &&\Rightarrow \uparrow \quad \text{if } \exists i.\ s@d_i \Rightarrow \uparrow \\
&\text{one}(s)@[d] &&\Rightarrow \uparrow \\
&\text{one}(s)@c(d_1 \cdots d_n) &&\Rightarrow c(\cdots d'_i \cdots) \quad \text{if } \exists i.\ s@d_1 \Rightarrow \uparrow \wedge \cdots \wedge s@d_{i-1} \Rightarrow \uparrow \wedge s@d_i \Rightarrow d'_i \\
&\text{one}(s)@c(d_1 \cdots d_n) &&\Rightarrow \uparrow \quad \text{if } s@d_1 \Rightarrow \uparrow,\ldots,s@d_n \Rightarrow \uparrow \\
&\text{adhoc}(s, a)@d &&\Rightarrow a@d \quad \text{if } a : t \text{ and } d : t \\
&\text{adhoc}(s, a)@d &&\Rightarrow s@d \quad \text{if } a : t \wedge d : t' \wedge t \neq t'
\end{aligned}
$$

Identities

[unit] $s \equiv \text{seq}(\text{id}, s) \equiv \text{seq}(s, \text{id}) \equiv \text{choice}(\text{fail}, s) \equiv \text{choice}(s, \text{fail})$

[zero] $\text{fail} \equiv \text{seq}(\text{fail}, s) \equiv \text{seq}(s, \text{fail}) \equiv \text{one}(\text{fail})$

[skip] $\text{id} \equiv \text{choice}(\text{id}, s) \equiv \text{all}(\text{id})$

[nested type dispatch]

$\text{adhoc}(\text{adhoc}(s, a), a') \equiv \text{adhoc}(s, a') \quad \text{if } a : t \wedge a' : t$

$\text{adhoc}(\text{adhoc}(s, a), a') \equiv \text{adhoc}(\text{adhoc}(s, a'), a) \quad \text{if } a : t \wedge a' : t' \wedge t \neq t'$

$\text{adhoc}(\text{adhoc}(\text{fail}, a), a') \equiv \text{choice}(\text{adhoc}(\text{fail}, a), \text{adhoc}(\text{fail}, a')) \quad \text{if } a : t \wedge a' : t' \wedge t \neq t'$

Fig. 1. Specification of a guideline set of basic strategy combinators

Figure 1 shows a set of such basic strategy combinators, along with their operational semantics.

Using the basic strategy combinators, more elaborate ones can easily be constructed. Consider for instance the following definitions:

$$
\begin{aligned}
try(s) &= \text{choice}(s, \text{id}) \\
repeat(s) &= try(\text{seq}(s, repeat(s)))
\end{aligned}
$$

$$full\_topdown(s) = \mathsf{seq}(s, \mathsf{all}(full\_topdown(s)))$$
$$innermost(s) \quad = \mathsf{seq}(\mathsf{all}(innermost(s)), try(\mathsf{seq}(s, innermost(s))))$$

The *try* combinator takes a potentially failing strategy as argument, and attempts to apply it. When failure occurs, the identity strategy id is used to recover. The *repeat* combinator repeatedly applies its argument strategy, until it fails. The *full_topdown* combinator applies its argument once to every node in a term, in pre-order. Finally, the *innermost* strategy applies its argument in left-most innermost fashion to a term, until it is not applicable anywhere anymore, i.e. until a fixpoint is reached.

The challenge of combining strategic term rewriting with strong typing was first met by the Haskell-based Strafunski bundle [23], which we will use in this paper, and the Java-based JJTraveler framework [36, 19]. A formal semantics of typed strategic programming was constructed subsequently [20]. Further generalizations were provided in the Haskell context [22, 21].

Strategic term rewriting has several benefits over traditional term rewriting. The most important benefits derive from the fact that many applications require rewrite equations that together do not form a confluent and terminating TRS. A program refactoring system, for instance, may require equations both for "extract method" and for "inline method". A document processing system may include equations that change mark-up only inside the context of certain document tags. In a traditional term rewriting environment, the only option to obtain sufficient control over when and where equations are applied, is to switch to so-called 'functional style'. This means that every rewrite rule $t \mapsto \ldots s \ldots$ is reformulated to include function symbols to control rewriting: $f(t) \mapsto \ldots g(s) \ldots$. This way, the rewriting strategy in fact becomes explicit in the additional function symbols, but is thoroughly entangled with the rewrite equations. In strategic programming, the rewrite equations can stay as they are, the strategy can be specified separately, and both equations and strategies can be used and reused in different combinations to obtain different TRSs. So, apart from full control over when and where equations are applied, strategic rewriting enhances separation of concerns, reusability, and understandability.

In this paper, we will rely on strategic term rewriting to cleanly separate the individual conversion rules from the strategy of applying them to the abstract syntax terms. We will use the Strafunski bundle as strategic term rewriting environment in which to implement the conversion tool.

3   Database Design by Calculation

The calculation method which underlies our VDM-SL to SQL conversion tool finds its roots in a "data refinement by calculation" strategy which originated in [29, 30] and has been focussed towards relational database design more recently [31, 32]. Reference [28] describes its application to reverse engineering legacy databases.

3.1   Abstraction and Representation

The calculus consists of inequations of the form $A \leq B$ (read: *"data type B implements, or refines data type A"*) which abbreviates the fact that there is a surjective, possibly partial function $A \xleftarrow{\ F\ } B$ (the *abstraction relation*) and an injective, total relation $A \xrightarrow{\ R\ } B$ (the *representation relation*) such that

$$F \cdot R = id_A \qquad (1)$$

where id_A is the identity function on datatype A. (F is traditionally referred to as a *retrieve* function [17].) Since the equality $R = S$ of two relations R and S is bi-inclusion $R \subseteq S \wedge S \subseteq R$, we have two readings of equation (1): $id_A \subseteq F \cdot R$, which ensures that every inhabitant of the abstract datatype A gets represented at B-level; and $F \cdot R \subseteq id_A$, which prevents "confusion" in the representation process:

$$\langle \forall\, b \in B, a \in A \,:\, b\,R\,a : \langle \forall\, a' \in A \,:\, a'\,F\,b : a' = a \rangle \rangle$$

("Never forget whom you are representing".)

   Below we will present a series of particular $\leq$-equations which together specify a data model refinement calculus. The types of the refinement relations will be mapped onto rewrite rules in the implementation.

3.2   Preorder

It can be shown that $\leq$ is a preorder, reflexivity meaning that any datatype represents itself ($R = F = id$) and transitivity meaning that $\leq$-steps can be chained by sequentially composing abstractions and representations:

$$(2)$$

This suggests that one may *calculate* implementations from specifications

$$Spec = X \leq X' \leq X'' \leq \cdots \leq Imp$$

by adding implementation *details* in a controlled manner. This also makes sense wherever the representation of a parameter of a datatype needs to be promoted to the overall parametric datatype by *structural data refinement*:

$$(3)$$

where F is such a parametric type, e.g. set of A in VDM-SL notation. (Technically, F is named a *relator* [3].) This is valid also for parametric types of higher arity, such as those of standard VDM-SL:

 - binary product types $A \times B$ and n-ary ones $\prod_{i=0}^{n} A_i$, which can be specified in VDM-SL as (nested) tuples or via record types, (semantically equivalent modulo selectors). E.g. A*B or compose AB of a: A b: B end, respectively.
 - sum types $A + B$, which in VDM-SL are specified by writing A | B for suitably specified (disjoint) A and B, extensible to finitary sums $\sum_{i=0}^{n} A_i$.
 - finite mappings $A \rightharpoonup B$, written map A to B in VDM-SL, in which case the abstraction of the domain datatype is required to be injective (otherwise the outcome may not be a mapping).

3.3   Conversion Laws

It is often the case that the abstraction (resp. representation) relation is a (total) function, in which case it is an *injection* (resp. *surjection*). As an example of this we present law

$$A^{\star} \xbegin{array}{c} seq2index \\ \leq \\ list \end{array} \mathbb{N} \rightharpoonup A \qquad (4)$$

which indexes a finite sequence, for instance,

$$seq2index([a, b, a]) = \{1 \mapsto a, 2 \mapsto b, 3 \mapsto a\}$$
$$list(\{11 \mapsto a, 12 \mapsto b, 33 \mapsto a\}) = [a, b, a]$$

A more structural law is

$$A \rightharpoonup (B + C) \begin{array}{c} uncojoin \\ \leq \\ cojoin \end{array} (A \rightharpoonup B) \times (A \rightharpoonup C) \qquad (5)$$

whereby *mappings of sums* are represented as *products of mappings*. (Definitions for *cojoin* and *uncojoin* are easy to guess.) In a situation where the abstraction is also a representation and vice-versa we have an isomorphism $A \cong B$, a special case of the $\leq$-law which works in both directions. For example, the abstraction/representation pair of the following isomorphism

$$A \times (B + C) \begin{array}{c} distr \\ \cong \\ undistr \end{array} (A \times B) + (A \times C) \qquad (6)$$

(product distributes through sum) is well-known from set-theory.

The VDM-SL finite mapping *dom* function witnesses a very useful isomorphism between finite sets and partial finite mappings,

$$2^A \begin{array}{c} set2fm \\ \cong \\ dom \end{array} A \rightharpoonup 1 \qquad (7)$$

which expresses the equivalence between data models set of A and map A to nil. (The inhabitants of $A \rightharpoonup 1$, often called *right-conditions* [13], obey a number of interesting properties.) Another basic isomorphism tells us how "singleton" finite mappings disguise "pointers" (guess *opt-intro* and *opt-elim*):

$$A + 1 \begin{array}{c} opt\text{-}intro \\ \cong \\ opt\text{-}elim \end{array} 1 \rightharpoonup A \qquad (8)$$

The following isomorphism law

$$(B + C) \rightharpoonup A \quad \overset{unpeither}{\underset{peither}{\cong}} \quad (B \rightharpoonup A) \times (C \rightharpoonup A) \tag{9}$$

is a companion of (5).

Two important $\leq$-rules from [32] are still missing from our catalog: the representation function of one of these,

$$A \rightharpoonup (B \times (C \rightharpoonup D)) \quad \overset{unnjoin}{\underset{njoin}{\leq}} \quad (A \rightharpoonup B) \times (A \times C \rightharpoonup D) \tag{10}$$

enables us to infer *composite keys* out of nested finite mappings. (See [30, 31] concerning abstraction $njoin$ and representation $unnjoin$.) In the abstraction direction (from right to left) it merges two tables which share a common (sub)key.

The other rule missing has to do with datatype "derecursivation". Suppose we are given a recursive datatype definition $\mu F \cong F \, \mu F$ where F is polynomial [3, 30]. Then any "tree" in μF can be represented by a "heap" and a "pointer" to it,

$$\mu F \quad \overset{rec\text{-}elim}{\underset{rec\text{-}intro}{\leq}} \quad (K \rightharpoonup F K) \times K \tag{11}$$

for K a data type of *"heap addresses"*, keys or *"pointers"*, such that $K \cong I\!N$. For example, the binary tree on the left-hand side of (12) below will be represented — via (11) followed by (5) — by address 5 pointing at the tables on the right-hand side:

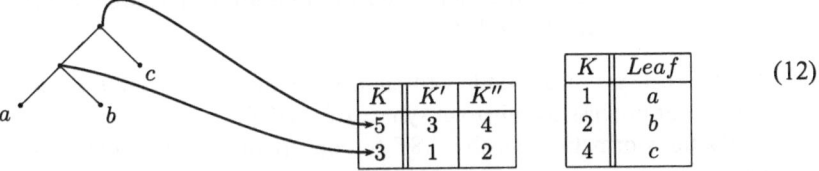

K	$Leaf$	
1	a	
2	b	
4	c	

K	K'	K''
5	3	4
3	1	2

$$\tag{12}$$

See [30, 31, 32] for several important details we have to skip at this point about this *generic* data representation technique, in particular in what concerns the complex abstraction invariant imposed by (11), which requires "well-founded heaps".

3.4   Normal Form

A pattern common to equations (4, 5, 7, 8, 9, 10 and 11) is that right-hand-sides do not involve functors other than product ($\times$) and finite mapping ($\rightharpoonup$). It so happens that these are exactly the functors admissible in the following abstract model

$$DB = \prod_{i=1}^{n} (\prod_{j=0}^{n_i} K_j \rightharpoonup \prod_{k=0}^{m_i} D_k) \tag{13}$$

of a relational database, whereby every $db \in DB$ is a collection of n relational tables (index $i = 1, n$) each of which is a mapping from a tuple of *keys* (index j) to a tuple of relevant *data* (index k). Wherever $m_i = 0$ we have $\prod_{k=0}^{0} D_k \cong 1$, meaning — via (7) — that we have a *finite set* of tuples in $\prod_{j=0}^{n_i} K_j$. (These are called *entity relationships* in the standard terminology.) Wherever $n_i = 0$ we are in presence of a singleton relational table. Last but not least, all K_j and D_k are "atomic" types, otherwise db would fail first normal form (1NF) compliance [24].

To derive such normal forms, the above calculation laws can be used in combination with appropriate laws for commutativity and associativity of tuples, and laws for introduction and elimination of empty tuples. To avoid these additional bookkeeping laws, we can generalize law (10) to:

$$A \rightharpoonup \left(\prod_i B_i \times \prod_j (C_j \rightharpoonup D_j)\right) \overset{\text{g-njoin}}{\underset{\text{g-unnjoin}}{\lessgtr}} \left(A \rightharpoonup \prod_i B_i\right) \times \prod_j (A \times C_j \rightharpoonup D_j) \quad (14)$$

In the implementation, we will make use of this generalization.

Thus, with this collection of calculation rules we are able to unravel (polynomial) recursive datatypes and decompose complex/nested mappings or sequences into tuples of simpler mappings, leading to models in relational normal form (13). In the upcoming section we will show how a term rewriting system can be constructed and implemented that performs such unraveling in a deterministic and confluent manner.

4   Design and Implementation of the VooDooM Tool

This section describes the implementation of the VooDooM tool, which uses strategic term rewriting to apply the refinement laws described above to VDM-SL source code. The overall architecture of the tool is shown in Figure 2. The architecture mirrors the phases needed to tackle the problem:

1. Recognize a specification file written in VDM-SL and convert it to a format that can be used for processing: abstract syntax tree (AST);
2. Apply transformations to the AST to convert the input model into its relational equivalent; and
3. Output the transformed specification either as VDM-SL or to SQL concrete syntax.

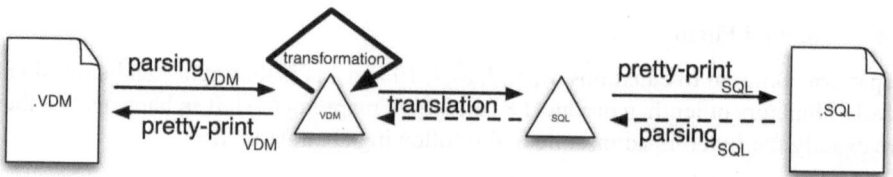

Fig. 2. Overall architecture of the VooDooM tool

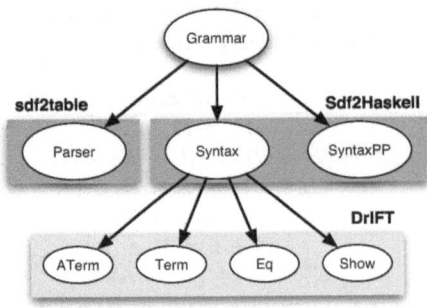

Fig. 3. Grammar-centric approach diagram

To handle each of these steps, the following modules were developed:

VDM-SL and SQL front-ends Deal with the language issues, namely parsing, pretty-printing and abstract representation.

Transformation engine Receives a VDM-SL AST representing the original specification and applies the calculation laws in order to compute a relational model that refines it (also a VDM-SL AST).

VDM-SL to SQL translator Maps a relational model in VDM-SL AST format to an equivalent SQL AST.

In the upcoming sections we will describe the implementation of these modules in more detail. We will use the following specification of a tiny bank account management system (BAMS) as example input[1]:

```
types
    BAMS       = map AccId to Account;
    Account    :: H: set of AccHolder
                  B: Amount;
    AccId      = seq of char;
    AccHolder  = seq of char;
    Amount     = int
```

4.1   Technology

We followed a grammar-centered approach to language tool development, where various kinds of functionality are automatically generated from concrete syntax definitions of the languages involved [18]. In particular, we relied on the Haskell-based Strafunski [23] bundle to generate parsers, pretty-printers, and support libraries for abstract syntax representation and traversal from SDF grammars of VDM-SL and SQL. Figure 3 illustrates this approach. SDF is the formalism in which both grammars are expressed. Parse tables are automatically generated by the *sdf2table* tool from the SDF software

---

[1] The intermediate steps will be presented in concrete VDM-SL syntax for clarity, although the tool actually uses ASTs.

Table 1. Catalog of rewriting rules. These rules are based on the various equations and inequations of the calculational data refinement theory presented in Section 3

Function	Rewrite rule	Law
seq2index	$A^* \Rightarrow I\!N \rightharpoonup A$	(4)
unconjoin	$A \rightharpoonup (B + C) \Rightarrow (A \rightharpoonup B) \times (A \rightharpoonup C)$	(5)
distr	$A \times (B + C) \Rightarrow (A \times B) + (A \times C)$	(6)
set2fm	$2^A \Rightarrow A \rightharpoonup 1$	(7)
opt-elim	$A + 1 \Rightarrow 1 \rightharpoonup A$	(8)
unpeither	$(B + C) \rightharpoonup A \Rightarrow (B \rightharpoonup A) \times (C \rightharpoonup A)$	(9)
unnjoin	$A \rightharpoonup (B \times (C \rightharpoonup D)) \Rightarrow (A \rightharpoonup B) \times (A \times C \rightharpoonup D)$	(10)
rec-elim	$\mu F \Rightarrow (K \rightharpoonup F\,K) \times K$	(11)

bundle, which corresponds to the *Parser* ellipses of Figure 3. The AST Haskell data type definition and the pretty-printer are generated with the *Sdf2Haskell* tool from Strafunski. They correspond to the *Syntax* and *SyntaxPP* ellipses from the picture.

From the abstract syntax, further components are generated in the form of Haskell Class instances, using the *DrIFT* tool. The *ATerm* instances support serialization to the ATerm format, which is used as interchange format between the generated parser and other components. The *Term* instances support generic traversal and strategic term rewriting over ASTs. The last two (*Eq* and *Show*), are not mandatory: they add comparison and printing functions to the Haskell data types.

As SQL grammar, we were able to employ a previously developed grammar. The VDM-SL grammar was developed by reconstructing the concrete syntax definition of the ISO standard [15] in SDF, as reported elsewhere [2].

4.2   Transformation

The transformation engine is the core module of the VooDooM tool. It is responsible for the refinement of the VDM-SL data types to a relational form, in accordance with the refinement laws presented above.

We make ample use of strategic term rewriting techniques in its implementation. The overall approach is as follows. First, we formulate individual term rewriting rules on the basis of the type signatures of the representation functions of the refinement laws. Table 1 lists these individual rules. Secondly, we use strategy combinators to compose these individual rules into a transformation engine that applies the individual rules in a way that a normal form is reached in a deterministic and confluent manner.

Before transformation begins, a single traversal is made over the AST that represents the complete VDM-SL input specification, to collect all sub-ASTs that represent data type definitions into a list. The transformation process itself operates on this collection. The transformation process is organized into the following sequential phases:

Inlining and Recursion Removal. The rewrite rules for conversion operate on datatypes, not on systems of named data type definitions. To avoid needing to perform lookups of data type names during transformation, we start by inlining, i.e. replacing all data type names by their definitions. This technique leads to the loss of the top level data type names, which in some cases are useful. To overcome this problem, singleton composes are introduced before inlining those types.

Of course, this substitution process would run into cycles if we did not treat recursive definitions differently. For this reason, the recursion removal rewrite rule *rec-elim* is used in combination with inlining. After these rules have exhaustively been applied, a set of non-recursive, independent datatypes is obtained that is amenable to further transformation. Exhaustive application is realized by using the *repeat* combinator.

After the inlining step, our example specification will look as follows:

```
types
  BAMS = map compose AccId of seq of char end to
              compose Account of
                H: set of compose AccHolder of seq of char end
                B: compose Amount of int end
              end
```

Though our example does not contain recursive datatypes, the tree example of Section 3 illustrates recursion removal. More examples are given in [30, 31].

Desugaring. We limit the language of data type definitions by removing those constructs for which we have a simple elimination rule: sets, sequences, and optionals. Sequences of characters are viewed as atomic and excluded from desugaring, because we want to map them to native SQL strings (varchar). Also, we rewrite all tuples to VDM-SL's compose construct. This desugaring step is performed by applying the rules *seq2index*, *set2fm*, and *optElim*, in a single traversal.

In the same traversal, we rewrite tuples to VDM-SL compose constructs. Alternatively, we could have desugared composes to nested tuples, but that would lead to the loss of names of composes and their fields. Of course, if all tuples are eliminated in favour of composes, this has the consequence that all calculation laws involving products should be mapped to rewrite rules involving composes. This has as additional benefit that various rules (e.g. 14) can be generalized, because composes are n-ary, rather than binary.

After desugaring, our example specification looks as follows:

```
types
  BAMS = map compose AccId of seq of char end to
              compose Account of
                H: map compose AccHolder of seq of char end to NIL
                B: compose Amount of int end
              end
```

This expression contains only maps and products (compose), but is not yet in relational form.

Conversion to Relational Form. After having the desugared structure, further transformation rules can now be applied. At this stage, the needed rules are *unconjoin*, *unpeither*, and the generalized version of *unnjoin*. In addition, a rule for flattening nested composes is needed to bring expressions into the best form to be rewritten with that

Table 2. Correspondence between VDM-SL and SQL92 data types

VDM-SL data type	SQL data type	SQL Constraint
bool	SMALLINT	CHECK (.. IN (0,1))
nat	INT	CHECK .. >= 0
nat1	INT	CHECK .. >= 1
int	INT	
rat	REAL	
real	REAL	
char	CHAR (1)	
token	VARCHAR (128)	
seq of char	VARCHAR (128)	

generalized rule. These rewrite rules need to be applied exhaustively throughout the AST. The *innermost* combinator is suitable for this.

After conversion, our example specification is in the relational normal form which follows:

```
types
  BAMS = compose mapAggr of
            map compose AccId of seq of char end
            to compose Amount of int end
            map compose tuple of
                         seq of char
                         seq of char
                    end
               to NIL
          end
```

Resugaring. Finally, sets are reintroduced into the expression, using the dom rule. Thus, any occurrence of the form map x to NIL is converted to set of x. This occurs when further simplification was not possible. This is justified, because these can be represented directly in SQL. When VDM-SL is targeted as output language, tuples are reintroduced where binary composes with anonymous fields occur.

4.3   SQL Translation

During transformation, an initial specification is transformed into a relational normal form. In the translation process these VDM-SL data types are converted to SQL tables and attributes.

The translation of normal forms to SQL is straightforward. The relational equivalent of a *map* is a table in which the domain of the map is the primary key. The relational counterpart of a *set* is a table with a compound primary key on all columns to guarantee uniqueness. The elements of maps and sets, which are products of elementary VDM-SL data types, are converted to SQL column attributes (that are also of elementary types).

Because basic VDM-SL and SQL data types are not compatible, a correspondence between them must be made. Table 2 shows the correspondence implemented in the

VooDooM tool. The table also shows constraints to be added to the SQL data model to better preserve the semantics of some VDM-SL data types. Only Standard SQL92 [16] data types were chosen, to provide a solution that works for all SQL vendor dialects.

The SQL generated for our running BAMS example is as follows:

```
CREATE TABLE table1 (              CREATE TABLE table2 (
  AccId VARCHAR (128) NOT NULL,      Attr1 VARCHAR (128) NOT NULL,
  Amount INT NOT NULL,               Attr2 VARCHAR (128) NOT NULL,
  PRIMARY KEY (AccId)                PRIMARY KEY (Attr1, Attr2)
)                                  )
```

As can be seen, a composite type (the outer compose) with a map and a set (reintroduced for map ... to NIL) is translated to two tables in SQL. Because none of the compose elements have tags, they have been automatically generated as table1 and table2. The fields of the inner composes have been converted to SQL attribute columns. In case of the map there are two tags: AccId and Amount. This led to the creation of two attributes with those names. The primary key of the generated table is AccID because it represents the domain of the map. In case of the set there are no tags, so attribute names are automatically generated: Attr1 and Attr2. These two attributes together form a compound primary key, because combined they represent the domain of the set.

Thus, table1 associates an amount to the identifier of each account in the system, while table2 uniquely relates accounts identifiers with account holders. These two tables implement the original specification in which account identifiers are mapped to accounts, and each account has a set of account holders and an amount. The actual retrieve function that witnesses the abstraction relation between the original VDM-SL specification and this pair of SQL tables is given in [1].

5   Concluding Remarks

A decade ago, Barros [5] referred to the derivation of database programs directly from formal specifications as an unsolved problem. By contrast, deriving the database structure was regarded as a trivial aspect. However, his specifications are Z schemata whose internal states are already close to the relational model (e.g. power-sets of products).

This is in contrast with our approach, in which the source data-model can be arbitrarily complex (as far as VDM-SL data constructors are concerned), including recursive datatypes. Our "derecursivation" law (rec-elim), which relationally expresses the main result of [37], bears some resemblance (at least in spirit) with "defunctionalization" [14], a technique which is used in program transformation and compilation.

On the other hand, our approach shares with [5] the view that database design should be regarded as special case of data refinement. It is orthogonal to [5] in the sense that we are not concerned with database dynamics (transactions, etc).

Another advantage of our approach is the prospect of synthesizing abstraction invariants generated by each refinement step, which is still in the to-do list of the project. These include abstraction / representation functions and concrete invariants. The former can be used for data-migration between the original VDM-SL source and the generated relational model, in a way similar to [28] and to what is done manually in [1]. The latter can be (at least in part) incorporated as SQL constraints.

Strategic term rewriting provides a realistic solution to database schema calculation when compared with previous attempts to animate the same calculus using *genetic algorithm*-based term-rewriting techniques [27].

5.1   Future Work

We plan to extend the VooDooM tool in several ways. Firstly, in addition to the conversion of VDM-SL to SQL, we want to support the reverse process of obtaining an algebraic set of datatypes from a relational model, as already suggested by the dashed lines in the architecture overview in Figure 2.

Reversing a database to VDM-SL is not a novelty. This problem was already tackled in [28], in which the authors describe an implemented functional prototype and its application using a real world example. However that implementation has several drawbacks. The process has to be assisted manually, the initial relational model must be specified in VDM-SL, the transformation rules were coded with explicit recursion, and all traversals were hard-coded leading to a inflexibility in the implementation. With the strategic term rewriting approach, the same problem can be solved in a more pragmatic way.

Secondly, we intend to offer better support for invariants to the tool. The transformation and translation processes in both directions lack support for VDM-SL invariants. To more accurately preserve semantics, invariants should be added during the transformation process when a data type is split in two or more. However, invariants pose some difficulties when performing transformations since the data definitions which they refer are changing. Thus, invariants need also to reflect this change. When the transformations are simple rearrangements of data fields this can be easy but, since invariants can be as complicated as any function mapping the type to a boolean, the general case is not. Transforming arbitrary functionality in an automated manner is a challenging subject which would involve investigation beyond the scope of this tool. However, we intend to develop some invariant support, namely to referential integrity constraints, by providing a small subset of VDM-SL that can be mapped into SQL constraints in an automated way.

Availability

The VooDooM tool is developed as open source software and is available from its project web page: http://voodoom.sourceforge.net/.

Acknowledgments

The work reported in this paper has been carried out in the context of the Eureka project Σ!2235 *IKF: Information Knowledge Fusion* funded by *Agência de Inovação S.A*, and of the project *Program Understanding and Re-engineering: Calculi and Applications (PURe)* funded by *Fundação para a Ciência e a Tecnologia*, grant number POSI/ICHS/44304/2002.

References

1. J.J. Almeida, L.S. Barbosa, F.L. Neves, and J.N. Oliveira. Bringing Camila and SetCalc Together — the bams.cam and ppd.cam Camila Toolset demos. Technical report, DI/UM, Braga, December 1997. [45 p. doc.].

2. T. Alves and J. Visser. Development of an industrial strength grammar for VDM. Technical Report DI-PURe-05.04.29, Universidade do Minho, 2005.

3. R.C. Backhouse, P. de Bruin, P. Hoogendijk, G. Malcolm, T.S. Voermans, and J. van der Woude. Polynomial relators. In *2nd Int. Conf. Algebraic Methodology and Software Technology (AMAST'91)*, pages 303–362. Springer LNCS, 1992.

4. D. D. Baluta. A formal specification in Z of the relational data model, Version 2, of E.F. Codd. M. Sc. thesis, Concordia University, Montreal, QC, Canada, 1995.

5. R.S.M. de Barros. Deriving relational database programs from formal specifications. In Maurice Naftalin, B. Tim Denvir, and Miquel Bertran, editors, *FME '94: Industrial Benefit of Formal Methods, Second International Symposium of Formal Methods Europe, Barcelona, Spain, October 24-18, 1994, Proceedings*, volume 873 of *Lecture Notes in Computer Science*, pages 703–723. Springer, 1994.

6. D. Bjorner and C.B. Jones. *Formal Specification and Software Development*. Series in Computer Science. Prentice-Hall International, 1982. C.A.R. Hoare, ed.

7. H. Cirstea, C. Kirchner, and L. Liquori. The Rho Cube. In Furio Honsell, editor, *Foundations of Software Science and Computation Structures, ETAPS'2001*, Lecture Notes in Computer Science, pages 166–180, Genova, Italy, April 2001. Springer-Verlag.

8. E. F. Codd. *Missing Information*. Addison-Wesley Publishing Company, Inc., 1990.

9. E.F. Codd. A relational model of data for large shared data banks. *Communications of the ACM*, 13(6):377–387, June 1970.

10. J. Fitzgerald and P.G. Larsen. *Modelling Systems: Practical Tools and Techniques for Software Development*. Cambridge University Press, 1st edition, 1998.

11. J.S. Fitzgerald and C.B. Jones. *Modularizing the formal description of a database system*, volume 428 of *Lecture Notes in Computer Science*. Springer, 1990.

12. H. Garcia-Molina, J. D. Ullman, and J. D. Widom. *Database Systems: The Complete Book*. Prentice Hall, 2002. ISBN: 0-13-031995-3.

13. P. Hoogendijk. *A Generic Theory of Data Types*. PhD thesis, University of Eindhoven, The Netherlands, 1997.

14. G. Hutton and J. Wright. Compiling exceptions correctly. In Dexter Kozen and Carron Shankland, editors, *Mathematics of Program Construction, 7th International Conference, MPC 2004, Stirling, Scotland, UK, July 12-14, 2004, Proceedings*, volume 3125 of *Lecture Notes in Computer Science*, pages 211–227. Springer, 2004.

15. ISO. Information technology — programmming languages, their environments and system software interfaces — Vienna Development Method — specification language — part 1: Base language, Dec. 1996. (ISO/IEC 13817-1, Geneva).

16. ISO. *Information Technology – Database languages – SQL*. Reference number ISO/IEC 9075:1992(E), Nov. 1992.

17. C.B. Jones. *Software Development — A Rigorous Approach*. Series in Computer Science. Prentice-Hall International, 1980. C.A. R. Hoare.

18. M. de Jonge and J. Visser. Grammars as contracts. In *Proceedings of the Second International Conference on Generative and Component-based Software Engineering (GCSE 2000)*, volume 2177 of *Lecture Notes in Computer Science*, pages 85–99. Springer, 2000.

19. T. Kuipers and J. Visser. Object-oriented tree traversal with JJForester. In M. van den Brand and D. Parigot, editors, *Electronic Notes in Theoretical Computer Science*, volume 44. Elsevier Science, 2001. Proc. Workshop on Language Descriptions, Tools and Applications.

20. R. Lämmel. Typed Generic Traversal With Term Rewriting Strategies. *Journal of Logic and Algebraic Programming*, 54, 2003.
21. R. Lämmel and S. Peyton Jones. Scrap your boilerplate: a practical design pattern for generic programming. *ACM SIGPLAN Notices*, 38(3):26–37, March 2003. Proc. ACM SIGPLAN Workshop on Types in Language Design and Implementation (TLDI 2003).
22. R. Lämmel and J. Visser. Strategic polymorphism requires just two combinators! Technical Report cs.PL/0212048, arXiv, December 2002.
23. R. Lämmel and J. Visser. A Strafunski Application Letter. In V. Dahl and P. Wadler, editors, *Proc. of Practical Aspects of Declarative Programming (PADL'03)*, volume 2562 of *LNCS*, pages 357–375. Springer-Verlag, January 2003.
24. D. Maier. *The Theory of Relational Databases*. Computer Science Press, 1983.
25. C. Morgan. *Programming from Specification*. Series in Computer Science. Prentice-Hall International, 1990. C.A. R. Hoare, series editor.
26. C. Necco. Polytypic data processing. Master's thesis, Facultad de Cs. Físico Matemáticas y Naturales, University of San Luis, Argentina, 2005. (Submitted.).
27. F.L. Neves and J.N. Oliveira. ART — Um Laborat=rio de Reificatpo "GenTtica". In *IBERAMIA'98 — Sixth Ibero-Conference on Artificial Intelligence*, pages 201–215, Lisbon, Portugal, October 5-9 1998. (in Portuguese).
28. F.L. Neves, J.C. Silva, and J.N. Oliveira. Converting Informal Meta-data to VDM-SL: A Reverse Calculation Approach . In *VDM in Practice! A Workshop co-located with FM'99: The World Congress on Formal Methods, Toulouse, France*, September 1999.
29. J.N. Oliveira. A reification calculus for model-oriented software specification. *Formal Aspects of Computing*, 2(1):1–23, April 1990.
30. J.N. Oliveira. Software reification using the SETS calculus. In Tim Denvir, Cliff B. Jones, and Roger C. Shaw, editors, *Proc. of the BCS FACS 5th Refinement Workshop, Theory and Practice of Formal Software Development, London, UK*, pages 140–171. ISBN 0387197524, Springer-Verlag, 8–10 January 1992. (Invited paper).
31. J.N. Oliveira. Data processing by calculation, 2001. 108 pages. Lecture Notes for the 6th Estonian Winter School in Computer Science, 4-9 March 2001, Palmse, Estonia.
32. J.N. Oliveira. Calculate databases with 'simplicity', September 2004. Presentation at the IFIP WG 2.1 #59 Meeting, Nottingham, UK.
33. W.B. Samson and A.W. Wakelin. *Algebraic Specification of Databases: A Survey from a Database Perspective*. Workshops in Computing. Springer Verlag, Glasgow, 1992.
34. J. D. Ullman. *Principles of Database and Knowledge-Base Systems*. Computer Science Press, 1988.
35. E. Visser and Z. Benaissa. A Core Language for Rewriting. In C. Kirchner and H. Kirchner, editors, *Proc. International Workshop on Rewriting Logic and its Applications (WRLA'98)*, volume 15 of *ENTCS*, Pont-à-Mousson, France, September 1998. Elsevier Science.
36. J. Visser. Visitor combination and traversal control. *ACM SIGPLAN Notices*, 36(11):270–282, 2001. Proceedings of the ACM Conference on Object-Oriented Programming Systems, Languages, and Applications (OOPSLA 2001).
37. E. G. Wagner. All recursive types defined using products and sums can be implemented using pointers. In Clifford Bergman, Roger D. Maddux, and Don Pigozzi, editors, *Algebraic Logic and Universal Algebra in Computer Science*, volume 425 of *Lecture Notes in Computer Science*. Springer, 1990.
38. A. Walshe. *NDB: The Formal Specification and Rigorous Design of a Single-User Database System*. Prentice Hall, ISBN 0-13-116088-5, 1990.

Synthesis of Distributed Processes from Scenario-Based Specifications

Jun Sun and Jin Song Dong

School of Computing, National University of Singapore
{sunj, dongjs}@comp.nus.eud.sg

Abstract. Given a set of sequence diagrams, the problem of synthesis is of deciding whether there exists a satisfying object system and if so, synthesize one automatically. It is crucial in the development of complex systems, since sequence diagrams serve as the manifestation of use cases and if synthesizable they could lead directly to implementation. It is even more interesting (and harder) if the synthesized object system is distributed. In this paper, we propose a systematic way of synthesizing distributed processes from Live Sequence Charts. The basic idea is to first construct a CSP specification from the LSC specification, and then use CSP algebraic laws to group the behaviors of each object effectively. The key point is that the behaviors of each object can be decided locally without constructing the global state machine.

Keywords: LSC, CSP, Synthesis.

1 Introduction

Sequence diagrams have been a popular means of specifying scenarios of reactive systems for decades. They have found their ways into many methodologies, e.g. Sequence Diagrams in Unified Modelling Languages (UML [12]), Messages Sequence Charts (MSCs) in Specification and Description Language (SDL) [18]. They are used in the early stage of system development to describe possible communication scenarios. Given a set of sequence diagrams, the problem of synthesis is of deciding whether there exists a satisfying object system and if so, synthesize one automatically. The problem is crucial in the development of complex systems, as sequence diagrams serve as the manifestation of use cases and if synthesizable they could lead directly to implementation. The problem has been long recognized as a hard problem and tackled by many researchers [2, 1, 21]. The conclusion is that for reactive distributed systems, synthesizing a distributed object system with precisely the set of behaviors is in general impossible. Detailed discussions on why distributed systems are hard to synthesize and why unspecified behaviors are unavoidable can be found in [24] and [1] respectively.

Live Sequence Charts (LSCs) are proposed by Damm and Harel [8]. They are rapidly recognized as a rather rich and useful extension of MSCs. A rich set of constructs are provided for specifying not only possible behaviors, but also mandatory behaviors. For instance, a universal chart, possibly preceded with a pre-chart, specifies mandatory behaviors globally, i.e. once the system behavior matches its pre-chart, the

J.S. Fitzgerald, I.J. Hayes, and A. Tarlecki (Eds.): FM 2005, LNCS 3582, pp. 415–431, 2005.

subsequence behavior must follow the chart. On the level of a chart, events and conditions and locations are also labelled with modalities. LSCs also provides structuring constructs, like sub-charts, branching and iterations, to build scenarios hierarchically. In a nutshell, LSCs provide a far more powerful means for setting requirements for complex system than classic sequence diagrams. Therefore, they serve as the basis of tool supporting analysis of scenarios, for example, the study of the synthesis problem.

The synthesis problem of LSCs is discussed by Harel and Kugler in [14], in which they tackled the problem by defining the notion of consistency between LSCs. Their approach starts with constructing a **global system automata** and decompose it by different means (refer to [14] for details). Their approach suffers from the state explosion problem due to the construction of the **global system automata**, which is often of huge size because of the distributed nature of LSCs and the underlying weak partial ordering semantics. In this paper, we present a systematic way of synthesizing distributed processes directly from LSCs. The basic idea is to first construct a Communicating Sequential Process (CSP [17]) specification from the LSC specification, and then use CSP algebraic laws to group the behaviors of each object effectively. The key point is that the behaviors of each object can be decided locally without constructing the global state machine. In our previous work [27], we explored the semantic-based equivalence relations between CSP and LSCs. We prove that we may capture the semantics of LSC specifications using CSP. The practical implication is that CSP supporting tools like FDR [10] can be reused to validate LSC specifications. The construction of CSP specifications in this work, however, is different because our aim is to synthesize refinements of consistent LSC specifications. Only distributed processes that are not only consistent with the LSC specification but also regular (so that they lead to finite state machine implementations) and minimally restrictive (if possible) are interested. Our work in [27] can be viewed as a necessary precedence of this work. Our approach is experimented with an automated tool developed using JAVA and XML.

We remark that the same result can be derived using Büchi Automata [6] with a painfully complicated procedure. In [3], Bontemps and Heymans use Büchi automata to define the language expressed by a set of LSCs. They claim that standard algorithm for automata can be used to check consistency and refinement and etc. As one of the future works, they mentioned the synthesis of state-based implementations from LSCs. However, as Büchi automata are low-level and not structured, flattening high-level LSCs into automata suffers from the state explosion problem. Whereas CSP provides a rich set of compositional constructs. Therefore, our work preserves the structure of the LSC specification and avoids constructing the global state machine both at the chart level or globally. In [4], Bontemps and Schobbens and Löding discussed the synthesis problem for a small subset of LSCs (LSCs without conditions, structuring constructs, modalities on locations and messages). They proposed a game-based semantics for LSCs, which leads to the notion of consistency between their LSCs. However, their discussion on the problem of synthesis is limited to a single universal chart. In our approach, almost all LSC constructs are supported except timing constructs, which we leave to the future works. In addition, there is the work described in [19], which synthesizes a timed Büchi Automata from a single chart only. What makes our goal both harder and more interesting is in the treatment of a set of charts, not just a single one. As far as the limited case of classical MSC goes, there have been quite some works on formalizing and then synthesizing from them. This includes the works by Alur mentioned earlier and others, evidenced in [20, 21, 22, 16].

The rest of the paper is organized as follows. Section 2 introduces LSCs and CSP. Section 3 presents our approach to synthesize distributed processes from a set of LSC universal charts. Section 4 discusses relevant issues of the synthesis, i.e. how to handle modalities on locations. Section 5 concludes the paper with possible future works.

2   Background

2.1   Live Sequence Charts

MSCs are widely used to describe scenarios of interaction between processes or objects. However, MSCs suffer from the rather weak partial-order semantics that makes it incapable of capturing many kinds of behavioral requirements. LSCs are introduced in [8] to overcome the shortcomings of MSCs by adding liveness or universality, i.e. something desired must be observed.

There are two kinds of charts in LSCs. Existential charts are mainly used to describe possible scenarios of a system in the early stage of system development, i.e. the same role played by classic MSCs. In later stage, knowledge becomes available about when a system run has progressed far enough for a specific usage of the system to become relevant. Universal charts are then used to specify behaviors that should always be exhibited. In this work, we assume that an LSC specification consists of a set of universal charts, and existential charts are used to specify test cases. A universal chart may be preceded by a pre-chart, which serves as the activation condition for executing the main chart. Whenever a communication sequence matches a pre-chart, the system must proceed as specified by the main chart. Due to pre-charts, a system run may activate a universal chart more than once and some of the activation might overlap [23].

Each chart is associated with a set of visible events. Only the set of visible events are constrained by the chart. A chart typically consists of multiple instances, which are represented as vertical lines graphically. Along with each line, there are a finite number of locations. A location carries the temperature annotation for progress within an instance. A location may be labelled as either cold or hot. A hot location means that the system has to move beyond. Whereas the system may stay at a cold location forever. Similarly, messages and conditions are also labelled. A hot message must be received, whereas a cold one may get lost. A hot condition must be met, whereas a cold condition terminates the chart if it is evaluated to false.

Example 1. We introduce a mobile phone system as a running example to explain and illustrate the main ideas and results. This example is partially inspired by the phone system specification presented in [7]. The system consists of six participating objects, a *user*, the *cover*, the *display*, the *speaker*, the *chip* and the environment where the incoming calls are from. Due to the page limit, we only introduce a self-containing set of scenarios. Scenario **OpenCover** illustrates the interaction between the objects when the *user* opens the *cover*, i.e. the *chip* is notified that the *cover* is opened, it then requests the *display* to display the menu. The *display* then carries out a local action

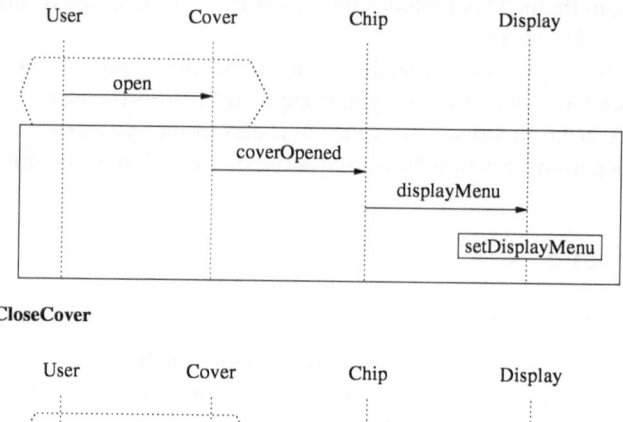

Fig. 1. Mobile Phone System Scenario: OpenCover, CloseCover

setDisplayMenu to initialize the menu screen. The upper chart in Figure 1 illustrates the scenario. Figure 1, 2 illustrates the scenarios where the user closes the cover, an incoming call arrives and the user picks up the phone and talk. These scenarios are self-explanatory. Note that all vertical lines in the charts are dotted, which means that all locations along the lines are cold and, therefore, the system may pause at any point of execution forever. This is possible because unexpected events like the battery runs out or the system breaks down may occur at any time. The set of visible events for each chart are exactly those appeared in the diagram except the scenario **Talk**, which includes a forbidden event *close*. We remark that the message from the user to the cover *close* is forbidden in the scenario **Talk**, i.e. in order to carry out the scenario successfully, the user should not close the cover before the scenario completes. Figure 3 illustrates the typical usage of the phone. Note that implicit assumptions are captured by hot locations, for example an incoming call will eventually trigger the ring, the user will eventually pick up the call and hand up the call and etc.

LSCs also support advanced MSC features like co-region, hierarchy and etc. Symbolic instances and messages are adopted to group scenarios effectively. For a detailed introduction on a complete list of features of LSCs, refer to [15]. LSCs are far more expressive than MSCs, which makes them capable of expressing complicated scenario-based requirements. However, we remark that the ability to specify hot and cold messages, i.e. whether a message is required to be received or may get lost, is redundant

Receive

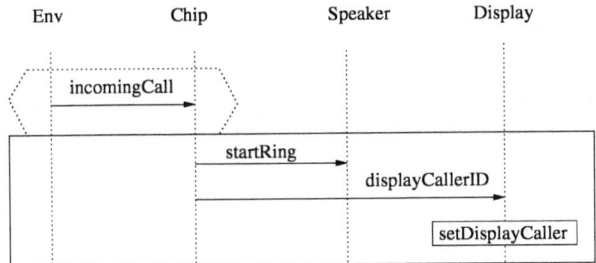

Talk

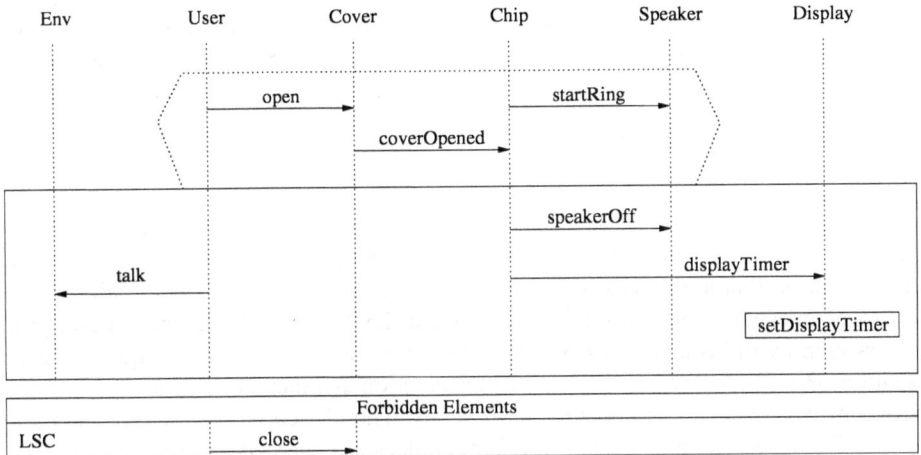

Fig. 2. Mobile Phone System Scenario: Receive, Talk

Phone

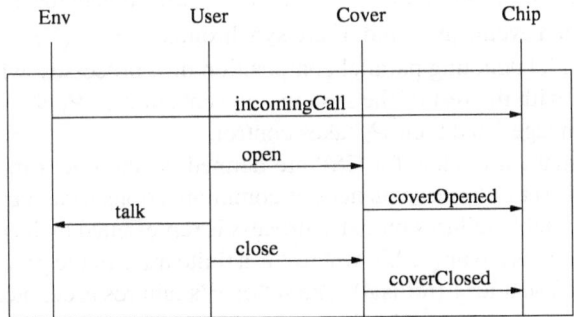

Fig. 3. Mobile Phone System Scenario: Phone

because of the facility for describing hot and cold locations. Essentially, the temperature of the locations takes precedence over the temperature of messages, so whether or not the message is received is determined entirely by the temperature of the message input. This questionable feature of LSCs is recognized by Harel and Marelly who list the possible cases and conclude that the temperature of the message has no semantical meaning [15]. Thus, in the following discussion, the temperature of all messages is discarded.

2.2   Communicating Sequential Process

Hoare's CSP [17, 25] is a formal specification language where processes proceed from one state to another by engaging in events. Processes may be composed by operators which require synchronization on events, i.e. each component must be willing to participate in a given event before the whole system makes the transition. A CSP process is defined by process expressions. Let $\mathcal{P}$ denote all possible CSP processes. The relevant syntactic class of process expression is defined as:

$$\mathcal{P} ::= RUN_{\Sigma} \mid \text{STOP} \mid \text{SKIP} \mid \mathcal{P}_1 \sqcap \mathcal{P}_2 \mid \mathcal{P}_1 \Box \mathcal{P}_2 \mid \mathcal{P}_1; \mathcal{P}_2 \mid \mathcal{P}_1 \mid\mid\mid \mathcal{P}_2 \mid$$
$$\mathcal{P}_1 {}_X\mid\mid_Y \mathcal{P}_2 \mid \mathcal{P}_1 {}_X\mid\mid_Y \mathcal{P}_2 \mid \mathcal{P}_1 \triangledown_e \mathcal{P}_2 \mid \cdots$$

CSP defines a rich set of operators to create processes. RUN_{Σ} is a process always willing to engage any event in Σ. STOP denotes a process that deadlocks and does nothing. A process that terminates is written as SKIP. A process $e \rightarrow \mathcal{P}$ is initially willing to engage in event e and behaves as $\mathcal{P}$ afterward. CSP allows a hierarchical description of a system by offering various operators to compose processes. The sequential composition, $\mathcal{P}_1; \mathcal{P}_2$, behaves as $\mathcal{P}_1$ until its termination and then behaves as $\mathcal{P}_2$. A choice between two processes is denoted as $\mathcal{P}_1 \mid \mathcal{P}_2$. The choice is made either internally $(\mathcal{P}_1 \sqcap \mathcal{P}_2)$ or externally $(\mathcal{P}_1 \Box \mathcal{P}_2)$. Often, choices are guarded by prefixing or conditionals. A choice that depends on the truth value of a boolean expression b is written as $\mathcal{P}_1 \langle b \rangle \mathcal{P}_2$. If b is true, this process proceeds as $\mathcal{P}_1$, otherwise $\mathcal{P}_2$. Parallel composition of two processes is denoted as $\mathcal{P}_1 \parallel \mathcal{P}_2$, where common events are synchronized. If X is an empty set, the two processes interleaves, denoted as $\mathcal{P}_1 \mid\mid\mid \mathcal{P}_2$. The generalized form of synchronization is denoted as $\mathcal{P}_1 {}_X\parallel_Y \mathcal{P}_2$, the alphabetized parallel composition where common events in X and Y are synchronized. $\parallel_{k=1}^{n} (\mathcal{P}_k, \Sigma_k)$ is a replicated alphabetized parallel denoting parallel composition of n processes, where each process $\mathcal{P}_k$ synchronizes with the rest of the system on events in Σ_k. $\mathcal{P}_1 \triangledown_e \mathcal{P}_2$ behaves as $\mathcal{P}_1$ until event e is engaged and then $\mathcal{P}_2$ takes control.

Three mathematical models for CSP are defined. In the traces model, a process is represented by the set of finite sequences of communications it can perform, denoted as $traces(\mathcal{P})$. In the stable failures model, a process is represented by its traces and also by its failures. A failure is a pair (t, Σ), where t is a finite trace of the process and Σ is a set of events it can refuse after t (refusal). The set of P's failures is denoted as $failures(\mathcal{P})$. In the failures/divergences model [5], a process is represented by its failures, together with its divergences. A divergence is a finite trace during or after which the process can perform an infinite sequence of consecutive internal actions. Failure/divergence model and stable failure model make no difference for divergence-free systems. A detailed discussion on the three semantics models can be found in [25]. The well-established failure semantics is used to establish equivalence relations between processes by appeal to algebraic laws of CSP. We quote the relevant laws below. The proof of each law can be found in either [17] or [25].

$$
\begin{array}{lll}
\mathcal{P} \,|[\, \Sigma \,]|\, RUN_{\Sigma} & = \mathcal{P} & \text{[L1]} \\
\mathcal{P} \,\|\, \text{STOP} & = \text{STOP} & \text{[L2]} \\
\mathcal{P} \,\|\, \mathcal{P} & = \mathcal{P} & \text{[L3]} \\
\mathcal{P}_1 \,{}_X\|_Y\, \mathcal{P}_2 & = \mathcal{P}_2 \,{}_Y\|_X\, \mathcal{P}_1 & \text{[L4]} \\
(\mathcal{P}_1 \,{}_X\|_Y\, \mathcal{P}_2) \,{}_{X \cup Y}\|_Z\, \mathcal{P}_3 & = \mathcal{P}_1 \,{}_X\|_{Y \cup Z}\, (\mathcal{P}_2 \,{}_Y\|_Z\, \mathcal{P}_3) & \text{[L5]}
\end{array}
$$

The following laws are derived. Law [L6] is a directly consequence of law [L4] and [L5]. Law [L7] is the generalized form of law [L6].

$$
(\mathcal{P}_1 \,{}_X\|_Y\, \mathcal{P}_2) \,{}_{X \cup Y}\|_{Z \cup W}\, (\mathcal{P}_3 \,{}_Z\|_W\, \mathcal{P}_4) = (\mathcal{P}_1 \,{}_X\|_Z\, \mathcal{P}_3) \,{}_{X \cup Z}\|_{Y \cup W}\, (\mathcal{P}_2 \,{}_Y\|_W\, \mathcal{P}_4) \quad \text{[L6]}
$$

$$
\Big\|_{i=1}^{m} \Big(\Big\|_{j=1}^{n} (\mathcal{P}_i^j, \Sigma_i^j), \bigcup_j \Sigma_i^j \Big) = \Big\|_{j=1}^{n} \Big(\Big\|_{i=1}^{m} (\mathcal{P}_i^j, \Sigma_i^j), \bigcup_i \Sigma_i^j \Big) \quad \text{[L7]}
$$

3   Synthesizing Distributed Processes

Our discussion in this section assumes that the LSC specification is well-formed and consistent, i.e. the weak event relation is acyclic, existential charts trace-refine the universal charts and etc. Additional assumptions are discussed in the following. We assume that all locations are cold and all conditions are distributed. The former is due to the lack of "liveness" in the original CSP semantics. This problem is addressed in Section 4. The latter gets rid of shared condition, which we think is a problematic feature of LSCs. In LSCs, a condition is a boolean expression over the visible variables of the chart. Therefore, some form of global variables is presupposed. This doesn't match the reality of distributed system. Indeed, objects in distributed systems have their own state space (local variables) and all communication between objects would be via messages. Therefore, we are only interested in local conditions in this work. However, shared condition can be (partially) supported by rewriting it to a set of distributed condition with additional proper synchronization. Without loss of generality, we also assume that no co-region is allowed and all messages are synchronized. There is nothing interesting about co-region except it complicates the presentation of the synthesis. Asynchronous message passing is supported by explicitly modelling the behavior of the buffers, e.g. FIFO. A consequence of this assumption is that a message loss is captured by an infinitely long delay of the forwarding by the buffer instead of a traditional *lost message* symbol.

The principles of the synthesis are that, the synthesized processes should be minimally restrictive (if possible) so that further refinement is possible, the global state machine should never be constructed so that state explosion is avoided, and above all, the synthesized processes should be consistent with the LSC specification. The basic idea of our approach is to first construct a CSP specification from the LSC specification (a refinement), and then use CSP algebraic laws to group the behaviors of each object effectively. The key point of our synthesis is that the behaviors of each object can be determined locally and, therefore, the global state machine is never constructed. In the following, we present the synthesis in a bottom-up fashion using synthesis rules (**SR**).

The most primitive building blocks of LSCs are locations. Along an instance in a chart, there are a finite number of locations. A location contains exactly one event and an optional condition. Let S be an LSC specification. Let c, i be a chart and a participating object (instance) in S respectively. Let *Location*, *Condition*, *Event* be all locations, condition and events respectively. Let $cond : Location \rightarrow Condition$ be the condition observer. Let $event : Location \rightarrow Event$ be the event observer. We denote the process synthesized for the location l on instance i in the main chart of chart c as $MainLoca_c^i(l)$. Let $MainLoca_c^i(l+1)$ be the process synthesized for the next location.

- **SR1**: The condition labelled with location l is cold and location l is not the last. If the condition labelled with l evaluates to true, the system engages the event and proceeds to the next location, otherwise, its engages a special event α_c to signal all other instances in the chart before termination. Processes for all other instances in the chart are interrupted by α_c and terminate so that the chart terminates.

$$MainLoca_c^i(l) \mathrel{\hat{=}} (event(l) \rightarrow MainLoca_c^i(l+1)) \mathbin{\langle\!\langle cond(l) \rangle\!\rangle} (\alpha_c \rightarrow \textsc{Skip})$$

- **SR2**: The condition is cold and the location is the last. After engaging the event, a special event γ_c is synchronized by all instances in the chart before any of them terminates.

$$MainLoca_c^i(l) \mathrel{\hat{=}} (event(l) \rightarrow \gamma_c \rightarrow \textsc{Skip}) \mathbin{\langle\!\langle cond(l) \rangle\!\rangle} (\alpha_c \rightarrow \textsc{Skip})$$

- **SR3**: The condition is hot and the location is not the last. A special event β_c is engaged if the hot condition is violated so that all other instances in the chart are signaled and deadlock.

$$MainLoca_c^i(l) \mathrel{\hat{=}} (event(l) \rightarrow MainLoca_c^i(l+1)) \mathbin{\langle\!\langle cond(l) \rangle\!\rangle} (\beta_c \rightarrow \textsc{Stop})$$

- **SR4**: The condition is hot and the location is the last.

$$MainLoca_c^i(l) \mathrel{\hat{=}} (event(l) \rightarrow \gamma_c \rightarrow \textsc{Skip}) \mathbin{\langle\!\langle cond(l) \rangle\!\rangle} (\beta_c \rightarrow \textsc{Stop})$$

Each chart is associated with a set of visible events. Let Σ_c be the set of visible events of chart c. Let Σ_c^i be the set of events associated with Instance i in chart c, including forbidden events. Special events are added to Σ_c^i to carry out the synthesis systematically. The number of special events is bounded by the number of charts if we are only interested in regular implementations (discussed later). In particular, we associate each chart with three special events, $\alpha_c, \beta_c, \gamma_c$. Event α_c is engaged only when a cold condition is violated, either in the pre-chart or the main chart. Event γ_c is used to synchronize the entering or exiting of a chart or a sub-chart among all participating instances. For example, in the above construction, a γ_c event is engaged when the last location has been traversed. Event β_c is engaged only when a hot condition is violated so as to force the system to fail. This reflects the semantics of hot conditions. However, this is slightly problematic as the intention of hot conditions is to make sure they are never violated in the scenario. A hot condition is violated either because there is inconsistency in the LSC specification, i.e. wrong implementation of the local action and etc., or the system is insufficiently specified. A model checker, e.g. FDR, would help refine LSC specifications step by step so that all hot condition holds all the time [27].

A location could be a structuring construct, e.g. a sub-chart or a branching. We remark that all LSC structuring constructs have their exact images in CSP, e.g. choice in CSP for branching, process reference for sub-charts and etc. This is a clear advantage why CSP is better than unstructured automata for our discussion.

Similarly, we may synthesize the process for a location l in the pre-chart. We denote the process synthesized for the location l on instance i in the pre-chart of chart c as $PreLoca_c^i(l)$. An instance not in the pre-chart is treated as if it is in the pre-chart with one empty location.

- **SR5**: Location l is neither the first location nor the last. If the condition evaluates to false, then the process signals all other instances in the chart and terminates. Otherwise, if the expected event is engaged, the process proceeds to the next location, else, the process engages the unexpected event and puts no further constraints on the system ([L1]). Note that we do not distinguish hot or cold condition in pre-charts as hot conditions have no semantical meaning in pre-charts.

$$PreLoca_c^i(l) \; \widehat{=} \; ((event(l) \to PreLoca_c^i(l+1))$$
$$\Box \; (\Box \; e : \Sigma_c^i \setminus \{event(l), \alpha_c, \beta_c, \gamma_c\} \to RUN))$$
$$\triangleleft cond(l) \triangleright (\alpha_c \to \text{Skip})$$

- **SR6**: The location is not the first location but is the last. After engaging the event, the instance waits for the synchronization for termination and proceeds to the first location of the main chart.

$$PreLoca_c^i(l) \; \widehat{=} \; ((event(l) \to \gamma_c \to MainLoca_c^i(0))$$
$$\Box \; (\Box \; e : \Sigma_c^i \setminus \{event(l), \alpha_c, \beta_c, \gamma_c\} \to RUN))$$
$$\triangleleft cond(l) \triangleright (\alpha_c \to \text{Skip})$$

- **SR7**: The location is the first but not the last. A new process is forked whenever an expected event is engaged. This way, we allow system runs that may trigger multiple overlapping activation of the same chart. Note that the special events are not synchronized between different activation.

$$PreLoca_c^i(0) \; \widehat{=} \; ((event(0) \to PreLoca_c^i(1) \, \| [\, \Sigma_c^i \setminus \{\alpha_c, \beta_c, \gamma_c\}\,] \| \, PreLoca_c^i(0))$$
$$\Box \; (\Box \; e : \Sigma_c^i \setminus \{event(0), \alpha_c, \beta_c, \gamma_c\} \to RUN))$$
$$\triangleleft cond(0) \triangleright (\alpha_c \to PreLoca_c^i(0))$$

- **SR8**: The location is the only location of the instance in the pre-chart.

$$PreLoca_c^i(0) \; \widehat{=} \; ((event(0) \to$$
$$(\gamma_c \to MainLoca_c^i(0)) \, \| [\, \Sigma_c^i \setminus \{\alpha_c, \beta_c, \gamma_c\}\,] \| \, PreLoca_c^i(0))$$
$$\Box \; (\Box \; e : \Sigma_c^i \setminus \{event(0), \alpha_c, \beta_c, \gamma_c\} \to RUN))$$
$$\triangleleft cond(l) \triangleright (\alpha_c \to PreLoca_c^i(0))$$

- **SR9**: The chart is not preceded with a pre-chart.

$$PreLoca_c^i(0) \; \widehat{=} \; MainLoca_c^i(0)$$

Whenever a chart is activated by a system run, the subsequence behavior of the system is constrained by both the process and the newly forked process and, therefore, remains valid. However, the process $PreLoca_c^i(0)$ allows, in general, irregular languages that cannot be realized by finite state machines. A similar problem is recognized by Harel and Kugler [14]. We may synthesize systems with possible overlapping activation of the same chart using the above set of rules. Nevertheless, in most cases, only regular processes which lead to finite state implementations are interested. If we assume that activation of the same chart never overlaps, i.e. the chart is not re-activated till its completion, we may augment **SR1-2, SR4-8** as the following so that a chart can be re-activated only after its completion. The same assumption is made by Harel and Kugler in [14].

SR1': $MainLoca_c^i(l) \mathrel{\widehat{=}} (event(l) \rightarrow MainLoca_c^i(l+1)) \mathbin{\{\!\!\{} cond(l) \mathbin{\}\!\!\}} (\alpha_c \rightarrow PreLoca_c^i(0))$

SR2': $MainLoca_c^i(l) \mathrel{\widehat{=}} (event(l) \rightarrow \gamma_c \rightarrow PreLoca_c^i(0)) \mathbin{\{\!\!\{} cond(l) \mathbin{\}\!\!\}} (\alpha_c \rightarrow PreLoca_c^i(0))$

SR4': $MainLoca_c^i(l) \mathrel{\widehat{=}} (event(l) \rightarrow \gamma_c \rightarrow PreLoca_c^i(0)) \mathbin{\{\!\!\{} cond(l) \mathbin{\}\!\!\}} (\beta_c \rightarrow \text{STOP})$

SR5': $PreLoca_c^i(l) \mathrel{\widehat{=}} ((event(l) \rightarrow PreLoca_c^i(l+1)) \;\square$
$$(\square\, e : \Sigma_c^i \setminus \{event(l), event(0), \alpha_c, \beta_c, \gamma_c\} \rightarrow PreLoca_c^i(0)))$$
$$\mathbin{\{\!\!\{} cond(l) \mathbin{\}\!\!\}} (\alpha_c \rightarrow PreLoca_c^i(0))$$

SR6': $PreLoca_c^i(l) \mathrel{\widehat{=}} ((event(l) \rightarrow \gamma_c \rightarrow MainLoca_c^i(0)) \;\square$
$$(\square\, e : \Sigma_c^i \setminus \{event(l), event(0), \alpha_c, \beta_c, \gamma_c\} \rightarrow PreLoca_c^i(0)))$$
$$\mathbin{\{\!\!\{} cond(l) \mathbin{\}\!\!\}} (\alpha_c \rightarrow PreLoca_c^i(0))$$

SR7': $PreLoca_c^i(0) \mathrel{\widehat{=}} ((event(0) \rightarrow PreLoca_c^i(1)) \;\square$
$$(\square\, e : \Sigma_c^i \setminus \{event(0), \alpha_c, \beta_c, \gamma_c\} \rightarrow PreLoca_c^i(0)))$$
$$\mathbin{\{\!\!\{} cond(l) \mathbin{\}\!\!\}} (\alpha_c \rightarrow PreLoca_c^i(0))$$

SR8': $PreLoca_c^i(0) \mathrel{\widehat{=}} ((event(0) \rightarrow \gamma_c \rightarrow MainLoca_c^i(0)) \;\square$
$$(\square\, e : \Sigma_c^i \setminus \{event(0), \alpha_c, \beta_c, \gamma_c\} \rightarrow PreLoca_c^i(0)))$$
$$\mathbin{\{\!\!\{} cond(l) \mathbin{\}\!\!\}} (\alpha_c \rightarrow PreLoca_c^i(0))$$

Rule **SR1-2,4** are augmented so that the process proceeds to the first location after completing the last location or whenever a cold condition is violated. Rule **SR5-8** are augmented so that the initial event which may activate a chart ($event(0)$) is not engaged before the chart completes. As a result, no new processes need to be forked under our assumption. For simplicity, the subsequent discussion assumes that there is no overlapping activation of the same chart. The process synthesized for instance i in chart c is denoted as $Instance_c^i$.

- **SR10**: The process terminates whenever a cold condition is violated in the chart, and deadlocks whenever a hot condition is violated. Both are captured using interrupt operators.

$$Instance_c^i \mathrel{\widehat{=}} (PreLoca_c^i(0) \;\triangledown_{\alpha_c}\; Instance_c^i) \;\triangledown_{\beta_c}\; \text{STOP}$$

Each chart consists of a finite number of interacting instances. Let $Chart_c$ be the process for chart c.

- **SR11**: The process is an alphabetized parallel of the processes of all instances in the chart. Note that in case a hot condition is violated, the process deadlocks and, therefore, the system deadlocks (**L2**). In case a cold condition is violated, the process restores to its initial state.

$$Chart_c \mathrel{\widehat{=}} \left\|_i (Instance_c^i, \Sigma_c^i)\right.$$

An LSC specification consists of a finite number of universal charts, each constraining a set of visible events. Let $\mathcal{I}$ be the process synthesized from the LSC specification.

– **SR12**: $\mathcal{I} \mathrel{\widehat{=}} \left\|_c (Chart_c, \Sigma_c)\right.$

We claim that $\mathcal{I}$ is an implementation of $\mathcal{S}$. From the construction of $Chart_c$, it is clear that only behaviors satisfying the chart are allowed. Therefore, $\mathcal{I}$ only allows behaviors that satisfies all the charts (because of the parallel composition). Moreover, $Chart_c$ only constraints its visible events (as it is alphabetized) and, therefore, other events are free to occur. We skip the case-by-case proof in this paper. The main result of our work is that we may group the behaviors of an object in the system effectively by transforming $\mathcal{I}$ using CSP algebraic laws, in particular, the distributivity law of alphabetized parallel composition.

$$\mathcal{I} \mathrel{\widehat{=}} \left\|_c (Chart_c, \Sigma_c)\right. \mathrel{\widehat{=}} \left\|_c (\left\|_i (Instance_c^i, \Sigma_c^i), \Sigma_c\right.)\right. \qquad \textbf{[SR11,12]}$$

$$\mathrel{\widehat{=}} \left\|_i (\left\|_c (Instance_c^i, \Sigma_c^i), \bigcup_i \Sigma_c^i\right.)\right. \qquad \textbf{[L7]}$$

We remark that the underlying portion of the process is the behavior of an object in isolation, and $\bigcup_i \Sigma_c^i$ is its alphabet with a number of special events. Thus, the behaviors of each objects can be determined locally without ever constructing the global state machine. Each object is composed with the rest of the system by alphabetized parallel composition. There is a subtle difference between alphabetized parallel composition and traditional common event synchronization between state machines. For the former, an event in the alphabet but not in the process indicates a forbidden event. Whereas the alphabet of a state machine always contains exactly the set of events in the state machine. Other than that, the process of each object is realized by traditional finite state machines straightforwardly.

Example 2. We show the synthesized processes for the lower chart in Figure 2 (as it is the most complicated one) in detail. For the **talk** scenario,

$$Instance_{Talk}^{Env} \mathrel{\widehat{=}} (\gamma_{Talk} \to talk \to \gamma_{Talk} \to Instance_{Talk}^{Env}) \,\square\, (talk \to Instance_{Talk}^{Env})$$

$$Instance_{Talk}^{User} \mathrel{\widehat{=}} (open \to \gamma_{Talk} \to talk \to \gamma_{Talk} \to Instance_{Talk}^{User})$$
$$\square\, (talk \to Instance_{Talk}^{User}) \,\square\, (close \to Instance_{Talk}^{User})$$

$$Instance_{Talk}^{Cover} \mathrel{\widehat{=}} (open \to coverOpened \to \gamma_{Talk} \to \gamma_{Talk} \to Instance_{Talk}^{Cover})$$
$$\square\, (coverOpened \to Instance_{Talk}^{Cover}) \,\square\, (close \to Instance_{Talk}^{Cover})$$

$$Instance_{Talk}^{Chip} \mathrel{\widehat{=}} (startRing \to coverOpened \to \gamma_{Talk} \to speakerOff \to$$
$$displayTimer \to \gamma_{talk} \to Instance_{Talk}^{Chip})$$
$$\square\, (coverOpened \to Instance_{Talk}^{Chip}) \,\square\, (speakerOff \to Instance_{Talk}^{Chip})$$
$$\square\, (displayTimer \to Instance_{Talk}^{Chip})$$

$$Instance_{Talk}^{Speaker} \mathrel{\widehat{=}} (startRing \to \gamma_{Talk} \to speakerOff \to \gamma_{Talk} \to Instance_{Talk}^{Speaker})$$
$$\square\, (speakerOff \to Instance_{Talk}^{Speaker})$$

$$Instance_{Talk}^{Display} \mathrel{\widehat{=}} (\gamma_{Talk} \to displayTimer \to setDisplayTimer \to$$
$$\gamma_{Talk} \to Instance_{Talk}^{Display})$$
$$\square\, (displayTimer \to Instance_{Talk}^{Display})$$
$$\square\, (setDisplayTimer \to Instance_{Talk}^{Display})$$

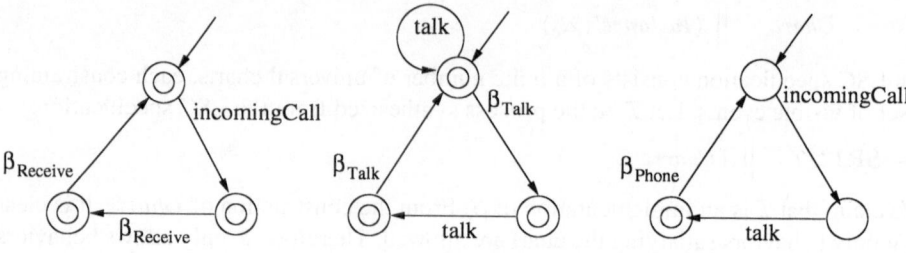

Fig. 4. Finite State Machine Implementation of Env

Before the main chart is activated, all visible events are free to occur (captured by the external choices). Once the instances synchronize the entering of the main chart, only event sequences specified by the main chart are allowed. This example also illustrates how forbidden events are handled. For instance, event *close* is in the alphabet of $Instance_{Talk}^{User}$ and $Instance_{Talk}^{Cover}$. It can occur before the main chart is activated but not after. Similarly, we may synthesize the processes for the instances in the other charts. The behavior of the same instance is then composed using an alphabetized parallel operator as discussed. The following example shows the behaviors of the Env instance in the system.

$$Instance_{Receive}^{Env} \mathrel{\hat{=}} incomingCall \rightarrow \gamma_{Receive} \rightarrow \gamma_{Receive} \rightarrow Instance_{Receive}^{Env}$$
$$Instance_{Talk}^{Env} \mathrel{\hat{=}} (\gamma_{Talk} \rightarrow talk \rightarrow \gamma_{talk} \rightarrow Instance_{Talk}^{Env}) \,\square\, (talk \rightarrow Instance_{Talk}^{Env})$$
$$Instance_{Phone}^{Env} \mathrel{\hat{=}} incomingCall \rightarrow talk \rightarrow \gamma_{phone} \rightarrow Instance_{Phone}^{Env}$$

$$Instance^{Env} \mathrel{\hat{=}} Instance_{Receive}^{Env} \parallel Instance_{Talk}^{Env} \parallel Instance_{Phone}^{Env}$$

The behaviors of Env in **Receive**, **Talk**, **Phone** are captured by the three processes above. The finite state machine implementation of the Env instance is illustrated in Figure 4. The three state machines are running concurrently, where common events are synchronized. We remark that all the synthesized processes are regular and, therefore, can be implemented by finite state machines.

4   Discussion

In Section 3, we ignore the modalities on locations because CSP lacks the expressiveness to capture liveness, i.e. certain events must be observed in the future. Globally, a system run satisfies an LSC specification only if no instance is stuck at a hot location. In this section, we amend the traditional CSP failure semantics with "signals" to capture liveness. We show that modalities on locations can be captured naturally using signals and the result in Section 3 remains. That is, we show that global behaviors satisfying liveness condition associated with locations can be determined locally.

The name, "signal", is suggested by Davies [9], where signal are used to express broadcast effectively in CSP and they must be observed in the future. In this work, signals are simply events that must be observed in the future. Naturally, events on hot locations are mapped to signals. In the following discussion, we focus on failure semantics only because there could be nondeterminism in LSCs (therefore trace semantics is insufficient) and there is no hiding operator in LSCs (therefore the synthesized processes are divergence-free). If we use $\widehat{\Sigma}$ to denote the set of all signals, then the set of all events is given by $\widetilde{\Sigma} \cong \Sigma \cup \widehat{\Sigma}$. For each event a in Σ, we add a signal $\widehat{a}$. We remark that except they must be engaged eventually, signals play the same role as ordinary events, e.g. synchonizing with signals or events obeying the CSP rules. The set of extended processes is denoted as $\widetilde{\mathcal{P}}$. To ease the discussion (i.e. ensure type consistency), we assume that a process in $\widetilde{\mathcal{P}}$ is uniquely identified by a set of failures.

$$\widetilde{\mathcal{P}} == \mathbb{P}\,\mathbb{P}(\widetilde{\Sigma}^* \times \mathbb{P}\,\widetilde{\Sigma})$$

To ensure the additional constraint caused by signals, we define a filter function to eliminate behaviors from the original CSP failure definitions so that the mature semantic models of CSP are maintained. The filter function $\mathcal{F} : \widetilde{\mathcal{P}} \to \mathbb{P}\,\widetilde{\mathcal{P}}$ satisfies the following condition:

$$\forall p : \widetilde{\mathcal{P}};\; s : \widetilde{\Sigma}^*;\; E : \mathbb{P}\,\widetilde{\Sigma} \bullet$$
$$(s, E) \in \mathcal{F}(p) \Leftrightarrow (s, E) \in p \wedge \exists (s, E') : p \bullet \widehat{\Sigma} \subseteq E'$$

This axiom insists that any observation that can be extended by engaging a signal must be extended into the future. This way, we augment CSP semantics with a simple fairness condition. Intuitively, it captures the idea that events labelled with a hot location must be engaged. The failures calculation for the compositional CSP constructs remain unchanged and, therefore, the relevant algebraic laws remain valid, including the associativity and symmetry laws for alphabetized parallel ([L4,L5]) and, therefore, law [L6,L7]. The goal of our discussion is to show that the modalities associated with locations can be captured using signals by the processes in a distributed fashion, so that a local process can be implemented by a finite state machine with a set of accepting states. Equivalently, we want to show that in our context the following laws hold.

$$\mathcal{F}(\widetilde{\mathcal{P}_1} \,{}_X\|_Y\, \widetilde{\mathcal{P}_2}) = \mathcal{F}(\widetilde{\mathcal{P}_1}) \,{}_X\|_Y\, \mathcal{F}(\widetilde{\mathcal{P}_2}) \qquad \text{[L8]}$$
$$\mathcal{F}(\big\|_{i=1}^{m}(\big\|_{j=1}^{n}(\widetilde{\mathcal{P}}_i^j, \widetilde{\Sigma}_i^j), \bigcup_j \widetilde{\Sigma}_i^j)) = \big\|_{j=1}^{n}(\mathcal{F}(\big\|_{i=1}^{m}(\widetilde{\mathcal{P}}_i^j, \widetilde{\Sigma}_i^j)), \bigcup_i \widetilde{\Sigma}_i^j) \qquad \text{[L9]}$$

Intuitively, if two traces, one for each component, both cannot be extended by engaging a signal, then the composed trace cannot be extended with the signal either. The reserve is not true in general (counter example in Appendix A). However, if a shared signal is always ready to be engaged or refused by both components, then the reverse is also true and, therefore, law [L8, L9] are true. The proof is left to Appendix A. We remark that for consistent LSC specifications, the assumption is safe because graphically a message output event is always connected to a message input events and vice versa due to the absence of *lost message* symbol. The above result is crucial to our work because it guarantees that equipping the global process with liveness conditions is equivalent to equip the liveness conditions locally. Behaviors of each component, therefore, can be decided locally.

Example 3. For example, the CSP process synthesized from *Env* instance in the chart presented in Figure 3 is the following:

$$Instance_{Phone}^{Env} \mathrel{\widehat{=}} \widehat{incomingCall} \to \widehat{talk} \to \gamma_{phone} \to Instance_{Phone}^{Env}$$

Processes with signals can be implemented as finite state machines equipped with simple fairness conditions, namely, accepting states. A state is accepting if there is no outgoing transition labelled with a signal. For example, in the right-most state machine in Figure 4, only the state after the *talk* event is accepting, indicated by a double-lined circle. A global accepting state is a state where all its components' states are accepting.

5   Conclusion and Future Works

The main contribution of our work is that we present a systematic way of synthesizing distributed processes from LSC specifications. The key point of our method is that the global state machine is never constructed. Therefore, our method can handle system with complicated interactive behaviors. By constructing a CSP specification first and then rewriting it using CSP algebraic laws, we address some of the challenges of such synthesis discussed in [24, 1, 14]. For instance, we prove that the behaviors of each object can be determined without ever constructing the global state machines [14]. We guarantee that no unspecified behaviors are allowed by using only CSP equivalence laws [1]. Moreover, we developed a JAVA application to automatically synthesize CSP expression from LSCs. The tool extends the one reported in [27] with the new way of constructing CSP processes.

There are a couple of possible extensions to our work. First, we may investigate whether our result holds for LSCs with qualitative timing behaviors. Timed CSP [26] seems to be a promising media to carry out the discussion. We may as well transform the synthesized CSP processes to executable models, e.g. SystemC [11], Statechart in Rhapsody [13], so that users may execute the distributed implementations.

Acknowledgements

We thank Steffen Andersen and Dines Bjørner and Steffen Holmslykke for their insightful comments and discussion on early versions of this paper.

References

1. R. Alur, K. Etessami, and M. Yannakakis. Inference of Message Sequence Charts. In *Proc. of the 22nd International Conference on Software Engineering*, pages 304–313. ACM Press, 2000.
2. R. Alur and M. Yannakakis. Model Checking of Message Sequence Charts. In *Proc. of the 10th International Conference on Concurrency Theory*, pages 114–129. Springer-Verlag, 1999.
3. Y. Bontemps and P. Heymans. Turning High-Level Live Sequence Charts into Automata. In *ICSE'02 Workshop: Scenarios and State Machines: Models, Algorithms and Tools*, 2002.
4. Y. Bontemps, P. Schobbens, and C. Löding. Synthesis of Open Reactive Systems from Scenario-Based Specifications. *Fundamenta Informaticae*, 62(2):139–169, July 2004.

5. S. D. Brookes and A. W. Roscoe. An Improved Failures Model for Communicating Processes. In *Proc. of the Pittsburgh seminar on concurrency LNCS 197*, pages 281–305, 1985.
6. J. R. Buchi and L. H. Landweber. Solving Sequential Conditions by Finite State Strategies. *Trans. on American Math. Soc.*, 138:295–311, 1969.
7. D. Harel and R. Marelly. *Play-Engine User's Guide*, 2003.
8. W. Damm and D. Harel. LSCs: Breathing Life into Message Sequence Charts. *Formal Methods in System Design*, 19(1):45–80, 2001.
9. J. Davies. *Specification and Proof in Real-Time CSP*. Cambridge University Press, 1993.
10. Formal System Europe. Failure Divergence Refinement. http://www.fsel.com/, 2003.
11. T. Grotker, S. Liao, G. Martin, and S. Swan. *System Design with SystemC*. Kluwer Academic Publishers, 2002.
12. UML Group. OMG UML v1.5. http://www.uml.org/, June 2002.
13. D. Harel and E. Gery. Executable Object Modeling with Statecharts. *Computer*, 30(7):31–42, 1997.
14. D. Harel and H. Kugler. Synthesizing State-Based Object Systems from LSC Specifications. In *Proc. of CIAA*, volume 2088 of *LNCS*, pages 1–26, 2001.
15. D. Harel and R. Marelly. *Come, Let's Play - Scenario-Based Programming Using LSCs and Play-Engine*. Springer-Verlag, 2003.
16. Ø. Haugen and K. Stølen. STAIRS C Steps to Analyze Interactions with Refinement Semantics. In *Proc. Sixth International Conference on UML (UML'2003)*, volume 2863 of *LNCS*, pages 388–402, 2003.
17. C. A. R. Hoare. *Communicating Sequential Processes*. International Series in Computer Science. Prentice-Hall, 1985.
18. ITU. *Message Sequence Chart(MSC)*, Nov 1999. Series Z: Languages and general software aspects for telecommunication systems.
19. J. Klose and H. Wittke. An Automata Based Interpretation of Live Sequence Charts. In *TACAS*, pages 512–527, 2001.
20. P. Kosiuczenko and M. Wirsing. Formalizing and Executing Message Sequence Charts via Timed Rewriting. *Electr. Notes Theor. Comput. Sci.*, 25:1–25, 1999.
21. K. Koskimies and E. Mäkinen. Automatic Synthesis of State Machines from Trace Diagrams. *Softw. Pract. Exper.*, 24(7):643–658, 1994.
22. X. S. Li, Z. M. Liu, and J. F. He. A Formal Semantics of UML Sequence Diagram. In *Australian Software Engineering Conference*, pages 168–177. IEEE Computer Society, 2004.
23. R. Marelly and H. Kugler. Multiple Instances and Symbolic Variables in Executable Sequence Charts. In *Proceedings of OOPSLA'02*, pages 83–100, 2002.
24. A. Pnueli and R. Rosner. Distributed Reactive Systems are Hard to Synthesis. In *Proc. of 31st IEEE Sypm. on Foudation of Computer Science*, 1990.
25. A. W. Roscoe. *The Theory and Practice of Concurrency*. Prentice-Hall, 1997.
26. S. Schneider, J. Davies, D. M. Jackson, G. M. Reed, J. N. Reed, and A. W. Roscoe. Timed CSP: Theory and practice. In *Real-Time: Theory in Practice*, volume 600, pages 640–675. Springer-Verlag, 1992.
27. J. Sun and J. S. Dong. Model Checking Live Sequence Charts. In *ICECCS'05, to appear*, 2005.

Appendix A: Proof of L8

Given two processes $\widetilde{\mathcal{P}_1}$ and $\widetilde{\mathcal{P}_2}$ and their alphabets X, Y respectively, the alphabetized parallel composition is denoted as $\widetilde{\mathcal{P}_1} \; {}_X\|_Y \; \widetilde{\mathcal{P}_2}$.

$$\widetilde{\mathcal{P}_1} \, {}_X||_Y \, \widetilde{\mathcal{P}_2} = \{(u, M \cup N) : (X \cup Y)^* \times \mathbb{P}(X \cup Y) \mid$$
$$u \in traces(\widetilde{\mathcal{P}_1} \, {}_X||_Y \, \widetilde{\mathcal{P}_2}) \wedge M \setminus (X \cap Y) = N \setminus (X \cap Y)$$
$$\wedge \, (u \restriction X, M) \in \widetilde{\mathcal{P}_1} \wedge (u \restriction Y, N) \in \widetilde{\mathcal{P}_2}\} \qquad \text{[Def1]}$$

An event sequence u is a trace of $\widetilde{\mathcal{P}_1} \, {}_X||_Y \, \widetilde{\mathcal{P}_2}$ if and only if there exists a trace $s :$ $traces(\widetilde{\mathcal{P}_1})$ and $t : traces(\widetilde{\mathcal{P}_2})$ such that $u \in s \, {}_X||_Y \, t$. The definition of $s \, {}_X||_Y \, t$ can be referred in [25].

Lemma 1. $\forall (s, E) \bullet (s, E) \in \mathcal{F}(\widetilde{\mathcal{P}_1}) \, {}_X||_Y \, \mathcal{F}(\widetilde{\mathcal{P}_2}) \Rightarrow (s, E) \in \mathcal{F}(\widetilde{\mathcal{P}_1} \, {}_X||_Y \, \widetilde{\mathcal{P}_2})$

Proof. $(s, M \cup N) \in \mathcal{F}(\widetilde{\mathcal{P}_1}) \, {}_X||_Y \, \mathcal{F}(\widetilde{\mathcal{P}_2})$
$$\Rightarrow s \in trace(\mathcal{F}(\widetilde{\mathcal{P}_1}) \, {}_X||_Y \, \mathcal{F}(\widetilde{\mathcal{P}_2})) \wedge M \setminus (X \cap Y) = N \setminus (X \cap Y)$$
$$\wedge \, (s \restriction X, M) \in \mathcal{F}(\widetilde{\mathcal{P}_1}) \wedge (s \restriction Y, N) \in \mathcal{F}(\widetilde{\mathcal{P}_2}) \qquad \text{[Def1]}$$
$$\Rightarrow s \in trace(\widetilde{\mathcal{P}_1} \, {}_X||_Y \, \widetilde{\mathcal{P}_2}) \wedge M \setminus (X \cap Y) = N \setminus (X \cap Y)$$
$$\wedge \, (s \restriction X, M) \in \widetilde{\mathcal{P}_1} \wedge \exists (s \restriction X, M') : \widetilde{\mathcal{P}_1} \bullet \widehat{\Sigma} \subseteq M'$$
$$\wedge \, (s \restriction Y, N) \in \widetilde{\mathcal{P}_2} \wedge \exists (s \restriction Y, N') : \widetilde{\mathcal{P}_2} \bullet \widehat{\Sigma} \subseteq N' \qquad \text{[Def. of } \mathcal{F}]$$
$$\Rightarrow (s, M \cup N) \in \widetilde{\mathcal{P}_1} \, {}_X||_Y \, \widetilde{\mathcal{P}_2}$$
$$\wedge \exists (s, M' \cup N') : \widetilde{\mathcal{P}_1} \, {}_X||_Y \, \widetilde{\mathcal{P}_2} \bullet \widehat{\Sigma} \subseteq M' \cup N'$$
$$\Rightarrow (s, M \cup N) \in \mathcal{F}(\widetilde{\mathcal{P}_1} \, {}_X||_Y \, \widetilde{\mathcal{P}_2}) \qquad \text{[Def. of } \mathcal{F}]$$

Intuitively, this lemma states that if both components cannot engage a signal (all signals are refused) at certain point of execution, then the composition cannot engage a signal either. Unfortunately, the reverse is not true. The following illustrates a counter example where $\widetilde{\mathcal{P}_1}$ can be extended by engaging a shared signal and $\widetilde{\mathcal{P}_2}$ cannot.

$$\mathcal{P}_1 \mathrel{\widehat{=}} (\widehat{a} \to \text{STOP} \,\square\, b \to \text{STOP}) \qquad X \mathrel{\widehat{=}} \{\widehat{a}, b\}$$
$$\mathcal{P}_2 \mathrel{\widehat{=}} c \to \text{STOP} \qquad\qquad\qquad Y \mathrel{\widehat{=}} \{\widehat{a}, c\}$$

It is easy to verify that $(\langle\rangle, \{\widehat{a}\})$ is in $\mathcal{F}(\widetilde{\mathcal{P}_1} \, {}_X||_Y \, \widetilde{\mathcal{P}_2})$ but not $\mathcal{F}(\widetilde{\mathcal{P}_1}) \, {}_X||_Y \, \mathcal{F}(\widetilde{\mathcal{P}_2})$. However, if we assume that whenever the two components agree on the set of refused local events, they also agree on the set of shared events, i.e. if one component is ready to engage a shared event, the other is ready too and vice versa, then the reverse is true. Formally, we assume

$$\forall (s, M) \in \widetilde{\mathcal{P}_1} \wedge (t, N) \in \widetilde{\mathcal{P}_2} \bullet M \setminus (X \cap Y) = N \setminus (X \cap Y) \Rightarrow M = N$$

Lemma 2. $\forall (s, E) \bullet (s, E) \in \mathcal{F}(\widetilde{\mathcal{P}_1} \, {}_X||_Y \, \widetilde{\mathcal{P}_2}) \Rightarrow (s, E) \in \mathcal{F}(\widetilde{\mathcal{P}_1}) \, {}_X||_Y \, \mathcal{F}(\widetilde{\mathcal{P}_2})$

Proof. $(s, M \cup N) \in \mathcal{F}(\widetilde{\mathcal{P}_1} \, {}_X||_Y \, \widetilde{\mathcal{P}_2})$
$$\Rightarrow (s, M \cup N) \in (\widetilde{\mathcal{P}_1} \, {}_X||_Y \, \widetilde{\mathcal{P}_2}) \wedge \exists (s, E') : (\widetilde{\mathcal{P}_1} \, {}_X||_Y \, \widetilde{\mathcal{P}_2}) \bullet \widehat{\Sigma} \subseteq E' \text{[Def. of } \mathcal{F}]$$
$$\Rightarrow s \in trace(\widetilde{\mathcal{P}_1} \, {}_X||_Y \, \widetilde{\mathcal{P}_2}) \wedge M \setminus (X \cap Y) = N \setminus (X \cap Y)$$
$$\wedge \, (s \restriction X, M) \in \widetilde{\mathcal{P}_1} \wedge (s \restriction Y, N) \in \widetilde{\mathcal{P}_2}$$
$$\wedge \exists (s, E') : (\widetilde{\mathcal{P}_1} \, {}_X||_Y \, \widetilde{\mathcal{P}_2}) \bullet \widehat{\Sigma} \subseteq E' \qquad \text{[Def1]}$$

From the healthiness conditions of CSP, there exists $(s \restriction X, M')$ in $\widetilde{\mathcal{P}_1}$, and $(s \restriction Y, N')$ in $\widetilde{\mathcal{P}_2}$ with maximal refusal set. By the definition of the alphabetized parallel composition, $M' \setminus (X \cap Y) = N' \setminus (X \cap Y)$ and, therefore, by our assumption $M' = N' = E'$.

$\Rightarrow s \in trace(\widetilde{\mathcal{P}_1} \,_X||_Y\, \widetilde{\mathcal{P}_2}) \wedge M \setminus (X \cap Y) = N \setminus (X \cap Y)$
$\quad \wedge (s \upharpoonright X, M) \in \widetilde{\mathcal{P}_1} \wedge (s \upharpoonright Y, N) \in \widetilde{\mathcal{P}_2}$
$\quad \wedge (s \upharpoonright X, E') \in \widetilde{\mathcal{P}_1} \wedge \widehat{\Sigma} \subseteq E' \wedge (s \upharpoonright Y, E') \in \widetilde{\mathcal{P}_2} \wedge \widehat{\Sigma} \subseteq E'$ [By assump.]
$\Rightarrow s \in trace(\widetilde{\mathcal{P}_1} \,_X||_Y\, \widetilde{\mathcal{P}_2}) \wedge M \setminus (X \cap Y) = N \setminus (X \cap Y)$
$\quad \wedge (s \upharpoonright X, M) \in \mathcal{F}(\widetilde{\mathcal{P}_1}) \wedge (s \upharpoonright Y, N) \in \mathcal{F}(\widetilde{\mathcal{P}_2})$ [Def. of $\mathcal{F}$]
$\Rightarrow (s, E) \in \mathcal{F}(\widetilde{\mathcal{P}_1}) \,_X||_Y\, \mathcal{F}(\widetilde{\mathcal{P}_2})$ [Def1]

Thus, by Lemma 1 and 2 we conclude **L8**. Law **L9** is a direct consequence of law **L8** and the symmetry and associativity laws of alphabetized parallel.

Verifying Scenario-Based Aspect Specifications

Emilia Katz and Shmuel Katz

Department of Computer Science,
The Technion, Haifa 32000, Israel
{emika, katz}@cs.technion.ac.il

Abstract. Software systems specifications are often described as a set of typical scenarios. Some of the desired scenarios are crosscut by other requirements, called *aspects*, also naturally described as scenarios. Aspect descriptions are independent of the description of the non-aspectual scenarios, but the crosscutting relationship between them has to be specified, so for each aspect a description of its *join-points* is provided. When aspectual scenarios are added to the system, we need to prove that every execution is equivalent to one in which the aspectual scenarios occur as blocks of operations immediately at their join-points, and all the other operations form a sequence of non-aspectual scenarios, interrupted only by the aspectual scenarios. We extend an existing method of automatic verification for non-aspect systems to the case of systems with scenario-based aspect specifications. A prototype implementation based on Cadence SMV is also extended accordingly.

Keywords: Aspects, scenarios, model-checking, conformance, convenient executions.

1 Introduction

1.1 Scenario-Based Specifications

Often, when describing a system, it is natural to think of its desired behavior as a collection of finite sequences of events, called *scenarios*. That can be done by using use-cases or sequence charts of UML [12], or the variant of Live Sequence Charts (LSCs) defined in [3]. For example, let us think of an ATM system of a bank, consisting of one central computer with a database, asynchronously communicating with several ATM machines. It would be natural to describe the system behavior as possible scenarios, such as money withdrawal, bill payment, or checking the account balance. System computations in which only the described scenarios occur, one after another in some order, obviously satisfy such a specification, and will be called *convenient* (using the notation of [1], [2]). However, an execution of the system does not have to consist of the scenarios only, because sometimes computations differ only in that independent operations occur in a different order. Moreover, often operations of one computation can be re-ordered by exchanging places of independent operations, in such a way that a convenient execution is obtained. In that case the original execution and the

J.S. Fitzgerald, I.J. Hayes, and A. Tarlecki (Eds.): FM 2005, LNCS 3582, pp. 432–447, 2005.

obtained convenient one are considered *equivalent*. A system *conforms* with a scenario-based specification if every computation is equivalent to a convenient one.

1.2   Aspects and Scenarios

When stating requirements for a system behavior, it is often the case that some of the requirements crosscut the others. Those crosscutting requirements are called *aspects*. The best way to deal with crosscutting requirements is to model them separately from other requirements, and then weave them into the main system in programming notations like AspectJ [7]. For each aspect, a set of *join-points*, called a *pointcut*, is defined, identifying the states where the aspect code (called *advice*) should be executed. When it is natural to describe a system by a scenario-based specification (e.g., for communication protocols, or electronic funds transferring systems), aspects such as security, privacy, or monitoring are also naturally described as scenarios. This approach is seen in [6] and also used here. Thus, a specification of a system is a set of scenarios, and aspectual and non-aspectual scenarios are described independently.

In our bank system example above, several aspectual scenarios might be needed. For example, we might need to count all the ATM operations for every account, in order to make the client pay for the operations performed. This concern is naturally solved by introducing an aspect scenario that will be run any time an ATM operation is completed successfully. The join-points of this scenario will be all the places in the system executions at which the last operation of the money-withdrawal scenario, the bill payment, or the scenario of checking the account balance is performed. To treat this aspect, the state of the system will be extended by a new variable - a counter. Applying the aspect scenario changes only the value of the counter and does not affect the projection of the state on the previously defined ATM system: if the scenario is applied at some state s of the system execution, after the aspect finishes to run, the system will pass to a state $s\prime$ that differs from s by the value of the counter only. Such an aspect is called *spectative*, as defined in [14].

Another example of a cross-cutting requirement might treat communication failures: when a failure is detected, the interaction of the user with the relevant machine is stopped, the magnetic card is returned, and a warning message appears. After applying this scenario the ATM system will not return to the state it was before, but will return to its initial state - waiting for a magnetic card to be inserted. Thus it is a *regulative* aspect, changing the control of the system.

Aspects can also be categorized as *invasive*. Such an aspect changes the state of the original system, but if it appears in the middle of some non-aspectual scenario, the scenario proceeds after the advice finishes. That is the case, for example, if we want the user to immediately pay for every ATM operation. After applying such a scenario, the amount of money in the user's account will change, but the interrupted scenario will proceed from the place where it was interrupted.

We are interested in the verification of systems containing aspects, i. e., systems in which the code implementation of aspects is already woven in. Actually, it would be better to separate the aspects from the base system, both in the description and in the verification, but unfortunately, sometimes this is impossible. One example of such a situation is a system that does not use any aspect-oriented language at the implementation stage. Another possibility is that our goal is to check the weaver itself, and thus we need to examine the result of its application, which is the system with the aspect code woven in. Also when there are complex interactions between the aspect code and the original program, techniques do not exist to separately analyze the aspect. In those cases the verification of the augmented system as a whole is necessary.

For such an augmented system, the definition of the convenient executions should be refined. The new convenient executions are those in which the aspectual scenarios appear always as a block of operations, and exactly at the place they are needed. The non-aspectual scenarios also appear as a block, but with one difference: each block can be interrupted with blocks of the appropriate aspectual scenarios. Depending on the aspect description, the interruption can either cancel the continuation of the interrupted scenario (then it will be called *strict* interruption), or let the scenario proceed, possibly after some invasive changes (then it will be called a *weak* interruption). In a general execution the operations of an aspectual scenario might not appear immediately after a join-point, and could be interleaved with some other operations of aspectual or non-aspectual scenarios. So in order to prove that a system conforms with a scenario-based specification that includes aspectual scenarios, it is enough to show that every computation is equivalent to a convenient one (where the definition of the convenient executions is refined as above).

We extend the model-checking approach and the CNV tool in [2] (described below in Section 2) with key modifications to automatically verify conformance of systems containing aspects with scenario-based specifications. Note that unlike some attempts for verification of aspects that restrict themselves to spectative aspects only [8], we do not pose such a restriction, but in this version we do not treat the case of aspects applied on other aspects. Our method consists of three parts. First of all, the join-points of the aspectual scenarios are found. Then the appearance of the scenarios is predicted at those points. This kind of prediction will be fulfilled only if the needed aspect scenario indeed appears somewhere in the continuation of the execution, and it could have appeared immediately at the join-point (i.e., all the operations of the aspect scenario are independent of all the other operations occurring between the join-point and the actual occurrence of the aspect operations in the advice). To treat the strictly-interrupting aspects, additional legal scenarios are defined: for each previously specified scenario some prefix of which ends by a possible last operation of a pointcut, a new scenario will be defined as that prefix in which the last operation is indeed the last operation of that pointcut. The third part of the verification is to show that if we ignore the appearance of the aspectual scenarios in the executions, the operations left can be organized as blocks of non-aspectual scenarios.

This paper is organized as follows: In Section 2 the existing method of verification for non-aspect systems is described, and some basic definitions needed for equivalence-based verification appear. In Section 3 we present our method of verification for systems with aspects, and outline the soundness proof. An application example appears in Section 4, and we conclude in Section 5.

2   Background: Verification of Conformance for Non-aspect Systems

In [2], the CNV tool for automatically verifying conformance with non-aspectual scenario-based specifications has been presented. In CNV, the original system is automatically augmented by additional constructions and temporal logic assertions, converted to the input-format of Cadence SMV [10], and then model-checked. When all the properties are verified by the model-checking, it follows that every computation of the original system is equivalent to some convenient one, and thus the original system conforms to the specification. Although the method is sound, it is incomplete, and a negative answer does not necessarily mean the original system does not conform to the specification.

The verification is based on proving equivalence of executions, so before describing the method, we list the formal definitions needed for such a proof. The definitions are taken from [2]. The systems we are working on are Fair Transition Systems (FTS), as defined in [9].

Definition 1. *A computation of FTS M is an infinite sequence of state-transition pairs $\sigma = (s_0, \tau_0), (s_1, \tau_1), \ldots$ such that s_0 satisfies the initial state condition of M, $\forall i : s_{i+1} \in \tau_i(s_i)$, and the fairness requirements are not violated in σ (i.e., for each weakly fair transition τ it is not the case that τ is continually enabled beyond some position j in σ, but not taken beyond j).*

Definition 2. *Transitions τ_1, τ_2 are* conditionally independent *in state s (denoted $CondIndep(s, \tau_1, \tau_2))$) iff $\tau_1 \neq \tau_2 \wedge \tau_2(\tau_1(s)) = \tau_1(\tau_2(s))$.*

Definition 3. *Let $\sigma = (s_0, \tau_0), (s_1, \tau_1), \ldots$ be a computation of M, such that for some i, $CondIndep(s_i, \tau_i, \tau_{i+1})$ holds. Then the sequence $\sigma\prime = (s_0, \tau_0), \ldots, (s_i, \tau_{i+1}), (\tau_{i+1}(s_i), \tau_i), (s_{i+2}, \tau_{i+2}), \ldots$ is also a legal computation of M, and we say that σ and $\sigma\prime$ are one-swap-equivalent ($\sigma \equiv_{1sw} \sigma\prime$). We also define the* swap-equivalence *($\equiv_{sw}$) relation as the reflexive-transitive closure of one-swap-equivalence.*

Now let us give a more detailed description of the method for systems without aspects. Given a fair transition system M, together with the list of the desired scenarios and the independence relation between the operations of M, an augmented system $M\prime$, called the *transducer*, is built. The transducer is a composition of M with a bounded *history window* H - a queue of fixed length L, and an ω-automaton C, called the *chopper*, which reads its input from H and accepts only the desired scenarios. $M\prime$ also has an *error* flag, initially false. The initial state of $M\prime$ is the state in which M is at its initial state, H is empty, and *error* is false. The chopper has only one state, in which it is waiting for the next scenario to be formed at the head of the history. The transitions of $M\prime$ are as follows:

- All the transitions of M. When a transition of M, τ, is performed at a state s of M, the state of $M\prime$ changes according to τ, and the pair (s, τ) is inserted into H. If there is no place in the history, the insertion is impossible, and the *error* flag is raised. Once raised, it never goes down again.
- *chop* operation. If some scenario appears at the head of the history, it can be removed from the queue.
- *swap* operation. A pair of consecutive entries of H, (s_1, τ_1) and (s_2, τ_2), can be swapped, if τ_1 and τ_2 are conditionally independent at the state s_1, and the states at those entries are updated according to the result of applying the operations, so that the two entries become (s_1, τ_2), $(\tau_2(s_1), \tau_1)$.
- *predict* operation. Sometimes there is only one way to complete the prefix of the history to a whole scenario. Then we may *predict* the remaining operations and chop the prefix of the scenario from the history. (The cases when such prediction is possible are defined by the user.) The prediction is done by inserting to the history the *anti-transitions* of the remaining transitions of the scenario after its prefix, in the reversed order, with appropriate states. Then the anti-transitions are swapped backwards in the history by the *swap − pred* (see below) operation to meet the remaining transitions of the scenario and to annihilate together with them after the *cancel* operation.
- *swap − pred* operation. Swapping two consecutive entries in H, (s_1, τ_1) and (s_2, τ_2), such that τ_1 is the anti-transition of τ (denoted $\overline{\tau}$), and τ_2 is some transition of M that is independent of τ at s_2.
- *cancel* operation. Removing a pair of consecutive entries of H, (s_1, τ_1) and (s_2, τ_2), such that τ_1 is the anti-transition of τ_2.

Now let us describe the added temporal assertions to be checked for the transducer by SMV. (We will give only a brief verbal description here, a fuller version is in [2].)

1. Legal progress of the computation is guaranteed: it is always possible to proceed without overflow of the history queue, by chopping one more scenario, and a place can always be reached at which the already performed prefix of the computation is equivalent to some convenient one.
2. The predictions are correct: whenever a prediction is made, it is always fulfilled.
3. No operation is "lost": Every action performed in the computation appears in the convenient computation built, i.e., whenever an operation enters the history, it is eventually chopped (either explicitly - as a part of the head of the history queue, or implicitly - as a part of some prediction).
4. The user-defined independence relation is legal: the operations that are declared independent indeed satisfy the *CondIndep* condition, and their swapping preserves the values of the enabling conditions of operations so that a fair computation can be equivalent only to another fair computation.

This system is proven to be sound: if $M\prime$ is the above augmentation of M, and all the above assertions hold in $M\prime$, it implies that every computation of M is equivalent to some convenient one.

3   Verification of Systems with Aspects

First, we give a more formal definition of aspects. An aspect consists of two parts: a *pointcut* and an *advice*, where the *advice* is a scenario that should be executed whenever the pointcut occurs, and the pointcut is defined as follows:

Definition 4. *A* pointcut *is a sequence of operations* $op_1, \ldots, op_n$ *together with an LTL past formula* φ. *An occurrence of the pointcut in a computation* π *is a sequence of states of* π, $s_1, \ldots, s_n$ *(possibly interleaved by other states) such that:*

- op_i *is the operation performed at the state* s_i
- φ *holds at the state* $op_n(s_n)$

Our verification problem consists now of three parts, treated separately:

- To recognize the appearance of the pointcuts in the computation.
- To ensure that the operations of the appropriate aspect advice can be brought to appear as a block immediately at the pointcuts.
- To examine the computation we get after arranging all the aspect advice as blocks, and show that all the non-aspectual scenarios can also be arranged in blocks of consecutive operations interrupted only by advice blocks.

We extend the CNV system to provide automatically generated solutions to the problem. In fact, the changes mostly arise from the last two parts, because some known techniques (partly described in Section 3.1) already exist for pointcut recognition, and we will assume that the given system M has already been pre-processed by one of them. The main change to the CNV system is the automatic creation of a new module, the *advisor*, as a part of the augmented system, $M\prime$. The advisor is in charge of arranging the aspect advice. Some changes to the swapper module are also needed for that purpose - as will be seen in Section 3.2, the swapping of the end-of-pointcut operations should differ from the regular one. Finally, as will be seen from Section 3.3, arranging the non-aspectual scenarios requires changing the chopper module.

3.1   Recognizing the Pointcuts: Three Options

Cross-Product Automaton. If φ is the past formula of a pointcut, we may build a finite automaton A_φ that recognizes φ, as in [9] or [11], and take the cross-product of $M\prime$ with A_φ. In this new system, each time a transition is inserted into the history, the automaton updates its state. If an accepting state is reached, a pointcut is recognized in that state, and the state becomes a join-point of the appropriate aspect. This is obviously a correct solution, but also a very costly one. Several optimizations are possible, all based on pre-processing of the system M in order to mark the states that are join-points.

Static Analysis. One possibility is to perform static analysis, as in [13]. The pointcuts are restricted to be described by regular expressions over the call stack. Such expressions are called *pointcut designators* (*PCD*s). The call graph of the system is built: the set of paths from the start vertex v to a node representing procedure call p is the set of all possible call stacks at point p during program execution. For each procedure call p, if all the possible stacks satisfy a PCD of some advice a, then this procedure call is recognized as a place where a should always be applied, and if none of the possible stacks satisfies the PCD of a, this procedure call is recognized as a place where a should never be applied. The advantage of this approach is its simplicity and relative cheapness, but there are many cases when the analysis is inconclusive. Moreover, the class of the possible pointcuts recognized is rather narrow.

Model-Checking Analysis. This approach is proposed by [8]. Here the pointcuts are described by temporal logic formulas. The algorithm is based on model-checking using future time CTL over a modified program state machine with reversed transitions (arrows). The result of the model-checking is identifying the states corresponding to each join-point. A state is marked as a join-point if there is an execution in which this state is the join-point, even if there is another possibility of reaching this state, in which the pointcut does not occur. Thus, this algorithm detects *potential* pointcuts, rather than real ones. So, in cases in which the previous algorithm would be inconclusive, this algorithm will give a positive answer, which might be wrong for the concrete computation we are interested in, but in the cases in which the previous algorithm was able to give an answer, this algorithm will give a correct answer too. The advantage of the model-checking algorithm is the ability to deal with a much wider class of pointcuts than the previous one can handle. It is also efficient, though less simple than the static analysis algorithm.

3.2   Ensuring the Appearance of the Aspects

Let us suppose a pointcut p of the aspect a was recognized as described above. Let t be its last transition, performed at a state s of M. We will modify $M\prime$ in such a way that in the above case when t is performed by M,instead of inserting the pair (s, t) into the history, the pair (s, t_ptc) will be inserted. The transition t_ptc is automatically created for every t that is the last transition of some pointcut. The t_ptc has the same enabling condition as t, and changes the state of M in the same way as t does. The only difference between t and t_ptc should be that whenever t_ptc occurs, we should be able to ensure the following:

- It is followed by the advice of a, σ_a, somewhere later in the computation.
- The operations of σ_a can be brought by legal *swap* operations to appear as a block immediately after t_ptc.

Let $\sigma_a = a_1, \ldots, a_n$ be the advice of a. To ensure the first property above, we make a prediction of σ_a immediately after inserting the t_ptc entry to the history, i.e., the anti-transitions $\overline{a_n}, \ldots, \overline{a_1}$ are inserted into the history after the t_ptc entry. If some predicted transition does not appear later in the computation, or can not be brought to the place where prediction was made, then the prediction fails. Thus the first property is guaranteed. The prediction mechanism also would be enough to ensure the second property, if we knew that t_ptc would never be swapped with any other operation. But if t_ptc is swapped with some transition τ, we need to show that all the operations of σ_a can be swapped with τ in the same direction, to be re-unified with t_ptc, because even if it is swapped with some independent operation, t_ptc continues to be the last operation of the pointcut, due to the correctness of the independence relation. Let us show two examples when such a swapping is needed:

- Let σ_1, t, σ_2 be a legal scenario. Let the following sequence of operations be a prefix of H: $< \sigma_1, \sigma_2, t\_ptc, a_1, \ldots, a_n >$, such that σ_2 and t are independent in the state where σ_2 appears. In order to chop the scenario σ_1, t, σ_2 from the history, we need the sequence $< \sigma_1, \sigma_2, t\_ptc, a_1, \ldots, a_n >$ to be equivalent to the convenient sequence $< \sigma_1, t\_ptc, a_1, \ldots, a_n, \sigma_2 >$. Thus we would like to enable the swap of σ_2 with t_ptc only if σ_2 is independent of t and of all the a_i-s at the relevant states.
- Let σ_1, σ_2, t be a legal scenario. Let the following sequence of operations be a prefix of H: $< \sigma_1, t\_ptc, a_1, \ldots, a_n, \sigma_2 >$, such that σ_2 and t are independent in the state where t_ptc appears. In order to chop the scenario σ_1, σ_2, t from the history, we need the sequence $< \sigma_1, t\_ptc, a_1, \ldots, a_n, \sigma_2 >$ to be equivalent to the convenient sequence $< \sigma_1, \sigma_2, t\_ptc, a_1, \ldots, a_n >$. Thus again the swap of t_ptc with σ_2 is possible only if t and all the a_i-s are independent of σ_2 at the relevant states.

As we see from the examples above, the independence relation of t_ptc should be different from the one of t.

If the sequence $\langle (s_1, \tau), (s, t\_ptc) \rangle$ appears in the history in some computation of M', we would like to enable the swap of τ_1 and t_ptc only when the following sequence of swaps is possible: first, the swap of τ and t, and then the swap of τ with each of $a_1 \ldots a_n$. Thus we will say that τ and t_ptc are independent at s_1 ($I(s_1, \tau, t\_ptc)$) iff the following conditions hold:

1. $I(s_1, \tau, t)$ is true
2. $I(t(s_1), \tau, a_1)$, $I(a_1(t(s_1)), \tau, a_2)$ and
   $\forall (2 \leq i \leq n - 1).I(a_i(\ldots(a_1(t(s_1)))\ldots), \tau, a_{i+1})$.

If the sequence $\langle (s, t\_ptc), (s_2, \tau) \rangle$ appears in the history, we would like to enable the swap of t_ptc and τ only when the following sequence of swaps is possible: first, the swap of each of $a_n \ldots a_1$ (notice the reversed order!) with τ, and then the swap of t with τ. There are two possible cases. The first possibility is that τ occurred after t_ptc in the original computation of M. This case is handled by the prediction of σ_a, because τ could be brought to appear next to t_ptc in the history only if it was possible to swap τ with the prediction of σ_a first. The remaining possibility is that τ occurred before t_ptc in the original computation of M. This case is already handled by the treatment of the case when τ preceded t_ptc in the history: to bring t_ptc to occur before τ in the history, we had to swap them, and now we just swap them back, bringing t_ptc closer to the place at which σ_a was originally predicted. (Notice that there is no contradiction here with the second example of needed swapping: in the example, σ_2 will never occur next to t_ptc if the swapping of $a_n \ldots a_1$ with σ_2 is not possible.) Thus, to swap t_ptc with a following operation, no strengthening is needed beyond the prediction, and we have that $I(s, t\_ptc, \tau)$ iff $I(s, t, \tau)$.

3.3   Arranging Non-aspectual Scenarios

If a given computation g is swap-equivalent to some computation c in which each aspect advice appears only immediately after its pointcut, then each time an advice operation enters the history, its anti-transition already appears somewhere in the tail of H and will be brought to it by the $swap - pred$ operations of $M\prime$, so that both operations will annihilate. Thus, none of the advice transitions will appear inside any prefix of the history examined by the chopper. Due to that fact, and also because the recognition of the scenarios by the chopper is based only on the operations appearing at the head of the history (and not on the states corresponding to those operations), we can, for the purpose of scenarios recognition, ignore the advice transitions in the executions. Now there will be two types of scenarios to be recognized by the chopper: the regular scenarios specified by the system M, and the prefixes of regular scenarios that are cut by strictly interrupting aspects. Thus we will add those prefixes to the list of legal scenarios to be recognized by the chopper, by the following algorithm:

> For every aspect advice a that is defined as strictly interrupting
> > For every scenario $\sigma = \langle op_1, \ldots, op_n \rangle$
> > > For every $1 \leq i \leq n$
> > > > If $op_i = t$ where t is the last operation of the pointcut of a then
> > > > > add scenario $\sigma\prime = \langle op_1, \ldots, op_{i-1}, t\_ptc \rangle$ to the scenario list.

Note that the new chopper recognizes prefixes of scenarios as legal scenarios only if they are indeed cut by some strictly interrupting aspect advice, because only in that case was t_ptc substituted for t.

3.4   Proving Soundness

First of all, let us give some definitions needed to state and prove the soundness of the system. Here we ignore predictions added by non-aspectual scenarios, since they can be shown equivalent to a version without predictions, but with a longer history.

Definition 5. *A computation $g\prime$ of $M\prime$ follows a computation g of M if the error flag is never raised in $g\prime$, and g is the projection of $g\prime$ on M, $proj_M(g\prime)$ (i.e., g is obtained from $g\prime$ by deleting all the operations that are not operations of M, and all the assignments to state variables that are not defined in M).*

Given a computation $g\prime$ that follows g, we can say that any moment i in $g\prime$ naturally divides all the operations of $g\prime$ to three subsequences: $chopped(g\prime, i)$ -

the sequence of operations already chopped, $h(g\prime, i)$ - the contents of the history, and $suffix(g\prime, i)$ - all the rest of $g\prime$. Now let us look at a sequence of executions $R(g\prime) = \{r_i\}_{i=0}^{i=\infty}$, where $r_i = chopped(g\prime, i) \cdot h(g\prime.i) \cdot proj_M(suffix(g\prime, i))$. We have $r_0 = g$ and the only difference between r_i and r_{i+1} can be one swap of consecutive independent operations, so $\forall i.r_i \equiv_{1sw} r_{i+1}$. $R(g\prime)$ is a special case of a *reduction sequence* from g, which is defined as a sequence of swap-equivalent executions starting from g. We will say that a reduction sequence $\{r_i\}_{i=0}^{\infty}$ *converges* to some computation c iff for any prefix of c, we can find an index j such that for every $i \geq j$, every r_i will have the same prefix.

We also need to define formally equivalence of infinite computations. For that we will first define that $c \sqsubseteq g$ for infinite computations g, c iff from every finite prefix c_1 of c there exists a continuation h such that $c_1 \cdot h \equiv_{sw} g$.

Definition 6. *Two infinite computations g and c are* conditional trace equivalent *($c \approx g$) iff $c \sqsubseteq g$ and $g \sqsubseteq c$.*

Notation: Let g be a computation of M. Let $g\prime$ be any computation of $M\prime$ that follows g. We will denote by g^{-a} the sequence of history entries that are added to the history during the run of $g\prime$, excluding all the entries corresponding to the operations of aspect advice.

Note that g^{-a} is well defined, since for all the computations of $M\prime$ that follow g the same entries are added to the history, and in the same order. However, the sequence g^{-a} does not necessarily represent a legal computation of M in case some of the removed aspect advice subsequences are non-spectative. For example, let the following sequence be a part of g: $\ldots, (s_1, t_1), (s_2, a_1), \ldots, (s_{n+1}, a_n), (s_{n+2}, t_2), \ldots$ where $\sigma = a_1, \ldots, a_n$ is an invasive aspect advice. Then when passing from g to g^{-a}, σ is removed from the computation, and we get the following subsequence in g^{-a}: $(s_1, t_1), (s_{n+2}, t_2)$. Since σ was invasive, it can be the case that $s_{n+2} \neq t_1(s_1)$, and thus g^{-a} is not a legal computation of M.

Definition 7. *A computation g of M is* convenient *iff the following holds:*

- *whenever a pointcut appears in g, it is immediately followed by the corresponding aspect advice, and no operations of the system appear between the operations of the aspect*
- *g^{-a} is comprised of blocks of (non-aspectual) scenario operations.*

Clearly, by construction, if the chopper recognizes a sequence, it is comprised of blocks of (non-aspectual) scenario operations, including prefixes added earlier. In order to show the soundness of the new system, we need to prove:

Theorem 1. *When $M\prime$ is the transducer defined from M, and the convenient executions are defined as in Definition 7, the temporal assertions described in Section 2 imply that every computation of M is conditionally trace equivalent to some convenient one.*

Here we will bring the outline of the proof to show a key property - the existence of a convenient computation c such that $c \sqsubseteq g$. First we will show that we can restrict our discussion only to the case when in g whenever a pointcut occurs it is immediately followed by the corresponding aspect advice as a block (Step1 of the proof outline). Then we will show that if the non-aspectual part of g, g^{-a}, is reducible to some sequence c_1 recognized by the chopper ($c_1 \sqsubseteq g^{-a}$), then there exists a convenient computation c as needed (Step2). Finally, we will prove that in our case there indeed exists a sequence c_1 recognized by the chopper such that $c_1 \sqsubseteq g^{-a}$ (Step3: Lemma 1).

Step1: Let $g\prime$ be a computation of $M\prime$ that follows a computation g of M. The *CorrectPredictions* property holds in $M\prime$, and whenever a pointcut occurred in $g\prime$ the appropriate aspect advice was predicted. Thus there exists a computation $g\prime\prime$ of $M\prime$ such that $g\prime\prime \approx g\prime$ and whenever a pointcut occurs in $g\prime\prime$ it is immediately followed by the appropriate aspect advice as a block. Let g_1 be the computation obtained from $g\prime\prime$ by deleting all the operations that are not operations of M (notice that in g_1 all the aspect advice are applied correctly). The error flag is never raised in $g\prime\prime$, as it is a computation of $M\prime$, and $M\prime$ satisfies the first property from Section 2. Thus, $g\prime\prime$ follows g_1. As $g\prime\prime \approx g\prime$, we have that also $g_1 \approx g$, and so it is enough to show that there exists a convenient computation c such that $c \sqsubseteq g_1$. It follows that we indeed can assume that in the original computation g all the aspect advice are applied correctly.

Step2: Here we will extract the blocks of the aspect advices from the computation, and show that the resulting sequence, g^{-a}, can be brought by legal swap operations to one recognized by the chopper, c_1 ($c_1 \sqsubseteq g^{-a}$). Analogously to the proof in [2], it can be shown that given a computation g_1 of M without any aspect advice operations, if there exists a computation $g_1\prime$ of $M\prime$ that follows g_1, then there exists a computation c_1 recognized by the chopper such that $c_1 \sqsubseteq g_1$. Let us notice that this statement stays true also for operation sequences that are not legal computations, because the chopper recognizes scenarios only by their operations, and the problem of detecting swap-equivalence of computation sequences with missing aspect advice operations was treated in the definition of the independence relation for t_ptc, which took the aspect advice into account. Our sequence g^{-a} is followed by the sequence $g\prime\prime^{-a}$, so we can apply the above statement and thus, indeed, there exists c_1 recognized by the chopper such that $c_1 \sqsubseteq g^{-a}$.

Step3: The following lemma completes the proof of the existence of the convenient computation needed.

Lemma 1. *Let g be a computation of M such that whenever a pointcut appears in g, it is immediately followed by the corresponding aspect advice, and no operations of the system appear between the operations of the aspect. Let us also suppose that $c_1 \sqsubseteq g^{-a}$ for some c_1 recognized by the chopper. Then there exists a convenient computation c such that $c \sqsubseteq g$.*

Proof. As $c_1 \sqsubseteq g^{-a}$, there exists a reduction sequence R starting from g^{-a} that converges to c_1. Let us build a reduction sequence $R\prime$ starting from g and following R:

1. $r\prime_0 = g$; last used step of R is 0.
2. If the last built element of $R\prime$ is $r\prime_i$, and the last used element of R is r_k,
   - If in the swap performed to obtain r_{k+1} from r_k no last operation of a pointcut is involved, then the same swap is performed to pass from $r\prime_i$ to $r\prime_{i+1}$. The last built element of $R\prime$ becomes $i + 1$, and the last used element of R becomes r_{k+1}.
   - Otherwise, let t and $t\prime$ be the swapped operations, and let t be the last operation of a pointcut, and $a = a_1, \ldots, a_n$ be the aspect advice that follows t. Then not only t and $t\prime$ are swapped, but also $t\prime$ is swapped with every a_j, $1 \leq j \leq n$. After that the last built element of $R\prime$ becomes $i + n + 1$, and the last used element of R becomes r_{k+1}. If $t\prime$ is also the last operation of some pointcut, then the operations of its advice are also swapped with t and $a_1, \ldots, a_n$, and the index of the last built element of $R\prime$ is updated accordingly.

From the definition of the independence relation it follows that the last operation of a pointcut is independent of some operation op only if all the operations of the corresponding advice are also independent of op in the relevant states. Thus all the swaps performed while building $R\prime$ were legal, and thus $R\prime$ is indeed a reduction sequence from g. We are left to show that $R\prime$ converges to some convenient computation c. The construction of $R\prime$ followed that of R, and at every step i the "frozen" part of $r\prime_i$ was at least as long as that of r_i, thus, $R\prime$ indeed converges to some computation c. It is also seen from the construction, that the only difference between c and c_1 is that in c blocks of aspect advice operations are added whenever the corresponding pointcut occurs. Thus we have that c is indeed a convenient computation (with $c^{-a} = c_1$ recognized by the chopper). Q. E. D.

Now the soundness theorem will follow if the other direction, $g \sqsubseteq c$, holds. This is true, because from the temporal properties in Section 2 it follows that all the operations of g are either chopped or predicted, so the operations performed in c are exactly the operations that appear in g.

4   Example

We return to the example of the ATM system, and describe the part of the system involved in money withdrawal in more detail. Let the system consist of two ATM machines and one server. First let us give a list of operations of the system. The operations of a user will appear in *italic* style, the operations of a machine - in **bold**, and the operations of the server - in ***bold italic***.

- user operations: *ic* - *insert card and code*; *es*(*sum*) - *enter sum*.
- machine operations: **cm** - send "check code" message to the server and update connection status (boolean variable "cs");
  wm(sum) - send "**withdraw**(sum)" message to the server and update cs;
  mr - perform money return and eject card;
  ec - eject card;

fm - send "take fee" message to the server and update cs;

rf - print report on communication failure between the ATM and the server;

- server operations: **gc** - check the code, send "**g**ood **c**ode" message to the machine, update cs;

bc - check the code, send "**b**ad **c**ode" message to the machine, update cs;

gs - check that the sum can be withdrawn leaving a non-negative balance, update the balance, send "**g**ood **s**um" message to the machine, update cs;

bs - check the sum, do not update the balance, send "**b**ad **s**um" message to the machine, update cs;

tf - **t**ake management **f**ee from an account;

pc - **p**romote by 1 the operations **c**ounter for the relevant account;

The non-aspectual system behavior can be described by the following scenarios:

- Successful withdrawal: ⟨ *ic*; **cm**; **gc**; *es*(sum); **wm**(sum); **gs**; **mr**⟩
- Erroneous code: ⟨ *ic*; **cm**; **bc**; **ec**⟩
- Erroneous sum withdrawal:⟨ *ic*; **cm**; **gc**; *es*(sum); **wm**(sum); **bs**; **ec**⟩

The aspectual scenarios are:

- Operations fee: Applies whenever an ATM operation is completed successfully, in order to take the fee for the operation performed from the relevant account. It is a weakly interrupting aspect. In the above described scenarios, there is only one possibility for its application - the case when **mr** is performed. Thus the pointcut is (⟨**mr**⟩,$\varphi = (op = \mathbf{mr}1 \lor op = \mathbf{mr}2)$). The advice is ⟨**pc**; **fm**; **tf**⟩.

- Communication failure: Applies whenever a communication failure between an ATM and the server is detected, in order to stop the current interaction with the ATM machine (but when the communication is restored, the next user will be able to interact with the machine). It is a strictly interrupting aspect. The *cs* variable is updated by the message-sending operations, thus the pointcut here is (⟨**cm** or **wm** or **fm** or **gc** or **bc** or **gs** or **bs**⟩,$\varphi = (cs = false)$). The advice is ⟨**ec**; **rf**⟩.

Let us consider some examples of executions, and check their equivalence to convenient ones. When it is necessary to explicitly specify the account and/or the user relevant for some operation, they appear in parentheses: op(user,acc). When there is more than one participant of some kind (for example, two ATM machines), their operations will be indexed, e. g., an operation *op* of the first machine will be written as *op*1.

Example1. In this example we have a computation in which two "successful withdrawal" scenarios start one after another. The scenario for user1 and acc1 is completed when the remainder of the scenario for user2 and acc2 (starting from the second operation) is performed, and then the aspectual scenarios of taking the operation fee are executed - first for acc1 and then for acc2.

$\langle ic(user1, acc1); ic(user2, acc2); \textbf{cm1}(user1); \textbf{\textit{gc}}(user1); es(user1, sum1);$

$\textbf{wm1}(acc1, sum1); \textbf{\textit{gs}}(acc1); \textbf{mr1}; \textbf{cm2}(user2); \textbf{\textit{gc}}(user2); es(user2, sum2);$

$\textbf{wm2}(acc2, sum2); \textbf{\textit{gs}}(acc2); \textbf{mr2}; \textbf{\textit{pc}}(acc1); \textbf{fm1}(acc1); \textbf{\textit{tf}}(acc1);$

$\textbf{\textit{pc}}(acc2); \textbf{fm2}(acc2); \textbf{\textit{tf}}(acc2) \ldots \rangle$

Let us show that this computation can be brought to a convenient one.

1. The operations of the "successful withdrawal" scenario for user1 and acc1 enter the history, but are mixed together, so the scenario cannot be chopped immediately. Immediately after the $\overline{\textbf{mr1}}$ operation enters the history, the prediction $\overline{\textbf{\textit{tf}}(acc1)}, \overline{\textbf{fm1}(acc1)}, \overline{\textbf{\textit{pc}}(acc1)}$ is inserted.
2. The accounts acc1 and acc2 are different, thus the operation $ic(user2, acc2)$ can be swapped with all the operations of the "successful withdrawal" scenario for acc1, including the pointcut $\textbf{mr1}$ (as it is also independent of the operations of "operations fee" advice for acc1).
3. Now the operations of the "successful withdrawal" scenario for acc1 appear as a prefix of the history, and are chopped. What is left in the history is only the operation $ic(user2, acc2)$ followed by the prediction of the 'operations fee" advice for acc1.
4. The operations $\textbf{cm2}(user2); \textbf{\textit{gc}}(user2); es(user2, sum2); \textbf{wm2}(acc2, sum2);$ $\textbf{\textit{gs}}(acc2); \textbf{mr2}$ enter the history. Immediately after the $\textbf{mr2}$ operation the prediction $\overline{\textbf{\textit{tf}}(acc2)}, \overline{\textbf{fm2}(acc2)}, \overline{\textbf{\textit{pc}}(acc2)}$ is inserted.
5. The accounts acc1 and acc2 are different, thus all the operations of the "successful withdrawal" scenario for acc2 (again, including the pointcut $\textbf{mr2}$), can be swapped with the prediction of the "operation fee" advice for acc1.
6. After the swapping is performed, the "successful withdrawal" scenario for acc2 appears as a prefix of the history, and is chopped.
7. The operations of the advice of "Operations fee" aspect for account 1, $\textbf{\textit{pc}}(acc1); \textbf{fm1}(acc1); \textbf{\textit{tf}}(acc1)$, enter the history one after another, are swapped with the prediction of the advice of "Operations fee" aspect for account 2, and cancelled with their prediction.
8. The operations of the advice of "Operations fee" aspect for account 2, $\textbf{\textit{pc}}(acc2); \textbf{fm2}(acc2); \textbf{\textit{tf}}(acc2)$, enter the history one after another, and are cancelled with their predictions. The history becomes empty, as needed.

Example2. Consider a computation identical to the previous one except that the same account number acc1 is used by the two withdrawals, and the account balance of acc1 is initially equal to $(sum1 + sum2)$. Let us show that this computation cannot be brought to a convenient one.

1. The history develops as previously, until the operation $\textbf{\textit{gs}}$ of the second withdrawal enters the history. It is successfully swapped with $\overline{\textbf{fm1}}, \overline{\textbf{\textit{pc}}}$, but it cannot be swapped with $\overline{\textbf{\textit{tf}}}$. The reason is that after $\overline{\textbf{\textit{tf}}}$ is performed, the account balance becomes smaller than the sum needed for the second withdrawal, and thus $\textbf{\textit{gs}}$ is not enabled any more. Thus the chop operation

cannot be performed and the history will never become empty during the execution, which violates the property of never "losing" operations, and means that this execution cannot be brought to a convenient one.

Example3. In this example, user1 starts a "successful withdrawal" scenario at ATM1, and it is interrupted by communication failure. Meanwhile, user2 performs an "erroneous code" scenario at ATM2.

$$\langle ic(user1, acc1); ic(user2, acc2); \mathbf{cm1}(user1); \mathbf{cm2}(user2); \mathbf{gc}(user1);$$

$$es(user1, sum1); \mathbf{bc}(user2); \mathbf{ec2}; \mathbf{wm1}(sum1)[cf = false]; \mathbf{ec1}; \mathbf{rf1}; \ldots\rangle$$

This computation can be brought to a convenient one:

1. The operations of the interrupted "successful withdrawal" scenario at ATM1 are independent from those of the "erroneous code" scenario at ATM2, and they will be swapped so that the interrupted "successful withdrawal" scenario will appear at the head of the history. It will be chopped, as its last operation is marked as the last operation of the pointcut, and it was added to the chopper scenarios when $M\prime$ was constructed. The operations of the advice will be predicted immediately after it, and the prediction will immediately be fulfilled.
2. Only the head of the "erroneous code" scenario at ATM2 now appears in the history. Then the tail of the scenario will arrive, and be chopped.

Note that the modified CNV system automatically checks all possible computations of the transformed system as part of the model checking tasks, and would list the second example above as a counter-example to the properties to be checked.

5   Conclusions

Formal methods will be useful for software development only if they both deal with specification methods actually used, and treat real languages and programming techniques. Software model checking systems such as Bandera [4] or Java Pathfinder [5] already can turn Java code into input for standard model checking. In this paper, we show how specifications based on scenarios, like those seen in UML, can be extended to treat aspect scenarios, and how systems with aspects woven into them (e.g., the result of the AspectJ precompiler into Java bytecode) can be proven to conform with such a specification using model checking. The model produced by a software model checker applied to a woven system actually is a machine M which is the input to our system.

The efficiency of the resultant model checking tasks is an obvious problem, due to the extended state of the transformed model. However, optimization techniques described in [2] can be used to separate this task into several smaller stages. This work thus provides another step towards the goal of integrating formal methods into practical software development.

References

1. M. Glusman and S. Katz, *A mechanized proof environment for the convenient computations proof method*, Formal Methods in System Design **23** (2003), 115–142, Available at `http://www.cs.technion.ac.il/Labs/ssdl/pub/conv_PVS`.

2. _____ , *Model checking conformance with scenario-based specifications*, Computer-Aided Verification, (CAV'03) (W.A. Hunt and F. Somenzi, eds.), LNCS, vol. 2725, Springer-Verlag, 2003, pp. 328–340, Full version and system at `http://www.cs.technion.ac.il/Labs/ssdl/pub/CNV`.

3. D. Harel and R. Marelly, *Come, let's play : Scenario-based programming using LSC's and the play-engine*, Springer-Verlag, 2003.

4. J. Hatcliff and M. Dwyer, *Using the Bandera Tool Set to model-check properties of concurrent Java software*, Proc. 12th Int. Conf. on Concurrency Theory, CONCUR'01 (K. G. Larsen and M. Nielsen, eds.), LNCS, vol. 2154, Springer-Verlag, 2001, pp. 39–58.

5. K. Havelund and T. Pressburger, *Model checking Java programs using Java PathFinder*, International Journal on Software Tools for Technology Transfer (STTT) **2** (2000), no. 4.

6. J.Arajo, J. Whittle, and D. Kim, *Modeling and composing scenario-based requirements with aspects*, The 12th IEEE International Requirements Engineering Conference (RE2004) (Kyoto, Japan), September 2004, pp. 58–67.

7. G. Kiczales, E. Hilsdale, J. Hugunin, M. Kersten, J. Palm, and W. G. Griswold, *An overview of AspectJ*, Proceedings ECOOP 2001, LNCS 2072, Jun 2001, `http://aspectj.org`, pp. 327–353.

8. S. Krishnamurthi, K. Fisler, and M. Greenberg, *Verifying aspect advice modularly*, SIGSOFT FSE, 2004, pp. 137–146.

9. Z. Manna and A. Pnueli, *The temporal logic of reactive and concurrent systems - safety*, Springer-Verlag, 1995.

10. K. L. McMillan, *Getting started with SMV*, Cadence Labs, March 1999.

11. D. Peled, *Software reliability methods*, Springer-Verlag, 2001.

12. J. Rumbaugh, I. Jacobson, and G. Booch, *The Unified Modeling Language reference manual, second edition*, Addison-Wesley, 2004.

13. D. Sereni and O. de Moor, *Static analysis of aspects.*, AOSD, 2003, pp. 30–39.

14. M. Sihman and S. Katz, *Superimposition and aspect-oriented programming*, BCS Computer Journal **46** (2003), no. 5, 529–541, Available at `http://www.cs.technion.ac.il/~katz/cj.ps`.

An MDA Approach Towards
Integrating Formal and Informal Modeling Languages

Soon-Kyeong Kim, Damian Burger, and David Carrington

School of Information Technology and Electrical Engineering,
The University of Queensland, St. Lucia, 4072, Australia
{soon, damian, davec}@itee.uq.edu.au

Abstract. The Model Driven Architecture (MDA) involves automated transformations between software models defined in different languages at different
abstraction levels. This paper takes an MDA approach to integrate a formal
modeling language (Object-Z) with an informal modeling language (UML) via
model transformation. This paper shows how formal and informal modeling
languages can be cooperatively used in the MDA framework and how the transformations between models in these languages can be achieved using an MDA
development environment. The MDA model transformation techniques allow us
to have a reusable transformation between formal and informal modeling languages. The integrated approach provides an effective V&V technique for the
MDA.

1 Introduction

Integration between formal and informal or semi-formal visual modeling (or specification) languages is a well-known topic in the literature [8, 11, 12, 14]. There are
many advantages to be gained from integrating formal techniques with informal or
semi-formal approaches in the field of software development. Integration can make
formal methods easier to apply and informal methods more precise, aiming towards
"the best of both worlds". Despite the potential for taking benefits from both types of
techniques, the integrated approach is seldom used in practice. Several drawbacks we
have identified are: transformations between formal and informal models are often not
explicitly defined [1, 8, 13, 14, 15, 23], which makes it difficult to know on what semantic basis the transformation has taken place, whether semantics of models are preserved during the transformation and whether the transformation is complete and consistent. Also a lack of tool support for the actual transformation is a drawback in this
area. In order to contribute to this area, this paper presents an MDA approach towards
the integration of a formal modeling language Object-Z [4] with the Unified Modeling Language (UML) [19], a semi-formal visual modeling language.

The Model Driven Architecture (MDA) [18] is a new software development
framework that aims to separate business logic from underlying platform technology.
It involves automated transformations between software models defined in different
languages. In MDA, a Platform Independent Model (PIM) of a system is specified
and a Platform Specific Model (PSM) is derived from the PIM using transformations.
MDA model transformation can be applied to the integrated approach. In the MDA,

J.S. Fitzgerald, I.J. Hayes, and A. Tarlecki (Eds.): FM 2005, LNCS 3582, pp. 448–464, 2005.

models are integrated by their common basis in the Meta Object Facility (MOF) [16], which is the meta-language standard for UML and the other OMG modelling languages. That is, each modeling language is defined in terms of a metamodel using the MOF. Given the metamodels of different modeling languages, a set of transformation rules is defined explicitly using a transformation language, which is also a MOF model. Actual transformations are then achieved automatically using a transformation tool that understands the transformation language. In this paper, we use this reusable MDA transformation framework for modeling language integration with Object-Z and UML. For this, we first define Object-Z in terms of a metamodel based on the MOF. Given the metamodels of UML and Object-Z, we then define transformation rules using a transformation language[1]. The metamodel-based MDA transformation framework allows us to define transformations precisely and explicitly in terms of transformation rules, which is critical for rigorous model evolution from informal to formal and vice-versa. It also allows us to have a reusable transformation that can be applied to any models in the two languages. Actual transformations are achieved using tools supporting MDA.

Additionally our integrated approach can deliver benefits to MDA. To get the full potential of the MDA, the MDA transformation infrastructure (currently being standardized [18]) should include the ability to use modelling notations that are the most appropriate to capture different aspects of a system, and should have a capability of transforming between models in these different notations. Also there must exist efficient ways to check the models for properties such as consistency and correctness. Currently UML is proposed as the central modelling language by OMG in the MDA. However, using only UML has limitations to provide these capabilities required for the MDA. Our integrated approach with formal and informal modeling techniques can contribute to this area. For example, it provides the convenience to choose appropriate modeling techniques to capture different aspects. Formal techniques provide effective means to check models providing increased quality for both specification and implementation. In this integrated MDA modeling framework, models are corrected and evolved via model transformation from informal to formal and vice-versa. In fact, the integrated approach can be a V&V technique for the MDA. For example, an Object-Z model derived from a UML model is a V&V model of the UML model. Any formal reasoning techniques available for Object-Z can be used to validate the UML model.

It should be noted that in this paper it is not our intention to present a complete definition of Object-Z or UML, or a complete set of transformation rules between the two languages. Rather we focus on explaining how the MDA model transformation framework can be applied to the integration of the two languages. The transformation presented in this paper should pave the way for others to follow the same transformation approach towards integrating different formal and informal modeling languages.

The structure of the rest of this paper is as follows. Section 2 discusses relevant background information. Section 3 presents the model transformation environment

---

[1] In this paper, we use the Distributed Systems Technology Centre (DSTC)'s transformation language [3] that has been submitted to respond to the OMG's MOF 2.0 Query/Views/Transformations (QVT) Request for proposals [17], and its transformation engine Tefkat [2]. Once the OMG finalizes a standard transformation language, the transformation rules can be converted into the standard language.

used in this work and its rationale. Section 4 discusses the transformation itself in detail with an example. Finally, Section 5 concludes and discusses further work.

2 Background Information

In this section, we present a metamodel of Object-Z and a metamodel of UML. The Object-Z metamodel presented in this section is an enhanced version of the one presented in [9, 10]. The UML metamodel presented in this section is a simplified version of UML 2.0 [19].

2.1 Object-Z Metamodel

Figure 1 is a UML class diagram showing core model elements in Object-Z and their structure (we add OZ to the names of the model constructs to distinguish them from the UML modeling constructs). Figure 2 shows types in Object-Z (see [10]).

OZElement is a top-level metaclass from which all possible model elements in Object-Z can be drawn. OZNamedElement represents all model elements with names (e.g. attributes, classes, operations, and parameters). OZNamespace is an element that can own other named elements (e.g. classes or operations).

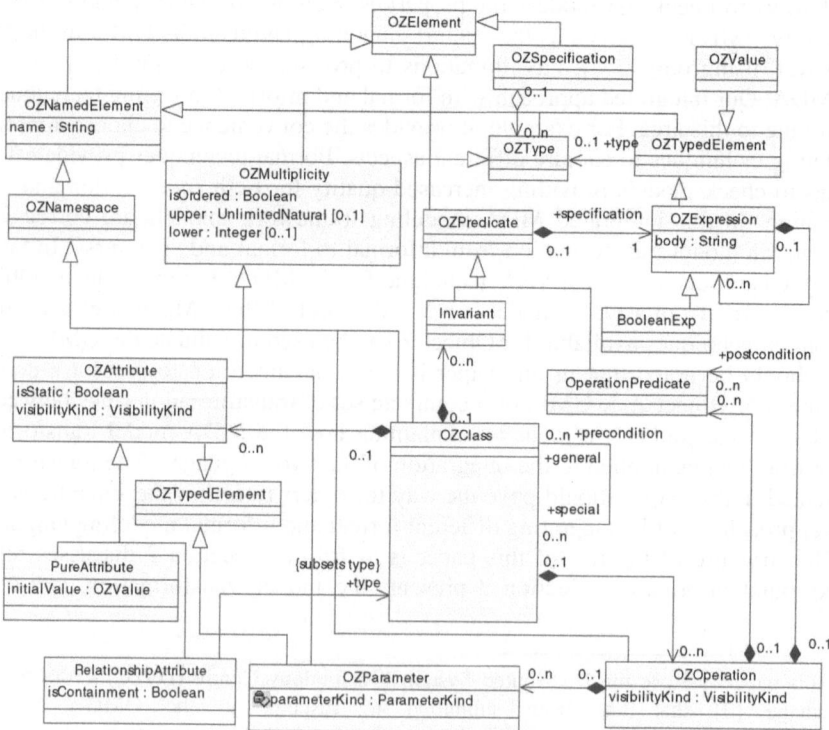

Fig. 1. Object-Z model elements

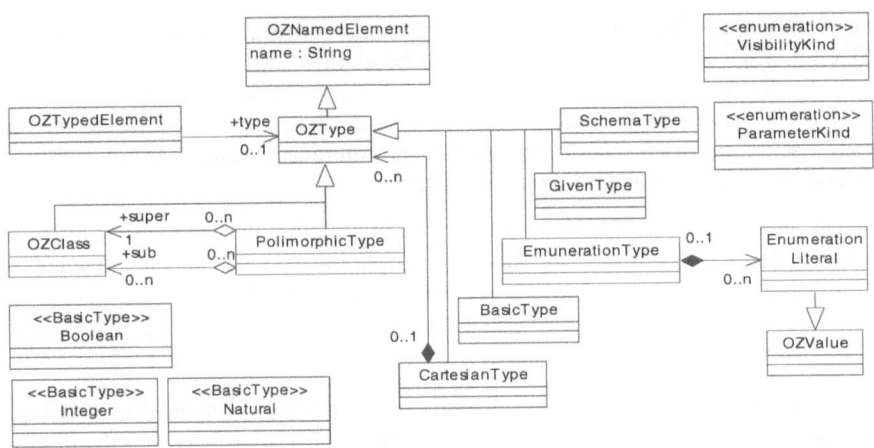

Fig. 2. Object-Z types

OZTypedElement presents elements with types (e.g. attributes and parameters) and the type of a typed element constrains the set of values that the typed element may refer to. OZMultiplicity is an abstract metaclass of elements with multiplicity information that specifies the allowable cardinalities for an instantiation of the elements (e.g. attribute values and parameter values). It also has an attribute (isOrdered) to define whether the values in an instantiation of this element must be ordered.

OZPredicate is a metaclass to define a condition in classes or operations. Conditions defined in a class are invariants and conditions defined in an operation are either a precondition or a postcondition of the operation. Predicates contain expressions that will have a set (possibly empty) of values when evaluated in a context. Boolean expressions are one type of expression in Object-Z.

UML is a visual modelling language and does not provide a language for specifying expressions al-though OCL [19] is recommended as a constraint language for UML by OMG. Consequently UML treats expressions as an uninterpreted textual statement (see the meta-class OpaqueExpression in the UML metamodel) and the semantics of expressions depends on the language. For this reason, we do not further clarify expressions in Object-Z in this paper focusing on transforming the structural constructs of the two languages and leave this issue as further work to map Object-Z expressions to a specification language such as OCL.

Classes: In Object-Z, classes are the major modeling construct for specifying a system. A Class is a template for objects that have common behaviors. A Class has a set of attributes (PureAttribute) and a set of operations. Each attribute has a name, a type, a visibility and an attribute (isStatic) specifying whether the attribute is static. By specializing multiplicity element, an attribute supports a multiplicity that specifies valid cardinalities for the set of values associated with the attribute. An operation has a name, a visibility and a set of parameters, each of which also has a name, a type and the multiplicity information for the set of values associated with the parameter.

Relationships and instantiation: Classes can be instantiated in other classes as attributes. In Object-Z, instantiation is used as a mechanism for modeling relationships between objects, which in UML is modeled using a separate modeling construct, Association. Objects that instantiate other classes as their attributes (RelationshipAttribute) can refer to the objects of the instantiated classes. The values of these attributes are object-identities of the referenced objects. Each relationship attribute has an attribute (isContainment) specifying whether the referenced objects are owned by their referencing object (a containment relationship).

Inheritance: Classes in Object-Z can be used in defining other classes by inheritance. A class can inherit from several classes (multiple inheritance). In the Object-Z metamodel, inheritance is defined with an association between classes.

2.2 A Simplified UML Metamodel

Figure 3 presents class modeling constructs in UML. In this paper, we are concerned with only a subset of the UML modeling constructs that are relevant to the discussion of transformation with Object-Z. For a full description of the UML 2.0 metamodel refer to [19].

Classes: A class in UML is a descriptor of a set of objects with common properties in terms of structure, behavior, and relationship. Class is a kind of classifier whose features are attributes and operations. Attributes of a class are represented by instances of Property that are owned by the class. Some of these attributes may represent the navigable ends of binary associations. An attribute has a name, a visibility, a type, and amultiplicity. An operation also has a name, a visibility and parameters. Each parame-

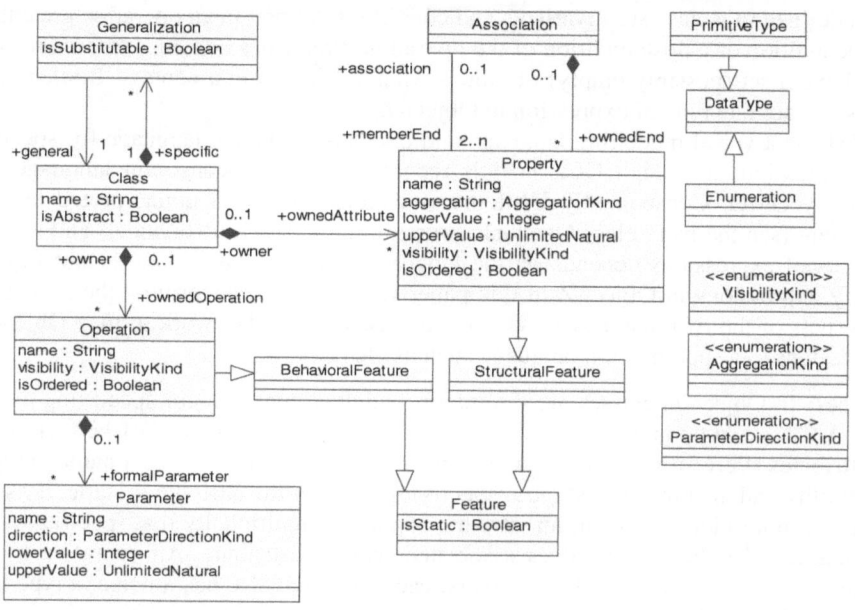

Fig. 3. A simplified UML metamodel

ter of an operation has a name and a given type. Attributes and operations have a visibility. Visibility in UML can be private, public, or protected.

Associations: In UML, relationships between classes are represented as associations. An association specifies a semantic relationship that can occur between typed instances. It has at least two ends represented by properties, each of which is connected to the type of the end. When a property is owned by an association, it represents a non-navigable end of the association. In this case the property does not appear in the namespace of any of the associated classifiers. When a property at an end of an association is owned by one of the associated classifiers, it represents a navigable end of the association. In this case the property is also an attribute of the associated classifier. Only binary associations may have navigable ends. A property of an association has attributes indicating whether the property has an aggregation (aggregation) and if it is compositionally aggregated (isComposite).

Generalizations: In UML, a generalization is a taxonomic relationship between a more general class and a more specific class. Each instance of the specific class is also an indirect instance of the general class. Thus, the specific classifier inherits the features of the more general class. An attribute, isSubstitutable, indicates whether the specific class can be used wherever the general class can be used.

3 Transformation Environment

Sendal and Kozaczynski [20] identify a number of challenges in model transformation. Most importantly, defining a model transformation requires a clear understanding of the abstract syntax and the semantics of both the source and target models. In the metamodel-based approach, each modelling notation is precisely defined in terms of its metamodel (using the OMG's MOF). Model transformations are then defined in terms of the relationship between a source MOF metamodel and a target MOF metamodel. Previously the authors defined a set of formal mapping functions between Object-Z and UML 1.4 based on their metamodels [9]. We implement these formal mapping functions using a transformation language in a MDA development environment. This section covers background information of the implementation.

3.1 DSTC Transformation Language Overview

In 2002, OMG issued a Queries, Views and Transformations (QVT) Request For Proposals (RFP) [17] and is currently in the process of selecting a standard MDA model transformation language. Several proposals have been submitted to the request. The Distributed Systems Technology Centre (DSTC)'s transformation language [3] is one of them and is used in this paper to define mappings between UML and Object-Z.

Figure 4 illustrates how an Object-Z model is transformed into a UML model using the DSTC's transformation language. At the meta-level, we have four metamodels: the UML metamodel, an Object-Z metamodel, a Transformation metamodel defining the concepts in the DSTC's trans-formation language and a Tracking metamodel defining the mapping relationships between model elements in Object-Z and UML. The diagram in Figure 5 is a Tracking metamodel used in our work.

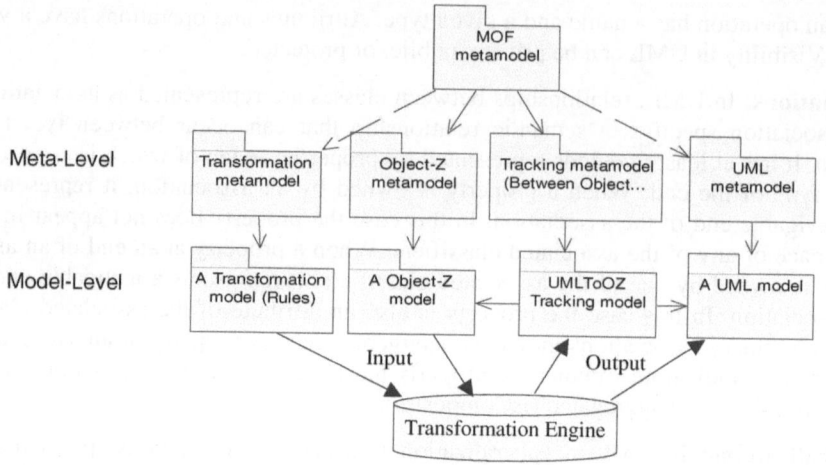

Fig. 4. Model Transformation with the DSTC's Transformation Language

For example, an Object-Z class maps to a UML class, an Object-Z attribute maps to a UML attribute, an Object-Z operation maps a UML operation and an Object-Z attribute modelling a relation maps to an association in UML. Since both the languages share common concepts in object technology, mappings between these two languages are mostly straightforward.

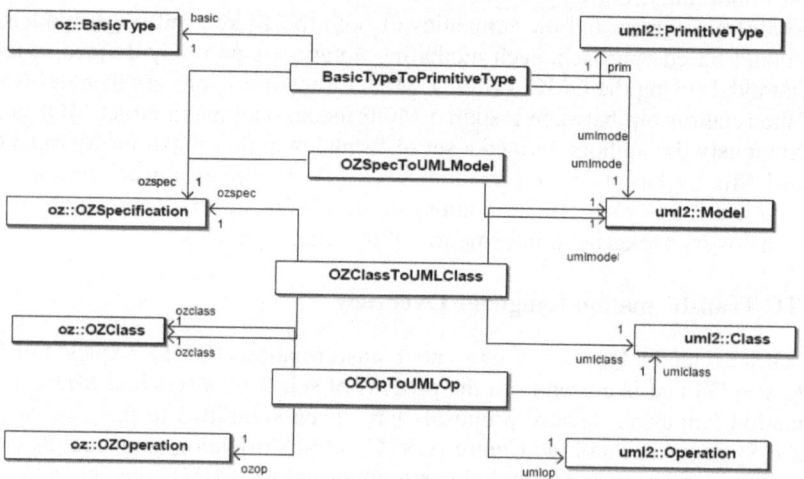

Fig. 5. Tracking model for UML and Object-Z

At the model-level, an Object-Z model (an instance of the Object-Z metamodel) and a transformation model are input to a transformation engine. The transformation model includes a set of transformation rules specifying how to convert an Object-Z element into a UML model element. These rules are based on the mapping relationships defined in the Tracking metamodel. Then the transformation engine populates a target UML model based on the source model according to the transformation rules. During the transformation, a tracking model is created and used to store correspondences between source elements and target elements. These correspondences can then be used to link transformation rules together. For example, the OZClassToUMLClass tracking class records the corresponding UML class for each Object-Z class. This is stored so that the UML class generated from a particular Object-Z class can be looked up from other transformation rules. For example, a UML operation generated for an Object-Z operation can be inserted into the right UML class by querying the tracking model.

The DSTC's transformation language consists of three major concepts: pattern definitions, transformation rules, and tracking relationships [3]:

- Pattern definitions can be used to define common structures to be reused throughout a transformation.
- Transformation rules are used to describe the elements to be created in a target model based on the elements in a source model. Transformation rules can be extended or superseded allowing for modularity and reusability.
- Tracking relationships are used to associate target elements with the source elements that led to their creation, important for rule reuse.

Currently the DSTC's Transformation language uses a concrete syntax in the style of SQL [3]. An example transformation rule (OZSpec2UMLModel) in the DSTC transformation language is given below. It simply maps each Object-Z specification to a UML Model. Line 1 declares the rule name and variables to be used in the rule. Lines 2 and 3 then express that for each Object-Z specification found in the source model (FORALL statement), a UML Model should be created in the target model (MAKE statement). Line 4 preserves the tracking relationship between the UML Model that was created and the Object-Z specification it was created from. This is done by using a LINKING...WITH statement and setting the ozspec and umlmodel references of the tracking model class OZSpecToUMLModel (see Figure 5). This tracking will allow other rules to find the corresponding UML Model for an OZ specification. We present other rules in detail in Section 4.

```
1    RULE OZSpec2UMLModel(ozs, umlm)
2    FORALL   OZSpecification ozs
3    MAKE     Model umlm
4    LINKING OZSpecToUMLModel WITH ozspec = ozs, umlmodel = umlm;
```

3.2 Model Transformation Tool Environment

Figure 6 shows the overall tool architecture used in our work. The Eclipse Platform [5] is a universal tool platform – an IDE that allows tool developers to add functionality through tool plug-ins. It is used as a tool integration environment for transformation. The plug-ins we use are: EMF [7] and Tefkat [2].

3.2.1 Eclipse Modeling Framework (EMF)
EMF is a Java framework for building applications based on simple class models [7]. It allows developers to turn the models into customizable Java code. EMF plays a

very important role in our transformation tool architecture as it is used to construct the metamodels and instances that are used as input to the Tefkat Transformation Engine.

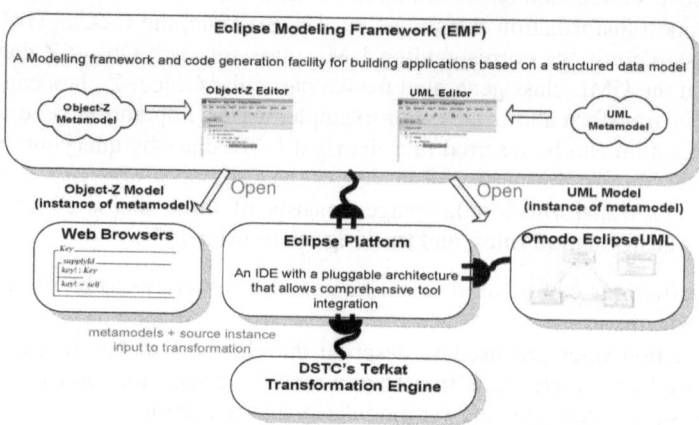

Fig. 6. Tool Architecture used in this work

The metamodels for Object-Z and UML defined using EMF are Ecore models (e.g. the Object-Z metamodel Object-Z.ecore, the UML metamodel UML2.ecore[2], and the Tracking metamodel OZToUMLTracking.ecore), which then allows the automatic generation of an editor to create Object-Z (instance) models, stored in XMI format, to be transformed into UML. The Ecore language used to create models in EMF is a core subset of the OMG's MOF [16] that provides a common basis of models in the MDA. However, to avoid any confusion, the MOF-like core meta model in EMF is called Ecore. In fact, EMF can generate an Ecore model from Rational Rose (.mdl file), which is the approach taken in this paper to construct the Object-Z metamodel. Alternatively, we could create an Ecore model using an EMF supporting tool such as Omondo EclipseUML [6] which is a visual modelling tool that allows users to visually create and edit both UML and Ecore models, or from XML schema and other inputs.

Figure 7 shows the editor generated by EMF from the Object-Z metamodel presented in Section 2.1. When we click on the right button at the top of the tree editor, we can see all the model elements definable at the Object-Z specification level such as classes and data types. To create an Object-Z class instance, we simply choose Class from the list and fill in properties such as name in the property window. Once an instance of an Object-Z class is created, we can define attributes and operations using the editor. Once an Object-Z instance specification is created, EMF will generate an output in XMI that is an input to the Tefkat transformation engine. The example Object-Z model created using the editor in Figure 7 specifies a key system containing four classes resulting in the KeySystem.oz file. To view the Object-Z model in its concrete syntax (see Figure 8), we need to map the abstract syntax to a concrete syntax such as [21]. This work is under investigation.

---

[2] In this work, we use the UML2.ecore file supplied by the UML2 project [22].

3.2.2 Tefkat Transformation Engine

Tefkat is DSTC's prototype model transformation engine [2]. It is built on EMF, in that it works with Ecore models and corresponding XMI instances, and implements the DSTC's transformation language [3].

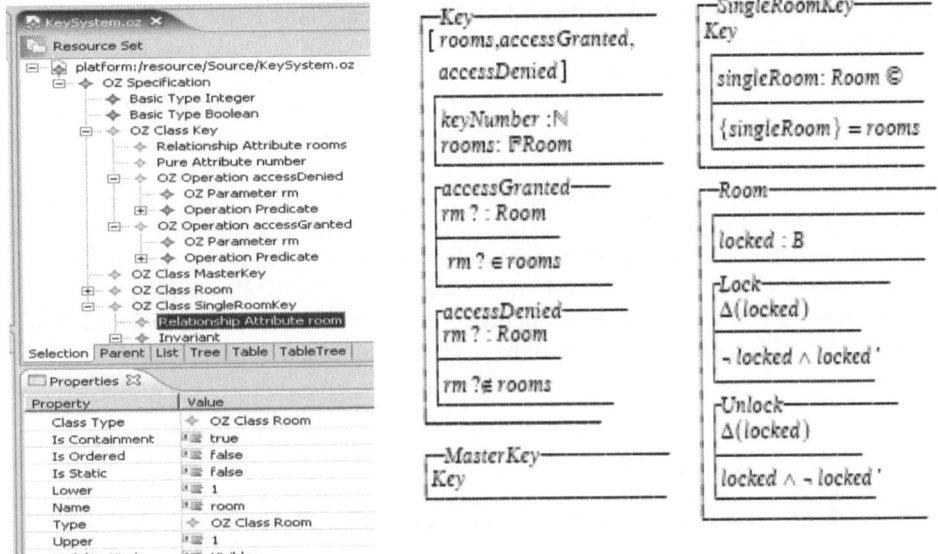

Fig. 7. Object-Z editor generated by EMF   **Fig. 8.** Object-Z model in its concrete syntax

The user creates a Tefkat project containing the required Object-Z and UML metamodels, Object-Z source model, transformation rules file and possibly a tracking model. Tefkat includes a configuration editor which is used to create a configuration file specifying the locations of the required files. The transformation is set to run automatically each time the project is updated, creating a target UML instance. Tefkat also provides a textual editor for transformation rule files (.qvt), which highlights syntax and dynamically reports any syntax errors in the Eclipse Problems View.

4   Transformation Rules from Object-Z to UML

In this section, we describe how to convert Object-Z constructs to UML constructs using the DSTC transformation language and its Transformation Engine. The mapping is based on the metamodels of Object-Z and UML, and the tracking model defined in previous sections. Currently the DSTC's transformation language does not support bi-directional transformations [3]. For this reason, in this paper we define a set of transformation rules from Object-Z to UML, but the rules will be readily redefined when the transformation language supports the bi-directional feature.

4.1 Transformation Rule for Object-Z Classes

Semantically, an Object-Z class represents a set of objects of that class. This semantics is the same as that of a UML class, so we convert an Object-Z class to a UML class. The OZClass2UMLClass rule implements this mapping by creating a UML class for each OZClass. Line 5 declares the rule name and variables to be used in the rule. Line 7 introduces a WHERE...LINKS statement. This is the way in which the tracking relationship created in the OZSpec2UMLModel rule presented in Section 3.1 can be queried in order to find the correct UML model into which to place the created UML Class. Lines 7 and 8 effectively find the Object-Z specification that is containing the source Object-Z class (ozc.owner), and then look up and store the corresponding UML model (umlm) for use later in the rule. Line 9 creates the target UML class, while Line 10 introduces a SET statement, which is used to set the attributes and references of created target elements. In this case, the UML class name is set to the same name as the Object-Z class, and the UML class is added to the UML model. Note that umlc is being added to the ownedMember collection of the UML model, umlm[3]. Line 11 preserves the tracking relationship, also storing the corresponding Object-Z specification and UML model as these will be used in other rules.

```
5    RULE     OZClass2UMLClass(ozs, umlm, ozc, umlc)
6    FORALL   OZClass ozc
7    WHERE    OZSpecToUMLModel LINKS ozspec = ozs, umlmodel = umlm
8    AND      ozc.owner = ozs
9    MAKE     Class umlc
10   SET      umlc.name = ozc.name, umlm.ownedMember = umlc
11   LINKING  OZClassToUMLClass WITH ozclass = ozc, umlclass = umlc,
                  ozspec = ozs, umlmodel = umlm;
```

4.2 Transformation Rule for Object-Z Operations

Each Object-Z operation is converted to a UML operation. The OZOperation2UMLOperation rule implements this mapping. This rule has a similar structure to OZClass2UMLClass, except that a UML Operation is created for each OZOperation and placed inside the correct UML Class (Line 19). However, the rule is different in that it demonstrates the use of two patterns in Lines 14 and 16. Many rules presented in this paper need to find the corresponding UML class for an Object-Z class. The lookupClass pattern on Line 21 simplifies this by defining the common WHERE...LINKS statement as a pattern so that it can be used in many rules. Also the pattern convertVisibility in Line 24 matches visibilities in both languages and it is used in the rules presented in this paper[4].

```
12   RULE     OZOperation2UMLOperation(ozc, umlc, ozo, umlo, vis)
13   FORALL   OZOperation ozo
14   WHERE    lookupClass(ozc, umlc)
15   AND      ozo.owner = ozc
16   AND      convertVisibility(ozo.visibilityKind, vis)
17   MAKE     Operation umlo
18   SET      umlo.name = ozo.name, umlc.ownedOperation = umlo,
                  umlo.visibility = vis
```

---

[3] In the DSTC transformation language the syntax is the same for setting the value of a single-valued attribute or reference as it is for adding an element to a collection.

[4] Due to the page limits, we omit details of some pattern definitions.

```
19    LINKING OZOpToUMLOp WITH ozop = ozo, umlop = umlo,
              ozclass = ozc, umlclass = umlc;
20    // look up correct UML classes
21    PATTERN lookupClass(ozc, umlc)
22    WHERE   OZClassToUMLClass LINKS ozclass = ozc, umlclass = umlc;
23    // convert Object-Z visibility kinds into UML visibility kinds
24    PATTERN convertVisibility(ozvis, umlvis) …;
```

4.3 Transformation Rule for Object-Z Operation Parameters

Prior to describing the transformation of parameters, we explain how to convert data types. While types of attributes and parameters in UML are a language-dependent specification of the implementation types, those in Object-Z are language-independent specification types. For this reason, we define a rule to match only those types that are common in both languages such as Integer and Boolean (see the rule OZBasicType2UMLPrimitiveType) and we do not define a specific rule for other data types in Object-Z.

```
25    RULE    OZBasicType2UMLPrimitiveType(bt, pt, ozs, umlm)
26    FORALL  BasicType bt
27    WHERE   OZSpecToUMLModel LINKS ozspec = ozs, umlmodel = umlm
28    AND     bt.owner = ozs
29    MAKE    PrimitiveType pt
30    SET     pt.name = bt.name, umlm.ownedMember = pt
31    LINKING BasicTypeToPrimitiveType WITH basic = bt, prim = pt;
```

Due to the differences in data types in both languages, we apply different rules for parameters with different types. OZBasicParam2UMLParam is the rule to map the parameters of Object-Z operations with basic types to UML operation parameters with primitive types. Again, a WHERE...LINKS statement is used to find the correct UML operation for the created UML parameter in Line 34 and 35; to check the type (using the pattern isBasicType in Line 36); to find the correct matching UML type (using the pattern lookupBasicType in Line 37); to find the correct matching UML parameter kind (using the pattern convertParamKind in Line 38). Parameters in both languages have several equivalent properties that are mapped including name, isOrdered and upper and lower multiplicity values. The LiteralInteger and LiteralUnlimitedNatural classes must be used to set the upper and lower multiplicity values of the UML parameter because they are the types of the lowerValue and upperValue references respectively in the MultiplicityElement class of the UML2 metamodel (UML2.ecore).

```
32    RULE    OZBasicParam2UMLParam(ozo, umlo, ozp, umlp, int, nat,
              pkind, umltype)
33    FORALL  OZParameter ozp
34    WHERE   OZOpToUMLOp LINKS ozop = ozo, umlop = umlo
35    AND     ozp.owner = ozo
36    AND     isBasicType(ozp.type)
37    AND     lookupBasicType(ozp.type, umltype)
38    AND     convertParamKind(ozp.parameterKind, pkind)
39    MAKE    Parameter umlp, LiteralInteger int,
              LiteralUnlimitedNatural nat
40    SET     umlp.name = ozp.name, umlp.isOrdered = ozp.isOrdered,
              umlo.ownedParameter = umlp, int.value = ozp.lower,
              nat.value = ozp.upper, umlp.lowerValue = int,
              umlp.upperValue = nat, umlp.direction = pkind,
              umlp.type = umltype;
41    // convert Object-Z parameter kinds into UML parameter kinds
42    PATTERN convertParamKind(ozparkind, umlparkind)…;
43    // match OZ basic types with UML primitive types
44    PATTERN lookupBasicType(oztype, umltype)
```

```
45    WHERE    BasicTypeToPrimitiveType LINKS basic = oztype,
               prim = umltype;
46    // check Basic types
47    PATTERN isBasicType(oztype)
48    FORALL  BasicType oztype;
```

Rules for transforming parameters with other types are very similar to this rule except for the mapping of types. We omit these rules due to the page limits.

4.4 Transformation Rule for Object-Z Pure Attributes

Object-Z pure attributes (attributes with types that are not class types) are converted to a UML attribute. The OZBasicPureAttr2UMLProperty rule implements the mapping of pure attributes with basic types, setting the name, isStatic, isOrdered, lowerValue and upperValue properties of the created UML Property appropriately. Again a WHERE...LINKS statement is used to find the corresponding UML class for an Object-Z class in Line 51; to check the type in Line 52; to find the correct matching UML type in Line54; to find the correct matching UML visibility kind in Line 55.

```
49    RULE     OZBasicPureAttr2UMLProperty(ozc, umlc, oza, umlp, int,
               nat, vis, umltype)
50    FORALL   PureAttribute oza
51    WHERE    lookupClass(ozc, umlc)
52    AND      isBasicType(oza.type)
53    AND      oza.owner = ozc
54    AND      lookupBasicType(oza.type, umltype)
55    AND      convertVisibility(oza.visibilityKind, vis)
56    MAKE     Property umlp, LiteralInteger int,
               LiteralUnlimitedNatural nat
57    SET      umlp.name = oza.name, umlc.ownedAttribute = umlp,
               int.value = oza.lower, nat.value = oza.upper,
               umlp.isStatic  =  oza.isStatic,  umlp.isOrdered  =
               oza.isOrdered, umlp.lowerValue = int, umlp.upperValue =
               nat, umlp.visibility = vis, umlp.type = umltype;
```

4.5 Transformation Rule for Relationship Attributes

Object-Z RelationshipAttribute defines relationships between objects. This semantics of relationship attributes in Object-Z maps to that of associations in UML. The OZConRelAttr2UMLAssoc rule implements the mapping of relationship attributes with a containment property to UML Associations. Lines 60 - 62 are required to find the corresponding UML classes for the Object-Z class owning the relationship attribute and also the Object-Z class that is the type of that attribute (oza.classType). Line 63 matches the visibility, and Lines 64 and 65 match the containment property. An Association and two Properties are created as a result of the transformation rule. When an Object-Z class has a relationship attribute, the attribute is navigable by the owning class. In this rule, the nav property represents the navigable end of the association, while the non property is the non-navigable end. The SET statement in this rule accomplishes the following:

1. The name of the navigable end of the association is set to be the same as the name of the relationship attribute.
2. The type of the navigable end is set to the UML class corresponding to the Object-Z class that is the type of the relationship attribute.
3. The isStatic, isOrdered, lowerValue and upperValue properties of the navigable end are matched with the corresponding properties of the relationship attribute.

4. The type of the non-navigable end is set to the UML class corresponding to the Object-Z class that is the owner of the relationship attribute.
5. The navigable end property is added to the attributes of the UML class corresponding to the Object-Z class that is the owner of the relationship attribute. This is done because in the UML2.0 [19], a navigable end property of an association is also an attribute of the associated UML class.
6. In UML an Association has at least two memberEnd properties representing the ends of the association, and non-navigable ends are owned by the Association. This is accomplished at the end of Line 67 as both association ends are added to the memberEnd collection of the Association and the ownedEnd is set to the non-navigable end.
7. Finally, the new association is placed in the UML model by adding it to the ownedMember collection.

```
58   RULE    OZContRelAttr2UMLAssoc(ozc, umlc, umlm, oza, umla, non,
             nav, umlt, int, nat, vis, agg)
59   FORALL  RelationshipAttribute oza
60   WHERE   lookupClass(ozc, umlc)
61   AND     oza.owner = ozc
62   AND     OZClassToUMLClass LINKS ozclass = oza.classType,
             umlclass = umlt, umlmodel = umlm
63   AND     convertVisibility(oza.visibilityKind, vis)
64   AND     isContainment(oza)
65   AND     convertContainment(oza.isContainment, agg)
66   MAKE    Association umla, Property non, Property nav,
             LiteralInteger int1, LiteralUnlimitedNatural nat1,
             LiteralInteger int2, LiteralUnlimitedNatural nat2
67   SET     nav.name = oza.name, nav.type = umlt,
             nav.isStatic    =    oza.isStatic,    nav.isOrdered   =
             oza.isOrdered,   int1.value  =  oza.lower,  nat1.value  =
             oza.upper, nav.lowerValue = int1, nav.upperValue = nat1,
             nav.visibility = vis, non.aggregation = agg,
             int2.value = 0, nat2.value = 1,
             non.lowerValue = int2, non.upperValue = nat2,
             non.type = umlc, umlc.ownedAttribute = nav,
             umla.ownedEnd = non, umla.memberEnd = nav,
             umla.memberEnd = non, umlm.ownedMember = umla;
68   // check containment property
69   PATTERN isContainment(ozattr)
70   WHERE   ozattr.isContainment = true;
```

The rule for mapping relationship attributes with a non-containment property is basically the same as this rule except for the mapping of the containment property.

4.6 Transformation Rule for Inheritance

In Object-Z, inheritance is a mechanism to incrementally extend an Object-Z model. Sub-classes inherit all features defined in its super classes. We convert Object-Z inheritance to generalization in UML. The OZInherit2UMLGeneral rule achieves this mapping. For each pair of Object-Z classes where one is a superclass of the other, a UML Generalization is created. The lookupClass pattern is used twice to find the corresponding UML classes in Line 73 and 74. In the UML2.0 [19], a Generalization has specific and general references to store the subclass and superclass respectively, and the Generalization itself is owned by the subclass. These values are set appropriately in the SET statement. Since inheritance in Object-Z does not support subtyping automatically, we leave the isSubstitutable property of the generalization undefined.

```
71  RULE    OZInherit2UMLGeneral(ozc, umlc, ozg, umlg, umlgen)
72  FORALL  OZClass ozc, OZClass ozg
73  WHERE   lookupClass(ozc, umlc)
74  AND     lookupClass(ozg, umlg)
75  AND     ozc.general = ozg
76  MAKE    Generalization umlgen
77  SET     umlgen.specific = umlc, umlc.generalization = umlgen,
            umlc.generalization.general = umlg;
```

4.7 Transformation Example

Figure 9 shows the target UML model generated from the example source Object-Z model presented in Figure 8 according to the transformation rules defined in this section. The actual output (KeySystem.uml2) is in XMI but we visualize it using a UML class diagram.

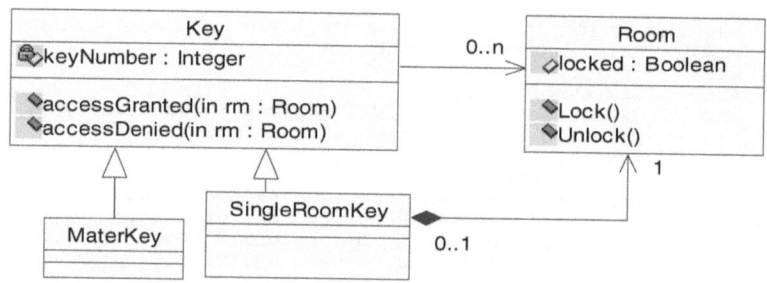

Fig. 9. A target UML model

5 Conclusion and Future Work

This paper has presented an MDA approach to integrating formal and informal modeling languages within the Eclipse tool integration environment. Using the MDA model transformation approach, we define a metamodel of Object-Z using the MOF. Given the metamodels of UML and Object-Z, we then define transformation rules using a transformation language, the DSTC's Transformation Language.

The metamodel-based MDA transformation framework allows us to define transformation rules precisely and explicitly, which is essential to be able to know the semantic basis of the transformation, to check the completeness and consistency of the transformation, and to provide the traceability of notations. It also allows us to have a reusable transformation that can be applied to any models in the two languages. Finally we achieve an automatic transformation using existing tools supporting MDA. In addition, the integrated approach with formal and informal techniques incorporates an effective V&V mechanism into the MDA and it supports model evolution that is concerned with correcting errors in the model.

The transformation rules presented in this paper are from Object-Z to UML. When the transformation language supports multi-directional transformation, the rules will be refined accordingly to support the bi-directional transformation between the two languages. Mapping the abstract syntax of Object-Z to its concrete syntax and converting Object-Z expressions to OCL expressions are under investigation.

Acknowledgements

This research is funded by an Australian Research Council Discovery Grant: DP0451830. We wish to thank Keith Duddy, Michael Lawley and other DSTC staff for their assistance with their transformation language [3] and their Tefkat tool [2].

References

1. S. Dascalu and P. Hitchcock, An approach to integrating semi-formal and formal notations in software specification, ACM symposium on Applied computing, pp. 1014–1020, 2002.
2. DSTC, Tefkat: The EMF transformation engine. http://www.dstc.edu.au/Research/Projects/Pegamento/tefkat/index.html
3. DSTC Transformation Language, MOF query/views/ transformations: Second revised submission, 2004. http://www.omg.org/docs/ad/04-01-06.pdf
4. R. Duke and G. Rose, Formal Object-Oriented Specification Using Object-Z, Macmillan, 2000.
5. Eclipse Foundation. http://www.eclipse.org/
6. EclipseUML, Omondo http://www.eclipsedownload.com/
7. EMF, The eclipse modeling framework. http://download.eclipse.org/tools/emf/scripts/docs.php?doc=references/overview/EMF.html
8. R. France, J. Wu, M. M. Larrondo-Petrie, and J.-M. Bruel, A Tale of Two Case Studies: Using Integrated Methods to Support Rigorous Requirements Specification, Proc. BCS FACS Methods Integration Workshop, 1996.
9. S-K. Kim and D. Carrington, A Formal Mapping between UML Models and Object-Z Specifications, ZB2000, LNCS 1878, pp. 2-21, 2000.
10. S-K. Kim, A Metamodel-based Approach to Integrate Object-Oriented Graphical and Formal Specification Techniques, PhD Thesis, ITEE, The University of Queensland, 2002.
11. R. Laleau and F. Polack. Coming and going from UML to B: A proposal to support traceability in rigorous IS development. Proc. ZB'2002, LNCS 2272, pp. 517–534, 2002.
12. K. Lano, D. Clark and K. Androutsopoulos, UML to B: Formal Verification of Object-Oriented Models, Proc. IFM'04, LNCS 2999, pp. 187 - 206 2004.
13. J. Lilius and I. P. Paltor, Formalizing UML state machines for model checking, Proc. UML'99, LNCS 1723, pp. 430-445, 1999.
14. W. McUmber and B. Cheng. A General Framework for Formalizing UML with Formal Languages. in IEEE Conference on Software Engineering, pp. 433–442, 2001.
15. M. Y. Ng and M. Butler. Tool Support for Visualizing CSP in UML. Proc. ICFEM'02, LNCS 2495, pp. 287–298. 2002.
16. OMG, Meta Object Facility (MOF),1.4, OMG Document ad/02-04-03, 2002.
17. OMG, MOF 2.0 Query/Views/Transformations RFP, OMG Document ad/02-04-10, 2002.
18. OMG, MDA Guide Version 1.0.1, 2003. http://www.omg.org/docs/omg/03-06-01.pdf
19. OMG, UML 2.0 Superstructure Specification, OMG Document ptc/03-08-02. http://www.omg.org/docs/ptc/03-08-02.pdf, 2003.
20. S. Sendall and W. Kozaczynski, Model Transformation: The Heart and Soul of Model-Driven Software Development, IEEE Software, pp. 42-45, Sep/Oct 2003.

21. J. Sun, J. S. Dong, J. Liu, and H. Wang. Z family on the web with their UML photos. http://nt-appn.comp.nus.edu.sg/fm/zml/
22. UML2, The eclipse UML2 project. http://www.eclipse.org/uml2/
23. R. Wieringa, E. Dubois, and S. Huyts. Integrating Semi-formal and Formal Requirements. in Advanced Information Systems Engineering, LNCS 1250, pp. 19-32, 1997.

Model-Checking of Specifications Integrating Processes, Data and Time*

Jochen Hoenicke[1] and Patrick Maier[2]

[1] Universität Oldenburg, Department für Informatik, 26111 Oldenburg, Germany
hoenicke@informatik.uni-oldenburg.de
[2] MPI für Informatik, Programming Logics Group, 66123 Saarbrücken, Germany
maier@mpi-sb.mpg.de

Abstract. We present a new model-checking technique for CSP-OZ-DC, a combination of CSP, Object-Z and Duration Calculus, that allows reasoning about systems exhibiting communication, data and real-time aspects. As intermediate layer we will use a new kind of timed automata that preserve events and data variables of the specification. These automata have a simple operational semantics that is amenable to verification by a constraint-based abstraction-refinement model checker. By means of a case study, a simple elevator parameterised by the number of floors, we show that this approach admits model-checking parameterised and infinite state real-time systems.

1 Introduction

Complex computing systems exhibit various behavioural aspects such as communication between components, state transformation within components, and real-time constraints on the communications and state changes. This observation has led research to combine and semantically integrate specification techniques. In [13] and [14] we introduced CSP-OZ-DC, the combination of three well-investigated specification techniques: CSP [11], Object-Z [21, 22] and Duration Calculus [26, 25]. Due to its expressiveness, however, CSP-OZ-DC is not suited for automated verification.

In this paper, we present an approach to automatically verify CSP-OZ-DC specifications by model-checking. To this end, the specifications are translated to *transition constraint systems* (transition systems whose transitions are labelled by constraints expressed in first-order logic), which are model-checked using constraint-based symbolic techniques [5] plus predicate abstraction [9] with counterexample-driven abstraction refinement [3, 10, 4].

The translation from CSP-OZ-DC to transition constraint systems is via a novel class of timed automata, called *phase event automata*, providing an essential prerequisite for model-checking: an operational semantics for CSP-OZ-DC specifications. These automata describe the behaviour of instantaneous events that stem from the CSP

---

* This work was partly supported by the German Research Council (DFG) as part of the Transregional Collaborative Research Center "Automatic Verification and Analysis of Complex Systems" (SFB/TR 14 AVACS). See www.avacs.org for more information.

world, states with durations that model the Object-Z state variables, and clocks used for real-time constraints defined by Duration Calculus. The translation to phase event automata is compositional, i. e., the translation of a CSP-OZ-DC specification is a parallel product of several automata, each corresponding to one part of the specification. Thus, our phase event automata provide the first compositional operational semantics for (a subclass of) CSP-OZ-DC.

The translation from phase event automata to transition constraint systems follows an "old-fashioned recipe for real-time" [1, 15] by splitting continuous runs into discrete sequences of intervals. Moreover, the translation is compositional with respect to parallel products. All in all, the process of translating CSP-OZ-DC specifications via phase event automata into transition constraint systems and model-checking these systems can be automated completely. In all steps the structure of the original specification is preserved, so that counterexamples found by the model-checker can easily be translated back to the CSP-OZ-DC world.

For being able to model-check, we have to pay a price. We have to restrict the CSP-OZ-DC specifications such that the CSP part is finite state, the constraints in the OZ part fall into a decidable class, and the DC part consists of so-called *counterexample formulae* only. Nevertheless, this subclass of CSP-OZ-DC still admits non-trivial specifications, as we show in a small case study.

The paper is organised as follows. Section 2 introduces the main constructs of CSP-OZ-DC via a case study. Section 3 describes phase event automata. Section 4 sketches the translation from CSP-OZ-DC to phase event automata. In section 5 we will introduce transition constraint systems and give the translation from automata to transition constraints. Section 6 presents the results of applying our approach to the case study and verifying an invariant. Finally, we conclude with section 7.

2   Case Study

In this section we introduce the combined formalism CSP-OZ-DC [13] and the case study of a controller for an elevator, see Fig. 1. The case study is kept very simple and only contains the core of the controller. It is separated into three aspects, each of which is specified in one of the three languages. The control and communication aspects are specified with CSP and encompass the interaction with the environment abstracting from concrete values transmitted. Data aspects specified with Object-Z involve the calculation of current and goal floor. The real-time behaviour is specified with Duration Calculus.

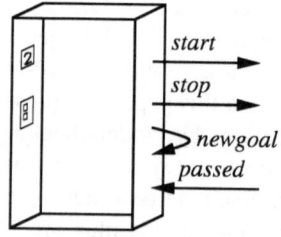

Fig. 1. Elevator

Communication Aspects. are described with CSP [11], a language for communicating sequential processes. It is used to define the admissible sequences of events:

$$\text{main} \stackrel{c}{=} newgoal \rightarrow start \rightarrow Drive$$
$$Drive \stackrel{c}{=} (passed \rightarrow Drive) \ \square \ (stop \rightarrow \text{main})$$

The elevator has a cyclic behaviour switching between the processes `main` and *Drive*. The keyword `main` names the process that will be entered initially. The elevator first chooses a new goal floor, then it starts the engine and switches to the *Drive* process. It can then either pass a floor and keep on driving, or stop and return to the `main` process. The symbol □ denotes an external choice, which means that the environment determines which of these event will be taken. In this case it is determined by the interaction with the Object-Z and Duration Calculus part of the specification.

Data Aspects. The representation of data state and the algorithmic part of the elevator is described with Object-Z. The floors are modelled by integers ranging from the constants *Min* to *Max*. No concrete values for the boundaries are given but the only requirement is $Min < Max$. These bounds can be seen as parameters of the elevator. In Z these constants are declared in a so called axiomatic definition. The internal state of the elevator is given by the following state schema. It contains two variables for *current* and *goal* floor and a variable *dir*, which describes the direction the elevator is heading to (1 for upwards, -1 for downwards). The initial values for the variables are given by a schema with the special name `Init`.

$$
\begin{array}{|l}
Min, Max : \mathbb{Z} \\
\hline
Min < Max
\end{array}
\qquad
\begin{array}{|l}
current, goal : \mathbb{Z} \\
dir : \{-1, 0, 1\}
\end{array}
\qquad
\begin{array}{|l}
\underline{\;Init} \\
goal = current = Min \\
dir = 0
\end{array}
$$

In CSP-OZ-DC the link between events and states is established by communication schemas. By naming convenience, the following schema describes the change that the *passed* event induces:

$$
\begin{array}{|l}
\underline{\;com\_passed} \\
\Delta(current) \\
\hline
current' = current + dir
\end{array}
$$

The Δ list on the first line mentions the variables that are changed by the operation. In this case only *current* is changed by adding the value of *dir*, which increases or decreases the floor counter depending on the value of *dir*.

For simplicity the set of requested floors and the algorithm to choose the next goal floor is abstracted from. Instead the goal floor is chosen non-deterministically from the range of all floors except the current one. When the elevator starts, it will choose the direction in accordance with the position of the new goal floor. Finally the elevator is not allowed to stop before reaching the goal floor. This can be stated by a communication schema with an empty delta list. These schemas are given Fig. 2.

Real-Time Aspects. are described with Duration Calculus (DC). This is a logic that allows specifying real-time behaviours. Unfortunately the full logic of Duration Calculus is too powerful to be checked automatically. Therefore only a restricted class of formulae, called *counterexample formulae*, may be used in CSP-OZ-DC specifications[1].

---

[1] In [13] we used implementables for Duration Calculus but that are just abbreviations for certain counterexample formulae.

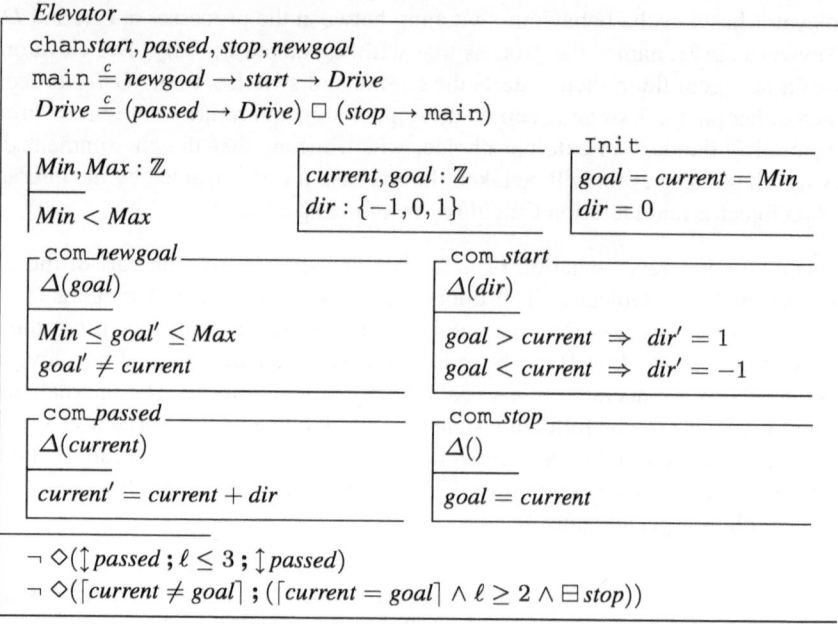

Fig. 2. Elevator specification

A counterexample formula describes a specific undesired behaviour in form of a linear trace. This formula is negated as it is a forbidden behaviour. Restricting ourself to these types of formulae makes over-specification less likely: It is easy to see that a certain behaviour should not occur and this is all the formula states.

The general shape of a counterexample formula is as follows:

$$\neg \Diamond(phase_1 ; \ldots ; phase_n)$$

Here the formula $\Diamond F$ states that there is a subinterval (DC formulae describe the shape of trajectories in a given time interval) where F holds. This interval is then chopped up into n subintervals (this is denoted by ;) each satisfying $phase_i$, which must be a simple formula restricting the current state of the system, the events that may or may not occur during this interval, and either the minimum or the maximum length of this interval. The whole formula is negated as it is a counterexample.

To restrict the state of a variable the standard Duration Calculus notation is used: For example, $\lceil dir = 1 \rceil$ holds for intervals satisfying $dir = 1$. For each event a new Boolean variable is introduced that changes every time the event occurs. The formula $\updownarrow ev$ holds for a point interval, at which the Boolean variable ev changes[2]. The formula $\boxminus ev$ states that an event does not occur during a non-empty interval[3].

In the case study real-time properties are used to ensure that the elevator stops when it reaches the goal floor before passing the next floor. To achieve this, a minimum time

---

[2] It is defined as $\updownarrow ev = \uparrow ev \vee \downarrow ev$ with the operators $\uparrow, \downarrow$ as defined in [25]
[3] It is defined as $\boxminus ev := \lceil ev \rceil \vee \lceil \neg ev \rceil$

of three seconds between two adjacent *passed* events is demanded. This is expressed by a negated counterexample where two *passed* events occur after each other, with an interval in between that has a duration (denoted by ℓ) of at most three seconds.

$$\neg \Diamond (\updownarrow passed \,;\, \ell \leq 3 \,;\, \updownarrow passed)$$

Furthermore it is claimed that the elevator stops within two seconds. The following formula states the impossibility of the stop event not occurring even after the goal has been reached for more than two seconds.

$$\neg \Diamond (\lceil current \neq goal \rceil \,;\, (\lceil current = goal \rceil \wedge \ell \geq 2 \wedge \boxminus stop))$$

The complete specification of the elevator is shown in Fig. 2. The specification is framed and given a name. It starts with the interface specification that lists the names of the communication events. The interface is followed by the CSP and Object-Z part. Then follows the DC part, which is separated by a short horizontal line.

The property to verify for this specification is $Min \leq current \leq Max$. Note that it is not obvious that this property holds at all, as there is no such check in com_*passed*. It only holds because of the interaction between the CSP process, the data transformation and the real-time properties of the specification. As a matter of fact, every single line of the above specification contributes to this property. In the remainder of this paper this combined specification is translated into a certain kind of timed automata and the invariant property above is proven.

3   Phase Event Automata

In this section a new type of timed automata is introduced, so called *phase event automata*, that can characterise the behaviour of state- and event-based systems. These automata serve as a bridge between CSP-OZ-DC described in section 2 and transition constraint systems that will be described in the next section. They possess the notion of events, variables and clocks.

Fig. 3 shows an example of a phase event automaton. This automaton corresponds to the second Duration Calculus formula of the case study specifying that the automaton should stop when the destination floor has been reached. Initially it can be either in

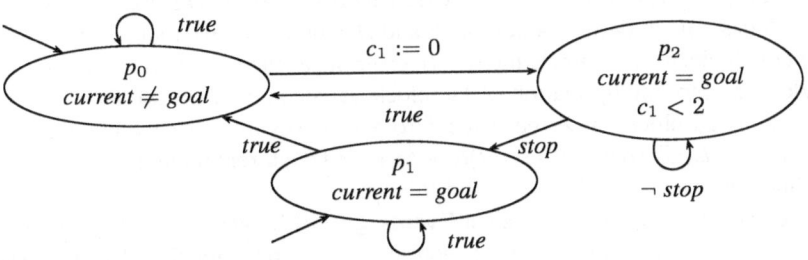

Fig. 3. A phase event automaton

phase p_0 (if *current* $\neq$ *goal* holds) or in phase p_1 (otherwise). There are no restrictions of what may happen next. As soon as a change from *current* $\neq$ *goal* to *current* = *goal* occurs, the automaton switches to phase p_2, resets the clock c_1 to zero and makes sure that the elevator will stop within two seconds. Due to the invariant $c_1 < 2$, phase p_2 must be left in time. One possibility is to back to p_1, which can only be done if *current* $\neq$ *goal* holds. The other possibility is by a *stop* event.

3.1   Notation

The states of the systems are described by first-order formulae. We work in many-sorted first-order logic with equality denoted by $\approx$. The set of variables is denoted by $\hat{V}$. With each variable $x \in \hat{V}$ a sort $type(x)$ is associated, which restricts the possible values for x. The logic uses typed functions and predicate symbols. From this terms and formulae are defined inductively. By $\mathcal{L}$, we denote the class of first-order formulae that are allowed in the specification. $\mathcal{L}(V)$ denotes the set of those formulae in $\mathcal{L}$ that only refer to variables in $V \subseteq \hat{V}$. To be able to formulate the translations in Section 5, we demand that $\mathcal{L}$ contains at least the class of quantifier-free formulae involving only Booleans variables and linear arithmetic expressions over the reals. For the case study, $\mathcal{L}$ should moreover contain linear arithmetic expressions over the integers.

The set of variables $\hat{V}$ is partitioned into two disjoint sets V and V' such that V' is a copy of V. We call the variables in V' *primed*, those in V *unprimed*. The unprimed variables refer to the state before a transition while the primed variables refer to the post state.

Semantically, variables are interpreted by valuations and all syntactic symbols except variables by a fixed algebra. Given a subset $V \subseteq \hat{V}$, a V-valuation α is a mapping that assigns a value in $U_{type(x)}$ to each variable $x \in V$, the domain of that type. Sometimes, we denote a V-valuation α by the expression $\{x \mapsto \alpha(x) \mid x \in V\}$. The set of all V-valuations is denoted by $Val(V)$. Given two subsets $V_1, V_2 \subseteq \hat{V}$ and a V_1-valuation α, we denote the restriction of α to a $(V_1 \cap V_2)$-valuation by $\alpha|_{V_2}$. Given two subsets $V_1, V_2 \subseteq \hat{V}$, a V_1-valuation α_1 and a V_2-valuation α_2 with $\alpha_1|_{V_2} = \alpha_2|_{V_1}$, we write $\alpha_1 \cup \alpha_2$ to denote the $(V_1 \cup V_2)$-valuation α with $\alpha|_{V_1} = \alpha_1$ and $\alpha|_{V_2} = \alpha_2$. Given a subset $V \subseteq V$ and a V-valuation α, we write α' to denote the V'-valuation with $\alpha'(x') = \alpha(x)$ for all $x \in V$. Given a V-valuation α and a formula φ with $free(\varphi) \subseteq V$, we write $\alpha \models \varphi$ to denote that α satisfies φ. We write $\models \varphi$ to denote that φ is valid.

To introduce the timed automata notion of clocks, we distinguish a sort Time, interpreted by the (non-negative) real numbers. Let **Clocks** $\subseteq V$ be a set of time variables, i.e., $type(c) =$ Time for all $c \in$ **Clocks**, which we call *clocks*. Let $C \subseteq$ **Clocks** be a set of clocks. Given two C-valuations α and β, a non-negative real number $t \geq 0$ and a subset of clocks $X \subseteq C$, we define $\alpha + \beta$, $\alpha + t$, $t\alpha$ as the C-valuations that are obtained by addition resp. multiplication of the clock values and $\alpha[X := 0]$ as the C-valuation that assigns all clocks in X the value zero and leaves all other unchanged. We call a formula $\varphi \in \mathcal{L}(C)$ *convex* if $(1 - t)\alpha + t\beta \models \varphi$ for all real numbers $0 \leq t \leq 1$ and all C-valuations α and β with $\alpha \models \varphi$ and $\beta \models \varphi$.

The *events* are modelled by a set **Events** $\subseteq V$ of boolean variables, i.e., $type(e) =$ Bool for all $e \in$ **Events**. However, here events are not modelled by changes of this variable, but the variable is true if the event occurs, false otherwise. Let $E \subseteq$ **Events** be a set of events. By χ_E, we denote the characteristic function of E, i.e., the mapping from **Events** to $U_{\text{Bool}} = \mathbb{B}$ such that for all $e \in$ **Events**, $\chi_E(e) = true$ iff $e \in E$. Note that χ_E is an **Events**-valuation.

3.2   Formal Definition

A *phase event automaton (PEA)* is defined as a tuple $\mathcal{A} = (P, V, A, C, E, s, I, P_0)$ of the following components:

- P is a set of states (phases).
- $V \subseteq \mathcal{V} \setminus (\textbf{Events} \cup \textbf{Clocks})$ is a finite set of (state) variables.
- $A \subseteq$ **Events** is a finite set of events.
- $C \subseteq$ **Clocks** is a finite set of clocks.
- $E \subseteq P \times \mathcal{L}(V \cup V' \cup A \cup C) \times \mathbb{P}(C) \times P$ is a set of edges. An edge $(p_1, g, X, p_2) \in E$ represents a transition from phase p_1 to phase p_2 under guard g. All clocks in X are reset when this transition is taken.
- $s : P \rightarrow \mathcal{L}(V)$ is a labelling function that associates each phase with a predicate that must hold during this phase.
- $I : P \rightarrow \mathcal{L}(C)$ is a function assigning to each phase a clock invariant that has to hold while the automaton is in this phase.
- $P_0 \subseteq P$ is a set of possible initial phases.

We impose the extra requirements that

- for all $p \in P$, the clock invariant $I(p)$ is convex, and
- for all $p \in P$, E contains a stuttering edge $(p, \neg e_1 \wedge \ldots \wedge \neg e_k \wedge v_1 = v'_1 \wedge \ldots \wedge v_j = v'_j, \varnothing, p)$ for some particular $\{e_1, \ldots, e_k\} \subseteq A, \{v_1, \ldots, v_j\} \subseteq V$.

To make the intuitive meaning of phase event automata precise we define the traces of an automaton as sequences of variable and clock evaluations, time delays and communicated events. Let $\mathcal{A} = (P, V, A, C, E, s, I, P_0)$ be a PEA. A *state* of $\mathcal{A}$ is a triple (p, β, γ) of a phase $p \in P$, a V-valuation β and a C-valuation γ. A *duration* is a positive real number. A *run* of $\mathcal{A}$ is an infinite sequence

$$\langle (p_0, \beta_0, \gamma_0), t_0, Y_0, (p_1, \beta_1, \gamma_1), t_1, Y_1, \ldots \rangle$$

alternating states (p_i, β_i, γ_i), durations t_i and sets of events $Y_i \subseteq A$ such that the following holds:

1. $p_0 \in P_0$.
2. For all $c \in C$, $\gamma_0(c) = 0$.
3. For all $i \geq 0$, $\beta_i \models s(p_i)$.
4. For all $i \geq 0$ and all $0 \leq \delta \leq t_i$, $\gamma_i + \delta \models I(p_i)$.
5. For all $i \geq 0$ there is an edge $(p_i, g, X, p_{i+1}) \in E$ such that
    (a) $\beta_i \cup \beta'_{i+1} \cup (\gamma_i + t_i) \cup \chi_{Y_i} \models g$ and
    (b) $\gamma_{i+1} = (\gamma_i + t_i)[X := 0]$.

We denote the set of runs by $Run(\mathcal{A})$. We call a state (p, β, γ) *reachable* if there is a run $\langle(p_0, \beta_0, \gamma_0), t_0, Y_0, (p_1, \beta_1, \gamma_1), t_1, Y_1, \ldots\rangle$ of $\mathcal{A}$ such that $(p, \beta, \gamma) = (p_i, \beta_i, \gamma_i + \delta)$ for some $i \geq 0$ and $0 \leq \delta \leq t_i$. By $Reach(\mathcal{A})$, we denote the set of reachable states of $\mathcal{A}$.

The stuttering edge $(p_i, \neg e_1 \wedge \ldots \wedge \neg e_k \wedge v_1 = v_1' \wedge \ldots \wedge v_j = v_j', \varnothing, p_i)$ is required to make the definition invariant against stuttering. This simplifies the definition of parallel composition, because automata can step synchronously.

Lemma 1. *Let $\mathcal{A}$ be a PEA and $r = \langle(p_0, \beta_0, \gamma_0), t_0, Y_0, (p_1, \beta_1, \gamma_1), t_1, Y_1, \ldots\rangle$ a run of $\mathcal{A}$. Then for all $i \geq 0$, stuttering the i-th state in r yields another run of $\mathcal{A}$; more precisely for all $0 < \delta < t_i$, replacing the subsequence $\langle(p_i, \beta_i, \gamma_i), t_i, Y_i\rangle$ in r by $\langle(p_i, \beta_i, \gamma_i), \delta, \varnothing, (p_i, \beta_i, \gamma_i + \delta), t_i - \delta, Y_i\rangle$ yields a run of $\mathcal{A}$.*

Given a run $\langle(p_0, \beta_0, \gamma_0), t_0, Y_0, (p_1, \beta_1, \gamma_1), t_1, Y_1, \ldots\rangle$ of $\mathcal{A}$, we call the infinite sequence $(\beta_0, t_0, Y_0, \beta_1, t_1, Y_1, \ldots)$ a *trace* of $\mathcal{A}$, i. e., a trace is a sequence alternating V-valuations, durations and sets of events. By $Trace(\mathcal{A})$, we denote the *trace language* (i. e., set of traces) of $\mathcal{A}$.

3.3 Parallel Composition

To build a larger system from multiple automata a parallel composition operator has to be defined. Here, it also plays an important role in defining semantics for CSP-OZ-DC. Each part is translated separately into an automaton and they are put in parallel. In [13] the CSP and Object-Z part are joined by the CSP synchronised parallel operator and the Duration Calculus part is joined with logical conjunction. To define equivalent semantics with phase event automata the parallel composition is required to have the same property. To achieve this, the automata are synchronised on both events and states: An event that is in the alphabet of both automata may only be taken if both automata agree, which is the same as CSP synchronisation. Likewise a variable of both automata may only be changed if both automata allow it, which corresponds to logical conjunction. The clocks need to be disjoint, so they do not interfere with each other. The *parallel composition* $\mathcal{A}_1 \parallel \mathcal{A}_2$ *of two automata* $\mathcal{A}_1$ *and* $\mathcal{A}_2$, $\mathcal{A}_i = (P_i, V_i, A_i, C_i, E_i, s_i, I_i, P_{0i})$, is the PEA $\mathcal{A} = (P, V, A, C, E, s, I, P_0)$ defined as follows:

- $P := P_1 \times P_2$. This is a standard product automata construction.
- $V := V_1 \cup V_2$.
- $A := A_1 \cup A_2$. The new alphabet is the union of the two alphabets.
- $C := C_1 \cup C_2$ and $C_1 \cap C_2 = \varnothing$. The clock set is the disjoint union of C_1 and C_2, that is clocks that appear in both sets need to be renamed.
- $s((p_1, p_2)) = s(p_1) \wedge s(p_2)$. The states are labelled with the conjunction of the corresponding state predicates in $\mathcal{A}_1$ and $\mathcal{A}_2$.
- $I((p_1, p_2)) = I(p_1) \wedge I(p_2)$. Likewise the clock invariant is the conjunction of the clock invariants in $\mathcal{A}_1$ and $\mathcal{A}_2$.
- $P_0 := P_{01} \times P_{02}$.
- The set of edges E contains $((p_1, p_2), g_1 \wedge g_2, X_1 \cup X_2, (p_1', p_2'))$ for each two edges $(p_i, g_i, X_i, p_i') \in E_i, i = 1, 2$ in the corresponding automata $\mathcal{A}_i$. Note that the stuttering edges of one automaton allow the other automaton to do a step independently from the first automaton. This is the reason why stuttering edges are required.

This is a product automaton construction. Both automata must agree on the state space and events must occur synchronously, therefore the state predicates and transition guards are the conjunction of the predicates for the two automata. It is obvious from this definition that parallel composition is commutative (modulo renaming of phases) and that it preserves the extra requirements of convexity and stuttering edges. The traces of the parallel automaton are exactly those that are allowed by both automata:

Lemma 2. *Let $\mathcal{A}_1$ and $\mathcal{A}_2$ be PEA. Then $\langle \beta_0, t_0, Y_0, \ldots \rangle \in Trace(\mathcal{A}_1 \parallel \mathcal{A}_2)$ if and only if $\langle \beta_0|_{V_1}, t_0, Y_0 \cap A_1, \ldots \rangle \in \mathcal{A}_1$ and $\langle \beta_0|_{V_2}, t_0, Y_0 \cap A_2, \ldots \rangle \in \mathcal{A}_2$.*

This can be easily seen by comparing the runs of the three automata. This lemma suggests the following verification method for properties that are satisfied if they hold for every trace. To prove such a property for a system of automata $\mathcal{A}_1 \parallel \ldots \parallel \mathcal{A}_n$, one can choose some automata that seem to be related to the property. The hope is that for this small subsystem it is much easier to prove than for the full system. If the smaller subsystem satisfies the property, the complete system does also, because it has only fewer traces. Otherwise the model-checker gives a counterexample that can be examined. If it is prevented by one of the remaining automata the automaton is added to the parallel product and the model checking is repeated.

4   PEA Semantics for CSP-OZ-DC

In this section we will give semantics for CSP-OZ-DC based on phase event automata. They are equivalent to the semantics given in [13]. The semantics is compositional: The CSP, Object-Z and Duration Calculus part are translated separately into phase event automata and then run in parallel. The semantics of the complete elevator specification is

$$\mathcal{A}(Elevator) = \mathcal{A}(CSP_{Elevator}) \parallel \mathcal{A}(OZ_{Elevator}) \parallel \mathcal{A}(DC_{Elevator})$$

Translation of CSP. The translation of the CSP part to a phase event automaton is straightforward. The operational semantics of CSP [17] is used to construct an equivalent phase event automaton. The phases are labelled by CSP processes, the alphabet A is the alphabet of `main`. There are no state variables V and no clocks C. For each transition $p \xrightarrow{a} p'$ of the operational semantics there is an edge $(p, a \wedge \bigwedge_{e \in A \setminus \{a\}} \neg e, \varnothing, p') \in E$, which allows only event a and forbids all other events in the alphabet. For a τ transition $p \xrightarrow{\tau} p'$ the corresponding edge is $(p, \bigwedge_{e \in A} \neg e, \varnothing, p')$ communicating no events. And finally there is the stuttering edge $(p, \bigwedge_{e \in A} \neg e, \varnothing, p)$ for every $p \in P$. The initial phase is the phase corresponding to the `main`-process. Fig. 4 shows the phase event automaton for the CSP process given in section 2.

Translation of Object-Z. The Object-Z part is translated into a two-phase automaton. The initial phase restricts the state with the predicates in `Init`. This phase is connected with the main phase by a single edge allowing no events or variable changes. The main phase has one edge for each event that allows exactly this event, keeps all variables not in the Δ-list constant, and restricts the variables in accordance with the communication schema. Every phase further has the stuttering edge, disallowing all events and variable changes.

Translation of Duration Calculus. Despite their expressiveness it is possible to translate each DC counterexample formula to a phase event automaton. The basic algorithm is the same that is used for negating a finite automaton, namely the power set construction. As defined in section 2, a counterexample formula consists of several phases $phase_1$; ... ; $phase_n$. The idea is to remember for each of these phases, whether the time interval from the start of the system to the current time satisfies the formula

$$true ; phase_1 ; \ldots ; phase_i, \quad 1 \leq i \leq n$$

A phase of the PEA is labelled by a set of those phases of the counterexample, for which the above formula holds. For a phase with a lower bound on its duration there is an additional flag that signals if the above formula would only hold without the lower bound. Each phase $phase_i$ with a time bound needs a clock c_i that measures the duration of the phase. Because only either an upper or a lower bound on the duration is allowed it is obvious, when to reset those clocks (as often as possible for upper bounds; only when we have to reenter the phase for lower bounds).

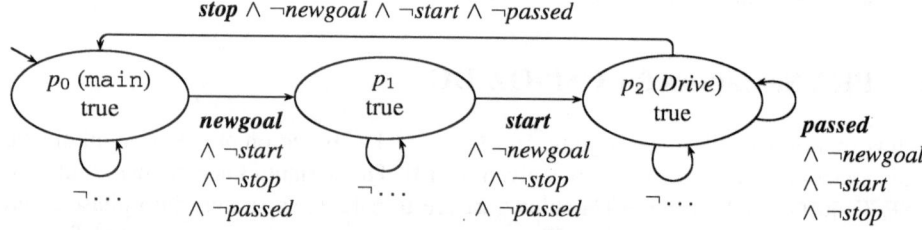

Fig. 4. Translation of CSP part

We implemented a tool that converts a counterexample formula into a phase event automaton. Due to space limitations the algorithm cannot be explained in full detail here. One of the resulting automata was already shown in Fig. 3. The automaton for the other formula is given in [12].

5   A Constraint-Based Semantics for PEA

To give semantics for CSP-OZ-DC (and phase event automata) in a domain where model-checking is possible, we use an "old-fashioned recipe for real-time" [1, 15]. The runs are described by sequences of states, where each state gives the values of all variables for a given time interval. Lamport adds one variable to denote the time since the start of the system. As we are not interested in absolute time, we have a variable len instead, denoting the length of the time interval. Events are represented by changes of Boolean variables as in section 2. Since we want to verify safety properties of phase event automata using a discrete time model checker, we translate the automata into discrete transition systems (with constraints) in such a way that the transition system generate as runs exactly the above sequences of interval states.

5.1   Transition Constraint Systems

A *transition constraint system* (TCS) $T = (Loc, Var, Init, Trans)$ is a 4-tuple such that

- Loc is a set (of locations),
- $Var \subseteq \mathcal{V}$ is a finite set of unprimed (state) variables,
- $Init : Loc \to \mathcal{L}(Var)$ assigns a (state) constraint to every location, and
- $Trans : Loc \times Loc \to \mathcal{L}(Var \cup Var')$ assigns a (transition) constraint to every pair of locations.

We can view *Init*, which is a vector of state constraints, as vector of sets of initial states of a transition system. Likewise, *Trans* is matrix of transition constraints, which can be viewed as a matrix of relations between pre-states (valuations of the unprimed variables) and post-states (valuations of the primed variables) of a transition system. See [12] for examples of transition constraint systems.

We define the *parallel composition* $T_1 \parallel T_2$ of two transition constraint systems T_1 and T_2 (where $T_i = (Loc_i, Var_i, Init_i, Trans_i)$, $i = 1, 2$) as the TCS $T = (Loc_1 \times Loc_2, Var_1 \cup Var_2, Init, Trans)$ such that for all locations $(\ell_1, \ell_2), (\ell'_1, \ell'_2) \in Loc_1 \times Loc_2$,

- $Init((\ell_1, \ell_2)) = Init_1(\ell_1) \wedge Init_2(\ell_2)$, and
- $Trans((\ell_1, \ell_2), (\ell'_1, \ell'_2)) = Trans_1(\ell_1, \ell'_1) \wedge Trans_2(\ell_2, \ell'_2)$.

Let $T = (Loc, Var, Init, Trans)$ be a TCS. A *state* of T is a pair (ℓ, α) of a location $\ell \in Loc$ and a Var-valuation α. Taking states as vertices, the TCS T can be viewed as a (potentially infinite) directed graph (where two states are connected by an edge if they satisfy the respective transition constraint). This graph gives rise to the usual notions of run and reachable state. Formally, a *run* of T is an infinite sequence of states $\langle (\ell_0, \alpha_0), (\ell_1, \alpha_1), \ldots \rangle$ such that

1. $\alpha_0 \models Init(\ell_0)$, and
2. for all $i \geq 0$, $\alpha_i \cup \alpha'_{i+1} \models Trans(\ell_i, \ell_{i+1})$.

We call a state (ℓ, α) *reachable* if there is a run $\langle (\ell_0, \alpha_0), (\ell_1, \alpha_1), \ldots \rangle$ of T such that $(\ell, \alpha) = (\ell_i, \alpha_i)$ for some $i \geq 0$. By $Reach(T)$, we denote the set of reachable states of T. As is easily seen, the notion of run is compatible with parallel composition.

Lemma 3. *For TCS* T^1 *and* T^2, $\langle ((\ell_0^1, \ell_0^2), \alpha_0), ((\ell_1^1, \ell_1^2), \alpha_1), \ldots \rangle$ *is a run of* $T^1 \parallel T^2$ *if and only if* $\langle (\ell_0^1, \alpha_0|_{Var^1}), (\ell_1^1, \alpha_1|_{Var^1}), \ldots \rangle$ *and* $\langle (\ell_0^2, \alpha_0|_{Var^2}), (\ell_1^2, \alpha_1|_{Var^2}), \ldots \rangle$ *are runs of* T^1 *and* T^2, *respectively*.

5.2   Translation of PEA to TCS

We now present a translation of a phase event automaton $\mathcal{A} = (P, V, A, C, E, s, I, P_0)$ into a transition constraint system $T(\mathcal{A}) = (Loc, Var, Init, Trans)$. There are two key features of this translation. First, continuous transitions of the automaton (which are implicit in the timed automata model) are translated into explicit discrete transitions. Second, the distinction between state and event variables is given up in favour of state variables; events are modelled by state change. To this end, we transform formulas $\varphi \in \mathcal{L}(V)$ into formulas $\varphi[e \not\equiv e'/e]_{e \in \mathbf{Events}} \in \mathcal{L}(V \cup \mathbf{Events}')$ by replacing each event variable $e \in \mathbf{Events}$ with a disequation $e \not\equiv e'$. Furthermore, we introduce two auxiliary variables, disc of type Bool (indicating whether the next transition is a discrete one) and len of type Time (recording the length of the time interval of a continuous transition). These auxiliary variables are reserved specially for translating PEA to TCS, therefore they may not be used by any PEA. Formally, the translation $T(\mathcal{A})$ is given by:

- $Loc = P$.
- $Var = V \cup A \cup C \cup \{\mathsf{len}, \mathsf{disc}\}$.
- For all $p \in P$,

$$Init(p) = \begin{cases} \neg\mathsf{disc} \wedge \bigwedge_{c \in C} c \approx 0 \wedge s(p) \wedge I(p) \wedge \mathsf{len} > 0 & \text{if } p \in P_0, \\ \mathit{false} & \text{otherwise.} \end{cases}$$

- For all $p_1, p_2 \in P$,

$$Trans(p_1, p_2) = \begin{cases} Inv(p_2)' \wedge \left(Cont \vee \bigvee\limits_{(p_1,g,X,p_2) \in E} Disc(g,X) \right) & \text{if } p_1 = p_2, \\ Inv(p_2)' \wedge \left(\bigvee\limits_{(p_1,g,X,p_2) \in E} Disc(g,X) \right) & \text{if } p_1 \neq p_2, \end{cases}$$

where the formulas $Inv(p_2)$, $Cont$ and $Disc(g,X)$ are given by:

$$Inv(p_2) = \mathsf{len} > 0 \wedge s(p_2) \wedge I(p_2)$$

$$Cont = \neg\mathsf{disc} \wedge \mathsf{disc}' \wedge \bigwedge_{c \in C} c' \approx c + \mathsf{len} \wedge \bigwedge_{x \in V \cup A} x' \approx x$$

$$Disc(g,X) = \mathsf{disc} \wedge \neg\mathsf{disc}' \wedge g[e \not\approx e'/e]_{e \in \mathbf{Events}} \wedge \bigwedge_{c \in X} c' \approx 0 \wedge \bigwedge_{c \in C \setminus X} c' \approx c$$

Here, $Inv(p)$ expresses the invariant constraints (state and clock) associated with phase p, $Cont$ relates pre- and post-states in a continuous transition, and $Disc(g,X)$ relates pre- and post-states of a discrete transition (with guard g and resetting the clocks in X). See [12] for samples of PEA translated to TCS.

5.3   Semantical Correctness of the Translation

We show that the translation $T(\mathcal{A})$ of a PEA $\mathcal{A}$ preserves the semantics in the sense that there is a correspondence between the runs of $\mathcal{A}$ and $T(\mathcal{A})$. Given a run $r = \langle (\ell_0, \alpha_0), (\ell_1, \alpha_1), \ldots \rangle$ of the TCS $T(\mathcal{A})$, we define an infinite sequence $r_\mathcal{A} = \langle (p_0, \beta_0, \gamma_0), t_0, Y_0, (p_1, \beta_1, \gamma_1), t_1, Y_1, \ldots \rangle$ such that for all $i \geq 0$, $p_i = \ell_{2i}$, $\beta_i = \alpha_{2i}|_V$, $\gamma_i = \alpha_{2i}|_C$, $t_i = \alpha_{2i}(\mathsf{len})$ and $Y_i = \{e \in A \mid \alpha_{2i+1}(e) \neq \alpha_{2i+2}(e)\}$. As the following theorem shows, this translation maps runs of the TCS $T(\mathcal{A})$ to runs of the PEA $\mathcal{A}$. Furthermore, the translation is surjective, so for every run of $\mathcal{A}$ there is a corresponding run of $T(\mathcal{A})$. See [12] for a proof.

Theorem 4. Let $\mathcal{A}$ be a PEA and $T(\mathcal{A})$ its TCS translation.

1. For all runs r of $T(\mathcal{A})$, $r_\mathcal{A}$ is a run of $\mathcal{A}$.
2. For every run r of $\mathcal{A}$ there is a run $\hat{r}$ of $T(\mathcal{A})$ such that $\hat{r}_\mathcal{A} = r$.

Note that the proof of the first half of the theorem requires convexity of the clock invariants of the PEA. In fact, without convexity, $T(\mathcal{A})$ might show runs that are artefacts of the translation and do not correspond to runs of $\mathcal{A}$.

As a corollary, we obtain a correspondence between the reachable states of $\mathcal{A}$ and $T(\mathcal{A})$, which justifies doing reachability analysis on the discrete system $T(\mathcal{A})$ instead of the timed automaton $\mathcal{A}$. To state the correspondence formally, we translate a state (ℓ, α) of $T(\mathcal{A})$ into a state $(\ell, \alpha)_{\mathcal{A}} = (\ell, \alpha|_V, \alpha|_C)$ of $\mathcal{A}$. The corollary claims that this translation is a surjective mapping from the reachable states of $T(\mathcal{A})$ to the reachable states of $\mathcal{A}$; see [12] for a proof.

Corollary 5. *Let $\mathcal{A}$ be a PEA and $T(\mathcal{A})$ its TCS translation.*

1. *For all states (ℓ, α) of $T(\mathcal{A})$, if $(\ell, \alpha) \in Reach(T(\mathcal{A}))$ then $(\ell, \alpha)_{\mathcal{A}} \in Reach(\mathcal{A})$.*
2. *For all states (p, β, γ) of $\mathcal{A}$, if $(p, \beta, \gamma) \in Reach(\mathcal{A})$ then there is state $(\ell, \alpha) \in Reach(T(\mathcal{A}))$ such that $(\ell, \alpha)_{\mathcal{A}} = (p, \beta, \gamma)$.*

Note that the translation of the reachable states of the TCS $T(\mathcal{A})$ ignores variables that are not state variables of the PEA $\mathcal{A}$, i. e., the event variables in A and the auxiliary variables disc and len. However, the reachable states of $T(\mathcal{A})$ are not more informative than the reachable states of $\mathcal{A}$, because the values of the event variables are irrelevant for reachability in $T(\mathcal{A})$.

6   Model Checking TCS

We verify temporal properties of CSP-OZ-DC specifications by translating them to transition constraint systems, which we can model check. In this paper, we confine ourselves to the verification of state invariants, i. e., to checking whether a set of unsafe states (violating the invariant) is reachable from the initial states. It is well known that this implies the ability to verify arbitrary safety properties by augmenting the system with suitable monitors or test-automata [6].

For verification, we decided to use the constraint-based model checker ARMC [18], because its constraint solver can handle linear arithmetic over the reals, which is crucial for our approach to real-time. The model checker takes as input a transition constraint system and a set of unsafe states (given as a vector of constraints, like the initial states). Going backwards from the unsafe states, it tries to determine whether the initial states are reachable by alternating the following two steps.

1. Over-approximating the reachable states using predicate abstraction (w. r. t. a current set of abstraction predicates) in order to disprove reachability, i. e., to prove the invariant.
2. Under-approximating the reachable states using a bounded (yet precise) symbolic backwards reachability analysis in order to prove reachability, i. e., to detect real counterexamples (and to refine the set of abstraction predicates to exclude spurious counterexamples).

In general, this abstraction-refinement loop may not terminate. However, in practice it does terminate on numerous examples after a small number of iterations.

We would like to stress that the effectiveness and the performance of the model checker crucially depend on the constraints in the input. Both steps in the abstraction-refinement loop, computing a predicate abstraction and doing a symbolic reachability analysis, require to decide satisfiability of formulae in $\mathcal{L}$. Therefore, $\mathcal{L}$ should be a decidable class of constraints, e. g., linear arithmetic over the integers and reals as in our case study. Moreover, the solver for $\mathcal{L}$ should be performant in practice, since one run of the model checker may trigger thousands of calls to the solver.

6.1   Verification of the Case Study

To demonstrate our approach, we verified that our parameterised elevator never drives below the lowest or above the highest floor, i. e., we verified the invariant

$$Min \leq current \leq Max \ . \tag{1}$$

In order to model check, we translated the CSP-OZ-DC specification according to section 4 into a parallel product of four PEA, one for the CSP part, one for the OZ part and one for each DC formula. As described in section 5, each PEA was translated to a TCS; see [12] for the details. The parallel composition of these TCS together with the negation of the invariant were fed into the model checker ARMC, which proved the invariant in about 2 minutes[4] with two iterations of the abstraction-refinement loop. Recall that the CSP-OZ-DC specification as well as the invariant were parameterised by the symbolic constants *Min* and *Max*. Thus, we have verified the invariant for all elevators that are instances of the specification, independent of the actual size the state space of those instances.

Note that even the simple invariant (1) is a real-time property, despite it does not contain timing constraints. However, the invariant does depend on the timing constraints enforced by the DC formulas; in fact, erasing any of the two DC formulas from the CSP-OZ-DC specification causes (1) to be violated, which ARMC can demonstrate with counterexample traces in less than 20 seconds.

7   Conclusion

We presented a technique to model-check a combined specification written in CSP-OZ-DC by translating it into phase event automata. The semantics of CSP-OZ-DC used here is equivalent to the original one given in [13], however, it is defined in a different way. The three parts of the specification are separately translated into phase event automata, which are then joined by parallel composition. These automata have the notion of events, data variables and clocks, which allows to represent these concepts without encoding. Their special parallel composition is equivalent to CSP synchronised parallel composition and logical conjunction in Object-Z and Duration Calculus. These automata are further translated into transition constraint systems that are then checked by a constraint-based model-checker using the abstraction-refinement paradigm. The

---

[4] Measured on a standard Linux PC (2.6 GHz Pentium 4, 512 MB RAM).

model-checker can work with symbolic values, thus admits checking parameterised specifications.

7.1 Related Work

In [13] we already presented a model-checking algorithm using the model-checker Uppaal for timed automata. However, it could only handle a very restricted set of Duration Calculus that could not refer to state variables. Also it could only handle finite system.

In [7] a translation from TCOZ, a combination of Timed-CSP and Object-Z, to Timed Automata is presented. In TCOZ timing behaviour is not separated but mixed with the CSP part and the translation closely follows the structure of the Timed-CSP part. This approach lacks support for infinite data.

A bounded model-checking (BMC) approach for checking validity of dense-time Duration Calculus was first presented in [8] and is the basis for the tool IDLVALID [19]. However, BMC can only find counter-examples upto a given length and also does not support infinite data.

Closest to our model of phase event automata are the timed automata of Kronos [24], which use the same model of clocks and the same synchronisation on events but lack the data part, and phase automata [23], where the idea of synchronisation over states is taken from. In many other automata models, e.g., state charts, there is a shared data space in the form of global variables, that can be read from and written to by any component. This leads to unexpected side-effects though, for example, if a component that writes to the variable is added later.

HyTech [2] can also check parameterised systems. However the approach used there is complementary: HyTech finds the parameter values for which the system is safe, while in our approach safety is checked for all possible parameters values. Also HyTech can only have parameters in timing constraints.

There exist a number of other abstraction-refinement model checkers, for example BLAST [10], MAGIC [4] and SLAM [3]. These model checkers are tailored to check properties of sequential or multi-threaded imperative programs, often operating systems code, and they generally deal well with arrays and linear arithmetic over the integers. However, to our knowledge, none of the above model checkers supports reals, which are essential for model checking real-time systems.

7.2 Future Work

Currently the model-checker can only check for reachability. We would like to use the technique of test-automata [6] to reduce model-checking of DC-formulae to reachability. In this approach a parallel automaton checks the formula and reaches a certain state if the formula is violated. We are currently researching the class of Duration Calculus formulae that can be checked by this approach. It is even larger than the set of counterexample formulae.

The above approach only allows safety properties. However, there exists an extension of ARMC, the model-checker used here, that allows to check liveness properties [16]. It can only check for fair termination, but with the idea of test automata it is possible to check for liveness properties given in Duration Calculus extended by liveness [20].

References

1. M. Abadi and L. Lamport. An old-fashioned recipe for real time. In *Real-Time: Theory in Practice*, volume 600 of *LNCS*, pages 1–27. Springer, 1992.
2. R. Alur, T.A. Henzinger, and P.-H. Ho. Automatic symbolic verification of embedded systems. *IEEE Trans. Software Engineering*, 22:181–201, 1996.
3. T. Ball and S. K. Rajamani. The SLAM toolkit. In *CAV'01*, pages 260–264. Springer, 2001.
4. S. Chaki, E. Clarke, A. Groce, S. Jha, and H. Veith. Modular verification of software components in C. In *ICSE'03*, pages 385–395, 2003.
5. G. Delzanno and A. Podelski. Model checking in CLP. In *TACAS'99*, pages 223–239, 1999.
6. H. Dierks and M. Lettrari. Constructing test automata from graphical real-time requirements. In *FTRTFT'02*, volume 2469 of *LNCS*, pages 433–454, 2002.
7. J.S. Dong, P. Hao, S.C. Qin, J. Sun, and W. Yi. Timed patterns: TCOZ to timed automata. In *ICFEM'04*, volume 3308 of *LNCS*, pages 483–498. Springer, 2004.
8. M. Fränzle. Take it NP-easy: Bounded model construction for duration calculus. In *FTRTFT'02*, volume 2469 of *LNCS*, pages 234–264. Springer, 2002.
9. S. Graf and H. Saïdi. Construction of abstract state graphs with PVS. In *CAV'97*, pages 72–83, 1997.
10. T.A. Henzinger, R. Jhala, R. Majumdar, and G. Sutre. Lazy abstraction. In *POPL'02*, pages 58–70. ACM Press, 2002.
11. C.A.R. Hoare. *Communicating Sequential Processes*. Prentice Hall, 1985.
12. J. Hoenicke and P. Maier. Model-checking of specifications integrating processes, data and time. Technical Report 5, SFB/TR 14 AVACS, http://www.avacs.org/, 2005.
13. J. Hoenicke and E.-R. Olderog. Combining specification techniques for processes data and time. In *IFM'02*, volume 2335 of *LNCS*. Springer, May 2002.
14. J. Hoenicke and E.-R. Olderog. CSP-OZ-DC: A combination of specification techniques for processes, data and time. *Nordic Journal of Computing*, 9(4), 2002.
15. L. Lamport. The temporal logic of actions. *ACM TOPLAS*, 16:872–973, 1994.
16. A. Podelski and A. Rybalchenko. Transition predicate abstraction and fair termination. In *POPL'05*, pages 132–144. ACM Press, 2005.
17. A.W. Roscoe. *The Theory and Practice of Concurrency*. Prentice Hall, 1998.
18. A. Rybalchenko. A model checker based on abstraction refinement. Master's thesis, Universität des Saarlandes, Saarbrücken, Saarland, September 2002.
19. B. Sharma, P.K. Pandya, and S. Chakraborty. Bounded validity checking of interval duration logic. In *TACAS'05*, volume 3440 of *LNCS*, pages 301–316. Springer, 2005.
20. J. U. Skakkebæk. Liveness and fairness in duration calculus. In *CONCUR'94*, pages 283–298, 1994.
21. G. Smith. *The Object-Z Specification Language*. Kluwer Academic Publisher, 2000.
22. J.M. Spivey. *The Z Notation: A Reference Manual*. Prentice-Hall International Series in Computer Science, 2nd edition, 1992.
23. J. Tapken. *Model-Checking of Duration Calculus Specifications*. PhD thesis, University of Oldenburg, June 2001.
24. S. Yovine. Kronos: A verification tool for real-time systems. *International Journal of Software Tools for Technology Transfer*, 1(1+2), October 1997.
25. C. Zhou and M.R. Hansen. *Duration Calculus: A Formal Approach to Real-Time Systems*. EATCS: Monographs in Theoretical Computer Science. Springer, 2004.
26. C. Zhou, C.A.R. Hoare, and A.P. Ravn. A calculus of durations. *Information Processing Letters*, 40(5):269–276, 1991.

Automatic Symmetry Detection for Model Checking Using Computational Group Theory

A.F. Donaldson* and A. Miller

Department of Computing Science,
University of Glasgow,
Glasgow, Scotland
{ally, alice}@dcs.gla.ac.uk

Abstract. We present an automatic technique for the detection of structural symmetry in a model directly from its Promela specification. Our approach involves finding the *static channel diagram* of the model, a graphical representation of channel-based system communication; computing the group of symmetries of this diagram; and computing the largest possible subgroup of these symmetries which induce automorphisms of the underlying model. We describe a tool, SymmExtractor, which, for a given model and *LTL* property, uses our approach to find a group of symmetries of the model which preserve the property. This group can then be used for symmetry reduction during model checking using existing quotient-based methods. Unlike previous approaches, our method can detect arbitrary structural symmetries arising from the communication structure of the model.

Keywords: Promela/SPIN; symmetry reduction; model checking; communicating processes; distributed systems; formal modelling; GAP; concurrency.

1   Introduction

Model checking [5] is an increasingly popular technique for the formal verification of concurrent systems. The application of model checking is limited due to the state-space explosion problem—as the number of components represented by a model increases, the size of the associated state-space grows exponentially. As such, models of realistic systems are often too large to feasibly check. Symmetry reduction techniques [3, 7, 15] can be used to combat this problem for models of systems with many replicated components. Symmetry in a system can result in portions of the state-space of a model of the system being *equivalent* up to rearrangement of component ids. If symmetry is known to be present in a model then model checking of certain properties can be performed over a quotient state-space, which is generally smaller than the full state-space of the model. Most

---

* Supported by the Carnegie Trust for the Universities of Scotland.

J.S. Fitzgerald, I.J. Hayes, and A. Tarlecki (Eds.): FM 2005, LNCS 3582, pp. 481–496, 2005.

work on exploiting symmetry during model checking assumes that symmetries of a model are either known *a priori* [7], or are coded into the model through the use of special keywords [3, 15]. Both approaches require the modeller to provide information on the presence of symmetry in a model. This is potentially error prone, and compromises the automation of model checking, which is one of its main strengths as a verification technique. The challenge of automatic symmetry detection is to infer symmetries of the state-space underlying a model *without* explicitly constructing the state-space. The inferred symmetries must be guaranteed to be valid, otherwise the results of symmetry-reduced model checking are untrustworthy.

In this paper we present a method for the automatic detection of symmetry directly from the source code of a model, requiring no additional input from the user. Our approach applies to models written using the Promela specification language (used as input to the SPIN model checker [14]). Given a Promela model, generators for a group of *candidate* symmetries are found by analysing the *static channel diagram* of the model. These generators are checked individually against the model to see if they induce valid automorphisms of the underlying state-graph. Starting with the set of candidate generators which are valid, the largest possible subgroup of candidate symmetries which are all valid is computed. Unlike previous approaches to specifying symmetry using *scalarsets* [3, 15], our method can detect *arbitrary* structural symmetries arising from the communication structure of a model. A scalarset can only be used to specify full symmetry between a set of components of a model. The symmetry group computed using our approach is, by construction, an invariance group for a specified linear temporal logic (*LTL*) formula (contained within the Promela model). As such, the group can be used safely for symmetry reduction during model checking. Static channel diagrams were introduced in previous work [11]. The significant additional contributions of this paper include some detailed theoretical results to determine *valid* automorphisms, and the implementation of our approach via a tool, SymmExtractor, which makes use of the computational group theory package GAP [13]. We provide experimental results for a variety of models, and discuss how our approach can be extended. We conclude by briefly discussing some of the issues which will be involved in future work, implementing symmetry reduction techniques into SPIN based on our approach to symmetry detection.

2   Preliminaries

Model checking involves checking the correctness of a temporal logic formula ϕ over a Kripke structure $\mathcal{M} = (S, R, L, s_0)$ and a set of atomic propositions AP, where S is a finite set of states, $R \subseteq S \times S$ is a total transition relation, $L : S \rightarrow 2^{AP}$ labels each state with the propositions that are true at the state, and $s_0 \in S$ is an initial state. The Kripke structure $\mathcal{M}$ represents a model of a concurrent system. In practice $\mathcal{M}$ is obtained from a high level specification $\mathcal{P}$ written in a language such as Promela [14].

2.1   Promela

Promela (**Pro**cess **me**ta **la**nguage) is a high level specification language for modelling concurrent, distributed systems, and Promela programs are used as input to the SPIN model checker [14]. A Promela program consists of a series of *proctype* definitions, global variable and channel declarations, an *init* process (used to initialise the model), and (optionally) a *never claim* process (used to verify a *LTL* formula). A *proctype* defines a parameterised process type, of which multiple copies can be instantiated by the *init* process. A *proctype* definition has the form `proctype name(param_list) {body}`. The body of a *proctype* consists of local variable declarations, as well as expressions and statements over local and global variables, and channels. A statement of the form

```
if :: seq_1
   :: seq_2
      ...
   :: seq_m
fi
```

is used to model nondeterministic branching (branching in which any executable sequence `seq_i` may be chosen). Similarly, a `do...od` statement is used to model repeated nondeterministic branching.

Global variables, and variables local to a *proctype* can be declared of type *bit, byte, short, int, pid, chan,* or *mtype*. A variable of type *chan* refers to a system channel, which has the form `[x] of {field_1,field_2,...,field_m}`, where $x \geq 0$ is the capacity of the channel, $m > 0$ is the number of fields which a message must contain to be sent on the channel, and for $1 \leq i \leq m$, $field\_i \in \{bit, byte, short, int, pid, chan, mtype\}$ specifies the type of the ith field of a message. A *send* operation on channel c is denoted $c!msg$, where msg is a list of values or variables, one for each field of the message. Similarly, a *receive* operation on channel c is denoted $c?msg$. Variables of type *pid* should only be assigned values that correspond to the instantiation number (process id) of an executing process. Each process has a predefined, read-only, local variable *_pid* which stores its instantiation number The value 0 may be used as a default value for variables of type *pid*. This is the instantiation number of the *init* process.

In this paper we consider models where all processes are instantiated simultaneously by the *init* process, and where processes do not themselves instantiate child processes (we discuss the implications of this in Section 5.5). In such models the *init* process has the form

```
init { atomic { run proctypename_1(params_1);
           ... run proctypename_m(params_m) } }
```

The keyword *atomic* ensures that the statements enclosed in the pair of braces immediately following the keyword are executed in sequence as a *single* transition of the system (provided that the statements do not block). In a Promela model, the *init* process is assigned process id 0 by default, and the other processes are assigned process ids in order, starting from 1. Two processes have the same

```
     chan box_1 = [1] of {pid,pid}; chan box_2 = [1] of {pid,pid};
     chan box_3 = [1] of {pid,pid}; chan box_4 = [1] of {pid,pid};
     chan box_5 = [1] of {pid,pid}; chan network = [5] of {pid,pid};
     pid received_from

     proctype mailer(chan in) {
       pid source, dest;
(1)    pid blocked_client = 3;
       chan out;
       do :: in?source,dest;
            if :: source==blocked_client -> skip
               :: else ->
                   if :: dest==1 -> out = box_1 :: dest==2 -> out = box_2
(2)                   :: dest==3 -> out = box_3 :: dest==4 -> out = box_4
                      :: dest==5 -> out = box_5
                   fi;
                   out!source,dest
            fi
       od
     }

     proctype client(chan in) {
       pid source, dest;
       do :: in?source,dest; assert(dest==_pid); received_from = source
          :: atomic { nfull(network) -> source = _pid;
(3)           if :: dest = 1 :: dest = 2 :: dest = 3 :: dest = 4 :: dest = 5 fi;
              network!source,dest }
       od
     }

     init {
       atomic {
(4)       run client(box_1); run client(box_2); run client(box_3);
          run client(box_4); run client(box_5); run mailer(network)
       }
     }

     never {     /* !([]  (received_from!=3)) */
     T0_init:
(5)    if :: (! (received_from!=3)) -> goto accept_all
          :: (1) -> goto T0_init
       fi;
     accept_all: skip }
```

Fig. 1. Promela model of an email system

process type if they are instantiations of the same *proctype*. To verify an *LTL* property, SPIN converts the *negation* of the property into a Büchi automaton, expressed as a *never-claim*. A never-claim is an additional process in the Promela model, specifying system behaviour that should *never* occur [14], i.e. behaviour which violates the given property.

Figure 1 shows Promela code for a model of an email system, adapted from [4]. The system consists of 5 instantiations of a parameterised *client* process, running in parallel with a *mailer* process. The *client* processes can send messages to each other via the *mailer* process, but all messages sent by the process with id 3 are blocked by the *mailer* process. Labels (1)—(5) have been added to the code for explanatory reasons and should otherwise be ignored. An example *LTL* property of interest for this model is:

Property 1. $[](received\_from \neq 3)$

which states that no *client* ever receives a message from *client* 3. Note that *received_from* is a global variable which is reset by a *client* process each time a message is received. The never-claim for Property 1 has been included at the end of the Promela code shown in Figure 1. As properties are included within the model in this way, the automorphism groups computed by our approach to symmetry detection are, by construction, property preserving (see Section 2.2).

Let $\mathcal{P}$ be a Promela program. Let Loc be the set of local variables, $Glob$ the set of global variables, and $Chan$ the set of channels of $\mathcal{P}$. Let D be the set of data values for the program. To denote a local variable of a process with process id i we write x_i where x is the name of the variable. For example, in the email example, $source_i$ denotes the local variable $source$ of a *client* process with process id i. If x_i is a local variable of process i, and if processes i and j have the same process type, then x_j is the corresponding local variable of process j.

We now define the set AP of atomic propositions for a Promela program. Let $AP_{local} = \{(x_i = val) : x_i \in Loc, val \in D\}$, the set of propositions relating to local variables, and define AP_{global} and $AP_{channel}$, the set of propositions relating to global variables and channels respectively, similarly. Then $AP = AP_{local} \cup AP_{global} \cup AP_{channel}$. The underlying Kripke structure $\mathcal{M}$ over AP for the program $\mathcal{P}$ is generated by exploring all possible behaviours of $\mathcal{P}$. States of $\mathcal{M}$ are uniquely identified by a labelling of atomic propositions, and transitions between states are derived from the statements of the program. Note that each process in $\mathcal{P}$ has its own *program counter* variable which indicates the statements which may be executed in the next transition. Thus two states, for which all other variables are assigned identical values, may be distinguished due to assignments of the associated program counters.

We say that two programs $\mathcal{P}_1$ and $\mathcal{P}_2$ are equivalent, and write $\mathcal{P}_1 \equiv \mathcal{P}_2$, if they are the same up to rearrangement of: options in `if...fi` and `do..od` statements; operands to commutative operators; and `run` statements within the `init{atomic{...}}` block. Equivalent programs have identical behaviour, and thus the underlying Kripke structures for equivalent programs are the same.

2.2   Group Theory and Symmetry in Model Checking

Let G be a group, and let $\alpha_1, \alpha_2, \ldots, \alpha_n \in G$. The smallest subgroup of G containing the elements $\alpha_1, \ldots, \alpha_n$ is denoted $\langle \alpha_1, \alpha_2, \ldots, \alpha_n \rangle$, and is called the subgroup *generated* by $\alpha_1, \alpha_2, \ldots, \alpha_n$. The elements α_i $(1 \leq i \leq n)$ are called *generators* for this subgroup. Let $X = \{\alpha_1, \ldots, \alpha_n\}$ be a finite subset of G. Then we use $\langle X \rangle$ to denote $\langle \alpha_1, \ldots, \alpha_n \rangle$, the subgroup generated by X.

Let H be a subgroup of G, and let $\alpha \in G$. The set $H\alpha = \{\beta\alpha : \beta \in H\}$ is called a *right coset* of H in G. The set of all right cosets of H in G partitions G into disjoint equivalence classes. In particular, for $\alpha \in H$, we have $H\alpha = H$ [16].

Let $\mathcal{M} = (S, R, L, s_0)$ be a Kripke structure. An *automorphism* of $\mathcal{M}$ is a bijection $\alpha : S \to S$ which satisfies the following conditions:

- $\forall s, t \in S, \ (s, t) \in R \Rightarrow (\alpha(s), \alpha(t)) \in R,$
- $\alpha(s_0) = s_0$

In a model of a concurrent system with many replicated processes, Kripke structure automorphisms usually involve the permutation of process identifiers of identical processes throughout all states of a model. The set of all automorphisms of the Kripke structure $\mathcal{M}$ forms a group under composition of mappings. This group is denoted $Aut(\mathcal{M})$. A subgroup G of $Aut(\mathcal{M})$ induces an equivalence relation $\equiv_G$ on the states of $\mathcal{M}$ thus: $s \equiv_G t \Leftrightarrow s = \alpha(t)$ for some $\alpha \in G$. The equivalence class under $\equiv_G$ of a state $s \in S$, denoted $[s]$, is called the *orbit* of s under the action of G. The orbits can be used to construct a *quotient* Kripke structure $\mathcal{M}_G$ as follows:

Definition 1. *The quotient Kripke structure $\mathcal{M}_G$ of $\mathcal{M}$ with respect to G is a tuple $\mathcal{M}_G = (S_G, R_G, L_G, [s_0])$ where:*

- $S_G = \{[s] : s \in S\}$ *(the set of orbits of S under the action of G),*
- $R_G = \{([s], [t]) : (s, t) \in R\},$
- $L_G([s]) = L(rep([s]))$ *(where $rep([s])$ is a unique representative of $[s]$),*
- $[s_0] \in S_G$ *(the orbit of the initial state $s_0 \in S$).*

In general $\mathcal{M}_G$ is a smaller structure than $\mathcal{M}$, but $\mathcal{M}_G$ and $\mathcal{M}$ are equivalent in the sense that they satisfy the same set of logic properties which are *invariant* under the group G (that is, properties which are "symmetric" with respect to G). For a proof of the following theorem, together with details of the temporal logic CTL^*, see [5].

Theorem 1. *Let $\mathcal{M}$ be a Kripke structure, G a subgroup of $Aut(\mathcal{M})$ and ϕ a CTL^* formula. If ϕ is invariant under the group G then*

$$\mathcal{M}, s \models \phi \Leftrightarrow \mathcal{M}_G, [s] \models \phi$$

Thus by choosing a suitable symmetry group G, model checking can be performed over $\mathcal{M}_G$ instead of $\mathcal{M}$, often resulting in considerable savings in memory and verification time [3, 7]. Consider Property 1 for our email example. The property explicitly refers to the id of *client* 3, so an invariance group for this property is any subgroup of $Aut(\mathcal{M})$ which fixes *client* 3.

If automorphisms of a Kripke structure can be identified in advance, then a quotient structure can be incrementally constructed using an algorithm given in [15]. This means that it may be possible to construct the quotient structure even if the original structure is intractable. In the next section we show that symmetries of the Kripke structure associated with a Promela program can be detected by analysing the *static channel diagram* of the program.

3   Finding Automorphisms via Static Channel Diagrams

In this section we define the static channel diagram $\mathcal{C}(\mathcal{P})$ associated with a Promela program $\mathcal{P}$, and show how automorphisms of the corresponding Kripke structure $\mathcal{M}$ can be obtained by finding the automorphisms of $\mathcal{C}(\mathcal{P})$.

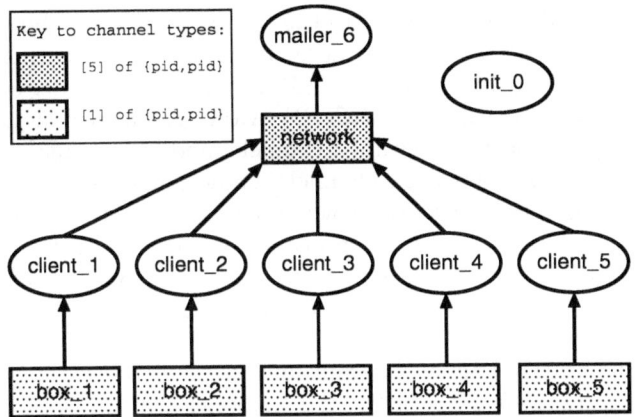

Fig. 2. Channel diagram of the message passing model

3.1   Static Channel Diagrams

Let $\mathcal{P}$ be a Promela program. A *static channel* of $\mathcal{P}$ is a channel which is declared globally, out of the scope of any *proctype* definition. Let V_P be the set of process identifiers for $\mathcal{P}$, and let V_C be the set of names of static channels of $\mathcal{P}$. For $i \in V_P$ let *proctype*(i) be the name of type *proctype* of which process i is an instantiation, and for $i \in V_C$ let *chantype*(i) denote the type of channel i (see Section 2.1).

Definition 2. *The static channel diagram of $\mathcal{P}$ is a coloured, bipartite digraph* $\mathcal{C}(\mathcal{P}) = (V, E, C)$, *where:*

- $V = V_P \cup V_C$;
- *For $i \in V_P$, $j \in V_C$, $(i, j) \in E$ iff process i has a send statement $j!msg$, $(j, i) \in E$ iff process i has a receive statement $j?msg$;*
- *For $x \in V$, $C(x) = proctype(x)$ if $x \in V_P$, and $C(x) = chantype(x)$ if $x \in V_C$.*

The static channel diagram of a program represents the potential communication links that can be detected from the program by considering only static channels. Figure 2 illustrates the static channel diagram for the email model of Figure 1. Processes are represented by ovals and channels by rectangles. The type of a process is indicated by the name preceding its process id in the diagram. The type of a channel is indicated by the shading of the rectangle. Note that although the *mailer* process sends messages to the client processes, it does so using its local channel, *out*, which is not a static channel. Thus this communication is not indicated in the static channel diagram.

An automorphism of the static channel diagram $\mathcal{C}(\mathcal{P})$ is a bijection $\alpha : V \to V$ which satisfies the following conditions:

- $\forall i, j \in V, \ (i, j) \in E \Rightarrow (\alpha(i), \alpha(j)) \in E$
- $\forall i \in V, \ C(i) = C(\alpha(i))$

Note that the second condition ensures that channels can only be mapped on to one another if they have the same capacity. It can be shown that the set of automorphisms of a static channel diagram $\mathcal{C}(\mathcal{P})$ forms a group under composition of mappings. We denote this group $Aut(\mathcal{C}(\mathcal{P}))$. Although our technique exploits the static communication declared within a Promela model, dynamic communication (in which messages are passed on channels whose names are received by other processes during program execution) which *cannot* be determined statically, is still permissible. This is because, if processes i and j are otherwise shown to be symmetrically equivalent (via static analysis), any dynamic communication involving process i will be reflected by corresponding dynamic communication involving process j.

Consider the static channel diagram for our email example, shown in Figure 2. Let $\alpha = (1\ 2)(box\_1\ box\_2)$, the mapping which swaps *client* 1 with *client* 2, and simultaneously swaps box_1 with box_2 in the diagram. Clearly α is an automorphism of $\mathcal{C}(\mathcal{P})$. In fact any permutation of the *client* processes and their incoming channels which leaves box_i connected to *client* i is an automorphism of $\mathcal{C}(\mathcal{P})$. The group $Aut(\mathcal{C}(\mathcal{P}))$ can be generated by the set $\{(1\ 2)(box\_1\ box\_2), (2\ 3)(box\_2\ box\_3), (3\ 4)(box\_3\ box\_4), (4\ 5)(box\_4\ box\_5)\}$.

We now show how the elements of $Aut(\mathcal{C}(\mathcal{P}))$ act on the source text of the Promela program $\mathcal{P}$, and on the Kripke structure underlying the program.

3.2   Action of $Aut(\mathcal{C}(\mathcal{P}))$ on $\mathcal{P}$

Let $\mathcal{P}$ be a Promela program with static channel diagram $\mathcal{C}(\mathcal{P})$, let $n > 0$ be the number of processes instantiated by $\mathcal{P}$, and let $\alpha \in Aut(\mathcal{C}(\mathcal{P}))$. The program $\alpha(\mathcal{P})$ is the same as $\mathcal{P}$, except that every applied occurrence of a static channel name c is replaced by the static channel name $\alpha(c)$, and every assignment statement of the form $x = val$, boolean expression of the form $x == val$ or $val == x$, where $type(x) = pid$ and $val \in \{1, \ldots, n\}$, is replaced by $x = \alpha(val)$, $x == \alpha(val)$ or $\alpha(val) == x$ respectively.

Consider the element $\alpha = (1\ 2)(box\_1\ box\_2) \in Aut(\mathcal{C}(\mathcal{P}))$ where $\mathcal{P}$ is our email example. Applying α to the code given in Figure 1 results in an identical program, except for the ordering of the options at labels (2) and (3), and the ordering of the *run* statements at label (4). Therefore $\mathcal{P} \equiv \alpha(\mathcal{P})$. If we take the element $\alpha = (2\ 3)(box\_2\ box\_3)$ then the programs $\mathcal{P}$ and $\alpha(\mathcal{P})$ are *not* equivalent, since the statement $blocked\_client = 3$ in $\mathcal{P}$ shown at label (1) of Figure 1 is replaced by the statement $blocked\_client = 2$ in $\alpha(\mathcal{P})$. Neither statement appears in both programs. Similarly, applying α to the expression $(!(received\_from\ ! = 3))$ shown at label (5) of Figure 1 results in the expression $(!(received\_from\ ! = 2))$. This inconsistency between $\mathcal{P}$ and $\alpha(\mathcal{P})$ shows that the given LTL property is not invariant under α.

For an element $\alpha \in Aut(\mathcal{C}(\mathcal{P}))$, we say that α is *valid* (for $\mathcal{P}$) if $\alpha(\mathcal{P}) \equiv \mathcal{P}$. We say that a subgroup H of $Aut(\mathcal{C}(\mathcal{P}))$ is valid (for $\mathcal{P}$) if every $\alpha \in H$ is valid.

3.3   Action of $Aut(\mathcal{C}(\mathcal{P}))$ on $\mathcal{M}$

For an element $\alpha \in Aut(\mathcal{C}(\mathcal{P}))$ we define a corresponding mapping α^* which is a permutation of the Kripke structure $\mathcal{M}$ underlying $\mathcal{P}$. For any $s \in S$, let

$L(\alpha^*(s)) = \{\alpha(p) : p \in L(s)\}$. For a proposition $p \in AP$, the proposition $\alpha(p)$ is defined as follows:

If $p = (x_i = val) \in AP_{local}$ for some $x_i \in Loc$, and $type(x_i) \in \{pid, chan\}$ then $\alpha(p) = (x_{\alpha(i)} = \alpha(val))$, otherwise $\alpha(p) = (x_{\alpha(i)} = val)$. If $p = (x = val) \in AP_{global}$ for some $x \in Glob$, and $type(x) \in \{pid, chan\}$ then $\alpha(p) = (x = \alpha(val))$, otherwise $\alpha(p) = p$. If $p = (c[i] = msg) \in AP_{channel}$ for some $c \in Chan$, i.e. msg is at position i on channel c, then $\alpha(p) = (\alpha(c)[i] = \alpha(msg))$. Here α acts on msg by permuting the value of each field of msg which has type pid or $chan$, and leaving all other fields unchanged.

The following theorem shows that in certain cases the permutation α^* of $\mathcal{M}$ defined by an element $\alpha \in Aut(\mathcal{C}(\mathcal{P}))$ is an automorphism of $\mathcal{M}$.

Theorem 2. *Let $\mathcal{P}$ be a Promela program with static channel diagram $\mathcal{C}(\mathcal{P})$ and associated Kripke structure $\mathcal{M}$. Let $\alpha \in Aut(\mathcal{C}(\mathcal{P}))$. If α is valid for $\mathcal{P}$ then $\alpha^* \in Aut(\mathcal{M})$.*

For a proof of this theorem see [11]. The theorem shows that automorphisms of the Kripke structure underlying a Promela program can be obtained by finding symmetries of the static channel diagram for the program. Note that for any LTL property ϕ under investigation, the never claim for ϕ is included with a model (see Section 2.1). It follows that ϕ is invariant under all valid automorphisms constructed in this way. Thus, by Theorem 1, the set of valid automorphisms is suitable for checking the property ϕ over a quotient structure.

The static channel diagram of a program is typically a small graph which can be easily extracted from the program. Additionally, checking for an element α of $Aut(\mathcal{C}(\mathcal{P}))$ whether or not $\alpha(\mathcal{P}) \equiv \mathcal{P}$, can be implemented efficiently (see Section 5.2). Thus, using Theorem 2, it is possible to quickly obtain a group of Kripke structure automorphisms, generated by the set $\{\alpha^* : \alpha \in S, \ \alpha(\mathcal{P}) \equiv \mathcal{P}\}$, where S is the set of generators for $Aut(\mathcal{C}(\mathcal{P}))$. However, this group may not be as large as possible. Consider the generating set for $Aut(\mathcal{C}(\mathcal{P}))$ given in Section 3.1, where $\mathcal{P}$ is the Promela description of the email example. The generators $(2\ 3)(box\_2\ box\_3)$ and $(3\ 4)(box\_3\ box\_4)$ are clearly not valid for $\mathcal{P}$. Let G be the group generated by the remaining generators. Thus $G = \langle (1\ 2)(box\_1\ box\_2), (4\ 5)(box\_4\ box\_5) \rangle$. Consider the group $G' = \langle (1\ 2)(box\_1\ box\_2), (2\ 4)(box\_2\ box\_4), (4\ 5)(box\_4\ box\_5) \rangle$. Each generator of G' is valid for $\mathcal{P}$, and $G \subset G'$ since $(2\ 4)(box\_2\ box\_4) \notin G$. Thus G is not the largest valid subgroup of $Aut(\mathcal{C}(\mathcal{P}))$.

4   Finding the Largest Valid Subgroup of $Aut(\mathcal{C}(\mathcal{P}))$

In this section we establish that, for a Promela program $\mathcal{P}$, there is a unique, largest valid subgroup of $Aut(\mathcal{C}(\mathcal{P}))$. We then present an algorithm to find this subgroup. First we state some preliminary results, omitting the (very straightforward) proofs for space reasons.

Lemma 1. *Let $\alpha, \beta \in Aut(\mathcal{C}(\mathcal{P}))$. Suppose α and β are both valid for $\mathcal{P}$. Then $\alpha\beta$ is valid for $\mathcal{P}$.*

Corollary 1. *Let S be a set of generators for $Aut(\mathcal{C}(\mathcal{P}))$. Let $S' = \{\alpha \in S : \alpha$ is valid for $\mathcal{P}\}$. Then $\langle S' \rangle$ is valid for $\mathcal{P}$.*

Corollary 2. *Suppose $H \leq Aut(\mathcal{C}(\mathcal{P}))$ is valid for $\mathcal{P}$. Let $\alpha \in Aut(\mathcal{C}(\mathcal{P})), \alpha \notin H$ be valid for $\mathcal{P}$. Then $\langle H \cup \{\alpha\} \rangle$ is valid for $\mathcal{P}$.*

Using Lemma 1 we can prove that there is a unique largest valid subgroup of $Aut(\mathcal{C}(\mathcal{P}))$.

Theorem 3. *There is a group $K \leq Aut(\mathcal{C}(\mathcal{P}))$ such that K is valid for $\mathcal{P}$, and for any $H \leq Aut(\mathcal{C}(\mathcal{P}))$ which is also valid for $\mathcal{P}$, $H \leq K$.*

Proof. Let $\mathcal{X}$ be the set of all valid subgroups of $Aut(\mathcal{C}(\mathcal{P}))$. Since $Aut(\mathcal{C}(\mathcal{P}))$ is finite, $Aut(\mathcal{C}(\mathcal{P}))$ has a finite number of subgroups, therefore $\mathcal{X}$ is finite. Let $K = \langle \bigcup_{H \in \mathcal{X}} H \rangle$. Since every generator of K is valid for $\mathcal{P}$, it follows by Lemma 1 that K is valid for $\mathcal{P}$. Clearly $H \leq K$ for every $H \in \mathcal{X}$, i.e. $H \leq K$ for every valid subgroup H of $Aut(\mathcal{C}(\mathcal{P}))$.

Our algorithm for finding the largest valid subgroup of $Aut(\mathcal{C}(\mathcal{P}))$ involves starting with a known valid subgroup H of $Aut(\mathcal{C}(\mathcal{P}))$, and adding valid coset representatives to the generators of H to obtain successively larger valid subgroups. The following lemma is used to determine when the largest possible valid subgroup has been found.

Lemma 2. *Suppose $H \leq Aut(\mathcal{C}(\mathcal{P}))$ and H is valid for $\mathcal{P}$. Let $\{\alpha_1, \alpha_2 \ldots, \alpha_k\}$ be a set of right coset representatives for H in $Aut(\mathcal{C}(\mathcal{P}))$, where $\alpha_1 \in H$, $\alpha_i \in Aut(\mathcal{C}(\mathcal{P})) \setminus H$ for $2 \leq i \leq k$ and $k = |Aut(\mathcal{C}(\mathcal{P}))|/|H|$. Suppose $\alpha_2, \ldots, \alpha_k$ are not valid for $\mathcal{P}$. Then H is the unique largest valid subgroup of $Aut(\mathcal{C}(\mathcal{P}))$.*

Proof. Let K be the unique, largest valid subgroup of $Aut(\mathcal{C}(\mathcal{P}))$. By Theorem 3, $H \leq K$. Suppose $H \subset K$. Then there exists $\alpha \in K$ with $\alpha \notin H$. So $H\alpha$ is a right coset of H in $Aut(\mathcal{C}(\mathcal{P}))$, $H\alpha \neq H$, and $\alpha_i \in H\alpha$ for some $2 \leq i \leq k$. By hypothesis, α_i is not valid for $\mathcal{P}$. However, $H\alpha \subseteq K$ and $\alpha_i \in H\alpha$, so we have $\alpha_i \in K$. This is a contradiction since K is valid for $\mathcal{P}$. Hence $H = K$.

Algorithm 1 shows how the unique largest valid subgroup of $Aut(\mathcal{C}(\mathcal{P}))$ can be computed.

Theorem 4. *Algorithm 1 computes the largest valid subgroup of $Aut(\mathcal{C}(\mathcal{P}))$.*

Proof. By Corollaries 1 and 2, the group H computed by Algorithm 1 is valid for $\mathcal{P}$. The group H is the largest subgroup of $Aut(\mathcal{C}(\mathcal{P}))$ which is valid for $\mathcal{P}$ by Lemma 2.

We discuss the implementation and efficiency of Algorithm 1 in Section 5.3.

5   The SymmExtractor Tool

Given a Promela program $\mathcal{P}$, the SymmExtractor tool finds the largest subgroup of $Aut(\mathcal{C}(\mathcal{P}))$ which is valid for $\mathcal{P}$. By Theorem 2 this group induces a group

Algorithm 1 Algorithm to find the largest valid subgroup of $Aut(\mathcal{C}(\mathcal{P}))$

$S :=$ generators of $Aut(\mathcal{C}(\mathcal{P}))$
$H := \langle\{\alpha \in S : \alpha \text{ is valid for } \mathcal{P}\}\rangle$
$C :=$ representatives of right cosets of H in $Aut(\mathcal{C}(\mathcal{P}))$ except H
while $C \neq \emptyset$ **do**
    $C := C \setminus \{\alpha\}$
    if α is valid for $\mathcal{P}$ **then**
        $H := \langle H \cup \{\alpha\}\rangle$
        if $|Aut(\mathcal{C}(\mathcal{P}))|/|H| < |C|$ **then**
            $C :=$ representatives of right cosets of H in $Aut(\mathcal{C}(\mathcal{P}))$ except H
        end if
    end if
end while

of automorphisms of the underlying Kripke structure which can be used for symmetry reduction while model checking.

Our tool parses a Promela model and stores its abstract syntax tree using a set of Java classes generated by the SableCC compiler generation tool [12]. The grammar for Promela given in [14] was used as input to SableCC, and the SPIN source distribution was used to resolve ambiguities in this grammar.

SymmExtractor operates in four stages. In the first stage the given program is type-checked to ensure that variables of type *pid* and *chan* are used appropriately: for example that *pid* variables should only be assigned to, or compared for equality with, other *pid* variables or values. These restrictions are similar to those applied to variables of type *scalarset* in previous work on symmetry [15]. In the second stage the static channel diagram $\mathcal{C}(\mathcal{P})$ is constructed. In the third stage, the *saucy* program [9] is used to compute a set of generators for $Aut(\mathcal{C}(\mathcal{P}))$. Finally each generator α is checked for validity. Using Algorithm 1, the largest valid subgroup of $Aut(\mathcal{C}(\mathcal{P}))$ is computed.

5.1 Obtaining Static Channel Diagram Automorphisms from a Promela Program

Extracting the static channel diagram from a Promela program is straightforward, and involves one pass over the abstract syntax tree. Each time a *proctype* definition appears in the program, the formal names of outgoing and incoming channels for that *proctype* are recorded. A new channel node is added to the static channel diagram for each static channel in the program. For each *run* statement, a new process node is added to the static channel diagram. The formal parameters of the *proctype* for the new process are substituted for the actual parameters provided in the *run* statement, and edges between processes and channels are added to the channel diagram according to the substituted outgoing and incoming channel names for the *proctype*.

Generators for $Aut(\mathcal{C}(\mathcal{P}))$ are computed using *saucy* [9]. The *saucy* program has been specifically designed for finding automorphisms of sparse graphs which correspond to instances of satisfiability problems. Since static channel diagrams are relatively sparse, the performance of *saucy* is generally very good.

5.2   Checking the Validity of an Element of $Aut(\mathcal{C}(\mathcal{P}))$

Applying a channel diagram automorphism α to $\mathcal{P}$ as described in Section 3.2 is trivial. Determining whether or not $\mathcal{P} \equiv \alpha(\mathcal{P})$ requires the use of a normalisation function. Recall that programs $\mathcal{P}_1$ and $\mathcal{P}_2$ are equivalent if they are identical up to rearrangement of: options in choice statements; operands to commutative operators; and run statements within the init{atomic{...}} block. The function *normalise* sorts the options in a choice statement, the operands of a commutative operator, and the sequence of run statements of the *init* process, using the natural ordering on strings. It is clear that if two programs are *equal* after normalisation then they are *equivalent*. The notions of equivalence and normalisation which we use here are basic but practical. It is easy to construct an example of an obscure program $\mathcal{P}$ such that an element $\alpha \in Aut(\mathcal{C}(\mathcal{P}))$ would not be deemed valid for the program, but would actually induce a valid automorphism of the Kripke structure for the program. However, for all Promela programs our lightweight approach to checking symmetries is safe and very fast, and is sufficient for sensibly written programs.

Checking the validity of an element α against $\mathcal{P}$ involves two passes over the abstract syntax tree for the program: one to apply the permutation, and one to normalise the program after the symmetry has been applied. The original program only needs to be normalised once when checking a set of generators.

5.3   Using GAP to Compute the Largest Valid Subgroup

The computational group theory package GAP is used to implement Algorithm 1. The Java and GAP components of the tool communicate using redirected standard input and output. Given a group G and a subgroup H of G, GAP provides a function to efficiently compute right coset representatives of H in G. The number of generators of $Aut(\mathcal{C}(\mathcal{P}))$ is typically small, and so initial generators for the valid group H are found quickly by checking each generator of $Aut(\mathcal{C}(\mathcal{P}))$ for validity against the program $\mathcal{P}$.

The algorithm performs badly if the initial group H is small, and $Aut(\mathcal{C}(\mathcal{P}))$ is very large. In such cases the number of right coset representatives to consider is, in the worst case, $|Aut(\mathcal{C}(\mathcal{P}))|/|H|$. Our implementation includes a heuristic which can be applied to try to combat this problem. If the size of the initial valid subgroup H can be increased, fewer coset representatives need to be considered. An initial approach involved taking a set X of random elements of $Aut(\mathcal{C}(\mathcal{P})) \setminus H$ and checking the validity of each element of X against $\mathcal{P}$, adding the valid ones to the generators of H. However, when $Aut(\mathcal{C}(\mathcal{P}))$ is large, the probability of a random element being valid for $\mathcal{P}$ may be small. In this case a better approach is, for each $\beta \in X$ and each generator α of H, to check the validity of the element $\beta^{-1}\alpha\beta$ (the *conjugate* of α by β), adding each valid element $\beta^{-1}\alpha\beta$ to the generators of H. Adding random conjugates to the generators of H works well in practice, because discarding invalid generators of $Aut(\mathcal{C}(\mathcal{P}))$ may result in a group which can permute disjoint sets of processes and channels, but cannot permute processes/channels which are in different sets. For example, if $\mathcal{P}$ is the email model, we found in Section 3.3 that the valid generators of $Aut(\mathcal{C}(\mathcal{P}))$

are $(1\ 2)(box\_1\ box\_2)$ and $(4\ 5)(box\_4\ box\_5)$. The group generated by these elements can swap processes 1 and 2, and processes 4 and 5 (similarly channels box_1, box_2 and box_4, box_5), but *cannot* swap e.g. process 2 with process 4 and box_2 with box_4, even though this permutation is valid for $\mathcal{P}$. The element $(2\ 4)(box\_2\ box\_4)$ is a valid element of $Aut(\mathcal{C}(\mathcal{P}))$ which bridges the gap between processes 1, 2 and 4, 5 (and their associated channels). While a random element drawn from $Aut(\mathcal{C}(\mathcal{P}))$ is unlikely to bridge this gap, a random conjugate of $(1\ 2)(box\_1\ box\_2)$ (for example) is more likely to do so, since a conjugate of an element which exchanges two processes (and associated channels) will also exchange two processes (and associated channels).

5.4   Applying SymmExtractor to the Email Example

Running SymmExtractor with our email example as input yields the following output:

```
>symmextractor email.pml
    Program is well typed.
    Finding the static channel diagram C(P).
    Computing the group Aut(C(P)) using saucy.
        Aut(C(P)) = <(box2 box4)(2 4),(5 4)(box4 box5),(box2 box3)(3 2),(3 1)(box3 box1)>
    H = <(box2 box1)(2 1),(5 4)(box4 box5),(box2 box4)(2 4)>
        is a valid group for symmetry reduction.
```

The generators of $Aut(\mathcal{C}(\mathcal{P}))$ found by SymmExtractor agree with our discussion in Section 3.1. Observe that the generator $(2\ 3)(box\_2\ box\_3)$ which we identified to be unsuitable for symmetry reduction in Section 3.2 does not belong to the group H of valid symmetries.

5.5   Extending SymmExtractor

As discussed in Section 2.1, our current approach only applies to models where all processes are instantiated by the *init* process: processes do not themselves instantiate child processes. Large classes of distributed systems can be modelled without dynamic process creation, so this restriction is not too limiting. However, the modelling of multi-threaded software applications often requires dynamic processes to model dynamic thread creation. Extending our approach to handle dynamic process creation will be challenging since the definition of a static channel diagram assumes a constant set of running processes. (Note that our approach *can* handle systems with dynamic *communication structures*, see Section 3.1.)

SymmExtractor cannot detect *data symmetries*, which arise as a result of indistinguishable data values in a protocol. We do not see this as a practical limitation. It is common practice when designing a verification model to abstract away from data [8] and to model only control messages. Indeed, a verification model which allows a range of data values to be communicated between processes, but for which the behaviour of processes is *independent* of the data values communicated, is usually a badly designed model [14].

Structural symmetries arising due to channel-based communication are detected by SymmExtractor. Promela also allows communication by shared variables. To capture symmetry between shared variables, the definition of a static channel diagram can be extended to include additional nodes for shared variables. In this case we add an edge from a process node to a variable node for each process that may write to the variable; and an edge from a variable node to a process node for each process that may read from the variable. The group $Aut(\mathcal{C}(\mathcal{P}))$ then indicates permutations of processes, channels, and shared variables which preserve the communication structure of the program $\mathcal{P}$. The check for validity described in Section 5.2 can be extended to deal with shared variables in a straightforward manner, and the group-theoretic approach of Section 4 can be used to find the largest valid subgroup of $Aut(\mathcal{C}(\mathcal{P}))$.

6 Experimental Results

We have tested SymmExtractor on a variety of Promela models of distributed systems in addition to the email example described earlier. These models include: a token ring network [18]; a client-server system with load balancing [2]; control flow in a three-tiered architecture [18]; and a resource allocation system with two priority levels [17]. Table 1 shows the time taken for symmetry detection in each model, and the size of the resulting symmetry group. Experiments were performed on a PC with a 2.4GHz Intel Xenon processor, 3Gb of available main memory, running Linux (2.4.18), with GAP version 4.3. In all cases, the time taken for symmetry detection would be an acceptable overhead before search. All models have non-trivial symmetry groups of significant order. The theoretical maximum factor of reduction which may be obtained through symmetry reduction with a group G is $|G|$, since the orbit of a state s under G may have at most $|G|$ elements. The results of Table 1 show that the theoretical maximum factors of reduction for the models we have tested are large, though the results do not indicate the factors of reduction which will be achieved in practice.

There is no clear relationship between the time taken for symmetry detection and the number of symmetries detected. This is because the approach to symmetry detection depends on the number of generators of $Aut(\mathcal{C}(\mathcal{P}))$ rather than on the size of $Aut(\mathcal{C}(\mathcal{P}))$, and there is no direct relationship between the size of a group and the size of its generating set. Symmetry detection for the resource allocator example took longer than for the other models due to asymmetry in the model resulting from priority levels. Applying our "random conjugates" heuristic for this model reduced the time for symmetry detection to 4.4s. The overhead of launching GAP in each experiment was less than 1s.

Table 1. Symmetry detection results for some example models

model	time (s)	$|G|$
Token ring	2.52	10
Load balancer	2.70	432
Three-tiered	3.56	144
Resource allocator	7.44	576

7   Related Work

The SymmSpin package [3] implements symmetry reduction techniques for SPIN based on an approach using *scalarsets* [15]. Symmetry reduction techniques for SPIN have also been implemented by adding extra keywords to the Promela language [10]. Neither approach to symmetry reduction can automatically detect symmetries of a model—the user needs to identify symmetry and annotate the model to indicate what symmetry is present. Our approach to symmetry detection is fully automatic. Deriving symmetry from the communication structure of a shared variable concurrent program is proposed, but not automated, in [6]. The idea of detecting symmetries by finding graph automorphisms has also been applied to boolean satisfiability problems [1].

In certain cases, *partial* symmetries of a model can be safely exploited to combat state-explosion during model checking [17]. Our tool cannot currently detect these partial symmetries.

8   Conclusions and Future Work

We have described an approach for detection of structural symmetry in Promela models, and presented a tool, SymmExtractor, to detect these symmetries automatically. Although our approach is specific to models specified in Promela, it can clearly be generalised to any graph-based modelling method.

Future work includes the implementation of symmetry reduction techniques based on these structural symmetries for the SPIN model checker. Although symmetry reduction packages for SPIN exist [3, 10], they are limited with respect to the kinds of symmetry they can exploit. Since our detection method can handle systems with arbitrary structural symmetries, it will be necessary to write a new symmetry reduction package for SPIN. In particular, techniques for efficiently computing orbit representatives during model checking will be required for arbitrary symmetry groups. The SymmSpin tool [3] makes use of various heuristics in systems where there is full symmetry between components. We plan to use a computational group theory package such as GAP to classify the symmetry group of a model so that a suitable heuristic for symmetry reduction can be chosen.

Acknowledgments

The authors would like to thank Simon Gay, Warwick Harvey and Colva Roney-Dougal for their useful comments on this work.

References

1. F. Aloul, A. Ramani, I. Markov, and K. Sakallah. Solving difficult SAT instances in the presence of symmetry. *IEEE Transactions on Computer Aided Design*, 22(9):1117–1137, 2003.

2. J. Balasubramanian, D. Schmidt, L. Dowdy, and O. Othman. Evaluating the performance of middleware load balancing strategies. In *EDOC'01*, pages 135–146. IEEE Computer Society Press, 2004.
3. D. Bosnacki, D. Dams, and L. Holenderski. Symmetric Spin. *International Journal on Software Tools for Technology Transfer*, 4(1):65–80, 2002.
4. M. Calder and A. Miller. Generalising feature interactions in email. In *Feature Interactions in Telecommunications and Software Systems VII*, pages 187–205. IOS Press, 2003.
5. E. M. Clarke, O. Grumberg, and D. Peled. *Model Checking*. The MIT Press, 1999.
6. E. Clarke, E. Emerson, S. Jha, and A. Sistla. Symmetry reductions in model-checking. In *CAV'98*, LNCS 1427, pages 147–158. Springer-Verlag, 1998.
7. E. Clarke, R. Enders, T. Filkhorn, and S. Jha. Exploiting symmetry in temporal logic model checking. *Formal Methods in System Design*, 9(1–2):77–104, 1996.
8. E. Clarke, O. Grumberg, and D. Long. Model checking and abstraction. In *POPL'92*, pages 343–354. ACM Press, 1992.
9. P. T. Darga, M. H. Liffiton, K. A. Sakallah, and I. L. Markov. Exploiting structure in symmetry detection for CNF. In *DAC'04*, pages 530–534. ACM Press, 2004.
10. F. Derepas and P. Gastin. Model checking systems of replicated processes with Spin. In *SPIN'01*, LNCS 2057, pages 235–251. Springer-Verlag, 2001.
11. A. Donaldson, A. Miller, and M. Calder. Finding symmetry in models of concurrent systems by static channel diagram analysis. In *AVoCS'04*, ENTCS 128(6), pages 161–177. Elsevier Science Publishers B.V, 2005.
12. E. Gagnon and L. J. Hendren. SableCC, an object-oriented compiler framework. In *TOOLS'98*, pages 140–154. IEEE Computer Society Press, 1998.
13. The Gap Group. *GAP–Groups Algorithms and Programming, Version 4.2*. Aachen, St. Andrews, 1999. http://www-gap.dcs.st-and.ac.uk/~gap.
14. G. J. Holzmann. *The SPIN model checker: primer and reference manual*. Addison Wesley, 2003.
15. C. Ip and D. Dill. Better verification through symmetry. *Formal Methods in System Design*, 9:41–75, 1996.
16. J. Rose. *A Course in Group Theory*. Dover Publications, 1964.
17. A. P. Sistla and P. Godefroid. Symmetry and reduced symmetry in model checking. *ACM Transactions on Programming Languages and Systems*, 25(4):702–734, 2004.
18. A. S. Tanenbaum and M. van Steen. *Distributed Systems Principles and Paradigms*. Prentice Hall, 2002.

On Partitioning and Symbolic Model Checking

Subramanian Iyer[1], Debashis Sahoo[2], E. Allen Emerson[1], and Jawahar Jain[3]

[1] University of Texas at Austin, Austin, TX 78712, USA
[2] Stanford University, Stanford CA 94305, USA
[3] Fujitsu Laboratoies of America, Sunnyvale CA 94085, USA

Abstract. State space partitioning-based approaches have been proposed in the literature to address the *state-space explosion* problem in model checking. These approaches, whether sequential or distributed, perform a large amount of work in the form of inter-partition (*cross-over*) image computations, which can be expensive. We present a model checking algorithm that aggregates these expensive cross-over images by localizing computation to individual partitions. It reduces the number of cross-over images and drastically outperforms extant approaches in terms of *cross-over* image computation cost as well as total model checking time, often by two orders of magnitude.

Keywords: Symbolic Model Checking, BDD, state partitioning, CTL.

1 Introduction

Model checking is performed by means of successive backwards image computations. Image computation becomes difficult as the data structures representing the state sets grow larger. Large state sets are a direct consequence of the *state-space explosion* problem. Model checking is unable to handle data structures when their size exceeds (roughly by an order of magnitude) what can be reasonably handled in main memory. This frequently happens when handling large designs.

From a practical standpoint, representing the state sets during model checking symbolically using BDDs fails due to this excessive memory requirement. Partitioned symbolic data structures have been proposed in the literature to handle this *memory explosion problem*. Partitioning of the state space is found to balance the trade-off between compactness and canonicity of symbolic BDD representations. In such a framework, each partition of the state space may obey a different variable order.

In a partitioned approach, the state space S is partitioned into subspaces $S_1, S_2, \ldots S_n$. This induces a disjunctive partitioning on the transition relation T into the parts T_{ij} which represents the set of transitions from states in a source partition i to states in the destination partition j. The size of each such transition relation can be further reduced by an implicitly conjoined implementation.

Each partition can be thought of as being the *owner* of a set of states. Transitions from each partition naturally comprise of two components - ones that

J.S. Fitzgerald, I.J. Hayes, and A. Tarlecki (Eds.): FM 2005, LNCS 3582, pp. 497–511, 2005.

are wholly local to individual partitions, and ones that span multiple partitions. Correspondingly, the computed image X comprises of a *local* component X_l and a *cross-over* component X_c. The states corresponding to X_l may be computed locally in each partition. On the other hand, the states in X_c arise out of transitions that originate at a state in one partition and terminate at a state in another, thus, "crossing over" into the destination partition.

Computing cross-over component of the image is often significantly more expensive than the local component for various reasons. Firstly, the cross-over component involves transitions into a potentially larger subspace. Secondly, this incurs the overhead of transporting these states to the partition that "owns" them. Thirdly, the source and destination partitions likely obey different variable orders, and therefore the communicated state set needs to be reordered, which is a known difficult problem as representation sizes become large. Hence even a small reduction in the number of cross-over images can result in a drastic reduction in the total amount of time spent in cross-over images. Our experimental results show that this is indeed the case.

The simplistic way of combining partitioning with the classical model checking algorithm [1, 5], for instance, the distributed model checking algorithm of [2], performs repeated exact images. Each such image computation requires a quadratic number of image computations during each cross-over image computation.

Notice that the set obtained by performing operation EX_l is a subset of the actual image, and in this sense, can be thought of as an under-approximation to EX. This allows for an efficient analysis of reachability [6] and a subset of CTL [3] by replacing a sequence of EX operations by a sequence of the less expensive EX_l operations, interspersed with an occasional EX_c to maintain completeness.

The problem is trickier with greatest fix-points, e.g. the EG operator. The EG operator and its dual AF are important in falsifying and verifying liveness properties. In this case, the final result is the conjunction of successively smaller supersets of the result. If operation EX_c is ignored in pre-image computations, then the result is a subset of the actual pre-image EX. Consequently, some states get pruned early in the greatest fix-point computation for computing the set EG. Since the convergence is on a sequence which is monotonically decreasing, these states pruned early may be lost for ever. Consequently, EX cannot be replaced by EX_l as it compromises on soundness. An important question arises as to how to compute greatest fix-points in the partitioned framework without having to perform repeated frequent cross-over image computations.

In this paper, we propose an alternative *piece-wise* algorithm for model checking CTL formulae in a partitioned setting that addresses these concerns. Our approach exploits the separability of the local and cross-over components of image computation. It performs a number of image computations locally within each partition, and synchronizes occasionally by doing cross-over image computations only when a fix-point is reached locally in each partition.

If during state space traversal, each partition requires many steps of image computation to reach a local fix-point, then the proposed algorithm shows significant gain (which is proportional to the depth of the fix-point).

In section 2, we recall the notions of state space partitioning and the definition of model checking. We present a simple partitioned version of the classical model checking algorithm in section 3. Section 4 describes our modified algorithm designed to localize computation by postponing cross-over image computations. In the final section, we present our experimental results documenting the increased efficiency of our technique.

Note that the set of states that are incorrectly pruned early in the above computation of EG comprises of states, each of which lies in a different partition from its predecessor, and can therefore be discovered only by performing the operation EX_c between partitions, which is expensive. Instead the algorithm maintains an over-approximation to EX_c in each partition. This superset of EX_c is used to calculate a superset of EX at every image. This superset is updated only when each partition reaches a fix-point with respect to local images EX_l. We prove that these over-approximations are monotonically decreasing, and therefore the computed set eventually converges to the desired set EG.

2   Preliminaries

In this section, we briefly look at some background related to state space partitioning and image computation, leading up to a description of the classical model checking algorithm in a partitioned framework.

2.1   State Space Partitioning

The idea of partitioning was used to discuss a function representation scheme called partitioned-ROBDDs in [4] which was further extensively developed in [7].
Definition. [7] Given a Boolean function $f : B^n \to B$, defined over n inputs $X_n = \{x_1, \ldots, x_n\}$, the partitioned-ROBDD (henceforth, POBDD) representation χ_f of f is a set of k function pairs, $\chi_f = \{(w_1, f_1), \ldots, (w_k, f_k)\}$ where, $w_i : B^n \to B$ and $f_i : B^n \to B$, are also defined over X_n and satisfy the following conditions:
1. w_i and f_i are ROBDDs respecting the variable ordering π_i, for $1 \leq i \leq k$.
2. $w_1 \vee w_2 \vee \ldots \vee w_k = 1$
3. $w_i \wedge w_j = 0$, for $i \neq j$
4. $f_i = w_i \wedge f$, for $1 \leq i \leq k$ The set $\{w_1, \ldots, w_k\}$ is denoted by W. Each w_i is called a *window function* and represents a *partition* of the Boolean space over which f is defined. Each partition is represented separately as an ROBDDs and can have a different variable order. Most ROBDD based algorithms can be adapted easily for POBDDs.

Partitioned-ROBDDs are canonical and various Boolean operations can be efficiently performed on them just like ROBDDs. In addition, they can be exponentially more compact than ROBDDs for certain classes of functions. The practical utility of this representation is also demonstrated by constructing ROBDDs for the outputs of combinational circuits [7].

In the rest of this paper, we only consider such *window-based state partitioning*. The reason for this is that this representation is canonical, and allows negation to be performed locally in each partition. Other schemes for dividing the state sets, notably that of [2], need to perform a global synchronization operation to perform negation and this can be expensive.

2.2   Model Checking

We omit the syntax of CTL as it is widely known and readily available in the literature. We shall only note that it is possible to express any CTL formula in terms of the Boolean connectives of propositional logic and the existential temporal operators EX, EU and EG. Such a representation is called the *existential normal form*.

Model Checking is usually performed in two stages: In the first stage, the finite state machine is reduced with respect to the formula being model checked and then the reachable states are computed. The second stage involves computing the set of states falsifying the given formula. The reachable states computed earlier are used as a *care set* in this step. These two stages can be performed either one after the other by -computing the reachable states first, or in an interleaved manner, where the reachable states are computed on demand. For the purpose of this paper, and to keep the discussion restricted to the model checking algorithm, we shall assume that the set of reachable states is computed and provided *a priori*.

Since there exist computational procedures for efficiently performing Boolean operations on symbolic BDD data structures, including POBDDs, model checking of CTL formulas primarily is concerned with the symbolic application of the temporal operators. EXq is a backward image and uses the same machinery as image computation during reachability, with the adjustment for the direction. $EpUq$ (resp. EGp) has been traditionally represented as the least (resp. greatest) fix-point of the operator $\tau(Z) = q \vee (p \wedge EXZ)$ (resp. $\tau(Z) = p \wedge EXZ$).

We now examine the classical model checking algorithm, modified for a partitioned representation of the state sets. This is a simple algorithm, along the lines of the distributed model checking algorithm of [2].

3   Classical Model Checking with Partitioning

First, a word on our terminology. Each partition *owns* states that are in its subspace, as defined by its window function. Conversely, such states *belong* to the partition. We say that a partition performs operations on sets that it owns. The result of such operations may lie in a different subspace and may then need to be transferred to one or more other partitions. It is important to make this distinction between the partition where the operation is performed and the partition to whom the result finally belongs, because they may obey different variable orders[1] and variable reordering is known to be expensive.

---

[1] Further, in case of a parallel implementation, such partitions may be physically on different processors. For now, we ignore this detail.

Since backward image computation is the basic unit operation in performing model checking, we first examine image computation in the presence of partitioning.

3.1   Partitioned Image Computation

Given a set of states, $R(s)$, that the system can reach, the set of next states, $N(s')$, is calculated using the equation $N(s') = \exists_{s,i}[T(s, s', i) \wedge R(s)]$. This calculation is also known as *image computation*. Similarly, the *backward image computation*, which calculates the set of states $N(s)$ from which the system can reach given set of states $R(s')$, uses the equation $N(s) = \exists_{s',i'}[T(s, s', i) \wedge R(s')]$. The computation of EXp can be done using the backward image computation. State space partitioning into n disjoint parts induces a partitioning of the transition relation T into n^2 parts T_{jk} consisting of transitions from a state in partition j to a state in partition k. We can derive T_{jk} by conjoining T with the respective window functions as $T_{jk}(s, s', i) = w_j(s)w_k(s')T(s, s', i)$. Thus we can express the transition relation $T(s, s', i) = \bigvee_j \bigvee_k T_{jk}(s, s', i)$ as an induced disjunctive partitioning.

ComputeEX(Set R, Transition Relation T) {
  foreach (partition j)
   foreach (partition k)
    $PreImg^{jk}(s) = \exists_{s',i}[T_{jk}(s, s', i) \wedge R_k(s')]$
    reorder BDD $PreImg^{jk}(s)$ from partition order k to order j
   end for
   $N_j(s) = \bigvee_k PreImg^{jk}(s)$
  end for
  output N
}

Fig. 1. Backwards Image Computation with Partitioning

Figure 1 shows how to calculate EXp separately on each partitions. Here the set R_j is the set of states that represent p in partition j, and the set N_j represents EXp in partition j which are computed by application of the transition relation $T_{jk}(s, s', i)$.

To compute the pre-image, the n^2 computations $T_{jk}(R_k)$ need to be performed, followed by n disjunctions as shown. Recall that when using a partitioned-BDD to represent the set of states, each partition is maintained separately in memory, under differing variable orders. It is therefore natural that the pre-image of states in partition k under the transitions leading to each partition j, i.e. the computation $T_{jk} \wedge (R_k)$, is performed in partition k. Each partition k thus computes states that potentially belong to every other partition. Subsequently the disjunction to obtain the pre-image lying with partition j, i.e. the computation of $\bigvee_k PreImg^{jk}$, is performed by partition j. As a consequence, the set $PreImg^{jk}$ needs to be transferred from partition k to partition j, when j and k differ.

We call these $n^2 - n$ computations as *cross-over image* computations, in the sense that the source and destination partitions are different. It must be emphasized that *Cross-over image computation is expensive* for various reasons: First, a quadratic number of image computations need to be performed as above and the BDDs need to be accessed from every partition. In the case of large designs, where the BDDs of even a single partition can run into millions of nodes, this usually means accessing stored partitions from secondary memory. Then, the BDD variable order of the computed image set must be changed from the order of the source partition to that of each of its target partitions, before the new states can be added to the reached set in the target. Reordering large BDDs can be very expensive. Finally, there may also be other overhead, for eg., in the case of a parallel implementation there is the overhead of physically transmitting a large number of these BDDs over the network.

Thus the cost of a cross-over image computation may be significantly greater than that of a local image computation.

Next, we consider a simple partitioned model checking algorithm for the fix-point operators.

computeEU(p, q) {	computeEG(p) {
$S := q$ and $S.old := \phi$	$S := p$
repeat	repeat
$S.old := S$	$S.old := S$
$temp :=$ computeEX(S)	$temp :=$ computeEX(S)
forall (partitions j)	forall (partitions j)
$S_j := q_j \vee (p_j \wedge temp_j)$	$S_j := p_j \wedge temp_j$
end for	end for
until$(S = S.old)$	until$(S = S.old)$
output S	output S
}	}
a) Least fix-point, $E(pUq)$	b) Greatest fix-point, EGp

Fig. 2. Classical Model Checking of Fix-points in presence of Partitioning

3.2   Partitioned Computation of Fix-Points

The classical fix-point algorithms for $E(pUq)$ and EGp as modified to use a partitioned data structure are illustrated in Fig. 2. Notice that these rely on the partitioned image computation and therefore perform one set of cross-over images in each iteration. In other words, each iteration until the fix-point is reached performs a number of image computations, quadratic in the number of partitions. As discussed in Section 3.1, this can get rather expensive.

In the next section, we present a model checking algorithm that localizes computation to individual partitions by postponing these cross-over image computations.

4   Partitioned Model Checking

In this section we present a new partitioned model checking algorithm which works by postponing cross-over image computations. When the design is defective and is falsified, this algorithm discovers bugs faster, by virtue of computations being localized to individual partitions. Even when the design is correct and is verified, this algorithm converges after fewer cross-over image computations. We show that in the worst case, this algorithm has at most as many cross-over image computations as the partitioned version of the classical algorithm, presented in the previous section.

Model checking of boolean connectives is well-known for the partitioned approach, so we will only describe the image and fix-point computations. It must however be mentioned that all boolean operations - conjunction, disjunction as well as negation - are local to individual partitions[2] and involve no interaction between them. Also, it suffices to consider the existential temporal operators EX, EG and EU, as these with the propositional connectives form a basis for all CTL formulae.

4.1   Image Computation

The main computation in the partitioned form of the classical model checking algorithm is image computation. As noted in the previous section, the computation of EXp from p comprises of n^2 image computations, re-orderings and state set transfers between partitions and this can get expensive. Even though our focus is on trying to avoid computing the entire image *at every step*, it may still be necessary to perform the full image computation in two cases – firstly, for the occasional cross-over images, and secondly, when the property is expressed in terms of the EX or AX operators. In this section, we look at some of the issues in computing the image.

We find that performing the cross-over images one partition at a time is memory intensive and often the intermediate BDDs get very large for many examples. Therefore, we advocate performing these cross-over image computations from each partition into many partitions at a time.[3]

In order to perform cross-over images efficiently, we maintain a *transfer manager* M. Given the set p, in order to compute EXp, each partition i computes the image $T_{ii}(p_i)$ which it keeps locally and the set of unowned states $U_i = T_{i\bar{i}}(p_i)$ which is communicated to the manager M. M uses the window functions w_j to calculate the sets $S_j = \bigvee_{i \neq j} U_i * w_j$ and then transmits the states S_j to partition j. Thus EXp is computed by doing $2n$ image computations and $2n$ transfers between partitions, although the number of re-orderings remains n^2.

It should be mentioned here that in a multiprocessor environment, such a manager can become a bottleneck, and should perhaps be dispensed with. But

---

[2] This is an important consequence of window-based partitioning.

[3] Here, it must be noted that we address the case of verification using uniprocessor systems. The partitioned approach easily extends to distributed and parallel computing environments and our improvements are expected to scale accordingly.

$\boxed{\begin{array}{l}\textbf{Compute}EX_l(R) \ \{\\ \quad \text{foreach (partition } j)\\ \quad PreImg^{jj}(s) =\\ \quad\quad \exists_{s',i}[T_{jj}(s,s',i) \wedge R_j(s')]\\ \quad N_j(s) = PreImg^{jj}(s)\\ \quad \text{end for}\\ \quad \text{output } N\\ \}\\ \\ \\ \quad\quad\quad \text{a) Local, } EX_lp\end{array}}$ $\boxed{\begin{array}{l}\textbf{Compute}EX_c(R) \ \{\\ \quad \text{foreach (partition } j)\\ \quad\quad \text{foreach (partition } k \neq j)\\ \quad\quad PreImg^{jk}(s) =\\ \quad\quad\quad \exists_{s',i}[T_{jk}(s,s',i) \wedge R_k(s')]\\ \quad\quad \text{reorder BDD } PreImg^{jk}(s)\\ \quad\quad\quad \text{from partition order } k \text{ to order } j\\ \quad\quad \text{end for}\\ \quad\quad N_j(s) = \bigvee_k PreImg^{jk}(s)\\ \quad \text{end for}\\ \quad \text{output } N\\ \}\\ \quad\quad\quad \text{b) Cross-over, } EX_cp\end{array}}$

Fig. 3. Local and Cross-over Components of Image Computation with Partitioning

the point is that, in each partition, only a constant number of image computations be performed, rather than a number linear in the number of partitions. Thus the total number of image computations is linear rather than quadratic in the number of partitions.

We call the fraction $T_{ii}(p_i)$ that is computed locally using T_{ii} as the ith projection of the local image EX_l. The rest of the images comprise the cross-over image EX_c. The algorithms to compute EX_l and EX_c are shown in Figure 3.

4.2   Fix-Point Computations

The main idea for model checking fix-points is that the computations can be significantly localized to individual partitions by postponing the cross-over image computations EX_c, which are then aggregated and performed infrequently. Accordingly, we define the fix-point operators in terms of two operations – local image computations EX_l and cross-over image computations EX_c, rather than the classical definition in terms of just the image computation operation, EX.

The algorithms for computing $E(pUq)$ and EGp are shown in Figure 4. The key idea is to create an under-approximation (resp. over-approximation) to EXp, which can be wholly calculated locally within individual partitions, so that the least (resp. greatest) fix-point computation can be localized.

Definition 1. *Each iteration of the outermost repeat-until loop in Algo.2 (shown in Fig. 2) and Algo.4 (resp. Fig. 4) is called a* phase *of the respective algorithm.*

From this definition, we note the following.

Lemma 1. *Every phase has one and only one cross-over image.*

We will show that Algo.4 terminates with the correct result and that the number of its phases is at most the number of phases in Algo.2. Since each such phase has precisely one cross-over image computation, we have that the number of cross-over images computed by the new algorithm is, in the worst case, no more than that for the existing algorithm. However in practice, the

computeEU(p, q) {	computeEG(p) {
$\quad S := q$	$\quad S := p$
$\quad S.old := \phi$	$\quad Border := p \wedge EX_c(S)$
$\quad$repeat	$\quad$repeat
$\quad\quad S.old := S$	$\quad\quad S.old := S$
$\quad\quad$forall (partitions j)	$\quad\quad$forall (partitions j)
$\quad\quad\quad$repeat	$\quad\quad\quad$repeat
$\quad\quad\quad\quad S_j.old := S_j$	$\quad\quad\quad\quad S_j.old := S_j$
$\quad\quad\quad\quad S_j := S_j \vee (p_j \wedge EX_l(S_j, j))$	$\quad\quad\quad\quad S_j := p_j \wedge (EX_l(S_j, j) \vee Border_j)$
$\quad\quad\quad$until$(S_j = S_j.old)$	$\quad\quad\quad$until$(S_j == S_j.old)$
$\quad\quad$end for	$\quad\quad$end for
$\quad\quad S := S \vee (p \wedge EX_c(S))$	$\quad\quad Border := p \wedge EX_c(S)$
$\quad$until$(S = S.old)$	$\quad$until$(S == S.old)$
$\quad$output S	$\quad$output S
}	}
a) Least fix-point, $E(pUq)$	b) Greatest fix-point, EGp

Fig. 4. Fix-point Computations localized by postponing cross-over images

new algorithm computes a number of "local" images in each phase. Therefore it has fewer phases than the algorithm of Fig.2 almost always. As noted before, even a small reduction in the number of cross-over images can result in a drastic reduction in the total amount of time spent in cross-over images.

Theorem 1. *a)[3] The procedure computeEU of Fig 4a, given the set of states corresponding to formulas p and q as inputs, terminates with the output S being precisely the set of states that model the formula $E(pUq)$.*
b) The number of its phases does not exceed the number of phases for Algo.2a.

Proof: Let the set of states S at the end of the ith phase be called S^i. The termination is guaranteed because the sequence of sets S^i is strictly monotonic increasing.

We first show the soundness of Algo.4a, i.e., at all times $S \models E(pUq)$. We show this by induction on the sets S^k. This clearly holds for any state in S^0, since every state in S^0 satisfies q and therefore $E(pUq)$. Assume that $S^i \models E(pUq)$. Consider a state $s \in S^{i+1} - S^i$. Then, by construction of S^{i+1} from S^i, we have $s \models p$. Either s is added in the local image computation EX_l for some partition j or in the cross-over image computations EX_c. In either case, $s \models p$. It remains to show that s is the predecessor of a state that models $E(pUq)$. In the first case, such a state is in the same partition as s and in the second case, such a state exists in partition k such that s was added in the cross-over image computation from k to j. Thus in either case, s models $EX(E(pUq))$. Consequently, Algo.3a is sound.

Next, we show completeness, i.e., that every state of $E(pUq)$ is indeed in set S. For every state $s \models E(pUq)$, there exists a sequence of states $s_0, s_1, \ldots, s_k$ that has the smallest length $k \geq 0$ such that $s_0 = s$, $s_k \models q$, $\forall i < k : s_i \models p$ and $\forall i < k : s_i \in EX(s_{i+1})$. This sequence of states is called a *witness* for the inclusion of s in $E(pUq)$, and k is its *length*. Let T^k be the set of states whose inclusion in $E(pUq)$ is witnessed by a path of length at most k. We prove by induction on k that $T^k \subseteq S$. In the base case, this trivially holds because $T^0 = q = S^0 \subseteq S$. Now, assume that $T^i \subseteq S$. For any state $s \in T^{i+1}$ consider the sequence of states $s_0 = s, s_1, \ldots, s_{i+1}$ that witnesses its inclusion in $E(pUq)$. The sequence $s_1, \ldots, s_{i+1}$ is a witness for s_1, therefore $s_1 \in T^i \subseteq S$. In particular, there exists a smallest j so that $s_1 \in S^j$. We know that $s \models p$ and $s \in EX(s_1) \subseteq EX(S^j)$. From the definition of S^j and Algo.4a, we have that $s \in S^{j+1}$, whereby $T^{i+1} \subseteq S^{j+1} \subseteq S$. By induction, this gives us $E(pUq) \subseteq S$.

This proves that Algo.4a terminates with the set $S = E(pUq)$. Notice that the set of states at the end of the kth phase of Algo.2a is precisely T^i. As above, $\forall i, T^{i+1} \subseteq S^{j+1} \subseteq S^{i+1}$. Hence Algo.4a has at most as many phases as Algo.2a.   ∎

Before proving an analogous result for the greatest fix-point operator EGp, we briefly motivate its construction. As $EX_l p$ is a subset of EXp, the result of localizing the computation by performing repeated EX_l operations yields an underapproximation at every step. Since the greatest fix-point operator converges by a sequence of monotonically decreasing sets, under-approximation leads to some states being pruned too early and being lost for ever. States that may be incorrectly pruned early in the computation of EG comprises of states, each of which lies in a different partition from its predecessor, and can therefore be discovered only by performing the operation EX_c, which is the expensive component of image computation.

Algo.4b compensates for this by maintaining a set *Border*, which is the set of all states which have a successor in a different partition than themselves. This is, clearly an over-approximation to EX_c in each partition. This superset of EX_c is used to calculate a superset of EX at every image. This *Border* is updated only once in each phase, when each partition has reached a fix-point with respect to local images EX_l. These over-approximations are monotonically decreasing, and so the computed set eventually converges to the desired set EG.

We now prove the following theorem.

Theorem 2. *a) The procedure computeEG of Fig 4b, given the set of states corresponding to formula p as input , terminates with the output S being precisely the set of states that model the formula EGp.*
b) The number of its phases does not exceed the number of phases for Algo.2b.

Proof: Again, let the set of states S at the end of the ith phase be called S^i. The termination is guaranteed because the sequence of sets S^i is strictly monotonic decreasing.

We first show the soundness of Algo.4b, i.e., the algorithm only deletes states which do not satisfy EGp. Note that a state can be deleted only in the two circumstances. The first is if it does not satisfy p and is deleted in the very beginning. We can therefore assume that all states under consideration satisfy p. The second way a state may be deleted is during some phase, when it is not a predecessor to any state in its own partition, and it is not on the Border, i.e., it has been determined previously that this state is not a predecessor to any state in another partition. Thus all successors to such a state satisfy $\neg p$, and therefore any deleted state is not in EGp.

Next we show completeness, i.e., the algorithm deletes all states that do not satisfy EGp. Consider a state $s \not\models EGp$. Then there exists a sequence of states $s_0, s_1, \ldots, s_k$, which is cycle-free that has the greatest length $k \geq 0$ such that $s_0 = s$, $s_k \models \neg p$, $\forall i < k : s_i \models p$ and $\forall i < k : s_i \in EX(s_{i+1})$. This sequence of states is called a *witness* for the exclusion of s from EGp, and k is its *length*. Now, let T^k be the set of states whose exclusion from EGp is witnessed by a longest cycle-free path of length at most k. We prove by induction on k that $T^k \cap S^k = \phi$. In the base case, this trivially holds because $T^0 = \neg q$ and $S^0 = q$. Now, assume that $T^i \cap S^i = \phi$. For any state $s \in T^{i+1}$ consider the sequence of states $s_0 = s, s_1, \ldots, s_{i+1}$ that witnesses its exclusion from EGp. The sequence $s_1, \ldots, s_{i+1}$ is a witness for s_1, therefore $s_1 \in T^i$, and therefore $s_1 \notin S^i$. In particular, there exists a smallest j so that s_1 was deleted in the jth stage of the algorithm. Two cases arise, either both s_0 and s_1 are in the same partition or they are in different partitions. If they are in the same partition, then s_0 is deleted in the jth stage also when a fix-point is computed locally in that partition. If they are in different partitions, then s_0 is in the border set for its partition, and is deleted from this border set at the end of the jth stage because its last successor s_1 is deleted and no other successors can exist because this is the longest witness. Therefore s is deleted in the $j + 1^{th}$ stage, as required to be proved.

This proves that Algo.4b terminates with the set EGp. Notice that the set of states T^i is precisely the set of states deleted in phase i of Algo.2b. As above, states in T_i have all been deleted by the end of i phases of the algorithm. Hence Algo.4b has at most as many phases as Algo.2b.   ∎

4.3   Comparison

In the worst case, Algo.4 requires at most as many phases as Algo.2. However, in practice, Algo.4 outperforms Algo.2, because when computing the least (resp greatest) fix-point by localizing computation to individual partitions, Algo.4 often discovers (resp. prunes) many more states than when performing just one image computation in each phase. Thus the postponement of cross-over images affords a significant benefit in overall faster convergence of the model checking algorithm, often reducing the number of phases.

We now analyze the benefit of reducing the number of cross-over images. Consider a simple model where the number of image computations performed is the same in each partition, say n. Further, assume the time for computing EX_l is L and that for EX_c is C.

Thus Algo.2 performs n phases, each with one computation of EX_l and EX_c, and incurs a total time $C_{old} = n * (L + C)$. Algo.4 needs potentially fewer phases, say $m \leq n$. Each such phase has one EX_c computation and a number of EX_l computations, for concreteness say there are $k \geq 1$ of them. This gives a total time $C_{new} = m * (k * L + C)$.

Recall from Section 3.1 that $C >> L$. Thus for reasonable k, the reduction in the number of cross-over images is directly reflected in the reduction of the total model checking time. Further, in the best case scenario, when $m * k = n$, the reduction may be by as much as a factor of k.

In practice a significant gain is observed, as borne out by the experimental results that are described in the next section.

If operation EX_c is ignored in pre-image computations, then the result is a subset of the actual pre-image EX, and this means that some states get pruned early in the greatest fix-point computation for computing the set EG. Since the convergence is on a sequence which is monotonically decreasing, these states pruned early may be lost for ever.

The new algorithm is shown in the following figure. Here preImgComm refers to the fraction of the pre-image that needs to be communicated via a communications manager EX_c and preImgPart refers to the fraction of the image that is computed locally within each partition EX_l.

5   Experimental Results

We implemented the algorithm of Fig. 3 on top of the CUDD package for BDDs using the VIS-2.0 verification environment, which is a state-of-the-art public domain BDD-based formal verification package. We have chosen VIS for its Verilog support and its powerful OBDD-package (i.e. CUDD [8]). As our techniques affect only the BDD-data structures and algorithms, they can – with moderate effort – be implemented in other packages as well. These techniques work with any method of image computation; all experiments here are conducted using the IWLS95 method.

We use the partitioning scheme detailed in [3] for performing reachability analysis. Once the reachable states are computed, the model checking algorithms use the same partitions created during reachability analysis.

Benchmarks

We chose the public domain circuits and their model checking properties from the VIS-Verilog [9] benchmark suite. For sake of brevity, results are omitted for some of the smaller examples.

Results

We notice that crossover image computation is indeed a bottleneck in verification. On a uniprocessor machine, in the VIS-Verilog benchmark suite, there are examples where the program runs out of memory while performing the crossover images. Thus a reduction in the number and frequency of such cross-over images is critical for the full utilization of computing resources in a multi-processor environment.

The run-times for our sequential implementation are shown in Table 1. The first column of Table 1 has the name of the circuit and the property being checked. This is followed by the data for cross-over image computation. Firstly, the number of cross-over images is shown for the Naive algorithm, labeled *Old* and for our proposed algorithm, labeled *New*. The next two columns show the respective time taken. This is followed by the speedup achieved by the proposed algorithm over the older one. The last two columns show the total time taken by the model checking, after reachability has finished.

Table 1. Comparison of existing and proposed algorithms for partitioned model checking CTL properties on circuits in the VIS Verilog benchmark suite. For each circuit and property, the first pair of columns shows the number of inter-partition cross-over images performed by the two methods, the second set shows the time required for these cross-over images, and the speedup achieved by the new method and the final set shows the total model checking time

Circuit_	Cross-over images					Model Checking time(sec)	
Property	Number		Time (s)				
	Old	New	Old	New	Speedup	Old	New
bpbs	4	1	24	1	24	398	313
gcd_1	15	7	19.11	.7	27	68.97	108.07
gcd_2	15	7	18.27	.16	114	27.56	9.06
gcd_3	10	8	37.13	4.29	8.6	134.65	56.32
gcd_4	10	8	37.41	3.44	11	108.76	42.11
gcd_5	11	9	37.13	46.3	0.8	107.31	92.19
gcd_6	12	9	42.96	3.79	11	121.66	53.69
gcd_7	13	9	42.98	3.99	11	132.7	50.51
gcd_8	14	9	35.68	1.41	25	128.04	48.94
gcd_9	15	9	31.77	0.91	35	119.63	48.04
gcd_10	16	9	28.72	0.57	50	111.89	46.47
ghg	9367	6	166.12	0.15	1107	280.75	27.31
idu32_1	3	3	12.35	89.96	0.13	294.49	406.61
idu32_2	2	2	0.07	0.02	3.5	0.12	0.03
idu32_3	3	3	0.07	0.02	3.5	0.06	0.02
idu32_4	8	4	0.61	0.02	30	0.82	0.1
idu32_5	8	4	0.61	0.03	20	0.83	0.11
idu32_6	7	2	0.83	0.02	41	1.27	0.1
idu32_7	7	4	1.31	0.02	65	2.11	0.22
idu32_8	8	4	13.63	0.03	454	14.15	0.28
idu32_9	8	4	0.38	0.02	19	0.52	0.05
idu32_10	23	9	0.58	0.04	14	0.8	0.15
luckySeven	64	35	80.12	55.89	1.4	114.64	82.03
nosel	7	3	106.01	10.2	10	270.18	130.87
product	1	1	3	3	1	1798	418
s1269b_1	1	1	9.42	0.01	942	15	13
s1269b_2	8	8	67	1.01	67	93	1
soap_44	53	5	592.09	1.2	493	714.81	28.24
soap_45	80	8	106.76	1.86	57	224.19	104.11
soap_46	53	5	92.9	1.14	81	187.79	28.76
soap_47	52	5	41.87	1.11	37	94.89	31.83
soap_48	60	5	42.3	0.76	55	98.91	56.41
soap_49	79	9	94.68	1.61	58	207.18	73.78
soap_50	60	5	199.6	1.05	190	299.4	22.9
sppint2_1	5	4	86.26	45.06	1.9	100.39	58.26
sppint2_4	1	1	2.8	0.01	280	3.06	2.82
sppint2_5	7	3	4.4	0.01	440	4.94	0.75
sppint2_6	5	3	0.2	0.13	1.5	0.68	0.28
sppint2_7	16	6	4.23	0.7	6	24.66	2.27
sppint2_8	5	4	1.22	0.37	3.3	1.87	0.71
sppint2_9	14	6	1.29	0.74	1.7	5.01	1.81
sppint2_10	5	4	1.31	0.17	7.7	1.83	0.32
two	38	24	30.6	18.8	1.6	46	28
usb_phy_1	49	23	16	19	0.8	43	29
usb_phy_3	40	19	108.51	11.83	9	24.89	28.97
usb_phy_4	21	11	5.6	2.32	2.4	12.01	8.26
usb_phy_6	5	5	0.97	1.05	0.9	2	2.99
usb_phy_7	39	17	10.96	2.14	5	24.32	8.72

Experimentally, the proposed algorithm converges faster, both in terms of total time, as well as in terms of number of expensive cross-over image computations that are performed. Further, the time taken by cross-over images as a percentage of total time is reduced. These are demonstrated in the table that follows. In numerous cases (e.g. s1269, soap, ghg, etc.), we find that total cross-over image time is reduced by two orders of magnitude or more.

Using the data in Table 1, we can compare the total time taken for model checking by the two methods. Notice that the proposed algorithm reduces, often dramatically, the number of cross-over images and the proportion of the total time that is spent in doing them. In almost all the examples, this leads to a direct improvement in the total time.

6   Conclusion

We have presented a model checking algorithm in the presence of state space partitioning, that aggregates and postpones cross-over image computations, allowing for significant localization of image computations. This is also found in practice to reduce the number of iterations in fix-point computations.

If during state space traversal, each partition requires many steps of image computation to reach a local fix-point, then the proposed algorithm shows significant gain (which is proportional to the depth of the fix-point). In the worst case, this method would be identical to the naive one, with strict alternation between localized (EX_l) and cross-over (EX_c) image operations in every fix-point calculation. However, this is extremely unlikely because it corresponds to a case where every "path" corresponding to a formula comprises of states *each* of which lies in a different partition from its predecessor. This does not happen in practice when partitioning is done properly.

Our experiments have been conducted on uniprocessor machines, but this algorithm can be easily parallelized and we believe its benefits would scale to an implementation in a multi-processor environment.

We believe this algorithm can be generalized to more expressive logics like the full μ-calculus with a few modifications. A parallel form of the proposed algorithm can also provide better resource usage than existing distributed model checking algorithms.

References

1. E.M. Clarke and E.A. Emerson. Design and synthesis of synchronization skeletons using branching time temporal logic. In *Proc. IBM Workshop on Logics of Programs*, volume 131 of *Lecture Notes in Computer Science*, pages 52–71. Springer-Verlag, 1981.
2. Orna Grumberg, Tamir Heyman, and Assaf Schuster. Distributed symbolic model checking for μ-calculus. In *Computer Aided Verification*, pages 350–362, 2001.
3. S. Iyer, D. Sahoo, C. Stangier, A. Narayan, and J. Jain. Improved symbolic Verification Using Partitioning Techniques. In *Proc. of CHARME 2003*, volume 2860 of *Lecture Notes in Computer Science*, 2003.

4. J. Jain. On analysis of boolean functions. *Ph.D Dissertation, Dept. of Electrical and Computer Engineering, The University of Texas at Austin*, 1993.
5. Kenneth L. McMillan. *Symbolic Model Checking.* Kluwer Academic Publishers, 1993.
6. A. Narayan, A. Isles, J. Jain, R. Brayton, and A. Sangiovanni-Vincentelli. Reachability Analysis Using Partitioned-ROBDDs. In *Proc. of the Intl. Conf. on Computer-Aided Design*, pages 388–393, 1997.
7. A. Narayan, J. Jain, M. Fujita, and A. L. Sangiovanni-Vincentelli. Partitioned-ROBDDs - A Compact, Canonical and Efficiently Manipulable Representation for Boolean Functions. In *Proc. of the Intl. Conf. on Computer-Aided Design*, pages 547–554, 1996.
8. Fabio Somenzi. CUDD: CU Decision Diagram Package ftp://vlsi.colorado.edu/pub, 2001.
9. VIS. Vis verilog benchmarks http://vlsi.colorado.edu/ vis/, 2001.

Dynamic Component Substitutability Analysis*

Natasha Sharygina, Sagar Chaki, Edmund Clarke, and Nishant Sinha

Carnegie Mellon University
{nys, chaki}@sei.cmu.edu
{emc, natalie, nishants}@cs.cmu.edu

Abstract. This paper presents an *automated* and *compositional* procedure to solve the substitutability problem in the context of evolving software systems. Our solution contributes two techniques for checking correctness of software upgrades: 1) a technique based on simultaneous use of over and under approximations obtained via existential and universal abstractions; 2) a *dynamic* assume-guarantee reasoning algorithm – previously generated component assumptions are reused and altered on-the-fly to prove or disprove the global safety properties on the updated system. When upgrades are found to be non-substitutable our solution generates constructive feedback to developers showing how to improve the components. The substitutability approach has been implemented and validated in the COMFORT model checking tool set and we report encouraging results on an industrial benchmark.

Keywords: Software Model Checking, Verification of Evolving Software, Learning Regular Sets, Assume/Guarantee Reasoning.

1 Introduction

Software systems evolve throughout the product life-cycle. For example, any software module (or component) is inevitably transformed as designs take shape, requirements change, and bugs are discovered and fixed. In general such evolution results in the removal of previous behaviors from the component and addition of new ones. Since the behavior of the updated software component has no direct correlation to that of its older counterpart, substituting it directly can lead to two kinds of problems. First, the removal of behavior can lead to unavailability of previously provided services. Second, the addition of new behavior can lead to violation of global correctness properties that were previously being respected.

In this context, the *substitutability* problem has been defined [7] as the verification of the following two criteria: (i) any *updated portion* of a software system must continue to provide all *services* offered by its earlier counterpart, and (ii) previously established

---

* This research was conducted as part of the CMU/SEI IRAD project on Verification of Evolving Software and partially sponsored by the Office of Naval Research (ONR). The views and conclusions contained in this document are those of the authors and should not be interpreted as representing the official policies, either expressed or implied, of ONR, the U.S. Government or any other entity.

J.S. Fitzgerald, I.J. Hayes, and A. Tarlecki (Eds.): FM 2005, LNCS 3582, pp. 512–528, 2005.
© Springer-Verlag Berlin Heidelberg 2005

system *correctness properties* must remain valid for the new version of the software system.

Model checking can be used at each stage of a system's evolution to solve both the above problems. However, conventionally model checking is applied to the entire system after every update irrespective of the degree of modification involved. The amount of time and effort required to verify an entire system can be prohibitive and repeating the exercise after each (even minor) system update is therefore impractical. In this article we present an *automated* framework that *localizes* the necessary verification to only modified system components, and thereby reduces dramatically the effort to check substitutability after every system update. Note that our framework is general enough to handle changes in the environment since the environment can also be modeled as a component.

In our framework a component is essentially a C program communicating with other components via blocking message passing. An assembly is a collection of such concurrently executing and mutually interacting components. We will define the notion of a component's behavior precisely later but for now let us denote the set of behaviors of a component C by $Behv(C)$. Given two components C and C' we will write $C \sqsubseteq C'$ to mean $Behv(C) \subseteq Behv(C')$.

Suppose we are given an assembly of components: $C = \{C_1, \ldots, C_n\}$, and a safety property φ. Now suppose that *multiple* components in C are upgraded. In other words, consider an index set $\mathcal{I} \subseteq \{1, \ldots, n\}$ such that for each $i \in \mathcal{I}$ there is a *new* component C'_i to be used in place of its *old* version C_i. Our goal is to check the substitutability of C'_i for C_i in C for every $i \in \mathcal{I}$ with respect to the property φ. This paper presents a framework that satisfies this goal by establishing the following two tasks:

Containment. Verify, for each $i \in \mathcal{I}$, that every behavior of C_i is also a behavior of C'_i, i.e., $C_i \sqsubseteq C'_i$. If $C_i \not\sqsubseteq C'_i$, we also construct a set $\mathcal{F}_i$ of behaviors in $Behv(C_i) \setminus Behv(C'_i)$ which will be subsequently used for feedback generation. Note that the upgrade may involve the removal of behaviors designated as errant, say B. In this case, we check $C_i \setminus B \sqsubseteq C'_i$ since behaviors of B will clearly be absent in C'_i.

Compatibility. Let us denote by C' the assembly obtained from C by replacing the old component C_i with its new version C'_i for each $i \in \mathcal{I}$. Since in general it is not the case that for each $i \in \mathcal{I}$, $C'_i \sqsubseteq C_i$. Therefore, the new assembly C' may have more behaviors than the old assembly C. Hence C' might violate φ even though C did not. Thus, our second task is to verify that C' satisfies the safety property φ (which would imply that the new components can be safely integrated).

Note that checking compatibility is non-trivial because it requires the verification of a concurrent system where multiple components might have been modified. Moreover, this task is complicated by the fact that our goal is to focus on the components that have been modified.

The component substitutability framework is defined by the following new algorithms: 1) a technique based on simultaneous use of over and under approximations obtained via existential and universal abstractions for the containment check of the substitutable components; 2) a *dynamic* assume-guarantee algorithm developed for the compatibility check. The algorithm is based on automata-theoretic learning for regular sets. It is dynamic in the sense that it learns appropriate environment assumptions for the new components by *reusing* the environment assumptions for their older versions.

The framework uses an iterative abstraction/refinement paradigm for both the containment and compatibility check procedures. The abstraction-based approach is essential since it not only enables the extraction of finite-state models from software programs but also reduces the complexity of software verification. Details of the abstraction procedure and the abstraction/refinement process are beyond the scope of this article and can be found in [4]. In summary, the developed component substitutability framework has several advantageous features:

– It allows *multiple* components to be upgraded simultaneously. This is crucial since modifications in different components often interact non-trivially to maintain overall system safety and integrity. Hence such modifications must be analyzed jointly.
– It identifies features of an old component which are absent in its updated version. It subsequently generates feedback to localize the modifications required to add the missing features back.
– It is completely automated and uses *dynamic* assume-guarantee style reasoning to scale to large software systems.
– It allows new components to have more behaviors than their old counterparts in order be replaceable. The *extra* behaviors are critical since they provide vendors with flexibility to implement new features into the product upgrades. Our framework verifies if these new behaviors do not violate previously established global specifications of a component assembly[1].

We employ state/event-based modeling techniques [5] to model and reason about both the data and communication aspects of software. In particular we use the state/event computational structures, called Doubly Labeled Automata (DLA) to model, as well as to specify, software systems. We have implemented the substitutability framework as part of the COMFORT [6] reasoning framework, which is based on the C model checker MAGIC [4, 15]. We experimented with an industrial benchmark and report encouraging results in Section 7.

2   Related Work

Related projects often impose the restriction that every behavior of the new component must also be a behavior of the old component. In such a case the new component is said to refine the old component. For instance, de Alfaro et al. [11, 8] define a notion of interface automaton for modeling component interfaces and show compatibility between components via refinement and consistency between interfaces. However, automated techniques for constructing interface automata from component implementations are not presented. In contrast, our approach automatically extracts conservative DLA models (which are similar to finite state interface automata) from component implementa-

---

[1] Verification of these new features remains a responsibility of designers of the upgraded systems.

tions. Moreover, we do not require refinement among the old components and their new versions.

Ernst et al. [16] suggest a technique for checking compatibility of multi-component upgrades. They derive consistency criteria by focusing on input/output component behavior only and abstract away the temporal information. Even though they state that their abstractions are unsound in general, they report success in detecting important errors. In contrast, our abstractions preserve temporal information about component behavior and are always sound. They also use a refinement-based notion on the generated consistency criteria for showing compatibility.

The application of learning is extremely useful from a pragmatic point of view since it is amenable to complete automation, and is gaining rapid popularity [14] in formal verification. The use of learning for automated assume-guarantee reasoning was proposed originally by Cobleigh et al. [10]. The use of learning along with predicate abstraction has also been applied in the context of interface synthesis [1] and various types of assume-guarantee proof rules for automated software verification [3].

This work is related to our earlier project [7] that solves the component substitutability problem in the context of verifying *individual* component upgrades. A major improvement of the current work is that it is aimed at verifying the component substitutability in the presence of *simultaneous upgrades of multiple components*. Another distinction of this work is that it provides an innovative *dynamic* assume-guarantee reasoning framework for the compatibility check. The dynamic nature of the compatibility check allows reusing previously computed assumptions to prove or disprove the global properties of the updated system.

Additionally, this paper gives a new solution to the containment check problem presented in [7]. In our earlier work, the containment step is solved using learning techniques for regular sets and handles finite-state systems only. In contrast, the new approach is extended to handle infinite-state C programs. Moreover, this paper defines a new technique based on simultaneous use of over and under approximations obtained via existential and universal abstractions.

3   Background and Notation

Let $\bullet$ denote the concatenation operator over sequences and X^* denote zero or more applications of $\bullet$ over X as usual. For any two sets X and Y we will denote the set $\{x \bullet y \mid x \in X \land y \in Y\}$ by $X \bullet Y$.

Definition 1 (Words and Traces). *Given an alphabet Σ and a set of atomic propositions AP we often say that (Σ, AP) is a state/event (SE) alphabet. For an SE alphabet $\widehat{\Sigma} = (\Sigma, AP)$, the set of words over $\widehat{\Sigma}$ is denoted by $Word(\widehat{\Sigma})$ and defined as $Word(\widehat{\Sigma}) = (\Sigma \bullet 2^{AP})^*$. The set of traces over $\widehat{\Sigma}$ is denoted by $Trace(\widehat{\Sigma})$ and defined as $Trace(\widehat{\Sigma}) = 2^{AP} \bullet Word(\widehat{\Sigma})$.*

Thus a word or a trace is an alternating sequence of subsets of AP and elements of Σ. However a word always begins with an action and ends with a set of propositions and can be empty. In contrast, a trace begins and ends with a set of propositions and cannot be empty.

Definition 2 (Doubly Labeled Automaton). *A doubly labeled automaton (DLA) is a 7-tuple $(S, Init, AP, \mathcal{L}, \Sigma, \delta, F)$ such that: (i) S is a finite set of states, (ii) $Init \subseteq S$ is a set of initial states, (iii) AP a finite set of (atomic) state propositions, (iv) $\mathcal{L} : S \to 2^{AP}$ a state-labeling function, (v) Σ a finite set of events or actions (alphabet), (vi) $\delta \subseteq S \times \Sigma \times S$ a transition relation, and (vii) $F \subseteq S$ is a set of final or accepting states.*

For any DLA with transition relation δ we write $q \xrightarrow{\alpha} q'$ to mean $q' \in \delta(q, \alpha)$. A DLA is said to be deterministic (DDLA) iff for any $q \in S$, $\alpha \in \Sigma$ and $p \subseteq AP$ there is at most one $q' \in S$ such that $q \xrightarrow{\alpha} q'$ and $\mathcal{L}(q') = p$. DLAs are not more expressive than standard finite automata since propositional labelings can always be rewritten in terms of actions [9]. However, we choose to use the DLA formalism for the sake of simplicity since it captures the essence of the state/event-based notation.

Definition 3 (Language). *Let $M = (S, Init, AP, \mathcal{L}, \Sigma, \delta, F)$ be a DLA and $\widehat{\Sigma} = (\Sigma, AP)$. A trace $t \in Trace(\widehat{\Sigma})$ is accepted by M iff $t = p_1, \alpha_1, p_2, \ldots, \alpha_{n-1}, p_n$ and there exists a sequence $s_1, s_2, \ldots, s_n$ of states of M such that: (i) $s_1 \in Init$, (ii) $s_n \in F$, (iii) for $1 \leq i \leq n$, $\mathcal{L}(s_i) = p_i$, and (iii) for $1 \leq i < n$, $s_i \xrightarrow{\alpha_i} s_{i+1}$. The language of M is denoted by $\mathbb{L}(M)$ and defined as the set of all traces accepted by M.*

A language is said to be regular iff it is accepted by some DLA. The set of regular languages is closed under union, intersection and complementation. DDLAs are equivalent to DLAs as far as language acceptance is concerned. In other words for any regular language L there is a DDLA M such that $\mathbb{L}(M) = L$. Also every regular language L is accepted by a unique (up to isomorphism) minimal DDLA.

Definition 4 (Abstraction). *Given two DLAs M_1 and M_2 we say that M_2 is an abstraction of M_1, denoted by $M_1 \sqsubseteq M_2$, iff $\mathbb{L}(M_1) \subseteq \mathbb{L}(M_2)$.*

Definition 5 (Parallel Composition). *Let $M_1 = (S_1, Init_1, AP_1, \mathcal{L}_1, \Sigma_1, \delta_1, F_1)$ and $M_2 = (S_2, Init_2, AP_2, \mathcal{L}_2, \Sigma_2, \delta_2, F_2)$ be two DLAs. The parallel composition of M_1 and M_2, denoted by $M_1 \parallel M_2$, is the DLA $(S_1 \times S_2, Init_1 \times Init_2, AP_1 \cup AP_2, \mathcal{L}, \Sigma_1 \cup \Sigma_2, \delta, F_1 \times F_2)$, where:*   (i) *$\mathcal{L}(s_1, s_2) = \mathcal{L}_1(s_1) \cup \mathcal{L}_2(s_2)$, and (ii) δ is such that $(s_1, s_2) \xrightarrow{\alpha} (s_1', s_2')$ iff:*

$$\forall i \in \{1, 2\} \centerdot (\alpha \notin \Sigma_i \wedge s_i = s_i') \bigvee (\alpha \in \Sigma_i \wedge s_i \xrightarrow{\alpha} s_i')$$

In other words, DLAs must synchronize on shared actions and proceed independently on local actions. This notion of parallel composition is derived from CSP [19].

Definition 6 (Weakest Assumption). *For any DLA M, and any safety property, expressed as a DLA φ, there exists a weakest (w.r.t. the $\sqsubseteq$ preorder) DLA WA with the following property: for any DLA E, $M \parallel E \sqsubseteq \varphi$ iff $E \sqsubseteq WA$ [12]. In fact it can be shown that WA is a DLA accepting the language $\mathbb{L}(\overline{M \parallel \overline{\varphi}})$.*

4   Containment

Recall that in the containment step we verify for each $i \in \mathcal{I}$, that $C_i \sqsubseteq C_i'$, i.e., every behavior of C_i is also a behavior of C_i'. If $C_i \not\sqsubseteq C_i'$, we also construct a set $\mathcal{F}_i$ of behaviors in $Behv(C_i) \setminus Behv(C_i')$ which will be subsequently used for feedback generation. This containment check is performed iteratively and component-wise as depicted in Figure 1 (CE refers to the counterexample generated during the verification phase). For each $i \in \mathcal{I}$, the containment check proceeds as follows:

1. Abstraction. Construct finite models M and M' such that **(C1)** $C_i \sqsubseteq M$ and **(C2)** $M' \sqsubseteq C_i'$. Note that M is an *over-approximation* of C_i and can be constructed by standard predicate abstraction [13]. However M' is constructed from C_i' via a modified predicate abstraction which produces an *under-approximation* of its input C component. We give an overview of predicate abstraction and then the modified predicate abstraction. Complete details of our predicate abstraction procedure can be found elsewhere [4].

Predicates and Valuations. Suppose we are given a set of predicates (pure C expressions) $\mathcal{P}$. Each valuation $\mathcal{V}$ of $\mathcal{P}$ is simply a mapping from $\mathcal{P}$ to $\{0, 1\}$. Thus if $\mathcal{P} = \{x < 1, y \geq 0\}$ then the set of valuations of $\mathcal{P}$ is $\{(0, 0), (0, 1), (1, 0), (1, 1)\}$. Let $\mathcal{P} = \{p_1, \ldots, p_n\}$ and $\mathcal{V}$ be a valuation of $\mathcal{P}$. Then the concretization of $\mathcal{V}$ is denoted by $\gamma(\mathcal{V})$ and defined as: $\gamma(\mathcal{V}) \equiv \bigwedge_{i=1}^n X_i$ where $X_i = p_i$ iff $\mathcal{V}(p_i) = 1$ and $\neg p_i$ otherwise. For example consider $\mathcal{P} = \{x < 1, y \geq 0\}$ and $\mathcal{V} = (0, 1)$. Then $\gamma(\mathcal{V}) = \neg(x < 1) \wedge (y \geq 0)$.

Predicate Abstraction. Suppose that C_i comprises of a set of C statements $Stmt = \{st_1, \ldots, st_k\}$. Without loss of generality we assume that each statement of C_i is either an assignment, an if-then-else or a goto. Also we are given a set of predicates $\mathcal{P}$ with set of valuations Val. The general idea behind predicate abstraction is to represent a set of concrete states symbolically using a formula. Thus the predicate abstraction

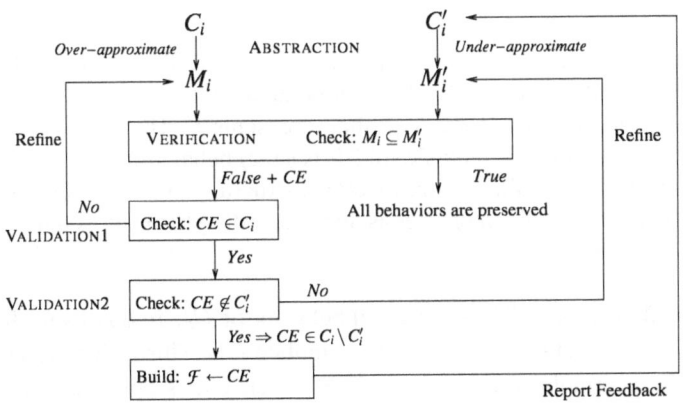

Fig. 1. The containment phase of the substitutability framework

C_i w.r.t. $\mathcal{P}$ is an DLA M whose set of states = $Stmt \times Val$. Intuitively each state $s = (st, \mathcal{V})$ of M represents the set of all concrete execution states c of C_i such that st is the next statement to be executed at c and the expression $\gamma(\mathcal{V})$ is satisfied by the memory configuration at c. In such a case we often say $c \in s$ to highlight the fact that each state of M can be thought of as a set of concrete execution states of C_i.

The transitions of M are defined such that M is an over-approximation of C_i via *existential* abstraction. For example, let $s_1 = (st_1, \mathcal{V}_1)$ and $s_2 = (st_2, \mathcal{V}_2)$ be two states of M such that st_1 is an assignment. Then M contains a transition from s_1 to s_2 if there is a transition from *some* concrete state $c_1 \in s_1$ to some concrete state $c_2 \in s_2$. It turns out that this is equivalent to: (i) st_2 being the next statement to be executed after st_1, and (ii) the formula $WP\{\gamma(\mathcal{V}_2)\}[st_1] \wedge \gamma(\mathcal{V}_1)$ being satisfiable where $WP\{\gamma(\mathcal{V}_2)\}[st_1]$ denotes the weakest precondition of $\gamma(\mathcal{V}_2)$ w.r.t. st_1. Other kinds of statements are handled analogously.

Modified Predicate Abstraction. In contrast our modified predicate abstraction constructs an under-approximation of the concrete system via *universal* abstraction. More precisely suppose C_i' comprises of a set of C statements $Stmt'$ and we are given a set of predicates $\mathcal{P}'$ with set of valuations Val'. Then the modified predicate abstraction of C_i' w.r.t. $\mathcal{P}'$ is an DLA M' whose set of states = $Stmt' \times Val'$. The correspondence between the states of M' and the execution states of C_i' is exactly as in the case of predicate abstraction. The difference is in the way the transitions of M' are defined. More precisely, let $s_1 = (st_1, \mathcal{V}_1)$ and $s_2 = (st_2, \mathcal{V}_2)$ be two states of M' such that st_1 is an assignment. Then M' contains a transition from s_1 to s_2 if there is a transition from *every* concrete state $c_1 \in s_1$ to some concrete state $c_2 \in s_2$. This is equivalent to: (i) st_2 being the next statement to be executed after st_1, and (ii) the formula $\gamma(\mathcal{V}_1) \implies WP\{\gamma(\mathcal{V}_2)\}[st_1]$ being valid. Other kinds of statements are handled analogously. The satisfiability and validity of formulas are checked using an automated theorem prover.

2. Verification. Verify if $M \sqsubseteq M'$ (or alternatively $M \setminus B \sqsubseteq M'$ if the upgrade involved some bug fix and the bug was defined as a DLA B). If so then from **(C1)** and **(C2)** above we know that $C_i \sqsubseteq C_i'$ and we terminate with success. Otherwise we obtain a counterexample CE.

3. Validation 1. Check if CE is a real behavior of C_i. To do this we first compute the set S of concrete states of C_i that can simulate CE. This is done via symbolic simulation and the result is a formula ϕ that represents S. Then CE is a real behavior of C_i iff $S \neq \emptyset$, i.e., iff ϕ is satisfiable. If CE is a real behavior of C_i, we proceed to the next step. Otherwise we refine model M by constructing a new set of predicates $\mathcal{P}$ and repeat from Step 2. The refinement step is done according to the procedure implemented in the MAGIC [4] tool.

4. Validation 2. Check if CE is *not* a real behavior of C_i'. To do this we first compute the set S' of concrete states of C_i' that can simulate CE. This is done as above and the result is again a formula ϕ that represents S'. Then CE is not a real behavior of C_i' iff $S' = \emptyset$, i.e., iff ϕ is unsatisfiable. If CE is not a real behavior of C_i', we know that $CE \in Behv(C_i) \setminus Behv(C_i')$. We add CE to $\mathcal{F}_i$ and stop. Otherwise we refine M' by constructing a new set of predicates $\mathcal{P}'$ and repeat from Step 2. This refinement step is an antithesis of standard abstraction-refinement since it *adds* the valid behavior CE back to M'. However it is conceptually similar to standard abstraction-refinement and we omit its details in this article.

Note that the above process terminates as soon as it adds a single behavior to $\mathcal{F}_i$. However it can be extended to generate a set of behaviors in $\mathcal{F}_i$ as follows. First a set of counterexamples $\widehat{CE}$ is constructed in Step 2. Then each element of $\widehat{CE}$ is processed via Steps 3 and 4 and every counterexample which belongs to C_i but not to C_i' is added to $\mathcal{F}_i$. The use of $\mathcal{F}_i$ to provide feedback to developers showing how to correct the updated components is discussed in Section 6.

5   Compatibility

Recall that the compatibility check is aimed at ensuring that the upgraded system satisfies global safety specifications. Our compatibility check procedure involves two key paradigms - *dynamic* regular set learning and assume guarantee reasoning. We first present these two techniques and then describe their use in our overall compatibility algorithm.

5.1   Dynamic Regular Set Learning

Central to our compatibility check procedure is a new *dynamic* algorithm to learn regular languages. Our algorithm is based on the L^* algorithm developed by Angluin [2]. The compatibility check uses a state/event version of the L^* that is a straight forward extension of the original algorithm (for simplicity we will refer to both as L^*). The detailed description of the state/event L^* algorithm and the proof of its correctness and complexity analysis can be found in [20]. We will first present the state/event learning algorithm and then describe a *dynamic* version of it that we actually use for checking compatibility. We will denote the symmetric difference of two sets X and Y by $X \oplus Y$, i.e, $\rho \in X \oplus Y$ iff $\rho \in X \setminus Y$ or $\rho \in Y \setminus X$.

The L^* Algorithm. Let U be an unknown regular language over some SE alphabet $\widehat{\Sigma} = (\Sigma, AP)$. In order to learn U, L^* interacts with a *minimally adequate teacher* MAT for U, which can provide Boolean answers the following two kinds of queries:

1. *Membership.* Given a $\rho \in Trace(\widehat{\Sigma})$, MAT returns TRUE iff $\rho \in U$.
2. *Candidate.* Given a DDLA D, MAT returns TRUE iff $\mathbb{L}(D) = U$. If MAT returns FALSE, it also returns a counterexample trace $w \in \mathbb{L}(D) \oplus U$.

Given an unknown regular language $U \subseteq Trace(\widehat{\Sigma})$ and a MAT for U, the L^* algorithm *iteratively* constructs a minimal DDLA D such that $L(D) = U$. It maintains an observation table (S, E, T) where: (i) S is a prefix-closed set over $Trace(\widehat{\Sigma})$ labeling the rows of the table, (ii) E a suffix-closed set over $Word(\widehat{\Sigma})$ labeling the columns of the table, and (iii) $T : (S \cup S \bullet \widehat{\Sigma}) \times E \to \{0, 1\}$ is the valuation of the table entries such that:

$$\forall s \in S \cup S \bullet \widehat{\Sigma} \, . \, \forall e \in E \, . \, T[s, e] = 1 \iff s \bullet e \in U$$

Additionally, for any $s \in S \cup S \bullet \widehat{\Sigma}$, let us define a function r_s as follows:

$$\forall e \in E \centerdot r_s(e) = T[s, e]$$

Given a trace $t \in \mathit{Trace}(\widehat{\Sigma})$ we write $Last(t)$ to mean the last set of propositions in t. L^* always ensures that the following invariant holds on the table: for any two distinct $s_1, s_2 \in S$ either $r_{s_1} \neq r_{s_2}$ or $Last(s_1) \neq Last(s_2)$. The table is said to be *closed* if for every $t \in S \bullet \widehat{\Sigma}$, there exist an $s \in S$ such that $r_s = r_t$ and $Last(s) = Last(t)$.

Let us denote the empty word by λ. Then L^* starts with a table (S, E, T) such that $S = 2^{AP}$, $E = \{\lambda\}$ and in each iteration proceeds as follows. It first updates the table using membership queries till it is closed. Next L^* builds a candidate DDLA D from the table and makes a candidate query with D. If the MAT returns TRUE to the candidate query, L^* returns D and stops. Otherwise, L^* updates E with a single word (constructed from the CE returned by the candidate query) and proceeds with the next iteration. The complexity of L^* is expressed by the following theorem [2, 20].

Theorem 1. *If n is the number of states of the minimum DDLA accepting U and m is the upper bound on the length of any counterexample provided by the MAT, then the total running time of L^* is bounded by a polynomial in m and n. Moreover, the observation table is of size $O(m^2 n^2 + mn^3)$.*

Dynamic L^*. Normally L^* initializes with: $S = 2^{AP}$ and $E = \{\lambda\}$. This can be a drawback in cases where a previously learned candidate (and hence a table) exists and we wish to restart learning using information from the previous table. In the following, we show (Theorem 2) that if L^* begins with any non-empty *valid* table then it must terminate with the correct result. In particular, this allows us to perform our compatibility check dynamically by restarting L^* with any previously computed table by *re-validating* it instead of starting from an empty table[2].

Definition 7 (Agreement). *An observation table (S, E, T) is said to agree with a regular language U iff: $\forall (s, e) \in (S \cup S \bullet \widehat{\Sigma}) \times E$, $T(s, e) = 1$ iff $s \bullet e \in U$. Also, (S, E, T) agrees with a candidate DDLA D if it agrees with $\mathbb{L}(D)$.*

Definition 8 (Validity). *An observation table $T = (S, E, T)$ is said to be valid for a language U iff (S, E, T) agrees with U. We say that a candidate derived from a closed table T is valid if T is valid.*

Theorem 2. *L^* terminates with a correct result for any unknown language U starting from any valid table for U.*

Proof. Let n be the number of states in the minimal DDLA M_U such that $\mathbb{L}(M_U) = U$. Note that both Theorem 1 and Lemma 5 from Angluin's correctness proof for L^* [2] hold for valid and closed tables and candidates consistent with them. It follows from Theorem 1 and Lemma 5 that L^* can always make a valid table closed and hence is

---

[2] A similar idea was also proposed in the context of *adaptive* model checking [14].

able to construct a candidate, say D, with at most n states. We now show that every subsequent candidate must have at least one more state than D.

A candidate query with D either returns TRUE or a counterexample $CE \in \mathbb{L}(D) \oplus U$. Note that the table must agree with D since D is consistent with it. Also since the table is valid, it must agree with U. Therefore, $CE \notin (S \cup S \bullet \widehat{\Sigma}) \bullet E$ and will be added to S. Again, a valid and closed table (S', E', T') must be obtained eventually after adding CE. Let D' be the corresponding candidate.

Now, D' is consistent with T since T' extends T. Also D' agrees with M_U as far accepting CE is concerned while D does not. Hence D' is inequivalent to D and by Theorem 1 in Angluin's proof, must have at least one more state than D. Hence, starting from D, L^* can make at most $n - 1$ incorrect candidates, since the number of states is initially at least one, always increases monotonically and may not exceed $n - 1$. Since L^* must keep making new candidates as long as it is running, it must terminate with a correct candidate M_U.   □

Suppose we have a table T which is valid for an unknown language U and we have a new unknown language U' different from U. Suppose we want to learn U' by starting L^* with table T. Note that in general T will not be valid for U' and hence starting from T will not be appropriate. However, we can first *validate* T against U' and then start L^* from the validated T. Theorem 2 provides the key insight behind the correctness of this procedure. As we shall see, this idea forms the backbone of our dynamic compatibility check procedure (cf. Section 5.3).

5.2   Assume-Guarantee Reasoning

Along with dynamic L^*, we also use assume-guarantee style compositional reasoning to check compatibility. Given a set of component DLAs $M_1, \ldots, M_n$ and a specification DLA φ, the following non-circular rule **AG** [17] can be used to verify $M_1 \parallel \cdots \parallel M_n \sqsubseteq \varphi$:

$$\frac{M_1 \parallel A_1 \sqsubseteq \varphi \qquad M_2 \parallel \cdots \parallel M_n \sqsubseteq A_1}{M_1 \parallel \cdots \parallel M_n \sqsubseteq \varphi}$$

In the above, A_1 is an DLA representing the assumption about the environment under which M_1 is expected to operate correctly. As also observed by Cobleigh et al. [10], the second premise is itself an instance of the top-level proof-obligation with $n - 1$ component DLAs. Hence, **AG** can be applied to decompose it further.

5.3   Compatibility Check for C Components

The procedure for checking compatibility of new components in the context of the original component assembly is presented in Figure 2. Given an old component assembly $C = \{C_1, \ldots, C_n\}$, and a set of new components $C' = \{C'_i \mid i \in \mathcal{I}\}$ (where $\mathcal{I} \subseteq \{1, \ldots, n\}$), it checks if a safety property φ holds in the new assembly. We first present an overview of the compatibility procedure and then discuss its implementation in detail. The procedure uses a **DynamicCheck** algorithm, and is done in an iterative abstraction refinement style as follows:

1. Use predicate abstraction to obtain finite DLA models M_i, where M_i is constructed from C_i if $i \notin \mathcal{I}$ and from C_i' if $i \in \mathcal{I}$. The abstraction is carried out component-wise. Let $\mathcal{M} = \{M_1, \ldots, M_n\}$.
2. Apply **DynamicCheck** on $\mathcal{M}$. If the result is TRUE the compatibility check terminates successfully. Otherwise we obtain a counterexample CE.
3. Check if CE is a valid counterexample. Once again this is done component-wise. If CE is valid, the compatibility check terminates unsuccessfully with CE as counterexample. Otherwise we go to the next step.
4. Refine a specific model, say M_k, such that the spurious CE is eliminated. Repeat from Step 2.

Overview of DynamicCheck. We first present an overview of the algorithm for two DLAs and then generalize it to an arbitrary collection of DLAs. Suppose we have two old DLAs M_1, M_2 and a property DLA φ. We assume that we previously tried to verify $M_1 \parallel M_2 \sqsubseteq \varphi$ using **DynamicCheck**. The algorithm **DynamicCheck** uses dynamic L^* to learn appropriate assumptions that can discharge the premises of **AG**. In particular suppose that while trying to verify $M_1 \parallel M_2 \sqsubseteq \varphi$, **DynamicCheck** had constructed an observation table $\mathcal{T}$.

Now suppose we have new versions M_1', M_2' for M_1, M_2. Note than in general it could be that either M_1' or M_2' is identical to its old version. **DynamicCheck** will now reuse $\mathcal{T}$ and invoke the dynamic L^* algorithm to automatically learn an assumption A' such that: (i) $M_1' \parallel A' \sqsubseteq \varphi$ and (ii) $M_2' \sqsubseteq A'$. More precisely, **DynamicCheck** proceeds iteratively as follows:

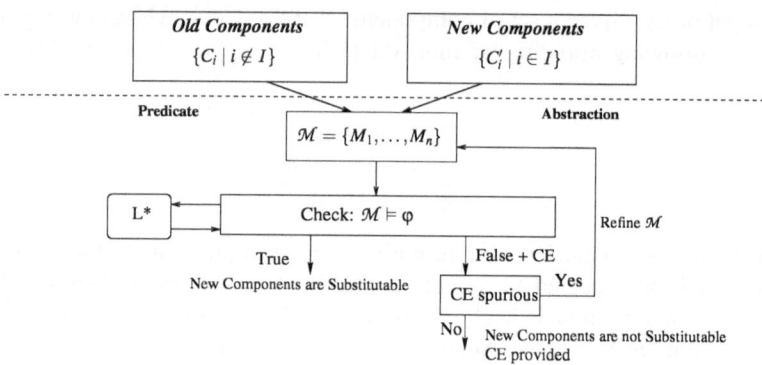

Fig. 2. The compatibility phase of the substitutability framework

1. It checks if $M_1 = M_1'$. If so, it starts learning from the previous table $\mathcal{T}$, i.e., it sets $\mathcal{T}' := \mathcal{T}$. Otherwise it re-validates $\mathcal{T}$ against M_1' to obtain a new table $\mathcal{T}'$.
2. It derives a conjecture A' from $\mathcal{T}'$ and checks if $M_2' \sqsubseteq A'$. If this check passes it terminates with TRUE and the new assumption A'. Otherwise it obtains a counterexample CE.

3. It analyzes CE to see if CE corresponds to a real counterexample to $M_1' \parallel M_2' \sqsubseteq \varphi$. If so, it constructs such a counterexample and terminates with FALSE. Otherwise it updates T' using CE.
4. It makes T' closed by making membership queries and repeats from Step 2.

Generalized DynamicCheck. We first describe the key ideas that enable us to reuse the previous assumptions and then present the complete **DynamicCheck** algorithm for multiple DLAs. Note that due to its dynamic nature, the algorithm will be able to *locally* identify the set of assumptions that need to be modified to re-validate the system.

Incremental Changes between Successive Assumptions. Recall that the L^* algorithm maintains an observation table (S, E, T) corresponding to an assumption A for every component M. During an initial compatibility check, this table stores the information about membership of the current set of traces in an unknown language U (i.e., the language of the *weakest assumption* for M). Upgrading the component M modifies this unknown language for the corresponding assumption from U to say, U'. Therefore, checking compatibility after an upgrade requires that the learner must compute a new assumption A' corresponding to U'. In most cases, the languages $L(A)$ and $L(A')$ may *differ only slightly* and hence the information about behaviors of A is *reused* in computing A'.

Table Re-validation. The original L^* algorithm computes A' starting from an empty table. However, as mentioned before, a more efficient algorithm would intend to reuse the previously inferred set of elements of S and E to learn A'. The result in Section 5.1 (Theorem 2) precisely enables the L^* algorithm to achieve this goal. In particular, since L^* terminates starting from any *valid* table, the assumption learner first obtains a valid table by reusing words in S and E: update T by asking membership queries w.r.t. U' for each $\rho \in (S \cup S \bullet \widehat{\Sigma}) \bullet E$. The valid table (S, E, T') hence obtained is subsequently made closed and then learning proceeds in the normal fashion. This allows the compatibility check to restart from any previous set of assumptions by *re-validating* them. The **GenerateAssumption** module implements this feature.

Overall DynamicCheck Procedure. The **DynamicCheck** procedure instantiates the AG rule for n components and enables checking multiple upgrades simultaneously by reusing previous assumptions and verification results. In the description, we denote the previous and the new versions of a component DLA by M and M' and the previous and the new versions of a component assemblies by $\mathcal{M}$ and $\mathcal{M}'$ respectively. For ease of description, we always use a property, φ, to denote the right hand side of the top-level proof obligation of the compositional rule. We denote the modified property[3] at each recursion level of the algorithm by φ'. The old and new assumptions are denoted by A and A' respectively.

Figure 3 presents the pseudo-code of the algorithm **DynamicCheck** to perform the compatibility check. Lines (1-4) describe the case when $\mathcal{M}$ contains only one component. In Line 5, an assumption A' corresponding to M' and φ' is generated using

---

[3] Note that under the recursive application of the compatibility check procedure the updated property φ' corresponds to an assumption from the previous recursion level

DynamicCheck $(\mathcal{M}', \varphi')$ **returns** counterexample or TRUE
1:   **let** $M' = first$ element of $\mathcal{M}'$;
2:   **if** $(\mathcal{M}' = \{M'\})$
3:        **if** $(M \neq M'$ or $\varphi \neq \varphi')$ **return** $(M' \sqsubseteq \varphi')$;
4:        **else return** $M \sqsubseteq \varphi$;
5:   $A' := $ **GenerateAssumption**(M', φ');
6:   **if** $(A \neq A'$ or $\mathcal{M} \setminus M \neq \mathcal{M}' \setminus M')$
7:        $CE := $ **DynamicCheck**$(\mathcal{M}' \setminus M', A')$;
8:   **else** $CE := $ **DynamicCheck**$(\mathcal{M} \setminus M, A)$;
9:   **while**$(CE$ is non-empty)
10:      **if** $(M' \parallel CE \sqsubseteq \varphi')$
11:           $A' := $ **UpdateAssumption** (A', CE);
12:           $A' := $ **GenerateAssumption** (M', φ');
13:           $CE = $ **DynamicCheck** $(\mathcal{M}' \setminus M', A')$;
14:      **else return** a witness counterexample CE to $M' \parallel CE \not\sqsubseteq \varphi'$;
15: **return** TRUE;

Fig. 3. Pseudo-code for efficient compatibility check

dynamic L^* such that $M' \parallel A' \sqsubseteq \varphi'$. Lines (6-8) describe recursive invocation of **DynamicCheck** on $\mathcal{M} \setminus M$ against property A'. Finally, lines (9-15) show how the algorithm detects a counterexample CE and updates A' with it or terminates with a TRUE/FALSE result. The salient features of this algorithm are the following:

- **GenerateAssumption** (line 5) does not generate new assumptions every time **DynamicCheck** is invoked. Instead, it reuses (by re-validating if necessary) the assumption A computed in the previous compatibility check. When CE is used to update A, **GenerateAssumption** (line 12) does not need to re-validate A since it must be validated previously.
- Verification checks are repeated on a component M' (or a collection of components $\mathcal{M}' \setminus M'$) only if it is (they are) found to be different from the previous version M ($\mathcal{M} \setminus M$) or if the corresponding property φ has changed (lines 3,7,12). Otherwise, the previously computed result is re-used (lines 4,8).

The correctness of **DynamicCheck** follows from the following theorem.

Theorem 3. *Given modified* $\mathcal{M}'$ *and* φ', **DynamicCheck** *algorithm always terminates with either* TRUE *or a counterexample* CE *to* $\mathcal{M}' \sqsubseteq \varphi'$.

We use the notion of weakest assumptions in proving the correctness of **DynamicCheck**. We know that for any DLA M, there must exist a weakest environment assumption DLA WA such that $M \parallel E\varphi$ iff $E \sqsubseteq WA$. Suppose, we have a system of components $M_1, \ldots, M_n$ and a global property φ. Consider rules of form $M_i \parallel A_i \sqsubseteq A_{i-1} (1 \leq i \leq n - 1, A_0 = \varphi)$ and $M_n \sqsubseteq A_{n-1}$ as used in our recursive procedure to show that $M_1 \parallel .. \parallel M_n \sqsubseteq \varphi$. It is clear that a weakest assumption WA_1 exists such that $M_1 \parallel WA_1 \sqsubseteq \varphi$. Given WA_1, it follows that WA_2 must exist so that $M_2 \parallel WA_2 \sqsubseteq WA_1$. Therefore, by induction on i, there must exist weakest assumptions WA_i for $1 \leq i \leq n-1$, such that $M_i \parallel WA_i \sqsubseteq WA_{i-1} (1 \leq i \leq n-1, WA_0 = \varphi)$

and $M_n \sqsubseteq A_{n-1}$. Also, by Theorem 2, **UpdateAssumption**(A, CE) must terminate starting from any valid assumption A' with respect to U' and a counterexample $CE \in L(A') \oplus U'$.

Proof. Suppose, without loss of generality, that component DLA M', is upgraded. Note that after an upgrade, a weakest assumption WA' (possibly different from WA) must exist for every $M' \in \mathcal{M}'$. We proceed by induction over the size k of $\mathcal{M}'$. In the base case, it is clear that we need to model check M' against φ' only if either M or φ changed (line 3). This either returns a counterexample to $M' \sqsubseteq \varphi'$ or the previous $M \sqsubseteq \varphi$ (line 4) result holds.

Assume for the inductive case that **DynamicCheck**$(\mathcal{M}'\backslash M', A')$ terminates with either TRUE or a counterexample CE. It is clear from its definition that A' computed by **GenerateAssumption** (line 5) is valid. If line 6 holds, i.e, $A' \neq A$ or $\mathcal{M} \backslash M \neq \mathcal{M}' \backslash M'$ then by inductive hypothesis, execution of line 7 terminates with either a TRUE result or a counterexample CE. Otherwise, the previously computed CE result is used (line 8). It remains to be shown that lines (9-15) compute the correct return value based on this result.

If this result is TRUE then it follows from the soundness of the assume-guarantee rule that $\mathcal{M}' \sqsubseteq \varphi'$ and **DynamicCheck** returns TRUE (line 15). If $M' \parallel CE \not\sqsubseteq \varphi'$ (line 10), then by set-theoretic arguments based on the definitions of A' and CE, we know that $\mathcal{M}' \not\sqsubseteq P'$ and a suitable witness CE' (line 14) is returned by the algorithm. Otherwise, since A' is valid, both **UpdateAssumption** (line 11) and **GenerateAssumption** (line 12) must terminate by learning a new assumption, say A'', such that $M' \parallel A'' \sqsubseteq \varphi'$. It follows from the proof of correctness of L^* that $|A'| < |A''|$ and from the definition of weakest assumptions that $|A''| \leq |WA'|$. Also, by inductive hypothesis, line 13 must terminate with the correct CE result. Hence, lines 9-13 of the **while** loop may be executed only a finite number of times until $|A''| = |WA'|$, when (by set-theoretic arguments) either the result is TRUE (line 15) or a witness counterexample CE' (line 14) for $\mathcal{M}' \not\sqsubseteq P'$ is returned.

$\qquad\qquad\qquad\qquad\qquad\qquad\qquad\qquad\qquad\qquad\qquad\qquad\qquad\qquad\qquad\qquad\qquad\qquad$ □

Further optimizations. Recall that our procedure reuses assumptions generated during previous compatibility checks. We further optimize it by identifying a subset of assumptions that have to be re-validated at the initialization of the next check. This optimization is enabled by the following lemma whose proof follows directly from Theorem 3 and definition of weakest assumptions.

Lemma 1. *Let* $\mathcal{M} = \{M_1, \ldots, M_n\}$ *be an assembly of components,* $A = \{A_1, \ldots, A_{n-1}\}$ *be a set of previously computed assumptions and* $\mathcal{I} \subseteq \{1, \ldots, n\}$ *be an index set. Also, let* $\{M_i' \mid i \in \mathcal{I}\}$ *be the set of new components. If k is the minimum index of $\mathcal{I}$, then it is sufficient for* **DynamicCheck** *to re-validate only the assumptions in the set* $\{A_j \mid j \geq k \wedge j \leq n\}$.

6   Feedback

Recall that for some $i \in \mathcal{I}$, if our containment check detects that $C_i \not\sqsubseteq C_i'$, it also computes a set $\mathcal{F}_i$. Intuitively each element of $\mathcal{F}_i$ represents a behavior of C_i which is not a behavior of C_i'. We now present our process of generating feedback from $\mathcal{F}_i$. In the rest of this section we will write C, C' and $\mathcal{F}$ to mean C_i, C_i' and $\mathcal{F}_i$ respectively.

Consider any behavior π in $\mathcal{F}$. Recall that π is a trace of a DLA M obtained by predicate abstraction of C. By simulating π on M, we construct an alternating sequence $Rep(\pi) = \langle s_1, \alpha_1, \ldots, s_n \rangle$ of states and actions of M corresponding to π. Recall from our earlier discussion of predicate abstraction (cf. Section 4) that each s_i is of the form $(st_i, \mathcal{V}_i)$ where st_i is a statement of C and $\mathcal{V}_i$ is a predicate valuation. Thus, $Rep(\pi) = \langle (st_1, \mathcal{V}_1), \alpha_1, \ldots, (st_n, \mathcal{V}_n) \rangle$.

We also know that π represents an actual behavior of C but not an actual behavior of C'. Thus, there is a prefix $Pref(\pi)$ of π such that $Pref(\pi)$ represents a behavior of C'. However any extension of $Pref(\pi)$ is no longer a valid behavior of C'. Note that $Pref(\pi)$ can be constructed by simulating π on C'. Let us denote the suffix of π after $Pref(\pi)$ by $Suff(\pi)$. Since $Pref(\pi)$ is an actual behavior of C' we can also construct a representation for $Pref(\pi)$ in terms of the statements and predicate valuations of C'. Let us denote this representation by $Rep'(Pref(\pi))$.

As our feedback we output, for each $\pi \in \mathcal{F}$, the following representations: $Rep(Pref(\pi))$, $Rep(Suff(\pi))$ and $Rep'(Pref(\pi))$. Note that such feedback allows us to identify the exact *divergence* point of π beyond which it ceases to correspond to any concrete behavior of C'. Since the feedback refers to program statement, it allows us to understand at the source code level why C is able match π completely but C' is forced to diverge from π beyond $Pref(\pi)$. This makes it easier to modify C' so as to add back to it the missing behavior π.

7   Implementation and Experimental Evaluation

We implemented and evaluated the compatibility check phase for checking component substitutability in the COMFORT framework. COMFORT extracts abstract component DLA models from C programs using predicate abstraction. It also serves as a *MAT* (cf. Section 5.1) for learning assumptions in the compatibility check. If the compatibility check returns a counterexample, the counterexample validation and abstraction-refinement modules of COMFORT are employed to check for spuriousness and do refinement, if necessary.

We validated the component substitutability framework while verifying upgrades of a benchmark provided to us by our industrial partner, ABB Inc. (http://www.abb.com). The benchmarks consist of seven components which together implement an interprocess communication (IPC) protocol. The combined statespace is over 10^6.

We used a set of properties describing functionality of the verified portion of the IPC protocol. We used upgrades of the *write-queue* (ipc_1) and the *ipc-queue* (ipc_2 and ipc_3) components. The upgrades had both missing and extra behaviors compared to their original versions. We verified two properties (P_1 and P_2) before and after the upgrades. We also verified the properties on a simultaneous upgrade (ipc_4) of both the components. P_1 specifies that a process may write data into the *ipc-queue* only after it obtains a lock for the corresponding critical section. P_2 specifies an order in which data may be written into the ipc-queue. Table 1 shows the comparison between time required

Table 1. Comparison of times required for original verification (T_{orig}) and verification on upgrade (T_{ug}) by **DynamicCheck**. $\#Mem.$ $Queries$ denotes the total number of membership queries made during verification of the original assembly

Upgrade#(Prop.)	# Mem. Queries	T_{orig} (msec)	T_{ug} (msec)
$ipc_1(P_1)$	279	2260	13
$ipc_1(P_2)$	308	1694	14
$ipc_2(P_1)$	358	3286	17
$ipc_2(P_2)$	232	805	10
$ipc_3(P_1)$	363	3624	17
$ipc_3(P_2)$	258	1649	14
$ipc_4(P_1)$	355	1102	24

for initial verification of the IPC system with the time taken by **DynamicCheck** for verification of upgrades. We observed that the previously generated assumptions in all the cases were sufficient to prove the properties on the upgraded system also. Hence, the compatibility check succeeded in a *small fraction of time* (T_{ug}) as compared to the time for compositional verification (T_{orig}) of the original system.

8   Conclusions and Future Work

We proposed a solution to the critical and vital problem of component substitutability consisting of two phases: *containment* and *compatibility*. The compatibility check performs compositional reasoning with help of a *dynamic* regular language inference algorithm and a model checker. Our experiments confirm that the dynamic approach is more effective than complete re-validation of the system after an upgrade. The containment check detects behaviors which were present in each component before but not after the upgrade. These behaviors are used to construct useful feedback to the developers. We observed that the order of components used to discharge the assume-guarantee rules has a significant impact on the algorithm run times and hence needs investigation. We would further like to investigate a modification of it based on a more efficient L^* algorithm by Rivest et al. [18] in order to improve the performance of **DynamicCheck**.

References

1. R. Alur, P. Cerny, G. Gupta, P. Madhusudan, W. Nam, and A. Srivastava. Synthesis of interface specifications for Java classes. In *Symp. on Principles Of Programming Languages (POPL)*, 2005.
2. D. Angluin. Learning regular sets from queries and counterexamples. In *Information and Computation*, volume 75(2), pages 87–106, 1987.
3. S. Chaki, E. Clarke, D. Giannakopoulou, and C. S. Pasareanu. Abstraction and assume-guarantee reasoning for automated software verification. Technical Report 05.02, Research Institute for Advanced Computer Science (RIACS), 2004.

4. S. Chaki, E. Clarke, A. Groce, J. Ouaknine, O. Strichman, and K. Yorav. Efficient verification of sequential and concurrent C programs. *Formal Methods in System Design*, 25(2–3), 2004.
5. S. Chaki, E. Clarke, J. Ouaknine, N. Sharygina, and N. Sinha. State/event-based software model checking. In *Integrated Formal Methods*, volume 2999, pages 128–147. LNCS, 2004.
6. S. Chaki, J. Ivers, N. Sharygina, and K. Wallnau. The ComFoRT reasoning framework. In *Proceedings of Computer Aided Verification (CAV)*, 2005.
7. S. Chaki, N. Sharygina, and N. Sinha. Verification of evolving software. In *3rd Workshop on Spec. and Ver. of Component-based Systems, ESEC/FSE*, 2004.
8. A. Chakrabarti, L. de Alfaro, T. A. Henzinger, M. Jurdzinski, and F. Y. C. Mang. Interface compatibility checking for software modules. In *Proceedings of the 14th International Conference on Computer-Aided Verification*, pages 428–441. LNCS 2404, Springer-Verlag, 2002.
9. E. Clarke, O. Grumberg, and D. Peled. *Model Checking*. MIT Press, 1999.
10. J. M. Cobleigh, D. Giannakopoulou, and C. S. Pasareanu. Learning assumptions for compositional verification. In *Tools and Algorithms for Construction and Analysis of Systems*, volume 2619. LNCS, Springer-Verlag, 2003.
11. L. de Alfaro and T. A. Henzinger. Interface automata. In *Proceedings of the Ninth Annual Symposium on Foundations of Software Engineering*. ACM Press, 2001.
12. D. Giannakopoulou, C. S. Pasareanu, and H. Barringer. Assumption generation for software component verification. In *Proceedings of the ASE*, 2002.
13. S. Graf and H. Saïdi. Construction of abstract state graphs with PVS. In *Proceedings of Computer Aided Verification*, 1997.
14. A. Groce, D. Peled, and M. Yannakakis. Adaptive model checking. In *Tools and Algorithms for Construction and Analysis of Systems*, pages 357–370. Springer-Verlag, 2002.
15. MAGIC. http://www.cs.cmu.edu/ chaki/magic.
16. S. McCamant and M. D. Ernst. Early identification of incompatibilities in multi-component upgrades. In *ECOOP 2004 — Object-Oriented Programming, 18th European Conference*, Oslo, Norway, 2004.
17. A. Pnueli. In transition from global to modular temporal reasoning about programs. In *Logics and Models of Concurrent Systems*, pages 123–144, New York, NY, USA, 1985. Springer-Verlag New York, Inc.
18. R. L. Rivest and R. E. Schapire. Inference of finite automata using homing sequences. In *Information and Computation*, volume 103(2), pages 299–347, 1993.
19. A. W. Roscoe. *The Theory and Practice of Concurrency*. Prentice-Hall Int., 1997.
20. Learning for software. http://www.sei.cmu.edu/staff/chaki/publications/learn-se-trace.pdf.

Floating-Point Verification

John Harrison

Intel Corporation, JF1-13, 2111 NE 25th Avenue,
Hillsboro OR 97124
johnh@ichips.intel.com
http://www.cl.cam.ac.uk/users/jrh

1   Introduction

Only in a few isolated safety-critical niches of the software industry (e.g. avionics) is any kind of formal verification widespread. But in the hardware industry, formal verification is widely practised, and increasingly seen as necessary. We can perhaps identify at least three reasons:

- Hardware is designed in a more modular way than most software, with refinement an important design method. Constraints of interconnect layering and timing means that one cannot really design 'spaghetti hardware'.
- More proofs in the hardware domain can be largely automated, reducing the need for intensive interaction by a human expert with the mechanical theorem-proving system.
- The potential consequences of a hardware error are greater, since such errors often cannot be patched or worked around, and may *in extremis* necessitate a hardware replacement.

To emphasize the last point, an error in the FDIV (floating-point division) instruction of some early Intel® Pentium® processors in 1994 resulted in a charge to Intel of approximately \$475M. Given this salutary lesson, and the size and diversity of its market, it's therefore understandable that Intel should be particularly interested in formal verification.

Moreover, it is not surprising that a considerable amount of effort has been in the floating-point domain, not just at Intel [17, 10, 9], but also at AMD [15, 19] and IBM [9]. Floating-point algorithms have proven themselves difficult to get right. Yet in marked contrast to some other targets for formal verification, it is not hard to come up with widely accepted formal specifications of how floating-point operations *should* behave. In fact, many operations are specified almost completely by the IEEE Standard governing binary floating-point arithmetic [12]. However, in some other respects, floating-point operations present a difficult challenge for formal verification.

2   The Role of Theorem Proving

In many other areas of verification, significant success has been achieved using highly automated techniques, usually based on a Boolean model of the state of the system.

J.S. Fitzgerald, I.J. Hayes, and A. Tarlecki (Eds.): FM 2005, LNCS 3582, pp. 529–532, 2005.

For example, efficient algorithms for propositional logic [1, 5, 21] and their aggressively efficient implementation [16] have made possible a variety of techniques ranging from simple Boolean equivalence checking of combinational circuits to more advanced model checking of sequential systems [3, 18, 2, 20].

But it is less easy to verify non-trivial floating-point arithmetic operations using such techniques. The natural specifications, including the IEEE Standard, are based on real numbers, not bit-strings. While simple adders and multipliers can be specified quite naturally in Boolean terms, this becomes progressively more difficult when one considers division and square root, and seems quite impractical for transcendental functions. So while model checkers and similar tools are of great value in dealing with low-level details, at least some parts of the proof must be constructed in general theorem proving systems that enable one to talk about high-level mathematics.

There are many theorem proving programs,[1] and quite a few have been applied to floating-point verification, including at least ACL2, Coq, HOL Light and PVS. We will concentrate later on our own work using HOL Light [6], but this is not meant to disparage other important work being done at Intel and elsewhere in other systems.

3   Examples

We will now give a brief overview of some of our verification projects using HOL Light. Of course, a significant component is the formalization of background theories of pure mathematics [7] and floating-point arithmetic [8]. We will not dwell on that in much detail, but it is an essential prerequisite for the verifications that are described.

Division

The Intel® Itanium® architecture performs division in software or microcode using sequences of 'fused multiply-adds', an approach pioneered by Markstein [14]. There are numerous variants depending on the required performance and accuracy characteristics (e.g. IEEE double-precision division with maximum throughput), and quite a few recommended sequences are made available by Intel so that they can be inlined by compilers, used as the core of mathematical libraries, or called on as macros by assembly language programmers. We have verified a large number of such algorithms [10], giving a much higher degree of assurance than had been provided by earlier hand proofs. A particularly gratifying experience was that as part of the process of formalization we observed that one of the hypotheses in a key theorem of [14] was stronger than necessary. As a result, we were able to design some more efficient algorithms [13].

Square Root

Similarly, the Intel® Itanium® architecture defers square roots to software, and we have verified a number of sequences for the operation [11]. The process of formal verification

---

[1] See `http://www.cs.ru.nl/~freek/digimath/index.html` for a list, and `http://www.cs.ru.nl/~freek/comparison/index.html` for a comparison of the formalization of an elementary mathematical theorem in several.

follows a methodology established by Cornea [4]. A general analytical proof covers the majority of cases, but a number of potential exceptions are isolated using number-theoretic techniques and dealt with using an explicit case analysis.

Proofs of this nature, large parts of which involve intricate but routine error bounding and the exhaustive solution of diophantine equations, are very tedious and error-prone to do by hand. In practice, one would do better to use *some* kind of machine assistance, such as *ad hoc* programs to solve the diophantine equations and check the special cases so derived. Although this can be helpful, it can also create new dangers of incorrectly implemented helper programs and transcription errors when passing results between 'hand' and 'machine' portions of the proof. By contrast, we perform all steps of the proof in HOL Light, and can be quite confident that no errors have been introduced.

Transcendentals

We have also proven rigorous error bounds for implementations of several common transcendental functions [9]. It is here that we really start to see the need for non-trivial mathematics. This proof, for example, involves verifying the accuracy of polynomial approximations to transcendental functions (optimal Remez polynomials rather than simply truncated Taylor series), precisely bounding rounding errors in sophisticated floating-point computations, and even diophantine approximation theory in order to deal with difficult cases where the input number is close to a multiple of $\pi/2$.

4   Conclusions

Formal verification in this area is a good target for theorem proving. The work outlined here has contributed in several ways: bugs have been found, potential optimizations have been uncovered, and the general level of confidence and intellectual grasp has been raised. In particular, two key strengths of HOL Light are important: (i) available library of formalized real analysis, and (ii) programmability of special-purpose inference rules without compromising soundness. Subsequent improvements might focus on integrating the verification more tightly into the design flow as in [17].

References

1. R. E. Bryant. Graph-based algorithms for Boolean function manipulation. *IEEE Transactions on Computers*, C-35:677–691, 1986.
2. J. R. Burch, E. M. Clarke, K. L. McMillan, D. L. Dill, and L. J. Hwang. Symbolic model checking: 10^{20} states and beyond. *Information and Computation*, 98:142–170, 1992.
3. E. M. Clarke and E. A. Emerson. Design and synthesis of synchronization skeletons using branching-time temporal logic. In D. Kozen, editor, *Logics of Programs*, volume 131 of *Lecture Notes in Computer Science*, pages 52–71, Yorktown Heights, 1981. Springer-Verlag.
4. M. Cornea-Hasegan. Proving the IEEE correctness of iterative floating-point square root, divide and remainder algorithms. *Intel Technology Journal*, 1998-Q2:1–11, 1998. Available on the Web as http://developer.intel.com/technology/itj/q21998/articles/art_3.htm.

5. M. Davis, G. Logemann, and D. Loveland. A machine program for theorem proving. *Communications of the ACM*, 5:394–397, 1962.
6. J. Harrison. HOL Light: A tutorial introduction. In M. Srivas and A. Camilleri, editors, *Proceedings of the First International Conference on Formal Methods in Computer-Aided Design (FMCAD'96)*, volume 1166 of *Lecture Notes in Computer Science*, pages 265–269. Springer-Verlag, 1996.
7. J. Harrison. *Theorem Proving with the Real Numbers*. Springer-Verlag, 1998. Revised version of author's PhD thesis.
8. J. Harrison. A machine-checked theory of floating point arithmetic. In Y. Bertot, G. Dowek, A. Hirschowitz, C. Paulin, and L. Théry, editors, *Theorem Proving in Higher Order Logics: 12th International Conference, TPHOLs'99*, volume 1690 of *Lecture Notes in Computer Science*, pages 113–130, Nice, France, 1999. Springer-Verlag.
9. J. Harrison. Formal verification of floating point trigonometric functions. In W. A. Hunt and S. D. Johnson, editors, *Formal Methods in Computer-Aided Design: Third International Conference FMCAD 2000*, volume 1954 of *Lecture Notes in Computer Science*, pages 217–233. Springer-Verlag, 2000.
10. J. Harrison. Formal verification of IA-64 division algorithms. In M. Aagaard and J. Harrison, editors, *Theorem Proving in Higher Order Logics: 13th International Conference, TPHOLs 2000*, volume 1869 of *Lecture Notes in Computer Science*, pages 234–251. Springer-Verlag, 2000.
11. J. Harrison. Formal verification of square root algorithms. *Formal Methods in System Design*, 22:143–153, 2003.
12. IEEE. Standard for binary floating point arithmetic. ANSI/IEEE Standard 754-1985, The Institute of Electrical and Electronic Engineers, Inc., 345 East 47th Street, New York, NY 10017, USA, 1985.
13. P. Markstein. *IA-64 and Elementary Functions: Speed and Precision*. Prentice-Hall, 2000.
14. P. W. Markstein. Computation of elementary functions on the IBM RISC System/6000 processor. *IBM Journal of Research and Development*, 34:111–119, 1990.
15. J. S. Moore, T. Lynch, and M. Kaufmann. A mechanically checked proof of the correctness of the kernel of the $AMD5_K86$ floating-point division program. *IEEE Transactions on Computers*, 47:913–926, 1998.
16. M. W. Moskewicz, C. F. Madigan, Y. Zhao, L. Zhang, and S. Malik. Chaff: Engineering an efficient SAT solver. In *Proceedings of the 38th Design Automation Conference (DAC 2001)*, pages 530–535. ACM Press, 2001.
17. J. O'Leary, X. Zhao, R. Gerth, and C.-J. H. Seger. Formally verifying IEEE compliance of floating-point hardware. *Intel Technology Journal*, 1999-Q1:1–14, 1999. Available on the Web as http://developer.intel.com/technology/itj/q11999/articles/art_5.htm.
18. J. P. Queille and J. Sifakis. Specification and verification of concurrent programs in CESAR. In *Proceedings of the 5th International Symposium on Programming*, volume 137 of *Lecture Notes in Computer Science*, pages 195–220. Springer-Verlag, 1982.
19. D. Rusinoff. A mechanically checked proof of IEEE compliance of a register-transfer-level specification of the AMD-K7 floating-point multiplication, division, and square root instructions. *LMS Journal of Computation and Mathematics*, 1:148–200, 1998. Available on the Web via http://www.onr.com/user/russ/david/k7-div-sqrt.html.
20. C.-J. H. Seger and R. E. Bryant. Formal verification by symbolic evaluation of partially-ordered trajectories. *Formal Methods in System Design*, 6:147–189, 1995.
21. G. Stålmarck and M. Säflund. Modeling and verifying systems and software in propositional logic. In B. K. Daniels, editor, *Safety of Computer Control Systems, 1990 (SAFECOMP '90)*, pages 31–36, Gatwick, UK, 1990. Pergamon Press.

Preliminary Results of a Case Study: Model Checking for Advanced Automotive Applications

Stefan Eisler[1], Christian Scheidler[1], Bernhard Josko[2],
Guido Sandmann[3], and Joachim Stroop[4]

[1] DaimlerChrysler AG, Alt-Moabit 96A,
D-10559 Berlin, Germany
{Stefan.Eisler, Christian Scheidler}@DaimlerChrysler.Com
[2] OFFIS, Escherweg 2,
D-26121 Oldenburg, Germany
Bernhard.Josko@Offis.de
[3] OSC - Embedded Systems AG, Industriestraße 11,
D-26121 Oldenburg, Germany
Guido.Sandmann@osc-es.de
[4] dSPACE GmbH, Technologiepark 25,
D-33100 Paderborn, Germany
jstroop@dspace.de

Abstract. Model checking is a promising formal verification technique success-fully applied in several industrial environments, such as in chip design and in the telecommunication industry. In this paper, preliminary results of an automotive case study are presented as performed in the context of the European project EASIS[1].

1 Introduction

The formal verification technique model checking (MC) was initially proposed by Clarke and Emerson [1] to check the complete state space of a finite state machine and to determine if a certain property is true or false. In contrast to *testing*, model checking provides exhaustive coverage of all possible input scenarios for a formally specified requirement. The requirements may be straightforward Boolean expressions or more sophisticated ones expressing temporal and causal properties.

2 Embedded*Validator*™

Embedded*Validator* (EV) is a commercial tool suite for performing model-based automatic formal verification by model checking for reactive embedded systems. EV is distributed by OSC-ES [2], a spin-off of the OFFIS Institute at the University of Oldenburg, Germany. EV is a fully integrated solution for the tool chain of The

---

[1] EASIS – Electronic Architectures and System Engineering for Integrated Safety Systems - is partly funded by the European Commission under contract No IST-507690.

J.S. Fitzgerald, I.J. Hayes, and A. Tarlecki (Eds.): FM 2005, LNCS 3582, pp. 533–536, 2005.
© Springer-Verlag Berlin Heidelberg 2005

MathWorks and dSPACE (Stateflow/Simulink/TargetLink) and is based on two established proof engines:

- VIS [3] has been developed jointly at the University of California at Berkeley, the University of Colorado at Boulder, and the University of Texas, Austin. The VIS engine provides *complete* model checking, meaning that the system is explored with regard to all reachable system states. Only when all reachable states have been visited does the verification procedure terminate.
- Prover, distributed by Prover Technologies [4], is a *bounded* engine which explores the system states only up to a user-defined number of steps. Counterexamples detected within this number of steps are design errors of the complete system. Errors which require a larger number of steps cannot be considered. This implies that if a counterexample is not detected within the given range, it cannot be concluded that the model fulfills the requirement.

Both technologies have their advantages and shortcomings. The complete technology suffers from complexity problems to a greater extent than the bounded one does. On the other hand, the bounded one only detects errors and cannot certify an implementation regarding a specification, as the complete engine can. EV supports two types of verification methods, referred to as *Robustness Checks and Standard Analyses* and *Proofs*:

1. The Robustness Checks and Standard Analyses cover checks like Drive-to-States, Drive-to-Configuration, Drive-to-Property and Range Violation. These verifications are very simple to use and require no knowledge of temporal logic.
2. Proofs address the formal verification of user-defined system properties. For ease of use, a Pattern Template Library for specifying temporal-logical requirements is provided. Eight-teen core proof patterns, like `inv_P`, `P_implies_Q_X_steps_later` or `Q_not_before_P` are supported. The abstract variables P and Q used in the formulas have to be substituted by concrete expressions of states and/or variables of the system model. The Pattern Template Library cannot be extended by the user. However, first experiences show that the given patterns cover a broad spectrum of proofs. More than 70 proofs have been already performed based on the current Pattern Template Library (see chapter 3).

The compilation of the model behavior into the verification language is based upon generated C code by TargetLink. The benefit of this approach is a smaller semantic gap between the "proven unit" (generated C code) and the "final system" (ECU), compared to the alternative method of getting the model data out of the Simulink model files (*.mdl). However, additional costs for the TargetLink code generator have to be considered.

3 Evaluation

For the purpose of evaluation, an advanced automotive assistance system, which will come to market in 2006, has been chosen as DaimlerChrysler Pilot Application #1. For confidentiality reasons, only limited information about this application can be given in this publication. The system model of Pilot Application #1 offers several advantages:

- Pilot Application #1 is an in-house development; therefore all artifacts of this application (requirements, models, etc.) are available at DaimlerChrysler.
- The main control flow logic of the application is represented explicitly in Stateflow state charts, which is a fundamental prerequisite for model checking.
- The system model is represented as TargetLink fix-point model, which is a requirement of the EV (see chapter 2).
- Textual requirements associated with state charts exist already, which eases the preparation of system properties to be proven.

However, the model is not purely based on Stateflow subsystems, which raises the limitations of the model checking technology. Several parts of the application are represented by Simulink subsystems that consist of TargetLink blocks not supported by EV and hence cannot be analyzed. These subsystems have to be verified by conventional testing technologies.

The evaluation requires the following steps. Firstly, relevant Stateflow subsystems of the system model and all related requirements have to be identified. Secondly, the extraction procedure of EV has to be started. Floating-point numbers have to be converted to fix-point representations; here the TargetLink property manager can be applied. Finally, analyses and proofs can be configured. The configuration of proofs is the intellectually most demanding task. Some experience is needed to transform textual requirements into temporal logic formulas.

We would like to distinguish between *methodology* and *tool* evaluation. Criteria for methodology evaluation are:

- *Maturity* - covering the size/ type of system models which can be analyzed,
- *Limitations* - typically characterized by system models which cannot be analyzed due to their size,
- *Process conformity* - how to integrate the methodology into an established system engineering process.

Typical criteria for tool evaluation are:

- *Usability* – covering all GUI aspects, like user friendliness, etc.,
- *Ease of formalization* – how much expert knowledge on formal methods/model checking, respectively, is needed to prove a certain requirement,
  Maturity – absence of bugs, etc.

Table 1 covers preliminary yet promising results of the automotive case study. Sixty-seven requirements associated with four different subsystems have been already analyzed; sixty-two requirements have been proven successfully. Five requirements have been disproven; the counterexamples bring up slight mismatches between requirements specification and system model. None of these counterexamples could have been found easily using conventional testing technologies; which demonstrates the power of model checking technology. However, the effects found are negligible, because they do not change the system behavior in such a way that can be experienced by the driver/customer.

Table 1. Preliminary results of the case study

State chart	No. of re-quirements	Provable (Requirement represented in model)	TRUE	FALSE (counterexample exists)
#1	9	6	5	1
#2	17	14	14	0
#3	16	11	11	0
#4	39	36	32	4
Sum	81	67(83%)	62(93%)	5(7%)

Four counterexamples are associated with a minimal change of the timing behavior, which might be illustrated by state chart #1. The disproven requirement says *"that the system has to go to the inactive state if a certain kind of driver activity has been sensed."* This property holds in nearly all cases; however, there is one input sequence where the activation of the inactive state is delayed by two steps, causing a decelerated system behavior. This effect is associated with the Stateflow clock rule, because the delayed path corresponds to an out transition of a superstate, which is of higher priority than the out transition corresponding to the direct path to the inactive state.

4   Summary and Outlook

Preliminary yet promising results of an automotive case study for model checking have been presented. We can conclude that the methodology and the supporting tool fit to the model-based development process, which has become a de-facto standard in the automotive domain. Future short-term activities cover the proof of further Stateflow subsystems in Pilot Application #1 and the analysis of the semantic gap between the proven C code and the C code compiled for the target ECU. The comparison of the methodology model checking and testing is a further research issue. Here we would like to examine whether model checking substitutes or complements conventional testing. A fundamental problem of model checking is the lack of traceability in the case that a property has been proven. Here, concepts are needed to increase confidence in model checking results.

References

1. Clarke, E.M., Emerson, E.A.: Design and synthesis of synchronization skeletons using branching-time temporal logic. Lecture Notes in Computer Science, Vol. 131. Springer-Verlag, Berlin Heidelberg New York (1981).
2. http://www.osc-es.de
3. The VIS Group: VIS: A system for Verification and Synthesis. Proceedings of the 8th International Conference on Computer Aided Verification. Lecture Notes in Computer Science, Vol. 1102. Springer-Verlag, Berlin Heidelberg New York (1996) 428-432.
4. Prover Technologies. http://www.prover.com/, 2003.

Model-Based Testing in Practice

Alexander Pretschner

Information Security, ETH Zürich, 8092 Zürich, Switzerland

1   Introduction

Testing comprises activities that aim at showing that the intended and actual behaviors of a system differ, or at gaining confidence that they do not. The goal of testing is failure detection: observable differences between the behaviors of implementation and specification. Classical estimates relate one half of the overall development effort to testing. Even if Fagan [1] suspects that this percentage includes activities such as finding the causes of failures in the code and removing them, testing is an important and expensive activity in the development process.

Model-based testing (MBT) relies on models (specifications) that encode the intended behavior of a system. Runs of the model are interpreted as *test cases* (in this paper, *tests* for short) for a system under test (SUT): input and expected output. Activities in MBT have attracted a major interest in the past years. In addition to the appeal of the concept, we see the major reasons (a) in a gain of momentum of model-based languages and technologies (UML, MDA) and their seemingly direct connection to testing activities, (b) in the increasing popularity of test-centered development processes such as TDD or XP, and (c) in the possibility of promoting research activities and results under the umbrella of "lightweight" formal methods. Yet, despite numerous efforts in the area, it is not clear if the use of this technology pays off and, if so, in which niches.

This overview paper summarizes the ideas, promises, assumptions, and evidence of the benefits of MBT in Sec. 2. Sec. 3 argues for empirical studies.

2   Model-Based Testing

We describe the fundamentals of MBT, convey the appeal of the concept, pin down assumptions for successful deployment, and report on evidence.

Fundamentals. Testing consists of three stages: generation of tests, execution of tests, and derivation of verdicts. When applied to non-deterministic systems, the first two stages are likely to collapse. Models are used for the generation of tests and test harnesses. Since tests already comprise input and expected output we do not need models for assigning verdicts. Test harnesses are pieces of code that actually execute tests. Models that can be used to derive test harnesses are usually of a structural nature. These are not the subject of this paper; we will focus on behavior models instead.

J.S. Fitzgerald, I.J. Hayes, and A. Tarlecki (Eds.): FM 2005, LNCS 3582, pp. 537–541, 2005.

The number of possible tests is normally very large or even infinite. For economical reasons, it should be reduced to a minimum. For quality reasons, it must be sufficiently high as to reduce the number of remaining failures in the field to an acceptable number. This means that test case generation, be it model-based or not, must face the problem of selecting "good" tests in the following sense. They are cheap to derive and cheap to execute; they are cheap to evaluate in that they help detecting faults on the grounds of failures; they find all "serious" and "frequent" failures.

Respective selection criteria can be divided into structural, functional, fault-based, and stochastic criteria. *Structural criteria* require that, upon execution of the SUT or the model, a certain coverage of data domains and of the nodes and edges in control flow and data flow graphs be obtained. Their ability to detect failures is subject to ongoing disputes [2], and particularly so when compared to random testing. On the other hand, structural criteria lend themselves to the automated generation of tests (test selection criteria are also quality indicators [3]), and they are measurable. This is relevant from a management point of view. *Functional criteria* try to capture isolated functionalities or requirements of a system, and define tests accordingly. This is usually achieved by defining models of the environment, or by other dedicated constraints on the set of all executions of the model. In general, MBT is hence concerned with models of both the SUT and the environment. Alleviating the task of defining concrete functional criteria seems to be possible from a methodological perspective, but not from a technical point of view. *Fault-based criteria* rely on knowledge of typically occurring failures. Finally, *stochastic criteria* rely on input probability distributions. If the distribution is uniform, then testing is random. Other distributions are based on user profiles [4] which is particularly appealing from an economic point of view since it caters for the frequency of potential failures.

Given a model and an adequately operationalized test selection criterion— constraints or environment models—a test case generator, human or automatic, then derives traces of the model, i.e. tests for the SUT. Test case generators use the technologies of model checkers, symbolic execution, satisfiability checkers, or deductive theorem provers. In addition to the practical difficulties with verifying large systems, model checking or theorem proving of the programs alone are not sufficient because these activities cannot transcend the assumptions on the environment (hardware, operating systems, legacy systems).

Methodologically, MBT makes sense only if the model is more abstract than the SUT. Otherwise, the effort of validating the model would exactly match the effort of validating the SUT itself. This implies (a) that only behavior encoded in the model can be tested and (b) that the different levels of abstraction must be bridged [5]: the input part of the test is concretized before it is fed into the SUT, and the output of the SUT is abstracted before it is compared to the expected output part of the test. For instance, the output of a model can be as abstract as "exception thrown" or "not thrown". Concretization and abstraction are performed by dedicated driver components. Coming up with the adequate abstraction continues to be an art.

Testing requires redundancy. Except for stress and performance testing, it is questionable to use one single model for the generation of both tests and code: the model would be tested against itself. In such a setting, only assumptions on the environment of the SUT and the code generator can be tested [5].

Promises and Benefits. Then dubbed "specification-based testing", the ideas of MBT have been around for about three decades. Traditionally, engineers form a vague understanding of the system by reading the specification. They build a mental model. Inventing tests on the grounds of these mental models is a creative process that is often implicit, barely reproducible, not motivated in its details and bound to the ingenuity of single engineers. Proponents of MBT claim that by making the mental model explicit, it is possible to generate sufficiently many tests of a sufficient quality at an acceptable cost in a structured manner. Even if it is rarely explicitly stated, the claim is that MBT yields better and cheaper tests than strategies that do not rely on explicit models (we do not discuss the relationship with reviews here; McConnell as well as Rombach and Endres have compiled studies that relate them to traditional testing [6, 7]).

The mere act of building behavior models in itself helps understand and clarify the requirements. This is because one is forced to thoroughly think about the system. In this vein, MBT can be seen as add-on to an activity the benefits of which usually go unchallenged, at least if cost is not an issue.

Assumptions. We will now make explicit three major assumptions that, usually concealed, go along with the first promise of the last paragraph.

The first assumption concerns models as abstractions. We have argued above that some loss of information is methodologically indispensable. The assumption consists of two parts. (1) Because models are simplifications, they are simpler to check than the SUT. (2) Sufficiently large parts of the omitted information can be re-inserted by the driver components that perform concretizations and abstractions: complexity can be distributed among model and driver.

The second assumption is concerned with the cost-effectiveness of the approach. It reads as follows. When compared to traditional forms of testing, the resulting high quality of a SUT that was tested on the grounds of a model justifies the cost of building the model and generating tests.

The third assumption concerns reuse. Recognizing the high cost of building models, it comes in two forms. One states that changes in the model as a consequence of changing requirements are (1) easy to validate, and, provided that MBT is a push-button technology, (2) re-generating tests is cheaper than changing existing test suites. The second form states that reusing models and test selection criteria in product lines automatically implies a reuse of tests.

Evidence. As far as we know, there is no published evidence that the promises of MBT are kept. Horstmann et al. have recently provided a compilation of case studies [8]. Roughly, all report on successful applications of MBT with automated test case generation in that "failures were found". With the exception of a recent study [2], comparative studies do not exist: MBT is not measured against random or manual testing (in fact, some studies do vaguely state that "model-based tests covered hand-written tests", without explicitly stating what exactly this means). Subject of the cited study [2] is the comparison of several test suites generated automatically/manually/randomly, all with and without a model. Comparison was done w.r.t. the number of detected failures, model coverage, and implementation coverage (condition/decision coverage). The main results of that study are (1) with a distinction between programming and specification errors, model-based tests detect significantly more specification errors than the other suites, (2) hand-crafted model-based tests detected roughly as many failures as a significantly larger number of automatically generated tests, and (3) inconclusive findings on the relationship between coverages and failure detection. The study is concerned with one single embedded system only, and it does not take into account the cost of building the model.

3   Conclusions

The ideas of MBT are appealing, in particular when testing is just one activity in an overall model-based development process. Numerous studies have shown that MBT does help with revealing errors, even in products that have been in the field for several years. We are convinced that MBT is a promising technology, but most studies leave the following questions open. (1) How many errors were detected during the modeling phase and before testing, i.e. during the careful review of the requirements or specification documents? (2) How many errors were detected by competitive technologies, in particular, testing without models and MBT with manual derivation of tests? (3) How do cost and benefits relate?

It is true that not all successful technology had had prior empirical evidence on its side (e.g. OO technology). To date, the question of whether or not structural test selection yield "better" tests than random tests remains undecided. We are convinced that an array of empirical studies on MBT for single systems will help find out where the technology is promising from a cost-benefit point of view, where it is not, and why. Further, comparative studies that take into account different technical approaches to MBT as well as different (kinds of) systems will help with identifying potential areas of successful application of MBT. This is even if the design of such studies is intricate, and even if, in sum, results of comparable work in the domain of error classifications are rather inconclusive [6]. A suite of benchmark problems with manually derived tests, known errors, and known cost of these errors could be a starting point.

References

1. Fagan, M.: Reviews and Inspections. In: Software Pioneers–Contributions to Software Engineering, Springer Verlag (2002) 562–573
2. Pretschner, A., Prenninger, W., Wagner, S., Kühnel, C., Baumgartner, M., Zölch, R., Sostawa, B., Stauner, T.: One evaluation of model-based testing and its automation. In: Proc. 27th Intl. Conf. on Software Engineering. (2005) To appear.
3. Zhu, H., Hall, P., May, J.: Software Unit Test Coverage and Adequacy. ACM Computing Surveys **29** (1997) 366–427

4. Musa, J.: Software Reliability Engineering. AuthorHouse, 2nd ed. (2004)
5. Pretschner, A., Philipps, J.: Methodological Issues in Model-Based Testing. Springer LNCS 3472. In: Model-Based Testing–a tutorial volume. (2005) 281–291
6. McConnell, S.: Code Complete. Microsoft Press (1993)
7. Endres, A., Rombach, D.: A Handbook of Software and Systems Engineering— Empirical Observations, Laws and Theories. Pearson Addison Wesley (2003)
8. Horstmann, M., Prenninger, W., El-Ramly, M.: Case Studies. Springer LNCS 3472. In: Model-Based Testing–a tutorial volume. (2005) 439–461

Testing Concurrent Object-Oriented Systems with Spec Explorer

Extended Abstract

Colin Campbell, Wolfgang Grieskamp, Lev Nachmanson,
Wolfram Schulte, Nikolai Tillmann, and Margus Veanes

Microsoft Research, Redmond, WA, USA

Abstract. We describe a practical model-based testing tool developed at Microsoft Research called Spec Explorer. Spec Explorer enables modeling and automatic testing of concurrent object-oriented systems. These systems take inputs as well as provide outputs in form of spontaneous reactions, where inputs and outputs can be arbitrary data types, including objects. Spec Explorer is being used daily by several Microsoft product groups. The here presented techniques are used to test operating system components and Web service infrastructure.

Transition Systems Formalize Reactive and Distributed Systems. Reactive and distributed systems are inherently nondeterministic. No single agent (component, thread, etc.) controls all state transitions, and even external entities like the operating systems scheduler or the network may play a role.

A practical and theoretically sound way to test the evolution of semi-independent state spaces is to use a kind of transition system known as an interface automaton [3]. *Interface automata* make a distinction between input transitions and output transitions. In some states, input is enabled and we can drive the system forward by giving it new things to do; at other times the system and its environment choose what happens next. This is like a game where players take turns. Sometimes it is our turn to make a move; sometimes it is the systems.

To illustrate how this works we will use a network-based chat system as an example. In the chat system there are multiple clients that may post messages. The system delivers pending messages in FIFO order with local consistency. Figure 1 shows a typical scenario of the chat systems' behavior as an interface automaton. The nodes of the graph represent distinct states of the system. The arcs represent actions that change the systems state. Each state in the graph is either input enabled or output enabled. The states drawn with ovals represent *active, input-enabled states* where a client may give the system new work to do. States drawn with diamonds are *passive, output-enabled states* where the system reacts to input or spontaneously makes a move of its own choosing. The Post *action* is said to be *controllable* because it can be invoked by a user to provide system input. The Deliver action is only *observable*; that is, it is an output message. The names of observable actions in the graph are prefixed by the ? symbol. Note that in some passive states there is a race between what the user may do and what the system may do. The Timeout transition, here represented by a transition that carries no label, indicates that no output was seen in the time the user was willing to wait. This causes a transition from an output-enabled state to an input-enabled state.

J.S. Fitzgerald, I.J. Hayes, and A. Tarlecki (Eds.): FM 2005, LNCS 3582, pp. 542–547, 2005.

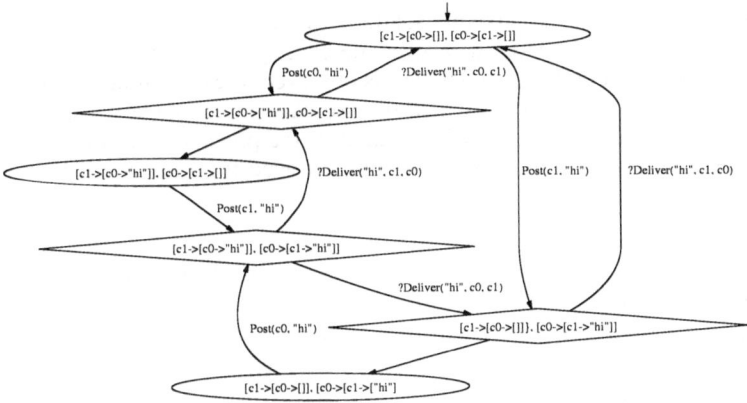

Fig. 1. Exploration of the Chat model with two clients (c0 and c1), a fixed message ("hi") under the restriction that at most 1 message from each sender must still be delivered to a client

Model Programs Compactly Encode Large Transition Systems. Interface automata describe fixed scenarios. But we are not only interested in modeling and testing a fixed scenario; we want to have a general description for a protocol, like a chat server. This is where model programs can help. Rather than coding our system description directly as a transition system, we use a *model program* to express system behavior as an "abstract state machine". Tools like Spec Explorer that analyze the states of the machine can produce the transition system needed for testing.

Here is a model program that describes the chat system shown above, written in the Spec# language. The state of the system consists of instances of the class `Client` that have been created so far, and a map `Members` that for each client specifies the messages that have been sent but not yet delivered to that client as sender queues. Each sender queue is identified by the client that sent the messages in the queue. In the initial state of the system there are no clients and and `Members` is an empty map.

```
class Client
type Message = string;
type SendersQueue = Map<Client,Seq<Message>>;
type MemberState = Map<Client,SendersQueue>;

MemberState Members = new Map();
```

We give two actions of the system. Actions are methods with preconditions that say in which state of the system they may occur and for which input parameters. A member of the chat session may post a message for all members except himself to receive. When a sender posts a message, the message is appended at the end of the corresponding sender queue of each of the other members of the session.

```
void Post(Client sndr, Message msg)
  requires sndr in Members && Members.Size > 1;
{ foreach(rcvr in Members)
    if (rcvr != sndr) Members[rcvr][sndr].Add(msg); }
```

A message being delivered from a sender to a receiver is an observable action or a notification callback that occurs whenever the chat system forwards a particular message to a particular client. When a delivery is observed, the corresponding sender queue of the receiver has to be nonempty, and the message must match the first message in that queue or else local consistency is violated. If the preconditions of the delivery are satisfied then the delivered message is simply removed from the corresponding sender queue of the recipient.

```
void Deliver(Message msg, Client sndr, Client rcvr)
  requires rcvr in Members && sndr in Members[rcvr];
  requires Members[rcvr][sndr].Length > 0 &&
           Members[rcvr][sndr].Head == msg;
{ Members[rcvr][sndr] = Members[rcvr][sndr].Tail; }
```

When a client joins the session, the related message queues are initialized appropriately.

To encode a specification of the system's intended behavior in machine-executable form is not the same as writing a second implementation. The model program does less than the implementation. Its purpose is to capture the states of the system that affect the observable behavior of interest.

Exploration can Reveal the Interface Automaton of a Model Program. The interface automaton defined by a model program is a complete unwinding or expansion of the program. An *explicit state model checking algorithm* is used to compute the (possibly infinite) space of all possible sequences of method invocations that 1) do not violate the pre- and postconditions and invariant of the system's contracts and 2) are relevant to a user-specified set of test properties [4].

If the model is infinite state, unwinding doesn't terminate. Spec Explorer thus includes practical features that control how the state space is explored. We mention two of these: *State groupings* allow the exploration to prune away states that are distinct but indistinguishable under a user-provided equivalence relation [1]. Avoiding isomorphic cases that differ in the choice of input but have identical runs results in a body of tests with a better chance of detecting a conformance discrepancy. *State-dependent parameter generation* allows to compute the parameter domains of each action with respect to the current state. This can make exploration more efficient by reducing the search for input parameters to feasible cases.

Interface Automaton Provides the Basis for Model-Based Test Case Generation. Test cases can be automatically generated by *traversing the graph* of the interface automaton. The graph also serves as a *test oracle*: a test fails if observed transitions of the implementation under test do not match transitions in the graph. Additionally, successful test runs must begin in the *initial state* and terminate in an accepting state. *Accepting states* are states that satisfy a user-specified logical condition that says whether the system is in a final, deinitialized state. In this example, the accepting state occurs whenever the message queues are empty.

Differences between the predicted and actual system behavior are called conformance failures. What constitutes a difference is mathematically defined in terms of alternating refinement of interface automata. *Alternating refinement* means that the system under test must accept at least as many inputs as the interface automaton defines (it may accept more inputs) and that, conversely, the test harness must accept at least as many outputs as the system may produce (it may accept more outputs than the system is capable of producing) [2].

Our test graphs are also used to *automatically harness* the implementation for conformance testing. Spec Explorer can instrument a .NET assembly and cause implementation methods corresponding to model actions to be invoked as needed.

Running a test results in a trace log that shows a comparison of expected versus actual behavior. Here is an example:

Step	Invocation	From State	To State	Status
1	Post(c0, "Hi")	S0	S1	Succeeded
2	?Timeout	S1	S1'	Succeeded
3	Post(c0, "Bye")	S1'	S7	Succeeded
4	?Deliver("Bye", c0, c1)	S7	S2	FAILED: observed Deliver("Bye", c0, c1), expected Deliver("Hi", c0, c1)

This test run observed that the particular chat system implementation being tested did not deliver messages in the order posted, as required by the specification. The server delivered in LIFO order instead of FIFO.

Game Strategies Help Achieve Test Goals. Although any traversal of the graph is a possible trace of the system, we can only choose moves in the active states (i.e., those drawn as ovals in the graph). A state where the system can choose from among more than one move represents nondeterminism from the observers point of view. This means a test case is not a just sequence of actions but a tree of actions and possible system responses. Executing a test is like a so-called *game against nature* where a players opponent chooses moves randomly. Spec Explorer implements game strategies using Markov decision processes as a technique for intelligently choosing input actions that broaden the coverage of nondeterministic tests [5].

On-the-Fly Conformance Checking Scales to Very Large State Spaces. When dealing with model programs that have very large state spaces, we can combine the state exploration and test case generation into an online algorithm called *on-the-fly testing* [6].

When testing in its on-the-fly mode, Spec Explorer's exploration makes moves based on the observed history of the test run. This allows it to omit exploration of nondeterministic branches that were not taken by the implementation during the test run. It can also be run in a way that attempts to match the distribution of actions exercised during testing to an application profile given as input.

Spec Explorer users rely on both pre-generated, offline tests with complete behavioral coverage over a restricted domain of system inputs and online tests generated on the fly which randomly sample a larger number of system inputs.

Empirical Evidence Shows that Spec Explorer is Effective. Spec Explorer was internally released in summer 2004. Since then approx. 100 testers use it on a daily basis. In fact, most of Microsoft's forthcoming Web service infrastructure was tested with Spec Explorer and so are components of the Windows operating system.

For instance, recently the Windows test team split a feature set into 4 components and decided to test 2 of them traditionally and 2 with Spec Explorer. The modeling team build (1) a system-level object-model consisting of approx. 200 and another one (2) of approx. 3500 lines of non-blank Spec# code. The multi-threaded implementations under test have 2000 and 20000 lines of non-blank C++ code respectively.

In this particular setting, the model-based approach helped to discover 10 times more errors than traditional test automation. Also the kind of bugs discovered were deep system-level bugs (i.e. bugs that were only found after the system performed many steps), for which manual test cases would have been hard to construct.

The effort in developing the models took roughly the same amount of time as developing the traditional test automation. The biggest impact that the modeling effort had was during the design phase, the process helped to discover and resolve 2 times more design issues than bugs that were found afterwards.

Microsoft developers typically can only check in code, which unit tests achieved already more than 60% feasible branch coverage. It is the testers task to improve this coverage. For (1) and (2) the testers refined the models so that they achieved 100% and 70% feasible branch coverage, respectively. While this improved the statistics, it does not reflect on how well a concurrent implementation is tested. In most cases when bugs were found, at least two or more threads and a shared resource were involved, although the same code coverage could often be achieved with a single thread.

When developing new versions of the code, models need to be adjusted, but such changes are typically local, whereas manual test cases have to be redesigned and sometimes completely rewritten. We have repeatedly observed that this is where model-based testing substantially reduces test case development time.

But caution: When customers discover discrepancies between model and implementation using our tool, typically about half of them originate from the informal requirements specification, the model, or bugs in the test harness, and half are due to coding errors in the implementation under test. But so far every team agreed that the modeling effort was helpful – not only for test, but also, and in particular for design.

References

1. C. Campbell and M. Veanes. State exploration with multiple state groupings. In D. Beauquier, E. Börger, and A. Slissenko, editors, *12th International Workshop on Abstract State Machines, ASM'05, March 8–11, 2005, Laboratory of Algorithms, Complexity and Logic, University Paris 12 – Val de Marne, Créteil, France*, pages 119–130, 2005.

2. L. de Alfaro. Game models for open systems. In N. Dershowitz, editor, *Verification: Theory and Practice: Essays Dedicated to Zohar Manna on the Occasion of His 64th Birthday*, volume 2772 of *LNCS*, pages 269 – 289. Springer, 2004.

3. L. de Alfaro and T. A. Henzinger. Interface automata. In *Proceedings of the 8th European Software Engineering Conference and the 9th ACM SIGSOFT Symposium on the Foundations of Software Engineering (ESEC/FSE)*, pages 109–120. ACM, 2001.

4. W. Grieskamp, Y. Gurevich, W. Schulte, and M. Veanes. Generating finite state machines from abstract state machines. In *ISSTA'02*, volume 27 of *Software Engineering Notes*, pages 112–122. ACM, 2002.

5. L. Nachmanson, M. Veanes, W. Schulte, N. Tillmann, and W. Grieskamp. Optimal strategies for testing nondeterministic systems. In *ISSTA'04*, volume 29 of *Software Engineering Notes*, pages 55–64. ACM, July 2004.
6. M. Veanes, C. Campbell, W. Schulte, and P. Kohli. On-the-fly testing of reactive systems. Technical Report MSR-TR-2005-03, Microsoft Research, January 2005.

ASD Case Notes: Costs and Benefits of Applying Formal Methods to Industrial Control Software

Guy H. Broadfoot

Verum Consultants BV
guy.broadfoot@verum.com

1   Introduction

Software is now an essential component that is embedded in an ever-increasing array of products. It has become an important means of realising product innovation and is a key determinant of both product quality and time-to-market. For many businesses, software has become *business-critical* and software development is a *strategic* business activity. At the same time, software development continues to suffer from poor predictability. Existing development methods appear to have reached a quality ceiling that incremental improvements in process and technology are unlikely to breach. To break through this ceiling, a different, more formal approach is needed, but one which can be introduced within existing development organisations.

In this extended abstract, we summarise the costs and benefits of applying Analytical Software Design (ASD), an approach that combines formal techniques with existing industrial methods, to an industrial software development project.

2   An Overview of ASD

ASD uses the Sequence-based Specification method (SBS) [PP03] to specify functional requirements and designs as total black box functions mapping every possible sequence of input stimuli to a response. SBS partitions the domain into a finite set of equivalence classes, each of which is characterised by a minimal length sequence called a *canonical sequence*. This approach differs fundamentally from informal methods using exemplary sequences, for example based on Sequence Diagrams or Use Case analysis, by guaranteeing completeness. The specifications are fully traceable to the original requirements specifications and because they are free from mathematical notation, they remain completely accessible to critical project stakeholders and existing project teams. This satisfies the industrial requirement that existing project personal retain a key role in verifying and controlling the specifications. At the same time, the specifications provide the degree of rigour and precision necessary for subsequent mathematical analysis.

The ASD Model Generator generates CSP [Hoa85, Ros98] models from these specifications and designs automatically and these can be formally analysed and verified using the model checker FDR [For03]. For example, we use the model checker to verify (i) whether a design satisfies its functional requirements; and (ii) whether the design uses other components according to their external functional specifications.

J.S. Fitzgerald, I.J. Hayes, and A. Tarlecki (Eds.): FM 2005, LNCS 3582, pp. 548–551, 2005.

The ASD Code Generator can generate significant amounts of program source code in C++, C or other similar languages automatically from these specifications. The major advantage of code generation is correctness; the code is generated automatically from specifications already formally verified. The percentage of the total code that can be generated this way varies from project to project. Experience suggests this is typically between 70% and 90%, leading to significant efficiency gains.

3   The Case: The MagLev Stage

The MagLev Stage is a new product developed by the Department of Mechatronics of Philips Applied Technologies in the Netherlands. It is a subsystem designed to be incorporated in a variety of industrial systems that require medium speed, highly accurate positioning, scanning or contouring for applications in a broad range of semiconductor related environments. The control software coordinates the actions of two multi-axis controllers and provides an Application Program Interface (API) to customer-developed domain specific application software. Due to the complexity of the software and the high defect rate of an earlier "proof of concept" version, ASD techniques were applied to develop a production quality version.

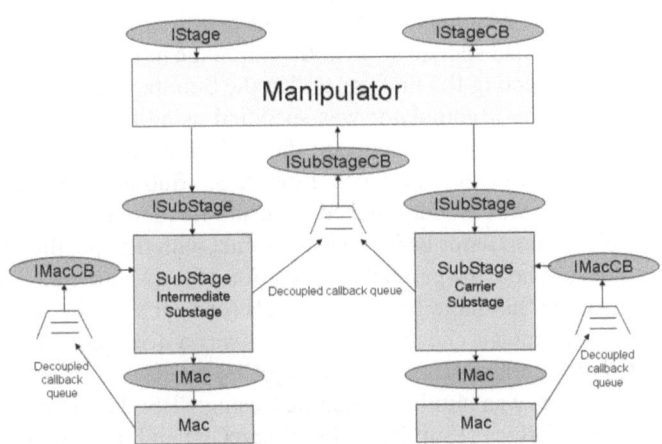

Fig. 1. MagLev Software Overview

3.1   Technical Details

The MagLev Stage consists of two *substages* called the *Intermediate Substage* and *Carrier Substage*. Each substage is controlled by its own dedicated multi-axis controller (MAC). Figure 1 shows the overall organisation of the software into two major components, namely the *Manipulator* and the *SubStage*. In the diagram, software components are depicted by rectangles; major interfaces are depicted by the labelled ovals.

The diagram shows two instances of the SubStage component, one controlling the Intermediate Substage and one controlling the Carrier Substage. The SubStage component is responsible for controlling a single substage via its dedicated MAC. The Manipulator component coordinates and controls the two substages. All actions that are specific to a single MAC are implemented in the SubStage component; all actions requiring coordination between the substages, such as most movements and all exception and error handling, are implemented in the Manipulator component.

The Manipulator component implements its client API (IStage), sending asynchronous call-back notifications to the client application (IStageCB), using the SubStage API (ISubStage) and receiving notifications from the two substages via the ISubStageCB interfaces. All the ISubStageCB events are routed to the Manipulator via a queue and are executed under the context of a separate deferred procedure call (DPC) server thread. The SubStage implements the ISubStage and ISubStageCB interfaces and accesses its MAC via the IMac and IMacCB interfaces. Notifications from the MAC are received asynchronously via the IMacCB interface and decoupled via a queue.

ASD was applied as follows: firstly, sequence-based specifications (SBS) were made of the MAC interface (IMac and IMacCB) and the Client interface (IStage and IStageCB). During this process, a significant number of interface ambiguities, omissions and inconsistencies were uncovered and resolved with the domain experts. The resulting black box functions were plotted as state transition diagrams and reviewed by the team.

The architecture was then developed, partitioning the major functions of the control software between the Manipulator component and the two instances of the SubStage component and an SBS specification of the SubStage interfaces (ISubStage, ISubStageCB) was made, reflecting the first "guess" at the SubStage abstraction.

Next, the design of the Manipulator was specified using the SBS method and the ASD Model Generator was used to generate the CSP models of the client interfaces (IStage, IStageCB), the SubStage interfaces (ISubStage, ISubStageCB) and the Manipulator design. The design was model checked to ensure freedom from internal inconsistencies (for example, Manipulator behaviour in conflict with the specified SubStage Interface) and deadlocks. Then, the parallel composition of the Manipulator design model plus two instances of the SubStage Interface models (one each for the Intermediate and Carrier SubStages) was model checked to ensure it was a divergence free, failures refinement of the Client Interface (IStage and IStageCB) model.

The SubStage design was similarly specified using SBS. The implemented interface is the SubStage interface (ISubStage, ISubStageCB) and the used interface is the MAC interface (IMac, IMacCB). The CSP models were generated and model checked to verify that the parallel composition of the SubStage design model and the MAC interface (IMac, IMacCB) was a divergence free, failures refinement of the same SubStage interface (ISubStage, ISubStageCB) model used to verify the Manipulator design.

When both the Manipulator and SubStage designs were completed and verified by model checking, the C++ code of both the Manipulator and the SubStage was generated using the ASD Code Generator.

3.2   Results

The specification of the MAC interfaces, the client API interface and the SubStage interface took about 2 weeks. The design and verification of the Manipulator took about 4 weeks to complete. Due to its complexity, the Manipulator design was hierarchically decomposed into a top level design together with 3 significant lower level sub-designs. The design has 1,700 transition rules and 28 canonical sequences. This hierarchical design structure was carried through into the generated CSP models and the generated C++ code, providing full traceability between these different views. During the design verification, about 200 errors were detected by model checking. Most of these fell into one of two categories: i) internal inconsistencies where the design violated the interface specifications of the used components or was unable to react correctly to notifications arriving asynchronously from the used interfaces; ii) complex race conditions.

The ASD design and verification of the SubStage took about 4 weeks to complete. Due to its complexity, the design was hierarchically decomposed into a top level design plus 5 lower level sub-designs. The design has 4,700 transition rules and 84 canonical sequences. More than 100 errors were detected by model checking and removed.

In total 18,000 executable lines of C++ were generated, representing 90% of the code. The hand written code was either concerned with domain specific issues such as coordinate transformations or "glue" code interfacing the software to the rest of the run-time environment.

4   Conclusions

Applying ASD to the specification and design phases of this project was cost neutral as compared to conventional specification and design methods. That is, there was no additional cost. Including all specification, design, design verification, coding and testing effort, this project produced 18,000 executable lines of code in 35 man weeks of effort, which equates to a production rate of 12 executable lines of C++ per hour, more than a factor three increase over the typical rate for an equivalent project.

In addition, the delivered code commanded very low defect rates; nearly 400 defects were removed during design verification before programming started. On a similar project developed in the conventional way, 60 defects were discovered during initial integration testing. So far, testing on the MagLev stage has detected 5 defects (hand written code errors, under-specification issues), all of which were simple to find. This is a defect rate of 0.28 defects per thousand lines of delivered code.

References

[For03]   Formal Systems (Europe) Ltd. *Failures-Divergence Refinement: FDR2 User Manual*, 2003. See http://www.fsel.com.

[Hoa85]   C. A. R. Hoare. *Communicating Sequential Processes*. Prentice Hall, 1985.

[PP03]   S. J. Prowell and J. H. Poore. Foundations of sequence-based software specification. *IEEE Transactions of Software Engineering*, 29(5):417–429, 2003.

[Ros98]   A. W. Roscoe. *The Theory and Practice of Concurrency*. Prentice Hall, 1998.

The Informal Nature of Systems Engineering

Gerrit Muller

Embedded Systems Institute, Den Dolech 2, 5612 AZ Eindhoven
gerrit.muller@esi.nl
http://www.extra.research.philips.com/natlab/sysarch/

Abstract. This is a position paper about the relation between Formal Methods and Systems Engineering for complex computerized systems. We will argue that Formal Methods are well suited to prescribed homogeneous domains, and that systems engineering, which integrates more specialized engineering disciplines, is inherently much more informal.

We will use the waferstepper as a typical complex computerized system, the case is described at the beginning. Next we explain the discipline of Systems Engineering. In a short intermezzo the overloaded meaning of the word "formal" is discussed. The real positioning is given in two steps: first we elaborate the informal nature of Systems Engineering and then we discuss the relation to Formal Methods.

1   An Example of a Complex Computerized System

The development of a new generation of wafersteppers, the ASML Twinscan family, is used as illustrative case. A waferstepper is a large (ca. 30 m^3), costly (ca. 10M USD) and complex system used in the lithographic process of a semiconductor fab. The main function of the system is to replicate a circuit pattern many times on a wafer, by stepwise exposing the wafer. The early wafersteppers exposed fields sequentially, where the wafer is not moving during the exposure. The actions are then simply to move, stop, and expose. The most recent wafersteppers use the scanning principle. Scanning is based on exposure through a slit, while the reticle with the original and the wafer move harmoniously. Time and position are much more directly coupled in the scanning exposure.

The key drivers of lithography are Critical Dimension (CD) control, overlay, and productivity. CD control is the variation of the line width or gate size, for 130 nm line width a typical CD control value is 10 nm. Less variation is better, minor variations may cause a significant power consumption problem in the final integrated circuit. Overlay is typical 45 nm for 130 nm line width. Smaller overlay values are better, allowing a denser design and hence more chips per wafer. Productivity for these systems is expressed in terms of exposed wafers per hour, typical 100 300 mm wafers per hour. The productivity of the waferstepper is directly related to the cost effectiveness of the semiconductor fab, the value of the waferstepper is more or less proportional with the productivity.

Characteristic for the semiconductor equipment market is the fast evolution, expressed in Moore's law. The exponential performance improvements dictated

J.S. Fitzgerald, I.J. Hayes, and A. Tarlecki (Eds.): FM 2005, LNCS 3582, pp. 552–556, 2005.

by this law translate in exponential improvements of CD control and overlay. A twofold improvement is required every four years.

The customer level performance is achieved by budgeting the most important performance targets. For example the overlay budget for wafersteppers in 1997 was decomposed in 5 decomposition steps in individual contributions. For instance tracking error contributions and stability requirements are specified in nanometers. Such a budget is an abstraction of the actual machine behavior. A typical overlay budget contains about 25 numbers, while hundreds of components and parameters have somehow impact on the final overlay.

2   Systems Engineering

The Systems Engineering discipline, see [2], is an integrating discipline. Systems Engineering integrates and guides mono-disciplines, such as mechanical engineering, electrical engineering, and software engineering, to create reliable systems. The Systems Engineering discipline comprehends multiple approaches:

- well defined formalized Systems Engineering methods
- strong process focused
- "common sense", based on human experience and intelligence

A balance of these three approaches yields successful products. In this document we will discuss this balance and especially the, often underrated, informal side of Systems Engineering.

3   What Is "Formal"?

Industrial discussions about the use of *formal* methods often derail due to the ambiguity of the word *formal* itself. In industrial context formality is often used in organizational sense: what are the formalized processes, responsibilities, roles, et cetera. Formalized processes facilitate well-known problems of heterogeneous nature. The scientific based *formal* methods use the mathematical sense of formality. Science based *formal* methods facilitate specialized well-known problems of homogeneous nature. These *formal* methods provide proven solutions to problems fitting in the limited specialized area covered by the method. For instance Rate Monotonic Scheduling guarantees real-time performance for repetitious tasks with well-defined processing times and deadlines.

The Systems Engineering community is strongly focused on (formal) processes. However, most system level problems are ill defined and very heterogeneous. The overlay specification of 45 nm, for example, sounds quite well defined. However, this specification is only valid in unique well-defined measurement circumstances. The realized overlay in actual production lots is a function of hundreds or thousands of parameters. Customer satisfaction is determined by actual overlay performance, not by the artificially defined acceptance specification. We will discuss the consequences of these characteristics in relation with *formal* methods.

4   The Informal Side of Systems Engineering

The key performance of the waferstepper, in terms of CD control, overlay and productivity and the design choices depend on many context aspects, such as the production environment, the business, the human stakeholders, and the many involved technical disciplines.

The yield and productivity of a lithography cell depends on the waferstepper, but also on many other aspects in the context of the waferstepper. For example, the wafer and the reticle themselves influence the performance as well as the measurement, processing and logistics of wafers and reticles.

In the business context a balancing act is performed between yield and CD control with a significant impact on the final chip performance (power and speed). The business context is a complex playing field with many players, such as equipments vendors, system integrators, lease companies, fab designers, consultants, mask makers, resist makers, and wafer makers and many different kinds of customers: design houses, foundries, and vertical integrated companies.

The human context is full of stakeholders, both internal as well as external. According to IEEE 1471 [3] all stakeholders have their particular concerns. We add on top of concerns that stakeholders also have their particular interests, rhythms, and contributions. The design emerges from a complex psychosocial interaction between all these stakeholders.

Problems arising from the complexity of this context become visible in a rather late stage of development: during integration or worse in the customer's fab. The dynamics, the uncertainties, the unknowns and the heterogeneity of these systems engineering aspects do not fit with rigorous formal methods. Informal, "common sense" and experience-based methods are used mostly here. See also the Systems Architecting book by Rechtin [1].

5   Where Do Systems Engineering and Formal Methods Meet?

In industrial practice some huge gaps exist between tools and methods of the involved disciplines. Worse is that the involved engineers are often unaware of these gaps and use their own frame of reference in the discussion with other disciplines. For example, software people claim to have a proven implementation, but at the same time cannot answer the simple, but crucial, question how much time is needed per function. The ideal situation would be that disciplines have sufficient mutual understanding to communicate and cooperate. The gap between Systems Engineering and Formal Methods in Software Engineering in industrial practice is rather large at this moment.

Conventional disciplines, such as mechanical engineering, electrical engineering, and computer science, have a rich collection of formalisms, techniques, tools and methods. The elements in this collection work on well defined problems in a well-defined manner. In product creation less well-defined problems occur when multiple disciplines jointly realize some functionality. Techniques, tools and methods exist at the multi-disciplinary level. These techniques, tools and methods are less well defined than at the mono-disciplinary level. When the focus is limited to a single objective the problems and means are well defined, but soft. At the system level, where multiple objectives have to be achieved simultaneously, the problems are ill defined and the methods become rather soft. The natural habitat of formal methods is in the category of well-defined problems, while Systems Engineering is heavily involved with the ill-defined problems, with multiple objectives and many contributing disciplines. Systems Engineering and formal methods can be complementary, when formal methods remove risks of well-defined problems.

A system can be described and analyzed at different levels of abstraction. The static description of today's embedded systems contains tens of millions of details, such as lines of code, components, and connections. The challenge of product creation is to translate a few key requirements in several design steps in the tens of millions details at the lowest level of abstraction. The most detailed design steps are mono disciplinary, for example transforming an interface and behavior specification of a class into hundreds to thousands lines of code. However, at a higher abstraction level design trade-offs are made to allocate functionality to technologies and components, typical multi-disciplinary design. System engineers have the responsibility for the integral system performance and functionality: the integration of multi-disciplinary components and subsystems into a system. For example the system engineer reasons at the highest abstraction level about exposure in terms of a light source, reticle, lens and wafer, and about system functionality in terms of 3 key parameters: overlay, CD control, and productivity. The higher-level abstraction is transformed into models and budgets with tens of contributing elements. Finally, the waferstepper contains 10 million lines of code to realize the required system behavior and performance.

In the following postulates we position formal methods in relation to systems engineering. The purpose of this positioning is to create mutual understanding of the contribution of these disciplines.

Postulate 1: Formal Methods in industrial context work only at the more detailed mono-disciplinary abstraction levels, with well-defined problems. Examples are communication protocols and scheduling strategies.

Postulate 2: Inventors of formal methods are capable to apply their personal strengths also at a much higher abstraction level. These inventors are: analytical, structural, firm of principle, and consistent. The formal methods themselves do not really contribute to the Systems Engineering means; the personal strength of formal people can contribute.

The research field of multi-disciplinary design is tackled with three research approaches. The *scientific* approach is to extend the existing body of knowledge with small increments. Every increment is well founded. A lot of the methods and techniques available in the existing body of knowledge can be used with adaptations at the multi-disciplinary design level. We call this approach *borrow & adapt*. The third approach is *heuristic*: observe the system engineers in the industrial context and make the implicit experience explicit. Based on the consolidation of the state-of-practice many research questions can be formulated. Such a consolidation starts with observations and descriptions, and in the long term, after a lot of research, will be turned into well-structured methods with clear fundaments.

6   Conclusions

Systems engineering takes place in a very heterogeneous environment, Systems engineering is the art of ignoring details. Formal Methods provide a systematic and accurate approach, and works on well-defined homogeneous problems.

Systems engineering can use formal thinking: *borrow & adapt.* An example is System Level modeling; systematic and structured like formal methods, but not proven or very accurate due to the inherent uncertainties at the system level. Formal methods, applied at specific homogeneous niches, provide input to Systems Engineering work at multi-disciplinary level. Systems Engineering sets, the other way around, the boundaries for the application of Formal Methods for partial system problems.

References

1. Rechtin, Eberhardt and Maier, Mark W., The Art of Systems Architecting CRC Press (1997)
2. Martin, James N.: Systems Engineering Guidebook A Process for Developing Systems and Products. CRC Press (1996)
3. Architecture Working Group (AWG): IEEE Recommended Practice for Architectural Description of Software-Intensive Systems The Institute of Electrical and Electronics Engineers, Inc. (2000)

Author Index

Lecture Notes in Computer Science

For information about Vols. 1–3481

please contact your bookseller or Springer

Vol. 3530: A. Prinz, R. Reed, J. Reed (Eds.), SDL 2005: Model Driven. XI, 361 pages. 2005.

Vol. 3528: P.S. Szczepaniak, J. Kacprzyk, A. Niewiadomski (Eds.), Advances in Web Intelligence. XVII, 513 pages. 2005. (Subseries LNAI).

Vol. 3527: R. Morrison, F. Oquendo (Eds.), Software Architecture. XII, 263 pages. 2005.

Vol. 3526: S.B. Cooper, B. Löwe, L. Torenvliet (Eds.), New Computational Paradigms. XVII, 574 pages. 2005.

Vol. 3525: A.E. Abdallah, C.B. Jones, J.W. Sanders (Eds.), Communicating Sequential Processes. XIV, 321 pages. 2005.

Vol. 3524: R. Barták, M. Milano (Eds.), Integration of AI and OR Techniques in Constraint Programming for Combinatorial Optimization Problems. XI, 320 pages. 2005.

Vol. 3523: J.S. Marques, N. Pérez de la Blanca, P. Pina (Eds.), Pattern Recognition and Image Analysis, Part II. XXVI, 733 pages. 2005.

Vol. 3522: J.S. Marques, N. Pérez de la Blanca, P. Pina (Eds.), Pattern Recognition and Image Analysis, Part I. XXVI, 703 pages. 2005.

Vol. 3521: N. Megiddo, Y. Xu, B. Zhu (Eds.), Algorithmic Applications in Management. XIII, 484 pages. 2005.

Vol. 3520: O. Pastor, J. Falcão e Cunha (Eds.), Advanced Information Systems Engineering. XVI, 584 pages. 2005.

Vol. 3519: H. Li, P. J. Olver, G. Sommer (Eds.), Computer Algebra and Geometric Algebra with Applications. IX, 449 pages. 2005.

Vol. 3518: T.B. Ho, D. Cheung, H. Liu (Eds.), Advances in Knowledge Discovery and Data Mining. XXI, 864 pages. 2005. (Subseries LNAI).

Vol. 3517: H.S. Baird, D.P. Lopresti (Eds.), Human Interactive Proofs. IX, 143 pages. 2005.

Vol. 3516: V.S. Sunderam, G.D.v. Albada, P.M.A. Sloot, J.J. Dongarra (Eds.), Computational Science – ICCS 2005, Part III. LXIII, 1143 pages. 2005.

Vol. 3515: V.S. Sunderam, G.D.v. Albada, P.M.A. Sloot, J.J. Dongarra (Eds.), Computational Science – ICCS 2005, Part II. LXIII, 1101 pages. 2005.

Vol. 3514: V.S. Sunderam, G.D.v. Albada, P.M.A. Sloot, J.J. Dongarra (Eds.), Computational Science – ICCS 2005, Part I. LXIII, 1089 pages. 2005.

Vol. 3513: A. Montoyo, R. Muñoz, E. Métais (Eds.), Natural Language Processing and Information Systems. XII, 408 pages. 2005.

Vol. 3512: J. Cabestany, A. Prieto, F. Sandoval (Eds.), Computational Intelligence and Bioinspired Systems. XXV, 1260 pages. 2005.

Vol. 3511: U.K. Wiil (Ed.), Metainformatics. VIII, 221 pages. 2005.

Vol. 3510: T. Braun, G. Carle, Y. Koucheryavy, V. Tsaoussidis (Eds.), Wired/Wireless Internet Communications. XIV, 366 pages. 2005.

Vol. 3509: M. Jünger, V. Kaibel (Eds.), Integer Programming and Combinatorial Optimization. XI, 484 pages. 2005.

Vol. 3508: P. Bresciani, P. Giorgini, B. Henderson-Sellers, G. Low, M. Winikoff (Eds.), Agent-Oriented Information Systems II. X, 227 pages. 2005. (Subseries LNAI).

Vol. 3507: F. Crestani, I. Ruthven (Eds.), Information Context: Nature, Impact, and Role. XIII, 253 pages. 2005.

Vol. 3506: C. Park, S. Chee (Eds.), Information Security and Cryptology – ICISC 2004. XIV, 490 pages. 2005.

Vol. 3505: V. Gorodetsky, J. Liu, V. A. Skormin (Eds.), Autonomous Intelligent Systems: Agents and Data Mining. XIII, 303 pages. 2005. (Subseries LNAI).

Vol. 3504: A.F. Frangi, P.I. Radeva, A. Santos, M. Hernandez (Eds.), Functional Imaging and Modeling of the Heart. XV, 489 pages. 2005.

Vol. 3503: S.E. Nikoletseas (Ed.), Experimental and Efficient Algorithms. XV, 624 pages. 2005.

Vol. 3502: F. Khendek, R. Dssouli (Eds.), Testing of Communicating Systems. X, 381 pages. 2005.

Vol. 3501: B. Kégl, G. Lapalme (Eds.), Advances in Artificial Intelligence. XV, 458 pages. 2005. (Subseries LNAI).

Vol. 3500: S. Miyano, J. Mesirov, S. Kasif, S. Istrail, P. Pevzner, M. Waterman (Eds.), Research in Computational Molecular Biology. XVII, 632 pages. 2005. (Subseries LNBI).

Vol. 3499: A. Pelc, M. Raynal (Eds.), Structural Information and Communication Complexity. X, 323 pages. 2005.

Vol. 3498: J. Wang, X. Liao, Z. Yi (Eds.), Advances in Neural Networks – ISNN 2005, Part III. XLIX, 1077 pages. 2005.

Vol. 3497: J. Wang, X. Liao, Z. Yi (Eds.), Advances in Neural Networks – ISNN 2005, Part II. XLIX, 947 pages. 2005.

Vol. 3496: J. Wang, X. Liao, Z. Yi (Eds.), Advances in Neural Networks – ISNN 2005, Part II. L, 1055 pages. 2005.

Vol. 3495: P. Kantor, G. Muresan, F. Roberts, D.D. Zeng, F.-Y. Wang, H. Chen, R.C. Merkle (Eds.), Intelligence and Security Informatics. XVIII, 674 pages. 2005.

Vol. 3494: R. Cramer (Ed.), Advances in Cryptology – EUROCRYPT 2005. XIV, 576 pages. 2005.

Vol. 3493: N. Fuhr, M. Lalmas, S. Malik, Z. Szlávik (Eds.), Advances in XML Information Retrieval. XI, 438 pages. 2005.

Vol. 3492: P. Blache, E. Stabler, J. Busquets, R. Moot (Eds.), Logical Aspects of Computational Linguistics. X, 363 pages. 2005. (Subseries LNAI).

Vol. 3489: G.T. Heineman, I. Crnkovic, H.W. Schmidt, J.A. Stafford, C. Szyperski, K. Wallnau (Eds.), Component-Based Software Engineering. XI, 358 pages. 2005.

Vol. 3488: M.-S. Hacid, N.V. Murray, Z.W. Raś, S. Tsumoto (Eds.), Foundations of Intelligent Systems. XIII, 700 pages. 2005. (Subseries LNAI).

Vol. 3486: T. Helleseth, D. Sarwate, H.-Y. Song, K. Yang (Eds.), Sequences and Their Applications - SETA 2004. XII, 451 pages. 2005.

Vol. 3483: O. Gervasi, M.L. Gavrilova, V. Kumar, A. Laganà, H.P. Lee, Y. Mun, D. Taniar, C.J.K. Tan (Eds.), Computational Science and Its Applications – ICCSA 2005, Part IV. LXV, 1362 pages. 2005.

Vol. 3482: O. Gervasi, M.L. Gavrilova, V. Kumar, A. Laganà, H.P. Lee, Y. Mun, D. Taniar, C.J.K. Tan (Eds.), Computational Science and Its Applications – ICCSA 2005, Part III. LXV, 1340 pages. 2005.